THE DEBT COLLECTOR'S HANDBOOK

DAVID J. COOK

COLLECTING DEBTS, FINDING ASSETS, ENFORCING JUDGMENTS, AND BEATING YOUR CREDITORS

Cover design by Tamara Kowalski/ABA Publishing.

Printed in the United States of America.

18 17 16 15 14 5 4 3 2 1

Library of Congress Cataloging-in-Publication Data

Cook, David J., 1949- author.

The debt collector's handbook : collecting debts, finding assets, enforcing judgments, and beating your creditors / By David J. Cook, Esq.; Solo, Small Firm, and General Practice Division, American Bar Association

pages cm

Includes bibliographical references and index.

ISBN 978-1-62722-495-6 (alk. paper)

1. Collection laws--United States. I. American Bar Association. Solo, Small Firm and General Practice Division, sponsoring body. II. Title.

KF1024.C66 2014

346.7307'7--dc23

2014009348

Discounts are available for books ordered in bulk. Special consideration is given to state bars, CLE programs, and other bar-related organizations. Inquire at Book Publishing, ABA Publishing, American Bar Association, 321 N. Clark Street, Chicago, Illinois 60654-7598.

www.ShopABA.org

I dedicate this book to my father who made me the person that I am. I also dedicate this book to Fred Goldman who gave me a life beyond my expectations.

Acknowledgments

Call this page the GUILT PAGE. The author feels guilty about all the business associates, buddies and family members who the author abused in transforming the book from an ephemeral dream in the wee hours of the morning to a 640 pages of hard text at the crack of dawn. The author pestered everyone in getting the book proofread. Please read it. Please make your corrections. I will name the book after you. I will make you co-author. Some authors can be a total and complete jerk. Super jerk.

The author shoved the manuscript in front of everyone. Some authors really feel bad about browbeating a lot of folks into helping write book including the basic research. The author wanted friends and family to read a manuscript that crawled out the literary critical care unit. The author would say, "Please please and please read my book. Pretty please with sugar on top. Please tell me that I am the rival to Stephen King which is a total lie. Tell me anything. I will give you my first born. No, I will give you my dog. Take the dog, which is a better deal."

An acknowledgment page shows the world that the author is a decent, kind and wonderful human being. This is another total lie. The author has to express that the book is the product of many folks, not few, and without their help, the book would be cooked, fried, fricasseed and burn to the crisp. The book might look good as a crispy critter. Yum Yum. Tastes like chicken. The author needs to sound, look and appear, I know that this is impossible, like a kind and grateful human being. Gadzooks!

The acknowledgment page thanks everybody who nursed the tome along. Kinda. The author thanks competing authors for their insights. Is this sincere? No, silly. Are you nuts? The author thanks his (or her) lucky stars that the number #1 mucky muck in the field didn't publish the super duper blockbuster that would blot everyone including the penitent author. Had Mr. Super Duper beaten the author to the punch, his first run would languish on sidewalk for "free." Did you know that the world still needs two pound door stops? What a Godsend for some books.

The author thanks libraries, universities, research tanks for access to their archives. Is this genuine? Maybe. The running joke is that the chair occupied by the scholars in the study room to examine the materials (you can't take them out—that would be theft, folks) is still warm to the touch from the last fellow who sat in the same chair and studied the same materials. Crap. A warm chair means that the author better get this book out the door to the publisher before a competitor beats the author to the punch. Why should the book appear in someone else's rear view mirror? Mr. Super Duper's blockbuster book would wipe the author off the face of the earth. The author would certainly learn what Number 5,000,000 means on the Amazon list. Any ranking less than 100,000 are bread crumbs on the publishing floor. Any ranking less 500,000 falls between the cracks on the publishing floor. Any ranking less than 2,000,000 needs an electron microscope.

How about thanking members of the office or staff for proof reading, typing or researching the manuscript? "I thank my administrative assistant, Joe, for his herculean effort in proofreading my manuscript." What the author meant to say was that the first draft was impenetrable. This sucker would stop a .45 bullet. Joe spent months translating the book into commonly understood English. Joe introduced the author to grammar, spelling and syntax. Too bad, but Joe retired on disability which was based double cataracts, which is awful given that Joe is 30. "I thank my secretary Mary for her diligence." Her diligence consisted of parading one excuse after another to avoid coming to the phone so the author could finish the manuscript.

How about thanking the family? "I thank my wife because I was able to hide in the study for 6 months, took a big hit in income, and never took a vacation." "How many books are you going to sell? Can we take a trip on the proceeds? Are you channeling Hemingway, Steinbeck, Shakespeare or Louis L'Amour? Is this "Stranger in a Strange Land, the Sequel?"

As *your* author, I am going to pass on the lot. Who do I thank? I am going to thank Carol Mann of Mann Literary Agency. I circulated a précis of the OJ Chapters, which kicked the literary doors wide open. She grabbed me before I fell into literary oblivion. I also thank the American Bar Association and particularly Richard Paszkiet in giving me an unbelievable opportunity to publish this book. Call this book my literary life jacket. I'll do better than Jack Dawson. Rick is my hero.

The other object of my gratitude are a place and the persons who inhabit the place. I am grateful to the English Department of the University of California at Los Angeles who gave me a classical education. I am grateful to the academic staff, but among everyone else, the most important was Professor George S. Rousseau who taught 18th Century English literature and particularly Alexander Pope. I guess that Professor Pope had my number. Professor Rousseau clued me into the fact that while I might not succeed in in academia but that I might have a crackerjack career in engineering and maybe, as you can imagine, law.

Contents

Introduction

Tales of Chicken Delight

Every college student has a part-time job, and more than one. Mine was off the beaten path. I was a Chicken Delight driver for the outlet located in Beverly Hills. The store was located on South Doheny right off Olympic Blvd and adjacent to the famous zip code of 90212 that introduced the "Tupperware" as the moniker for plastic surgery's new look. The Beverly Hills and West Los Angeles crowd loved Chicken Delight. I spent a year delivering boxes of fried chicken.

Located in the hills overlooking Los Angeles, some customers were accessible through long and steep driveways. This is the delivery business that required that I physically deliver the boxes of chicken to their front door. No problem, save and except my car, and everything I wore, smelled of fried chicken. I was the cat's meow. Literally.

About five days every year, Los Angeles gets rained out. After a couple of days, you'd think that Noah and the Ark took up station at Griffith Park to evacuate everyone. On one very rainy night, my job was to deliver chicken to a home on the very top of the Hollywood Hills. I found the address off the mailbox at the bottom of the steep driveway, turned the car into the driveway and hit the gas. The rain was so bad that the car's rear wheels spun around and failed to get traction. I was going nowhere. Hit the gas again, and still going nowhere. I thought about running up the hill. No, that would not work because the food would be drenched. Crap. No, the food would be crap. Soggy fried chicken sucks. My boss was a total screamer and would charge me back for the cost of the meal. (Legal or not, who cares).

Was I screwed without being kissed? Aside from Hugh Hefner's catalogue, what did 19-year-old boys read? Answer: *Car and Driver Magazine*. [Circa 1968]. I remember reading that a car's reverse gear had more torque (power) than the forward gear, especially for a small car with an automatic transmission. Taking a page from the *Car and Driver* playbook I turned the car around, leaned out the driver's side window to see where I was going, and hit the gas. This was a very narrow driveway, and I remember thinking that I might careen off the roadway and tumble down the hillside into the gully below. [This is what I feared: "Jack Cook? Are you the father of David Cook? This is the Los Angeles Police. We found your son at the bottom of a ravine buried under a pile of fried chicken. Amazingly, the chicken was still warm to the touch. Your son? Not so much."]. Low and behold the rear wheels dug into the pavement and the car bolted up the hill until I got to the top. I jumped out of the car, with the box of chicken in hand, and knocked on the door. Behind the door was "who's there" and I said "Chicken Delight," and presto gizmo, the door opened. I delivered the fried chicken and collected the $2.50 plus tip for a total haul of $3.00. (You read that right). I could have been the Jack the Ripper, but "Chicken Delight" opened any door.

This story is the theme of the book. Every revelation is a Chicken Delight moment. You are about to enter the world of high end enforcement, treasure hunting and recovering assets, worth millions which are cloaked under layers of Byzantine tapestry woven by very clever lawyers. You are about to engage in a high risk venture, confront all stout obstructions, and, don't forget, your adversaries are smart, quick and very determined Your adversaries hate you and make it their life's goals to beat you. Chicken Delight teaches you never be deterred, nor disheartened but be resourceful. Never give up when confronted with an obstacle. Think about the Chicken Delight solution to every problem. Try a backdoor scenario. Try anything and everything. Never take no for an answer, and try again. In my case, when in doubt, turn the car around and go up the hill backwards. At least I was pointed in the right direction going down the hill.

Section 1

Hors D'oeuvres

Chapter 1

Arrows and "Xs" on the Treasure Map

I am here to share my experiences as a hard-bitten and overly aggressive enforcement and collection lawyer. You will have the benefit of my 39-plus years of chasing down debtors tarred by credit card bills to debtors buried under $20 million jury awards. I am going to tell you how to find and read the treasure. You will learn, or may already know, that bad people hide their assets when they are fleeing from their debts and judgments. Bad people hide their money even when they present financial statements to qualify them for low-interest loans, government grants, and settlements based on financial distress. This is a true cookbook that offers the recipes of uncovering hidden assets. This book is your treasure map.

I am going to explain their schemes, show you the tricks of the trade, and tell you what schemes work and what sputters. This book will show you how to find money hidden by the debtor and reach that money. Call this the toy in the cereal moment. Remember those moments when your five-year-old tore into the $6 cereal box, rolled up her sleeve, and shoved her arm in the corn flakes to retrieve the toy? Upon the retrieving the toy, and with a smile on her face, she abandoned the destroyed box and ruined the cereal for you. Some of us learned to love that cereal. Welcome to your childhood.

This book also offers you the grand tour of Dante's financial hell. Consider this book the modern-day Virgil on the downward spiral through the nine levels. Don't mind the smell of fried chicken; it is aromatic. Eau de Poultry. Borrowing from *Apocalypse Now*: "I love the smell of fried chicken in the morning . . . Smells like . . . victory." I remind you that enforcing judgments against individuals who have perpetrated horrific acts that earned them a multimillion-dollar damages award are evil people, and when passing from this life to the next, they will never see the face of God but will reside in the bosom of Hell. What do you expect of me after reading years of Christian literature as an English major at UCLA?

Like all good cookbooks, we will teach the basics called CSI business and law basics. We will teach you the CSI Enforcement Basics. How can you dig for buried treasure without having a good shovel, pick and pair of tongs, and Robin at your side?

The ordinary cookbook teaches you how to make sauces, set the right temperature, and be aware of food safety. Our cookbook teaches the basics of civil remedies, real estate, finance, and sleuthing, which are all needed to unearth the hidden treasures. We will make you a CSI detective, and you can proudly wear a digital trench coat, gray fedora, and police .38 special. Don't forget the digital bottle of whiskey hidden in the desk drawer, and, of course, the digital moll draped over the desk. We will show the power of bluff and the outer parameters of threat, or when a threat becomes extortion, and when to take a hike. That's right. Sometimes you have to walk away.

You will also learn lesson #1. Ask more questions. The only stupid question is the question not asked. Ask the same question again, and you might get a different answer, Mr. Poirot. Never stop asking questions, and never leave any clue unresolved. For example, why is the debtor writing a check for crop insurance when the debtor denies owning any farm property? Checks don't fall from the sky.

Welcome to pottery shards, wobbling stars, and dinosaur fingernails. You will learn how to scrounge up treasure maps, grab big-time assets, and topple the most recalcitrant debtors, even ones defended by lawyers hailing from national law firms. You will learn to love bills of lading, debit cards, freight bills, Google, and Yelp. You will learn how to cook the other guy's goose or rescue your goose from a deep fryer full of bubbling duck fat. Offshore debtors are no longer immune, nor are the ne'er-do-wells who look you in the face when hiding under a rock that has been kicked over. Or maybe these folks are immune. Call this the open season for everyone: you, me, and them. You will come away very prepared, and never forget this sage advice: Chance favors the prepared mind, Mr. Pasteur. Become Themistocles, the famous Greek general, who built up a world-class navy that defeated the Persians at the battle of Salamis. Without Themistocles's foresight, we would all be speaking Farsi today.

Lesson #2. Don't presume that you know the answer to question #1. Read everything that you can about your debtor, every hearing transcript, every pleading, every deposition, every declaration, every public record, and anything you can find about the debtor on the Internet. If you are uncertain about the debtor's business, read everything you can. If you don't know anything about the debtor, ask the client and the trial lawyer. I have some bad news for you if you take the case from the trial lawyer. You are not getting the whole story, and better yet, you are getting a lot of half-truths about the debtor or the case itself. If you are going to chase someone down, you are looking at a multiyear experience and spending some $5,000 to $100,000 of someone's money and that might be your money. Know your debtor, know your client, and know what you want to do. Failing to answer any of these inquiries can be very painful.

The biggest risk is failing to grip the level of malice, perniciousness, anger, or violence of your debtor. You will soon become the tip of the sword and the object of this person's uncontrollable psychotic rage. This is an acceptable risk if you are prepared to face this challenge, assuming that you know what you will be facing. You might find yourself face to face with a domestic terrorist, who faces a million-dollar judgment that has destroyed his future. Be careful. Enforcement of high-end judgments is a tough business, and I don't wish this business upon anyone, including my family members. "Why don't you answer the door . . .? That person doesn't look too dangerous. I'll wait here."

We have seen it all, including physical violence, bank robberies, embezzlements, and Ponzi schemes. I have heard stories that are gruesome, gory, and retching—eyes gouged out, heads shot to a stump, bodies dismembered, and hands slashed in half. Pedophiles even say hello. These folks are very scary and unpredictable.

This book will offer some war stories, but you did not pay good money to hear about tales of grandeur or degradation, well, unless they are really entertaining or make a point. Rather, you will learn something that can help you out of that rut or, should you be the target of someone's ire, keep the other person in the rut.

This book represents the synthesis of a postdigital world of how to find hidden assets and where you find information that would assist you in this arduous and terrible quest. We start this book with O. J. Simpson and the historic judgment in favor of Fred Goldman against Simpson for the wrongful death of Ronald Goldman. Collecting this judgment, which is still continuing, runs the gamut of enforcement and information required to fuel those efforts. Collecting the judgment became a carnival of enforcement. We got O. J. Simpson's movie money from *The Naked Gun, Frogman, Capricorn One,* and *Towering Inferno*. Paramount's royalty checks are in Technicolor®. We got the acquittal suit that sits with Newseum, which is the museum dedicated to news and located in Washington, D.C. The suit was turned over in a settlement conference in which the settlement judge called O. J. Simpson, while parked in prison, to get his final signoff. We got the book, *If I Did It*, which the Goldman family published.

We missed on Hall of Fame ring, O. J.'s Miami house, and his video slasher money. According to news reports, O. J. Simpson claimed that he lost the Hall of Fame ring on the golf course. I don't believe that for a second. Others are searching for that ring. We got the fake Rolex watch, but I had to give it back. I wore the watch through security at LAX. We got part of the $800,000 book advance that O. J. Simpson received from HarperCollins, which paid down the mortgage on his Florida home. This recovery originated from the trustee of Lorraine Brooke Associates bankruptcy (who held the book rights) who sued the bank and got back a portion of the money that was distributed to Fred Goldman and the Nicole Brown Simpson family. This judgment is historic because the civil judgment substituted for a botched criminal trial when O. J. Simpson walked out a free man even though he committed a double murder.

In writing this book, I have provided you enough law and procedure so that you can see how this business works. If you are looking for money, you can ask the right questions, recognize deals that implicitly protect the other party from the consequences of a default, or if postdefault, lawsuit, and the inevitable judgment shields the person's asset from enforcement. With lessons learned from this book, you scribble over a proposed contract a new legal but precise term: No, Never, or Never in a Million Years. If you are at the butt end of the contract default or face a zillion-dollar tort judgment, whether intentionally or otherwise, you will better grasp the perils of default and a strategy to exit from the financial calamity. You will be reading about key court decisions, and nearly all of these cases are online, and most of them are straightforward. The law has become very democratic, and you read most cases by typing in the search site, the case name, or the citation to the case.

You don't need to be a collection lawyer or even have any collection experience to understand law here. There is no hocus-pocus here, nor the dreary explanation of legal principles. This book is about collecting debts, finding assets, enforcing judgments against difficult people, or, should you be so inclined, beating out your creditors. This book is not about winning in the courtroom. We leave that topic to others who can tell you what shoes to wear, where to buy your clothing, and how to smile. Here and now, we can encapsulate the bibliography of winning court cases with the "B" word: Be prepared, Be truthful, Be aware of the defenses to your case, Be on time, Be humble, Be realistic, Be respective to all, and most importantly, Be prepared to settle. Follow these rules, and you will emerge unscathed from the rigors of civil litigation.

Be honest to yourself and others. Be truthful to yourself. Some folks who walk into court are self-intoxicated and near delusional. Self-intoxicated means that a litigant has fallen in love with his or her own lies. These individuals start to believe falsehoods that they believe will get them out of their mess, such as "No, I didn't sign the agreement," when five witnesses say to the contrary. "No. I didn't touch her. She just fell in to my arms." The bruised and torn clothing? "I guess it's a modern fashion statement." Whatever the claim, the jury will find these lies repulsive and will clobber the defendant with a big-dollar judgment. Litigants who "fall in love with their own lies" rarely survive litigation. What is the antidote? Answer: "A come to Jesus meeting." Trial counsel should enshrine the conference room as a church, with crucifix, altar, and stained glass. Why? All clients who fall in love with their own lies necessarily encounter a come-to-Jesus meeting and a "dollop of candor" that tops their coffee.

This book is written for the quintessential America lawyer who confronts collection and enforcement issues on a daily basis and needs a down-to-earth guide of what to do. What questions do you ask? Where do you look? Where is the money? What are you doing? Is this case really worthwhile? What can you expect from a judge? How far can you go?

Chapter 2

A Preview

The book offers you the cocktail of business, real estate, established business practices, and a significant body of law. Shaken, and not stirred, Mr. Bond.

Your mission, Mr. Hawke, should you choose to accept this assignment, is advising a client whether to accept any one of the following offers: (1) settle a $10,000,000 judgment for $500,000 in cash; (2) accept a community property settlement based on a 30-year marriage that cycled through $10,000,000 but the wife gets only $500,000; (3) accept a policy-limits offer of $500,000, and release the defendant of $10,000,000 liability including a claim for wrongful death, or (4) shelve a $10,000,000 judgment because the client believes, and you advise, that the judgment is uncollectable. Everyone and everybody are counting on your skills to properly advise the client. Don't cock it up, Bond.

Suppose you ask for, and receive, a detailed financial statement from the debtor's lawyer that is executed under penalty of perjury. The debtor denies ownership of any real property, discloses near-poverty earnings, and lists marginal assets. Believing what you are seeing, any settlement is better than no settlement, and you are prepared to accept the debtor's representation that his family will raise the money to bail out their miscreant relative. You hire a private investigator who advises that he is unable to locate any real property in the name of the defendant. The $500,000 offer looks even better. However, well-versed in Shakespeare and supremely paranoid, you mutter "something is rotten in the state of Denmark," Horatio. What is wrong with this picture? You think, "I am staring at what appears to be a supremely successful businessman who claims abject poverty but is aided by an angel who is willing to lend $500,000 to resolve his financial crisis. What is wrong with this picture? 'Wake up, Little Suzie.'"

The answer is changing the channels and looking at another picture. The first picture is the debtor's credit report. A common credit report reveals the debtor's liabilities, not assets. The usual suspects are credit card, department store, and gas company credit card balances. These are called revolving balances. Financial institutions that make real estate loans are disclosed as "installment" obligations, the length of the maturity (360 months, or a 30-year loan), whether the loan is current, late, defaulted, or charged, off, the unpaid balance and rated. The credit report lists five *separate* installment loans that each exceeds $2,000,000, and all are current. Some of these lenders are local (your state, such as First Bank of Beverly Hills) and others are out of state or clearly regional (such as First Bank of Seattle).

Remember this rule: "Security follows the debt." Debt, like a real estate loan, is secured by the real property. Find the security, and you will find the debt. The flip side of this rule is "find the debt, and you will find the security that encumbers the collateral." With knowledge that the credit report reflects secured debt in which the debtor is the obligor, and with a little elbow grease, you can find the real property when you cycle through the grantor/grantee index of the local county recorder in which the property sits. If the name of the bank is First Bank of Beverly Hills, chances are the property is located in Los Angeles County.

What are you going to find? First, you are going to find the deed of trust (or mortgage) in the name of the debtor, which is not released or refinanced in the name of another. You will probably find a transfer instrument (grant or quitclaim deed) from the debtor to someone who bears the same last name or a newly formed limited liability company. The grant deed is handwritten, and the upper-left corner provides a return address of the debtor, and not the putative buyer. The grant deed for each parcel (five in all) is dated with the same date and recorded in serial order by the debtor (as the claimed seller) just before the offer of settlement. You do not see any earmarks of an escrow, such as an escrow number. You see cross-outs on the deeds. The notary, whom you can trace, works out of a Mail Box Etc. You don't find a refinance of the property when sold to the current buyer. You cycle through the multiple listing service (MLS), and never find that the property was listed for sale. You don't find a jump in the real property tax assessment, which is common in a rising market. The sale of real property authorizes the county tax assessor to reassess the property based on the current sales price, which arises from a bona fide sale, and prompts a reassessment, which appears in the public records of the county tax collector (not recorder). The county (or city) likewise collects transfer taxes upon the sale of property at the rate of $1.10 per thousand, which is likewise a public record.

Most, if not all, buyers purchase real property subject to their own "new financing," and rarely acquire property subject to existing financing. The reason is that the buyer in these cases brings better financing to the table; moreover, the sale of the property triggers the "due on sale" clause of the existing deed of trust that enables the lender to promptly foreclose. You do not find any new financing.

You come to the conclusion that the evidence suggests that the debtor still owns the five parcels of valuable real property, despite the denial, given the lack of an apparent escrow, no listing through the MLS, no new financing, no jump in the real estate taxes, no transfer fees, no transfer to a relative, and no serial recordings recorded in the face of the settlement offer for about $.05 on the dollar of the liability. You are staring at five living and breathing fraudulent conveyances, which, if recovered, might generate a million-dollar recovery for the client and for you, a big fee and the undying gratitude of the client. When you come to the realization that you spotted these fraudulent conveyances, avoid shouting out, "It's alive. It's alive," or at least until everyone has left for the day.

Let's keep in mind that the debtor denies ownership of property to convince you to take the settlement because the debtor lacks big assets that are vulnerable to enforcement. You can see attributes of them, such as checks for property taxes or insurance or maintenance, or loan payments to a bank. I can't see the property in the name of the debt, but I see attributes of ownership and infer that property exists and therefore reject the small-dollar settlement.

Do you advise the client to take the offer or reject the offer and hold out for a lot more? You can do the math.

This story tells it all. For the price of this ABA book, you can save yourself an eternal heartache, and maybe a lawsuit from the client, and may even make very good money if charged with the duty to recover these fraudulently conveyed properties.

By the way, you don't need the credit report to dig up the deeds of trust (or mortgages). These instruments are recorded documents and are readily accessible. March forward through this book to discover other ways to locate that secured credit instrument, which might be accompanied by a candid credit application executed by the debtor as a part of the credit due diligence.

Section 2

The Foundations

Chapter 1

The Basics of Law and Business—Civil Law, Practice, and Procedure

All cookbooks teach the foundations. What is the temperature of the oven? How do you dice and slice onions? How do you make couscous without turning it into mush? How do you blanche asparagus? How to slice an expensive cut of meat? What wine should be served with lamb, salmon, or pasta?

Learning the ropes of unearthing assets that are secreted in bank accounts that are cloaked by newly minted entities requires a course in the foundations. Some of this information is new, some is old, some is tried, but all is true. Take a seat, grab the coffee, and highlight what you want in yellow marker. We are going to offer various techniques, lessons of law and business, the rules of the legal and business road, the lingo of the experts, the rudiments of enforcement, and the deep, dark secrets of hiding money. I will show you the money, Tom.

We are going to expand your lexicon. You are going to talk the talk, do the walk, and ask questions that show that you know your "stuff." Do you know why most folks decline to ask questions when they should? Answer: They don't want to look stupid. This section of the book is going to provide you with a basic education of business, real estate, and law. After your read this section, you will know when to ask the question. Better yet, you can phrase the question that will generate a meaningful answer, and you will not look like a total dunderhead.

Consider this information the tools in your Craftsman® tool chest. This chapter will provide you with the language of law and business that enables you to recognize an arrow or "X" on the map. Let's put a name to the face.

We are going to march through the rudiments of law and business. Many of you are lawyers, paralegals, legal secretaries, and businesspeople experienced in the law; however, we will get reacquainted with these basic principles through the prism of collection and enforcement and discover what is important and what is a waste of time. Don't get mad if the basics here are too basic, but they are a good starting point.

Genesis starts with "In the beginning, God created the heaven and the earth," and we start with "In the beginning, someone is going to sue." Whatever the injury—broken contract, auto accident, slip and fail, or other claim—the aggrieved party will hire a lawyer who files a lawsuit. The lawyer will serve the lawsuit. The defendant has about 30 days to respond. If the defendant does not respond, the lawyer will move the court for a default judgment that spells out compensation due the plaintiff. A judgment is a piece of paper. Although most defendants settle the lawsuit when served, or pay judgment when entered, some defendants refuse to pay the judgment. A civil judgment is not an order directed to the defendant to pay money, but a declaration that the judgment creditor is owed the money.

Judgments are not self-executing. Bad news: a judgment will not spring off its hind legs and bite the debtor, no matter how much you'd wish that. The big judgment might be pretty, but absent money, beauty is skin deep. All those zeros dazzle.

Enforcement requires that do you do something. Do everything. This is lesson number #1, and this book is lesson #2. This means that a judgment creditor necessarily must enforce the judgment, which means that the judgment debtor can ignore the judgment until pushed. Call the recalcitrance of the debtor the middle-finger treatment. Some debtors will pay the judgment because a judgment will damage their credit and might bar them from a job that requires a good financial history or even a government job that requires a background check or security clearance. Every so often, the FBI calls us to inquire whether a judgment was paid and to learn the circumstances of the case.

Enforcement means that the judgment creditor can legally, and involuntarily, separate the defendant from property that the sheriff can sell and remit the proceeds of the sale to the plaintiff. Enforcement means that the judgment creditor can garnish wages, bank accounts, or receivables. Enforcement means that the judgment creditor can record or file liens that will encumber the defendant's property, which if sold, might produce payment. Enforcement also means that the defendant, or third parties, are compelled to disclose assets and the identity of person, such as a bank, who holds the assets. This process can take months, years, or decades. Some states allow an aggrieved party to attach the assets of a defendant before judgment; this legal process is called an attachment.

When faced with a lawsuit, some defendants will hire a lawyer who usually will respond with an answer to the lawsuit. Sometimes the lawyer might ask the court to change venue (where the lawsuit was filed) to a new venue that is more convenient or advantageous to the defendant. Typically, the answer denies the allegations of the complaint and sets up affirmative defenses, such as the statute of limitations. Sooner than later (and depending upon the states), plaintiff and defendant will go to trial. The judge or jury will decide the case. Despite *Law and Order,* trials offer parties the opportunity to tell their stories to the trier of fact (a judge or jury). The trier of fact can believe or disbelieve the witnesses, interpret ambiguous documents in a contorted manner, or just feel sorry, or truly hate, one of the parties. Juries do have evil eyes. Here is the standard trial pabulum: Juries vote for the party they like most. Here is a better slice of realty: Juries vote for the side that they hate the least.

Trials are tests of legal skills, professional presentations to the jury, and just plain old luck. Details are a big deal. Urban legend suggests that lawyers should drive Camrys and not Porsches to court, wear Timex watches and not Rolexes, and always shine their shoes. Dump the tasseled loafers and try the mahogany-hued wingtips. Postmodern claims of discrimination, workplace harassment, credit and bank policies, and apartment rental, all based upon race, color, creed, national origin, or sexual orientation, launch thousands of lawsuits. Companies with all white, *male* managers invite lawsuits, Mr. Wal-Mart. That is true. However, jurors view litigants and their lawyers commensurately through this same prism, whether good, bad, or horrific.

The aggrieved litigant can appeal; this action might lead to a reversal (unlikely if a jury verdict), but would certainly accrue expenses and fees. If the defendant loses, and appeals, but does not post a bond, the plaintiff is free to execute on the judgment. The fact of an unbounded judgment is worrisome to the plaintiff because the fact that the defendant could not post the bond means that the defendant might lack the financial ability to pay the judgment. Appeal bonds are collateralized, which means that the defendant must deposit cash, stocks, or other collateral equal to the face of the bond. An appeal bond is one-and-a-half times the face amount of the judgment. If the judgment is in the amount of $1,000,000, the bond amount is $1,500,000, and hence the collateral demanded by the bonding company. Large companies can post a bond without collateral based on their net worth. Bonding companies charge a premium anywhere between 0.5 percent and 5 percent, depending upon the defendant and his or her financial net worth. If the paintiff won at the trial court, and the defendant posts a bond, you are the creditor, and you should not have bought this book.

If the claim is an auto accident, slip and fall, or industrial accident, the defendant probably has insurance that pays off the plaintiff. These cases tend to settle, but not always, as insurance companies find that an aggressive defense to marginal claims sends the message that the plaintiff is going to huff and puff till blue in the face before seeing any money, if any. Big-time injuries, class actions, employment discrimination, wrongful deaths, commercial contracts and leases, toxic torts, Ponzi schemes, and financial frauds cycle through this civil process, including megatrials, which might produce multimillion-dollar judgments.

These big cases are not cheap. Lawyers (or parties) can invest hundreds of thousands in costs and charges, in addition to fees if the lawyer is working by the hour. In antitrust cases, lawyers can readily invest many millions. If a million-dollars is required to finance the lawsuit and collection or settlement is not guaranteed, counsel (or the financier) might hesitate before filing suit, no matter how righteous the injury, the gargantuan size of the judgment, or even the notoriety through the media. Nobody wants to work for free, or worse, go into the hole. At least Marie Antoinette's subjects ate cake. No matter how the plaintiff got there, if the plaintiff wins the case, but the defendant declines payment, the parties change their name and status. The plaintiff becomes the judgment creditor, and the defendant becomes the judgment debtor.

Let our games begin.

Chapter 2

The Basic Terms of Real Estate, Bankruptcy, Accounting, and Law

The law of enforcement sits tall in the saddle of business, Duke. You cannot be a financial detective without knowing the terms of art, the language of business and real estate, and basic investigative techniques. Knowledge of law and business enables you to spot the arrows and "Xs" on the treasure map. Chicken Delight can only rescue you if you have your foot on the gas and fried chicken as your wingman. Let's embrace the fact that enforcement enables the judgment creditor to reach the assets of the debtor. Successfully wresting the asset out of the hands (or claws) of the debtor requires a legacy knowledge of personal and real property principles, the rudiments of business and law. If you want to grab patent royalties, understanding how a patent works amps up your chances of grabbing the patent, or at least frightening the living daylights of the debtor by the fact that you might succeed. If the debtor believes that you can snare the patents that are the core of the business, the debtor might affix the pen to the instruments of surrender, which is called a check.

Other challenges confront you. So your debtor owns a valuable trademark? What is the difference between a patent and trademark? What if your debtor owns a home? Ejecting Mother Hubbard from her shoe is expensive and cumbersome. Figuring out whether the shoe is above or below water might save you time, money, and effort. This is knowledge that should enter your business wheelhouse, no greater or lesser than the law of enforcement. If you are going to threaten putting Ms. Hubbard on the street, at least learn the business and legal principles to get it right. Unrelated to this problem is the definition of a well-done steak: When steak is served to you, and you flip over the meat and see the brand name: Florsheim.

Now if you really want to frighten the bejesus out of your debtor, crank up the machinery to grab the domain name and trademark. This is delicious. This takes a little knowledge of anticyber-squatting. If you can grab the trademark and succeed in acquiring it, you might need to engage in the same business as the debtor so that you can grab the domain name because the domain name squats on your newly acquired trademark. Do you want to put the fear of God in the heart of the debtor? Launch a campaign to seize the trademark, domain name, and patents. Think Berlin in May 1945 if you succeed. Let's start with the basic terms, buzzwords, key concepts, and the lingo. At least we will sound good.

Chapter 3

Real Estate Buzzwords

I am going to spend a fair amount of time talking about real estate because real estate is the reservoir of wealth for most Americans. Absent states such as Florida and Texas, homes are subject to liens and levies. Nonresidential homes are subject to enforcement. Despite your debtor playing tiddlywinks with the title to forestall enforcement, real estate remains a target of any enforcement. Call real estate the "fat cow" of enforcement.

If you want to part the debtor from his or her assets, these next sections explain real estate ownership and finance. You have to know the language of real estate if you are going to seize property from the debtor. Real estate finance offers lots of clues that lead to hidden assets. Before you can unwind the debtor's fingers from the title to the $5,000,000 home, you first need to understand the language of finance and real estate first.

Let's start with the basics. Monthly mortgage payments are called debt service, which means the principal and interest payment necessary to keep the loan current over the life of the loan. Low- or no-money down financing compels the borrower to pay amounts equal to property taxes and insurance to the lender. This is called an impound, which means that the monthly payments include the debt service, taxes, and insurance.

A person who gets the loan qualifies as a borrower up to a certain amount and is subject to a down payment of unencumbered money, such as savings. To qualify for the loan, the borrower must have sufficient income to pay the debt service on a monthly basis. The person approving the loan is sometimes called the underwriter. Contrary to pop culture, loans are scored on a computerized basis. In seeking a loan, the borrower has a right of rescission, which is the three-day period between signing the loan papers and the closing of the deal. On the West Coast, title companies offer title insurance, and nearly all deals go through a professional escrow holder. On the East Coast, lawyers do title work and act as escrow holders. As we all know in 2013, *underwater* means that the loan balance exceeds the value of the home.

Chapter 4

Deeds of Trust and Mortgages, Title Insurance, and the County Recorder

Let's talk about consensual liens on real property. A deed of trust means that the lender holds the debtor's title as collateral through a third party (the trustee) to insure that the borrower pays the lender. Upon default in the loan, the trustee can foreclose by having the trustee sell the property after the notice of default and upon the notice of sale. The deed of trust is recorded with the county recorder and reveals the names of the debtor, the trustee, and the beneficiary who is also the lender. Most deeds of trust show the loan balance and the maturity date of the loan. A foreclosure under a deed of trust does not require supervision by a court.

A mortgage is a loan where the lender has a lien on the property to secure the debt. In the event of a default, the lender must file a lawsuit, and if the paperwork is perfect, the judge will order the property sold to pay the secured lender. Mortgage lawsuits require proof of default via affidavits, hence, as we all know the word: "robosigners." Security follows the debt. A deed of trust, or mortgage, untethered (or detached) from a live note, debt instrument, or other obligation, is illusory. Whether a deed of trust or a mortgage, these instruments secure a live debt.

Where do you get this information about deeds of trust or mortgages? Parties to a real estate transaction record deeds, mortgages, easements, and other instruments with the county recorder who maintains a public and permanent record called the county record. With the exception of Los Angeles County, nearly all California and other states county recorders are online and offer line-item information that identifies the parties to the recorded documents, the date of recording, and the serial number. Some recorders provide actual copies of the recorded documents, or detailed summaries. Most title companies offer customer service departments that will produce copies of the recorded documents by PDF or fax and charge a nominal amount or sometimes nothing at all. Other commercial services offer recorded documents for a reasonable price. Of course, you can buy copies at the offices of the county recorder.

You can also purchase a litigation guaranty that is nearly identical to a title report. Remember that litigation guaranties and title reports are contracts of insurance. If you are intending to move against the property, and the title is paramount, you can purchase insurance against recorded but undisclosed documents. If, on the other hand, you are surveying the territory to obtain a preliminary read on the state of title, you can purchase a litigation guaranty for $500 to $1,000 with $10,000 worth of insurance. If you rely on the litigation guaranty and the title company missed a recorded document, the maximum recovery for this error is $10,000.

Why is this information important to know? In considering whether to pursue a debtor, you might cull through the county recorder and discover a flurry of recorded mortgages, some older in time, and some more recent. Some deeds of trust identify banks, hard money lenders, or commercial credit grantors as the beneficiary. With the help of customer service offered by the local title company, you can pull down these deeds of trust, add up the total amount, and conclude that the debtor is underwater and walk from the case.

The fact that the debtor is genuinely underwater or worse, that the legitimate lenders are commencing a foreclosure (note recorded notices of default or notices of sale) is key information in valuing the case, taking a settlement, or deciding to pursue the matter any further. Chances are that a debtor who can't keep a roof over his or her head probably cannot pay the civil judgment. This assessment depends on many other factors. You might also spot recorded abstracts of judgment, tax liens, and even *lis pendens* that alert you that another person has an interest in the property. Underwater means that the total due on the secured loans exceeds the value of the property. I did make one error in the real estate market. I could have sold California real estate brokers, bankers, and lawyers tons of scuba gear, snorkels, fins, and wetsuits. Why, you might ask? Answer: Because the entire Central Valley was underwater (as of 2009).

Chapter 5

Real Estate Titles and Why They Are Important

If you are planning to enforce the judgment against the real property, securing a "good" and "marketable title" after the enforcement of judgment is paramount. *Good title* means that the owner has title or ownership according to the recorded documents. The most common title is fee simple, which means that the person is the owner of 100 percent of the legal and beneficial interest in the property. A person with a life estate is entitled to the ownership, and beneficial use, during his or her life. Life estates are estate planning devices that vest title in a surviving spouse who is usually spouse #2, and upon that person's death, the property goes to the children of the original owner. *Marketable title* means that the title insurer is willing to write a policy of title insurance to a person who is going to buy the property. What is marketable title? Answer: The property is free of defects, blemish, clouds, or irregularities and enables the title company to write a policy for the buyer.

What is the standard blemish? Let's say that about 100 years ago, a railroad company held an easement (a right way of the real property course in law school) that crosses your backyard. The railroad company is now long bankrupt, but that easement still sits on title. Another common scenario is that you are buying the property from the seller whose family held title over many generations. Blemishes are common in generational transfers because the family members reject a third-party sale or commercial refinance. Some 50 years ago, "Uncle Harry," a fractional owner of the property with his brother Joe, another fractional owner, died without a will and no probate followed. Years later, Harry's wife, Aunt Louise, died likewise without a will, and no probate. Joe and his wife Mary die without a will and no probate. Facing these remote but unresolved fractional interests in the property, the title company for the prospective buyer might suffer heartburn and decline to issue a policy of title insurance. Purchasing the property with exceptions on the title policy would be a disaster because, in turn, the buyer would not have been able to sell the property. A refinance of the property would be impossible because no financier, such as a bank, would accept blemished title as security.

Enforcing a judgment and acquiring title through a sheriff's or receiver's sale reposes the title in the name of the judgment creditor as the probable buyer at the sale or a third-party buyer who is a bidder at the sale. Whether the judgment creditor or a third-party buyer, the title in their name must be good and marketable; otherwise, no bona fide downstream buyer, or financier, would buy or lend against the property as collateral for a loan or refinance given flawed title. The title report at the outset would tell you what blemishes, clouds, or defects burden the title. If you find that the property is buried under a dozen blemishes of any type, you should reconsider your strategy and spool up a plan to clean up the title. Be alert to common names because some title companies will list as a potential lien holder any creditor, including the IRS, that has a lien claim against everybody with a same name.

Title reports are very informative and require attention to detail. You might also spot a few insider deeds of trust in favor of family members, offshore trusts, recently formed (or out-of-state or offshore) corporations, or limited liabilities companies. What a mess, you'd think. Shearing away this cavalcade of liens is going to accrue big expense and fees, and worse, the insiders (really) of the debtor are going to battle out the liens and claim that the debtor borrowed "family money" to finance living expenses. Every lien is a new claim, and multiple liens are multiple claims. As you will see later, you might win these battles, but at some ridiculous cost. Liars are guaranteed their day in court.

Before going further down the rabbit hole of real estate law and practice, I am going to pass along what I was told in law school by a very sharp lawyer. He said that when you do a real estate loan secured by the real property, the last document in the file is the posttransaction title report. What is a posttransaction title report? Answer: After the deed of trust (mortgage) has been recorded, run another title report to insure that the recorder's records reflect the recording and the contractual position. If the deal calls for a first position, the postrecording title report would show that first position. This title report showing the recording is the "last document" and the title report is "dated down." Dating down means that the title report shows all transaction up to the present date, as opposed to a date one, two, or even three weeks earlier. A title report that is effective, say, three weeks ago means that you have not the slightest clue what the debtor did in the last 21 days. What could the debtor do? You shall see.

Chapter 6

Phony Baloney Mortgages, Liens, and Lies

The starting (and ending point) of the quest to strip these false and fraudulent liens from title to the property is always the basic maximum: Security follows the debt. If the creditor cannot prove up a debt, the security evaporates. In any court battle with the insiders, the fact of an "insider," "family," or other collusive transaction compels the court to apply a strict and precise standard of evidence to prove up the existence of the debt. This standard does not quite shift the burden of proof to the alleged secured creditor, but the secured creditor must prove the existence of the debt, with more than "Sure, the debtor gave me security for my loan." These battles border on beauty contests, Oscar®-winning performances on the witness stand, and credible excuses as to why the secured party lacks any scratch of paper to prove the debt. These phony deeds will collapse in the face of a determined onslaught, but you will incur a significant expense. The fact of the phony deeds becomes part of the information mix in valuing the case, that the debtor perceived that the property has value that the debtor seeks to protect by these liens, and that the debtor is throwing up roadblocks to deter enforcement. This is information that aids your valuing the case, a settlement, the fees and charges that the client might have to pay, and the length of time (and misery factor) in collecting the judgment.

How do you get rid of these phony liens? When you pull the Uniform Residential Loan Application (URLA), credit report, tax returns (if possible), accountant's working papers (more likely), and, most importantly, bank statements, you will find out. For example, what do the bank statements tell you? A lot. If the claim is that the debtor borrowed money from the creditor, you would find at least two banking transactions. The first transaction is the check written from the account of the lender. The account might be a bank account, stock account, or account with a mutual fund, credit union, or other institution. Whatever the institution, we start with an account statement and paper or electronic check, better known as a wire transfer, or Automated Clearing House (ACH).

On the other side of the equation is the fact that the debtor received these funds and deposited the funds in a bank, stock, credit union, or other account. The debtor spends these funds by writing checks on the loan proceedings. This is more paper. The total sum of paper at the minimum would be the statements of the borrower (your debtor) and the lender (the family member), the check written by the lenders, and the checks written by the debtor disbursing the funds. This transaction would involve four or more pieces of paper. Chances are that the debtor will claim that the lender did not write a check, but handed over cash. For what purpose? Why would the lender warehouse huge amounts of cash? Is the lender hiding cash from the government to avoid payment of taxes? If the lender earned the money and paid taxes, the lender would readily hand over the money and, without any guile or hesitation, park the money in a bank account. If the lender handed the cash over to the debtor, why would the debtor hide the cash? Worse, the debtor could never deposit the cash because of money-laundering requirements. A transaction built on cash that lacks the slightest paper trail would never pass the smell test, particularly if the cash loan is six figures, and the deed of trust securing the loan is recorded ahead of the judgment.

Security follows the debt is part of this treasure map. Debtors load themselves up with liens to look unattractive or to claim that their assets are immune. The liens mean nothing without the debt and imbue this little homily with legal punch. Review a title report of the debtor's property, which shows multiple liens in favor of banks, commercial lenders, and family members. It looks bad, and the debtor apparently has no equity. Now compare the title report to a sworn financial statement (the URLA—see later discussion), and you might find that the debts represented by those liens are paid, paid down, or don't exist at all because they are not listed. "Security follows the debt" is just another arrow on the treasure map pointing you to the treasure.

Chapter 7

Amortization Tables

Old Math Is Good

I love amortization tables. There, I said it. When I was a budding real estate agent, my father taught me real estate. In buying commercial property, which generates rents that pay for the debt service, the initial trick is to determine monthly payments for debt service because the rent income is fairly fixed. Yes, new prospective owners tend to jack up the rents, but generally, the business model (maybe) is that current owner is charging the tenants the maximum rents.

Let's take a spin. If the sale price for a building is $100,000 and the standard down is 20 percent, a financial institution would finance the balance. Interest rates and the terms of the loan would be fixed, and we would figure out the monthly debt in the amortization book. These books had columns of numbers for the amount of the loan, the term, and the rate of interest. All predigital, all manual, and accurate to the penny. These tables, now digital, spell out the monthly payments. Title companies handed these little green books in which the papers were tissue thin. Mine is buried in the back of the desk drawer and probably next to my slide rule and pocket protector.

What does amortization mean to you, and why are amortization tables important to you? Amortization means the gradual pay down of a debt that bears interest that is usually fixed. Title companies, lenders, and third-party websites offer online amortization tables that are more flexible than the paper versions and are accurate to the penny.

Let's go through an example. Start with a $1,000,000 loan. We know this amount from the face of the deed of trust (or mortgage) because the recorded documents state that the deed of trust secures performance under the promissory note in the amount of $1,000,000 and other advances. Many deeds of trust reveal that the note provides for a 10-, 15-, or 30-year payout. If the lender is a nationally recognized bank, such as Bank of America, Wells Fargo, Chase, or Citibank, we can intuit by the date on the loan what the prevailing interest was.

Let's presume that the date of the loan is January 2, 2005, and that the focal point in time is January 2, 2012 (seven years). The amortization table shows that the monthly payments are in the sum of $5,368.22 and that the balance as of January 2, 2012, is $879,450.15. From Zillow.com, we can calculate probable value as of January 2, 2012, which is $1,200,000; therefore, you would ascertain an equity spread of $320,549.85. That's not bad for the postdigital Dick Tracey, the financial geek.

The recorder does not show a notice of default, or notice of sale, which is evidence of a loan default. Presume that the debtor is current on the loan. Mind you that many lenders hold thousands (or more) of default loans in their portfolio and decline to proceed with a foreclosure. Why? Foreclosure proceedings reduce the value of the property and hinder the homeowner's ability to sell or refinance the property. For nearly all, the fact of a long-standing default sufficiently motivates the homeowner to sell the property to realize some equity, or at least cycle through a short sale. However, the fact of a recorded notice of default or sale, or the absence of their recordings, deflates, if recorded, and inflates, if not recorded, the value of property. Let's mention credit reports. Assuming a traditional lender, the credit report would reveal the existence of the loan and would also indicate whether the loan was current or in default. We are going to presume that the loan is current and bears interest at five percent, which was the prevailing rate at the time of the loan. This information is ready online as business and government sites track the historic movement of interest rates. The credit report buttresses the probable balance due, the status of the loan (current or in default), and inferentially the amount due under the loan (if current).

An amortization table is another arrow on the treasure map that lays out the balance of the loans secured by the property and therefore the equity available for enforcement. The table also spells out the monthly payments. If the debtor claims total poverty but the amortization tables show monthly payments of $10,000 and the loan is current per the credit report, something is deathly wrong. Who is making these payments? The tooth fairy, the fairy godmother, or Don Corleone? The amortization table hands you the arrow on the map that spells out the debtor's stated income at least at the time of the loan and probable throughout the loan.

Before running to the next section, I have a tooth fairy story. Like all dutiful parents, I wanted to ensure that my daughter enjoyed the complete "kid experience." Disneyland, Great America, and Universal City were not missed. I got to love Happy Meals and the itty bitty toys. But what about little nuances like the tooth fairy? I thought to myself, "What can I do to ramp up that kid's experience? What? The drill is to leave a quarter under the pillow. Okay, that's a little chintzy today, but so what? Nope. I was going to challenge the tooth fairy. One tooth falls out, and I left the following: "Dear Gabriella, your tooth fell out. I ran out of coins. This is my IOU note. Signed, Mr. Tooth Fairy." Next time: "Do you take a check?" Nope. I tried this: "Do you take Visa, Master Card, or American Express? How about Discover card?" Don't cringe.

The kid went to summer camp and never wrote home. Out of desperation and to ensure that the wood fairies wouldn't kidnap the kid, I gave her prestamped, self-addressed postcards. She was 8 years old at the time. She only had to check the boxes—"Having a Good Time: yes or no," "Camp is Fun: yes or no," "Food is Good: yes or no," and "I am Alive"—and deposit them in the camp mail slot. Not one card got to me. I wonder why. It must have been something about a grudge.

Chapter 8

Residential Lending Standards and the Foreclosure Process

Let's learn about the basic standards in making real estate loans. The starting point is that a lender, usually a bank, must look first to the real property as the source of payment. In the event of a default, the bank will commence a nonjudicial foreclosure process (or if a mortgage, a judicial process). This means that the bank will record and serve the debtor with a notice of default that informs the debtor of the arrearage and gives the debtor 90 days to bring the loan current. Absent bringing the loan current, the bank will record and serve a notice of default that gives the debtor 21 days to pay off the loan; otherwise, the bank, through a trustee's sale, will sell the property on the courthouse steps. Absent the insane real estate frenzy from the 1990s to about 2006, most foreclosed properties rarely sell for cash equal to the bank's loan, and most times, the bank will bid on the loan as the purchase price at the foreclosure sale. The property is now called "bank owned," or Real Estate Owned (REO). Post 2012 values have skyrocketed. You might see some surplus sales.

After the 2000 real estate meltdown, the banks meticulously harvested their portfolio of defaulted loans in an effort to slow down the tidal wave of foreclosed properties on the market, lest the market prices of REOs would plummet. Here is where loan-to-value ratios become important. As a matter of recently discovered prudence, the bank would lend only 75 percent (or maybe 80 percent) of the appraised value to the borrower. What does this mean? If the borrower is buying the home, the presumption is that the sales price represents the fair market value. Cautious banks demand an appraisal from an independent appraiser to determine the "appraised value," which typically is near the sale price. If the appraiser value is $1,000,000, and the loan-to-value ratio is 75 percent/100 percent, the face of the loan is $750,000. The bank requires that the borrower put down unrestricted money of $250,000 and demands a sworn statement (and proof) that the down payment is not borrowed, and in fact belongs to the borrower. The reason for the down payment is that the borrower is more likely to continue to make payments to the bank when the borrower has a financial stake in the property.

Why is this information important to you? Answer: Assuming a traditional lender and postmeltdown, the loan amount represents 75 percent of the appraised value; therefore, with the help of eighth-grade algebra, the purchase price is $1 million. These numbers are confirmed by transfer taxes imposed by the city or county based on the sale price, which should match, dollar for dollar, the reconstruction of the sales price through the loan. The payments under this loan are about $5,368.22 (absent property taxes, insurance, and maintenance). The standard banking rule of thumb is that loan payments should equal about 25 percent of the borrower's gross monthly income or 33 percent of the net. This rule of thumb greatly fluctuates, given the real estate market at the time (1999 to 2006), whether the borrower has a track record with the bank, the amount of the down payment, whether the borrower has other sources of income aside from wages, whether the borrower has a high net worth, and the relationship of the borrower to the bank.

Let's try bigger numbers, and see what you get. The face of the deed of trust or mortgage shows the loan amount and maturity date. For example, the deed of trust discloses a loan of $1,200,000 and the due date (15- or 30-year term). At the time of the loan, the bank had well-known rates, such as 4.5 percent and the monthly payment would have been about $6,080. Given current banking practices, here the probable loan-to-value ratio is about 80 percent/100 percent. Maybe. This means the loan is 80 percent of the appraised value, and the bank appraised the house at $1,500,000. Add annual property taxes (at 1.22 percent) of $18,300. Nice homes need nice insurance costing about $5,000.00 annually. Add the following: $6,080 plus $1,941.66 for taxes and insurance, the total "nut" for the home is $8,021.66. Add another $200 to $600 a month for Homeowner's Association (HOA) fees or maintenance. To qualify for the loan, the borrower must have earnings of about $20,000 to $30,000 a month (all earners), depending upon the bank, the terms, whether the initial loan or refinance, the points, and the rate of interest. The annual income could range between $240,000 to $360,000, depending upon the bank.

Lending standards, along with the amortization tables, craft an analysis of the debtor's income and expenses. Also, postmeltdown real estate lender standards fix the value of the property and, as such, are arrows that suggest whether property is subject to enforcement.

Chapter 9

Appraisals and Transfer Taxes

Let's learn the rudiments of real estate appraisal. In appraising a home (a single-family residence), the usual method is comparables. Properties are appraised given their physical proximity to the "target," the closeness in date to the fixed date for the appraisal (now or a prior date), the condition of the house, the positive and negative amenities, the swings (up and down) of the market, the square footage, the deferred maintenance, the special tax issues (e.g., bond or sewer assessments), the school district, and the proximity to fire and police stations, parks, libraries, shopping centers, public transportation, and views, among other factors. The Internet has revolutionized appraisals through comparables. For example, type in 123 Oaks Road, Anytown, California 90000. In a nanosecond, you will find that that the neighbor property went for $600,000 (and get a picture to boot), that the property across the street went for $650,000, and that the property three doors down went for $585,000. What is the value of the subject house? Answer: Confirm that the subject house is comparable in number of bedrooms, number of bathrooms, lot size, and square footage; then average the comparables to discover the value of the property. Prudence dictates that if you have multiple nearby sales, you should ignore the highest and lowest and average the median prices.

If the property is income property, the appraisal is partially an income approach, but is recalibrated for the location. The four-unit apartment building located north of Wilshire in Beverly Hills which breaks even (i.e., no positive cash flow) is appraised at much greater price than the eight units in Modesto (Stanislaus county), even with a $5,000 monthly income. The standard is the use of a "multiplier of the gross". The Beverly Hills four-unit property has a greater multiplier than the property located in Modesto. Investors would readily pay two to three times more for the fourplex in Beverly Hills than Turlock, given the stability of the market, the prospect of appreciation, and the quality.

Appraisals for agricultural property are a hybrid of the comparable and the income approaches. For example, that the property is income producing, that the crops are subject to market and seasonable variables and other unknown factors, that the changing market tastes might increase the value of the crop (pomegranates, almonds, and Cuties are popular), and that farming costs (water, pesticides, fertilizer, etc.) are the variables. The key drivers of value are the water, the condition of the current crops, and the soil.

The other method is the cost approach. With the aid of an experienced contractor (or builder), the appraisal would value the property based on the cost of reconstruction. This method is common for fire, flood, earthquake, or other insured disasters in which the insured is entitled to rebuild.

Banks lend at the lower end of appraised value, postmeltdown, and the appraised value clearly indicates equity. The appraisal is another arrow on the treasure map.

Most states permit the county or city to impose a 1 percent (or more) transfer tax when property is sold. Counties or cities impose this tax upon the sale of real estate. This tax is on the "new value" paid by the buyer. In California, the average county tax is about 1.1 percent, which translates into $1.10 per $1,000 of new value and potentially a higher city tax. What is the transfer tax for $5,000,000 sale in California? Los Angeles: $28,000; San Jose: $22,000; Santa Monica: $20,500; San Francisco: $37,000. The transfer tax calculus provides for the sales price, which is highly accurate. Given that the face of the deed of trust shows the amount of the bank loan (assuming that the purchases price was in part financed) and that the probable loan-to-value ratio is 75 percent/25 percent, you can readily calculate the purchase price, figure out the amount of the down payment, and reconstruct the monthly debt service and probably monthly income of the debtor. Transfer taxes are based on the sale price of the home and are, therefore, a near-airtight indicator of the purchase price paid by the debtor to acquire the home. If the debtor is the seller of the home, the transfer informs you of the sale price and profit from the sale. Transfer taxes are another "X" on the treasure map to identify equity (if the debtor is a buyer), or profit (if the debtor is the seller).

Chapter 10

Stated Income Loans

Let's talk about stated income loans. The new buzzword for the real estate meltdown is a stated income loan, which means that the borrower can state income, assets, or personal history with little or no verification. Stated income loans created false statements of income and qualified individuals for loans beyond their financial ability. Many borrowers promptly defaulted, all which snowballed into the real estate meltdown. Today's real estate loan packages have long left the ebullient days of 2003 when national banks slurped up "stated income loans," and lent at 125 percent of value. Banks readily lent on stated income application in which each borrower boasted incomes exceeding six plus figures. Who knew that mariachi players bagged $250,000 a year?

Postmeltdown, loan underwriting compels detailed disclosures for all outstanding debts, verification of assets and income, ownership, copies of driver's licenses, and attestations of the purpose of the loan. You are not who you are, but what you tell your creditors or taxing authorities.

Why is this important to you as a creditor? It is important because as a creditor you are attempting to determine whether high-end enforcement is worthwhile and what you might collect. Loan packages reveal what the debtor has (or claims to have) and add more information, real or imagined, into the mix.

With knowledge of real estate, and particularly true value, you need to know the fair market value in determining whether you can sell the property, whether the debtor has a viable homestead right that might bar, or deflect, any enforcement, or whether you can bluff your way through the process. This is part and parcel of the information cocktail.

Chapter 11

The URLA Is the Treasure Map

I promised you a treasure map. Here it is. A treasure map reveals where the treasure is buried. Predigital, the treasure maps came in waterlogged parchment varieties, and where, as always, "X" marked the spot. These maps were always folded. Very cool. Even though we live in a postdigital age, the techniques used to hunt for treasure maps are still the same. Today's treasure map is the Uniform Residential Loan Application (URLA), which is a form of financial statement mandated by the Freddie Mac and Fannie Mae or its equivalent.

Most debtors refinance their real estate to cash out of the property or lower the rate of interest. The lender compels the debtor to complete a URLA. The URLA is more than just a five-page preprinted form; it incorporates the entire loan package, such as the attachments, lists, and verifications for bank accounts, stock, bonds, wages, and self-employment. The URLA demands that loan applicants list their assets and liabilities as follows:

> This Statement and any applicable supporting schedules may be completed jointly by both married and unmarried Co-Borrower if their assets and liabilities are sufficiently joined so that the Statement can be meaningfully and fairly presented on a combined basis; otherwise, separate Statements and Schedules are required. If the Co-Borrower section was completed about a non-applicant spouse or other person, this Statement and supporting Schedules must be completed about that spouse or other person also.

The debtors sign the URLA as a sworn statement under federal law, which means that the person who signs and tenders a fraudulent URLA is guilty of multiple federal crimes. ("I/We fully understand that it is a Federal crime punishable by fine or imprisonment, or both, to knowingly make any false statements concerning any of the above facts as applicable under the provisions of Title 18, United States Code, and Section 1001, et seq.") For the true devotees of *NCIS*, Title 18 is the federal code that spells out federal crimes. Federal sentencing compels persons to serve their entire sentence. Ouch! Better yet, the URLA opens the door to rigorous cross-examination and an explanation of what happened, or who has the assets listed on the URLA, and might even prompt the hapless debtor to ponder his or her rights under the Fifth Amendment.

Incidentally, URLAs and their vast baggage train of bank statements, tax returns, and supporting documentation find their way into divorce, partnership dissolutions, bankruptcy, insolvency, enforcement proceedings initiated by a creditor, tax, probate, and other proceedings. These proceedings compel parties to locate assets and confirm financial representations made to the courts, parties, lawyers, insurance companies, and judges. If you are the person advising a creditor whether to accept a compromise based on the debtor's financial condition, the URLA would shape your advice, or the client's informed decision, to accept a "pennies on the dollar" settlement or to kick off the campaign to dismantle the hastily constructed asset protection. The URLA tells all.

The URLA also reflects the debtor's liabilities. You pull a title report that is dated down. You double-check the grantor/grantee index to catch any last-minute transfers, mortgages or deeds of trusts, judgment or tax liens, or anything else dreadful. That's a good start. The title reports a first deed of trust (or mortgage) to Bank of America, which reflects the date that the loan was taken out, which is slightly before the date of the recording of the recording. Using the amortization tables, you can guess the loan balance down to the dime. Using appraisal standards, you can guess the value buttressed by Zillow. Using transfer taxes, you can approximate the purchase price paid by the debtor to acquire the property. You can buttress the estimate of the purchase price through the transfer tax by reconstructing the value based on the 75 percent loan-to-value ratio employed by most banks. Now, you spot deeds of trust in favor of family members, LLCs, offshore trusts, or corporations in which the debtor is a principal. These are all large amounts of money, even numbers, and recorded one after the other. The total of this secured debt exceeds the equity in the house, which you correctly estimated. How do you know that the junior liens are all fraudulent? You have a divining rod (yeah, that's right—the rod that leads you to water), which is the URLA. The URLA compels the borrower to list all assets and all liabilities. The debtor is obligated to list all loans in Section VI. Moreover, the URLA commands the debtor to list the secured debts, such as these insider loans secured by the junior lien in Section VI "Schedule of Real Estate Owned." If the debtor claims to make payments, check out Section V "Monthly Income and Combined Housing Expenses" under "Other Financing." If the debtor proceeds with a refinance that takes out the prior home loan and substitutes a new loan, typically to take money out of the property or to reduce the interest rate, the debtor would reveal the loans and corollary junior liens. The usual excuse for the debtor is that the loans due the insiders are "paid," or "contingent," in explaining away their omission in the URLA, but these secured insider loans eat, breathe, and poop when revealed during enforcement as a way to encumber real property and render the valuable equity immune from any enforcement brought a judgment creditor.

The first cousin to the URLA is the credit application issued by debtor in any capacity who seeks commercial credit. Nearly commercial credit grantors (manufacturing, wholesale, distribution, leasing, or any financing transactions) demand a credit application that incorporates an abbreviated financial statement. Larger-dollar transactions compel the disclosure of business and personal financial statements, tax returns, stock, and/or bank statements. These credit applications and accompanying financials disclose the ownership of the business and typically the financial condition of principals. Lessors, whether a true lease or finance lease, factors, finance companies, hard money lenders, purchasers of credit card drafts, or anybody else extending credit, a line of credit, or other financial accommodation demand extensive disclosures.

Laying a subpoena on every financier, creditor, lender, leasing company, supplier, landlord, or anybody else holding a financing statement (Uniform Commercial Code or UCC) would produce detailed financials that reveal an entire array of assets and ownership of other assets. These credit grantors are easy to find because they are listed on the debtor's website as "partners" or on the debtor's website as "featured products." Run a UCC search to verify. Sometimes, for a small fee, you can reach these vendors in a commercial credit report if available.

In its reigning glory, the URLA boasted entrenched assets and virtually no big debt, denied any lawsuits or judgments, failed to reveal a potential separate property claim, and described the borrowers as married, all for the purpose of convincing the lender of their vast community property estate, financial stability, and big net worth. This grand representation enable the borrowers to score the home loan at a very competitive rate of interest.

When faced with a deepening financial crisis, the debtor will tell you that he or she owes money to family members. The typical claim is that the family members lent money for the business and that the loans were in cash or that the files were lost, destroyed in a fire (but no fire report or insurance claim is on file), or washed away in a flash flood (in Irvine, California, no less). As we will explain later, in the midst of enforcement, the debtor will produce a quitclaim deed, deed of trust, grant deed, or mortgage and claim that the deed is the collateral for the family loan, even though the deed was never recorded. If the URLA does not list the insider loans under the liability section or lien section attached to the list of real property "owned," you can conclude that the relatives never lent the money to the debtor and that the debtor manufactured the newly minted deed. You can conclude that the newly found liens on the property, post-URLA, to secure the phantom debt are also fraudulent if these liens secure loans that should have been disclosed on the URLA. Remember that security follows the debt and that if there is no debt, there is no security. Once the alleged inside debts collapse, so do the liens. The URLA is your guide.

A credit report rides shotgun with the URLA, Chris. Insiders do not report their loans to the credit-reporting agencies, so the fact that the insider loans do not appear on the credit reports means nothing. However, the credit report reveals other commercial and consumer lenders, and particularly car loans, car leasing, unsecured personal loans, commercial loans, lenders holding guaranteed obligations, and even judgments and lawsuits. These lenders, revealed by the credit report, or county recorder or secretary of state, if a recorded lien or recorded UCC, might possess additional financial disclosures, including other URLAs, sworn financial statements, tax returns, and commercial loan applications. These financials would reveal the existence or, more likely, the nonexistence of these insider loans. Given that security follows the debt, the report of this debt, if secured, immediately announces the existence of an asset, whether as security for the debt or as an expenditure on behalf of the asset.

Chapter 12

Community Property

Let's briefly visit community property, which is the law in nine states and varies significantly from state to state. In California, community property is subject to the enforcement of a debt incurred by either spouse, even if the spouse is not the debtor. By the way, we all learned about community property when Eddie Murphy described the first words spoken by his new African bride as "HALF!"

A discussion of community property is important because community property law, depending upon the particular state, renders property of the community vulnerable to an event though only one spouse is civilly liable on the debt. A characterization of property in the Uniform Residential Loan Application (URLA), financial statements, or loan applications enables, or disables, a creditor from enforcing the judgment against community property. In applying for a loan, few applicants represent property as "jointly held," which is a fancy buzzword that the property jointly held by the couple is separate property. Generally, the creditor cannot reach the separate half of the nondebtor spouse. Only the separate interest of the debtor spouse is subject to enforcement, which renders the property judgment proof. Why? If the property is subject to a homestead, the court might not order the sale, unless the sale price equals payment of the liens encumbering the separate half and the homestead. This is very unlikely because the buyer is only acquiring half the property. Second, few buyers would ever buy a partial interest in a home because the buyer would face a near-impossible task of commercial resale. Facing enforcement, nearly every couple will swear up and down on 50 bibles that they hold property in joint tenancy and, therefore, separate property. You can litigate this claim from here to eternity and might even win, but you will face the unified chorus of the husband and wife who will recite from the same playbook of title ownership.

Classifying property as community, or jointly held (i.e., separate), can open, or foreclose, the gates of any enforcement. The URLA and most other loan applications compel a disclosure of the property as being community or separate. Getting these documents in hand is now a very big deal.

Let's go to court. This is what you can expect. Facing enforcement of a large-dollar judgment, the husband and wife will claim in court that they are legally separated, aside from disputing that the property is community. When parties legally separate, the assets acquired postseparation or the appreciation postseparation is now separate property and not community property, assuming a community interest in the first place. You can also expect that the debtor and spouse will claim that they separated before debt accrued. Better yet, the parties could have filed an action for legal separation. In cases from the Planet Vega, Mr. and Mrs. E. T. now claim, and can even prove, that they got divorced, and have always been divorced, and that all assets are separate, and not community. In other cases, the parties will manufacture a premartial agreement that characterizes the assets as separate and not community. Of course, the URLA, or any other loan paperwork, never discloses this premarital agreement or, for that matter, any agreement that property is held as separate for any reason. The reason is that the lender will downgrade the borrower if the property is held as separate, given an immediate downgrade by 50 percent of the asset base. Wages are community. If the parties advise the lender that everything is held as separate and not community, the lender will base the loan on the loan applicant's income and not the combined income. To enhance the loan, the nonapplicant spouse will cosign the loan or conceal (possibly because it never existed) the premarital agreement.

Chapter 13

Asset Protection Makes Its Debut

Asset protection means hiding assets from creditors. "Presto gizmo! Now you see it, and now you don't." You didn't like that? Sorry, but this homily says it all.

Asset protection makes assets in the name of the debtor disappear. After reading this chapter, you will have to thank me. Really. I am going to save everyone big bucks here. First, skip the asset protection books available for sale on Amazon.com. Why? They all peddle identical transformative schemes that coerce the creditors to abandon the judgment because they don't want to spend big money to chase down the debtor's assets. These schemes are exceedingly pernicious. These schemes, mostly written by lawyers no less, say to the plaintiff: You got ripped off by some hoodlum. Too bad he robbed you. Too bad he murdered your son or father. Too bad he molested five children in broad daylight. Too bad he made one thousand lewd and lascivious phone calls that would inflict the maximum amount of damage. Too bad he pushed some woman to the ground and kicked out her eye. She saw the tip of the shoe coming. We shall talk more about this story. Don't go anywhere.

Skip the $5,000 seminar because speakers peddle limited liability companies, offshore trusts, captive insurance companies, transfer schemes, unbundling schemes, and fraudulent liens. Asset protection is transformative of title but not of beneficial access to the property. Typically, asset protection transforms an asset from the estate of the debtor, and accessible enforcement, to the estate of a surrogate and inaccessible to the enforcement, but it still reposes in beneficial access to the debtor. "Aaron [the debtor] heard Malis [purveyor of asset protection] state at the asset protection seminar that he could 'own nothing but control everything' and he adopted this mantra as his own." In Re Hymas, U.S. Trustee v. Hymas, 2010 WL 39320142, p. *12 (USBC, D. Idaho, 2010). This is the mantra of asset protection, which is to transform title but not control and benefit.

Let's explore some examples to give you a flavor of what you can expect. Our debtor's name is John Smith. Form JohnSmithLLC. Have JohnSmithLLC open a bank account at Wells Fargo Bank. Withdraw funds on deposit with Bank of America in the debtor's own name, John Smith, and deposit the funds in the name of JohnSmithLLC in which John

Smith is the sole signatory. Would a garnishment seeking the accounts of John Smith, an individual, reach these funds? Answer: Probably not, because the names on the accounts are different. Would the bank produce records of the JohnSmithLLC account if the subpoena sought the records of John Smith? Probably not. If the question at the debtor's examination was "Do you have a bank account?" and the answer is "No," that answer might be accurate. Asset protection transforms title, but not beneficial interest.

Let's start with doctors who face huge risks in the practice of medicine. Despite the movies, television shows, and popular myths, most doctors truly fear legal liability. Doctors shade into the right wing, bear strong signs of paranoia when coming into proximity with lawyers (any lawyer), and practice medicine very defensively as they should. Some patients are nutcases, or very vindictive and mean-spirited individuals, and blame their doctors for just about everything and anything. "You promised me that I would look like a young Elizabeth Taylor, and not the late Roger Ebert. The Bride of Chucky looks better." (Honest to God, you have to Google Roger Ebert, which is particularly painful if you cycled through the PBS series At the Movies with the late Gene Siskel.)

Asset protection appeals to a doctor in a high-risk practice, or for that matter, any professional engaged in any high-risk business, and who is, therefore, vulnerable to lawsuits. These professions are major consumers of asset protection. Let's start with the standard sales pitch that offers assets protection:

> Our #1 goal is to deter and prevent lawsuits. Our powerful system acts as a legal fortress around your vulnerable assets. This prevents predator lawyers from taking cases they would not have otherwise considered. With our program in place, it is simply not worth the time, effort and resources for anyone to pursue a case against you. We are highly effective in denying unwanted access to your valuable assets without removing beneficial ownership and distributive rights to those assets. In cases where you are already involved in a lawsuit, we can offer a strategy that might help you minimize the effects of a poor outcome.

What is a poor outcome? It means that the doctor lost and lost big. An extreme example of a "poor outcome" is Andy Warhol, who was admitted to a New York hospital for gallbladder surgery and exited dead. "What happened to Mr. Warhol?" asks the lawyer for the Warhol estate. Asset protection enables doctors to protect their assets and render them immune from enforcement, who would face fewer (or no) lawsuits because the plaintiff can never collect. Neither the plaintiff, nor the lawyer most likely, would want to sue and never collect. In the face of asset protection, malpractice litigation would be futile, and any investment is costly and time is wasted.

This ad got it right. Lawsuits cost big bucks. Medical malpractice cases chew up $200,000 in a heartbeat. Other cases are not cheap. Asbestos litigation can accrue $50,000 to $150,000 of costs per case. Class action lawsuits chew up millions in costs alone. Major business litigation requires seven-figure investments. Why invest millions in expenses and time when you can't collect?

Asset protection usually retitles the asset in an LLC, a partnership, a corporation, or even a family member, which is controlled by the debtor, who retains access and beneficial ownership. This is the theme of all asset protection. Put the asset in the name, or shell, of another entity, but retain financial control and access to the asset. That's it. We are done. You don't need to buy the $50 book, which I did and I regretted that purchase to no end. Worse, the book was a total eye-glaze.

You can spend $50,000 with some lawyer offering his "asset protection packages." I know people who laid out that type of money. I did have a nice lunch with the guy who made the investment. Thank God he picked up the tab.

Why does asset protection work and immunize the debtor from the rigors of enforcement? Answer: Enforcement to reach the assets costs big bucks. Somebody has to finance the enforcement and spend the time, money, effort, and energy to unwind the asset protection schemes. Asset protection means that the debtor will do anything to make the creditor accrue an expense, effort, or risk in reaching an asset of the debtor. This is called the misery factor. Asset protection does not make the assets bulletproof, judge- or lawyer-proof, but it does make the asset very expensive to reach.

Let's take a brief tour of asset protection. Cashing receivable checks payable to the debtor from its customers or depositing the checks from the customers in nondebtor bank accounts stymie the creditor reaching the debtor's accounts because the money is parked in someone's bank account. Better yet, another stunt is contacting the customers of the debtor who would offer a big discount to pay early before the creditor levies these accounts through a writ of execution. "I will be down in ten minutes to pick up the check." Asset protection is cashing account receivable checks at the customer's bank.

How about assets protection on the cheap? Closing out the local bank account and reopening an account across the street, across town, in another city or state, or in another country is classic asset protection. Opening up a bank account in the maiden name of the wife, or newly formed LLC where the wife using her maiden or ethnic name is listed the managing member and dumping the money in that account. Adding spouses, children, or others to real property titles is an act of asset protection. Transferring a business from the debtor to a family partnership is an act of asset protection as is filing a marital separation action to convert community property into separate property. What about storing inventory in a storage locker? Or, let's try changing the corporate name of the business to another like corporate name, or cycling out a corporate name for a limited liability company of the same name. Emptying out the bank account and burying the money in the backyard is asset protection. Well, the money is in the garbage bags, Carmella.

How do I know? I know. When we levy on the last known account, inevitably the answer is the following: "Account closed." When the judgment comes down, the first advice that the debtor receives is to "CLOSE OUT THE ACCOUNTS," before the creditor levies the accounts to death. Days, hours, and minutes count because the debtor is busy running around closing out bank accounts and opening up new bank accounts.

You need three ingredients for the asset protection brew: A very angry, well-financed and motivated creditor; a very angry, somewhat financed and motivated debtor; and something worth some money that the debtor wants to hide and protect. Asset protection means putting a new title on an asset, but permitting the debtor to have beneficial access to the asset.

We are going to visit the leading case, and case that you should memorize is *In Re Bernard,* 96 F. 3rd 1279, 1283 (9th Cir. 1996). This case held that converting an account with a financial institution into cash is a transfer under fraudulent conveyance law. This quote is worth the ink: "Instead of owning money sitting in their accounts, the Bernards owned claims against their bank. When they withdrew from their accounts, they exchanged debt for money (which, more than incidentally, was more difficult for the Sheaffers to acquire). Thus, when the Bernards made their withdrawals they parted with property, satisfying the Code's definition of transfer." Cashing out an account is a transfer under fraudulent conveyance laws. This case is worth reading, and you can find it online.

Let's briefly review the gallery of the of fraudulent transfer cases from bankruptcy courts:

1. *In Re Wilbur,* 211 B.R. 98, 104 (USBC, M.D. Fla., 1997). After hearing of an adverse judgment, and prior to bankruptcy, the debtor withdrew $49,000 from his accounts and purchased $20,000 worth of traveler's checks, which he cashed five months after their purchase. The cashing of the checks is a fraudulent conveyance.
2. *In Re High Strength Steel Inc.,* 269 B.R. 560 (USBC, D. De., 2001). The corporate debtor's records reflect a $9,000,000 accounts receivable due from a related party. The debtor "reconciles the books," which eliminates the $9 million receivable from the books. The purging of the $9 million receivable from the books is a transfer under fraudulent conveyance law.
3. *In Re Pullman,* 279 B.R. 916 (USBC, M.D. Ga., 2002), *In Re Schafer*, 294 B.R. 126, 128 (USDC, ND, CA, 2003). In the face of an attachment upon a bank account, the debtor opened an account at a new bank to warehouse the company funds.
4. *In Re Marra*, 308 B.R. 628, 629 (USDC, D. Conn., 2004). In the midst of execution on a bank account, the debtor created a new LLC, established an account at the same bank that held his personal accounts, and deposited funds into the LLC's account and used the account to pay business and personal expenses. The establishment of the bank account in the name of the LLC, for the benefit of the debtor, and insulate from enforcement against the debtor is a fraudulent conveyance.
5. *In Re Perpinan,* 2007 W.L. 2345019 (BAP, 9th Cir., 2007). In the face of litigation,

and subsequent divorce, the debtor sold the family residence, received a check from the title company for $109,279.45, which he converted into cashier's checks and money orders. The debtor did not deposit these items in an account. The act of converting the title company check into the cashier's checks and money orders is a fraudulent conveyance.

6. *In Re Ryan,* 2009 W.L. 2822452 at *1 (USBC, ND, CA, 2009). In the face of an eviction and rent action, the debtor withdrew $41,000 from three bank accounts at Westamerica Bank and three days later deposited the funds into a new account at Bank of the West. The act of emptying one bank account and opening a new bank account across town is a fraudulent conveyance. This particular case is a big deal because all lawyers tell their clients who are facing active enforcement to close out their bank accounts and establish new accounts out of town, out of county, out of state, or out of the country.
7. *Hines v. Marchetti,* 436 B.R. 159, 162–163 (USDC, M.D. Alabama, 2010). In the face of arbitration claims that amounted to $667,000.00 and the bankruptcy, the debtor transfer the assets of his wholly owned medical corporation to a newly formed LLC that bears nearly the same name. He dissolved his medical corporation within days of the bankruptcy. The transfer of the assets from the medical corporation to the medical LLC is a fraudulent conveyance.
8. *In Re Haag*, 2012 WL 446535 (P. *2) (BAP, 9th Cir., 2012). Facing a large judgment, the debtor withdrew $120,000 in cash from a bank account at Bank of Tucson, and placed the money in a joint safe deposit box at Wachovia Bank. Some of the funds were deposited into the bank account of the debtor's spouse to pay family and business expenses. The transfer of the money from the bank account to cash in another bank and deposit into the wife's checking account is a fraudulent conveyance.
9. *In Re Caimano*, 2013 WL 2016406 (P. *8) (USBC, D. South Carolina, 2013). In the face of a restraining order, the debtor transferred money out his accounts and sold securities in other accounts. The liquidation of the account and sale of securities are fraudulent transfers.
10. *In Re Nascarella,* 492 B.R. 914, 915–916 (USBC, M.D. Fla., 2013). About six months before and during a major lawsuit, the debtor transferred $117,580.22 from his personal checking account to his wife's checking account. This is a fraudulent conveyance.

Playing pinball with money is a fraudulent conveyance. Mind you, these cases arise from the Bankruptcy Code § 727(a)(2)(A), which takes away the debtor's discharge if the debtor commits a fraudulent conveyance within one year before the bankruptcy filing.

The core of these cases is that the court found a transfer under fraudulent conveyance law because the debtor sought to transform the title, character, or physical form of the assets. In nearly all cases, the debtor still had access to the money, or it was even still in his or her possession, but the debtor changed the character or title, which made execution or attachment upon the property far more difficult, or even impossible. Converting sale proceeds from the sale of a house into cashier's checks and money orders nearly makes the money vanish in thin air. Playing a shell game with the bank accounts makes enforcement impossible because the creditor, absent a levy on every bank, will never find the money in the new bank account. Extracting the money from one entity and dumping it into another is near-perfect protection unless the creditor can latch onto the new entity and convince the judge or sheriff to reach the money in the new entity, of course, without tipping off the debtor. Call asset protection financial sleight of hand.

Chapter 14

Legal Asset Protection

Exemptions, Immunities, and Legitimate Strategies

Every state, and even federal law, declares certain assets that are exempt and immune from any enforcement. Certain states limit enforcement completely. These rules are important. If the debtor legitimately possesses only exempt assets, the debtor is a turnip. You can huff and puff, but you will never blow the exemption house down. Collect your wits and go home. Let's let this hombre ride off into the sunset. Now that does not mean that you give up, but you grip the reality that you are tilting at windmills, Mr. Quixote. Do remember to renew the judgment because the fate, time, and fortune might restore your debtor to financial health, or at least to a step above a subsistence existence.

Assets come in three flavors: exempt means that the creditor cannot reach the asset such as a home in Florida, a pension and most retirement accounts, and Social Security or disability payments. Partially exempt means that the exemption is for a dollar amount (e.g., the first $100,000 of equity in a home) or a dollar limit (e.g., $7,500 for tools of the trade). Nonexempt means that the property is subject to enforcement. The typical assets are stocks and bank accounts, business assets, and interest in an estate, patent, copyright, and other intellectual property (unless classed a tool of the trade). Corporations, limited liability companies, trusts (if the debtor), and partnership are not entitled to exemptions.

Some debtors bungle their exemption through hypercreative asset protection stunts. Woe befalls the clever debtor who fraudulently conveys the home to a trust, loses the property to the creditor who topples the conveyances, and likewise forfeits any complete or dollar-amount exemption. Worse, the creditor and credit bid (buy) the home at the sheriff's sale, and eject the debtor and family from the home.

Some states forbid wage levies with very limited exceptions (Pennsylvania and three other states). Like Florida, Texas renders a residence immune from enforcement. Other states render community property immune from enforcement unless both husband and wife are the judgment debtors (Arizona). The Employee Retirement Income Security Act (a federal pension law) makes all pensions immune from any enforcement.

Legal exemptions and immunities are blotches on the treasure map. Certain assets are off limits.

Chapter 15

Leaving Town Is Another Form of Asset Protection

As a respite, welcome to pop culture, which percolates in this book: What song personifies hiding asset and getting out of Dodge? Answer: "Cause I'm leavin' on a jet plane. . . Don't know when I'll be back again." Getting out of Dodge is a good strategy.

Is this for real? Yes, here we go. Go where? No self-respecting author would fail to tell everyone that the best asset protection is getting out of town. That's right. Pull up stakes and skedaddle. Leave, go away, and don't come back. But go where? Liquidate everything. Answer? (I know that you know the answer.) Try Florida or Texas, and preferably Florida. Absent limited circumstances, homes in Florida are judgment-proof. If the debtor has millions of nonexempt dollars at hand, the debtor can buy the million-dollar home in Florida free of creditor's claims and enforcement. Plough every dime into the home. Ask O. J. or any number of other scoundrels, including some of the refugees from Enron. He moved to Florida, which is the nation's haven for crooks and scoundrels.

Now folks, you can't rob a bank and bury the money in the house. Nice try, but that money comes back. The court is going to quash any manufactured homestead rights.

Leaving the state is smart, Albert. Why? Most states offer the creditor the power to hale the debtor into the courtroom to examine the debtor regarding assets and liabilities. These examinations can take days and days. The lawyer can motor through a detailed list of assets, financial statements, and the debtor's tax returns. At the end of the hearing, the creditor can seek from the judge an order compelling the debtor to surrender to the sheriff money, titles, or other property that the sheriff can matriculate or sell. Issued by the court at the time of the debtor's examination and with the judgment debtor present, these turnover orders enable the creditor to reach property in the debtor's possession or control, property that the debtor has placed in the hands of a surrogate, or most importantly, property, such as money, that is parked in offshore accounts. Given that the debtor has actual notice of the order, and, moreover, a "return date" to confirm compliance with the order, the court can hold the debtor in contempt in the event of noncompliance. Contempt has two components: punitive contempt, which is usually five days in the county jail, or coercive contempt, which is incarceration until the debtor complies. The debtor faces a big chunk of lawyer's fees.

While the creditor might be able to seek a turnover by filing papers before the court and serving the defendant; however, if and when the court hands down a turnover order, the creditor is going to face a tough time in enforcement if the debtor is out of state and dodges the process servers or local constable who would serve the order, or order to show cause re: contempt. Even if the debtor is held in contempt, the court would issue a bench warrant for the debtor's arrest. Bail might range from $1,000 to the face amount of the judgment. The sheriff is going to have a very difficult time in arresting a debtor who moved out of state and an impossible time if he or she moved offshore.

Getting the debtor in front of the judge is the key to coercive power of the court to recover secret, hidden, and difficult-to-reach assets, which are primarily out-of-state or off-shore bank accounts. In getting out of town, the debtor deflects the coercive power of the court. Of course, you can docket the judgment in the state where the judgment took up residence. Unfortunately you will face another set of attorney's fees due local counsel. Also the debtor gets the advantage of new state's exemption laws.

Chapter 16

Why Does the Debtor Pay and Why Does the Creditor Give Up?

Let me introduce to you to the Efficient Market Hypothesis. The Efficient Market Hypothesis states that the price of a good or service is based upon the total sum of all knowledge, whether real or imagined. Price has no relationship to intrinsic value, utilitarian purpose, or whether the objects (goods) are real or counterfeit. However, the fact that the object has intrinsic value bears some utilitarian purpose (some purpose) or is genuine and not a counterfeit is just information.

Let me prove my point. About five years ago, a rumor that Steve Jobs was dead (he died last year and he was in bad health for years) was circulating. The rumor caused Apple stock to drop by 20 points in a flash, and the price was restored when the Apple rebuked the rumor. However, did Apple deserve to forfeit about $60 billion of net worth in 10 seconds? Answer: Absolutely. The rumor is part of the market mix information, real or imagined, and necessarily reset the stock price at a 20 percent discount in a flash. How about women's undergarments? Victoria's Secret sells racy undergarments at $60 a pop. Let's say that Lady Gaga wore the underwear on stage, and better yet, sweated through them, what would be the price? Is there a difference between undergarments sitting on the shelf in a Victoria's Secret store, or lying on Lady Gaga's dressing room floor? Let's try $10,000 or more, as Lady Gaga's cone brassieres went for $60,000. The undergarments are the same, but the information (real or very imagined) is different.

The Efficient Market Hypothesis imbues the undergarments with enormous value because the buyer believes that Lady Gaga wore them; they bear a unique quality and, as such, are more valuable to the buyer. By the way, the fact that the Lady Gaga undergarment might be a fake is just more information that would affect value. During the Clinton years and just after the bruising impeachment battle, an auction house sold President Kennedy's side chest of drawers for about $30,000 (or more). President Clinton quipped that, for that money, he'd sell his furniture. President Clinton was deep in debt due to the legal battles including his impeachment trial, criminal investigation, Whitewater debacle, and more. The Efficient Market Hypothesis inflates President's Kennedy's furniture and deflates President Clinton's furniture to a lower number. Is there any innate difference between the two physical objects of furniture? Not really.

Let's take a stroll through the marketplace. Along skid row, you will see row upon row of pawn shops whose windows are lined with guitars. If the prior owner was another homeless person, the value is near zero, but if the prior owner was John Lennon, the value is astronomical. Is the guitar any different? No, because the belief (or rumor based on fabricated evidence that John Lennon owned the guitar) would inflate the price of the guitar. Even the rumor that John Lennon owned the guitar would bump up its value well in excess of six figures.

Conversely, value based on quality or usefulness adds to the price of the object or service if the market perceives that quality or usefulness would attract a higher price. Driven by information, whether real or imagined, Adam Smith's invisible hand of the marketplace is the foundation of the Efficient Market Hypothesis. Consumers are driven to pay greater or lesser sums of money to buy goods or service based on the information available in the marketplace itself, real or imagined. Movie marketing is the paradigm, and the king (or queen) is James Bond. Heineken paid some $45 million (maybe inflated) for the privilege of James Bond (Daniel Craig) quaffing a beer, as opposed to a dry martini, shaken and not stirred. What did this $45 million buy? Answer: Aside from about $1 billion worth of advertising, Heineken infused its beer with the mystic that James Bond drinks this beer. The Efficient Market Hypothesis sets the price of art including fine and modern art. The claim of "fake," can destroy a $50 million investment in some art, such as a Jackson Pollock, Van Gogh or Andy Warhol work. Whether or not the painting is a fake is not the issue, but what is important is that somebody is spreading the claim "fake."

The Tea Party, and its standard bearers, such as Michelle Bachman, Richard Santorum, Rick Perry, and Donald Trump injected into the 2012 presidential election an entire raft of absurd claims about President Obama. These claims ranged from the accusations that the president was born in Malaysia, that his birth certificate was forged, that the President spent $200,000,000 [no typo, folks] a day on an overseas trip, that the President opened the borders to terrorists, that the President is a secret Muslim, and that the President is leading the country into socialism. Congresswoman Bachman, have I missed anything? Please tell me.

Are any of these rumors vaguely true, Congresswoman? Of course not, and perish the thought. But many millions of American believed that these rumors were true and paid for the "goods" when they voted for Mitt Romney. Every time that Michelle Bachman ascends the digital lectern, courtesy of Fox News, and lambastes President Obama as a socialist or terrorist, her followers contribute to her political war chest. Money is the milk that runs through the veins of American politics. These contributions, based on lies, half-truths, and fantasy, prove that the total sum of all knowledge, real or imagined, sets the price of the good or service. If Ms. Bachman generates $2,000,000 in campaign contributions because she convinces the fringe right that President Obama is an Egyptian radical, the political currency is worth $2,000,000 because she can use these funds to finance the other political and issue campaign. Many decent Americans voted against Obama because they truly believed that Obama was a Muslim, opened the borders to terrorists, was born in Indonesia, and, post-Newtown, will confiscate everyone's guns.

This book will show you that an aggressive, noisy, and rambunctious campaign to collect a judgment, including near-irrational conduct, wild threats or boasts, or tactics unknown to the legal community injects information into the calculus that faces the debtor whether to pay the judgment, offer a decent settlement, flee, or file bankruptcy. This campaign might stampede the debtor into payment. Making the debtor believe that you will stop at nothing, and I mean nothing on God's green earth, in enforcing the judgment is the total sum of all knowledge and might compel the debtor to pay the judgment. Learn to spell "Messianic" without the benefit of spell-checker. Learn from Ms. Bachman. I don't know whether she believes that she is telling the American people the truth. This does not matter. What matters is that the American people listen to her and believe sufficiently in the truth of what she is saying to contribute money to Ms. Bachman's political war chest, say, in the $20,000,000 range. If truth is money and money is truth, Michele Bachman places first. The sole difference between Ms. Bachman and judgment enforcement is that the debtor, instead of financing the far-right agenda, pays a judgment. There is the same outcome, the same strategy, and the same rationale.

The thesis of this book is simple: Every step taken by you or the debtor is another layer of information, real or imagined, which is imparted to both debtor and creditor who necessarily ponder what the outcome might be. If your step includes finding and exploiting clues leading up the discovery and seizure of the key assets, the debtor is going to recognize the risk that the creditor is going to lift the veil of asset protection and get paid.

Enforcement is more than taking property away from the judgment debtor. A successful enforcement lies in the accumulation of all knowledge, whether real or imagined, of the debtor's assets and true liabilities, and the debtor's belief, rational or irrational, that you can or will reach those assets. The successful defense against enforcement is the mirror image of successful enforcement. The debtor accumulated sufficient information, whether factual or lies, real or imagined, that deters the creditor from prosecuting enforcement. The deterrence might constitute the horrendous expenses and fees confronting the creditor in seeking to topple an asset-protection scheme; the distaste in dealing with an unpleasant, hostile, or violent debtor (or lawyer); or the risk that years of enforcement and big-time expense might be wasted or barely effectual. The debtor's decision to pay and the creditor's decision to abandon the suit is based on their perception of risk and reward, which is based on the information known to them, whether real or imagined. In this business, bluffing, lies, obstruction, threats, and counterthreats count. Marching through the land of arrows and "Xs" tells the debtor that you are on the hunt and may well find the treasure.

The Efficient Market Hypothesis leads you to these basic questions: Will the debtor ever pay? If not, why not? What amount of money will the debtor pay to the creditor? How much money will the creditor invest in this process? What is the claim or judgment really worth?

Let me put this perspective. If the debtor believes that you have all the money, energy, and initiative in the world to drive the debtor into the ground, and will stop at absolutely nothing, save and except committing a crime, the debtor might scrounge up the resources and pay you. We call this an instrument of surrender analogous to the surrender of the Japanese Imperial Empire on the deck of the *USS Missouri,* September 2, 1945. Intimating in a phone call to the debtor's lawyer that you can grab the debtor's cargo off the high seas would motivate just about anyone to surrender. I know this works. Marching down the field with a motion to seize the debtor's trademark, patents, and domain name would put the fear of God in anyone.

If on the other hand, the creditor believes that the debtor has all the time in the world, some money, and a burning hatred toward the creditor or lawyer and will stop at nothing, including committing lots of crimes, the creditor is going to walk from the case, given the surreal investment, hopeless quest, and personal risk. Whether or not these beliefs are well founded or irrational is not the point. The point is that parties engage in a duel to the death based, sometimes, on their beliefs. Here is where propaganda really works. Many a smart debtor hires a lawyer to write a letter that says the creditors will never collect, the money is hidden in a far-off land, and the judgment is uncollectable. The lawyer offers pennies on the dollar and intimates that the few dollars available for settlement might well evaporate. "Take what you can, before the money disappears." Expect these letters.

When will the debtor surrender? When will the creditor quit? The answer might be found in law and practice guides and, upon the advice of counsel, accountants and financial experts. The Efficient Market Hypothesis better answers these questions: The debtor will pay, or the creditor will abandon the quest to collect (or continue endlessly) based upon the information known to the parties, even though the information is real, imagined, or some combination thereof. Of course, it helps to have that treasure map at hand.

Chapter 17

Don't Be a Dunce or a Victim

Be Sane, Be Smart, Be Conservative, Be Prepared, and Be Insured

Not all losses are inevitable. This is important to know, because debts and judgments originate from base human conduct and misconduct committed by base individuals. If you are tasked with the engagement of chasing down a hoodlum, cretin, or crook, let's keep in mind that the loss arose to both sides of the equation and hence to this section.

Insurance is the number one safeguard against a disaster. There are policies for malpractice, general comprehensive liability (premises and persons), worker's compensation, auto insurance if you have a true company car, a crime policy and the umbrella policies. Where can money be saved (or lost)? Malpractice is now competitive and the savings rise (or fall) on the deductible and the limits, or whether the policy is burning limits, or first dollar. The primary driver of cost is the deductible and policy limits (assuming that the insured does not bring to the table a litany of horrors). Accept a $50,000 deductible and you will pay less than you would for a $10,000 deductible, but don't cry when the bills climb to $50,000.00. Commercial General Liability (CGL) policies are also competitive and with some flexibility on deductible, scope of coverage, and exclusions or endorsements. Worker's compensation is now highly competitive, and a safe workplace environment is certainly paramount. A well-lit workplace, with well-placed furniture and injury-free workstations and offices, will save an enormous sum of money. Injuries will bump up the rates.

The best policy is the crime policy. This will cost you about $2,000 to $5,000 and protect you against employee theft and embezzlement, third-party theft and loss, and an entire anagram of horrors. Every year I get calls from a business owner who was destroyed when the bookkeeper embezzled millions. These losses routinely exceed $1,000,000 and, given the destruction of the records by the bookkeeper, are difficult to tally. Not all is lost here. The bookkeeper will routinely destroy records and render reconstruction very expensive. The destruction is to destroy the evidence and conceal the scope of discovery. The victim can approximate the loss based on the decreased cash flow, missing cash at hand, or better yet, the gain of the debtor. If money is gone and records are destroyed, but the debtor, a bookkeeper, making $70,000 a year, pulls into the company parking lot with a $100,000 fully paid Mercedes Benz coupe, you now can measure loss. By the way, don't forget that the embezzler's coworkers were probably enablers, conspirators, and aiders and abettors. Getting rid of the lot might clear the department of the conspirators, but it might spawn a pot of employment claims.

Common sense, maturity, and good sense of personal security are the line of defense. Events are not serendipitous in this business save and except the "Acts of God." Fred Goldman did not wake up one morning with the expectation that by nightfall his son would exit this life as the victim of O. J. Simpson's rage. Parents in Newtown will never come to grips with the reality of their losses. Absent turning kindergarten schools into armed camps, nothing could have saved those children.

If, however, you look at the train of events, they will make sense to you. Let's take one case. The defendant, or better stated, the defendant's president, is a groper. This is not a type of fish, which is a grouper, but an employer who has a hard time understanding that the laws of the domicile state and the laws of the United States prevent him from sexually harassing or molesting his employees. These people are called "gropers." Employees are to be seen and not touched. The consequences of this maltreatment is a lawsuit, and in fact, a big, messy, expensive, and ugly lawsuit that puts before the jury a female employee who gets on the witness stand and describes in graphic detail what amounts to be a sexual assault. "He put his hands on my buttocks. Many times and I couldn't stop him. He hurt me. I started to cry and locked myself in the bathroom. I lost sleep. I couldn't care for my children. I was driven crazy with fear." What can the employer say? Answer: Not much. If the employee is to be believed, and depending upon the jury pool, six-figure judgments are routine, and seven figure awards are no big deal. After Rena Weeks's in the *Baker McKenzie* case, in which she scored a million-dollar judgment, upheld on appeal, every employer wised up to the fact that employees are no longer fair game, and Monday through Friday is not open season. Common sense tells you that all gender, race, wage and hour, discrimination, sexual harassment, or misconduct claims are readily avoidable. Stated more simply: Adults warped in a middle-school mind get sued.

Chapter 18

Liar, Liar, Pants on Fire

You Cannot Sue a Liar for the Lies in Court

"In war, truth is the first casualty," said Aeschylus. Sorry, Dorothy, the Wizard of Oz is a big, fat liar. Here is the mindset of the debtor facing enforcement of a large judgment in which the creditor has just crossed the Rubicon: Promise the lawyer for the creditor anything, something, some lie or half-truth to stop the process. Tell the lawyer any lie to get the lawyer to release the bank account. "I will sign anything, say anything, promise anything, and swear to anything, to unwind this horror." "I will sell my first, second and third born. No problem." "I will sign any contract, agreement, or note." "I will get up on the witness stand and promise the judge anything. I don't care."

Embrace, and expect, the tsunami of lies to wash over everyone in a campaign to dissolve writs and levies. So, Dorothy, you just found out the Wizard of Oz took off and left you on the tarmac? Oz looks nice, but a life with the Munchkins might be unsettling. EHarmony.com with the stature challenged?

Disappointed and little frustrated to say the least? Can you sue for lies? Can you sue the debtor's lawyer? If you gave up your liens and levies, or stopped enforcement, the asset evaporated, are you history? The answer to that question depends on which court. If you are in state court (California to make this easy) and want to sue for fraud, given the fat lie, the change of position, and damages, you are officially and legally out of luck. Your lawsuit against the debtor's lawyer, or debtor, goes down the pot. Goodbye Mr. Fraud Lawsuit. Why? The law says that the communications during a judicial proceeding are immune from civil liability (a lawsuit). As long as the statement has something or anything to do with the case, even if the statement is a lie, falsehood, or perjury, you cannot sue for damages.

Let's visit *Portman v. George McDonald Law Corporation* (1979) 99 Cal. App. 3rd 988. Great facts: The defense counsel told plaintiff's counsel that the defendant was "financially sound as a dollar," which convinced plaintiff to forgo a bond. This decision was an ugly mistake. The defendant, an insurance company, tanked and left the plaintiff with an empty judgment. The plaintiff sued the defense counsel for negligent misrepresentation which died on the vine. The court dumped the case because the statements by the defense counsel, good, bad, or odious, were privileged under Civil Code § 47(b)(2), which means in plain English that whatever is said in court is immune from civil liability. Here is the body of law: Absent the most extreme, the lies in court just sit there. If you are the target of lies in court, suck it up.

Here is a better case. *Kachig v. Boothe* (1971) 22 Cal. App. 3d 626. Forged documents or perjured testimony are introduced in a civil trial that caused defendant to lose. Defendant uncovered the lies and sought revenge in a lawsuit against the lawyer and plaintiff based on the fraud. Without breaking any judicial sweat, the court again shows a litigant the courthouse door by holding that perjured testimony and forged documents are privileged.

In English: Lawyers lie.

Who do you think is our best president post-World War II? Truman, Eisenhower, Kennedy, Johnson, Nixon, Ford, Carter, Reagan, Bush (either one), Clinton (pre- or post-Monica), or Obama? Which one? My vote is Ronald Reagan. Why? Here is the reason: Trust but verify. You cannot sue for the lies, fraud, or any altered documents. You are stuck with the damage caused by these lies. It's too bad and very sad. If you are a party, and make a deal on these lies based on the advice of your lawyer, you might be able to sue your lawyer for negligence. If you are the lawyer, remind your client that whatever the debtor tells you is inherently unreliable and just a pack of lies.

Are you wandering in the desert of lies? Maybe not. If your debtor tumbles into bankruptcy, you might be able to bar his discharge and make this person liable for your debt forever, if you can prove fraud. Bankruptcy Code § 523(a)(2) says that debt based on fraud is nondischargeable and would survive the discharge. You might win that lawsuit, but collecting that claim postbankruptcy will be a bear. Your debtor just filed bankruptcy, and the sole source of payment is the postbankruptcy earnings. Good luck.

Chapter 19

The 50¢ Primer on Alter Ego Liability

What is alter ego? This is the legal proposition that the court can lift the veil of a phony-baloney corporation who is the party to the loss and pin the loss on the corporation principals. This is a tedious subject, but lawyer blogs and online articles kick this topic to death.

Here is the standard set of facts. The creditor sues a corporation who might or might not defend and wins at the end. The lawyer cycles through the debtor's examination and discovers that the corporation is a shell where assets leaked out, books and records are gone or cooked, and corporate formalities evaporated or that the corporate is a shell with nothing more. This is an awful result because the creditors already spent a boatload of money getting the judgment, and the judgment is worth ZERO. The number zero as the determination of value is, again, based on the Efficient Market Hypothesis, which is the total sum of all knowledge, real or imagined, at the time.

Whose fault is this? Well, first the creditor presumptively entered into an agreement with the debtor, but he did not demand a personal guaranty. Presto gizmo, you get the default judgment because nobody is home, and nobody cares. Is the debtor at fault for this debacle? Well, sure, but the debtor's saving grace is that the debtor exploited an advantageous situation, that is, taking the goods or services without any personal liability. Isn't this the American formula? Exploit every advantage God, or a careless person, handed you. Is the lawyer at fault? Could he or she be?

So here's the scoop. The creditor can file a new lawsuit against the corporate principals and claim that the corporation was a shell or sham, which is the technical jargon for phony-baloney. If the case was tried, the creditor can file a motion to amend and add the principals as judgment debtors. This is readily doable.

Let me summarize this body of law. A corporation that is a shell has no assets, no formalities, no stock, no records, and just a name which is only subject to judicial peeling. Is "peeling" a word that judge's really use? No, but the message is the same. The judge is going to peel back the patina of the corporation and expose the principals inside the corporate can to personal liability if the corporation is nothing more than a thin veneer of tin-foil. If you don't like peeling, you can use "unraveling." The lawyers reading this will call the process "piercing the corporate veil." Getting paid is another expression.

This body of law is well entrenched. *Associated Vendors, Inc. v. Oakland Meat Co.* (1962) 210 Cal. App. 2d 825, 836–843 is the oldie and goodie. This is the total jackpot case and cited today in the appellate opinions. While this case dates from 50 years ago, this case is bedrock and aggregates most of the fact patterns.

> The basic rule stated by our Supreme Court as a guide in the application of this doctrine is as follows: The two requirements are (1) that there be such unity of interest and ownership that the separate personalities of the corporation and the individual no longer exist, and (2) that, if the acts are treated as those of the corporation alone, an inequitable result will follow . . . . With respect to the second requirement, it is sufficient that it appear that recognition of the acts as those of a corporation only will produce inequitable results. The general rule is thus stated as follows: "Before a corporation's acts and obligations can be legally recognized as those of a particular person, and vice versa, it must be made to appear that the corporation is not only influenced and governed by that person, but that there is such a unity of interest and ownership that the individuality, or separateness, of such person and corporation has ceased, and that the facts are such that an adherence to the fiction of the separate existence of the corporation would, under the particular circumstances, sanction a fraud or promote injustice."
>
> The gist of the cases that have considered the doctrine is that both of these requirements must be found to exist before the corporate existence will be disregarded; that such determination is primarily one for the trial court and is not a question of law; and that the conclusion of the trier of fact will not be disturbed if it be supported by substantial evidence . . . . It should also be noted that, while the doctrine does not depend on the presence of actual fraud, it is designed to prevent what would be fraud or injustice, if accomplished. Accordingly, bad faith in one form or another is an underlying consideration and will be found in some form or another in those cases wherein the trial court was justified in disregarding the corporate entity . . . .
>
> A review of the cases which have discussed the problem discloses the consideration of a variety of factors which were pertinent to the trial court's determination under the particular circumstances of each case.
>
> Among these are the following: Commingling of funds and other assets, failure to segregate funds of the separate entities, and the unauthorized diversion of corporate funds or assets to other than corporate uses . . . . The treatment by an individual of the assets of the corporation as his own . . . ; the failure to obtain authority to issue stock or to subscribe to or issue the same . . . ; the holding out by an individual that he is personally liable for the debts of the corporation . . . ; the failure to

> maintain minutes or adequate corporate records, and the confusion of the records of the separate entities . . . ; the identical equitable ownership in the two entities; the identification of the equitable owners thereof with the domination and control of the two entities; identification of the directors and officers of the two entities in the responsible supervision and management; sole ownership of all of the stock in a corporation by one individual or the members of a family . . . ; the use of the same office or business location; the employment of the same employees and/or lawyer . . . ; the failure to adequately capitalize a corporation; the total absence of corporate assets, and undercapitalization . . . ; the use of a corporation as a mere shell, instrumentality or conduit for a single venture or the business of an individual or another corporation . . .; the concealment and misrepresentation of the identity of the responsible ownership, management and financial interest, or concealment of personal . . .; the disregard of legal formalities and the failure to maintain arm's length relationships among related entities . . . ; the diversion of assets from a corporation by or to a stockholder or other person or entity, to the detriment of creditors, or the manipulation of assets and liabilities between entities so as to concentrate the assets in one and the liabilities in another . . . ; the contracting with another with intent to avoid performance by use of a corporate entity as a shield against personal liability, or the use of a corporation as a subterfuge of illegal transactions."

You'd think that a guy like me would never lose one of these fancy alter ego lawsuits, that that batting score would put Ted Williams to shame. No, siree. Instead of offering eye glaze, a legal case, or some dreary story of *sturm und drang*, I will repeat what an arbitrator who ruled against me said: "Look, the plaintiff gave the debtor a line of credit without any meaningful credit check. Worse, the plaintiff knew that the corporate enterprise consisted of two women bakers who have just opened a small bakery with marginal capital. Nobody was keeping a secret here. I think that the plaintiff made a calculated decision to sell products without the safety net of a personal guaranty and with full knowledge that the collapse of the bakery would doom any repayment of the debt. I am not going to retroactively rewrite the credit terms to impose personal liability when the creditor could have demanded a personal guaranty or sold on a C.O.D. basis. Nice try. My job is to render justice, not fix someone else's mistakes." These cases might be predigital, but the templates are alive and well. How about the AlterEgo App I like CommonSense App.

Gee, suing the corporation insider for the company debt does not sound too tough. The law and practice are carved in marble, and clearly the insiders victimized the creditor because this person is holding a big judgment against a shell company. Terrific, when can we celebrate? Answer: When the client ponies up about $10,000 to $100,000 in up-front costs. Why? Absent the most fortuitous set of facts, you have to depose the corporate insiders and the accountant, subpoena the bank records, gather up financial statements that are in the hands of third parties, and hire a very expensive expert. You can spend $25,000 and only get halfway through the case. You can spend $25,000 for a forensic accountant. You can spend $5,000 on courtroom electronics and exhibits.

What about a reverse alter ego? What is that, you might ask. Here is the typical scenario. You scored a big judgment against Joe Ne'er-Do-Well, who declines payment, even a payment program. Joe makes defiance of the judgment his life's goals. He read a book that told him that if he has anything in his name, the creditor can reach the property. Instead, Joe forms a dozen LLCs, each with interlocking ownership and membership, in which the membership shares are held by an offshore entity which he controls. This is an expensive ploy and accrues enormous expense to topple. Are these entities his alter egos? You bet. Some jurisdictions, such as California, reject the claim that the LLCs (or corporation) are the alter ego for the debtor and represents another entity by which he does business. Not all is lost. The appropriate remedy is to sue the LLCs or corporation on a fraudulent conveyance and resulting trust theory that asserts that the money and property held by these entities is held in trust for and due to the debtor.

Chapter 20

Judges?

How about the judge who hears your case? What is the role of the judge postjudgment? Are judges all the same? Peas in a pod? They all look alike in the black robes. If you are litigating your claim, the judge is a major participant because most collection cases are heard by a judge and not a jury. The judge is a trier of law and a trier of fact, which means that the judge will listen to your case and rule who is telling the truth and who is lying. Getting along with the judge, being respectful and truthful, enhances your chances of victory. Lying gets you nowhere.

The core role of the judge is to apply the law to the facts. The job of the lawyer is to put in front of the judge both the law and the facts. Getting the law in front of the judge requires some level of writing skill, scholarship, and management to get the brief filed on time. Getting the facts in front of the judge requires the skill of the lawyer to discover the facts, assemble them in a coherent fashion, and get these facts admitted into evidence. That's not so tough. Despite the whining and moaning on cable news when some judge runs off the rails, judges usually get it right. If not, an appellate court might correct the error. If the appellate court botches the case, the state supreme court or U.S. Supreme Court will fix the mess. Before leaving this little foray, supreme courts have anywhere between five and nine justices. Given today's political schism, five-to-four decisions are common. When one justice dies or retires, the replacement justice might tip the ideological balance and upset an entire body of law. Does that mean that the justices in the minority were wrong, ill-informed about the law or the facts, or uneducated? No. The four justices were in the minority.

You won your case after trial or won your case by default because the debtor failed to respond to the lawsuit. What is the role of the judge after the judgment? Are you done with Mr. or Ms. Judge (collectively Mr. Judge)?

The answer is that the judge only becomes involved if you want, or need, judicial intervention. Enforcement is in the barrel of the writ of execution, which is enforced through the sheriff. Absent enforcement against a foreign state, once the plaintiff wins the case, the plaintiff becomes a judgment creditor can enforce the judgment against the assets of the judgment debtor without prior judicial order or supervision. You do not need the judge's permission to take the property of the debtor, subject to limited exceptions for third-party garnishments in certain states. You can paint the town red with enforcement without a peep from Mr. Judge. Absent grabbing the wrong person's asset, overcollecting, or needing some special relief, the creditor can seize the debtor's property through the levy process, which means that the creditor deposits the writ, instructions, and fees with the sheriff, who executes on the writ, seizes warehouses, liquidates the asset, and turns over the proceeds to the plaintiff. In many states such as California, the sheriff can empty the debtor's bank account and turn over the proceeds to the plaintiff. In other states, including most of the Eastern Seaboard, the South, and even the Southwest, the sheriff serves a garnishment upon the banks or third-party account, who in turn holds the funds and files an answer that funds are held pending a court order. Here, you do need Mr. Judge. The creditor files papers with the court in which the debtor, or interested third parties, is named and seeks an order compelling the bank to turn over the funds to the creditor absent a valid objection, exemption, or claim of third-party ownership.

If you want to examine the debtor in state court, the judges oversee the debtor's and third-parties' examinations to discover assets. At the conclusion of the hearing, the judge can order the debtor to turn over property to the sheriff for liquidation and impound other assets, pending service of writ and appointment of a receiver. At the examination of a third party, the court can likewise order the turnover of property, or payment of the debt due the debtor, to the sheriff; impound assets, appoint a receiver, or even conduct a trial, and enter judgment based on the third party's claim of interest or ownership.

If the debtor files a claim of exemption, the creditor can petition the court to adjudicate the exemption or limit the amount of the claimed exemption. These are minitrials. Many debtors file outlandish claims of exemption and seek to exempt (protect) any assets levied from enforcement. For example, California law provides that the debtor can seek to exempt all wages, salaries, and commissions on the basis that the debtor needs 100 percent of the income to pay for necessary living expenses, such as housing, food, transportation, and other necessaries. Many claims of exemption are fraudulent on their face, and the debtor is betting that the creditor will stumble over the technical process in setting a trial for these exemptions, or if going to trial, hoping that the judge will cut the debtor a big break. If an individual, the debtor can seek to exempt other assets, such as tools of the trade, personal family heirlooms and works of art (limited to about $6,700), a motor vehicle ($7,500), an IRA and retirement accounts, and other assets. The filing of the fraudulent claim of exemption gives the debtor a bargaining chip in reducing the wage levy, or limiting enforcement, because the creditor might fear that the judge might favorably rule on the exemption claim. This fear befalling the creditor that the judge might take pity on the debtor, whether rational or irrational, is relevant. The creditor recalibrates the value of the judgment based on the risk, not reality that the judge might render the debtor wages or other assets exempt and potentially render the judgment very hard to collect. In the creditor's eyes, the phony claim of exemption and the inherent risk of loss depreciate the value of the judgment. Settlement becomes a viable option. The filing of the exemption claim, even if false or fraudulent, is an act of asset protection.

If the creditor sues to set aside a fraudulent conveyance or grab property held by a bailee, family member, or the maws of a family trust, partnership, or LLC, the judge will preside over a trial and adjudicate the rights of the parties. Judges conduct these trials without the benefit of a jury unless you are seeking money damages. Even though these trials appear more mundane and far less sexy than the humongous toxic dump trial that seeks to impose millions in liability upon the hapless polluter, these trials open or close the door to reaching an asset and therefore compensation.

If the debtor conveys every asset to an LLC, which the debtor controls and has beneficial access, but for some unfathomable reason, the judge rejects claims of a fraudulent conveyance, the judgment becomes worthless because the creditor is unable to reach any assets. The awful result of the legal proceeding to unwind the conveyance renders immune the debtor's assets and therefore dooms the judgment and deprives the victim of any justice.

If the creditor seeks a receivership, assignment order, or charging order, files a creditor's suit, or seeks the sale of the debtor's home or other sophisticated relief, the judge becomes the sole authority for this relief. These proceedings do not ask the judgment for the proverbial "Do I win or lose," but rather "Can I reach this asset through this remedy?"

High-end civil enforcement is common in the big city courts in which the community features major financial institutions, venture capitalists, hedge funds, or major contractors. Absent the most bizarre, most judges have heard and considered the broad spectrum of postjudgment remedies. High-end enforcement in smaller courts, or courts that sit in a domicile, lacking a huge financial base, will be a challenge as the creditor is going to educate the judge in a meticulous, unbiased, and complete manner. If the hearing starts off with, "Counsel, I spent the last 20 years of my life as a career prosecutor. This is all new to me. So, let's take this from the very top, statute by statute, right by right, and remedy by remedy, so I get this right. I hear that you do enforcement and I would expect no less." In one case, I kicked off enforcement with a broad-based assignment motion. In response, with a full house in the courtroom, the court reconvened the matter to chambers. When everyone was sitting down, the judge himself launched the proceedings with the statement that his experience with collection matters was representing clients who fell behind on their bills. No harm, no foul, and everything worked out, but the moral of this tale is "know your judge," and if you have choice of court to enforce a judgment, pick your court very carefully.

Which judge and which court? This needs a touch of discussion.

You might have a choice, something like "He loves me . . . he loves me not." Federal courts generally designate one judge to hear your case from beginning to end. The district court judge might delegate routine matters to the magistrate judge, who in turn makes recommendations that the district judge might adopt. Some state courts likewise provide for a single assignment, and in other cases, some courts offer specialized departments.

Federal courts offer some leeway in finding a home for enforcement. Picking a venue takes a good-faith supportable belief that assets are located in the district. That's not much of a burden, mind you. Federal judges leave a more transparent slipstream of their judicial bent because trial court decisions become readily accessible if they are published through the West Reporter series of law books known as F. Supp., which is now F. Supp. 2d., or through West citing series for decisions of lesser import. These decisions are found as follows: *Jones v. Smith* etc., 2013 WL 333333 (USDC, SD NY, 2013). This stands for United States District Court, Southern District of New York and the year of the decision is 2013.

Google is your best friend forever (BFF) because you can type in "Judge John Jones," which might spin out tens or even hundreds of decisions. If you have a Westlaw subscription, you can download nearly every decision in the Westlaw archive. Believe me, in the space of three minutes, you will know who or what you are getting as a judge. If the federal bench has multiple trial judges, which is the case in nearly all districts, the court computer randomly assigns judges.

Unlike the federal courts, some states allow a party to disqualify a judge based on the claim of "prejudice." This means that a party can reject the first assigned state judge for virtually no reason and hope that the next judge is more to the party's liking. Maybe. Unless the parties and their lawyers are all local, out-of-town lawyers will research the first assigned judge to determine if the judgment is "proplaintiff," or "prodefendant." Given that a judge has wide latitude in making a decision in a postjudgment proceeding and moreover that these discretionary decisions are very difficult to reverse, the trial court is virtually the "court of first and last resort" in manner that allows a discretionary decision, or decisions based on the testimony of a person and his or her truthfulness and demeanor to be the kiss of death. This sounds all very abstract, but let me give a concrete example. We had a modest collection case in Stockton (San Joaquin County) about 15 years ago. Our client was probably the oldest continuous steel distributor in California. The family founded this company pre-Civil War 1848. The client suspected that a customer was about to skip town and leave a pile of debts. We mounted an expedited attachment to seize assets. At the outset of the hearing, and after settling down in his chair, the judge did not address his attention to me, or adverse counsel, but to my client, "Henry, tell me what this case is about." If the judge addresses adverse counsel with "How was your vacation?" you might have picked the wrong court. Tell your client to settle if the other side belongs to the same Moose, Elks, or Rotary Club as the judge.

Here is the punch line. In state court, and even sometimes in federal court, whom you hire is a very big deal. The "who" lawyer is more than just hiring the smartest, toughest, or most experienced lawyer. The "who" might be the lawyer who possesses the greatest familiarity, access, or personal relationship with the particular judge. Lawyers who routinely sit next to the judges on the panels for legal seminars are the big catches. Sitting next to a sitting judge is like sitting next to the seat of power.

In rural communities, close-knit communities, or even specialized courts, the bench maintains an active relationship with the local bar association, including the specialized bar associations (bankruptcy, tax, immigration, probate, etc.). These courts are based on a commonality of specialized areas of law, remote geographical areas, regional or local matters such as agriculture or other specialized industries, and any other strong bond. The president of the bar association is probably the lawyer who has the most contact with the bench in setting up "bench bar seminars," the year-end cocktail parties, and "judge's dinners" liaison with the local bar in formulating local rules. Some of these bar associations hand out a yearly award to the "jurist of the year." These awards enhance the judge's resume and ease entry in the lucrative practice of private judging (arbitration and mediation) when the judge retires. This is called the alternative dispute resolution business. The person handing that award is a big deal. Everybody wants the words, "Winner of BLAH BLAH Award for Judge of the Year." The bar association president might even have been a former partner with the judge, litigated against the judge in private practice, or even gone to school with the judge. Whatever the relationship, the local bar association president is the person to hire, along with outside counsel. The bar association president deflects the risk of being "home-towned" and, better yet, can provide the "read of the land" and avoid the potholes along the way. If you are out-of-town counsel, sitting shoulder to shoulder with the current bar association president who just attended last evening's bench bar annual dinner, and awarded the "jurist of the year award," to your trial judge is priceless. Forget Clarence Darrow.

Hire the local big-cheese lawyer. Your new-found local friend, who is sitting in the front row and who might be responsible for the elevation of his fellow lawyer to the bench, is worth every dollar (or a lot more) that you pay. We call these lawyers door openers because they will literally open the door of the courtroom and introduce you to the judge. These lawyers will get you access before a judge because they appear before this judge on a daily basis. We are not talking about Harvard, class of 1965, cum laude with 5 or 50 Supreme Court arguments and a former U.S. Attorney. This is not the lawyer who wrote the Supreme Court brief upholding Obamacare. We are talking about a lawyer, graduate of State University Law School, who maintains an active civil, collection, subrogation, personal injury, or routine practice that compels the lawyer to make near daily court appearances and become known, respected, and ever-beloved by the judges.

I am the poster child of the person in need of local counsel. A zillion years ago, I found myself in the midst of terrible litigation in which I sought the Preliminary Change of Ownership Report (PCOR) that would reveal true title to fraudulently conveyed property. The buyer of property must complete the PCOR form that discloses whether the buyer paid good money for the property in a straight sale and so is subject to property tax reassessment or the buyer is a trust entity and the transfer is in name only so that no tax is owed. I was in the process of examining the escrow holder who held the PCOR but refused to release it. I asked my local guy, assisting in the case, for help. He immediately got out of his chair in the deposition room, walked us down to the judge, who was the duty judge, physically opened the courtroom doors for me and introduced, me to the judge, and briefly explained the problem. The judge heard from me and the other side, and ordered the turnover of the PCOR. This is true access to power.

If you are not local and your adversary is the former (or present) president of the local bar association, hire someone local. Don't be a stranger in a strange land, Mr. Heinlein. This is paramount in remote rural courts in which the judges hear from the same group of lawyers on a daily basis; highly specialized courts, such as bankruptcy, tax, probate, or most of the federal administrative tribunals; or courts tethered to a unique community, such as San Diego. Partnering with local and reputable counsel will save the day and level the playing field by offering invaluable access and vitiate the hometown advantage of the adverse party.

Parties win cases and sometimes collect difficult judgments because a judge makes favorable rulings. Lawyers present the case to the judge. Absent the most bizarre case, nearly every body of law is well known and well understood. Real property law dates back nearly 1,000 years, and common law, developed by the courts of England, dates back more than 500 years. Fraudulent conveyance laws date from the reign of Queen Elizabeth I. Law libraries, law books, and online services such as Westlaw or Lexis-Nexis offer any facet of law without a whole lot of effort. Texts in law school are generally the same, no matter the law school. What they teach and how they teach from law school to law school does not substantially vary.

What makes a lawyer successful as opposed to famous, however, is a slightly different matter. Aside from ambition, personal drive, and a gob of personal charm, lawyers succeed when they can marshal the facts and discover key evidence such as documents, witnesses, and financial records. What makes a case, or difficult enforcement, is the evidence. Getting the facts in front of the judge is everything in this business and far more important than the pedigree of the lawyer.

Some judges will convene settlement conferences for the benefit of the parties. When Mr. Judge sits down with everyone at a conference table, looks the parties in the eye, and tells them that trial might take the wind out of their sails, the case might suddenly settle. I was graced with a settlement conference before a magistrate judge in the federal court. The defendant was a difficult person, and settlement was going nowhere. The judge saw us (myself and my client privately) as the custom. The judge asked me, "Well, what was the first offer you received?" My recollection was that the first offer had something to do with the phrase "Go - - - - yourself," which I could not bring to bear. I decided on a more gentle tact. "Well, Your Honor, the defendant gave the GPS offer." "What do you mean, GPS? Global Positioning Satellite?" "No, Your Honor." "What do you mean?" "Well Your Honor, what GPS means is Go Pound Sand." The case did not settle.

Let's walk back this discussion a bit. Nearly 99.99% of all judges want to "get it right," even though the attorneys got it wrong. Most states only require a bar passing grade of 70%. You could have a case where the attorneys on both sides fall into the 30% zone each. Ouch! Most judges do their best to avoid a miscarriage of justice, but sometimes Lady Justice gets thrown for a loop.

Chapter 21

Judgments

Judges hand down judgments, and your job is to collect the judgment or, if the debtor, evade payment. What type of judgments? That's a simple question, but a busy answer. Most money judgments are civil judgments from the civil court. The plaintiff sues, serves, and wins by default or trial. Judgments arise from the labor commissioner proceedings. The claimant files the claim that is served upon the employer who might respond. If the employee wins, the awards are converted into a civil judgment. Judgments flow from family courts. Family-law judgments incorporate the marital settlement agreement that provides for child, spousal, property settlement, or equalization agreements. Family-law courts daily churn out contested and uncontested judgments for spousal and child support.

Let's get this straight. A judgment is a declaration of the judgment that the debtor owes money to the judgment creditor for a specific amount of money. A judgment is deemed, nearly 90 percent of the time, the final pronouncement of the court. Upon signing the judgment, the judge is done, done, and very done, and absent an appeal, clerical error, or some fancy postjudgment motion, the judgment is cast in stone. If a party is unhappy with the judgment, the remedy is an appeal, and appeals are very time sensitive. States vary from 20 to 60 days by which to file an appeal. Federal court provides 30 days to file an appeal. Bankruptcy court is 10 days to file an appeal. These time limits are fixed and any variation is subject to very tight rules.

A family-law judgment is different because those judgments compel a spouse to affirmatively make payments. The failure to make payment gives rise to enforcement, contempt, and even criminal prosecution, depending upon the state. Failure to pay child support might even pull a law license. Although off the beaten path, criminal restitution orders are not civil judgments. Depending upon the state, the restitution order is a condition of probation. In the event of default under the restitution order, the probation department, or others, might initiate proceedings to resolve the probation order and arrest the defendant. If the probation period expires, the court forfeits the jurisdiction to incarcerate the defendant for a violation of the probation. If you are the victim of a crime, this is very important to you. Criminal victims mistakenly believe that the restitution order is theirs, or their civil judgment. This is typically wrong.

In many states, and the federal court, at the conclusion of criminal cases and at the time of sentencing, the criminal court can render a civil judgment in favor of the victim that awards the compensatory loss. See California Penal Code § 1214(b): "If the judgment is for a fine, including a restitution fine . . . , the judgment may be enforced in the manner provided for the enforcement of money judgments generally." Federal law and nearly every other state have the equivalent. A civil judgment entered as part of probation enables the victim to recover out-of-pocket damages, such as wage loss, medical expenses, and property damages. The victim must sue in civil court to recover for the personal injuries. The fact of the civil judgment in the criminal court and the civil judgment from civil court leads to the anomaly that the victim can have two civil judgments.

We do offer you a slight and sly trick and my favorites. The civil restitution judgment arrives early in the case and sometimes on the eve of the filing of the big-time civil damage action. For reasons unknown to nature, the debtor refuses to pay the civil restitution judgment. This is terrific, because you can immediately launch asset discovery, which includes a sit-down debtor's examination (e.g., what do you have, where it is, and what do you do with your assets?). Peruse the public records and dig up a Uniform Residential Loan Application from a loan secured by the debtor and compel its production at the debtor's examination. Demand financial records from the debtor. Lay a subpoena upon the debtor's lawyers for medium of payment.

With this portfolio of documents in hand, you now have a roadmap that opens up new vistas. You immediately can assess the debtor's net worth to better gauge the settlement value of the separate personal injury action. You can spot at the outset fraudulent conveyances before the assets disappear and link the fraudulent conveyance claims to the personal injury claims. Information of net worth from the discovery enables the plaintiff to prove up punitive damages, given proof of the defendant's net worth. You will learn further down in this book, that debtor's examination is a public proceeding.

Administrative agencies reduce their fines, penalties, and forfeiture into civil judgments. Out-of-state tax claims are converted into civil judgments in their own jurisdiction and therefore are "domesticated," in the new jurisdiction. Out-of-state judgments are routinely enforced under the Sister-State Judgment Act, and foreign judgments are the subjects of brand new lawsuits.

Before wondering down our primrose path of enforcement, should you strike pay dirt, counsel for the defendant will fly-speck your judgment to find some flaw in the proceeding. These flaws include a faulty or factually wrong proof of service, the default process that produced a judgment far different than the pleadings, and the lack of personal or subject-matter jurisdiction of the court.

The most common exit from a judgment is that the defendant claims to have bobbled the papers and seeks discretionary relief from the court under Federal Rule of Civil Procedure 60(b) (1) ("mistake, inadvertence, surprise, or excusable neglect"). In plain English: "Yes, I got served with the lawsuit, but the dog ate the papers." States have the same standard with only slight variations. Judges routinely grant these motions (the word is "routine," and not guaranteed). These motions tend to play upon the judge's sympathy that the defendant is entitled to his or her day in court.

Giving this topic short shrift here does not diminish the risks. The attacks upon judgments are plastered all over the Internet, law reviews, and journal articles and are subject to incessant blogs. Despite the insidious writings of the asset protection cadre, toppling the judgment for jurisdictional grounds is the best form of asset protection, aside from winning the case in the first place, or at least mitigating the damages. Motions to vacate a judgment based on discretionary grounds have a six-month to one-year life cycle, and thereafter these rights vanish. On your way to Oz, double-check the dates to better gauge whether kicking over the can might kick off a successful strategy prosecuted by the debtor to topple your house of cards.

Fly-speck the file yourself and assess any potential attack. Did the lawsuit allege a red, white, and blue contract, but default judgment seeks damages for a green, yellow, and tangerine contract? Changing horses in the middle of a stream might topple the judgment, President Lincoln. You look at the proof of service of the lawsuit and recognize that the address is patently wrong. Worse, the process server did not properly complete service by failing to mail the copy of the lawsuit to the defendant after leaving a copy with the person in charge of the business.

Expect a jurisdictional attack on your judgment. How do I know other than experiencing jurisdictional attacks up to and through the appellate courts, and even collateral lawsuit to topple a judgment? Yes, the debtor can file a brand new lawsuit to topple the judgment based on equitable grounds or lack of jurisdiction. This story is much better. I am standing in line at the clerk's office to issue a writ of execution on a modest dollar case. No big deal. I was standing behind a lawyer (I guessed) who was thumbing through the court's file. He was going through the file, page by page, and spending some time looking at the proof of service. I was standing right behind him and could see what he was doing. The fact that he had the file in front of him was not a big deal because some clerks will hand a file to the lawyer at the counter. After a second or two, I realized that he was perusing my file in which I was seeking execution. Lo and behold, the lawyer filed a motion to vacate the default, which stalled the enforcement of my judgment.

Don't forget that judgments accrue interest. Depending upon the jurisdiction, the rates range from 8 percent to 12 percent. Some states provide for compounding interest, which increases the effective rate of interest to nearly 20 perrcent over a passage of years. Federal rates of interest are less than 1 percent and fluctuate. When a judgment is renewed, the accrued interest is added to the principal of the judgment, which means that the renewed judgment is the total. The total of the renewed judgment is subject to interest that leads to effective compounding. Payments are received as first applied on account of interest and the balance to principal.

As a rule of thumb, judgments double in dollar value every 10 years. Judgments that require the judgment creditor to calendar the judgment must be renewed and renewed in a timely manner. This is not difficult, but it requires a modest amount of skill to renew the judgment and preserve the judgment liens that probably encumber real property.

Chapter 22

Rudiments of Fraudulent Conveyance Law

What body of law lets you reach the property that was fraudulently conveyed, hidden, concealed, or secreted? All states have enacted fraudulent conveyance laws under the title of Uniform Fraudulent Transfer Act (UFTA), save some states such as New York, which operates under its predecessor, the Uniform Fraudulent Conveyance Act (UFCA). The first type of conveyance is one made without fair and equivalent consideration and the debtor was insolvent or rendered insolvent. California Civil Code § 3439.05: "A transfer made or obligation incurred by a debtor is fraudulent as to a creditor whose claim arose before the transfer was made or the obligation was incurred if the debtor made the transfer or incurred the obligation without receiving a reasonably equivalent value in exchange for the transfer or obligation and the debtor was insolvent at that time or the debtor became insolvent as a result of the transfer or obligation." This is called constructive fraud or balance sheet fraud. Bring the forensic accountant, appraisers, and lots of charts and graphs to court. This relief protects only creditors that arose before the conveyance. To dispel any uncertainty, the date that the tort arose (i.e., the theft, injury, accident, or harm) is the date that the "claim arose," even though suit was filed later.

The other type of conveyance is a conveyance made with the intent to hinder, delay, or defraud any creditor including a creditor that arose after the conveyance. These cases are built on circumstantial evidence and called "badges of fraud." No, this is not Eagle Scout badge. Fraud badge, anyone?

Here is the law in its greatest glory: California Civil Code § 3439.04 (a) provides that a transfer made or obligation incurred by a debtor is fraudulent as to a creditor, whether the creditor's claim arose before or after the transfer was made or the obligation was incurred, if the debtor made the transfer or incurred the obligation as follows: (1) With actual intent to hinder, delay, or defraud any creditor of the debtor. (2) Without receiving a reasonably equivalent value in exchange for the transfer or obligation, and the debtor either: (A) Was engaged or was about to engage in a business or a transaction for which the remaining assets of the debtor were unreasonably small in relation to the business or transaction. (B) Intended to incur, or believed or reasonably should have believed that he or she would incur, debts beyond his or her ability to pay as they became due. (b) In determining actual intent under paragraph (1) of subdivision (a), consideration may be given, among other factors, to any or all of the following: (1) whether the transfer or obligation was to an insider. (2) Whether the debtor retained possession or control of the property transferred after the transfer. (3) Whether the transfer or obligation was disclosed or concealed. (4) Whether before the transfer was made or obligation was incurred, the debtor had been sued or threatened with suit. (5) Whether the transfer was of substantially all the debtor's assets. (6) Whether the debtor absconded. (7) Whether the debtor removed or concealed assets. (8) Whether the value of the consideration received by the debtor was reasonably equivalent to the value of the asset transferred or the amount of the obligation incurred. (9) Whether the debtor was insolvent or became insolvent shortly after the transfer was made or the obligation was incurred. (10) Whether the transfer occurred shortly before or shortly after a substantial debt was incurred. (11) Whether the debtor transferred the essential assets of the business to a lien holder who transferred the assets to an insider of the debtor.

Wake up, Little Susie, wake up. This recitation of the law is about the same in every state with only some slight variations. Even though this statute is pure eye-glaze, it is important eye-glaze. Commit this statute to memory.

No two cases are precisely alike. Fraudulent conveyances case are not like peas in a pod, sliced bread, or rows of barbecued chicken at Costco. These cases are terribly fact driven and are based on the motives of the transferor (i.e., the debtor). The fact that the debtor was solvent is not a defense or even that something of value was given to the debtor for the transfer. Again, the Internet is full of detailed articles on this subject, but keep in mind that the core of a case that you are seeking to build on the basis of "intent to hinder, delay and defraud," depends upon the debtor's state of mind, which is always circumstantial. Keep the e-mails that declaim: "You will never collect. You are wasting you money. If you hire a lawyer, you will owe more to a lawyer that what might be collected. Take pennies on the dollar."

You do have friends that all reside in the evidence code of virtually every state. The evidence code and case law offer various presumptions. Some are famous: If planes fall from the sky, the airline is at fault. Here are the relevant presumptions in fraudulent conveyance cases:

1. A thing delivered by one to another is presumed to have belonged to the latter.
2. The things that a person possesses are presumed to be owned by him.
3. A person who exercises acts of ownership over property is presumed to be the owner of it.

Fraudulent conveyances transfer the title of property from the debtor to another entity (or person) in which the debtor retains equitable benefit in the property. Put the money in the wife's name, but the debtor (the husband) has possession of the checkbook and the ATM card. Put the home in the name of a trust, but the debtor and family reside on the property and pay for the debt service, insurance, and property taxes. The debtor writes off the interest and property taxes on the IRS 1040. In the face of the big judgment, the debtor transfers his company FOODLE DOODLE INC. to DOODLE FOODLE INC. It has the same address, telephone number, fax number, Internet address, bank accounts, logo, trademark, P. O. box, customers, vendors, and product line.

These evidence code presumptions enable the litigant to vacate the fraudulent conveyance because the debtor retained control and possession over the property even though title changed hands. Let's keep in mind that fraudulent conveyances shield assets because they accrue expense to reach the assets as opposed to some hocus-pocus impermeable barrier.

In plain English: He who has it, owns it, notwithstanding claims of new title. Dad was right: Possession is nine-tenths of the law.

P.S. In some states changes are afoot to fraudulent conveyance law. Consider these changes legislative plastic surgery. What do you expect? Fraudulent conveyance law dates back 500 years. Consider these changes nip, tuck and lift.

Chapter 23

Introduction to Insolvency

"Insolvency" is a fancy word, but it has not quite the panache of "intellectual property." What does insolvency mean and why is this important? Insolvency means that the debtor owes more money to creditors than the debtor has available assets. Balance sheet insolvency means adding up the due and payable debts, subtracting the available assets, and coming up with a negative number. Postmeltdown, we call this underwater.

Insolvency also means that the debtor is generally failing to pay liabilities as they become due. That is ugly because when those liabilities become due, they become debts and further become fodder of debt collection, lawsuits, judgments, and liens. The creditors record liens that encumber the debtor's real and business personal property. The first to record is probably the first to get paid, if the property is sold. The last to record is the person who gets nothing. Taxes, wages, and government claims might take priority in insolvency proceedings such as a bankruptcy, receivership, or assignment for the benefit of creditors, which means that the debtor turns over assets and liabilities to a third person who liquidates the asset and pays creditors with the proceeds but only priority claim.

Bankruptcy is just another form of insolvency. Stuff goes in: stuff comes out. Let's wear the hat of debtor's counsel. Taxes, alimony, child support, government fines, penalties and forfeitures, and others debts pass through bankruptcy untouched, which means that the debtor is highly motivated to apply assets to satisfy these evergreen debts. Bankruptcy discharges (wipes out) commercial and personal loans, trade and bank debts (unsecured), credit card debts, and just about every other routine bill or debts. The debtor walks away from these debts: "I am free!" The debtor is going work real hard to pay off the nondischargeable evergreen debts given the debtor risk of near perpetual enforcement.

If you hold a dischargeable commercial debt (not based on malevolent conduct), the debtor lacks an incentive to pay you given this singled-minded drive to pay nondischargeable debts. The only incentive is to pay a dischargeable debt secured by real property (or personal property), which might move up the totem pole an unsecured nondischargeable debt and render that debt secured.

What does this information mean to you? Don't be miserable. Don't feel sorry for yourself. Start asking questions. First, run the debtor through the free grantor/grantee index, get a title or UCC report, run an invasive search through a commercial search company, and ascertain the total debt structure if publically available. If you find your debtor buried under millions in priority tax liens and claims, the likelihood of your getting paid, absent heroic enforcement, is low. If you find your debtor free of any other claims, suits, judgments or liens, knock yourself out, go to town and march to Atlanta, General Sherman.

Chapter 24

Technology

Let's get past the "oohs and ahhs" of technology. It's nice chatter, but unhelpful. What do you really need to succeed? Here is the answer: You need a first-rate smartphone or tablet (brand not important) that enables you to enjoy access to all statutes and case books via a subscription to Westlaw and its many competitors. When you are in court, in a meeting, in a deposition, on the road, in a panic at 3:00 a.m., your smartphone can offer immediate legal research that can answer any question. Is this technology really that important? Answer: You bet because your competition made the investment. Lawyers born after 1985 are wired. They solely rely on electronic access to research materials. Their last contact with true written materials was the first year of law school, which offered them a tour of the law library.

You think that I am kidding? Law libraries maintain stacks of law reviews that are bound in hardbound books. The better law schools offer the *Harvard Law Review* probably from its earlier publication date. We are talking about a lot of dusty books. Next time that you visit your alma mater, check out the section that houses the law reviews. Grab a volume or two and see if anyone ever cracked open the book. I'd bet you good money that few human hands ever touched that book other than putting it on the shelf. I'd bet you even more money that you are the only person among the law review stacks. Why is this important to you? Answer: Aside from the fact that few law review articles are actually read, Westlaw, among others, offers online subscription for all law reviews, journals, and legal magazines. Tablets are very helpful because they can hook into a printer.

Aside from access to legal research materials, a very good smartphone provides access to the Internet and particularly Google. A smartphone enables you to have access to Facebook, among similar services. You can take pictures, including pictures of documents that you can forward to clients, other lawyers, and even adverse counsel.

Most, if not all, federal dockets are online. Some state appellate dockets are coming online. In California, counties are shifting to online dockets. Upon filing by anyone, you have will immediate access to the filing no matter where you are. You literally can take the electronic court with you anywhere. Even though having access to the document on a smartphone is an effort, access to the document on a tablet is very close to the experience of reading the documents as if on paper. Any lawyer engaged in a large-scale federal practice, such as class actions, antitrust, major bankruptcies, and copyright, patent, or trademark battles should have immediate access to the dockets, courtesy of smartphones or tablets. Running your new-found adversary through Google during the midst of a deposition is always enlightening.

What is the true purpose of a smartphone? Seriously, a phone is a phone. You can e-mail on a smartphone, but you can more easily e-mail on a Blackberry. Sure, you can take pictures, but taking pictures is old hat. What about this technology that drives buyers to rush out and snap up the latest gizmo and pay some silly price when the current gizmo is also just as good? Just so you know, even though Blackberrys are the digital clunkers, they are indestructible. Crash dummies crumple in head-on collisions, but the Blackberrys in their hands survive.

Let me pass along another secret. Half of America sleeps with their cell phones under their pillow. Thank you, my mental health is great, but if you ask anyone younger than age 35, and nudge a touch, they will confess that the last thing they see before shut-eye is their cell phone, and the first vision in the morning is their cell phone. I would ante up these numbers to 75 percent for the young Facebook, Twitter, and social media set who are out-and-out digital addicts.

Let me answer your question. Every so often you will go out to dinner with the important client, or your senior partner, or some big shot lawyer. The waiter hands you the menu that features appetizers and entrees that bear inexplicable descriptions. Do you really want to ask the waiter, "What is this?" or "What is that?" Not so much. This is what you do. When the waiter asks for your order, answer: "I want the Instagram entrees." "Excuse me, sir, what is it that?" Answer: "I want whatever people post on Instagram after they squeal 'ooh and ahh.'"

Section 3

Investigatory Techniques

Chapter 1

Set the Table

Distracted by the ringing cell phone, the driver took her eyes off the road to grab the phone. At that moment, a bicyclist darted in front the driver who promptly ran over the rider. The bicyclist, a medical student, was not wearing a helmet, and the medical examiner pronounced him DOA on the scene. The accident techs took hours to clean the brain matter out of the tires.

Walking down a local grocery store aisle, the shopper, big-boned, but short of stature, reaches for the chicken stock on the top shelf. Unable to retrieve the container, but barely out of reach, the shopper wedged her foot in the bottom shelf to generate the few inches of height. Under the weight of 180 pounds, the bottom shelf collapsed, and the shopper fell backward and tumbled to the hard floor. She laid supine for 10 minutes before the ambulance arrived. Three surgeries later, the shopper was still confined to a wheelchair. Her disability nearly ended her career as a prosecutor, which the American Disabilities Act saved.

Marylou had an exemplary work ethos. Early to work and late to leave was her personal style. "What can I do for you? Let me help," she would ask any coworker. Marylou was of Hispanic decent and religious and displayed a small devotional picture on the interior wall of her cubicle. Joe Ultra Redneck was Marylou's supervisor. Inconsistent with company policy, Joe vociferously objected to the picture, which nonetheless remained. Losing face in this clash of wills and in retaliation, Joe wrote up a derogatory performance report that quashed Marylou's chances of promotion. Frustrated by a job, but without a career track, Marylou quit and quickly embraced the local, state, and national antidiscrimination laws. Marylou was older than 50 when she quit and was so traumatized that she left the workforce, never to return.

These cases have the makings of a big-time, multimillion-dollar litigation. These cases start with a complaint, an answer by the defendant, the exchange of discovery, pretrial motions, a trial setting, a trial, and the verdict. These cases follow the same template. These cases are linear because they have a beginning (the incident), middle (the litigation), and an end (trial and verdict). No matter the claim, and absent the unusual such as mandatory arbitration for Marylou, most civil cases follow this linear track.

Enforcement is nonlinear. Enforcement is messy and slow. Enforcement is pursued in fits and starts, leaps and bounds, and crisscrosses itself. Some enforcement is futile. Grinding down the debtor at a postjudgment examination is the epitome of a dead end. "What do you have?" "Nothing." "How to plan to pay this judgment?" "I don't." "What happened to the assets that were listed on the financial statement presented to the bank, my client?" "I have no clue." "Who is paying for your living expenses?" "Friends." "Who is paying for $10,000 mortgage payments for the house you live in?" "My children." "Where do your children live?" "I don't know." "Do you have their phone numbers?" "Yes I do. The phone numbers are on my cell phone. I lost the cell phone yesterday."

This debtor's examination looks like a dead end. Let's find a find a new path. Here are your new tools.

Chapter 2

A Pottery Shard Is the Key to Financial Archaeology

Finding assets of the recalcitrant debtor commands the skill of a trained archaeologist. Let's go back to college and take Archaeology 101. Don't worry, this course is pass or fail, and spelling does not count. These exercises will teach you how to read the treasure map.

First, why are you reading this section? This section gives you the skills to identify the arrows, clues, and secrets that point to assets. Find the clue, and you will find the asset. Find the arrow, and you will find the asset. Find the courier, and you will find Bin Laden, the CIA targeter taught us. Financial archaeology is the science of locating assets based upon the clues found in financial statements, credit applications, credit narratives, credit reports, third-party lawsuits, websites, and anything else that might suggest or hint at the existence of an asset.

We start with the basics: a pottery shard. Pottery shards are great. They last for a long time. I mean many millennia. They are sometimes glazed, baked, or fire-hardened and always well made. Ancient societies lived off their pottery, amphorae, craters, huge jars, and other clay receptacles. Most important, pottery was cheap and plentiful, and all levels of society used pottery. When ancient ships sank, amphorae littered the ocean floor.

What information can the pottery shard deliver? What about the method of glazing, the chemical composition of the clay and paint, the shape the reconstructed pot, the contour of the lip, or the shape of the spout? These clues identify the age of the pot and necessarily the epoch of the civilization. The chemical composition and shape indicates the sophistication of civilization and the level of technology. The shard might harbor a trace of the liquid, such as olive oil, wine, or water that might establish a date for the agriculture, science, or industry. The writings, pictures, or colors might represent a story, art, or even an historical event and establish, confirm, or conflict with sources the date of the event, or even memorialize, or impeach the existence of an event. Pottery shards bearing some historical roots date key events and, for those individuals wed to their history, can be affirmation, or awful rejection, of their claim to the Holy Land.

In excavating a site, the location in the strata might date the pottery shard, and if equivalent to other strata whose dates are know, you might be able to date the shard. Conversely, if you can date the shard, you can date the strata and the artifacts, or human debris, located nearby. The shard standing alone offers limited information, but when found in its original surroundings might speak volumes of the date, date, and epoch. Find the known shard next to the resting King Muckity Muck, and chances are you can identify Mr. King and Mrs. King and maybe his proper place in the royal lineage. If that shard is buried above or below a strata of limestone or sedimentary rock, you might be able to conclude that the shard pre- or postdated a flood.

If buried above or below a stratum bearing the debris of a massive fire or earthquake, you might be able to date a great fire or natural disaster. If the stratum contains seashells, limestone, and debris consistent with a massive deluge, you might find the remnants of Noah's Ark. Let's just take one hypothetical. Let's say you found a Roman coin dated about A.D. 32 as part of an archeological dig. Coins are well understood and easily dated. Typically, coinage featured each emperor. If you know the date of the emperor's reign, you'll know the date of the coins. Find the coins in strata, and you'll date the strata and everything around. Dating the strata fixes the date of other objects in the strata. For example, on the same strata next to a coin is a pottery shard that bears an inscription reciting the sermons of a person offering bread and wine. Might that shard be important? How about the pottery shard above, or below, a wide strata full of sedimentary rocks, seashells, or crustacean remains? Does that stratum suggest a major flood that lasted for many years? Maybe.

Given carbon-14 dating, the pottery shard bearing an event, artwork, face, or even writing might represent an accurate snap-shot of history. The pottery shard might even provide a contemporaneous historical picture, given other artifacts in the same strata or the historical or biblical record. You hope, however, that the snapshot is not ancient Photoshop, which might suggest that that the artist altered the image to suit the tastes of the victorious party king. Churchill was right: Victors write the history books.

Other clues present themselves. If the pot is valuable, you might conclude that you also found a gravesite that contains jewelry and other valuables that might be buried nearby. Those valuables might identify whether the person might have been nobility or even furnish their actual identity and more precisely the time period when they lived. Other artifacts might offer a clue that sets the age or epoch of the find. If the shard, along with other evidence, confirms or rejects evidence of a king or other nobility, somebody's historical applecart might take a tumble. If that applecart belongs to someone in the Middle East, expect a ferocious academic battle or even personal conflict because the historical records support, or subvert, impassioned claims to very valuable real estate in which bloodshed is never-ending. Imagine finding any confirmation of the biblical prophets, much less Moses, King David, or King Solomon. The History Channel would go nuts.

The pot might have been used for food, oil, cheese, fruit, cooking, wine, beer, or ashes of a family member or the king. The pot swings open the door of history that resonates with the parties who identify with the history as their own cultural heritage. Pots, shards, jewelry, eating implements, or ashes in a fire pit might alter history or change its course. Did the American Indians originate from Asia and come over the Bering Sea when it was connected with the Asian land mass? Did the Polynesians originate from China or South America? Who owned the Promised Land, and who came first? Lots of people died and continue to die over the last question. Embrace shards (and whole pots if you can find them) as the methodology to reconstructing an ancient era. Each financial clue might lead to another clue and ultimately an asset. Reconstructing a person's financial affairs, as we shall see, is no different and employs the same skills. The pottery shard is a snapshot of human activity. For the CSI, the pottery shard is the clue on the map.

Okay, smart guy, here is the next story. We take the trip to Asia. We go to China, Japan, and Hong Kong, which is the world's greatest shopping destination. Like all good tourists, I am looking for souvenirs and knowing less than nothing, I am figuring that some Chinese vase would be the prize. We go from shop to shop, and I get the running spiels that I ought to plunk down about $1,000 for a vase from such and such late dynasty. I was not too sure that the vases were authentic and worse, I had a hard time gripping value for those dollars. Was that vase, looking like something from Macy's, really worth $1,000?

After tramping around for a good hour, we find this vase store with a wonderful selection of tall thin vases—very nice looking stuff. The price was about $200.00. I could live with that. My wife (originally from Taiwan) had a puckered look in her face. "Let's do it," I said. "No," she said. "I don't want them." "Why? They look nice. We can buy two of them." "No, no, and no." "Why not?" "These are funeral urns," she said, "and always bad luck."

Chapter 3

Dinosaur Fossils Teach Us the Power of Inductive Logic

Let's take a trip to the Badlands, which is part of Wyoming, the Dakotas, and Colorado. These are barren lands, but they are home to undulating fields of dinosaurs' fossils. You are walking along (non–Indian lands—big trouble if you retrieve any fossils from Indian-owned lands. First, the Indians own the land and the fossils; next, taking fossils is wrong; and third, if you do this knowingly, you can face criminal charges and need a high-priced lawyer.).

You are looking at the ground, and pick up a small rock. Well, this isn't a rock. It looks like a fingernail to a dinosaur. (If there is anybody with the slight background in paleontology, I can see many cringing faces. Forgive me.)

You look very carefully and see the striations running up and down. The lines might show age or the configuration of muscles. You immediately conjecture what the position, shape, or even purpose of the digit and extrapolate to the position or shape or purpose of the hand or claw. You take another leap of faith and conclude what the arm or leg might look like and then deduce the position and purpose of the arm or leg. You might conclude that the dinosaur has short arms or legs. With a little more guess and golly, you conclude that you just discovered the fingernail to a *T. rex* and, given the short arm, that the *T. rex* was a scavenger and spent most of the time with its nose to the ground looking for carcasses, opposed to the towering monolith in *Jurassic Park* ready to slaughter all living creatures. (My hearing is so good that I can hear the entire UCLA paleontology department chortling, or maybe cackling, at my conclusion. I get a D+ in scholarship and at least a B+ for entertainment.)

The moral of this tale is not to reveal my pitiful knowledge of Paleontology 101, but rather to emphasize that the smallest clue, if properly extrapolated, might lead to a stunning revelation.

Details count and might point the way to a probable outcome otherwise hidden from plain sight. The other examples are tire tracks found near the dead body. At the trial for the accused (the usual case is the dead girlfriend murdered by the jealous boyfriend), the "tire guy" from the FBI would testify the tire tracks found at the scene are *consistent* with the tire tracks of the defendant's automobile. The FBI has tire, typewriter, computer, hair, fingernail, paint, paper, or pen "guys."

Chapter 4

The Wobble of a Star Suggests a Planetary Companion

Let's use the analogy of looking for E. T. I am looking at Star X. No, this is not the nursery rhyme: "Starlight, star bright, the first star I see tonight." Nope, this star is a wobbler. One day the star shifts about one meter to the right, and the next day the star shifts a meter to the left. The next day, the star looks like it is one meter closer to me and the other day one meter away from me. I cannot see what is causing the star to dance the polka, but this star has better moves than Mick Jagger. This star should get busted by Officer Einstein for drunk wandering. So, given that I am a proud graduate of UCLA and took a course in Introduction to Astronomy, I have a clear memory of something like this. The star is stumbling around like a drunken sailor because some nearly invisible planet is orbiting the star. The planet exerts a gravitational field that makes the star wobble. Remember, Einstein's Theory of General Relativity holds that massive objects cause a dent in the time-space continuum. Consider a planet as a medium-sized bowling ball dropped on a trampoline and the far-heavier star situated nearby. The gravitational field of the planet causes a deflection in the star's movement. We can detect the wobbling through the Doppler effect. When the star is pushed farther away from me, the light waves from the star move to longer wavelengths (blue), and when the star is pushed closer to me, the light waves move to the shorter wavelengths (red). I can accurately measure the shift because the wavelengths at blue or red have different spectral lines. I actually never see the planet, but I know the planet exists (and might even guess its mass) because of the planet's gravitational effect in causing the star to wobble, which is measured Doppler spectroscopy that shows the star's movement. Through inductive logic, I conclude through the spectral lines that a gravitational object (the planet) is orbiting the star and causing the wobble. Hello, E. T., and I did pass the course. I did call an astronomy professor at the University of California at Berkeley to confirm my rudimentary science. I got a "pass" on a pass-fail test from him. Thank goodness for that. At least I remembered the science.

So, why is this important to a collection lawyer looking for assets? Pray we have an answer. Why, oh why? Hunting for assets is the same as hunting for planets. Answer: Life is double-entry bookkeeping. I can deduce the existence of the asset by its effect upon the debtor's finances or tax return. If the person owns the real property, he might have warehoused title in another name, so the property is invisible to me. But what is visible to me are the checks to the tax collector, lender holding the mortgage, homeowners association (HOA) fees (if part of an association), insurance and maintenance, and utilities such as electric, gas, water, cable television, Internet access, trash, and sewer. Gas and electric bills are forensic peeping toms. When the gas and electric bills fluctuate up or down, someone runs the appliances, uses a blow-dryer, watches TV, goes online, takes a shower, cooks food on a gas or electric range, or turns on (or off) the heating or air conditioning. Utility bills tell you that someone is at home.

Credit card bills sent to the home show that someone is at home and is regularly receiving bills. Magazine and newspaper subscriptions all appear with great regularity and show who is at home. Find the check payable to these parties or proof of payment for real estate-related ownership, and I can find the property on the map.

Chapter 5

Burning the Trash Leads to UBL

Does this scheme work in the real world? You bet. How did the CIA locate Osama bin Laden (UBL to the Navy Seals) to his safe house located in Abbottabad that was within miles of the Pakistan equivalent of West Point? Not in a million years would the CIA snap a picture of Osama bin Laden waving from the rooftop of his compound. However, the CIA latched onto the courier. What is a courier, all America asks? A courier is a confident, messenger, purveyor of intelligence, and general aide or maybe weapons. The courier is the eyes, ears, and voice of Bin Laden and is his conduit to the world. Without the courier, Osama bin Laden would have suffered virtual house arrest. Find the courier (the gravitational pull) and find the planet (Osama bin Laden).

What proof is there that the debtor owns the property? Title to the house? Shades of *Miracle on 34th Street* because mail is addressed to Osama bin Laden? Utility (water, gas, and telephone), cable, and newspaper and magazine subscriptions? Yes, that's well and good. The best is the garbage bill. It is so innocuous. When you sit down with the debtor in a deposition, at trial, or in an interview, always ask about the garbage bill. Whose name is it in? Your name? How much per month? How do you pay the bill? If the answer is "There is no garbage service" or "The garbage bill is $10.00 a month (bare minimum)," your next question is "What does the occupant, if you, do about the garbage?" The answer might be, "We don't have any garbage for pick-up." "Why is that?" "We take the garbage to the dump ourselves" or "We burn our own garbage."

What did that mean in the hunt for bin Laden? If the debtor tells you that they are taking the garbage to the dump themselves, that means the debtor does not want the police or private investigator hunting through the garbage for evidence. You are now face to face with a professional marijuana grower. If the person tells you that he burns the garbage, you are face to the face with Osama bin Laden. Read *No Easy Day* by Mark Owens who writes that occupants of the compound occupied by Osama bin Laden burned their garbage, which investigators immediately recognized as standard operating procedure to prevent law enforcement from retrieving key evidence from the garbage, whether world-class terrorists or home-grown dope growers. Whether police or a private detective, the term for diving into a dumpster to find evidence is called the dumpster dive. You have read the story of the dinosaur fingernail, wobbling stars, and pottery shards in this book. The fact the occupants of the walled compound in Abbottabad burned their garbage was the telltale sign that somebody desperately wanted to cover his tracks. This is a pure treasure hunt, and that fortress in Abbottabad was the treasure.

Call this piece of evidence a wobbling star: Find the burned trash, and you will find the person who wants to conceal his or her identity or presence or hide some type of activity. People who wants to "cover their tracks" are those who tell you that others are looking for those tracks, such as the targeters of CIA and Navy Seals. By the way, if you are hunting down a marijuana grower, always subpoena the utility for gas and electric, but more importantly the water company. Dope growers habitually bypass the electric meter to avoid telltale high power bills that suggest commercial use in a home. Dope growers, on the other hand, rarely touch the gas service based on the fear that they cause a gas leak and necessarily call in the utility company or incinerate themselves. The crispy critter texture is a fashion statement. Few dopers bypass the water bills. Water is cheap. However, growing dope uses a lot of water and far more that the *Ozzie and Harriet* family of four and might suggest commercial use as opposed to residential use. Residential use of water is flat, and commercial use widely fluctuates.

We have more pottery shards, dinosaur fingernails and wobbling stars. The moral of this tale: Trash is a gold mine of information. Anybody who burns their trash or disposes of their trash to hide or conceal evidence is covering up criminal or illegal conduct. Find the missing trash, and you find your bad guy.

Chapter 6

Denial Is Not a River in Egypt

Here is another scenario that teaches you the power of deductive logic. Embrace that the debtor will deny ownership of any vulnerable property. But we can see attributes of them (the dinosaur fingernails, tire tracks, or pottery shards) such as checks for the lenders holding the secured debt, the county property taxes, insurance, or maintenance. You can't see the property in the name of the debt, but you can see attributes of ownership and infer that property exists (more fingernails, wobbling stars, and pottery shards). These attributes tell you that the debtor owns the property, but all you have are hints, suggestions, and evidence of ownership, but not the property itself.

Let's get back to business. Financial archaeology is no different. One clue leads to another and, down the line, the discovery of some treasure. Pottery shards provide information that reveals the wealth, or poverty, of the owner, the epoch of the civilization, the history of the times, and even the foods. Dinosaur fingernails might upend 200 years of scholarship. Wobbling starts might reveal E. T.'s crib. All these forensic tools enable the explorer to deduce certain suppositions that turn into scientific inferences or even facts. In discovering assets, the investigator, whether the party, lawyer, prosecutor, or victim, hunts for information that might reveal clues that evidence ownership of assets.

How does this work on the simplest terms? Subpoena the debtor's records and hunt for checks payable to the county tax assessor for property taxes, the bank for a loan, the insurance company for residential insurance, or even Home Depots for a large purchase. Why? These payments represent the normal debt service, taxes, and indices of real property ownership.

Chapter 7

Learn How to Track Parallel Dockets

The Lawsuit and Recorder

Eat and breathe pottery shards, wobbling planets, and dinosaur fingernails. If you seek to collect a debt or enforce a judgment, stop what you are doing for a moment and rethink the history of the incident, the chronology of the litigation, and reconstruct what you think the debtor has done. Enforcing a judgment requires you to retrace the history of every real estate transaction, go back deed by deed, lawsuit by lawsuit and reconstruct what the debtor has done. In nearly every case, we pull up the court's docket and compare the events, such as the filing of the lawsuit, service of process of the summons and complaint, filing of an answer, the status conferences, motions and trial setting, trial and judgment with the corresponding events on file with the county recorder or secretary of state (financing statement filings—call UCC's filings).

In one case, every time that the plaintiff inched down the litigation field toward the goal line of judgment, the debtor incrementally dumped over another parcel of real property into a limited liability company or family member. For example, the court's docket showed the date that that plaintiff served the lawsuit. Pull up the recorder's docket and see what happened around that date. Chances are you might find a grant deed to the debtor's spouse, child, or LLC a few days later. Better yet, get a copy of the deed and carefully look at the signature and accompanying acknowledgment by the notary. You might find that the date of the notarial acknowledgment for the deeds is the date after service of the lawsuit. Better yet, and for fun, pull down a copy of the proof of service and find out when (what time) the defendant was served. Compare that time of service with the actual time when the deed was recorded.

Be on the lookout for the events at trial. The court dockets show when the trial starts, who the witnesses are, what orders were entered, and what evidence is introduced. The court's docket will also show when the judge made the final ruling on the record, the date of the filed statement of decision, and ensuing judgment. Compare these dates to any transaction in the recorder. As we had in one case, the judgment was entered on day one, the debtor signed grant deeds for a pending sale on the next day, and closed the real estate deal on the third` day. On day four, and one day too late, the creditor recorded the abstract of judgment (the lien) and lost out. Late in this business is an inconsolable loss. It is not a complete loss because the proceeds from the sale of the property went into the debtor's lawyer's trust account. The debtor tumbled into bankruptcy court, and the trustee sued the lawyer for a fraudulent conveyance. The moral of this tale: Match the court's docket with the recorder's docket, and you will be able to track parallel events.

Let's play Sherlock Holmes. The plaintiff sues the defendant for an unlawful eviction, which means that the defendant (a landlord) illegally booted the plaintiff out of her rent-controlled house. The house is worth describing. The house was really a cottage that sat on the back portion of a rare (and legal) double lot in San Francisco. Getting rid the tenant would enable the landlord to demolish the cottage and build a three-story "wedding cake" house. For those of you new to the world of real estate, a wedding cake house is house built by real estate speculators that completely fills the lot space up and to and abutting the "setback lines." A setback is the borderline on the lot that limits the outer shell of the structure. The purpose of the wedding cake design is to exploit the real estate to the greatest extent possible.

Shortly after the landlord yanked the plaintiff out of the house, the landlord (now Mr. Defendant because he was sued for wrongful eviction) transfers the house to a conspirator who is the named owner. The transfer appears on the recorder's website as part of the grantor/grantee index. The landlord also owns a condominium in town. The tenant hired lawyers who filed suit against the former landlord who in fact hired a lawyer and filed an answer. The lawyer for the tenant took the deposition of the landlord, which commenced at 10:27 a.m. and ran about two hours.

That day was a busy morning for Mr. Defendant. On the way to the deposition taken at the plaintiff lawyer's office, Mr. Defendant stopped by the county recorder and deeded the condominium to his mother. Deeds are time-stamped, down to the minute. The deposition transcript showed the time that the deposition commenced, down to the minute. The sequence of these dates shows that Mr. Defendant stopped by the recorder's office, offloaded the last piece of real estate in his name, and showed up, without a worry in the world nor property to his name, and ready to be grilled. Mr. Defendant did not care what he said, whether he was believed, or whatever happened because he dumped over the side all his real estate holdings. Match the dates on the deposition and the dates on the recorded deeds; you have now entered the world of Financial CSI.

As you can imagine, the landlord lost the unlawful eviction case. The plaintiff recovered a $683,000 judgment against Mr. Defendant but never collected. The plaintiff sued the conspirator and recovered damages in the sum of $143,000. To exit that debacle, the conspirator filed bankruptcy, and the plaintiff sued again to declare the debt nondischargeable for "willful and malicious conduct." That case died in the manger.

Like a good archaeologist, you can also track the progress of litigation with filings of the Uniform Commercial Code (UCC) liens with the secretary of state, formation of new corporations, limited partnership or limited liability companies. You can track parallel to the progress of the lawsuit with new filings of fictitious business names that mirror the debtor but show as the owner a newly formed out-of-state, offshore corporation or limited liability company.

Enforcement compels you to embrace settled expectation that the debtor will offload assets so that when the judgment creditor wins at trial and scores that million-dollar judgment, the cupboard is absolutely bare. Expect that result; any other expectation would be a fool's game.

Chapter 8

Sir Isaac Commands You to Watch for the Reaction

You really don't need to read dense law books. You need to read Sir Isaac Newton. One of Newton's great rules is "to every action, there is an opposite and equal reaction." This means that if an aggrieved victim of a fraud or an assault sues the perpetrator, the opposite and equal reaction is to hide or conceal property. Count on it, and do not anticipate that the debtor will sit there supine, ready for you to pounce, when the judge pounds down the gavel and hands over to you the $15 million judgment. In military terms, failure or success depends on the correct analysis of the enemy's capabilities and intentions, as opposed to your intentions or capacities and, under the watchful eye of Sir Newton, what action you anticipate the debtor will take to fend off enforcement. Will the money in the debtor's bank account flee offshore, or will some Bahamian trust take title to the home? Don't sit there and think what a great guy you are and that the debtor is a dimwit. Sit there and immediately strategize exactly what the debtor will do.

This is important because the debtor is proactive. Nobody is going to sit idle while General Sherman marches through the Georgia woods. Expect that the debtor is going to squirrel everything away. Newton would tell you that.

Chapter 9

Pottery Shards in the Credit Report

Why can't I get a credit report that spells out everything?

If you are the creditor, you might have access to the credit reports of the debtor if allowed by law. If you are an agency or lawyer, you might have access also. The gatekeepers are the state and federal Fair Credit Reporting Acts. Even if you do not qualify and you are going to negotiate with the debtor over a discount, you can demand that the defendant produce a credit report. Don't get yourself sued by overstepping the consumer protection laws. If a private investigator claims to have access to protected information, hire someone else.

Modern credit reports and commercial services downstream (CreditReport.com etc.) amalgamate and synthesize this information.

What are you looking for? How about the following line entry: "First Bank & Trust," $1,000,000, 2012, 360 mo. Installment, Current." This is a pottery shard that tells you that the debtor is indebted to the bank, making payments on a long-term installment obligation (i.e., the home loan), probably owns the home and, most importantly, has the earnings to pay the debt service on a million-dollar home loan. Better yet, the loan is current. This line item also tells you that the debtor reposed with the lender a Uniform Residential Loan Application or sworn financial statement, verification of income and assets, and three years of tax returns. The credit report tells you who has possession of the treasure map. Credit reports offer information, such as the line items for other installment obligations, suggesting a mortgage that likewise suggests that the debtor owns other property. The credit report is the pottery shard that provides information that frames the financial condition of the debtor and steers you to a lender who possesses the debtor's financial statements. If you are an astronomy buff, the credit report is the wobbling star. Do you really know that the debtor owns the home, when in fact the debtor denies ownership and worse, the recorder's office shows that another person (or entity) owns the home? Answer: Yes. The line items listing the loan obligation to the bank, which are current to boot, are the wobble, and the actual home loan owed by the debtor is the planet's gravitational force exerted upon the star.

The credit report that shows secured installment loans indicating that ownership of a house, car, or other assets is your treasure map. Never hesitate to legally lay your hands on a credit report. Credit reports provide lots of clues that lead you to an asset. Find an installment obligation, and find an asset. Find a revolving line of credit, find collateral and probably a home; find a bid unsecured line of credit, and find big net worth.

Chapter 10

Tax Liens Are the Wobbling Stars

Let's apply pottery shards to tax liens and see what the liens can tell us.

This is a 50¢ primer on tax liens, which are all publicly recorded with the county recorder or filed with the secretary of state. If the tax lien is for 1040 taxes, that means that the debtor failed to pay for income taxes. If the tax lien is for, say, $200,000 (without penalties or interest), that means that the debtor earned about $600,000 as income (round numbers, folks, and if some IRS guy is reading this, he or she is going to cringe—sorry!). If you are examining this person in a debtor's examination, you know immediately that this person had a big income, whether earned or not, and gives you a place to start asking smart questions. If the taxes are 941's, this means that the debtor failed to turn over trust funds that constituted the employee portion of their own income taxes. Let's say that the 941 tax lien is $200,000 (without the penalties or interest), the payroll would exceed $1,000,000 (more cringing). This is another place to start at the debtor's examination. The 941 tax lien would also identify the debtor as the "owner" or "responsible agent" and confirm ownership of the business, notwithstanding the claims that the "wife" owns the business. UCC filings are available through the secretary of state, commercial search services, or public records services, such as Westlaw, Lexis-Nexis, D&B, TransUnion, Equifax, and Experian, among many others.

Tax liens are likewise clues on the treasure map. Show me $1,000,000 of unpaid income taxes (1040s), and I will show you about $4,000,000 in unreported income. The bigger the tax debt, the greater the income. You can mathematically reconstruct the income from the amounts in the lien notice. Tax liens are more arrows on the treasure map.

Chapter 11

The Wizardry of Financial Statement

The Good, Bad, and Really Ugly

What is a financial statement? I know many of you are lawyers, experienced businesspeople, and professionals, and accounting is left for the bean counters. Here we are going to count and classify the beans, which is the science of accounting. Accounting makes sense of financial transactions and renders them understandable. For our purposes, a financial statement depicts the financial condition of the debtor at a very precise moment in time. This document represents the state of the debtor's finances, such as assets and liabilities and income and expenses, which is an accumulation of prior financial activity brought current to the date of the presentation of the statement. The balance sheet distills and aggregates all financial activity. If, for example, the financial statement shows inventory, that means the inventory on hand as of that date. If we start on day one with $1,000 of inventory, $700 in accounts payable due the vendor for the goods, $100 for freight charges, and no cash, and on day two, we sold $900 of inventory and paid the bills including the freight bill, the balance sheet would show $100 of inventory, no accounts payable, no freight charges, and $100 of cash on hand as profit. If we closed the books on that date, the profit would be posted as retained earnings. I pray I got this right. Really I do. If not, my e-mail, which is available through the website of the State Bar of California and on my own website, will receive one or more testy e-mails. "Did you take remedial accounting? What grade did you get?"

Businesses employ the cash or accrual method of accounting and sometimes a mixture. Cash accounting means the business does not account (another word for recognize) the transaction until cash is in hand, or cash for goods or services, or other event when something tangible comes in hand. Restaurants are on a cash basis. Sales represent the delivery of the food, and collection of the check. Large industrial concerns, such as auto, oil, or high-tech, recognize the sale when the buyer and seller entered into a contract, or maybe when the seller delivers the product (or services), even though the bill is due in 30-plus days. Writing down inventory, accounts receivable, or other assets means that the company recognized the asset as almost irretrievably worthless and takes a loss, which is a direct charge against earnings.

During the subprime crisis, the banks, stockbrokers, and hedge funds wrote down, or wrote off, their mortgage portfolio because the borrowers defaulted, and the underlying collateral (theirs) plummeted in value. These write-downs decreased their earnings and charged to retained earnings.

Is this important to you? You bet. If chasing down any business, the first demand is for financials to assess whether the debtor is viable or a rotting hulk. The financials start with a treasure hunt in locating assets or deciding that the debtor lacks any assets. If the debtor in an operating business proposes a payment program, the financials would reveal how much or whether the debtor can pay. If the financial statement shows a huge negative retained earnings and that the debtor is unable to pay current bills, the debtor is likely to default on the payment program and probably file bankruptcy, or face foreclosure from a secured creditor. If the debtor is paying an inordinate amount for inventory, rent, or debt service due to insider loans, something is rotten in the financials and the business itself. If the business stopped maintaining records or claims that the accountant "walked off the job" or that the entire accounting department quit or that no financials are available, don't speculate that the debtor is rotten because the rot permeates the debtor.

The insiders shield their inside theft by destroying or concealing records. Inadequate, incomplete, or incomprehensible records are the wobbling stars that broadcast financial fraud. Financial statements without backup records, such as contemporaneous accounting journals, ledgers, and source materials, are likewise near useless. The failure to turn over these core documents likewise announces financial fraud.

Retained earnings are a backward and forward crystal ball. If the financial statement shows "retained earnings," that column represents historically all gains and losses from the beginning to the end. If the retained earnings are negative, that means that the company has had a history of losing money and that the losses have exceeded the capital and is aggregating the losses. If the company has positive retained earnings, the company has been making money and likewise aggregating over the years profits. In the land of insolvency, a debtor corporation bears huge negative retained earning that show years of losing money. Call retained earnings, if accurate, the accounting scorecard. The appearance of the insider loan on the financial statements means that at that moment, and at only that moment, the books and records of the company reflect that transaction.

Let's peel back the financial statement. The financial statement presents the classification of financial information from the company ledger of accounts. The ledger of accounts is the assembly of each account, such as cash, accounts receivable, inventory, equipment, furnishing, or leasehold interest. The ledger is the totality of the account at a certain point in time only. Each individual account that appears on the ledger is supported by journal entries that are called debit and credit.

Before unlocking the secrets of debit and credit, here is the primer on financial statements, which comes in four flavors: audited, reviewed, compiled, and "management only." I know some Certified Public Accountant is going to squawk and write me a nasty e-mail saying that "compiled" and "management only" are the same thing. I disagree for purposes of this book. The word "audited" means that the CPA verifies that the financial statement fairly and accurately reflects the financial condition of the company. The CPA impliedly warrants that the CPA has done something to ensure that the financial representation is reasonably accurate in reflecting the condition of the company, not just the condition of the books.

Audited financial statements are required for nearly all public companies, and virtually any big company that seeks a major bank loan. Consider an audited financial statement "touchy feely." What in God's name does touchy feely mean here? Answer: It means that the CPA presumptively touched and felt the assets of the debtor to make sure they were there. What does that really mean? If the debtor sells women's high-end dresses, the accountant (probably an inventory service) counted the dresses, or at least, tested management count to ensure that the inventory was accurate.

Very extensive notes accompany nearly all audited financials and represent the auditor's opinions. The most famous is the going-concern statement as follows: "There are material uncertainties related to events or conditions that may cast significant doubt about the company's ability to continue as a going concern." This statement, and its many variants, are the functional equivalent of the doctor telling the cancer patient that "further tests are required," which is one step before the "Have you gotten your affairs in order?" question. Auditor's notes reveal related or interconnected loans, leases or sales, pending lawsuits and claims, contingencies that are material, or whether certain accounts might default. A publicly filed company produces quarterly and annual financials are all available on the U.S. Securities & Exchange website, EDGAR, and include reams of auditor's notes.

The next financial statement is "reviewed." This means that the CPA believes that the numbers are accurate but not necessarily reflective of the financial condition. The reviewed statement in the vernacular means "it looks okay to me, but beyond that, I'm not so sure." The CPA warrants that the numbers on the financial statement accurately came from the books and records and that they, therefore, reflect the books and records, whatever that might be. Reviewed financials rarely have extensive notes, or any notes, which means that you don't get any feel for whether the statement is an accurate representation of the financial affairs of the entity.

The next one is "compiled." What does compile mean? The CPA is telling you that the financial statements look nice. They are so pretty. They are so cute! The columns are straight, there are no typos, and the commas are all in the right place. Numbers are in the correct column, and they might even add up. Does the compiled statement reflect the financial condition of the company? God only knows, and don't bet on it. The fact that the CPA issues a compiled statement implicitly tells you that the CPA figured out that the records are just plain cooked, and that the best he can do is make everything look nice. Call a compiled financial statement a particularly ugly pig with lipstick. If you ever take the deposition of the CPA who produced one of these statements and ask, "How would you classify the financial statement you produced, whether audited, reviewed, or compiled?" Answer: Compiled. Question: Why compiled? Why not reviewed or audited? Answer: "The books were awful. No way would I stick my name to anything less than rearranging the chairs on the upper deck." This comes directly from one of the final scenes from the movie *Titanic* when the ship is about to go down and the deck hands were rearranging the deck furniture. Don't expect any notes to the financial statement, other than "I had nothing to do with these numbers."

The last category of financial statements isn't really a financial statement in the truest sense. It represents numbers on a page, which may have no relationship to the financial condition of the company. Call these financial statements "by guess and by golly." This calls for "management only." These documents are helpful and kick off a wealth of questions. Are these statements accurate? Who knows, but at least you have a place to start and no more.

Chapter 12

Finding Real Money in Old Financial Statements

Let me save you $60,000 on your MBA. Reading and understanding financial statements gives you the financial X-ray vision to see through a clear financial fraud. Lift the veil of false financial statements and find the assets on the map right in front of you. Let's take a tour of a financial statement and see what we can find.

The first lesson is that financial statements are the ongoing but individual snapshots of the business. The financial statement will reveal as of its date the company's assets and liability, income and expense, and cash application statements, which change from day to day. The financial statement is a historical document that frames the exact condition of the company at that moment. Now, mind you, Ms. Ma Ligned is looking at the financial statement because you are trying to collect her judgment against Foodle Doodle Company and might see only junk which is downright discouraging and for good reason. A bad financial statement might scare off anyone who might well believe that Foodle Doodle Company is devoid of any assets and insolvent. In plain English: Foodle Doodle Company looks deader than a doornail.

If you want to understand its business, ask for financials over a five-year period. Let's see why. You might find that five years ago, the insider (Mr. Doodle) borrowed big money from Foodle Doodle Company, which means that Mr. Doodle as the insider is the account obligor who owes money to the company. This line item appears on the asset side of the financial statement either as a short-term note receivable (less than one year) or in long-term assets (more than one year) as a note receivable.

Why does the insider owe money to his own company? Answer: If his company, which is a corporation, made big money, the insider, Mr. Doodle, did not want to take a salary because he would have to pay taxes on his income, and his company would pay payroll taxes. Typically, the net due a high-end employee is about 70 percent of the total compensation. Instead, Mr. Doodle claimed that his company lent him the money, and the total cash due the insider was 100 percent. Sounds good? Well, it's too good to be true because the IRS might deem the loan as disguised income and assess stupendous penalties for this distribution.

Foodle's current financials did not reveal this account receivable due the company from Mr. Doodle, and for good reason. Ms. Ma Aligned hired a fancy lawyer who told him that Mr. Doodle is an "account debtor," who owed the money to his company—and Ms. Ma Aligned, the judgment creditor. She could levy on Mr. Doodle, the account debtor owing money to the judgment debtor, and compel Mr. Doodle to pay his debt to the company (or to her). It's a neat trick if you can do this. In plain English: Money that Mr. Doodle owed his company is an asset, and if subject to levy, like a bank account, Mr. Doodle can be forced to pay Ms. Ma Ligned, the judgment creditor, the debt he owes Foodle Doodle Co. Mr. Doodle wanted to conceal the fact that he owes his company a bunch of money so he does not have to pay off Ms. Ma Ligned. Mr. Doodle is going to bury the accounting line items that showed he owed big money to his company—and therefore Ms. Ma Ligned, the judgment creditor.

What's the good news and what's the bad news? Mr. Doodle found an old Turkish oil lamp, which he tried to shine up, but out pops Mr. Jinni who offers Mr. Doodle three wishes. Mr. Doodle's first wish was to make the debt he owed to the company disappear. Call this a David Copperfield accounting moment. The second wish was to have Mr. Jinni do the accounting. Mr. Doodle told Jinni, "Write off the debt." Jinni said, "Yeah, sure. If you write off this debt, and we file a tax return, the company's books will show that the insider's debt was "written off," which will require an explanation and might prompt an audit. You owe this big debt to the company, and you got the money as a tax-free loan to avoid paying taxes on the money for yourself and for the company. How are you are going to explain this to the IRS?" Mr. Doodle answered: "Look, I contributed all sorts of stuff to the company, including money which equaled the debt." "What money and what stuff and where are bank statements and contemporaneous accounting recorders?" "I don't know. I don't have any records. Just recreate a bunch of accounting entries, and nobody, but nobody, will know the difference." Jinni fabricates an entire series of accounting transactions such as inventory, equipment, furnishing, and products that Mr. Doodle claimed to have contributed to his company; cash payments to third parties such as vendors of his company; and investment in refurbishing the premises in the form of cash, with no receipts for the company. Jinni entered all these compensating transactions at the end the fiscal year under the title of "adjusting entries," even though the alleged transactions took place over many prior years. For the green shade set, the expression "reconciling entries," is the correct accounting term. The problem with the word *reconciling* or *reconciliation,* is the inference that the accountant seeks to reconcile (or more aptly change) the books to reflect another narrative, which is patently false.

The amount of these later-day entries, which were credits to the "note receivable" owed by Mr. Doodle, reduced the Doodle's obligation owed to his company to zero.

Better yet, the current financial statement did not even disclose the note receivable due from the insider because the obligation is "zeroed out" and deemed paid through the prior offsets. Of course, the note receivable due from Mr. Doodle appears on the financial statements over the prior years but disappeared magically when the last-minute offsets were posted.

Here is another classic "reconciliation." Faced with declining and irreversible financial losses, Joe wants to sell his failing business and eke out some gain, as opposed to dumping the business into bankruptcy. Upon this ugly demise, the trade creditors, the bank, and the landlord would sue Joe on his personal guaranties, which would force Joe to likewise file bankruptcy. Two bankruptcies is a bad ending. Joe turns to his accountant, Mr. Quicken (whose wife, by the way, is Mrs. Quicken), to "reconcile the books." Let's take a super-quick spin. Quicken will print invoices. Just input the name and address of the customer and fill in the blanks, and before the Top Ramen is ready, the newly minted sale inflates the financial statement. Tally up the sales and reconcile the ledger account for "lately posted" sales, and we turn this puppy from a dead-bang loser to the star of Harvard Business School. Joe sells the business for big money and skates. The buyer gets stuck holding an empty bag. Of course, the buyer is going to sue everybody, including his or her lawyer, accountant, and broker for their negligence in failing to confirm the financials of the seller.

Jinni offered three wishes. The third wish was to make the prior financial statements and prior accounting records disappear. This wish might or might not succeed. Some folks such as Mr. Doodle could make records disappear and refuse access to the company records. This strategy could backfire because the refusal to turn over records is an admission that the records would reveal some prejudicial admissions or wrongdoing. Moreover, the prior financial statement such as the balance sheet might be in the hands of an accountant, or third party, which would reveal the debt owed by Mr. Doodle. If the CPA generated the financial statements over the years, you can serve the CPA with a broad-based subpoena and generate copies. Moreover, you can also gain access to the CPA's working papers and source materials, notes that supported the year-end reconciling entries and other debit and credits to individual line accounts.

How can Ms. Ma Ligned reach this receivable by Mr. Doodle, which he owes to Foodle Doodle Company? Easy. Serve Mr. Doodle with a simple garnishment. He will have answered "no money held," which is a complete lie. She can sue him for the recovery of the money as an account receivable due the Foodle Doodle Company, fraudulent conveyances, breach of fiduciary duty, money had and received, and resulting trust (money held in trust for the benefit of another). She can take Doodle's deposition and his accountant's deposition, and they will sing the same song: Nothing is owed to the company because Mr. Doodle paid off his debt with compensating advances of personal property for the company's benefit and cash advances to third parties. Of course, none of these compensating entries that sought to reduce the debt were contemporaneous as they were manufactured years later.

Let's apply our lesson to this example. You have the earliest financial statement in your hands that shows that Mr. Doodle owes his company some serious money. The financial statement lists this obligation as a note receivable on the assets side. The next year the financial statement still shows the note receivable. So far, so good. The third year is bad. Your client, Mr. Creditor, gets burned and files a lawsuit. The financial statement at the end of the year in which Mr. Creditor sued and won omits the note receivable owed by Mr. Doodle. They are gone, gone, and really gone.

You grab the accounting ledgers and journals for the year in which the note receivable disappeared and spot a slug of year-end reconciling entries that wipe out the account with consummate credits to the account (reducing the balance) and debit to miscellaneous items, such as "equipment," "goods," or "goodwill." These are all year-end entries, and lack any contemporaneous accounting entries. Nada, nada, and more nada accounting entries other than the year-end hodgepodge of entries.

You find the note receivable, which means that Mr. Doodle owes a pot of money to the company, which if paid, would pay off the creditor. The note receivable does not appear on the financial statement issued in the midst of litigation. You look for the reconciling entries, which make no sense. You attempt to tie them back to the date or dates when the transaction took place and do not find any contemporaneous entries.

Who is going to win this case and why? Here is the answer from *Pivirotto v. Belkin*, A077897, 1998 WL 35320928 at page *5 (Cal. App. 1st Dist. 1998): "The trial court determined that Belkin did not carry his burden of persuasion of showing that payments made to TCT were either received by the company or accepted as debt repayment. The ultimate finding is supported by substantial evidence that Belkin's debt to TCT was not offset. First, Belkin failed to provide contemporaneous records showing that TCT received $240,000. Such evidence would have shown the receipt of the sum in three installments (Belkin claimed that he paid the sum in installments), posting of the funds to the cash account, and application of the payments as a payment to the loan account. Second, Belkin argues that TCT received $240,000. However, the accounting records did not indicate receipt at the time. He proposes that TCT mistakenly credited the money to the ARC2 (Airline Reporting Corporation) sales account. However, Belkin presented no contemporaneous records that reflected receipt of $240,000 in three installments into the ARC account or the erroneous posting of the money to that account. Third, Belkin failed to show the correction of each claimed erroneous entry from the sales account into the Belkin debt account.

Belkin admitted that TCT's records might be in error and that the funds may have been erroneously posted. However, he produced no evidence, such as bank statements, showing the receipt of $240,000.

In addition, the testimony of plaintiff's forensic expert, Michael Berg, demonstrated the improbability that the funds were either received or mistakenly posted to the sales account. He pointed to the insufficiency of records that would show the activity of each account. Furthermore, records that were available were made only after a final accounting.

Berg testified that a $240,000 offset was "improbable." Berg explained that to make Belkin's case credible, TCT would have had to commit 36 separate accounting mistakes. Berg also testified that the ARC account would have to be out of balance for multiple months. Berg also said, "[We would be] actually reducing sales of ARC and decreasing the amount of money that Mr. Belkin owes the company, which is a pretty odd entry [o]n its face, and would require, I don't know, a bunch of mistakes to be made for that to occur." Berg concluded that Belkin owed TCT $379,709.31, the debt was not paid, TCT did not receive the sum of $240,000, and Belkin's claim was bogus." The footnote is the best: "[B]asically the offsets that he tries to take against the [$]379,000 plus debt that he had are inappropriate. They were bookkeeping entries that were made inappropriately. And he still owed that money as of the time of the writ of attachment."

The facts offer a great narrative when the insider to a business borrows money from his company to free himself from the burden of taxes, and when the company is burdened with a big money judgment, the insider will try to discharge his liability to the company with nonexistent offsets. After I figured out that he took out a tax-free loan, we served him with a garnishment. He answered and denied owing any money to his company. We sued him on the loan that he owed the company, sued for a fraudulent conveyance, and sued in the name of the company itself to recover the debt.

This case showed that the records were not contemporaneous (i.e., they are trumped up), that the final adjusting entries were unsupported in the historical accounting record, that many of the accounting entries were irrational or wrong, that the contemporaneous accounting records did not evidence the receipt of offsetting money or property, and that there were massively irrational or erroneous postings, and there are no banking records that show the receipt of money (as an offset).

The insider has the burden of persuasion to prove the offsets against the debt that he owed to the company. This is not a technical term (burden of persuasion) but a point of law. Why is this important, or really important? Here is an easy example. I am going to sue you for the $10 that I claim I lent to you. The court calls the case. I take the stand and tell the judge that you entered into a loan agreement, that I gave you $10, and that you promised to pay me on Tuesday, Popeye. I tell the judge that you did not pay me, and rest my case. Now, you might take the stand and tell the judge that I did not give you any money or that the money was a gift or that you paid me back. Either way, I must prove to the judge that I lent you the money in the first place, and your job is to convince the judge that the transaction did not occur or that you have some defense such a payment or an offset.

Instead of an arm's-length transaction, the lender is a company, and the borrower is the company president. The company owes its trade creditors (the butcher, baker, and candlestick maker) up and down the street. The creditors find out that the company emptied out its bank account in favor of the president. The president literally wrote himself a check for the total of the company's bank balance but claimed that the payment was to liquidate a personal loan owed by the company to the president.

The company is now dead broke, and the president has all the company money. When the creditors sue the president for a fraudulent conveyance, given that the president is an insider and has control over the company, the president has the burden of persuasion to convince the judge that the company legitimately owed him the money and that payment to him was authorized. In plain English: The battle in many cases is to see who has to prove their case. If the insiders are sitting on a big fat fraudulent conveyance, which consists of the company treasury, most states will compel the insiders to justify their haul by a preponderance of the evidence, or otherwise cough back the money.

Moral of this tale: The person stuck going first is the person stuck proving the case. Typically, insiders who received company property (i.e., the debtor) necessarily go first in proving why the transfer of the money (or property) to the insider is valid and the insider should beat out the creditors of the company.

Chapter 13

The Insider's Secured Loans Are an Asset Protection

You are presented with a financial statement that reflects on the liability side an insider long-term loan. The financial statement might be accompanied by notes, indicating that this loan is owed to an insider and secured by the company assets. Insider loans, supported by a security interest, enable an insider to claim all assets and render a corporate debtor immune from any enforcement. When the creditor levies on the debtor's assets, the insider claims that the insider's lien has priority and attempts to oust the levying creditor. Ejecting the creditor from common enforcement renders the debtor "judgment proof," and therefore renders the judgment uncollectable. Secured insider loans are the remedy of choice in fending off aggressive enforcement.

Insider loans appear on the liability side of the balance sheet which might even be an audited financial statement. Typically, the loan exceeds the value of the assets. The first step to unpeeling this alleged loan and security is to demand all prior financial statements going back five years. If this is a long-term loan, this loan should appear on the liability side for the last five years. Obviously, if this loan does not appear on the financial statement last year or the year before, the inference is that the insiders were cooking the books and that the line item for the insider loan and the loan documents are fraudulent.

Let's take a break here. You are staring at the company's financial statement consisting of a balance sheet and profit and loss statement for 2012. The balance sheet shows an insider-secured loan of $1,000,000 and assets of $250,000. You say to yourself, "Where did this come from?" The balance sheet for 2011 does not show this loan. Presto gizmo! You conclude the following. One, the 2012 financial statement is a fraud, or two, the loan was made in 2012. Let's walk though that conclusion. Look through the bank records for a bank deposit of $1,000,000 in one lump sum or installments and the contemporaneous accounting entries for debit cash, credit loans, or notes payable. If you do not find the deposits or the accounting entries, the loan is a fraud.

Always demand the accounting journals, ledgers, quarterly (or monthly) financials, copies of the bank statements, copies of deposit slips, copies of canceled checks for insider transactions, and all prior accountant's notes. These documents are source documents, or earlier periodic snapshots that might contradict the later financial statement that is presented to you. Unpeeling these loans lifts the veil and opens the door to an asset unencumbered by false and fraudulent loans.

Chapter 14

Olly Olly Oxen Free! Where Can You Find the Financial Records?

First, the debtor has them. Drop a subpoena on the debtor. That's a good place to start. If you are in state court, attach the subpoena to the debtor's examination. If you are in federal court, just drop the subpoena on the debtor.

Some financial statements are posted in EDGAR, if the debtor is a public company. Second, these records are in the hands of the debtor's accountants, and potentially its major lender, factor, leasing company, or financier. The major vendor may have some of these records. A major lender for any of the corporate principals might have these records. If you do not know who these major lenders are, you can run a Universal Commercial Code search, or alternatively, cull through the records of the county recorder.

Vendors are important because it is likely that the debtor provided much better-looking financial statements free of these insider loans or other derogatory information. Other financiers, such as the banks, factors, or major goods suppliers, might have declined the credit if the company was buried under secured debt. Nobody wants to lend money to an insolvent entity. Good credit practices demand a potential customer supply financial statements for the company and the guarantors who are usually the customer's inside principals.

Chapter 15

Read the Loan Documents of Third Parties

Third Parties Bar Insider Loans

A lender, such as a bank, factor, flooring lender, or anybody else with a major financial commitment, imposes noneconomic covenants as part of the loan agreement. These noneconomic covenants bar insiders from encumbering the assets to secure their insider loans. The encumbering of the asset for an insider would be a default that would freeze the loan account or prompt an acceleration or foreclosure by the lender. Another noneconomic covenant is to subordinate the insider loan to the bank's loan, bar junior liens to secure insider loans or any other loan or credit, and, moreover, bar the debtor from paying off the insider loan until the bank loan is paid. Again, this insider loan and payments per the insider loan might be the basis of a default under the loan. Other noneconomic covenants might include mandatory turnover of financial statements and periodic reporting of cash, inventory, profit, receivables, sales, or capital requirements.

The insider of the debtor therefore would be disinclined to represent to the major financier the fact of the insider loan, and obviously would support the conclusion that the "insider loan" is fictitious. In the current environment, the lender rarely or never waives this term.

In the deposition of the insider, one of the first lines of questioning is to see how the insider can reconcile this insider loan to the fact that these loans are barred or subordinated in favor of the financial institution. This is not all that arcane. Anybody with the slightest financial background would know that the primary lenders always, and without fail, demand that insiders subordinate their loans to the bank, bar junior liens, and bar payments to insiders of their insider loans, as long as the bank is unpaid. The reason for these prohibitions is to protect the senior lender from competing with the junior lender for assets and to bar the junior lender (i.e., the insider) from claiming that the bank mishandled the collateral in the event of a foreclosure. Consider the noneconomic term the financial version of a powerful nanny who prevents the insider from pilfering company assets through insider loans or from seeking to bleed out cash or other fungible assets through the ruse of a junior security interest and the claims of a default. Call the term's trip wire on the way to financial Armageddon, Bruce.

The best advice my father gave me while I was in college was to take courses in accounting. I had no idea until much later in life how enormously valuable that advice was. You can't be a lawyer, you can't be a businessperson, you can't hunt for assets, you can't do anything until you have a working knowledge of accounting principles. I am certain I would not pass the CPA exam, but I am certain that I understand accounting principles enough to unwind a fraudulent loan.

Chapter 16

Peek-a-Boo, I See You

Finding Hidden Gems in the Financial Records

Let's start with a $100,000 loan. The insider claims to have written a check for a $100,000 to his company or 10 checks at $10,000 or irregular amounts. In other cases, the insider is going to claim that he or she transferred "goodwill," inventory, equipment, leasehold interest, or leasehold improvements into the company. If the cash transfer supports the loan, demand the check (the original) that would identify the name of the endorser and the depositing bank, which might or might not be the debtor. The company accountant takes the check and deposits it in the company account. Get the deposit slip. Demand the bank account of the insider to show the source of the funds.

Let's go through the rudiments of double-entry accounting. We are all postdigital, which means that accounting programs post debits and credits as part of double-entry accounting. Every accounting transaction requires two entries. We debit assets, expenses, and dividends, which increases these items. A credit to these categories decreases them. When we debit liabilities, revenue (sales), and equity, these items are decreased. When we credit these categories, they are increased. Let's say we sell something for cash. Here are the entries: Debit cash, credit sales, debit costs of sale, credit inventory. What is important is that the entry transaction requires at least two, or four separate entities. (Pray I got this right.)

Let's focus on that insider loan. The insider claims to have given the company the $100,000 and secured the loan with a broad-based security interest in all the assets. Aside from a legal attack of self-dealing and unfairness, let's wade through the accounting records. Aside from bank records to show that the money hit the debtor's bank account and the insider's bank records to show the source of the money, here are the basic entries for the $100,000. Cash comes into the bank account: Debit cash for each installment or the total. The liability of the company increases: Credit liabilities for each separate alleged contribution or loan infusion. These two simple entries would be contemporaneous with the actual loan: debit cash, and credit the loan balance. Chances are the insider is going to claim that periodic contributions made up the $100,000 total loan and you see for each transfer the double entries. If the insider contributed inventory, equipment, or furnishings, each accounting entry would be "debit inventory," "credit liabilities." We would look for double entries for each contribution, no matter the form.

Bookkeeping entries should be entered at or near the transaction by individuals charged with that duty in a manner consistent with regular and regular and ordinary course of business. The fact that the entry exists contemporaneously suggests a high degree of truthfulness by individuals who have no bias, free of consideration of future events, and that the entry was regular on its face. Moreover, the fact that those entries and related other entries were done, supervised, or approved by a multitude of individuals further supports the integrity of the entry. However, if the entries are not contemporaneous, but cobbled up at a later date, the technical term authorized under generally accepted accounting principles (GAAP) for these types of entries is that they "suck."

Let's go back to the wobbling star analogy. The star wobbles because a planet orbits the star and exerts a gravitational pull on the star. This pull, no matter how slight, forces the star to wobble. Conversely, if there is no wobble, there is no gravitational pull and no orbiting planet. Let's apply that lesson to debit and credit for insider loans. Seeking to assert a secured position based on an insider loan, the insider claims to have lent the company millions secured by a blanket lien. The accounting records do reflect contemporaneous debits and credits that would evidence the alleged contribution of cash, inventory, or anything else of value. The answer is simple: No accounting entries that contemporaneously record the loan contributions and therefore no loan at all. The loan is a fiction. The security is void. How so? Remember that security follows the debt and that security without any debt is void.

If you are in court battling over the secured loan and assert that the loan is bogus and then win, the security should evaporates because security only secures a debt that is outstanding. Security follows the debt.

Your first witness would be the company accountant or company-outside CPA to prove the lack of any of these entries. I know that some of you are going to say that not everybody's books and records are perfect and that many businesspeople bring in the accountants at the end of the year to do a "cleanup." This is total malarkey. Today's accounting products, such as Quick Books, are so efficient and inexpensive that a year-end cleanup is not required. An avid accounting student, as I was, could figure it out. The issue is that these entries were done contemporaneously. This is a pottery-shard epiphany. The lack of contemporaneous accounting records, such as debit cash and credit debt at the time of the alleged loan, suggests that the transaction never took place. The debit and credit postings or their absence is the pottery shard to contradict, and even doom, the claim of the insider loan. Once the court unpeels the fraudulent layer of the insider loan, the creditor can liquidate the company and collect.

Financial records, supported now by good deal of Accounting 101 and 102, always points out to an asset.

By the way, if you are contemplating law as a career, take accounting courses in college or a community college. This is 100% worthwhile.

Chapter 17

If the Entity Is Still Alive, the Entity Might Have Assets

Let's apply these lessons to the basic investigation. The first question is whether the debtor is alive. If the debtor is a corporation, or LLC, "alive" means that the secretary of state lists the entity as active. Well, partner, that costs some money and time. Most states compel payment of annual taxes for these entities, and the yearly filings of statements of officers, or members. To keep these entities alive, some effort is required. Not too much, but someone has to invest time, effort, and energy to keep these entities from going stale (i.e., suspended in the secretary of state lingo).

The question is why? Why is the debtor entity still alive? You cannot find, so you think, any property, bank accounts, real estate, or anything else in the debtor's name. The entity looks like a bust. But entities that are without any assets still have a life. Here is where pottery shards, dinosaur fingernails, and wobbling stars are important. The reason why the entity is still alive is that the entity is still doing business with someone, somewhere, and somehow. Or, the entity is suing, going to be sued, or will sue someone. An entity that is deader than a doornail cannot enter into a contract, nor can it file or defend a lawsuit. The entity is kept alive because the entity is conducting some type of business, or engaging in some sort of litigant or claims proceedings that you cannot directly see. This is a wobbling planet moment.

Call the active but apparently dormant corporation or LLC an example of the blinking lights test. What does this mean if you are not a techie? A blinking lights test means that you turn on an electronic device, and the lights (usually red, blue, or white) start to blink. This means that the device is energized and that the circuits are "closed" (i.e., electricity flows through the device). If you are a Frankenstein fan, the response is, "It's alive! It's alive!" The lights blink.

Who knows whether the device works or what the status of the software or other functions may be, but at least the device is breathing electrons. How does the analogy apply here? Answer: If the secretary of state shows that entity is active, the lights are blinking.

Better yet, if the debtor's phone or fax number answers or the website is current or some activity is taking place, the entity might be engaging in some type of transactions. Completely dead entities cannot sue or enter into contracts. "If it's alive, the entity is doing business somewhere," says Mr. Wobbling Star. Moral of this tale: If the lights are on, somebody is at home. Who is at home might be another question.

The blinking lights test (an alive entity) is another clue on the map. If someone is paying good money to keep the entity alive, the entity is alive, well, and kicking; therefore, it is another arrow on the map.

Chapter 18

Yelp Is the New Sherlock Holmes

The new source of information is Yelp. Yelp is the universal critic of virtually all goods and services. Call Yelp the town meeting hall in which the participants rate products and services. We had one case in which the debtor was a professional caterer. Most people think that a caterer is the person who caters parties, weddings, conventions, and food to other sites that lack an organized kitchen facility. Wakes are even catered. What you might not know is that catering businesses provide full kitchen food service to schools and universities, institutional facilities, corporate dining halls, sporting events, arenas, convention halls, and entertainment venues such as opera, symphony, concert halls. We were staring at one debtor without the slightest clue of who the debtor's clients were. The debtor was a good-sized caterer with a fixed office and apparent staff. The caterer had fixed clients.

We ran the debtor up through Google and spotted the name in Yelp. We opened up Yelp and found a wonderful review by a customer raving over the food offered by this caterer at a local concert hall. Immediately, we came to the conclusion that this debtor was providing food service to the concert hall. We called the concert hall, and they confirmed; we got the fax number. We held an assignment order issued by the court. We call them pay-me orders, meaning pay me and not the debtor. We have a nice letter that accompanies them and explains that the account debtor or the judgment debtor ought to pay "me," which really means the judgment creditor, and not the judgment debtor. About 2:30 p.m., I faxed the letter and the order to the concert hall. About 3:00 p.m., I received a telephone call from the caterer asking me to calculate the final balance due and advising that the check would be in my hands on the next business day. I suspect that the caterer's contract with the concert hall contained noneconomic terms, meaning that the caterer would be in default of his contract with the concert hall if the caterer suffered a judgment, levy, or execution. Alternatively, I don't think the concert hall was looking forward to the prospect of us sending in the sheriff to take money out of the cash register operated by the caterer on the premises. Entertaining, yes, but it is not good for business. Money falls from the sky in interesting ways. A Yelp review is the classic arrow on the map.

Chapter 19

Teddy Roosevelt Charged Up San Juan Hill to Become President

The lesson for you is determination. This story is worth telling. During the Civil War, the South was looking for a war-winner to change the tide of war. The Confederate army and navy were highly motivated and manned by legions of trained men who had great courage. However, the South lacked natural resources and had a manufacturing base inferior to that of the United States. In both cases, the South understood that the United States would ultimately prevail and that the only variable was when and how. Each country sought a war winner. The war winner (we call it a wonder weapon or technological marvel) for the South was the former *USS Merrimack*, which had been converted into the *CSS Virginia*. On March 9, 1862, the *CSS Virginia* and *USS Monitor* dueled for four hours and scored many hits on each other. Neither sank, and the *CSS Virginia* escaped. Why didn't the *Monitor* sink the *Merrimack* and why is that answer relevant in 2012? Answer: The armaments for the *Monitor* were designed by Dahlgren and were fired at 50 percent of their normal gunpowder. The reason was that in a prior demonstration and a full load, a Dahlgren blew up and killed the secretary of state and secretary of the navy. Had the *Monitor* used a full shot and hit the same spot on the *Merrimack*, the *Monitor* might have summarily sunk the *Merrimack* and severally damaged the morale of the South. What does this have to do with the enforcement of judgments? Don't hesitate and keep pounding away until the other person sinks or surrenders. Honest to goodness, keep at it.

Here is another story. We were pursuing a large judgment against an offshore debtor. We flooded their US customers with subpoenas. The debtor and its U.S. distributor retained first-rate lawyers to enjoin us from this broad-based campaign, which included our threats of sending out many more subpoenas. My beloved son-in-law did this legwork to locate more customers who we would subpoena. The debtor's lawyers hailed out of Los Angeles, which just increased the expense. He wore Ivy League on his face. He filed superb paperwork in an attempt to quash our campaign. His paperwork was much better than mine. No, that is not true. His paper was better paper than mine. We had pending our motion to grab the debtor's patent and trademark, which was set about a month away. I am sure that the paper left our office with the correct spelling of the United Patent and Trademark office. In response to his motion to stop what we were doing, we countered by filing a motion to advance the patent and trademark motions, which had been set much later down the line. Take that, we said! The judge rejected the debtor's request for a stay of our wildly ineffective but very noisy enforcement, but advanced our patent and trademark motions to an earlier hearing date. What that meant in plain English is that the debtor could not put a stop to our needling discovery, and the court put our patent and trademark motion in the debtor's face. The debtor settled. Stony silence punctuated our ensuing phone calls to work out the details of the settlement with the other side.

Let's go back a second and repeat the *Monitor* and *Virginia* story. So nobody is confused, and worse complains to my editor or me, the *CSS Virginia* is the *USS Merrimack*. I told you that had the *Monitor* used a full powder charge and pounded away at the same spot on the *Virginia*, that the *Monitor* might have sunk the *Virginia*. The Civil War might not have ended earlier, but the victory that the *Monitor* might have achieved in sinking the *Virginia* would have had a profound effect on the Civil War and the conduct of naval warfare. Same result here. Pound away and do not walk away. When in doubt, call in family members—well, not all family members, only the ones you owe a favor.

Chapter 20

Personal Drive Will Get You What You Want

Let's talk about motivation and personal drive. My father taught me that the key character element is personal drive, and nothing less. Your debtor does not want to pay. Whether a $100 personal loan to a family member or the $6.0M personal injury judgment, a debt becomes the challenge enjoyed by the debtor in evading payment, and the eternal quest by the creditor in separating the debtor from assets.

Before my stint as a Chicken Delight driver, I was a short-order cook. I was taught how to cook a breakfast of eggs, bacon, hash browns, toast, and coffee and make sure that every ingredient was hot when delivered to the customer. You'd start with the hash browns followed by the bacon. These two items take the longest to cook and held for a few minutes on the grill. While the hash browns and bacon are still cooking, the next items are the eggs, which take less time. Shortly after the eggs hit the grill you'd start the toast so the eggs and toast come up together. The hash browns, and bacon, still sitting on the griddle, and eggs, just finished, hit the plate, accompanied by the toast, butter, and jam and served with the coffee, unless already on the table. The moral of this tale: Watch carefully what you are doing and pay enormous attention to detail. Be determined to get it right. Every detail is important.

Even though an order of two eggs sunny side up and with a side of bacon, hash browns, and toast is ubiquitous, getting it right is synonymous with getting everything right. The moral of this tale: Whatever you do, do it better than anybody else, no matter the task. The better moral of this tale: You don't have to be greatest short-order cook of all time; all you have to do is deliver the order just right.

As told to me, you don't have to be great at anything, but be good at everything and put gas in the car. You can't slay the dragon if you don't get to the battlefield on time. Be smart, be prepared, be on time, be alert, be well rested, and, of course, be you. If not, you might be gone.

Section 4

Dangerous and Crazy Persons Lurk Behind the Next Door

Chapter 1

This World Is Full of Crazy Characters, Dangerous Psychopaths, and Clever Lawyers, All of Whom Might Be the Same Person

"Even we paranoids have enemies," which is what Golda Meir told Henry Kissinger at the Arab-Israeli cease-fire conference of 1973.

This book also reveals the enforcement of massive judgments against awful people. You will confront all sorts of nutcases on all sides of the aisle. When money is at issue, everything is at issue, including the conduct of both debtors and creditors. Expect debtors and creditors to take extreme, odd, or stupid action to collect a debt. Don't be put off by the rough-hewn language, profanity, and vignettes of degradation featuring both the rational and irrational depicted in this book. This is a tough business and full of nutcases. Recognize that punitive damage judgments, huge civil judgments, family law orders, tort lawsuits, and Ponzi schemes arise from the vicious acts of predators, psychopaths, cheats, and liars who victimize others to satisfy their unrequited rage. Take these folks seriously and don't believe that your huffing and puffing is going blow these folks away. That would be a big error in your thinking.

Let's be frank. Lawyers, businesspeople, professionals, skilled workers, and just about everyone else rarely come into contact with crazy people. Sure, we witness lots of craziness on the nightly news and lately cable and television reality shows. Craziness in your face is another matter. Each case starts with some nutcase who engages in destructive behavior, campaigns to terrorize another person, and when confronted with legal process, and instead of backing down, continues the campaign of terror through the process of litigation. Inevitably, the person loses big and confronts a million-dollar judgment meted out as pure punishment. Now facing enforcement, the crazy continues to terrorize through a campaign of lies, threats, hatred, malice, and physical intimidation, or even makes attempts on the life of the lawyer and the client.

Even the most mundane collection brings out the monsters. I made a routine collection call upon a debtor and demanded payment of a commercial bill of $13,000 for the sale of meat and poultry products. Through a public record search, I discovered that the debtor was a serial entrepreneur which means in plain English that he creates and collapses entities to avoid payment. I found through the recorder a string of tax liens. Worse, the debtor issued a $5,000 check that bounced. I got him on the phone, and he started screaming at me, "This was stupid. Your client shouldn't have hired you. The corporation is dead. There is a new entity. You can't collect from me. I have nothing. *F--k you. I have nothing.* You will never collect." Nice introduction to this person who later called, and unable to reach me, cursed out the office accountant with more profanity. He called the next day and cursed out the office bookkeeper who earned that string of profanity by just picking up the phone. In the great Korean War movie, *The Bridge of Toko Ri*, the ending line was, "Where do we get such men?" which was repeated by President Reagan. Let's find out.

We give these people credit for their vindictive conduct. Profanity and persistent and unbridled aggression made a debtor a particularly difficult and miserable person to confront. Unless you as the creditor relish confrontation, big and never-ending doses of profanity are tough to accept. You will find in many cases (as we have) that at the outset, and continuously, the debtor engages in an active campaign of attacking the parties and their lawyers. Letters, briefs, lawsuits, filings with the court, and outbursts in the courtroom, hallway, or even elevator overflow with viscious remarks, profanity, insults, and invective. It is endless and nonstop. This campaign of vitriol is a deliberate attempt to scare or deter parties from collection and lawyers from representing the party. Postdigital, a campaign of personal terror takes on the form of "flaming," in which the debtor (usually the party) will accuse the creditor and the lawyer of horrible and unspeakable conduct. This campaign is nonstop, bitter, and incessant. In every pleading, every letter, every e-mail, and every statement, the debtor is full of unbelievable invective all for the purpose of browbeating the creditor and counsel. Sometimes, and yes sometimes, the creditor and lawyer will walk away.

Accept that some debtors are crazy. They destroyed their lives. They have created their own debtor's prison because they can't or won't ever get a job. Beware of these folks.

Chapter 2

The Good Old Days Offered You Half a Hand

This is not the *Harvard Law Review*. When I was 25 and puberty was still visible in my rearview mirror, my next real job was with the Board of Trade of San Francisco, the oldest insolvency shop in California. When businesses failed, the Board would liquidate the assets and pay off creditors. The Board was an association of wholesale distributors who also pooled, preelectronic, their bad debt and put out a "bad debt" sheet every day. God help the retailer who becomes delinquent to one wholesaler and ends up on the street. The retailer's credit lines from every other distributor would evaporate. If the "pillar and stock treatment" did not work, the Board would accumulate the claims, make demands, and work out payments, or sue.

About the third day on the job, I was in the bullpen when a grocer came through with a paper bag. He opened the paper bag and pulled out a huge wad of cash as payment of the debts. Ones, fives, tens, and twenties. That didn't bother me. Dad routinely handled large sums of money. I looked more closely at the grocer's right hand. He was missing the two fingers and half of his right hand. He still had his thumb and the next two fingers. Someone had chopped his hand down the middle because the line was straight. I must have turned blue in the face. The Board liquidator (actually the person who took physical possession of a failing business and made arrangements to liquidate everything) was a former Marine, a big tough guy, and this was in 1975, just 30 years after World War II. He looked at me and said, "Gambling debt. Card club." What's more to say? Obviously, the creditor of this poor grocer had little patience for the justice afforded by the law courts of this state.

Chapter 3

Barbary Coast Justice

My experience with the Board of Trade was a time warp. The years of 1975 through 1978 were the dying sunset of the predigital, analog era. Inexpensive computers had yet to hit middle-sized businesses, and accounting was still done on 10-column green sheets. The Board of Trade still had 10-key punches (mammoth accounting machines the size of cash registers), a full-time PBX operator (for those of you under 30, that means a telephone-answering person who operated a switchboard), and rotary dial phones. In my prior job in the early 1970s, the dictation machines were using rubber belts. That meant that you would dictate into a recording device that recorded the sound in a belt-like object that was circular and three inches wide. Those faded out and were replaced by cassettes, which have lasted in various incarnations even up to this date. Sorry for the trip down memory lane. Monthly lunch was with the retired lawyer who worked in the law department in the 1930s.

Due process is a novel concept from the viewpoint of a 1930s lawyer. Better stated, due process was a luxury not necessarily available to everybody. Here is the story. In those days, some liquor store owner would fall behind on his bills owed to the wholesaler selling hard spirits. On Monday, the wholesaler would phone in the claim to the Board of Trade. On Monday night, the letter went out to all of the other wholesalers advising them that the liquor store owner defaulted on one of his trade debts. In the next day or so, the liquor store owner came in for a meeting at 9:00 a.m. The case manager and the in-house lawyer met with the liquor store owner who balked at payment. Right after the failed meeting, the lawyer prepared a summary complaint, writ, and cut a check for a few dollars. He walked it over to the court, and the clerk immediately issued a writ of attachment. Immediately thereafter, the lawyer went upstairs to the sheriff's office, dropped off the writ and a check for a sheriff's keeper, and in about two hours, the sheriff showed up. Needless to say, the case settled promptly. Was this fair or legal in the face of due process? Does it matter and to whom?

Chapter 4

Getting an Eye Gouged Out

The saddest case was the story of an older African American woman who parked her car in front of a house in a residential section. Parking is tough in this town, and many residents park their car on front lawns (actually concrete). She legally parked on the street, but blocked the front yard of a home. The owner confronted the woman and demanded that she move her car. She refused. They got into a shoving match, and he knocked her to the sidewalk. Not well enough to savor that moment, he kicked her in the face and his shoe smashed into her eyes blinding her in one eye. Somebody called the cops. He was arrested and pled guilty to felony battery. She hired a first-rate trial counsel who filed a civil suit. This debtor did not want to pay anything, and he had only small-dollar insurance. He owned two homes, of which he manipulated the title to obstruct any efforts to reach them. I was hired to unwind this mess.

In the criminal case the court awarded her a civil restitution judgment as compensation for her out-of-pocket losses under Penal Code § 1214(b) (worth reading). I was in line waiting to file something in the civil clerk's office, but I could see her at the front counter trying to get civil process issued. For whatever reason, the clerk was giving her static, which exacerbated an ugly situation. She walked out in a huff before I could help her. But I did see her walk out. She had this large black eye patch on the right side of her face. What a way to live a life. Penal Code § 1214(b) permits the trial judge, sitting in the criminal court, to award the victim a civil judgment for "out of pocket" expenses and damages. These awards are some solace.

Horrors also lurk in martial arts studios. Years later, we were hired to collect on another large-dollar judgment. As a young man, the plaintiff was a student in a martial arts studio. One exercise with the instructor went berserk. The instructor punched out the student's eye. The cops arrested the instructor, but the criminal case evaporated because the jury acquitted the instructor. The civil suit followed, along with the large-dollar judgment. I reached the debtor on the phone: "Yes, that's me. Who are you, and what do you want?" "How about payment of this judgment?" "I won the criminal case.

This was an accident. You don't have anything. I am going to file bankruptcy. You will get nothing. Zero." This was an unadulterated "f--k you moment." My own kid went through six years of SF Ballet, and the biggest risk was sore feet, sharp elbows, and a bruised ego, including mine.

Section 5

Foraging for the Right Ingredients

Chapter 1

Who Is the Debtor and What Is the Debtor?

Twinkle, twinkle, little star.
How I wonder what you are.
How I wonder what you are.

You cannot collect unless you know who owes the money. You cannot seize assets unless you known who has possession of the assets. You cannot read a treasure map until you known who has the treasure.

Banks have it easy. Let's cycle through Banking 101. This is helpful in laying out the repository of information that your debtor handed over to someone else. In a business loan, the lender will demand and receive financial statements, a statement of identity, a copy of a driver's license or passport, corporate or LLC formation packages, tax returns, lawyer letters and opinions, deeds, and just about anything else that would identify the debtor. Demanding massive paperwork is paramount to ensuring that the lender is handing money over to a real person and not an imposter. These documents confirm ownership of assets that serve as collateral for the loan. The document bleeds out claim of hidden owners, conflicting interest and unmask third parties who might be criminals, robbers, or extortionists. If the lender is a bank, federal law demands extensive disclosure that complies with money-laundering regulations. Getting the parties and collateral right is a legal, moral, and financial imperative. The banks got this wired. The banks know their customer.

On the other hand, you might not know who or what is the liable party. Victims, and their family members, of massive torts, financial swindles, horrific auto accidents, falling elevators, employers moonlighting as rapists, and murderers lack any concrete information. Nada, nada, and nada is the name of the bad guy, or what they know about the bad guy. "Do you know anything about the defendant who did you harm?" is our opening question. "No, and that's why we want to hire you because we don't know anything." is the answer. "Do you know anything about this person other than the name on the judgment and police report?" "Nothing other than this person's name on the judgment and police report" is the answer.

Sometimes, but never every time, the hapless victims struggles to identify the wrongdoers, conspirators, compatriots, or enablers. This list will help in identifying the right party to sue, and if you won, the right person who could pay you. Sometimes, the creditor might sue and win by default against the wrong party, and discover this error when collecting because the wrong party lacks any assets.

As you walk down this primrose path, we need to sing a Broadway tune from *The King and I*: "Getting to know you, Getting to know all about you. Getting to like you, Getting to hope you like me." This is the soundtrack to this section.

Here is your initial strategy in approaching the campaign to collect a high-dollar judgment. Ask this question: Who are you? Let's find the answer.

Chapter 2

Secretary of State

Every state has a secretary of state that is the repository for corporation, limited liability, limited partnership, and related filings. This site identifies the debtor as a corporation, LLC, or limited partnership, and whether domestic, foreign, or nonexistent. The word "nonexistent" is very important because that means the debtor is not incorporated one way or another, but might be a natural person. Or, the entity is formed in another state. Or, worse, you don't have the right name, but a trade name, false name, or misspelled or corrupted name.

Many jurisdictions provide a statement of officers and directors, copies of articles of incorporation, and annual reports. Florida offers for cross-indexing of names, agents for service of process, and related parties. Commercial services culling through the secretary of state will provide cross-referencing of officers, directors, and agents that are important in linking the principals of the debtor to other entities that might be the debtor's shareholder, affiliate, or subsidiary.

Nevada offers annual reports online. Expect that the debtor is incorporated, even though the assets of the business are reposed in another entity, even a domicile or out-of-state corporation or LLC as another layer to obscure true ownership. Nevada is popular because the incorporator can use dummy addresses and surrogates to hide true ownership and management.

Many predators run genuine businesses with employees and inventory, lease the property or even own the building, pay taxes, and sell products. Corporate, limited liability, limited partnership, and their various cocktail combinations are pervasive in most businesses. The expectation should be that the wrongdoer is acting behind some type of corporate shield and has become part of the creditor's settled expectations.

The secretary of state will reveal the date of formation, the agent for service of process, the names of the officers or managing members, the name of the general partnership if an LLC, the domicile of the entity if a limited partnership, and whether the entity is active, suspended, forfeited, dissolved, or merged.

The information is important when compared to the case itself. For example, if the debtor is a corporation but the secretary of state shows that the debtor is now suspended, the inference is that the debtor terminated its own business operation and abandoned the corporate shell. However, the website is still up and running, someone is answering the phones, and if brick and mortar, the business still runs. How can this happen, particularly if the debtor is still doing business under the same name? The answer is simple. The debtor abandoned entity number #1, buried the entity into a corporate grave, and formed entity #2 under a very different and hard-to-find name. In sum, the entity takes out a fictitious business name in the name of the new entity.

Chapter 3

Fictitious Business Name Filings

As a condition of filing a suit, fictitious business name (FBN) statements are required. FBN statements are common filings that do not need a lawyer to complete, file, or publish. FBNs are filed with the county clerk and identify the party who claims the fictitious business name. FBN filings are online or available through nearly all commercial search services.

FBNs are signed by the holder of the fictitious name. The FBNs reveal the legal name of the registered owner, residence addresses, whether the business is conducted by individual, partnership, LLC, association, trust, husband and wife, joint venture, domestic partners, or LLP. An FBN is signed under penalty of perjury. This means that the FBN is fairly reliable. Better yet, the FBN is usually executed at the time that the business starts and identifies the parties operating the business without the ominous shadow of big-time liability.

The FBN is the initial test in identifying the person who is running the business. They are common and cheap to file.

Chapter 4

UCC Filings and Real Property Recordings

Demanding security for loans, credit facilities and credit sales, lenders, leasing companies, factors, financiers, hard money lenders, and major vendors file UCCs or record deeds of trust. Seeking to collect unpaid taxes, the taxing authorities file and record liens—lots of them. These documents identify the liable party and presumptively the owner of the business who took out the loan or operated the business accruing the taxes. As a condition of a loan, lenders demand a URLA or a sworn loan application, three to four years of tax returns, audited or unaudited financial statements, and proof of identity and ownership. The Uniform Residential Loan Application tells everyone who is the debtor, identifies a spouse, shows and confirms the association with the business, and even offers up a driver's license. The name on the UCC or real property instruments (a mortgage or deed of trust) reveals the probable debtor and the correct name, spelling, name of spouse and location. Banks rarely misidentify anyone.

Tax liens are the caboose on the tax train but identify the debtor. The businessperson needs a federal and state tax identification number (TIN) by which to file employment tax and income tax returns. If selling goods at retail, the debtor needs a state board of equalization tax identification number. When the debtor defaults in payment of the taxes, the taxing authorities dun the debtor and, absent payment, file or record tax liens that identify the debtor as the "tax payer" from the tax return and any application for the TIN, all who is and presumptively the owner and operator of the business that accrued the tax liability. Chance are, and without uncertainty, the person whose name appears on the tax liens for unpaid sales tax, employment trust taxes such as the failure to turn over tax deposits or the employer's share of taxes or the failure to pay an employment-related taxes or any other tax, owns and operates the business. The name on the lien notice is presumptively the owner and operator of the business. If the debtor on the tax liens is different (name, entity, spelling, or existence at all) from the person who caused the losses in the first place, something is very wrong and you need to get out of your chair. You might have discovered the right entity, a new entity, or the wrong person from the tax lien.

Chapter 5

State Board of Equalization

With the sales tax resale number, the State Board of Equalization (SBE) website ("verify" the permit) reveals the permit holder who is also the owner and operator. Most states require that the seller of goods have a resale permit unless the state (Oregon) does not collect sales tax.

Westlaw, or other services, offers the resale number. The SBE requires the execution of a detailed application, under penalty of perjury, revealing the name of the person selling "taxable" goods, subject to sales tax. Westlaw (People Map) and Lexis-Nexus might provide this information. An SBE number is particularly helpful in identifying the owner because the SBE requires a detailed sworn application that identifies the owner and operator. As a matter of law, the person who is the holder of the SBE permit is presumptively the person who is selling the products.

Like Alcoholic Beverage Control records, SBE records will reveal the name of the persons who signed for the sales tax permit. You might discover that the person is not just a person but a partnership in which the partners are individually liable. You might find a new SBE permit that was taken out after the claim arose; the new permit suggests that the debtor terminated the original business entity (no matter the structure) and established a new entity using the same name. You can readily conclude that the debtor took out a new sales permit in the name of new entity, but used the name of the old entity as a fictitious business name.

Chapter 6

Professional Licenses

The Department of Real Estate, State Bar of California, Department of Consumer Affairs, Contractors Licensing Board, and others identify the licensee who is the operator of the licensed business. Most professional licenses require a sworn application, a test and educational requirements, investigation of the applicant, and bond (contractor). We pray that only a licensee can operate the business (all professions), and typically the name on the wall (the license) is the owner and operator, including the eye doctor. Hopefully. These records are online.

Chapter 7

Liquor Licenses

Liquor licenses require a sworn statement, proof that the licensee is the owner of the business, evidence of source of funds, and a lease for the premises. The Alcoholic Beverage Control (ABC) will investigate the character of the applicant. Absent secret or split ownership, the name on the license is the owner and operator of the restaurant or bar. ABC records are online. A bar must also have a State Board of Equalization (SBE) permit for sales tax and there should be a match. If there is not, the business might bear split ownership.

Buying or selling a bar requires the filings of a Notice of Intended Transfer with the county recorder, which likewise identifies the buyer and seller and therefore the presumptive operator of the business. These are all public records.

Chapter 8

Regulator's Site for the Publically Held Companies

The U.S. Securities and Exchange Commission (SEC) has a vast online library of all public filings (EDGAR). Free of any charge, these sites offer corporate, financial, and business information that identifies the company and its subsidiaries, and better, lays out the insiders, transactions, and financial statements. You can spend hours reading thousands of pages that reveal the deepest and darkest secrets of U.S. corporations, multinationals, foreign companies, and governments that seek access to the U.S. debt and equities markets. Sarbanes-Oxley ensures (or should ensure) that this information is reasonably reliable or someone is going to jail.

These filings offer you audited financials in which the auditor's notes tell you all about the business, its prospects for success, insider loans, lawsuits, and just about everything else about the company. If the company is not doing well, you will note the auditor's opinion that "we have doubts about the company's ability to continue as a going concern." This admonition echoes the doctor intoning you that "more tests are required," which is the precursor to "getting your affairs in order." This site will identify officers, directors, and related divisions, subdivisions, and affiliates. This site will advise of major transactions such as mergers and acquisitions. At your fingertips you will get detailed financial information and the history of lawsuit and insider transactions. For the United Kingdom, the site is The Company House. For Canada, the site is SEDAR.

Debt offerings are filed with the SEC, even though the company might be private. This means that even though the company is not a public company, the company might have filed detailed financial disclosures with the SEC.

If your debtor is a public company, this is your first stop. Get yourself a cup of coffee, you will be here a spell.

Chapter 9

Public Utilities Commission

Public utilities commissions (PUCs) compel licensing, and therefore a signed application, for telecommunication providers, utility companies, trucking and moving companies, and taxis (try the police department also), likewise, identifies the correct party; all this information can be found online. This is another stepping stone, but if the debtor might be a regulated entity, the PUC might have a file on them.

If your debtor is a regulated entity, and assuming that your state provides for an open act, drop a state Freedom of Information Act (FOIA) request. If the debtor is an entity regulated by the federal commission that deals with utility, the initial foray is a FOIA request.

Chapter 10

U.S. Patent and Trademark Office and U.S. Copyright Office

If you see that the debtor owns a patent, trademark, or copyright, you can identify the debtor through the U.S. Patent and Trademark Office (USPTO) or U.S. Copyright Office, which offer online databases that identify the registered owners of patents, trademarks, trade dress (if registered), and copyrights. Google also has a searchable USPTO database. You can identify the debtor, confirm the correct name or spelling, determine if affiliated entities might own the valuable intellectual property (IP), and even determine that the IP is owned by an entity that is new to you.

This search is an imperative. You might find that the debtor does not own the IP, but that the IP is owned by the corporate principal who, upon questioning, claims that the principal licenses the IP to the debtor. This information might furnish grounds to pierce the corporate veil because the corporation (or LLC) is an empty shell without any assets, and that the corporation's use of the IP (and apparent ownership) is a fraud. Alternatively, you might conclude that the corporation lacks any viable assets and, absent a big litigation investment of money and time, walk from the case. Foodle loo is the technical term. Reaching the alleged IP license is a matter of whether your case is pending in federal court (no luck here: *Everex Systems, Inc. v. Cadtrak Corp.* (9th Cir. 1996) 89 F.3d 673, 679), or state court (patent license is reachable: *Farmland Irrigation Co. v. Doplmaier* (1957) 48 Cal. 2d 208).

Sometimes you literally have to take matters into your own hands. I was hired to collect a bankruptcy judgment against a South African maker of wind-up radios. The name on the judgment did not look right, and I could not confirm the name anywhere. This was an offshore entity that was a mystery to me. However, the debtor sold their products through Sharper Image, a novelty retailer that subsequently filed bankruptcy. I guess their products were a little too novel, hence the word "novelty." With $80 in hand, I bought two (one for me and other for the client). I popped the radio out of the box and discovered multiple U.S. patent numbers, trademark insignias, copyrights, and "patents pending." I looked up all this information through the USPTO and discovered that the name on the judgment was slightly wrong, but probably the same person given the address. With that information in hand, I started enforcement under the correct name, which was a motion for assignment directed at the correct party with the correct name. Upon service of the papers, the case settled. I still have the wind-up radio somewhere in the office.

This site is a pure treasure map. Applications to register a patent, copyright, or trademark disclose their owners or assignees, who in turn are the probable owners and operators of the business. Filing for a patent, copyright, or trademark requires the applicant to clearly identify themselves under penalty of perjury.

Trademarks are particularly helpful. If the name on the product is "Golden Bloom," the USPTO would reveal the owner of the mark who is usually the owners and seller of the goods that bear the mark. Unlike patents, copyrights, and domain names, trademarks attach to goods or services in the marketplace. Absent the extreme, the person who is the owner of the mark is the person selling the goods or services in the community. Absent the bizarre, the person who owns the trademark owns the business because the mark is attached to the goods sold by the business.

Are we about to tumble into the trademark rabbit hole? If the owner of the trademark is not your debtor, but a closely related entity, such as a parent corporation, subsidiary, or shareholder, again you have a decent "piercing the corporate veil" case on the basis that the entity, clearly associated with the debtor, is presenting itself to the public by its mark that is attached to the products. If the trademarked products caused the loss or damage, particularly in a personal injury case, the plaintiff might have a case against the holder of the mark on alter ego basis even though the holder would claim that the mark was licensed or transferred to a related entity.

Chapter 11

Courts and Other Tribunals (Administrative Agencies)

Most courts and administrative tribunals are now online and might offer direct access to filed documents (federal and some state courts). The Trademark Trial and Appeal Board (TTAB) of the USPTO is online. This is very interesting reading, and these cases are very expansive.

Other lawsuits might identify the person, partners, and related entities. If you pull up every document filed by the defendant, you might find out the actual structure, the officers, the shareholders and board, or the location or disposition of its assets.

Papers filed by the party as a plaintiff or defendant reveal the true names. Embrace another person's greed. Greedy people will say anything to anybody, even in court filings. Prior sworn statements against a party are admissible and highly probative of the truth (buzzword for accurate). Filed papers attach as exhibits contracts, letters, brochures, marketing materials, e-mails, and purchase orders that identify a party. Always, and I means always, try family law court. Divorce proceedings compel the parties to file extensive financial disclosures, such as a listing of all assets and liabilities.

Lots of general and niche courts are online, including the docket and the items (filings) on the docket. Tax Court, the trial and appeal courts for the USPTO, and nearly all other federal lower courts (administrative law judges and courts). The Federal Maritime Commission tribunal are online. These filings are available to the public without charge, which is slight different than Public Access to Court Electronic Records (PACER), which requires a subscription and small fee. Even though not every filing is under oath, a statement by a party directly or through a lawyer might be admissible in another proceeding. If the party is regulated by a federal agency, cull through the records of the adjudicatory tribunal and you might find scads of filings that disclose key information. Any adjudication by the agency might resonate in court judicial proceedings because a decision against a party in one proceeding might bind that party in other proceedings. This is called the offensive use of collateral estoppel. *Parklane Hosiery Co., Inc. v. Shore*, 439 U.S. 322 1979, supra and *Bank of America v. Bernhard*, 19 Cal.2d 807 (1942), supra.

Don't be shy. Call up the other lawyer for a party (not your debtor, Forrest) and ask if he or she is willing to hand over the discovery such as depositions. This might be a mutual trade, but if he took the deposition of your defendant, you just saved yourself about $3,000 and might even learn information otherwise inaccessible. We were chasing down a Japanese national who owned a cattle farm in northern California. I found that another party had sued and nearly resolved the case. I called up the other lawyer and offered $1,000 for the deposition transcript. He accepted and off went the $1,000 and return FedEx Air bill. The battle in my case was ownership of the real property, which was resolved in other person's case. My case settled in seven days after we received this deposition transaction on very favorable terms. If you cannot buy the cooperation of the lawyer, don't hesitate to subpoena the lawyers file. The lawyer knows full well that you have the power of subpoena which would compel the attorney to cough up the transcript. The attorney gets $35 and maybe copy costs. Or, for $1000 the attorney can sell the deposition. You do the math.

Administrative tribunals conduct "live trials," in which the testimony is recorded through tape, or digitally, as opposed to a court reporter. These are public hearings, and you are entitled to purchase a transcript.

Chapter 12

Credit Reporting Agencies and Search Services

Westlaw, Lexis-Nexis, D&B, TransUnion, Equifax, Experian, and others might offer commercial reports or public record reports that identify the party on a subscription or single-use fee. The first task in opening a file is to put this person through these search services. Immediately you will confirm whether the person filed bankruptcy, recently sold real property, or lost property to a foreclosure, buried under tax liens and levies. This five-minute task will save you five years of grief.

Search Google, Yahoo Finance, all social (LinkedIn, Hoovers, etc.) media websites to confirm names if publicly accessible. Online legal research (Westlaw, Lexis-Nexis, etc.) might report cases revealing names. Trade associations identify their members. The party's own website discloses the name in "About us," "Our history," or "Warranties." Try blogs.

Let's chat about LinkedIn. In the last five years, LinkedIn has become the digital marketplace for professionals who disclose enormous amounts of personal information including their job history, qualification, and publications. When in doubt, call the business or office to confirm a name. Ask for the owner.

Chapter 13

Checks, Sellers and Buyers of Products, Online Banking Services, and the Brick and Mortar Banks Are Clues, Arrows, and Even "Xs"

Checks have many clues. Checks are sometimes treasure maps. Checks tell you who is your debtor or who owes you the money. Checks tell you everything. However, before you divine the secrets of a check, you have to know how a check works.

Let's describe the parties to a check. The person who is the owner of the bank account and whose name appears in the upper-left-hand corner of the check is called the drawer because this is the person who "draws" on the account maintained by the drawee bank to pay the check. The Drawer "draws" on the account held by the Drawee. Post-9-ll, the banks are fanatical in identifying the drawer and demand a driver's license, corporate minutes to open a corporate bank account, and articles of incorporation.

The person signing the check is called the maker and might be an officer, an agent of the drawer, or just an authorized signer. The maker might be a principal of the drawer, relative, or employee. If the check bounces, the maker might be personally liable to the vendor who received the check for payment of a debt. The person to whom the check is written is called the payee. The person who deposits the check is called an endorser and probably the payee. The tenor of the check is the amount. Some checks are endorsed without recourse, which means that the next person down the line who takes the check for value cannot sue the endorser.

The bank that receives the check for purpose of deposit is called the collecting or depositing bank. The bank that pays the check is called the drawee or the paying bank.

Some banks issue checks in the name of fictitiously named entities, such as "Harry's Bar and Grill," when the name of the business is ABC Corporation.

Documents abound in routine business transactions that reveal the correct, new, or different name for the debtor. If a garment vendor or restaurant, the party purchases products from wholesalers or leases from a commercial landlord. As a buyer, the party signs credit applications, contracts, and SBE resale certificates or issues purchase orders. Checks and ACH (or outgoing wires) transmittals as payment reveal the name of the party. The check identifies the party as the drawer, which originates from the documents furnished to the bank to open the account. Letters promising payment reveal the name of the party.

In selling products, the selling party confirms the purchase orders, enters into supply agreements, or a prescreening agreement that identifies the party. Bills of lading, invoices, statements, and dunning notices disclose the name of the party. Letters and e-mails, promotional materials, and ACH instructions (or incoming wires) reveal the party. The payee on the buyer's check, or the information from the ACH (or wire) transmittals, disclosing the recipient, identifies the party. The endorsement on the backside of the check reveals the identity of the party. Business cards reveal the parties.

If the party is in the rag trade, subpoena the major retailers whose files disclose the legal names, trade name or trademark, and label, and might have a vendor application. In the Los Angeles market, garment vendors factor their receivables and execute an agreement disclosing the legal name, trade name, label, and trademarks that the factor transmits to the retailer. The UCC filed by the factor correctly identifies the vendor. Factors rarely err in identifying their clients. Inherent in the rag trade, the infringement actions correctly name the liable party along with the retailer. The trick in this business is to locate third parties who do business with your debtor. Third parties can demand and receive enormously, accurate, reliable, and, best yet, admissible documents that identify the debtor and out the debtor's assets and liability.

The garment business offers its own confusion. The trademark is "Autumn Sunrise." The trade name for the vendor is Fair Weather Fashions. The owner of the trade name, and trademark, is Fabulous Fabrics Inc., which presumptively appears to be a debtor in the UCC filed by the factor. The fictitious business name would reveal that Fair Weather Fashions is the trade name for the corporation.

Some merchants take PayPal, Google Wallet, or other forms of electronic payment. Subpoena the payment service that will disclose the identity of the party. Subpoena the credit card processing service. Checks are passé. Restaurants, retail business, high-end grocery stores (Whole Foods, etc.) take in much of their revenue through credit cards. Credit card processors are the major source of cash flow and subject to levy and subpoena. Subpoena AMEX, Discover Card, and Capital One as popular credit card issuers. Always subpoena the debtor's bank and grab the loan application (and Uniform Residential Loan Application), loan file, and supporting documents. This is another gold mine that will identify the debtor, the partners, and insiders.

PayPal, among other electronic financial services, are necessarily tied into a bank account. The first wave is for PayPal and seeking not only the banking information but also the e-mail colloquium that PayPal enables by and between its customer and the persons depositing or receiving funds. This information enables you to identify by name, e-mail address, and general contents of the e-mail who is dealing with the debtor, and a general description of the business transaction.

The anecdote to this malaise is straightforward. Rethink the strategy from the vantage point of the debtor, which is to conceal funds through various online or digital repositories, and be prepared to engage in a massive subpoena of everybody, or better stated, anything that might serve as a depository for funds. On more than one occasion, the service of 100 subpoenas will generate one hit, and that one hit might crack the case.

Chapter 14

Who Needs James Bond When the Federal Freedom of Information Act and State Sunshine Laws Offer You the Keys to the Kingdom?

FOIA Keys to the Federal Archives

Let's ratchet this up. So far, you have learned never to take a name on face value because free online services enable you to peel back that name to uncloak the identity of the true debtor who might sport deep pockets.

The next step is likewise at your fingertips. This is called The Freedom of Information Act, or better known as FOIA found at 5 U.S.C. § 552 et seq. This is the best headline: "Subject to specified statutory exclusions and exemptions, 5 U.S.C. § 552(b), (c), "the Freedom of Information Act requires federal agencies to make agency records available to the public upon reasonable request," *United We Stand Am., Inc. v. IRS*, 359 F.3d 595, 597 (D.C. Cir., 2004).

Most states have Sunshine Laws that open up state, county, and local agencies and the legislature and executive branch to documents demands. The California version is the Brown Act: Gov't Code § 5495054963 and the Open Records Law, Calif. Public Records Act: Gov't Code § 62506270. Many states now mandate "open meeting laws," which prevents agencies, semiautonomous agencies, legislative committees, local districts and other governmental entities from closed-door meetings, absent a compelling legal reason. State Sunshine Laws compel these open meetings and compel turnover of minutes and filings. These local districts might have direct contact with property owners, such as your debtor because these are districts that control land use, issue permits, and control water, sewage, fire, and police protection. These local agencies are customer friendly and tend to be responsive to local needs. These agencies are professional and legal pack rats in that they catalogue and archive all meeting, filings, and other paper (and electronic) submissions.

Let's introduce you to FOIA. FOIA is the foundation of modern investigatory journalism. When the print articles or TV or cable news reveal the "secret files," the true source is an FOIA request or state equivalent. Typical story fueled by FOIA: "Internal records reveal that the Agency squandered millions on annual bonuses, lavish holiday bashes and employee perks," or "Agency records disclose anchor bolts flunked stress test but installed in the bridge that replaces Galloping Gertie." "Secret archives" are FOIA fodder, Geraldo. Buried "eyewitness statements" are more FOIA product. If FOIA didn't unearth these buried gems, at least FOIA pointed the reporter to the source, who is typically a former employee who parked a seething memo in the government file and who relishes the opportunity to promote the grievances. Most investigatory news programs (probably *60 Minutes*, etc.) and news organizations (Reuters, AP, *Bloomberg*, *The New York Times*, *Wall Street Journal*, and nearly every news-driven media) have deep experience in FOIA and employ lawyers specialized in bringing actions against the agency to compel FOIA disclosures. FOIA has spawned a large legal and business bibliography. FOIA is big business.

Any business that routinely contracts with the government (defense, etc.) or is subject to government regulations (oil, transportation, drugs, and most media) maintains large FOIA staffs. FOIA hands you the federal archives, Anderson. FOIA and state Sunshine Laws grant access to the records of nearly all federal and state agencies, with certain exceptions that principally consist of documents statutorily exempt, immune, or privileged. Exempt are lawyer-client communication, current criminal investigators, national security, proprietary and confidential information, and any matter dealing with taxes, the military, most foreign affairs, and other legitimate government secrets. Despite these broad swatches of protected materials, and absent the extreme or bizarre, the federal, state, regional, county, and city governments are open books. All you need to do is ask, and hence, this section.

Let's start with FOIA (federal). An FOIA request could be used as a supplement or substitute for discovery in a civil proceeding. See, e.g., *Jackson v. First Fed. Sav.*, 709 F. Supp. 887, 889 (E.D. Ark. 1989); see also, *In re F&H Barge Corp.*, 46 F. Supp. 2d 453, 454–455 (E.D. Va. 1998). Other cases have been less sanguine in which courts have put a hold on an FOIA request, pending a whole host of issues. See illustrative, *Envtl. Crimes Project v. EPA*, 928 F. Supp. 1, 2 (D.D.C. 1995). (There are many cases on these issues.)

A court can enforce an FOIA request, and these cases make an FOIA request compulsory. "That is exactly so. With Major Lawrence, mercy is a passion. With me, it is merely good manners. You may judge which motive is the more reliable," are the famous lines uttered by King Faisal to Bentley. Why here? The motivation in coercing the agency to cough up records is an angry district court judge, and not adherence to the ethos of public disclosure. The secret to FOIA: Push hard. Pester these folks.

Buttressing discovery in civil litigation, an FOIA request at the beginning of the case gets the names rights, establishes the identities of the parties, and flushes out key reports or studies. FOIA requests are routine in major litigation, antitrust, large-scale class actions, mass tort, or any claim involving a governmental entity. You can initiate an FOIA request without the necessity of filing the civil suit, or you can initiate the FOIA request before filing suit. In fact, you can initiate an FOIA request for no reason at all. FOIA is not a part of civil discovery, or any legal proceeding, but is a pure fishing expedition. FOIA is an independent means to discover and retrieve information in the hands of an agency or state.

What can an FOIA request deliver to you? In the initiation and prosecution of any civil action, the records delivered through FOIA might identify the person who is liable to the plaintiff or person who has the financial resources to pay a settlement or respond to a judgment. Maybe. The secondary concern is the "flip side," which is that the person you have sued lacks those financial resources, and therefore a settlement is worthwhile. The FOIA request might also identify the principals of the judgment debtor who might be liable in satellite litigation on an alter ego theory, fraudulent conveyance claim, or successor liability. This information could be in your hands before you file suit against anyone, or it could help you craft the lawsuit. Maybe, or maybe not.

FOIA might identify "the man behind the curtain" and save the case from the oblivion of insolvency in offering another target of litigation. If you are still working up the case for the purpose of proving liability, FOIA might deliver accident or incident reports, studies, surveys, narratives, reports of litigation, recalls, safety violations, histories, third-party reports, eyewitnesses, internal agencies reviews, and potentially photographs, or other "readable materials." Should your defendant live in any of these archives, these materials are critical to your case, if the report from the Department of Transportation shows a history of 20 accidents involving your defendant's vehicle. Whatever is found in the agency is per se important.

Did your client die of bad drugs, bad design, faulty parts, airplanes falling from the sky, or any other disaster that an agency of the federal government might have investigated? The report might be yours for the asking. Did some truck driver run over your client, bash into a school bus, and crater into a building? Ask the Department of Transportation. Anything medical or health related might spawn reports, studies, and reports in a dozen agencies. Try the FBI for any conduct that might be criminal. The FBI has lots of reports. All studies, reports, scholarly articles, research papers, compilations, and e-mails are yours for the asking without a lawsuit being filed, permission of the court, or even knowledge of your adversary. In the anticipation of any major litigation involving bad drugs, airplane crashes, oil rig fires and expressions, or other catastrophes that involve any business that reports to the government, before suit is filed, the lawyers on all sides might initiate FOIA requests, Forrest. If your entity is regulated, reports to the government, files anything with the government, holds any permit, license, or certificate, or is subject to any inspection, prosecute an FOIA request. An FOIA compels the government to turn over these materials. FOIA is an affirmative force to open up the federal records.

How can FOIA or local Sunshine Laws help you? Take the simple problem of property ownership. You are enforcing a judgment against a debtor who denies ownership of the residence. At the debtor's examination, the debtor claims that the "wife," "trustee of the Bahamian Trust," "Protector under the Nevada Asset Protection trust," or someone else, but not the debtor, owns the property. The debtor even coughs up a recorded deed that identifies the owner as any of these suspects. By chance, the debtor's neighbor seeks to demolish his two-bedroom, one-bath claptrap on two acres of Beverly Hills real estate and erect a nouveau Taj Mahal, designed by Frank Gehry who would clad the property in aluminum sheathing. Did you know that the sun's reflection from burnished aluminum could nearly fry an egg? The neighbor necessarily would file for a permit that entitles the debtor to file a *written* protest and appear in a planning department hearing that considers the debtor's objection. The written objection probably identifies the debtor as the "property owner of the neighboring property."

Permit hearings are recorded, and the transcripts are archived in the records of the local agencies. State or county FOIA laws could make this archived testimony available. This testimony might feature your debtor on the record and an admission of ownership of property. For example, residents of upscale communities frequently oppose permits sought by their neighbors that obstruct light, air, and views. The testimony at the permit hearing, which is open to the public, is often like the following:

Chair of the Commission: "Mr. Clerk, swear in the witnesses." All witnesses are sworn, including the debtor.

Chair of the Commission "Calling the case of *Smith v. Neighbor*." The debtor ("Smith") appears at the witness table before the commission.

Chair of the Commission: "Your name, sir."

Debtor: "John Smith."

"Did you file the protest to the permit?"

"Yes."

"What is your relationship to the subject property?"

"I own the neighboring house."

"When did you acquire the neighboring house?"

"20 years ago."

"Do you live on the property currently?"

"Yes."

"Are you the sole owner?"

"No, my wife and I own the property."

"Is Ms. Smith here to testify?"

"Yes, she is sitting next to me."

This is sworn testimony. This is admissible in another proceeding, such as your case. Land use battles, and particularly permit hearings, are reported through a recording device or even a court reporter. Under the state Sunshine Laws, this testimony is readily available but potentially at a fee to transcribe, prepare, and deliver to you (About $1,000 to $2,000 depending upon the local prices and length of the hearing). Hearing dates, minutes, and rulings are frequently online and, if not, are subject to a state FOIA request. This transcript would directly rebut, if not topple, the claimed title in the name of the "wife," "trustee," or "asset protector."

Rural property owners have more frequent contact with irrigation, police, fire, and sanitation districts whose archives might contain objections and protests signed by the debtor, reports, summaries, maps, and surveys. Sanitation districts hold live hearings, and should your debtor object to a projected sewer pipe on tape, you might find a concession of ownership.

Kicking Open the FOIA Door

The procedural requirements for FOIA are straightforward. In 2007 the Open Government Act compels the agency to assist requestors and facilitate the *prompt* processing of FOIA requests. All FOIA requests must be in writing. Agencies will accept requests via fax, e-mail, or U.S. mail or via secure online forms, if available. The letter should be identified as a "Freedom of Information Request" at the top to ensure that the request is handled promptly. The letter should spell out the following:

1. The name, address, e-mail, and telephone number of the contact person on behalf of the requesting party.
2. A precise description of the records being sought: consumer complaints, accident reports, investigatory files, histories, narrative, summaries, third-party contracts, accountings, surveys, etc.
3. If the request seeks information about a company (e.g., a request sent to the Department of Transportation that ask about Boeing), provide accurate spellings and names, addresses, and other identifying information.
4. The relevant time period. If the case involves a claim of defects in a car, specify the relevant time to avoid delays from producing stale information.
5. The willingness to pay for applicable fees associated with the processing of the request.

FOIA requires agencies to assign tracking numbers, provide status information, and maintain an FOIA liaison to assist requestors. Agencies must establish a telephone line or Internet site where requestors can track their request. FOIA compels the agencies to ensure prompt compliance with requests, increase transparency, and assist with the resolution of disputes. Many agencies have a specific address for request including and most importantly a dedicated fax number and e-mail address. For example, the e-mail address for the FTC is "FOIA@FTC.gov. Most agencies have available a 20-page (online) booklet to walk through the steps.

What Is Required—Not Much

An FOIA request has two requirements for access to records: (1) the request must reasonably describe the records, and (2) it must be made in accordance with the agency's regulations. Ordinarily, a person need not title a request as an FOIA request, while good practices would suggest that clarity would be very helpful. The standard is whether the requested information contains a description that enables a professional agency employee familiar with the subject to locate the record with a reasonable amount of effort. Fishing expeditions through agency files that are overly broad, excessive, or extremely vague will be rejected. The key in determining whether the request is reasonably described is the ability of the agency staff to ascertain which records are requested and to locate them.

The agency has 20 days to make a determination on the request. The agency does not have to turn over the records, but it must make a decision. Assuming that the agency agreed to turn over the records, the requestor, depending upon the volume and complexity, should have the records shortly. The agency has grace of another 10 days to get the request to the right person to respond. The agency might be entitled to tolling: one time to obtain information from the requestor, and necessary to clarify fees issues from the requestor. The agency might ask the requester for an extension under unusual circumstances, such as the need to collect the material from separate offices, a voluminous request, or the need to consult with another agency.

A requester might be entitled to expedite the FOIA request for a compelling need, such as the threat to life or limb, or that the requestor (i.e., a member of the press) is a person engaged in disseminating information.

The agency is under an obligation to make a search that is subject to judicial enforcement. The test is reasonableness under the circumstances and is dependent upon the scope of the request itself. An FOIA request is enforced by the court, and the duty to search is subject to judicial decree. The duty to search includes the duty to search through databases, paper files, and various offices. FOIA compels the agency to make partial disclosures, which means that some material might be disclosed in part, that portions of the document might be redacted or that pages might be removed or altered. If you wish the battle to compel production of document, you might collect fees. *Judicial Watch Inc. v. United States Department of Commerce* 470 F.3rd 363 (CA, DC, 2006); 5 U.S.C. § 552(a)(4)(E). In plain English? Ask and you shall receive the documents. If not, the U.S. government pays the lawyers' fees if you win the case. Expect a big battle. Uncle Sam hates to write checks.

FOIA makes records available and is entitled to charge fees (i.e., costs associated with the search and for copying). Once the disclosure is made, the disclosure is in the public domain and is not subject to a protective order. In many instances, the agency provides copies or other medium of disclosure. A secret once said is a secret told.

Get Out Your Checkbook

Nothing is free, and the requestor might be liable for fees and charges associated with the search. The categories are commercial requesters, educational institutions, noncommercial scientific institutions, and representative of the news media, among others. The fees are set by the Office of Management and Budget Fee Guidelines. Fees consist of search fees, which encompasses the time looking for responsive documents. Agencies may charge for search time if they fail to locate the records.

Before we close the door on this subject, you can find general and specific information on a vast array of topics that involve litigation, personal safety and health products, and commercial and financial reports and analysis through the Congressional Research Services (CRS), which is the nonpartisan research facility of Congress. This site is very organized, and the quality of the product rivals any academic research paper. CRS offers a huge catalogue on a vast array of topics from history, the military, foreign affairs, and even standards of statutory construction.

Chapter 15

Transfers to Trusts Never Work; Transfers to Trust Always Work

Did you lose the lawsuit and the judge enters the big judgment for punitive damages? What can be done? First, hire an appellate lawyer; second, see a lawyer who specializes in asset protection. Where do you find them? The "local" section of the *Los Angeles Times* (usually Saturday), *Los Angeles Lawyer* (LA County Bar Magazine), *California Lawyer* (State Bar of California), and of course online. These people fall from the sky and into the lap of the nervous defendant. They offer the following formula: Transfer the home to an irrevocable trust, in which the trustee is an offshore entity, some relative, Nevada LLC, or corporation or fictitious "asset trust protector."

After the transfer to this new-fangled irrevocable trust, what about the mortgage payments, property taxes, insurance (or an impound), homeowner's association dues and fees, and maintenance? The debtor no longer owns the home, but continues to make these mandatory payments. The lawyer is going to tell the debtor to call these necessary payments "rent" and pay the money to the "asset protector," who in turn will disburse the money to the bank, tax collector, and insurance company. Tell the collection guy, says the lawyer, that "you sold your home to the trust, and you are now renting."

Do you like this? Is this swell? Is the million-dollar equity now safely ensconced in the bosom of the irrevocable trust? Does this work? Now have you beaten out the plaintiff in the escalating quest to collect the million-dollar-plus judgment? No.

Why? First, this transaction contravenes the basic tax ramifications of home ownership. Residential mortgage payments to the extent of interest are a tax deduction. Property taxes are a deduction for federal income taxes. Let's presume that the mortgage payment is $5,000 a month, which is all interest and is common for the initial years of any 30-year fixed home loan. The property taxes are in the sum of $12,000 a year and deductible. This means that the total monthly "nut," aside from insurance, maintenance, and special assessment fees, is $6,000 a month. Let's assume a tax bracket of 33 percent (both federal and state), and therefore the net deduction or tax benefit is about $1,998 per month, or

$23,976 per year as the total tax savings. The 33.3 percent is for clarity. Most Americans are able to buy a home specifically because the interest components of their home loan are deductible and lower the debt service borne by the homeowner.

If the debtor recasts the $6,000 as "rent," the debtor forfeits this monthly tax savings of $1,998 and annual tax savings of $23,976. The owner of the trust is the "trustee," who must file his or her own tax return. The taxes for the individual debtor increase $23,976 every year and forever, given the forfeiture of the interest and tax deduction. Let's round this number up to $24,000.

Bad news takes root. The asset protection lawyer necessarily created another tax-paying entity: the irrevocable trust. The trustee is now receiving $6,000 per month (the $5,000 payment due the bank and $1,000 due the county tax assessor) or $72,000 a year. The trust is a separate taxpayer and must pay taxes on the $72,000 annual income, less deductions for outgoing expenses. The expenses consist of interest paid to the bank and property taxes. This creates another level of expense in forming the new entity and filing annual returns. If this farce continues long enough, the trust might even incur an income tax liability because over the years, the interest portion of the loan would decrease and likewise the interest deduction to the trustee would decrease. Once the trust accrues a tax liability, given the complete wash-through nature of the funds, the debtor has to fund the tax liability of the trust plus pay the accountant for the tax returns.

It is incredibly stupid. The debtor forfeits tax savings of about $24,000 a year, accrues about $3,000 in accounting fees, and, worse, has to get new insurance for the house because the property is in the name of a trustee who needs insurance in his or her name.

Section 6

Marooned on a Desert Island

Chapter 1

Getting Stalled, Stayed or Facing a Bond: Robinson Crusoe Wears Wingtips

Someone steal your map? Are you marooned at sea? Are you stuck on some tropical island, Tom? This is the chapter that helps you around of the doldrums of a stayed judgment.

Did you win $60 million in federal court but are stuck with the 14-day stay for state court with a discretionary stay up to 70 days? Are you stuck in park while the defendant just hit the accelerator in the dash out of town with bags of money in hand? Or did the verdict for $60 million come down, but the judge delayed entry of judgment? Federal Rule of Civil Procedure Rule 62(a) gives the defendant an automatic 14-day stay of execution. Do you think that money is going be in the bank when the stay expires?

State courts have different rules, but many states follow the federal rules of civil procedure. For example, California has its own rules. California Code of Civil Procedure § 918(b) gives the defendant up to a 70-day (or more, absent notice of entry of judgment) stay of execution. Think that million-dollar nest eggs remain intact when the 70-day stay expires? I don't think so, nor should you or your client. This is serious business because the client invested a lot of money in getting the judgment and would become enraged if the defendant engaged in shenanigans to frustrate enforcement and destroy that financial investment.

What happens after the 14 days in federal court? In federal court, if the case is on appeal, longer stays are discretionary under Federal Rule of Civil Procedure Rule 62(d). This means that the court can hand down a stay beyond the 14 days that might last through the entire appeal. Federal appeals, or just about any appeal, are very unpredictable in assessing when the appellate court will render a decision. Some federal appeals turn around in 12 months, and other appeals can span 24 months or more.

The law of discretionary stays in the federal courts is well tread because everyone who loses that battle tends to raise the discretionary appeal as part of the main brief. There are many cases, but these cases are the most illustrative: See *Poplar Grove Planting and Refining Co. v. Bache Halsey Stuart Inc.*, 600 F.2d 1189 (5th Cir. 1979); *Federal Prescription*

Service Inc. v. American Pharmaceutical Association etc., 636 F.2d 755 (USCA, D.C. 1980) [burden is on the defendant to show entitlement of discretionary stay without the burden of posting a bond]. Do read these cases if your judgment is on appeal and you face a motion for a discretionary stay.

These federal cases tell you that the judge can consider the prospect of success on appeal, some security or assurances of payment due the plaintiff, the importance or significance of the defendant and services provided to the community such as a hospital, and the amount of the judgment. The temporary stays under federal or state law protect the assets from active enforcement, but potentially not passive liens. See *Yusov v. Yusul*, 892 F.2d 784, 785, note 1 (9th Cir. 1989).

Chapter 2

Beating Out the Stay

For whatever stupid reason, the defendant fails to score a stay and fails to post a bond, and even if the case is on appeal, the plaintiff can execute. If the plaintiff collects before the defendant secures the stay, the plaintiff keeps the money, as a stay will not unwind a completed levy. See *Gencorp v. Olin Corporation*, 477 F.3d 368 at 376 (6th Cir. 2007) and *Del Riccio v. Superior Court* 115 Cal. App. 2d 29 (2nd Dist. 1952) (possession is nine-tenths of the law—in plain English, the court cannot pry the money out of the hands of the plaintiff if the plaintiff actually collected the money). The moral of this message: If you win and absent the stay, put the pedal to the metal. This is more than lawyer talk. If you win and are free of a stay, paint the town red with writs. Run to the marshal's office. Have in hand all your paperwork. Make sure that the paperwork is perfect and that you have an order allowing a private process server to serve the levy. This is FRCP Rule 4.1(a) for the propeller heads.

What happens if you successfully garnished the bank but the funds are still waylaid with the bank or the sheriff, and before the funds come to you, the judgment debtor posts a bond? Can you hang onto the money? That's tough because you snatched the money out of the defendant's hands, but the money is still in the bank or sheriff pipeline. Is this a problem, Houston? Answer? You bet, and the answer is *California Com. Bank v. Super. Ct.*, 10 Cal. Rptr. 2d 418, 421 (Cal. App. 4th Dist. 1992), which returned the money to the defendant who filed the appeal and posted the bond.

This was not a happy day in the Land of Oz. You might consider, maybe, if and when the defendant posts the gazillion-dollar bond that jerks back the gazillions in tow, that you avoid calling your co-counsel and screaming in the phone: "That bastard. He posted a bond. HE TOOK MY TOY AWAY FROM ME! I want my TOY back! CRAP! What a jerk! Why did this have to happen to me? I was having so much fun. I am going to file a complaint with somebody." I personally believe that co-counsel might have ratted me out and told everyone in his office because the receptionist seems to know my voice when I call. I can detect a slight giggle in her voice.

The punch line is that if the garnished money is still in the pipeline and the judgment debtor posts a bond in the correct amount, the money goes back to the defendant. Most states require that the bond be in the amount of one and a half times the judgment. You will lose your toy.

Chapter 3

The Bond—Shaken and Never Stirred

An appeal bond promises the appellee payment of the judgment if the appellant loses. Facing a large-dollar judgment, the appellant will post a bond that forestalls enforcement of the judgment. In issuing the appeal bond, the bonding company will demand collateral, which usually consists of cash or a cash equivalent, or if the appellant is very creditworthy, might accept a written indemnity (promise to pay) should the bonding company pay off the judgment. If the appellant loses, the appellee can petition the court (by motion or new suit) to compel the bonding company to pay off the bond. These are the mechanics.

Aren't all bonds alike? No, the business of bond is extremely boring, unless the bond that indemnified you for payment of the judgment died on the vine.

Is this possible? Do I detect mischief? You do have the right to object to the bond and sometimes for very good reasons. First, never overestimate the denizens of the dark business. Few know what they are doing, and many fumble their way through this thicket. "How do I bungle a bond? Let me count the ways." Be patient now because I have a punch line. Bungle #1. The bond is incorrectly written. Here is the line in the bond: "Know all these present, that we, Schoondle Doodle Company, and Poodle Foodle Bond Company . . . are held and firmly bound unto Ms. Ma Ligned in the just and full sum of $1,561,934.50." Ms. Ma Ligned is the plaintiff and entitled to the money. Some lawyers swap out the plaintiff and swap in the court. That's bungle #1. No, this is a total blunder. (Author's note: Ma is the 14th most common Chinese ethnic name, information courtesy of my wife. The meaning of "Ligned" is lost in the mists of history.)

Bungle #2. The person who signed the bond is unusually a bond agent who signs as "lawyer in fact." To ensure that the signature is genuine, a power of attorney is attached to the bond and filed along with the bond and recorded with the county recorder. Everything is notarized. The bond of the notary is typically filed with the county clerk-recorder. Failing to attach to the bond the power of attorney (or filing with the clerk and recording with the county recorder depending upon the state) is bungle #2.

Bungle #3. How much is owed to the plaintiff? In most case, the judgment is for the principal, interest, costs, and—the big winner—fees. The whole kit and caboodle is bonded at one and a half times. The bond must expressly provide for payment of everything. This is bungle #3.

Bungle #4. Bonding companies can go bust. That might be a shock, but once in a blue moon, these fine fellows crap-out. Absent a bond posted by a major AAA-rated company, such as an insurance company listed on the New York Stock Exchange and whose financials are public (courtesy of the SEC website), you can object on the basis that the bonding company is a financial weakling. You do have the right to do some discovery to ensure that Poodle Foodle Bond Company can write the big check, as opposed to the big financial bomb. Don't be shy, and don't take the other lawyer's word for it. The plaque for the foundering bond company is down in bankruptcy court, Maverick. This is bungle #4, and it is the most fatal. If you are in need of a patron saint (we all are), try Saint Thomas the Apostle, better known as Doubting Thomas. He is our type of guy.

Some very shrewd defendants offer personal sureties, supported by financials, who promise to pay the judgment. These bonds are financial stink bombs and compel an immediate objection. Call these bonds Klaxon moments that cause people to bolt up in their chairs. The lawyer for plaintiff has 10 days to object, and if not, all objections are waived to the bogus surety. Does this mean that the Schoondle Doodle Company can gin up a phony financial statement, staple it to the affidavit, file the package with the court, pray the lawyer is out to lunch (or out of town), and pry the money out of the sheriff's grip? Answer: Enjoy the lemonade made with the lemons.

Why do all this? Is this process a total waste of time and effort? This is not the act of some nutcase, mind you. Well, not really. Well, maybe. I am not sure. You want an enforceable bond in the right name, the right amount, for the right case, but the bonding company is a zombie. (This is a highly technical bond term for the under 30 set.) Let's stop this show. The defendant now posts a bond because you latched onto his or her bank account and are about to pull out a bunch of money. Levy someone's bank account, and the checks payable to the vendors, landlord, utilities, employees, and tax deposits are going to bounce. We are talking about checks bouncing so high that they exit earth's gravity and start orbiting alongside the Hubble. How about bouncing 100 payroll checks? We are now talking about the labor commission, facing a mob of very angry employees, and calling the cops. The defendant is running around for an appeal bond to recapture the money and start funding the payroll checks, keep the doors open, and keep the police at bay. Well, Kimosabe, what do you do? We object to the bond. That's what we do.

Why and what would possess you to do that? Depending on the state, a filed objection to bond stays the bond's effectiveness, which means that the enforcement continues unabated and money continues to rumble down the sheriff's pipeline. God forbid, the money is not going back to Schoondle Doodle Company but might bound over the finish line in the hands of Ms. Ma Ligned courtesy of the unstayed sheriff's disbursement. Don't try this at home. Don't try this at all unless you want an open dance card at the holiday party because nobody is ever going to invite you to their annual soiree.

Chapter 4

Thrown Under the Judgment Bus

Without a bond, nothing stops the defendant looting the company and rendering the judgment worthless. Embrace this sad and very sorry tale in *Peacock v. Thomas*, 516 U.S. 349 (1996):

> Respondent Jack L. Thomas is a former employee of Tru-Tech, Inc. In 1987, Thomas filed an ERISA class action in federal court against Tru-Tech and petitioner D. Grant Peacock, an officer and shareholder of Tru-Tech, for benefits due under the corporation's pension benefits plan. Thomas alleged primarily that Tru-Tech and Peacock breached their fiduciary duties to the class in administering the plan. The District Court found that Tru-Tech had breached its fiduciary duties, but ruled that Peacock was not a fiduciary. On November 28, 1988, the District Court entered judgment in the amount of $187,628.93 against Tru-Tech only [citation omitted]. On April 3, 1990, the Court of Appeals for the Fourth Circuit affirmed. [Citation omitted]. *Thomas did not execute the judgment while the case was on appeal* and, during that time, Peacock settled many of Tru-Tech's accounts with favored creditors, including himself.
>
> *After the Court of Appeals affirmed the judgment, Thomas unsuccessfully attempted to collect the judgment from Tru-Tech.* Thomas then sued Peacock in federal court, claiming that Peacock had entered into a civil conspiracy to siphon assets from Tru-Tech to prevent satisfaction of the ERISA judgment. Thomas also claimed that Peacock fraudulently conveyed Tru-Tech's assets in violation of South Carolina and Pennsylvania law. Thomas later amended his complaint to assert a claim for "piercing the corporation veil under ERISA and applicable federal law." [Citation omitted]. (Pages 351–352)

The lesson of this tale: Plaintiff should have executed upon the judgment, or at least encumbered the assets. Sitting still is getting killed by the other side. The Supreme Court tossed the case based on jurisdictional grounds. You snooze, you lose is the moral here.

This case is very sobering and worth reading. The amount of money at issue is something south of $200,000, but the parties drove this modest case up to the Supreme Court. While the record does not reveal the amount of lawyer's fees, rest assured, the fees exceeded the value of the case. Somebody was bent out of shape, Rambo. Too bad, this case ended poorly.

Chapter 5

Shooting Yourself in the Foot Ouch!

Do you know why you have two feet? Now, you'd think that you would need two feet to walk, skip, or run. Two feet are important if you want to rumba, tango, or waltz. Two feet enable the shoemakers to sell you two shoes and not one. Two feet mean that you can wear two socks. Two feet mean that you stand on two feet and avoid looking like a flamingo. Two feet just look nicer. I have two feet.

Maybe not, and here's why. You just spent the last half hour learning that you can get the drop on your debtor if you can levy the bank account before the debtor scores a discretionary stay. The discretionary stay, if granted, will not unwind the levy. Only a perfected appeal which compels the debtor to post a bond and file the appeal, unwinds the levy. Hog-tying the debtor's bank account puts a big crimp on the debtor and might hobble the debtor's attempt to post the bond. Bonding companies require collateral at 100 percent of the face of the bond or more. The levy made the debtor's checks bounce like crazy and turned the business upside down.

This sounds terrific. The debtor is ready to capitulate. Grant is ready to accept Lee's sword and maybe too quickly. What happens if the debtor goes kaput and the money cycles through the sheriff to the creditor? Is this time for the victory dance? Well, yes and no. The creditor might forfeit postjudgment lawyer's fees and costs if the judgment is paid in full prior to the motion for fees and costs. Moral of this tale: If the debtor expires, and the sheriff collects and remits the total, the creditor might forfeit the right to recover postjudgment fees and costs. Two feet do look better. Shooting yourself in the foot by forfeiting postjudgment costs is no fun.

Chapter 6

Some Judgments Are Empty

Let's start with the classic phone call:

"I won." "What did you win?" "A $30 million judgment." "Wow. Congratulations. . . . What can I do for you? Did your case go to trial?" "Well, yes and no." "What do you mean by that?" "The defendant hired a lawyer throughout most of the case, but failed to respond to discovery and court orders. The lawyer withdrew close to trial." "Did you have a contested trial?" "No. I won by default." "You mean that the defendant did not participate in the trial at all." "Yes. Total no-show." "What is your true financial loss here? I mean, what money have you really lost?" "You mean money out of pocket?" "Yes, money that left your bank account and went into the defendant's bank account. Call this wealth transfer." "Hmmm. That's hard to say. If you mean what money that I lost in the transaction in counting dollars out the door, I guess nothing. Defendant ripped off our trade secrets, and the judge awarded us money damages." "What portion of the $30 million were the damages?" "Oh, about $27.5 million. Did you ask me about our out-of-pocket?" "Yes. That gives a better idea how to view this problem and what can be done here." "Now that you ask, I did suffer out-of-pocket damages. Real money that went out of our door." "What was that?" "$2.5 million." "That's a lot of money. How did you lose the $2.5 million?" "I didn't lose that money." "Well, what happened?" "That is what I paid our lawyers to represent us in the case. I lost $2.5 million." Find this lawyer's marketing guru. Hire this person: $2.5 million for an empty judgment?

"Let's get this straight. You sued a person who ripped off your trade secrets. You hired first-rate, but pricey intellectual property (IP) lawyers. The defendant hired counsel. You slugged it out for a couple of years, and at the end you spent $2.5 million for counsel, but wind up with an empty judgment. You could have bought the City of Stockton for that money." (The City of Stockton is presently in a municipal bankruptcy proceeding.) The $2.5 million could capture the Cities of San Bernardino and Stockton, which are both in Chapter 9 bankruptcies. "Why do you think that my judgment is empty? We blew our entire legal budget on this case every year that matter was open." "This is my educated guess. The defendant made the judgment empty." "I don't get it. Please tell me why you think the judgment is empty? "

"My answer? I said that the judgment is empty, and this is not my personal conclusion. It is the defendant's conclusion." "Who came to the conclusion? I still don't get it." "The result is preordained. Here is the answer. The defendant determined that the judgment would be empty. The defendant made the decision to make the judgment uncollectible, worthless, and meaningless. This decision destroyed the financial value of the fees paid to your lawyers and destroyed the financial value of the money judgment. That is why the defendant abandoned the litigation, dumped his own lawyers, and failed to show up at the trial. The defendant did not care whether the judge gave you a $3,000, $300 million, or $3 billion judgment."

"Let me explain this to you. Every time a bus blows up in Jerusalem, U.S. service personnel massacred or kidnapped, or other act of terrorism, the U.S. citizens sue in U.S.D.C. (D.C.) and routinely score billions (not millions) in default judgments against Iran. Iran always declines to defend, but will appear when, and if, the judgment creditor latches onto an asset. Absent assets located in the U.S. and used for a commercial purpose, or assets that have been blocked by the U.S. government, Iran is near judgment-proof. If judgment-proof, why defend? Why bother? *Who cares,* they think, and maybe for good reason. The docket for the United States District Court for the District of Columbia sports now $60 billion in judgments against Iran. Should the judgment creditor latch onto assets, Iran will come out of the woodwork and seek to retrieve the asset. Frequently, the U.S. State Department will enter an appearance on behalf of Iran.

Winning by default sets your hair on fire, friend. Why? The debtor did not care how much you won because the debtor executed a plan that obstructs your ability to collect. The fact of the default, particularly for a large-dollar case, tattooed this message on your forehead. "I have been screwed." If the judgment is for a million-dollars, the debtor executed a million-dollar plan, and you will need a million-dollar attorney to topple this plan. Money drives this business.

"What? Are you crazy? I hired the best lawyers in town." "No doubt you did, and thank you for asking, but my mental health is excellent. Let me explain. That judgment, and the numbers inscribed by the judge only has meaning if you can enforce the judgment. Enforcement means that you *involuntarily* separate the defendant from his assets. If you cannot, those numbers on the judgment are eye candy. Dazzling. Intoxicating. Blinding—bring out the Ray-Bans. Better yet, bring back Tom Cruise in a *Few Good Men*. You will need him because you can't stand the truth. We anorexics say empty calories."

The truth of the matter is that this judgment is worthless because the defendant hid, secreted, or now fraudulently concealed his assets so adroitly that the judgment is just another, shall we say, pretty face. Just to prove my point, I'd bet you that days before the trial, the defendant could have hired some kid out of law school. Any law school, including the institutions who advertise on a matchbook. Fee? $5,000 for the entire trial. In cash.

In plain English: These cases are more *Star Trek* moments: Go where no man has gone before and never return. See you on the other side of the moon.

Chapter 7

Best Asset Protection in Town

We kicked the asset protection can down the road. What is the world's best asset protection? Really? Hiding gold ingots in a safety deposit box resting in the bosom of some bank in San Jose, Costa Rica? A bond buried in the bowels of some bank in Basel, Switzerland? How about money stuffed in a coffee can in the backyard? My personal favorite is the gobs of money wrapped in trash bags dumped in the plastic cans, Carmella. What a scene. These are all great ploys, and the bibliography of asset protection might even tell you how to hide your dough via Bitcoin.

Nope, the best asset protection is to win the lawsuit in the first place. Don't have the dough to hire a first-class lawyer? Aw, shucks! Don't worry about the credentials of the lawyer. You need someone with a pulse. You read that right. You need someone to take the defense of the claim against you to trial. That's right. Go to trial. You might win. O. J. did. Why not you?

What is the lawyer's job? Breathe, object, breathe some more, object some more, and keep breathing and objecting. "I object." Make some noise. Any noise. Shuffle papers. Look confident. Call the adverse witnesses big-time liars: 'Liar, liar, pants on fire!" Jump up and down and wave arms. That's it. What would that do? You never know. Think of Luke's lucky shot in *Star Wars*. He should have missed—it would have been a better movie, but no sequels. *Romeo and Juliet* still brings down the house after 400 years, even though Romeo and Juliet died at the end.

Aside from O. J., think Robert Blake's and Phil Spector's first trials. How about John DeLorean's drug trial? Marion Barry's drug trial? John Hinckley's attempted assassination of President Reagan? Casey Anthony? Michael Jackson's molestation trial? Jody Arias, not so much. You never know. A lawyer whose sole qualifications are a pulse and law license would have knocked down your damages by 50 percent, just by asking.

These lawyers will object to everything, proffer absurd arguments, personally attack the plaintiff and lawyer, ridicule the witness, and file motions. Do they have a defense to the case? Absolutely not. Zero. Are they in court to waste everyone's time and effort? You bet. Goody, goody, goody. Accept the reality that some lawyers defend a case, without a defense, solely for the purpose of obstruction. Some creditors might not want to spend the money and might accept pennies on the dollar, or even take a big walk. If you don't have the money but can get a lawyer to duke it out in court, maybe your creditors might conclude that spending another $50,000 to recover a worthless judgment is a waste of money and time.

By the way, if you are suing the defendant for fraud and have your eye on a nondischargeability judgment, your adversary might know the same. The purpose of the lawyer for the debtor is not to beat you but to dump the fraud charge. Beware of hidden agendas.

Chapter 8

Why Bother Defending When the Defendant Has Nothing to Lose?

The defendant did not defend because he had done such a great job immunizing his assets from enforcement that spending even $5,000 was a waste of money, as opposed to your spending 100 times that amount. The defendant declined to invest $5,000 because the defendant did not believe that even $5,000 was at peril. Here is my attempt at the math: The lack of the defense intimates the lack of accessible assets. The fact that the defendant did not defend means that the defendant is pursuing plan B, which is to ensure that the assets are immune from enforcement.

The defendant measured risk at zero and spent zero. The defendant was the smartest person (in absentia) in the courtroom. This is a sound analysis from the insurance risk theory. Consumers buy insurance to protect their assets, whether tangible (stuff in hand) or intangible (future income or opportunities). A million-dollar business, house, building, or opportunity requires, you guessed it, a million-dollars worth of insurance. The $100,000 house requires $100,000 worth of insurance, and so on. The theory goes, if the insured has no assets, no future, and nothing to protect, why buy insurance? The defendant viewed the risk as zero and spent zero, keeping in mind that risk is not liability but the vulnerability to enforce high-value assets. The punch line here is how the defendant measures risk, the financial investment to thwart the risk, by the yardstick of vulnerability to enforcement.

This analysis is important to you on both sides. If you are a victim of crime, or a family member of a crime victim (alive or probably dead), a commercial creditor, or someone who has suffered a catastrophic financial loss at the hands of a scam artist, the fact that you won by default raises precisely the issue of whether you can collect. The defendant did not care because the defendant hid everything, gave everything away, parked whatever he had in a place far, far away, Luke, or had nothing.

Really, folks, what is the punch line here? Here we go. The client asked the Maria von Trappe question. You remember *The Sound of Music* and its music score? The best song is "Climb Every Mountain": "Climb every mountain, Search high and low, Follow every byway, Every path you know. Climb every mountain, Ford every stream, Follow every rainbow, 'Till you find your dream." A client asked me to collect a judgment against Mr. Impossible, whose life's dream is to die with the tombstone: "You Missed."

Forget the mountain, byway, path, and stream. Let's try $20,000 upfront for fees and costs. The client branched. No kidding. My response was "Look, take the $20,000 and instead handing me the money, go out and buy yourself a nice piece of art and have it over your credenza so you have something nice in your office." All was quiet on the Western Front; I heard nothing from the client for weeks. I visited one other business and am taken in this office. Right over his credenza was an original painting from a well-known local artist.

Kiss Me First, Al

We need to run through bad deals. This section will survey swindles, cheats, and frauds. Even though newspapers report swindles, examining the mechanics teaches you what to avoid. As they say on TV, don't try any of this at home or ever. By the way, "Al" is Al Pacino in *Dog Day Afternoon*.

Do I have favorites? Routine deals are seed, mezzanine, or bridge loans that are tied to equity to enable a fledging entrepreneur to finance a start-up. These deals involve hundreds of millions of dollars and offer high rates of interest. Advisors, accountants, and business associates shop these opportunities, but they rarely offer realistic financials to justify the risk. These deals are straight loans of money, but, more commonly, the borrower asks the private lender to guaranty a bank loan or line of credit, enabling the borrower to have direct access to the credit without the draconian constraints imposed by the private party as a direct lender. All too typically, the borrower exhausts the credit line, rebuffs requests for financial statements, and assuredly defaults on the credit. The bank calls on the guaranty, and the private lender, as the guarantor, pays off the debt. Payment to the bank converts the guarantor, formerly the investor, into the belligerent creditor pondering the collection of the credit owed by a teetering start-up with miniscule assets, many bills, and no future.

Chapter 7 arrives in all its glory. Any investment that just requires the investor to guaranty the bank loan is an investment that craters. At the outset, these deals are attractive because the investors get into the deal with "no money down" and assume "an equity position without a capital investment." There is no free lunch in this world.

Why? Because the borrower has nothing, you will never collect. No money, honey. (This is not a sexist term—this applies to everyone.) Your justice is in the paper, and not the money. Be happy with that outcome because that is the only outcome you will enjoy, and no more. Face it, folks, the bad guys do not even have two nickels to their name. Enjoy the paper judgment, and at least the court believes in the justness of your cause.

Here are other stupid deals: investing in a portfolio of factor accounts receivables or short-term business loans. Here is the pitch. "We finance business by buying their receivables. Business people regularly pay 33 percent for short-term loans and use their receivables to collateralize these short-term loans. You can make 25 percent a year. Try this one." Real estate is going crazy. "I have found the perfect building. I need five partners. I need $200,000 and your name will be on the deed." Here is another common one: "We are offering construction loans to contractors at 30 percent interest a year. We need a commitment of $100,000. They are all the same because these deals offer huge profits on common transactions that sound lucrative."

We had a real estate scheme to unwind. The defendant terribly oversold a downtown building to many investors who overpaid by five times. Our job was to examine (depose) the defendant in an attempt to ferret out his assets and liability. He showed up with a new lawyer in tow, who was not the lawyer of record. I sat across from the defendant and new counsel (who looked about 25) and shoulder to shoulder with trial counsel. After consulting with trial counsel, I stated on the record that the new lawyer cannot appear or participate because he was not the lawyer of record. Nothing happened. There was not a word from this guy. Did I go wrong? Did the English language fail me? I repeated myself and said the same thing, but I said it more slowly. No response. Is this guy a walking corpse? Creepy. He finally spoke up. "I have been a lawyer for three months. Believe me, I am not going to object to anything." I don't know what was said next in that room because the laughter drowned out every voice. The deposition proceeded apace.

Remember this maxim in investing: When the tide rolls in, the junk floats off the beach; when the tide rolls out, the junk settles into the sand.

Section 7

Finding a Right Home

"Home, home on the range
Where the deer and the antelope play,
where seldom is heard
a discouraging word from Mr. Judge

Chapter 1

The Choice Between Federal and State Court: Choose Wisely, Dr. Jones

If you found the asset and gear up enforcement, what court offers you the most favorable forum? Isn't one court as good as another? We shall see.

If you decide to prosecute enforcement of the federal judgment in federal court, federal courts follow local state court rules for enforcement of a judgment. F.R.C.P. 69(a). The levying officer is the U.S. Marshal. The duties of the Marshal are to protect the courts, apprehend fugitives, and serve civil process. Many Marshals decline to serve routine civil process, such as garnishments, and require the judgment creditor to use a private process server. You contact the marshal's office, who suggests that U.S. Marshal Samuel Gerard is busy chasing down Dr. Richard Kimble and might decline to levy the bank account of Joe Poodle's bong store which sold pirated Darth Vader T-shirts.

If you have a federal judgment and seek high-end enforcement, check with the local marshal to determine whether they can accommodate you. Don't be shocked, Inspector Renault, but some marshals are unable or lack meaningful facilities to execute upon a big judgment. If not, go back to "GO," and never collect your $200; file the federal judgment in state court and convert the federal judgment into a state court judgment to gain access to the service of the state court sheriff. That can cost you time and money; therefore, rethink this issue at the outset rather than wasting six months down the road and finding yourself face to face with a levying officer slow on the draw. Believe it not, the lack of access to the services of a levying officer, such as the marshal, is another form of asset protection because only the levying officer (or judicial order substitute, such as a receiver) can reach the assets of a debtor. A creditor is not entitled to self-help. That would be theft.

The inability of the U.S. Marshal to take immediate action impedes effective enforcement and necessarily protects assets from effective enforcement. If you cannot grab the assets, the assets are necessarily immune. Although this statement sounds odd, at best, the underlying premise is that the debtor will never voluntarily pay, make payments, or even communicate. This is a brutal business, as I told you, and in some cases, the creditor will only be paid if the creditor can involuntarily separate the debtor from his property, and nothing less. Lacking the coercive powers of the levying officer is a functional equivalent of letting the debtor walk away unscathed.

The U.S. Marshal requires the creditor to jump through extensive paperwork hoops. Many U.S. marshals require that the judgment creditor provide an issued writ of execution, a file-stamped copy of the affidavit in support thereof, a copy of judgment, a typed U.S. Marshal #285 (USM #285) form, all typed notices of levy, a prepared memorandum of garnishee, a list of exemptions, a letter of instructions, payment up front for the marshal's services and maybe a blank check to cover mileage.

Many U.S. Marshals decline to serve common garnishments upon bank accounts, which necessitates the judgment creditor to obtain an order under F.R.C.P. 4.1(a). Some judges will issue these orders predicated upon a "request form." Other judges are more inclined to expect the judgment creditor to submit a declaration in support, a memorandum, or a notice to the judgment debtor. The district court judge might even to refer the matter to a magistrate judge for a recommendation. This is a significant number of steps that would not be required in state law enforcement.

Why is this information important to you? Is this level of detail necessary? You cannot enforce a judgment; only the levying officer can. In legalese: Getting paid compels you to turn the wheel of justice, which postjudgment is access to the coercive powers of the levying officer. If you think the judge is tough, the marshal or sheriffs are tougher. Absent the extreme, the levying officer will tell you, "It's my way or the highway."

If the judgment debtor has announced that you will only collect when you pry the money from the judgment debtor's "dead cold hands," thanks to Charlton Heston, the person doing the actual prying is the levying officer and not you. To prove my point, we purchased a judgment out of the bankruptcy court in Minnesota and were specifically told by the court clerk to domesticate the case in state court if we wanted the judgment collected. The judicial term is "go way."

Dealing with the U.S. Marshal in Los Angeles requires a typewriter or very good handwriting as of 2012 to complete the USM #285 form, which is a five-part carbon-backed form that must be manually typed or handwritten. Call to see if this practice has changed. No kidding. To get the marshal to take any action, the judgment creditor must tender, among everything else, the USM #285 form. Any lawyer who intends to actively enforce federal judgments should invest in a memory typewriter, which is needed to efficiently fill out the USM #285 form. Don't forget the required maintenance contract because typewriters, with a million moving parts, require maintenance.

The county sheriff is a better deal. If you are facing high-end enforcement, file suit in the state court to convert the federal judgment to a state court judgment. The county sheriffs have greater facilities, staff, levying officers, and storage-to-storage facilities than the U.S. Marshal. Given that each county offers a county sheriff, and that all states have more counties than federal districts, there are numerically more sheriffs than U.S. Marshals who are tied to the federal district court. California has 58 counties that offer 58 separate sheriffs. California has four federal districts, which offers four U.S. Marshals.

The locale of the debtor's assets is the homing beacon for domesticating any judgment. If the debtor owns real property in Reno, domesticate the federal judgment in the state court in Washoe County because the sheriff of Washoe County can execute on that asset, but not the real property located in Clark County (Las Vegas). Keep in mind, however, that the sheriffs are busy, and if you really require expedited service, you need to appear at the sheriff's counter and plead your case. If you can have a process server perform the services (serve bank garnishments or levy real property), you should pursue that process server route, even if very expensive, because the sheriff sometimes can be slow. Sheriffs execute on property in their county. Keep in mind that a state court can issue a writ to any sheriff.

If your federal judgment originates out of state, and you want to bring the judgment into your state, you have the option of registering the judgment under 28 U.S.C. §1963, in Federal court, which offers registration of the judgment in the new district. Upon registration of the out-of-district federal judgment, the newly registered judgment can be enforced as if the judgment had been entered in the new district. If you anticipate a hardcore judgment debtor who will resist all enforcement, or compel you to actually seize and sell assets, file suit in the state court and convert the out-of-state district court judgment into a state court judgment.

Out-of-state and offshore arbitral awards could be confirmed in federal court based on the diversity jurisdiction of the federal courts. The fact that the complainant succeeded in winning an arbitral award and the respondent declined payment intimates that only enforcement will get the respondent to pay. Converting the arbitral award into a state court expands the quantity, quality, and price of enforcement remedies.

State courts offer more judges, who routinely preside over the debtor examinations, garnishment battles, and receivers to liquidate a debtor's assets. State courts offer more courthouses, which are sometimes closer to the debtor, although many districts have multiple courthouses in a district, such as district court houses for the Central District of California in Los Angeles, Riverside, and Santa Ana.

Let's end the debate of whether you get a better judge out of the federal courts. Buy a lawyer a drink, or two, and pop this question, where do you get a better judge? Here is the answer: Federal judges have greater control of the case. The federal rules and Supreme Court precedent imbues broad supervisory powers in the hands of the district court judge. At various hearings or trials, a federal judge makes decisive rulings. Moreover, in federal court, you get one judge from soup to nuts, which means that after a few hearings, your judge knows the case. In state court the case might migrate to another department.

Most cases ramp up to trial after a series of pretrial motions, which are heard on "law and motion day." Upon the filing of the papers (motion, opposition, and reply), some federal judges take the matter under submission and rule on the paper. In many cases, the judge does not hear oral argument from the lawyers. Perry Mason can lounge in Maui. Abe Lincoln can work on his railroad cases. On the other hand, state courts offer live law and motion on a nearly daily basis and offer "face time" with the lawyers.

Chapter 2

One Court Might Offer More Treasure

For one key asset, the federal and state courts differ greatly: patent licenses. California state law subjects a patent license to enforcement (*Farmland Irrigation Co. v. Doplmaier* (1957) 48 Cal. 2d 208), whereas federal law prohibits the involuntary transfer (i.e., bankruptcy or execution sale) of a patent license. Read *Everex Systems, Inc. v. Cadtrak Corp.* (9th Cir. 1996) 89 F.3d 673, 679 (*Everex*) [regarding nonexclusive licenses]; *In re Hernandez* (Bkrtcy. D.Ariz. 2002) 285 B.R. 435 [applying same logic to exclusive licenses]. If your judgment debtor holds the patent license to curing cancer, the license might fetch a pretty price in an enforcement proceeding. State court is your choice.

What if the debtor is offshore and the only enforcement is seizing cargo in transit? Can you garnish cargo from an ocean-going carrier arising from state court enforcement? As you will see later, the answer is uncertain in state court because the federal court has jurisdiction over admiralty and maritime matters.

Choose wisely, as they say in the movies. In federal court, you might snag the sage of the century but fumble the gold ring of the patent license. In state court, you might secure the services of the sheriff, score a higher rate of interest, and relish the bench accustomed to the rough and tumble of debtor-creditor but forego reaching the only asset of the debt if sitting on the deck of an ocean-going carrier.

Chapter 3

The Power of Discovery: Which Court Is Better?

Postjudgment discovery in federal court beats out discovery in state court because federal court provides for the panoply of full discovery postjudgment. In federal court, you serve depositions and interrogatories (questionnaires), ask for documents, gain entrance to property, and, if the debtor is uncooperative, file motions and seek sanctions. Have fun. On the other hand, state court postjudgment discovery is far more limited and does not allow the unlimited subpoena of records directed to third parties unless attached to a debtor or third-party examination in court. For example, in federal court, getting the bank, accounting, or financial records requires only a subpoena directed to the witness, but this is not the case for state court, where the subpoena must be attached to a hearing date for an examination of the debtor.

Let's stop the show for a second. Federal court does not require a court order as a condition of a subpoena. What does this mean to you in plain English? Absent the highly motivated debtor with money to burn on a motion for a protective order, you can serve every bank in town with a subpoena that might identify the debtor's bank accounts, loan files, safe deposit boxes, lines of credit, or secured loans in which the bank holds collateral. As you will see in our section on notices of levy, you can levy (garnish) the collateral that the debtor reposed to collateralize a loan. If the debtor pays off the loan, the collateral might revert to the debtor; in garnished the lender, the collateral might land in the hands of the levying officer under the garnishment.

Think your debtor has funds on account with a casino? That is very exciting. Casinos are suspected havens for secreted funds, whose identity is kept secret to fend off creditors, partnership, the IRS, and the ubiquitous ex-spouses. Absent a casino on an Indian reservation, serve (or garnish if you have the money) every casino in town. If you believe that the debtor parked money, or conducted a transaction, with a title or escrow company, lawyer, factor, hard money lender, or anyone else, serve them with a federal subpoena. Unless the debtor gets ambitious, nothing stops you from a mass subpoena or mass levy except running out of money to serve everyone.

In state court, you can send out interrogatories (a questionnaire) and request for production of document to the debtor, but expect that the debtor will ignore it. Look, if the debtor defaulted on the zillion-dollar lawsuit because the debtor didn't have the money or insurance, or did not care, don't expect the debtor to unlock the door to the royal treasury by answering postjudgment written discovery. No matter the low expectations, given the low expense, you should serve the discovery, but don't expect a response.

What does this mean in plain English? Paper the city with federal court subpoenas and serve every bank within 10 miles. Serve every customer. Serve the shipping lines; service anyone and everybody doing business with the debtor. Federal court lets you paint the town with subpoenas. Remember, the power of the subpoena is the power to compel the disclosure of information. Information is the arrows and the "X's" on the treasure map.

Let's talk tax returns. Federal courts and some state courts (i.e., California has different rules) are tough to reach. Tax returns are immune from pretrial discovery in California (*Sav-On Drug Stores v. Superior Court* (1975) 15 Cal. 3rd. 1, 6 [except family law court]), or federal court to case based on California law (*Lewis v. United States* (Ninth Circuit, 1975) 517 F. 2d 236, 237. Tax returns are discoverable in federal court even in private litigation. *St. Regis Paper Co. v. United States* (1961) 368 U.S. 208, 218; *Young v. United States* (USDC, SD, CA, 1993) 149 F. R.D. 199, 201. See also *Premium Service Corp. v. Sperry & Hutchinson Co.* (9th Cir. 1975), 511 F.2d 225, 229). These cases are worth reading. If the keys to the kingdom lie in the debtor's tax returns, you have the option of parking a claim, or judgment, in federal or state court; picking the right court is picking victory. This is a major issue because sometimes tax returns are the only source of information.

Chapter 4

Tent Pole Jurisdiction

If in federal court, everyone is fair game: Accountants, banks, lawyers, spouses, title companies, partners, and banks and finance companies that have information concerning the debtor are subject to the power of subpoena and the production of records at your office. Come one; come all. This is very convenient and all is fair game.

If your case is in state court, you can hale these folks into court (not your office) if tethered to a debtor's examination. This is called tent pole jurisdiction because the order for examination (OEX) (the debtor's examination) gives the court plenary jurisdiction over the defendant and compels him or her to appear. The OEX is a formal judicial proceeding, and order is the pole that holds up the judicial tent.

If the debtor is offshore, or out of state, an OEX is impossible, absent domesticating the judgment in the debtor's jurisdiction. If out of state, the U.S. Constitution mandate of "full faith and credit" compels the state where the debtor sits to recognize the judgment and allows you to domesticate the judgment and proceed with discovery. This procedure is easy and routine; however, this procedure accrues another set of lawyer's fees, expenses, and delays. If the debtor is offshore, domesticating the judgment offshore is very expensive and potentially inaccessible as many foreign states decline to recognize a default judgment, a judgment upon claims that are not recognized under local law, or a judgment for certain types of damages, such as punitive damages.

If your case is in a state court that bars broad-based discovery untethered to an OEX, and you cannot gin up an OEX directed to the debtor, what can be done? If you can identify, in good faith, someone who is doing business with the debtor, such as a person owing money to the judgment or holding property of the judgment debtor, you can initiate a third-party OEX that brings the third party into court. Once the court authorizes the third-party OEX and compels the third party to appear, you now have raised the tent pole to invoke the power of the court to hale into court witnesses such as banks, lawyers, and accountants. It is very Chicken Delight. Once the tent is raised, you can also hail into the financial, banking, and title records in the hands of witnesses, which will make the examination more productive. You can create pole jurisdiction through the third-party OEX.

Can you really haul into court anybody who has the debtor's financial records, Mr. Chicken? Let's try this one for size. In *Lee v. Swansboro Country Property Owners Ass'n* (2007) 151 Cal. App. 4th 575, 582, 59 Cal. Rptr. 3d 924, 927-28, the court stated as follows:

> Thus, the second method of obtaining the necessary documentation is to serve the debtor with both a notice of hearing and a subpoena duces tecum outlining the documents to be produced. [You don't need this stuff—you can read the case yourself.] While the order to appear at the examination can also include an order to produce documents [Citation omitted.], a creditor often files a subpoena duces tecum separate and apart from the application for examination. As this court has noted, "In preparation for the examination, discovery may be necessary as the actual examination is not so much a device to gather information as it is a tool to confirm the existence of certain assets. [More stuff dumped.] Thus, the use of a subpoena duces tecum to discover and inspect relevant documents is an accepted practice." [More gobbly gook omitted.] As one practice guide advises, "Thus, as far as practicable, counsel should investigate the debtor's assets and subpoena any documents showing ownership . . . into court at the time of examination." [Just dumped]

How about this? In *Mancinelli v. Siewak*, 2009 WL 924285, at p. *4, n. 6 (Cal. App. 4 Dist. 2009), the court stated in an unpublished opinion:

> Indeed, MacAdam seems to contain the seeds of an approach that would permit Mancinelli to obtain some of the materials sought by his subpoenas: pursuit of judgment debtor's examination under Section 708.110, with witness subpoena's under Section 708.130 to entities with documents relevant to the issues that will arise in the judgment's debtor's examination.... In accord: "*Enforcing Judgments and Debts*" Alan Ahart, Rutter Group, 2009, Par. 6:1282 (any person with knowledge leading to enforcement, "e.g., debtor's bookkeeper, accountant or non-debtor spouse," can be subpoenaed as a trial witness at OEX); see also Section 6:1301 (more effective examination if records are subpoenaed from non-party custodians, e.g., a bank, lawyer, accountant, title company brokerage firm or employer.)

Sorry about the fine print, but this is the law. If information kicks open the door to the debtor's treasure room, expect big-time resistance from the debtor, and hence these snippets from the court cases arm you for the battle. Sorry about the editing, but at least you have a place to start.

Section 8

Kitchen Implements and the Grand Techniques to Make a Soufflé

Chapter 1

The Writ of Execution—The Key to Power

The clerk issues a writ of execution that is an order to the sheriff to levy and execute upon the debtor's property. That means that the judgment creditor can direct the sheriff to physically take property from the debtor by force. The judgment creditor must identify the property and instruct the sheriff to seize the property. The clerk and sheriff do not identify the debtor's property. The sheriff (or U.S. marshal) requires a fee for services and demands significant deposits in advance. These costs can run from $35 to levy a bank account to tens of thousands of dollars to clean out a fully stocked warehouse.

Before we launch into stories of shock and awe, let's go through the physical procedure of execution. This is very important because law school does not teach law students the mechanics of enforcement. Even the mandatory enforcement seminar fails to explain the nuts and bolts. The first step is to locate a form of writ of execution that is online. Nearly every state, and even the federal courts, provide for a preprinted form of a writ of execution. Most forms are online, but others must be typed. The writ of execution lists the name of the debtor, the name of the creditor, the amount, and the county of the levying officer. The writ is an order issued by the court and directed to the sheriff, marshal, or constable to physically take the property of the judgment debtor and sell it for cash to pay the judgment.

The next step for some states (California) is to prepare the notice of levy. This notice informs the debtor or third party of what property the sheriff is seizing. The notice of levy puts the third party, such as the bank whose accounts are garnished, or customer of the debtor whose accounts payable are garnished, on fair notice of what property the sheriff seeks. In the body of the notice of levy, the form asks for a description of the property to be seized. Getting the description right on the notice of levy reaches the property. The description in the notice of levy tells the garnishee what property in the garnishee's possession is being sought. Don't leave this description to the levying officer, your clerk, your secretary, or your junior associate. This description imposes a lien upon the property, which is subject to your execution lien and a levy, if effective and older than 90 days, survives bankruptcy. Effective enforcement upon property beats out junior garnishees such as the

IRS or state agencies or your competitors. A broad description is the box of chocolate technique because you never know what you will seize.

In drafting up the notice of levy, the identity of the garnishee must be set forth with enormous clarity and, moreover, absolutely correct spelling. The secretary of state offers the correct spelling and name of the garnishee and, more importantly, the address where service can be effectuated. If the garnishee is a large, multinational corporation, rest assured that this entity does business through anywhere from 3 to 30 separate corporations, and each of them is legally distinct. If you are going to levy upon General Electric, you will soon be educated that GE offers a number of separate, legal variations. Entities such as defense, agricultural, manufacturing, export, or other large multinationals might do business through their subsidiaries, all of them separately incorporated. In many cases, the subsidiaries use the same agent for service of process, such as CT Corporation System (CT) or Corporate Service Company (CSC), which all have offices in major cities. Each levy is distinct and will require a separate levy fee with the sheriff or marshal and, moreover, a separate charge from the process server. Corporate counsel on behalf of the garnishee will not give you a break or overlook the fact that you may have levied on the wrong entity. Given this level of precision, you may have to levy upon the corporate "parent" and all subsidiaries that are most logically related to your debtor. You can spend an awful lot of money in chasing down this problem, but a misidentified garnishee is a total disaster because you notified the debtor that you are generally after this garnishee but have not reached the receivable or property held by the garnishee. This gives the debtor an immediate "heads up" of your game plan, thereby enabling the debtor to clear out the account or file some type of bogus UCC, which would create an impediment to your reaching the account held by the garnishee. A botched garnishment is worse than no garnishment at all because all you do is tip your hand. Rest assured that the response to a botched garnishment is the undying gratitude of your debtor.

We are going to go through each class of property subject to enforcement and explain this description from the viewpoint of the garnishee. The garnishee views the garnishment as an order from the court reaching the property described in the notice of levy and in the possession of the garnishee. The description therefore is very important.

Deposit accounts: A deposit account is an account maintained by a financial institution that enables the debtor to write a check (i.e., draw on the account). The general description is "deposit accounts, accounts, bank accounts, daily demand accounts, certificates of deposit, money market accounts, or any other account no matter how described in the name of, for the benefit of, due to, owed to, owned by, held for the name of, or payable to order of the judgment debtor XXXX."

Accounts: Accounts are sometimes synonymous with deposit accounts. However accounts also refer to any right to payment of money based on the sale and delivery of goods or the rendition of services in which the obligation of the obligor (the buyer) is to pay.

All rights to payment of money: Sometimes money is owed to the judgment debtor for any reason. This description covers just about everything.

Contract rights: This is generally a catchall for any right to payment of money due the debtor from a contract rights.

Rights due the debtor under merchant account or credit card clearing account: Many businesses accept credit cards, including professionals (doctors, dentists, and lawyers), wholesale distributors, nearly all Internet or mail order merchants, anybody in the food and hospitality business, and nearly all retail businesses.

Any obligation owed by the garnishee to the debtor: Another catchall category.

Installment obligations (rent or lease payments): This includes rental and lease payments, periodic payments due on a sale or installment agreement, and payments due from a purchaser of real or personal property. This category reaches the payments, streams of income, lease payments, or rental payments. If the obligation owed by the obligor is in the form of a negotiable instrument, the method of collection is the seizure of the promissory note. This category is best reached by an assignment order that reaches income streams over a period of time.

Royalty payments for any intellectual property: Patents are typically licensed. Copyright royalties, such as music or software, or residual rights in movies, television, and cable, are subject to garnishment. This requires services upon the person who is actually making payment, such as the Screen Actor's Guild. For music try ASCAP, BMI, or SESAC.

Royalty payments for any license: Aside from intellectual property, the debtor might have re-leased or subleased real or personal property. Payments due from the licensee are subject to garnishment.

Chattel paper: Chattel paper is personal property leases, whether a true lease or a finance lease. The paper is the obligation to make payments for the use of equipment. This obligation represents payment for the finance (rolling stock such as cars, tractors, trucks, trailers, railroad rolling trains, and cars) or a true lease (rolling stock, equipment, software, etc.)

Negotiable instrument: A negotiable instrument is the physical evidence of the debtor. If the debtor is the holder of the note, the creditor can collect the payments from the obligor. If the asset of the debtor is the note owed by a third party but in the hands of another party, the judgment creditor can reach the note and related security.

Warehouse receipt: A warehouse receipt is a receipt for goods, a contract between the bailor and the bailee and implicitly title to the goods. If the debtor is the owner of a warehouse receipt, garnish the third party who has possession. The twist is whether the debtor has goods in storage such as cold storage, consignment houses, and copacking plants (or others who hold inventory or equipment inventory). If the warehouse receipt is negotiable, you have to find the receipt and levy on the garnishee, or if in the possession of the debtor compel the debtor to turn over the receipt. If the warehouse receipt is nonnegotiable, you can levy on the bailee (i.e., the warehouse).

Bill of lading: A negotiable bill of lading is the de facto title to the goods described in the bill. The common carrier will deliver the goods to the person in possession and control of the negotiable bill of lading, assuming that the holder has title to the bill. If your debtor is the consignee under a negotiable bill of lading, you can reach this bill by having the sheriff take possession of it. Under court order, the sheriff can take possession of the goods by presentment to the common carrier. The notice of levy would describe the bill of lading as clearly as possible by the date, bill of lading number, name of consignee or consignor, and the name of the bailee. If non-negotiable, levy on the carrier. If F.O.B. shipping point, the consignee (buyer) presumptively owns the goods. If F.O.B. destination, the consignor (seller) presumptively owns the goods. Who is the debtor? Have fun.

Tangible personal property: Tangible personal property is anything in the hands of the garnishee. For example, the debtor pawned, hocked, or financed stock, jewelry, cars, or other valuable personal property that is in the hands of a finance company, pawnbroker, or even bank. These entities, commonly known as pledgees or bailees, hold the personal property as collateral for a loan. Under Article Nine of the Commercial Code, unless and until the debtor defaults and the secured creditor forecloses on the collateral by way of foreclosure sale, or other disposition, the debtor retains rights in the collateral. Those rights, which are in effect the rights of redemption or return of the personal property, are either the right to the personal property or the right to redeem the personal property. The right to redeem is probably a general intangible. The property, and therefore the right to redeem, should be described in the notice of levy as the following: Levy on the "10 carat diamond ring, encased in a platinum setting, bearing pawn ticket #1111, the right to redeem the property under pawn ticket number 3445, and the general intangible right to redeem and reclaim the pledged property in the event of payment of the underlying obligation thereof."

Credit card drafts: Absent the extreme, most credit cards are electronically accepted as opposed to the paper draft. Nonetheless, the general concept remains the same. A customer offers the credit card, which is the magnetically encoded card to the merchant as payment for the purchase. The merchant charges the card, or more technically communicates with its own bank (the merchant bank) that the customer authorized the merchant to charge the card. The information (digital, of course) is routed through to the customer's bank, which credits the customer's charge account and bills the customer at the end of the transaction. The credit card receivable due the merchant is a form of account, held in the merchant account, that entitles the merchant to draw down, just like a bank account. You can describe these accounts due from a merchant bank as "general intangible rights to payment based on any credit card or digital transaction." Some of this money might be held by a credit card clearing house that clears the credit card drafts and money due to the merchant. These entities are subject to garnishment. Some funds are directly deposited in the debtor's bank account.

General intangibles: This is a catchall of every possible obligation for any reason that the obligor might owe the obligee, who is the judgment debtor. A general intangible is some right including any right to payment of money, such as a tort, contract, or other claim or money. A general intangible could be a contingent right to turn over person property. A general intangible could be intellectual property of the debtor reposed in the hands of the assignee with a right of reversion. For example, the debtor might have licensed a patent or copyright to a third party with a right of reversion at a specific date or under specific circumstances.

Safe deposit box: Many banks still offer safe deposit boxes. Always include this list of assets subject to levy. Safe deposit boxes are the Forest Gump box of chocolates. You never know what you'll get. You can direct the sheriff to drill the box. You might find drugs, money, stocks and bonds, a gun (a loaded gun, no less), coins, or maybe nothing. Drilling a box is worth the entertainment value.

Certificates of deposit: A certificate of deposit is a piece of paper that evidences the deposit by the customer of a sum of money with the financial institution. In some instances, the certificate of deposit might constitute a negotiable instrument if meeting the requirements of negotiability. In the levy upon the bank, the key term if "certificates of deposit, time certificates of deposit, accounts that hold or contain T-Bills, T-Notes, or any other account that holds, warehouses or contains any a medium or form of money and all other instruments."

Notes: The garnishee might have in its possession negotiable or non negotiable instruments (such as a check, cashier's check, or note due the debt). If the instrument or note is negotiable, a levy to reach the "instruments and notes" is the correct description.

Money market accounts: A money market account might constitute an account that entitles the customer to write multiple checks but that is held under the title of money market account. Most money market accounts held by brokers warehouse cash, dividends, stock redemptions, or other rights. Unlike banks, a levy on one office of the broker is a levy upon all locations of the broker.

Trust accounts: Trust accounts are held by lawyers, accountants, employers, and professional trustees. These accounts are subject to garnishment because the account holder is the trustee. Some banks push back on these levies, but this is incorrect. The designation by the account holder as "trustee," or "trust accounts" is a title imposed by the account holder as opposed to independent relationship on the bank as part of the trust relationship.

Margin accounts: A margin account held by a broker is a line of credit secured by the stock itself. The common purpose of the margin account is to permit the customer to buy stocks on the "margin," with the expectation that the stock will increase in price. A levy on a margin account might, or might not, reach the rights of the customer to draw down on the account. As stated elsewhere, the right to draw down on a loan account, such as a line of credit is different than the right of the customer (i.e., the debtor) to write a check on an account. If you are very serious about reaching a margin account, you will need a very serious bank account to finance your battle all the way up to the U.S. Supreme Court or your state Supreme Court.

Don't expect the check as the proceeds of a levy based on a margin account. Expect that the garnishee will respond "nothing held." Sue the garnishee for the failure to draw down the margin account which will earn you years of grief.

Personal property held as collateral for any loan, credit, or advance of money: This is a catchall description that encompasses any collateral held by the garnishee as collateral for a loan. This could be certificates of deposit, stocks, negotiable bills of lading, warehouse receipts, valuable personal property, promissory notes, or nonphysical property such as accounts, accounts receivables, rights to payment money, or general intangibles. Expect pushback. Expect resistance.

Rights under any letter of credit: A letter of credit is the direct obligation to pay a third party a sum of money, when that third party tenders documents, such as shipping documents, consisting of "clean on board bills of lading," invoices, and the like, which represent the shipment of goods. The typical use of a letter of credit is that a U.S. manufacturer is selling product to an overseas entity. Understanding the credit risks and wishing to avoid a catastrophic loss, the U.S. manufacturer will demand that the offshore customer will have a U.S. bank, local to the U.S. manufacturer, and provide for payment when the goods are shipped. This is called a letter of credit. A letter of credit per se is the property of the beneficiary and not the offshore customer. The letter of credit is a contingent right to payment of money due the beneficiary under the letter of credit and only becomes due and payable under presentment of the document precisely required under the letter of credit. Precision is paramount, and spelling counts. Letters of credit are frequently collateralized. If you are chasing down the offshore entity and discover that the entity is selling to U.S. customers who are paid through U.S. banks, it is possible (but a little unlikely) that the offshore entity has parked collateral with the U.S. bank to ensure that they are repaid, with a profit, for honoring the credit facility. Therefore, the levy is director to all "deposits, accounts, rights to payment money, certificates of deposit, bonds, notes instruments, cash on hand, general intangibles and other rights, which serve as collateral for the issuance of any letter of credit, line of credit, credit facility, or loan made to and/or for and on behalf of the debtor." If the debtor is a beneficiary under the letter of credit, you might collect.

Rights under any line of credit: This is going to be very tough as discussed elsewhere. A line of credit is the promise by a lender to advance funds upon demand. Expect insurmountable pushback from the garnishee if you are going to seriously pursue enforcement against the debtor's line of credit with a financial institution. A typical line of credit is a home equity line of credit (HELOC), which permits the homeowner to borrow from the bank to pay common, everyday expenses. This looks, sounds, and walks like a common checking account, but the banks take the position that the bank is making a loan when clearing a check, as opposed to the customer drawing funds in an account with a positive (i.e., credit) balance. Eat a full and hearty breakfast before you charge up San Juan Hill in trying to levy a HELOC. Only the state supreme court will resolve this battle.

Stocks, bonds, and other securities: These physical items of property can be levied upon in the hands of the broker, bank, or third party who has physical custody or control. Possession is nine-tenths of the law.

Securities accounts: This requires a full recitation of UCC § 8112:

> § 8112. Creditor's legal process
>
> (a) The interest of a debtor in a certificated security may be reached by a creditor only by actual seizure of the security certificate by the officer making the attachment or levy, except as otherwise provided in subdivision (d). However, a certificated security for which the certificate has been surrendered to the issuer may be reached by a creditor by legal process upon the issuer.
>
> (b) The interest of a debtor in an uncertificated security may be reached by a creditor only by legal process upon the issuer at its chief executive office in the United States, except as otherwise provided in subdivision (d).
>
> (c) The interest of a debtor in a security entitlement may be reached by a creditor only by legal process upon the securities intermediary with whom the debtor's securities account is maintained, except as otherwise provided in subdivision (d).
>
> (d) The interest of a debtor in a certificated security for which the certificate is in the possession of a secured party, or in an uncertificated security registered in the name of a secured party, or a security entitlement maintained in the name of a secured party, may be reached by a creditor by legal process upon the secured party.
>
> (e) A creditor whose debtor is the owner of a certificated security, uncertificated security, or security entitlement is entitled to aid from a court of competent jurisdiction, by injunction or otherwise, in reaching the certificated security, uncertificated security, or security entitlement or in satisfying the claim by means allowed at law or in equity in regard to property that cannot readily be reached by other legal process.

Don't think that this is obscure if you are chasing down securities. While UCC Code § 8112 rarely comes across anyone's desk in a lifetime, the lawyers for mutual funds, stockbrokers, and generally the entire securities business have this code section memorized and so should you if you are chasing stock. If you want to levy on a stockbroker because you believe that the debtor has a big stock account, read this section because, trust me, the debtor's lawyer and lawyer for the broker will have memorized it. Before we leave this brief discussion, the portability of the judgment becomes imperative if you have to levy upon the issuer who might be a Delaware entity, or the chief executive offices who are throughout the United States and potentially Delaware. A federal judgment is readily portable, whereas a state court judgment is more difficult to replant in another jurisdiction, particularly New York, which does not adhere to the Uniform Sister State Judgment Act.

The simple summary of this section is the following. If the stock certificate has been issued, you have to reach the actual stock itself. If the stock has not been issued or is an uncertificated security, you can levy on the issuing party itself. When in doubt, you can seek the appointment of a receiver. Be prepared. Have a hearty breakfast.

Commissions: Commissions are common for real estate brokers who are typically independent contractors, automobile sales persons, manufacturer's representatives, and lawyers who work on a contingency fee basis. The levy is directed against "all rights to the payment of money, commission, earnings, revenue, salaries, contingent rights and other claims." The problem with a levy is that a levy only reaches the rights to payment of money that are due as of the time of the levy. If no funds are due the debtor, no funds are due under the levy. The better remedy is a turnover order, or an assignment order that is designed to reach accounts that are due now, due in the future, or contingent.

Any license to use personal property, such as a license to use IP: The license itself is general intangible. The licensor is the holder and owner, which in most cases, is a patent. The owner licenses the patent to the licensee who typically is a manufacturer and who incorporates the patent in the manufacturing process. Under federal law (and jurisdiction in federal court), a patent license in the hands of the licensee, your debtor, is not subject to enforcement. If the judgment lies in state court, the license is subject to enforcement. Smart patent lawyers provide for the cancellation of the patent in the event of a legal action such as a garnishment, turnover order, or receivership of the patent license to prevent the judgment creditor successfully from acquiring the patent license. Patent holders are near pathological in the control of their patents and would do almost anything to avoid that license getting in the hands of a competitor, or worse, another entity (as the buyer at an execution) who might exploit the market and dilute the value of the patent.

A reversionary right under a contract: This is general intangible, but this right is better reached under a receivership for purpose of administration. However, we reached the reversionary rights for *If I Did It* through a levy with the following general description: "Reversionary rights or general intangibles due O. J. Simpson for the book entitled *If I Did It* due from HarperCollins."

Rights under drilling oil or other mining (extraction from the earth rights) [drilling rights] due from the driller: These rights are contingent rights and reachable as "general intangible, rights to payment of money, revenue, income or stream of money." However, given the continuing nature of these rights, the better remedy is an evergreen assignment order, or a receiver.

Deposit held by garnishee to secure payment: This is a form of collateral that is the property of the debtor and can be reached as the "rights to payment of money, accounts, general intangible, or claim for payment of money or return of property, held as collateral, or security for a debt."

With the writ at hand, the judgment creditor can garnish the debtor's bank accounts, receivables, or debts owed by a third party. Some states provide for a writ of garnishment in reaching obligations owed by third parties. With the property identified and deposit in hand, the sheriff will take possession of debtor's personal and real property and sell it.

PayPal itself does hold funds in the name of its customers and will be receptive to a levy. You will get a much better result if you include in the notice of levy the last four digits of the debtor's Social Security number, TIN number, the debtor's e-mail address or URL, a current street address for mailing, or if you perceive that the debtor is doing business under a trade name, a certified copy of the fictitious business name filing, or like proof. Garnishees are known to ignore garnishments, even if valid on their face, that reach one of their customers if the notice of levy fails to include a Social Security number, taxpayer identification number (TIN), and if an online financial institution, an e-mail address or URL. The typical response from the uncooperative garnishee is, "Unable to locate with the information as provided . . . Nothing held."

The onus is on the creditor to offer the garnishee the maximum amount of information to readily enable the garnishee to identify its customer. If the customer has an extremely common name, the garnishee will probably decline to reach the account, given the fact that the garnishee cannot identify the customer who is described in the notice of levy. In some ethnic communities, some names are exceedingly common, which compels you to exercise maximum efforts to identify your debtor by any and every means possible.

A botched garnishment is a disaster, once again, because all you have done is notify the debtor that you probably have located the correct bank, but due to the bad description, failed to reach the bank account. The debtor has received paper notice of the levy, which prompts the debtor to electronically determine that the funds are still intact or, moreover, to close the account. This is a total disaster for the creditor, and it is even worse should the creditor have paid good money to crack the account.

Chapter 2

The Writ of Execution Is the Secret Discovery Tool

Let me start with the standard collection case. You win. You win by default. You win a fair amount of money, say, in the hundreds of thousands. Your judgment debtor is a corporation, and you do not have a guaranty. Your debtor saw you coming when you wrote the demand letter, filed the lawsuit, served it, and cycled through a whole bunch of legal process until you obtained judgment. They saw you coming. Do you think there is any money in the debtor's bank account? Maybe, or more likely, maybe not. The debtor's insiders emptied out the company bank account by distributing funds to themselves or paying vendors who held a personal guaranty or overpaying key vendors such as the landlord, utility company, tax deposit accounts, or even paying down secured loans that would be subject to a personal guaranty. This is not a guess but a settled expectation.

How about the receivables? The receivable checks would normally flow into the debtor's bank account at or near the first of the month. Given the financial collapse of the debtor, the insiders are retaining and depositing the debtor's check into their new bank accounts that bear the initials of the debtor, or better yet, in the personal bank accounts of family members. The money did not disappear, but the money is hither and yon. Call this a game of hide and seek.

The first remedy would be to serve a subpoena upon everybody, such as family members, adult children, spouses, and the closely related companies. You should do this in a heartbeat, but be prepared for pushback when this gaggle of people file motions to quash on the basis that the postjudgment discovery is the proverbial fishing expedition and the subpoena invades their privacy. Be prepared to show up in court and justify these subpoenas. Don't be surprised if the judge quashes the subpoenas because you don't have any hard evidence that shows that the insider's adult children are sitting on the debtor's money. Your suspicions might be right, but they might not win the day.

Are you out of luck? Did the other guy win? Are you going to tell your client that the jig is up and that the case is hopeless? This is a Chicken Delight problem. Oh, pray tell, what would Chicken Delight do for you, and particularly in this section of the book that discusses writs of execution and notices of levy?

The answer is that an execution is more than just service of the document entitled "Writ of Execution" and the accompanying the notice of levy that describes the property that is the subject of the enforcement. This levy package includes a memorandum of garnishee, or in other states, execution interrogatories that likewise compel the garnishee to answer questions whether property of the debtor is held. A garnishee is the person who is served with the levy and might have possession of the property due the debtor. In nearly every state, the garnishee has to answer these execution interrogatories:

> (1) A description of any property of the judgment debtor sought to be levied upon that is not delivered to the levying officer and the reason for not delivering the property.
> (2) A description of any property of the judgment debtor sought to be levied upon that is in the possession or under the control of the third party at the time of levy.
> (3) A statement of the amount and terms of any obligation to the judgment debtor sought to be levied upon that is due and payable and is not paid to the levying officer, and the reason for not paying the obligation.
> (4) A statement of the amount and terms of any obligation to the judgment debtor sought to be levied upon that is not due and payable at the time of levy.
> (5) A statement of the amount and terms of any obligation to the judgment debtor at the time of levy not sought to be levied upon.
> (6) A description of claims and rights of other persons to the property or obligation levied upon that are known to the third party and the names and addresses of those other parties.
> (7) A statement that the garnishee holds neither any property nor any obligations in favor of the judgment debtor. California Code of Civil Procedure § 701.030 (West)

Unlike service of a subpoena, which the subpoenaed party can move to quash, rarely if ever would a judge quash service of a levy that itself does not require a court order as a condition of service or good cause in identifying a potential garnishee. Nothing under most states' laws require any type of diligence, "reason to believe," or good cause before serving somebody with a garnishment. A garnishment requires a garnishee to answer these execution interrogatories which compel the garnishee to identify property in their possession or under their control. Even though compelling garnishees to answer these execution interrogatories is certainly not the same as a full-blown examination, the answers to these questions might disclose the fact that the third party, such as a family member, is sitting upon the debtor's assets. Of course, if the garnishee does not respond at all, for whatever reason, the judgment creditor would have a first-rate reason to launch a subpoena directed at that person, and hence, discovery.

The law has recently changed in many states. Now, for example, California law provides that levy upon the centralized location designated by a financial institution reaches all bank accounts of the judgment debtor, no matter where located in the state and regardless of the branch. This means that the memorandum of garnishee will identify the branch where the account is kept. This is an enormous sea change and converts the previously opaque banking system into a virtual open book in which the levy reveals where the account is kept. Given the obligation to disclose the account upon the levy, even though the account might be in a far-flung branch, the judgment creditor should levy upon virtually every large bank and potentially reach the account.

Chapter 3

Kicking Over the Log and Finding a Pile of Money

In looking for money to levy, the very clever strategy is to drop a subpoena upon the debtor's customers, landlord, utility company, garbage hauler, or, for that matter, any major supplier. The purpose of the subpoena is to obtain from the customers copies of their checks, which are written to the debtor, or from the vendors copies of the debtor's check written to pay the vendor's bills. The debtor, or more likely a third party, such as a family member, negotiated and deposited the customer check. The backside of the customer check will identify the bank account and, more importantly, the name of the endorser. The person who actually received the check and deposited it in his or her bank account, such as the debtor's insider or family member, would be a first-rate target of a direct levy to reach the customer's remittance.

Service of a subpoena upon the company's vendors (i.e., the landlord, etc.) would reach a copy of the checks given to the vendors for payment of routine services. Service of a subpoena upon customers of the debtor or the debtor's vendors will probably identify the debtor's bank account (or successor) on the front of the check.

Customers' checks will identify by virtue of the endorsement the person who actually received and deposited the check. This becomes very important. Let's say that the garnishee, such as the family member, or successor entity, denies possession of the debtor's assets, such as the collection proceeds of accounts receivable. In answering the memorandum or postjudgment interrogatories, the garnishee denies possession or receipt of the money however, the cashed check will reveal who got the check because you can see who endorsed the check.

Are you a TV watcher? If you are, you would have seen zillions of TV commercials that feature the Millennial set who are depositing checks through their cell phones. The commercials show a person who takes a picture of the check, which is seemingly deposited instantaneously. The inference from this commercial is that the customer would have immediate access to the funds without endorsing the check. None of this is true. Here's the reality. The customer can certainly seek to deposit the check through the medium of an image acquired through the cell phone. That much is true. Absent the most extreme, the customer must photograph the front and backside of the check, which includes the endorsement. Few banks, which would either be the customer's "depositing bank" or the drawer's (the person who gave the check to the customer) bank, could process a check that lacked an endorsement. The only exception would be if the check was payable to the customer who owned the cell phone and the check was going to cycle into the customer's personal bank account. The customer's bank might accept that check as a deposit to the customer's *own bank account*. This is a big maybe and depends on the bank. Remote deposits may have slightly changed the rules; nonetheless, banks can demand that a check for deposit bear an endorsement. It is also correct that banks accept checks without an endorsement if the check is deposited into the customer's account directly (for deposit only). This is somewhat rare and against general banking practices.

Let's stop the show for a second. You served a subpoena upon the debtor's biggest customer, who hands over banking records that show that the endorser on the check was the debtor's president or family members or new entity that was recently formed. You garnished the president, family members, or new entity who all denied possession of the debtor's assets. Aside from the fact that the garnishee laundered the debtor's assets through these new bank accounts, committed perjury based on the denials in the memorandum of garnishees, and conspired in a fraudulent conveyance in hiding the money, this garnishee drapes a big bull's-eye on his or her forehead to reach the debtor's assets.

Not to digress, but please allow me. Don't turn the page too quickly because I have a decent story. This is a story about checks. Absent the bizarre or unusual, banks do not double-check the endorsement on a check. If the check is payable to ABC Company, the paying bank (the bank upon whom the check was written and called the drawee bank) does not physically inspect the back of the check to confirm that the real ABC Company actually got the check, and personally endorsed the check. The customer of the bank (the drawer of the check) is responsible for inspecting its own checks to confirm that the payee got the check, endorsed the check, and deposited the check in its own bank account.

What if ABC Company is dying on the vine? If the payee is ABC Company, which is insolvent and hounded to death by creditors, the president of ABC seeks to capture the checks that are payment for the debtor's receivables and salvage something. Call this financial :get out of Dodge."

Let's see how this can be done. Mr. Principal forms an new LLC under the name of ABC LLC and opens up a bank account and deposits the checks. Nobody would know the difference. The bank properly opened an account in the name of ABC LLC. The customer (who is the drawer of the check) is paying to ABC Company, although ending up in ABC LLC. The principal is happy because he has snared the cash flow of ABC Company and parked the money in the account of another legally separate entity, ABC LLC. The ABC Co. bank account is bone dry. Levies ricochet off this account.

The other option is that Mr. Principal simply endorsed the checks "ABC Company, and deposited the check in his own bank account, or the bank account of his spouse, adult children, or other corporate entities. Once in a blue moon (and this does happen—I have cycled through this game) he will form a new entity under the name of CDE LLC., which will file and publish a fictitious business name of ABC COMPANY. With the duly filed fictitious business name registration in one hand and the duly issued limited liability certificate in the other hand, Mr. Principal will establish a new bank account and deposit checks payable to the original debtor, ABC, Company. Everyone, except the creditors who are left high and dry, is happy. The story does not end. Don't think that the money sat around. These funds went to China and never returned. Total money laundering boffo. This was a total winner because the principals made them very difficult to reach.

Credit card drafts are no different because the credit card deposits (i.e., the payments from the merchant bank for the consumer's use of his or her card) are directed to the new account under the control of the principals.

Sorry for the digression. Hang in there.

When the debtor is near the end of its useful life, but wishes to continue its business in another structure, which is the classic fraudulent conveyance, the conveyee will write checks on its own bank account to the vendors to maintain the key lines of credit and essential services. The landlord has received a check for the rent from the successor, which warehouses the debtor's cash flow. The check given to the landlord reveals the new entity's bank account.

You can levy and subpoena the new entity and its bank account. If the successor entity was formed within a few days, but pays tens of thousands of dollars to the vendors of the predecessor debtor, the source of the funds for these payments are the collections of accounts receivable due the predecessor debtor. Levy on the successor's bank account and scoop up all those funds, which are probably the proceeds of the debtor's receivables. Accompany the levy with a subpoena to reach all of the bank account records, which will certainly show that the deposit of receivable checks represents collection proceeds of the accounts receivable generated by the predecessor debtor and not the successor entity. Serve the levy upon the successor entity itself, the successor's principals who are the principals of your predecessor debtor, and, for good measure, any employees working for the new entity who used to work for the old entity, which probably includes family members. The successor entity, and its principals, are obligated to answer the memorandum of garnishee, which might identify other assets or jump-start additional discovery.

Should you latch on to any of this money, you can expect a firestorm of resistance, but timing is your friend.

Chapter 4

Separating the Debtor from Its Property

The sheriff can install a keeper in the debtor's place of business and scoop up the money at hand as it comes in the door or sit by the cash register and take money as it is received. Call this a till tap, keeper, or custodian—it's all the same. Some sheriffs show up in uniforms, with a gun on their hip and writ in hand. It's very impressive. Other sheriffs show up in plain clothes, still with a gun on their hip and writ in hand. Call these folks crowd pleasers. I was speaking in front of about 30 people, all of them the cream of the bankruptcy bar in Oakland, California. I have known most of these people for 30 years. I am going through my normal routine, including the discussion of keepers. I said to the group, "Okay, how many of you have ever installed a keeper?" Bankruptcy lawyers do collection work as part of their practice. I saw only one hand go up. That was the local bankruptcy judge. And the judge blurted out, "I used to do this for a living. What do you expect? I did creditor work." I have no idea what anybody said for the next two minutes, as everybody was giggling. It was clearly worth the price of the carfare for that presentation.

The sheriff can open the mail and take the checks. The sheriff can order the debtor to open the office safe. The sheriff can remove the entire contents of the debtor's business. We installed a keeper in a restaurant to collect a $14,000 debt. Normally, the owner would pay immediately. Not this time. No way. Hours pass, and there is no progress. The debtor was downright uncooperative. The creditor was downright insistent. The remedy? Clean out the place. We forked over $15,000 (no typo, folks) to the sheriff who immediately engaged a moving company to remove the contents of the restaurant and transport the personal property to the sheriff's storage facility. Upon seeing the strange people seizing the chairs, tables, pots, pans, plates and silverware, the debtor panicked and called 911. He got the sheriff. As the story goes, the chief civil officer was in the bull pen when the 911 call came in. An officer fielded the call in which the civil officer responded: "Him? That's mine."

Another Hare Krishna moment: We once enforced federal judgments in a collection against bars and taverns in Los Angeles. The U.S. Marshals, as the levying officers, wore plain clothes and went out in groups of fours or sixes. I received a panicked call that when the U.S. Marshals entered one bar to collect on my writ, the bar owner freaked and called the cops who show up in multiple squad cars.

Chapter 5

The Moose Club

The writ will allow the judgment creditor to seize virtually any nonexempt personal property. How do you collect from the Moose Club, which fails to pay for the liquor bill, Rocky? Grab the moose head. Engaged to collect $2,000 owed by a moose lodge, we sent in the sheriff to grab the money from the till. The sheriff came back empty-handed because the club lacked a cash register, used a chit system, and billed the customers at the end of the month. Fold on that round. Taking another round, we send in the sheriff with the instructions to seize the personal property. Half-opened bottles of liquor? Cheap wine? Warm beer? Dirty glasses? No, none of this stuff. We instructed the sheriff to bring a ladder, lay the ladder against the wall, ascend the ladder, and take the moose head. The sheriff was descending the ladder when the manager started to waive his arms and offer payment. You can't run a moose club without the moose head, Rocky.

Chapter 6

Storage Lockers

Storage lockers come in two varieties. The standard storage locker is a glorified landlord/tenant relationship in which the storage facility is renting space to the tenant. This is no more or no less than the standard month-to-month tenancy. To reach the contents of the storage locker would require that the sheriff levy on the contents, which means instructing the sheriff to padlock the storage locker pending an order to gain entrance, through a locksmith or other means. Chances are that the debtor has something of value in that storage locker, including money, artwork, and, depending upon the size of the storage locker, a car. The question is how to locate the storage locker. The answer is to serve every storage company within a 10-mile radius with a subpoena. This is not cheap, but if the judgment is enough money and you have a big enough budget and perceive that the debtor has assets that inexplicably are invisible to the naked eye, chances are the debtor stowed them in a storage facility.

In other cases, the storage facility holds the personal property of the debtor as a bailee under a bailment. In effect, the storage facility has taken the personal property in its name and custody and issued a warehouse bill of lading. Warehouse bills of lading are akin to air bills, straight bills of lading, and other documents of title. The general statement is that possession of any negotiable bill of lading gives the person the right to physical custody of the personal property covered by the bill. As will be covered under bills of lading, the general rule is that you can reach the personal property in the hands of the bailee and have the personal property turned over to the sheriff if the document of title is nonnegotiable. Negotiability means that the document is title to the personal property and that the person who holds the document is deemed to be the owner of the personal property. Negotiation of the bill of lading transfers title to the transferee free of any equities or defenses. A nonnegotiable document of title has no such effect.

Storage facilities such as cold lockers, which store large quantities of food and like products; storage facilities that hold inventory on consignment; and "fulfillment houses," which hold large quantities on behalf of retailers, issue both negotiable and more likely nonnegotiable warehouse receipts. If your debtor is an online merchant, chances are that its product line might be in the hands of one of these storage facilities and subject to enforcement.

When I started out with the O. J. Simpson case, I got a call every six months from someone offering to inform me of hidden storage lockers that contained O. J.'s hidden gems.

Chapter 7

God Is My Copilot

My other favorite story is the experimental single-engine airplane. The debtor's only visible asset was his single-engine airplane. The debtor built it himself from a kit, as I was told. Upon judgment, we located the plane, and by luck the sheriff, with our writ of execution in hand, levied on the airplane. Our client was an amateur pilot and kept needling me to gain access to the airplane, which the sheriff would decline. He was dying to take a spin, and I was dying to stay alive. In an attempt to convince me to badger the sheriff to facilitate access, he told me, "Look, I'll be the pilot and you can be the copilot." There was an experimental airplane owned by a judgment debtor whose idea of maintenance might have been nascent. My response: "You can be the pilot, and God will be your copilot; and trust me, He'll bring a parachute."

Locating an airplane takes numerous calls to local general aviation airports. I remember calling the airport local managers. All were cordial, we asked if "John parked his aircraft at the field." For some reason, pilots and airport personnel share a comradery and few secrets. Aircraft owners are a small segment, and their aircraft and where parked was never a mystery. Pilot's license and airplane registration are "online," and most search services, such as LexisNexis, will readily disclose this information. Seizing an airplane is very expensive because the sheriff might have to install a keeper on a 24-hour basis to secure the plane, or move the plane, if possible to a secure area. The keeper is a deputized civilian, such as a retired sheriff, marshal, firefighter, police officer, member of the armed service, or just about anyone else, who literally "babysits" the property. Paramount in levying against an airplane is to grab the maintenance, flight, and other logs.

An airplane without a current maintenance log has reduced value because the buyer is unable to determine whether the debtor has performed the legally required maintenance. Airplanes likewise bear greater or lesser value based on their avionics, which is a fancy word for their electronic portfolio. As a rule of thumb, avionics make up about 33.3 percent of the value of any aircraft. In seizing an airplane, should you discover that the debtor in an act of spite tore out or destroyed the avionics, you can expect a marginal return from a sheriff's sale. Knowledge of the avionics (for that matter, any type of electronic inbred feature of any modern product) is paramount to the judgment creditor. Frequently, the debtor might offer to hand over personal property as payment in satisfaction of the debt. In the smartphone world, the 2008 BlackBerry would have a negative value.

Chapter 8

Boats

Boats bear the same problems as airplanes, which is locating and securing the boat, determining the boat's electronic package, and providing for an orderly sale. Boats are particularly difficult given the competition for legitimate boat dealers, the saturation in the secondary market, and the expense and burden of boat ownership. The old saying rings true: The first happiest day of the boat owner is taking possession of someone's pride and joy, and the second happiest day is getting rid of that pride and joy. If you have nothing better to do one Sunday afternoon, scroll through Craigslist, and you will find many offerings for boats at rock-bottom prices near the point of giving the boat away. Nonetheless, absent a boat serving as a houseboat, and exempt from execution as a surrogate dwelling house, we have levied on boats with some limited success. With a writ of execution and at our directions, in one case we directed the sheriff to pick up a 25-foot pleasure cruiser. The sheriff missed, as the boat literally pushed off when the sheriff's squad car pulled up in the boatyard parking lot and the debtor allegedly waived at the officers on the way out of the harbor.

The sheriff will retain the services of professional boat repo guys, storage and warehouse docks, and related facilities. Many sheriffs charge between $5,000 and $10,000 to seize a large boat and pay for seizure, transportation, and storage. Should the debtor file bankruptcy on the eve of the sheriff's sale and bring the proceeding to a cold dead stop, the trustee or debtor can recover the boat in the hands of the sheriff. The creditor would forfeit the sheriff's fees and charges, which would only exacerbate a terrible loss. The creditor's only defense is that the creditor's enforcement liens exceed 90 days, which means that the trustee, or the debtor, loses the right to recover the property under the bankruptcy preference statute. Bankruptcy law provides that all payments on account of antecedent debt (i.e., old bills) or liens and levies are recalled within 90 days before the filing of the bankruptcy.

Chapter 9

As Long as the Property Is Not Per Se Immune, You Can Take Anything

The writ of execution offers the judgment creditor endless and sometimes the most amusing options to compel payment. You can take anything that is not automatically immune from enforcement, or property that statutorily is outside the scope of enforcement, such as a professional license. You can take any property of a corporation, partnership, limited partnership, or limited liability company. With some judicial relief you can seize the property of a trust, if the trustee incurred the debt in the ordinary course of the business, and if the trustee has a right of indemnity against the trust asset. Watch, however, for a spendthrift trust, which might defeat that claim. You can seize all nonexempt property of an individual, and in many states community property, even though the spouse is not personally liable. This is a very big deal because you would have the right to all community assets for debt owed by only one spouse.

For example, how do you collect from the convalescent home that fails to pay for good suppliers? Grab the beds. Talk about total creep-out when the sheriff walked up and down the facility with a clipboard in hand counting off the beds with people still in them. Collect from the radio station? Grab the (then) vinyl records or turntable!

Service of the writ does not require a precondition that the creditor has any belief that the garnishee has funds or property at hand. What does this mean? Answer: It's open season. Open fire. Levy everything and anything. With a large judgment, aggrieved creditor as a client, and costs at hand, the lawyer can engage in a campaign of enforcement rivaling the Russian conquest of Germany in 1945.

Here are more stories. We had one good-sized judgment against a lawyer in a midsized town. We had no idea of her bank account. We picked 10 of the largest banks on the east side of town and levied all of them. About six days later, I received a telephone call from her. She introduced herself and asked whether I was levying every bank due east of town. I told her yes, and she responded, "You missed." She paid anyway.

This levy might include every bank in town, all stockbrokers, and every potential customer of the debtor, or even the spouse and adult children. If the debtor is a retail merchant, or even a wholesale merchant, levy every credit card processor to reach the credit card receivables and, along with the banks, to reach the accounts. Levy directly AMEX (see Chapter 10) who runs its own merchant banking services and holds funds directly for the debtor.

Chapter 10

Credit Card Processors

A credit card processor is a commercial service that will forward the credit card "drafts" (what the customer signs for, electronically or otherwise) to the credit card company, such as the banks that issued the particular VISA, MasterCard, American Express, etc. The credit card processor would receive payment and remit directly to the customer's account. The charges range anywhere between .35 to 2 percent. These services are common, and most businesses contract with the processors. The credit card processors at any given time would owe money to the customer, who is presumptively your debtor. There are approximately 10 major credit card processors, and many banks likewise offer these services. Levy on every one. You should ask the debtor at the debtor's examination who is the credit card processor.

Credit card processing is a growing business and you can easily locate them on the "top 10 best list," or other lists. The levy on the credit card processor should generate real money.

Chapter 11

Selling Falling Water

How about selling real property through an execution? Let's go through two flavors—nonresidential and residential. The creditor can levy on nonresidential real property. If the property is raw land or does not have a residence, the sheriff will hold an auction in about 120 days from date of levy, plus another 30 days. The judgment creditor can "bid in" the judgment, which means that the judgment creditor can pay for the purchase at the sheriff's sale with the debtor. This is another bouncing ball moment. A credit bid means that the creditor does not need to come up with cash. The judgment creditor can bid in some (such as $10) or all of the judgment to acquire the property. Call this funny money.

Absent the bizarre or large-dollar judgment, the debtor is going to pay off the judgment and end the sale. Hypothetically, we were within 24 hours of selling a parking lot in downtown San Francisco when the debtor blinked and paid off the judgment. In another case, the debtor paid a judgment within 24 hours of our sale of 20 acres of open space. We sold one home in Watsonville, California. This property faced the beach and suffered substantial damage. The process runs the creditor about $2,500, which consists of the $1,500 for the sheriff, $500 for a title report, and the balance— typical lawyer waste of money. Another time the judge dealt us a judgment against a VFW lodge. We proceeded to levy on the property and per California law landed in court to get an order for sale. We showed up and, right in front of the courtroom, I spotted two very elderly individuals, one of them with a cane. I knew exactly who they were. They were the lodge representatives. I introduced myself, shook hands, and told them that they ought to take care of this and "how about 90 days to raise the money." Their response was "great," and they would work on it. After we concluded that, I turned to the slightly older gentlemen and asked, "Where did you serve and what service were you in?" Answer: "Marines. Okinawa." I asked the other gentlemen the same question. The answer: "Marines. Chosen Reservoir." What a round. Had we not settled, I had visions of kicking Private Ryan out of his easy chair.

If the property is residential, the creditor can levy on the real property but needs a court order for the actual sale. At the hearing for the order authorizing the sale, the creditor has to prove that the property can be sold at a floor price (i.e., in California, 90 percent of the appraised value), that the sale is for cash and must pay off the prior liens, and the homestead and pay something to the creditor. Between 1999 and up to about 2006, the Los Angeles sheriff had frequent sales of homes, given the explosion of equities. After the real estate crash, sales are few and far between due to the limits under California Code of Civil Procedure § 704.800(b) (see below). Even if you succeed in selling the home, expect mass vandalism (walls knocked down, garbage and waste in the frontyard and backyard, etc.). In a more gruesome case, when a house was transferred to the creditor, unknown individuals littered the house with buckets of animal parts and blood that attracted raccoons and rats. A 1960s Lincoln was in the garage. Vandals bashed in the windshield, ripped the upholstery, and gashed the steering column. Someone really spent a lot of time in destroying the car. Somebody was really enraged. In other cases, we saw that vandals ripped out the walls and floors and dumped a massive amount of debris throughout the structure. Some of these houses looked like they suffered a Category 5 hurricane. Hurricane Katrina pales in comparison.

Meet your roadblock. California Code of Civil Procedure § 704.800(b) enables a judge to bar the sale of a house by ascribing an enormous value to the property. This drill is worth repeating because snaking through the § 704.800(b) labyrinth gets you paid or you find yourself skunked. If you get lost in the labyrinth, don't complain if the Minotaur eats you for dinner. Yum yum!

So, the judge can fix a price for the house. The sheriff has to sell the house for 90 percent of appraised value, set by the judge. The sale is for property and for cash—no financing. The buyers are not entitled to a walk-through, inspection, assurances of title, financing, or other routine term of a traditional real estate deal. When the real estate market went nuts between 1999 and 2006, sheriff's sales attracted buyers by the droves, but between 2007 and 2012 they draw very few.

Here is the pig in a poke moment. (This pig wore really pretty, glow-in-the-dark lipstick.) Here is the story. San Francisco tightly controls the conversion of apartments into condominiums for fear of depleting the rental market and hence driving up rents. The other reason for these draconian restrictions is that more voters are apartment dwellers than property owners. The poor man's condominium is a tenants in common (TIC).

What is "tenants in common" ownership. This is very old. This means that two or more people jointly hold title to the property as opposed to separate units, like a condominium. That doesn't sound too bad. But it is bad, sometimes. TIC's invite legal trouble. Owners fight over maintenance (trimming the bushes), major repairs (the roof, the driveway, the walls, and the exteriors), common area appearances, personal hygiene (trash and garbage), or nothing. Parties sign a TIC agreement that provides for binding arbitration for all disputes and a lawyer's fee clause that awards fees to the winner. Is this important? Yes. In this the TIC owners were brothers. The TIC building was a six-unit San Francisco apartment building in very good shape and located centrally ("location, location, location").

For whatever reason TIC war broke out; the dispute headed to arbitration and a staggering award consisting of a small-dollar damage and big-time lawyer's fees in favor of one brother. Folks, these are brothers. We thought the case would settle. We were brought in to assist in the forced sale. After about 120 days of process, the judge signs the order for sale. This is not the home of either brother and is free of the 90 percent cash rule. The sheriff is not going to sell the building but only the judgment debtor's interest in the TIC. A buyer is not buying the property, just the TIC interest of the judgment debtor. Buying into a partnership, limited liability company, joint venture, or other common ownership is very risky. My father called these purchases "buying a lawsuit." The sheriff sets the TIC interest for a public sale in the San Francisco City Hall, which used to be the courthouse. I thought to myself, "What person would buy a partial ownership interest from a sheriff's sale with marginal title (see next note) without title insurance, an inspection, and for cash?" Answer: Lots and lots. The auction was packed with bidders. Some were tire kickers and opportunists. The sheriff sold the interest for something at near the judgment amount. The sale was for cash, and I watched the buyer hand over cashier's checks to the sheriff. (This pig wore really nice lipstick.) The sheriff was able to sell this TIC for good money only because of "location, location, and location." For whatever the buyer paid, today he could purchase vast acreage of raw land in the California Central Valley and have money left over.

Don't feel beaten. You have other tricks up your sleeve. Let's say the 90 percent release price is $4,000,000. Are you going to find a buyer for $4,000,000 in cash without an interior appraisal, physical inspection, title insurance, financing, and a final walk-through to ensure that the property has not been destroyed? It's not too likely, but it's not completely impossible. The reason why the likelihood of finding a buyer is very low is the fact that someone with $4 million to burn has lots of choices, including an equivalent property in an equal or even better neighborhood that is subject to the normal real estate safeguards and conditions of financing, title, walk-through, and inspection. Every property that is purchased is a property that is sold down the line. Today, sellers must disclose an enormous amount of information about the property, such as the presence of lead paint, asbestos, mold, rot, and termites, and whether there is some "secret story" (e.g., a prior murder) associated with the property. When the buyer goes to sell the property, disclosures to the downstream buyer may make the sale difficult, or even impossible. If the Sheriff's sale does not fetch a price equal to or in excess of the 90 percent release price but does generate a price equal to the senior liens, the homestead, and some portion of the judgment, you can ask the court for an order accepting the lower price or make a new order for sale. This outcome would topple everyone's expectations. First, if the 90 percent price and the reduced escape price bear a great disparity, speculators would come out of the woodwork and hopefully bid on the property notwithstanding the potential title, disclosure, and inspection issues at the new sale. The winning hand is that scads of buyers might appear at the new sheriff's auction for a chance to acquire the property. This risk of a viable sale might compel the debtor to resolve the case or face the total loss of the home to a speculator with very deep pockets and no hesitation to buy troubled property if the price is right. Getting the debtor to pay the judgment requires getting the debtor to believe that you can engineer the sale of the property to a bona fide buyer with real money at hand.

So, where do we find a buyer or two or three or more, or a whole flash mob? How can we come up with real money in hand or even the risk of real money in hand that would prompt the debtor to come up with money to pay the judgment? Answer: Put the house up for sale on eBay and Craigslist. You might even try real estate sites or a local multiple listing service. You might be enlisting the services of a real estate broker who might accept a listing of the property. Getting a broker involved would be tremendous given the fact that the market is now turning into a seller's market and not a buyer's market.

Chapter 12

Collecting Big Money for a $12 Investment

Let's talk about persistence here. Running down debtors is time-consuming, tedious, and occasionally downright boring. You can spend a lot of time typing up subpoenas. To prove my point, we were chasing down an offshore manufacturer and had a devil of a time reconstructing the debtor's client base. We knew that the debtor sold construction elevators and related parts and machinery. This is a major player. Elevators need permits, and the California Department of Industrial Relations maintained a very long list of licensed elevator operators. Dragooning my son-in-law, he spent a few days extracting the name and address of each licensed elevator operator or maintenance company and reduced the information to removable stickers (30 to a page). Talk about mind-numbing work. With stickers in hand and a very current list, we drafted a subpoena for records that would show what products or services the offshore debtor was selling to the California operators, stuck the stickers to the subpoenas, and mailed out 300 subpoenas. We got some information from the witnesses, who were helpful, but we got a bigger reaction from the debtor who thought that we went too far. We didn't go too far, but the debtor thought that was more than enough as the debtor believed that we would stop at nothing. That was true except I knew the limits and was not even close.

In getting the subpoenas out the door, we used a form subpoena that sought the contracts, bills, and accounting records that showed what money the witnesses owed to the debtor. These debts are titled accounts receivable. You can levy on the accounts receivable. We affixed the sticker in the "to the witness" spot on the subpoena, stuck on a nice cover letter, and mailed the subpoena to the witnesses. Most companies will respond to subpoenas even if mailed. The cost for this process: $2.00 in stickers and $10.00 in postage. This amount of postage will get you 22 subpoenas. Invest $100.00 in postage you will get 217 subpoenas out the door. Most of the records came by e-mail with little or no cost. Labor cost of son-in-law: Priceless.

You have other options. Most large entities use CT Corporation System or Corporation Service Company, which are major professional agents for service of process whose job is to receive legal process such as lawsuits, levies, and subpoenas. If you can mail the subpoenas to these services, typically the witnesses will supply you with the records. If you believe that a particular witness has relevant records, such as the financial or loan package, the Uniform Residential Loan Application, credit files, and bank records such as the debtor's bank account, you might want to personally serve the witness through a private process server and pay the witness fees. Process servers charge about $50 to $100 to serve process. Witness fees range from $35 to about $100 and maybe $50 to $100 for copy charges, depending on the volume. Bank records, such as voluminous loan files and bank records (bank statements, cancelled checks, wire transfers) can be more costly given their volume, and spending $1,000 is par for the course.

The fact that you can serve the subpoena by mail with a preprinted form subpoena is not critical. What is critical is the mailing list culled through legitimate public sources and the labor to assemble and mail the list. Nothing stops you from mailing out mass subpoenas as you make a faith effort to develop a census of witnesses who might have information that would reveal the debtor's assets. Don't be surprised if you draw a super duper motion to quash.

In this case, we also confirmed through the U.S. Patent and Trademark Office website that the debtor owned the key trademarks that identified their business and that the debtor owned multiple patents. We guessed at their banks and wildly guessed at their customer base. We filed and served a series of assignment motions (nine of them) and two receivership motions (the patents and the trademarks). We had fun. You can have fun.

Chapter 13

Kicking Grandpa and Grandma Out of Their Homestead—Almost

About 20 years ago, we were chasing down an 85-year-old debtor whose 87-year-old wife was infirm. He refused to settle or, for that matter, do anything to resolve the judgment. He just wasn't going to pay. He and his wife owned a $1,000,000 home in Atherton, California, which at this time probably would be closer to $15 million or more. The only known asset was the home, and we proceeded with an execution sale. The sheriff, after levying the real property, sent out the notice that we needed to get a court order that would authorize the sale. I properly filed the papers, and the judge set the case for trial to determine the value of the home. My appraiser valued the house at what it was worth, which was $1,000,000, and used all of the comparables. It was a very good appraisal with correct results. The physical house actually had very little value. This was nothing more than a three-plus-bedroom, ranch-style home, sitting on one acre of prime real estate. Anybody would raze the house and probably build a six-bedroom mansion. Some contractors would say that they would "scrap" the structure off the dirt. The debtor, through counsel, brought in his own appraiser. If you read my opening chapters, residential appraisals generally are done through comparables. This means that the appraiser will find homes that are comparable, by location, comparable sales in time, condition of the house, and other amenities, such as a swimming pool. If there are two peas in a pod, presumably they are worth the same.

The adverse appraiser was very good. I didn't know how good he was until the end of the case. His comparables included some similar homes, but his best comparable was the Flood Mansion. This was an historic, two-plus-story home in the heart of Atherton. This nine-bedroom house (San Mateo County) was built in 1941 and occupied 92 oak-studded acres. A staggering home, and not even close to the debtor's three-plus-bedroom, three-bath, ranch-style home, sitting on about an acre, which would never see the light of day after it was sold. The other appraiser estimated that the Flood Mansion had a value equal or exceeding $3 million. He was probably right and maybe low. On September 23, 2012, the *San Francisco Chronicle* broke the story that the Flood Mansion is on the market for $85,000,000. The current property tax, based on Prop. 13, is $18,019. We are going to talk later about the bump in the assessed value and increased property taxes. If the Flood Mansion sells for $85 million, the new property taxes will be about $927,605. The transfer tax is $1.10 per $1,000, which the seller pays. The transfer tax is $94,350.00.

The judge heard my case, and at the conclusion of the testimony, issued an order providing for the sale of the home at 90 percent of the appraised value. The appraised value was $3 million. He stated on the record that the most comparable house was the Flood Mansion. Not in the debtor's lifetime would I be able to sell the debtor's house for $3 million at that time.

The debtor did settle, and now the house is worth, as you can imagine, well in excess of that number.

The moral of this tale: The judge barred enforcement because he could not tolerate the prospect that two elderly people would be dumped out of their home, near the end of their lives, when in fact the judgment would be paid through probate. Is this the case of asset protection? You bet. Did our client get paid? Ultimately.

Chapter 14

What Is a Sheriff's Deed?

What type of title does the sheriff offer the buyer? Doesn't the sheriff give the buyer a sheriff's deed?

We are going to backtrack, and for you real estate speculators, you need to read this. A sheriff's deed is a quitclaim deed. The sheriff is not warranting that the debtor has any right, title or interest, if at all. But, if the debtor has any interest, the sheriff deeds that interest to the buyer. In this section, we are telling you that an unrecorded, and presumptively valid, deed or deed of trust (a mortgage) beats out a prior judicial lien. If on the day of suit, service, trial, or judgment, but before any judicial lien, the debtor sells or mortgages the property in favor of a bona fide buyer, or lender, the judgment creditor is screwed to the wall.

Secret but valid liens might survive a sheriff's sale. This is very scary. The buyer at a sheriff's sale only acquires the debtor's interest, whatever it might be, and it might be nothing says CCP §701.640. Now you see it. Now you don't.

CCP §701.630 wipes out the junior liens. Consider the sheriff's sale as dumping over the side those liens south of you. Toodle-loo and good riddance, you bums.

Got some money in your pocket and want to join the ranks of the real estate barons? Sounds good to me. Let me tell you this story. After three years of misery, the judgment creditor succeeds in forcing a sale of the debtor's rental house. This was not the debtor's home. The judgment creditor credit bid and acquired the property by bidding in part of the judgment. The sheriff duly executed a sheriff's deed. The judgment creditor put the house on the market and found a buyer at a very good price. So far, so good. The parties opened escrow, money was at hand, the champagne was chilling, and money should flow like milk and honey. "Whoa Nelly!" yells Mr. Title Officer, who declines to issue a title policy for the buyer. He says something to the effect, "I am not going to insure crap title." "Crap title" is the vernacular for, how shall I put it, crappy title, a well-known and well-understood technical term used by title companies when they are insuring junk title. Remember, folks, there is good title and marketable title. You can have good title all you like, but you can't sell or refinance the property without marketable title. Another explanation at this point is redundant. The reason is that the debtor, unknown to anyone, could have sold the property underneath everyone's nose, and the bona fide buyer or financier claim title to the property at a later date. Whether this claim is good, or bad, this claim is called a cloud on the title. A cloud on the title is very damaging because when the claimant pops up and asserts an interest in the property, and whether the claim is real or imagined, the property is impossible to sell. The only way to get rid of this cloud is to sue the claimant, or pay a ransom.

Not all is lost. Some title companies will insure a sheriff's deed. Some case authority upholds the position that a buyer at a sheriff's sale is a BFP. In English, what does that mean? Answer, my friend, is that bona fide buyer at a sheriff's sale will wipe out secret unrecorded liens and deeds. Eat a hearty breakfast because you are going to battle the prior claimant from now until the cows come home. Buy next year's calendar.

Chapter 15

Laundering Title Documents

Does this cloud on the title last forever? No. Let me introduce everyone to basic title law. Most states have "race-notice" recording laws. Wake up. Drink some black coffee. Sit up straight. Wipe your eyes. This is important. This means that a person without knowledge of the hidden lien or sale can record the deed or mortgage and wipe out (extinguish) the prior unrecorded deed or mortgage. Hence, the race is on. Without notice of the blemish to the title, the later buyer records first and beats out the prior deed or mortgage holder.

I know this, you know this, and Mr. Title Officer knows this. Mr. Title Officer told the seller (the judgment creditor, who acquired title at the sheriff's sale) to execute a general grant deed from himself (holding the sheriff's deed) to himself (as the grantee under the grant deed.) We call this recycling title. Maybe. A grant deed means the grantor warrants that title is good and affirmatively conveys "good title" to the grantee. As the holder of title under a grant deed, the judgment creditor warrants that title is good and prompts the title company to issue a title policy to the buyer. The niftier explanation is that when the judgment creditor, free of any knowledge of a blemish, records the grant deed and warrants good title, the transferee buyer becomes a bona fide buyer, and cuts off prior hidden deeds and mortgage. The grant deed cycling the title from a "sheriff's deed" to a "grant deed" held by the seller wipes out, hopefully, all prior defects in the title. Could be that the putative buyer takes title without notice of the prior hidden, latent defects—maybe.

Yes, this stuff is arcane, but it's important. If you buy and sell real estate acquired through a sheriff's sale, you need to know this.

Here is another story. Now gather around. The plaintiff wins an $800,000 rent judgment against the defendant, who owns a vacation home in Watsonville, California. We levy. The property is a dwelling house. We go to court and get an order for sale and claim that the property is a vacation home and free of the exemption burden. So far, so good, partner. In the midst of the execution sale, I punch up the Santa Cruz County Recorder's website and make a beeline to the grantor/grantee page. I plug in the debtor's name. All looks good as I see the vesting deed in his name, the lien for property taxes, the first deed of trust due a bank, our abstract of judgment, and our execution.

Everything is good in the land of milk and honey. I scroll down further and eyeball another line item. This is new. This is a new entry. What is this? What is this crap? The online site gives me the summary. Somebody, and I know who, recorded a grant deed signed by the debtor to the debtor's adult son. The deed was recorded after my execution and I'd think, so what. I got a copy of the deed from customer services through a local title company, and what a bad day. Crap all over place. Call the hazmat people. The grant deed was dated and notarized prior to the original recording of my abstract. This means that the debtor, postjudgment (which came from Hawaii) but prior to my abstract, deeded the property away, but held up the recording. Ugly. This was a fraudulent conveyance; the judge toppled the deed because the deed had too many earmarks of a fraudulent conveyance as no consideration changed hands.

This is a classic asset protection scheme because the debtor can manufacture deeds of trust, quitclaim deeds, grant deeds, and record them to defeat execution (and execution liens) and these passive liens. Hum the mantra: Wonders never cease: "Hare Krishna Hare Krishna Krishna Hare, Hare Rama Hare Rama Hare." You have to have lived through the 1980s. I just could not resist.

Chapter 16

Can You Seize Alimony?

Okay, what about somebody's alimony? Is alimony exempt? You read that right. Alimony is now called spousal support and means money paid typically by the ex-husband to the ex-wife. No ex-husband is happy about that. Perish the thought. About 20 years ago, I represented a mid-sized bank in the collection of their commercial and consumer accounts. We obtained a judgment against an older woman whose sole source of income was alimony payments. We looked through the Code books (law books) to find whether alimony was exempt and immune from enforcement and found nothing. So what did we do? We served the writ of execution on the ex-husband to grab her alimony payments. The ex-husband was a big-time doctor with a major practice in town. I am sure they suffered shock when I served the doctor with the levy. A few days later, the doctor's assistant called me and wanted to know how to make payment. I told her to write the monthly checks to the sheriff until the debt was paid. She asked for a little more information, such as the address and how to write the check, and I gladly accommodated her. Every month for the next 11 months, the doctor dutifully paid the amount to the sheriff that he would otherwise pay to the ex-wife. The debt was paid. On the 12th month, I received a call from the doctor's office wanting to know whether any additional funds would be due and whether they should be sent to the sheriff. My best recollection is there was a slight discussion whether or not any interest accrued or costs that needed to be paid. I believe I told the assistant that, no, everything was paid, and thank you very much. I believe that this person was extremely disappointed that no further funds were due on that judgment, and I sensed that the doctor was more than happy to keep paying, assuming that additional funds were due on that judgment. From the doctor's point of view, this was poetic justice.

Chapter 17

Monies Due from Factors, Financiers, Escrow Agents, Disbursement Agents

Factors purchase accounts receivables , which are usually generated by a manufacturer or distributor (i.e., your debtor). At the time of the purchase the factor owes money to the debtor. When the customer pays the receivables to the factor as the holder and assignee, the factor might remit further funds to the debtor as its "customer." Maybe. Any funds due to the debtor from the factor at the outset, or a later date, are subject to enforcement through a writ execution. These amounts are payable periodically and sometimes haphazardly. Typically a writ reaches any obligation that has matured, and it does so when the obligor is ready, willing, and able to pay, and not sooner or later. Therefore an early or late levy might not reach the amounts due payable to the debtor. The alternative remedy is an assignment order (see next paragraph) that reaches all debts due the debtor now and in the future. An assignment order would perennially reach all amounts due the judgment debtor no matter when accruing.

In construction, a bank, third-party manager, disbursement agent, or other party might disburse funds to the general contractor. The creditor of the general contractor could reach those funds payable from the third party with a levy on the right date and time. This is tough because the contractor could seek payment at any time, and certainly if the creditor is pounding at his door, the contractor would seek payment in a manner to hinder the creditors. Contractors are rarely known for the love of judgment creditors. The remedy is an assignment order that would reach all funds now and in the future. The judgment creditor can serve the assignment order on the third party, like a factor, and latch on to all funds due the contractor without the necessity of repeated service of process. Escrow holders and disbursement agents serve the same function of disbursing funds to the contractor. How do you find the factor, bank, disbursement agent, or financier? Answer: All of these creditors have filed a UCC with the secretary of state or recorded an encumbrance against the property to secure construction financing. Of course, these parties are subject to subpoena, along with an independent order of examination. Collecting the remittance is a treasure hunt. So much fun.

Chapter 18

Funds or Property Held by Bank as Collateral for a Loan or to Secure a Credit Facility

Banks, commercial financiers, factors, and third parties offer customers lines of credit, letters of credit facilities for international trade, and other credit accommodations. Most, if not all, of these facilities are secured by personal property through a UCC, and sometime through a pledge of a certificate of deposit issued by a bank. If the debtor pays off the liability supporting the credit facilities, the creditor is obligated to return the collateral. A typical example is the bank that issues a letter of credit as the "issuing bank." The bank receives about 125 percent of collateral, which might consist of deposits, certificates of deposit from another bank, stock, or something equivalent. If the debtor repays the bank, after the beneficiaries drawing down on the line of credit, the issuing bank is obligated to return the collateral to the debtor. The judgment creditor of the debtor would levy on the issuing bank to reach the right of the refund of the collateral due the debtor as its customer. The alternative remedy is the service of an assignment order to reach the refunds. Of course, a subpoena for records should accompany the writ of service of the subpoena or assignment order.

Collecting from a refund of the collateral due from the bank, assuming that the debtor pays off the bank on the letter of credit, is another successful treasure hunt.

Chapter 19

Can a Judgment Creditor Levy on a Line of Credit?

Can a creditor reach by garnishment or assignment funds from a financier under a credit line? This is a very big deal because many debtors live off their line of credit secured by their home. Many lenders would totally freak out if the lender were compelled to empty out a line of credit in favor of a garnishing creditor. If this were the law, the creditor could easily identify the line of credit based on the recording with the county recorder of the "line of credit" deed of trust (or mortgage) under its common name of home equity line of credit (HELOC). Once the judgment creditor gets a lead on the line of credit through the deed of trust, serve the bank with a garnishment that seeks to empty out or draw down the line. I can ever hear the howls. I can also imagine that every bank would be rushing to the state capitol to demand an immediate legislative change to bar direct enforcement (i.e., a levy) against a line of credit.

Howling is no joke. I was invited to a luncheon of the local bank lawyer's association. Some folks I knew, and others I did not. This was my presentation, and I went through the pitch of whether an assignment order could reach a bank account. What does no mean in English? An assignment order is a court order (see next paragraph) that assigns all debt owed to the debtor, such as a receivable, to the judgment creditor. An assignment order mirrors what a garnishment would do, except instead of service of writ of execution through the sheriff, the plaintiff serves the bank with the assignment order. This is great for the creditor because the creditor could serve a thousand assignment orders by mail upon the banks at the price of $500 as opposed to $35,000 through the sheriff. Better, the assignment order might reach banks that are out of state. I would describe reception to the service of assignment order upon the banks as downright frosty.

Next, I pitched that a judgment creditor would garnish the bank for the residual (undrawn) balance under the line of credit secured by the home. Do you remember as a kid the angry parents with daggers coming out of their eyes? I do. How about 12 sets of eyes with lots of daggers. They all thought that I had snakes coming out of my mouth.

I remember leaving intact. You will not be surprised to find that I have not received an invite for a return engagement. To this date my dance card is wide open.

Can a judgment creditor really levy on the residual undrawn balance of a secured line of credit? Let's take this problem from the top. The lender establishes a bank account that is solely funded by advances secured by the house.

It is sad to say, but the courts have already held that lines of credit are immune from direct enforcement. *In Re Southwestern Glass Co., Inc. (Southwestern Glass Co., Inc. v. The Bank of Arkansas*, 332 F.3d 513, 517–518 (8th Cir. 2003), the court held that judgment creditor could garnish the funds already advanced under the line of credit and parked in the debtor's bank accounts. Note the past tense. The court noted that creditors cannot garnish the actual line of credit itself, as opposed to funds disbursed under the line of credit and available to the debtor. This quote is worth the effort:

> "Id. at 518: "The Bank's most compelling argument is Wielder cannot garnish the amounts used to honor the checks drawn on the loan manager account because one cannot garnish or attach a line of credit. We are not persuaded by the Bank's argument. In both *Ocean focus* and *Sears*, a party attempted to attach or garnish a line of credit and to compel the lender to pay over the amount available on the line of credit. In both cases, the courts concluded the party could not attach or garnish the line of credit." (*citing to Ocean Focus Shipping, Ltd. v. Navarra Humboldt, S.A.*, 962 F.Supp. 1481, 1483–86 [S.D.Fla.1996][secured line of credit cannot be attached in an admiralty proceeding]; *Sears, Roebuck & Co. v. Romano,* 196 N.J.Super. 229, 482 A.2d 50, 54 [1984][line of credit for overdraft protection is not subject to levy]).

Under *Southwestern Glass*, funds in the debtor's bank account are subject to a garnishment or assignment even though the source is the consummated "drawn down," but not the unexercised right to draw down the line of credit.

Want to ratchet up the pressure? Nothing stops the creditor from serving an assignment order on the financier of the line of credit that would reach individual advances when actually drawn down, and received, by the debtor at the time. This means that when the customer draws down the amounts (i.e., writes the check on the home equity line of credit account), the assignment order directs that the "draw" goes to the creditor and not the debtor. An assignment order swaps out the judgment debtor from the contractual relationship with the third-party obligor (the HELOC lender) and substitutes in the judgment creditor who stands in the judgment debtor's stead. The assignment order extracts cash in the account but not the line of credit. Hopefully. Expect real pushback and bank resistance. Don't expect another luncheon date with the bankers. Your dance card will still remain open. So does mine.

Why shouldn't this work? *Southwestern Glass* proposes that a judgment creditor can levy the "paid out" proceeds of a line of credit in the debtor's bank account but not the line of credit itself (page 518). The assignment order as a substitute for a straight levy upon the *proceeds*, would not contravene the bar against a direct levy against the line of credit. Good luck.

Should you really run off and serve an assignment order on every bank in town offering a HELOC and thereafter file a creditor's suit against every bank on the basis that every advance is subject to an assignment order? Keep me posted, and I wish the best of luck before the supreme court of your state or even the U.S. Supreme Court because the banks will not pay you until the highest court rules in your favor. Should you win, Congress or the state legislature will snatch away your victory. Collecting on a drawn down under a line of credit is collecting treasure.

Chapter 20

Examinations of the Debtor and Third Parties (OEXs) and Postjudgment Discovery

Omnipotence Is Not Omniscience

The court (i.e., the judge) will issue an order that compels the judgment debtor to appear in court and testify in a public hearing as to assets and liabilities. The debtor forfeits the right of privacy. The service of the order of examination (OEX) imposes a lien upon the debtor's assets that might survive a bankruptcy. At the OEX hearing, the creditor (or lawyer) can rigorously grill the debtor and even compel the debtor to empty out a wallet or purse, turn over rings or watches, and face posthearing restraining orders. The creditor can examine third parties, such as the debtor's spouse, partner, or third parties who might owe money or hold property due the debtor. At these hearings, the judgment creditor can subpoena the witnesses, such as the debtor's accountant, advisers, the debtor's banks, partnerships, or other persons who might have a document or knowledge that would reveal the location of the debtor's assets. What about tax returns? Unreported California case law protects the debtor from producing tax returns. *Brannan v. Ghafouri*, WL 1067799 (2002). What is unpublished opinion? The practice guides tell you that the area of law is well tread and that the decision doesn't add anything; or the decision is correct but shouldn't be added to the general body of law; the case simply isn't that important.

By the way, these are public hearings and not depositions. *Nebel v. Sulak* (1999) 73 Cal. App. 4th 1363, 1366. They are held in open court. That's right. OEXs are public humiliations. Bring out the stocks. Getting your debtor to empty out his pockets in public is priceless. This is more than academic. The fact that the judgment debtor must go through their personal finances in open court is very embarrassing. Public disclosure of personal finances is its own form of punishment. No, you cannot take into court a camera phone to record your moment of humiliation inflicted upon the debtor when you ask the debtor to stand up and empty his pockets. It's great theater. If you do snap the picture and get away with it, don't post it on YouTube, despite the temptation.

What type of budget do you have? If the judgment is large enough and you have costs money at hand, serve every major bank in town with a subpoena. Random subpoenas might unearth the bank account, safety deposit boxes, or unsecured claims accompanied by a detailed financial statement. If the loan is secured, you could identify the bank through the UCC or county recorder filings. Even if you don't find the current account, you might find the closed accounts and follow the paper trial that might identify the final repository for the funds. If the claim arose in a small town, do not hesitate in serving every bank, stockbroker, and major accountant with a subpoena. If the defendant is in the agricultural business, or a farmer, serve every packing house or other wholesale buyer with a subpoena and levy. You are looking for the home loans or refinance and seek to capture the loan package, including the URLA, which is the grand prize. You are going to have fun.

Chapter 21

Can You Serve Hundreds or Thousands of Subpoenas? How?

How far can you go in serving subpoenas? Can you serve hundreds or thousands? In a lawsuit, you can serve a subpoena upon someone to obtain information that is reasonably calculated to lead to discovery of admissible evidence and has some bearing to the case. Yes, these subpoenas are fishing expeditions, and most judges will give you a pass if you prove that the fish you seek to hook has some relationship to the case, or might lead to evidence.

Postjudgment is different. The case is over. You are serving subpoenas to find assets or information that might lead to assets as opposed to proving your case or court or digging up evidence. If you don't know where the debtor banks, serve every bank in town with a subpoena. We did and found $50,000 of monies transferred 2 hours before the debtor murdered his tenant. If you don't know the debtor's customers but do know what products the debtor sells in the marketplace, subpoena every possible customer. You might want to check local state rules.

Are you chasing a manufacturer? Don't know which distributor carries the defendant's product line? Serve all distributors. If you can't tell which online financial service, such as PayPal, might hold the debtor's funds, serve everyone with a subpoena. Don't hesitate: serve everyone. Hit the gas.

Are you obligated to personally serve the subpoenas? Well, that is a very interesting question. Typically, you would have to personally serve the subpoena upon the person about whom you seek information and tender a witness fee of about $35 plus mileage. What if you want to serve 200 possible targets? The process server will charge about $100 per serve, and the witness fees are about, say, $50, for a total burden per witness of $150 times 200 witnesses, or $30,000. Will this investment of $30,000 guaranty you $30,000 or anything? No, not a plug nickel. How to solve this dilemma? Answer: Mail the subpoenas to the witnesses. That's right. Mail them with a cover letter. You will find that about 90 percent of the witnesses will willingly respond to a mailed subpoena and provide promptly whatever documents you seek. Post digital, you might receive these documents in a PDF. These documents will reveal bank and customer accounts. Now, before you mail off 1,000 subpoenas, the banks are tougher as well as require the service of a subpoena and might well demand a witness fee up front. In some cases, many large-scale businesses use CT Corporation System or other professional agents for service of process. You can serve these agents in mass less expensively through a process server, or as we do, just serve them by mail or FedEx. You can stuff in a FedEx envelope endless subpoenas and reach a huge census of persons who might have information revealing the debtor's accounts, financial statements, tax returns, proof of ownership, location of assets, sales contacts, offshore and onshore locations, and just about anything else in the hand of lenders, key customers, financial institutions, and primary vendors.

Expect a howl of protests from the debtor or the debtor's affiliates that the blizzard of subpoenas is making everybody's life miserable. You will hear endless tales, receive threatening letters and e-mails, or even find yourself on the butt end of a motion to quash, which seeks a gazillion-dollars of sanctions. For sure, you have to take all of this seriously, but as long as the subpoena seeks information that would ferret out assets, identify a repository, or produce information that might be productive in identifying assets, you should be able to survive this onslaught of protests. Sending out mass subpoenas, if reasonably well crafted, is not actionable, meaning nobody will sue you, and assuming that you did not accuse the debtor of mass murder, you should walk away unscathed. The service of subpoenas upon persons who in good faith might be the repository of information that would reveal assets is free of any liability.

Let's take a short stop here. Your target is a trucking company doing business with a large ocean-going carrier, trucking or transportation company, nonvessel-operating common carrier, ocean transportation intermediary, freight forwarder, logistics company, oil service provider, and large corporation. Many of these business use CT or CSC as agents. You can stuff in *one* FedEx envelope, addressed to CT or CSC, the subpoenas, assuming that the witness uses these services. Make sure that the subpoena says "records only," "respond by e-mail," and "will pay for copy charges." What is the cost of servicing the subpoenas? The cost of the FedEx envelope or about $20. If you identified a thousand likely witnesses, stuff a thousand subpoenas in one FedEx envelope. If your success rate is 10 percent, you have done a very good job. Can you get sued for that stunt? Go back to *Rusheen v. Cohen*, which protects you from civil liability for a lawsuit. Trust me, they taught this stuff in law school. This is true prospecting in your big-time search to dig up treasure. You will enjoy no greater personal satisfaction than discovering a million-dollar asset through a campaign of random subpoenas.

When the witness calls up and says, "We have records that show we owe money to your debtor," you will fall off your chair. After you have recovered your wits, I hope, don't forget to levy on the witness, or lacking an agent for service of process in California, and sue the customer for the debt owed to the debtor (the creditor's suit).

Chapter 22

Be Fearless and Not Fearful; Be Direct and Be Prepared

Bring a court reporter for the examination. Have a big breakfast. This is a full-body contact sport. Bring the practice guide that spells out the remedies if the debtor is uncooperative, such as tossing the debtor in jail. Bring energy bars, high-calories dried fruit, dates, figs, prune, dried apricots, no nuts, and bottles of water to keep you going. Don't bring a candy bar as the sugar will give an energy rush and within minutes leave you to crash and burn.

Threaten the debtor with jail if the debtor provides an evasive, incomplete, or partial answer. "I will seek to incarcerate you if you continue to provide me with answers that are incomplete, evasive, or an obstruction. You will be incarcerated unless and until you agree to provide me with this information. If you knowingly provide me with false information, I will not hesitate to file criminal charges. You have been ordered to appear here and testify truthfully as to your assets and liabilities." Read the law to the defendant. Speak slowly.

In one case, I told the defendant I would seek to incarcerate him for as long as necessary until he started to answer the questions fully, fairly, and completely. OEXs are not prejudgment depositions in which the lawyer seeks information about the case. The OEX is a court ordered examination in which the court orders the debtor to disclose information. The failure to comply with the order leads to contempt and jail. Don't let the debtor forget this. Pound at this person. Demand that the defendant pull out his or her wallet and go through all the credit cards (i.e., for the credit balances). Tell the defendant to empty all pockets—every penny, nickel, dime, and quarter. If the debtor's lawyer butts in, as expected, remind he or she that the lawyer is obstructing a lawful examination and that any obstruction is an act of contempt and that the lawyer might get tossed in jail.

These examinations are sometimes in the jury or conference room. Sometimes the parties undertake the examinations in the courthouse hallways. In one $12,000,000 enforcement, I am examining family members of the defendant. Instead of the examination taking place in the jury room, the judge orders us out to the hallway. No problem. The court reporter found herself a seat on the hallway bench. I, the witness, and the other lawyer stood up.

This was a tough case because the defendant murdered his tenant who ratted him out for child abuse, in which he was convicted on 56 counts. After we got going with the examination, the other lawyer stepped back, took out his cell phone and took a bunch of pictures. Too bad for me, because I wasn't quick enough to turn my head and smile. I am bent out of shape because I did not get a copy of photo. I would post the photo on my website. Duh!

What happens if the debtor fails to appear at the OEX? Some courts issue "bench letters" that inform the debtor to show up at a continued hearing date or face the issuance of a bench warrant. Other courts dispense with this formality and order a bench warrant in the amount of the judgment. Civil judgments now motor past $2,000,000, which might be the amount of the bail attached to the bench warrant. This is a lot of money. Before you cause the arrest of this person and let him sit in county jail for a few days, let's explore why this person did not show up. The first answer is that the defendant did not show up because he is a jerk. That may be. The second answer is that the process server did not serve the right person (or anyone for that matter), and service is bad. The classic term is "gutter service." Getting someone tossed into jail based on bad service of an OEX might prompt criminal prosecution against the lawyer. See CCP § 708.170(b): "A person who willfully makes an improper service of an order for an examination which subsequently results in the arrest pursuant to subdivision (a) of the person who fails to appear is guilty of a misdemeanor."

Let's talk more about no-shows. The ugly reason why the defendant declined to appear is that the person filed bankruptcy, and you might not know. Getting this person arrested would violate the automatic stay under Bankruptcy Code § 362(a) [The "Whoa Nelly" law], etc., and hands the defendant, now a plaintiff in an ugly lawsuit against you, a whole bunch of your insurance money. Let's not miss a beat. The filing of bankruptcy stays the collection of a debt or enforcement of a judgment. Any action in contravention of the stay is void. Dead. Stone cold dead. Whether you know or don't know about the bankruptcy, that does not matter. In re Schwartz, 954 F.2d 569 (9th Cir. 1991) says so. See later discussion. Do your homework, son.

Is this possible? We are cautious people. We had one debtor who was properly served with an OEX, but he failed to appear. The standard routine is to write the debtor a letter that states that he was sued and served and that a judgment was entered; he was served with an OEX (order and proof service attached) and because he failed to appear, we sent a letter explaining that a bench warrant might be issued. The letter asked that he call us. We received a response from one debtor. We opened the envelope and inside was a bankruptcy notice stapled to my letter.

Most bankruptcy notices get to the right person on time. I said "most." Some bankruptcy notices go sideways when they are sent to the creditor's "lock-box address," which is a post office box address for the creditor's bank. The personnel opening the mail might not be attuned to the importance of these notices or very slow in getting it to the credit department. Some notices go to the wrong address, a sales office, or the client and not the lawyer, which would create further delay. In the issuance of any bench warrant, look for any bankruptcy through PACER, and keep in mind the district where the debtor might have filed. Don't be quick to get people arrested. Patience is your BFF.

Whether in state or federal court, the creditor can serve interrogatories and a documents request that compels financial disclosures. In about 90 percent of the time, the debtor ignores this discovery. This arrogance comes with a price. If the debtor appealed the judgment but confronts and ignores a discovery order, the appellate court can dismiss the appeal. This is called disentitlement. Disentitlement means that the defendant violated a court order, fled the jurisdiction to avoid incarceration, fled the court with the children in hand to defy a custody order, but, as a result of this conduct, got kicked out of court and forfeits defense of the case or appeal. You cannot have your cake and eat it, too. Therefore, withholding information from the creditor has a big fat price.

Certainly the debtor is going to object on the basis of privacy, but the purpose of post-judgment discovery is to ferret out assets of the debtor, which necessarily invades zones of privacy. This case is best: In *Hooser v. The Superior Court of San Diego County*, 84 Cal. App. 4th 997, 1002, 101 Cal. Rptr. 2d 341 (Cal. App. 4 Dist. 2000) "A judgment debtor examination is intended to allow the judgment creditor a wide scope of inquiry concerning property and business affairs of the judgment debtor. . . . the purpose of the examination is 'to leave no stone unturned in the search for assets which might be used to satisfy the judgment.')"

If you find the funds have moved from one account to another account, subpoena the next level of banks for production at the OEX. The subpoena should also be attached to a levy. This means that the process server will serve the bank with the subpoena demanding records and the levy demanding money. If no money, at least the banks show up with the debtor's examination. If the debtor in fact closed out the account in anticipation of the levy, at least you will receive written confirmation and the paper trail in open court.

While under state law, the tax returns that were filed might be off limits, but the working papers and financial disclosures given to the accountant are fair game. There is no such thing as "accountant's privilege," and therefore whatever was said, noted, or e-mailed is likewise accessible. Documents given to the accountants are fair game. Accountant's notes, summaries, and calculations are fair game. Other than the final tax return that was filed with the government, everything is fair game.

If money is stolen or embezzled, examine the debtor's accountant, who knows where the bodies are buried. If the accountant did not know of the embezzlement and is honest, the accountant is going to claim "ignorance." Claiming ignorance might be a hard sell, if the embezzled funds ended up in a bank or stock account that pays interest. Going back to the prior example, if Bank of America issues a 1099INT for $10,000, but the defendant makes only $60,000 a year, the accountant might question the defendant about this $1 million bank account. The converse is helpful. If you know that the defendant embezzled $1 million, but the tax returns (or 1099INT) fails to disclose interest tied to a $1 million deposit (or something close), the funds never hit the bank account, and the defendant is warehousing the funds in gold, coins, cashier's checks, debit cards, paid credit cards, or offshore.

Reread the sections that suggest the federal court, if possible, is a better home for your case. Why you might ask. Answer, my new found friend, tax returns are fair game in federal court. Well most of the time. You can snare the debtor's tax returns in federal court.

Where do people really hide money? Aside from cashier's checks which they stuff in safety deposit boxes, and all sorts of prepaid plastic, most people hide their wealth in currency that they park in home safes, safety deposit boxes, and off-site storage facilities. This works to a limited degree because most people cannot pay bills in cash, and they need the medium of plastic or electronic means, or even an old-fashioned check. In short, as they say, "money makes the world go round," the better expression is "only so far."

Cash is dangerous, and when folks are known to have a hoard of cash in their homes, they are an immediate magnet to home invasion robberies, which tend to be violent and only leave cold mangled bodies in their wakes. Also popular is gold, usually taking the shape of gold coins, small ingots, and other forms of gold. Most people will take their gold and stuff it in a safety deposit box. That might work, unless the creditor levies on every safety deposit box in town. (We did that once.) Other folks open up bank accounts in asset-protection friendly countries, such as Costa Rica, Panama, and nearly every Caribbean Island nation. They open safety deposit boxes and park their gold. This all sounds very exciting, but it is extremely inconvenient. The upside to offshore wealth is that the wealth is offshore and inaccessible to creditors. The downside to offshore wealth is that the wealth is offshore, and almost as inaccessible to the debtor.

Chapter 23

Money Makes the World Go Round, Mein Herr

Let's get to the heart of the debtor's examination: Where are the bank accounts, expensive jewelry, antiques, Persian carpets, stock and bond accounts, and other assets? Many debtors lie through their teeth, feign ignorance, give misleading or incomplete answers, or complain of ill health. We had one debtor who won the Academy Award at a debtor's examination. I was going absolutely nowhere with this person, making zero progress. I hailed in front of the court commissioner and was about to ask that the judge order the judgment debtor to answer the questions that I posed. I walked up to the counsel table, and the debtor walked a few feet behind. As he approached the defense side, he pirouetted his body into a corkscrew and slowly fell down on the ground. Amazingly, he landed squarely face down. I am looking at this guy who isn't moving. Dead and gone to heaven? Not too likely. The commissioner immediately had the bailiff call 911. About two minutes later the ambulance showed up, the techs hauled out the gurney, hoisted the debtor on it, and drove away.

Nothing was wrong with this person, and miraculously he made a full recovery. Marvels of modern American medicine or that Oscar® belonged to him.

Let's get back to the heart of the problem. The debtor is going to lie big time and repeatedly. Expect that. Remember when I told you (or I hope that I told you) to anticipate that debtors will prosecute a strategy based on their capability, and not based on your perception of their intentions. Accept that reality. Embrace the misery factor. The most effective counterinsurgency strategy is to subpoena bank accounts, financial statements, and the loan, credit, or lease applications for all home loans, car loans, credit accounts or any other type of credit relationship that compelled the debtor to turn over tax returns or make any financial disclosure. Subpoena the tax accountant. With these materials in hand, instead of asking the debtor whether the debtor has a bank account, you can cycle through the current disclosures and confirm (a) that the debtor had the bank account at the time of the disclosure and (b) that the bank account is still active and the current balance. These disclosures enable you to quiz the debtor whether the assets existed at the time of the disclosure, and whether the assets, such as bank, securities, and mutual fund accounts still exist. We call these historic disclosures "baseline." Financial records reveal real property whose ownership is warehoused in a limited liability company or held in the name of a spouse, partnership, or out-of-state property, which is difficult to confirm.

Chapter 24

Subpoena the Lawyer for Records That Show Payment for Services

Lawyers do not come cheap. Absent the bizarre, lawyers do not work for free or at least not intentionally. Someone is paying the lawyer in the defense of your debtor. The fact that a debtor fends off enforcement through the machinations of a clever lawyer aggravates the judgment creditor to no end. How can this judgment debtor pay tens of thousands to some fancy law firm, but plead total poverty in a debtor's examination? Something is wrong in the state of Denmark, Horatio.

What can you do, Hamlet? Answer: Attach to the debtor's examination order a subpoena upon the lawyer for checks, cashier's checks, wire transfer transmittal and confirmation, proof of electronic payments, including PayPal (and others), and the written receipt for payment of fees by and between the lawyer and the client. If the debtor is paying the lawyer from a bank account, you now have the bank information including the locale of the bank account. If the debtor's original bank account was with Bank of America, but the check for fees payable to the lawyer reflects another bank, out of county or state, or offshore, you are staring at a fraudulent conveyance. You might conclude that the lawyer advised or arranged for the new bank account to ensure payment of fees and cheat you. Better yet, you have a new account to levy.

You read that the service of a debtor's examination imposes a lien upon the debtor's assets, which includes the money in a bank account. You can sue the lawyer for conversion and ruin this person's day. This is an enormous deal if you served the debtor with the examination, which imposed a lien, and the debtor still pays the lawyer's bill with money subject to your lien. You might even get to examine the lawyer as a third party who holds property that consists of the funds originated from the debtor, but subject to your lien. The third-party examination order also creates a lien upon the debtor's funds in the hands of the lawyer.

This is a pure Chicken Delight moment when you can leverage a simple debtor's examination into a big-time lawsuit against the opposing counsel. Of course, the opposing counsel would bear a conflict with the client because the lawyer bears an incentive to compel the debtor to pay the judgment, which would render moot the conversion lawsuit against the lawyer. Everyone is tumbling into a rabbit hole.

If the money paid to the lawyer originates from a new entity, family member, spouse, or offshore entity, you can chase down these entities on the basis that these entities are warehousing the debtor's cash, accounts, and other assets. The good faith belief is that the third party is holding the funds in trust for the debtor and might hold more funds.

Now, all of this said, how would you like to collect the judgment from the third party? We are going to escape the earth's gravity and orbit the earth. Let's start with the premise that the debtor is sitting on a bunch of money and refuses to pay the creditor. The creditor wants to get paid and would levy every bank in town. If the funds are held by the family member, or new entity, the levies would bounce off the bank warehousing the account in the name of the surrogate like BBs against a battleship. The transfer of the funds from the debtor to the third party (new entity, including the lawyer, spouse, family member, etc.) as a warehouse is a fraudulent conveyance because the debtor transferred the money with the intent to hide the money from the creditor, and hence with the "intent to hinder, delay and defraud." The third party was acting as a knowing conduit in passing the money along to the lawyer. You can sue the third party as a conspirator in facilitating a fraudulent conveyance and ask for monetary damages, including punitive damages. Toss the lawyer into that hopper. We are talking about one very big ugly mess. The lawyer will probably have to hire his or her own lawyer.

Do you think that your adversary is going to hand over copies of the debtor's checks that reveal the bank account that you can levy within 24 hours, or sue the lawyer and everyone else, for conversion, a fraudulent conveyance, and ruin everyone's lives? Believe it or not, the methods and means of payment are subject to discovery. Let's start with *Clarke v. Am. Com. Nat. Bank*, 974 F.2d 127, 129 (9th Cir. 1992), in which the court stated as follows:

> Not all communications between lawyer and client are privileged. Our decisions have recognized that the identity of the client, the amount of the fee, the identification of payment by case file name, and the general purpose of the work performed are usually not protected from disclosure by the lawyer-client privilege. [For the rest of this quote, you need to read the case yourself.]

More stuff can be found at *U.S. v. Blackman*, 72 F.3d 1418, 1424 (9th Cir. 1995); *Dougan v. United States*, 2011 WL 3568455 (USDC, E. D. Cal. 2011); and *Torney v. United States*, 840 F.2d 1424, 1426 (9th Cir. 1988). If you want your money, you should read the materials.

Answer: Checks, wire transfers, and other medium of payment are discoverable, along with the fee agreement. As they say in the movies: Follow the money. With banking information, you can convert a pig's ear into a silk purse with a few shekels inside. Read this stuff.

Chapter 25

Postjudgment Written Discovery—Federal and State Court

We kicked this around before, but this is the nuts and bolts of written postjudgment discovery. Is your debtor playing peekaboo with you? Is your debtor busy dodging process servers, sheriffs, and marshals? Here is a better one: The process server comes to the debtor's home, knocks on the door, waits, knocks on the door again, and Mr. Occupant comes to the door. The process server asks Mr. Occupant if he is the defendant in the lawsuit. Mr. Occupant, who might be the defendant, does not say squat. We got one alpha male staring down another alpha male. The process server asks Mr. Occupant again if he is the defendant in the lawsuit. Mr. Occupant responds: "What's it to you, bud." The process server says that he has papers to serve. Mr. Occupant says: "You are trespassing, and this is Texas. I suggest that you leave before I grab my pistol. The Marines gave me a marksmanship badge."

Let's try Plan B. You can serve postjudgment interrogatories and request for production of documents that seek the discovery of assets and liabilities. Most lawyers have canned forms. This procedure works in state and federal court. This procedure is easy, painless, and cheap. Try a 96 cent stamp. Nobody is pointing guns, nobody is running around, and nobody is staking out someone else.

This remedy sounds like a winner, yet it has one flaw. Most debtors ignore written discovery. Call it kindling. Who knows? Your debtor might answer the written discovery, but this is wishful thinking. If the debtor defaults, you might score a disentitlement order and knock the debtor out of court. You might gin up a motion to compel, which will spool out an order to compel discovery. The failure to respond to the discovery order might hand you a contempt order, which authorizes the sheriff to pick up the defendant and land him in the clink for a day or two. Maybe.

If the debtor is playing peek-a-boo, written discovery is your remedy, but don't expect the debtor to respond. At least your process server will not meet the same fate as St. Sebastian.

Chapter 26

Getting Tossed Out of Court by the Judge

Disentitlement and the Death of Appeals

Let's talk more about the law of disentitlement. This is a little known area of civil law, but it is important to anyone in the business of collecting from debtors who are downright ornery and uncooperative. The law of disentitlement converts the obstinacy of the debtor (and your frustration) into the debtor's forced exit from the courthouse. Disentitlement allows the court to eject the debtor from the judicial proceeding. This is a very big deal. Failing to appear at an order of examination (OEX) is a violation of a court order and might disentitle the defendant from defending any asset that might have been revealed at the OEX. Disentitlement is an equitable remedy that ousts the debtor from access to the courts, which would include appeals being dismissed, claims stricken, or a party barred from defending an asset. This is more than a rarified academic discussion. Judgment debtors routinely defy discovery orders, fail to appeal at debtor's exams, refuse to answer questions, refuse to turn over documents, and otherwise act like a complete jerk. Once a bully, always a bully.

Disentitlement converts this obstinacy into ouster. In *Blue Shield and Blue Cross v. Finkelstein*, 111 F.3d 278 (2nd Cir. 1997), the court dismissed an appeal brought by a debtor when the debtor fraudulently disposed of assets, dodged process servers and the marshal, and apparently fled. The court found that the conduct was so egregious and that the sole purpose was to undermine the jurisdiction of the court that the court authorized the dismissal of the appeal, the effect of which was to throw the debtors out the courthouse door and on their butts. If you are the creditor, you should propound discovery and hope that the debtor defaults. If the debtor defaults on the discovery order, you might be able to dump the appeal. If you are the debtor and wish to ensure access to the courts, don't default. You are asking for trouble and might find yourself shown the door by Mr. Judge, and told never to come back.

See *TMS v. Aihara* (1999) 71 Cal. App. 4th 377 [appeal dismissed when the appellant defaulted on postjudgment discovery order]. You can find online Roman Polanski's case, which explains civil and criminal disentitlement. *Polanski v. Superior Court* (2009) 180 Cal. App. 4th 507. The latter case is *In re MARRIAGE OF John M. HOFER and Lisa M. Hofer*, 208 Cal. App. 4th 454, 145 Cal. Rptr. 3d 697 (2nd Dist. 2012), in which the husband violated a court order, was stuck with a big-money judgment, and was disentitled from an appeal of an adverse family order. Arrogance comes at a big price. The court stated as follows:

> The disentitlement doctrine enables an appellate court to stay or to dismiss the appeal of a party who has refused to obey the superior court's legal orders. . . . "Dismissal is not ' "a penalty imposed as a punishment for criminal contempt. It is an exercise of a state court's inherent power to use its processes to induce compliance" ' with a presumptively valid order." . . . Thus, the disentitlement doctrine prevents a party from seeking assistance from the court while that party is in "an attitude of contempt to legal orders and processes of the courts of this state." . . .
>
> John cites criminal and civil cases in which the disentitlement doctrine applies, but argues the dissimilar facts in those cases compared to the facts here make his cases distinguishable. . . . [defendant was a fugitive from justice and was not entitled to an appeal]; . . . . [defendant twice disobeyed the court's order to pay specified funds to plaintiff, among other things]; . . . [defendant failed to appear for debtor's examination resulting in a warrant for his arrest]; . . . [defendants failed to comply with order to deposit income with a receiver]; . . . [father absconded with minor]; . . . [grandparents denied placement and guardianship and their counsel absconded with minor]; . . . [husband's appeal contesting wife's lawyer fee order was dismissed after he left the country with the couple's children in defiance of a custody order in favor of wife].

Federal cases, likewise, follow suit and include *Goya Foods, Inc. v. Unanue-Casal* (1st Cir. 2001) 275 F.3d 124, and *Empire Blue Cross/Blue Shield v. Finkelstein* (2d Cir. 2009) 111 F.3d 278. These cases provide for the dismissal of an appeal based upon the appellant's refusal to comply with postjudgment discovery. These cases have a strong record evidencing fraudulent conveyances and other asset protection (see *Goya Foods* at 131; *Finkelstein* at 282). Blowing off an out-of-state discovery order to compel disclosure of assets would justify the dismissal of an appeal of a form state. You can run but never hide from disentitlement says the court in *Stoltenberg etc. v. Ampton Investments Inc.* (2013) 215 C.A. 4th 1225 [Debtor gets tossed from appeal because debtor violates out-of-state discovery order].

Disentitlement exploits the defendant's recalcitrance into a strategic victory that might oust the defendant from the court of appeals and foreclose the prospect of an adverse but unexpected result. The nonjudicial vernacular for disentitlement: "Hit the road Jack and don't you come back no more, no more, no more, no more. . . . Hit the road Jack and don't you come back no more." Getting kicked out of court might not guarantee collection, but it clears the docket of absurd motions filed by the debtor that seek to fend off enforcement. Is it important? Yes, because you can rid yourself of an expensive and troublesome appeal based on the debtor's recalcitrance. If you can kick the debtor out of court, your chances of success go up dramatically.

We chased down an offshore asbestos manufacturer who refused to pay a judgment. After multiple rounds of discovery motions, the judge granted a motion that disentitled the debtor from defending against an asset that should have been revealed in the discovery. During the case, the State Bar of California asked me to meet with a delegation of Japanese law school academics who were researching postjudgment remedies in the United States. Apparently Japanese postjudgment remedies are arthritic, slow, and cumbersome, which led these academics to grace our door in search of wholesale reforms. I had a crash course in their remedies and grasped that the inefficiencies make the judgment unenforceable and inferentially shielded assets from enforcement. Making the remedies effective might compel a debtor to pay and therefore unlock billions in hidden capital. My meeting was about 3:00 p.m. At the outset the Japanese delegation first inquired about discovery, order of examination and what happens if the debtor is a no show or uncooperative. Does the person go to jail? Why? How long? Does this work? In my responding, I told the lead delegate who was a full professor at the Japanese equivalent of Harvard Law School about the asbestos case and the order of disentitlement. I was about to explain the case in detail when the professor cut me off: "Thank you, but you don't need to tell me the story. I heard this story from the judge in the case this morning."

Chapter 27

Blocking Statutes

The International Hurdle to Enforcement

I love "International Law." When I say those words, I just sound smarter. The same is true for "Intellectual Property." How about offshore enforcement? It gets my blood going. Did I mean to say that my blood is going cold? Offshore enforcement is tough because the debtor is offshore and inaccessible to discovery. You think that $10,000 a day in sanctions is going to compel the debtor to respond? Expect a catastrophic default of all discovery. If the debtor dumped junk in the U.S. market that maimed or killed a bunch of people, who won judgments that exceeded the gross domestic product of most countries. You also might encounter "blocking statutes," in pursuing discovery against the debtor.

"Knowledge is power," including knowledge of the debtor's financial affairs. In Latin, *scientia potentia est* is generally attributed to Sir Francis Bacon. See FRANCIS BACON, 8 NOVUM ORGANUM, PART I, APHORISM III. (Taggard & Thompson, 1863) at 67–68. Also, from Proverbs 24:5, "A wise man is strong, a man of knowledge increaseth strength." Cf. also, Ferdowsi, SHAHNAMEH (Book of Kings) (Persia, c. 1000 A.D.): "One who has wisdom is powerful." Knowledge of the debtor's U.S. customers or customer with a U.S. presence is getting paid.

Do you want to chase down some offshore debtor domiciled in a foreign country whose laws prohibit the disclosures of their financial affairs, such as its records and the assets? These cases cost a bundle and the initial costs can exceed $5000 or more just to get the case up and running (filing fees, transaction, costs of service of process through the Hague Convention, the initial and certain motion to quash, etc.). If the offshore debtor does not willingly write you a check, this investment (try closer to $25,000) is a total waste of capital, unless you proceed with very high-end enforcement such as asset discovery.

Expect that the offshore debtor will claim that their own local law prohibits any financial disclosure and relies on the local "blocking statutes." Blocking statutes are laws enacted in one jurisdiction to obstruct the local (extrajurisdictional) application of a law enacted in another jurisdiction. In *Société Nationale Industrielle Aérospatiale v. U.S. District Court for the Southern Dist. of Iowa*, 482 U.S. 522, 107 S. Ct. 2542 (1987) [worth reading], the blocking statute in question forbade disclosure of documents or information on economical, commercial, industrial, financial, or technical matters. Blocking statutes typically prohibit a defendant from revealing its own financial information or handing over documents demanded in litigation. Blocking statutes are used against both pretrial discovery and in posttrial disclosure of assets to aid in enforcement of the judgment. You have to battle, and battle hard, to get the judge to order the debtor to turn over this information. Expect further pushback when the debtor complies with the judge's order to produce discovery, usually those that would identify the assets and their location.

Blocking statutes might disentitle judgment creditors from access to offshore financial information that reveals assets subject to enforcement. Enforcement would be near impossible because the U.S. marshal (or any levying officer) requires instructions that adequately describe the property and identify the place, bailee, or custodian who has possession or control of the property. California Code of Civil Procedure § 687.010(a) states that "The instructions shall contain the information needed or requested by the levying officer to comply with this title, including but not limited to: (1) an adequate description of any property to be levied upon." California Code of Civil Procedure § 699.545 requires service of a notice of levy upon the third party who is holding the property of the judgment debtor. California Code of Civil Procedure §§ 700.110 to 700.170 state that a levy upon a chattel paper, bank account, account receivable, general intangible, safe-deposit box, negotiable document of title require services upon the third party in possession of the property. In simple English: you are your own bloodhound.

You can grab what you can find. You can grab property that you can identify, and moreover identify the person (a real-live breathing entity) who has possession of the property (fancy terms: bailee or garnishee). The sheriff is not going to play Dick Tracy, Sherlock Homes, or some CSI geek to figure you who has the debtor's property and what it is. That is your job. Three blind mice need not apply, and I don't care what the American Disabilities Act says. Blocking statutes seek to stop you for collecting on the judgment because these statutes entitle the debtor to escape discovery.

Blocking statutes prevent you from identifying the property of the debtor and moreover identify the person, such as the bank, who has possession of the property. If you are chasing down someone offshore and seek information through the courts, expect the barricades of blocking statutes that impede your trip toward the land of milk and honey.

Got this? Did I lose you? Well, in chasing down offshore entities, you can expect this pushback. Blocking statutes means that wherever the offshore entities hang their hats, local law bars financial disclosures to third parties. Is the local government protecting state secrets? No. Whether the offshore manufacturer of Sheetrock used defective materials is not the equivalent of the nuclear launch codes. The local domicile blocks financial disclosure to impede enforcement by the aggrieved judgment creditor.

Federal court cases fare no better, no matter how wonderful the seal on the writ looks. Rule 69(a)(1) compels the marshal to follow state practices and incorporate the state's code of civil procedure in the enforcement of judgments. Lawyers enforcing federal judgments might enjoy greater omnipotence, but not omniscience. Sorry to say lawyers, sheriffs, and marshals lack X-ray vision, Clark. Stick to reporting.

Chapter 28

Turnover Orders and Dead Cold Hands, Mr. Heston

At the end of the order of examination, or independently, the court can compel the debtor to turn property in the debtor's possession to the sheriff for the purpose of sale. Watches come off the wrist, and rings come off the fingers, which are deposited with the sheriff. Another common use of a turnover order is cash-on-hand, valuable personal property located in a home, bank accounts or accounts receivable, or notes due the debtor, which the court can freeze and order the debtor to turn over to the sheriff.

Let's get one thing out of the way. The judge can order the judgment debtor to turn over property, but only to the sheriff, absent the very bizarre. A court cannot order the judgment debtor to hand over its property to the judgment creditor, unless cash-on-hand and probably not. This is a no-no. I have met many judgment creditors who have this vision that they can walk off with the judgment debtor's jewelry, cars, and unique wearing apparel in hand. They have this vision of ousting the debtor from a home. That might be in their wildest dreams, but the courts have made it clear that the enforcement of judgments provides for payment of a money judgment, and not grand larceny. The best case is *Palacio Del Mar Homeowners Association v. McMahon*, 95 Cal. Rptr. 3d 445 (Cal. App. 4th Dist. 2009), which says that the court cannot hand over the debtor's property directly to the creditors. Dismemberment, drawing and quartering, or disembowelment are not recognized forms of civil enforcement. The next case is *Ho v. Hsieh*, 105 Cal. Rptr. 3d 17 (Cal. Ct. App. 2010) [same thing; can't hand over property to creditor but only to sheriff to sell and turn over proceeds to creditor]. Apparently, not everyone agrees. You should read *Sleepy Hollow Inv. Co. No. 2 v. Prototek, Inc.*, No. C 03-4792, 2007 WL 2701318 (N. D. Cal. Sept. 13, 2007) [turnover of property directly to creditor].

Congratulations, you confirmed that your debtor is holding a bunch of money, real dollars in an offshore account that is warehoused by an offshore financial institution. You cannot levy on this bank account. An assignment order, even if properly served, wouldn't even scratch the paint, Admiral Halsey. You cannot serve a third-party order of examination on the bank because the bank is offshore. You can huff and puff and blow down every other bank, but not this culprit.

You knew that I would get there. Money is parked offshore. Here is how you can get to the money. First, you can lasso the debtor into court and convince Judge Chamberlain Haller to order the debtor to turn over the money to the sheriff. Judge Haller will issue a turnover order that compels the debtor to turn over the money to the county sheriff. Absent compliance, which I personally guarantee, the judge can throw the debtor into jail until he complies. Orange is the new black. This might take some time and effort, and more than one hearing, but indeterminate incarceration will encourage your debtor to come to his senses and cough up the money. A violation of the court order also enables the judge to convict the debtor of punitive contempt, which lands the debtor in jail for even more time. Have fun.

What if you can't get the debtor served with the debtor's examination or the order to show cause regarding contempt, or the order to turn over the funds? We have a problem, Houston. Well, yes and no. Some states mandate personal service of everything, which is par for the course. Other states are looser, and you might get away with something less. Maybe, but do not count on it. Believe me, your debtor is going to hide under his bed, particularly if you take my advice and direct 10 process servers to serve him with the Order to Show Cause for Contempt, or the contempt order.

No go on the service. What's next? How do we cut this Gordian Knot, Oedipus? Answer: If you are reasonably sure that the bank is holding money due your debtor, and that the account is an offshore shame, sue the bank for the debtor's funds on hand, sue for a conspiracy, sue for fraud, sue for money laundering, and sue for the works. Take no prisoners, Colonel Lawrence.

Chapter 29

The Great Turnover

The Great O. J. Watch Story

Here is the O. J. watch story. The start of this story was that TMZ ran a photo showing O. J. wearing a Rolex Submariner watch. Nobody could tell from the photo whether the Rolex was real or fake. Harvey Levin called me and pointed out the photo on his website. I have to give Harvey credit. He lit the fuse. A fake fuse, but a fuse that was burning nonetheless. This fuse was closer to a "detonation cord," which is a flammable cord infused with an accelerant that burns at the rate of 100 feet per second. The short name is det cord and enters our lexicon as meaning any situation in which the outcome is explosive and compels the judgment creditor to move very expeditiously. We say that the det cord is lit, and don't waste time.

Normally to grab a watch, ring, or other items of personal property, the judgment creditor would have the judgment debtor in court at the OEX, and at the conclusion ask the judge for a turnover order. No, we didn't examine Mr. Simpson; however, the court did order O. J. Simpson to turn the watch over to us. This story is worth telling.

After Harvey Levin's call, I gave notice to Simpson's lawyer that I intended to show up in court and get a turnover order for the watch and other relief. The press knew that I would be in court. I remember personally typing up the paperwork and clearly understanding the media value of this stunt. This was also the hearing that compelled O. J. to turn over his tax returns, which laid out his annual income near $400,000 courtesy of his NFL and related pensions. At the hearing before Judge Rosenberg, the press packed the courtroom. Judge Rosenberg ordered O. J. through his lawyer (who had possession of the watch) to turn the watch over to me. At the hearing I announced I would get the watch appraised and report back to the court. I knew that I would be personally safeguarding the watch.

After the hearing, we went to O. J.'s lawyer's office. Peter Haven, my partner in the case, and I personally showed up at Ron Slate's office. We were greeted at the reception desk and escorted to Ron's private office. He knew that we were coming and was very cordial. Peter and I sat down and Ron had on his desk a small box, about 3 inches square.

He opened upon the box and handed me the gold "Rolex" Submariner watch. I confess that I own, but do not wear, a Rolex watch. Lawyer arrogance compelled me to buy that unwearable lummox. When I looked at O. J.'s watch and had it in my hand, I could tell from the heft that something was not right. Rolex watches bear this enormous gravitas. They are heavy but elegant in their own right. You don't need to be Harry Winston, the famous jeweler of New York City to tell the difference between a real and a fake Rolex.

As part of the court order, I was obliged to safeguard and appraise the watch. The court is in Santa Monica. My office is in San Francisco. I had to fly home courtesy of Southwest. Now what? I had to go through LA airport security. I could have put the watch in my briefcase, but I had always heard stories of thieves stealing briefcases from the airport X-ray machine. I could have put the watch in my pocket, but then the screening device would scream bloody murder and I would waste time through a body scan. So I wore it on my wrist. That took a second. I am at the Los Angeles Airport, snaking through the security line, with O. J. Simpson's Submariner in my pocket and contemplating whether to strap the watch to my wrist and go through the security gate. At that point in time, I said to myself, wear the blasted watch and enter (in the most perverted sense) O. J. immortality. I took O. J.'s Rolex out of my pocket, took off my current $39.95 Timex Expedition, and put on O. J.'s Rolex. Never in my wildest dreams did I imagine that I would be wearing O. J. Simpson's Rolex watch and go through airport security at the Los Angeles Airport.

Now, O. J.'s wrist is clearly thicker than mine, and his watch literally drooped from my wrist. We are talking about a watch that, when clasped, nearly exceeded the circumference of my closed hand. I walked through security. The Rolex failed to kick off the alarm. That was bizarre. The Rolex was huge and weighed a ton. Either I was very lucky, or something was really wrong. I remember holding up my hand way over my head going through the security gate. Even weirder was the fact that I was pondering my wrist size in comparison to that of O. J. Simpson's.

In court, I had told Judge Rosenberg that we would take the watch to Shreve & Company, the oldest jewelry store in San Francisco, for an appraisal. I knew that Shreve's had the biggest selection of Rolex watches in town just based on the Christmas advertising. The next day, we walked into Shreve's and found the service department in the rear of the store, where the manager was waiting for us. I handed over O. J.'s watch, which we and Shreve's photographed. After the preliminaries about the cost of the appraisal and when we would hear from them, we left the watch in Shreve's good care. The service department manager informed us that the appraisal would be ready at 5:00 p.m. that day.

At about 4:45 p.m. the next day, I called Shreve's. I got the service manager on the phone. He informed me that they had opened the watch case and found Chinese markings on the watch's movements. He told me that the watch is a fake. About a few minutes later, the press began calling. The calls started to pile up. I was ready with my precanned quotes. I wasn't going to let this opportunity slip out of my hand, no matter what. I told the press "It was made by the finest craftsmen in China" and "It's a people's Rolex." That quote was my favorite, because fake Rolexes have their own special place in America's heart. It's socially acceptable to wear a fake Rolex. I told everyone that the timepiece was "Value disabled."

At the ensuing court hearing, the courtroom was packed. Judge Rosenberg slowly read the appraisal report, paused, and said "Fake," causing the courtroom to erupt in peals of laughter. I could see, ever so slightly, Judge Rosenberg crack the thinnest of smiles when he finished reading the report while on the bench. I had to read the transcript for what the judge said next because no one could hear him through the laughter. We had a buyer for $15,000 from a big Hollywood celebrity and tried to facilitate a sale through the court. The court turned us down on the grounds that the watch has virtually no value, aside from the celebrity value, and had to be returned to Simpson.

Taking personal property off the debtor at an OEX is common. Judgment debtors have turned over cash, a fake Patek Philippe watch, and rings that pass for brass knuckles.

Chapter 30

Assignment Orders

The court can order that debts, accounts receivables, and even inheritances and obligations due the judgment debtor be assigned to the judgment creditors. Common obligations are real estate commissions, insurance receivables, notes receivables, or any other debts due the debtor. This remedy is analogous to a garnishment through a writ of execution, but instead of going through the sheriff, the judgment creditor can serve the obligors in person or through the mail. If the debtor is a dentist or doctor or operates any type of healthcare facility, the judgment creditor can mail the order to insurance companies (thousands of them). The ease and low cost of service of an assignment order enables the judgment creditor to reach an extremely broad range of assets. This is a campaign of enforcement.

A little greater explanation would be helpful here. Let's presume that the creditor is located in California. Let's presume that the debtor is located in the Dominican Republic, Puerto Rico, Guam, Canada, Mexico, or any other place. Let's presume that the debtor is a dentist, doctor, or anybody else who is paid through insurance, American Express, Discover Card, Capital One, PayPal, or any other conduit or financial institution that has a U.S. presence and, more specifically, a California presence.

Let's stop the movie here for a second. The debtor is offshore and the debtor probably banks with a local offshore bank, which means that bank account is probably inaccessible. Maybe. However, the debtor is paid through multinational financial institutions, all with a California or U.S. presence. An assignment order therefore would reach monies due from these financial institutions, which owe money to the debtor. The financial institutions are subject to the jurisdiction of the state upon which the court sits and vulnerable to an order. Stated succinctly, the financial institution is subject to the jurisdiction of the court that issued the assignment order. Therefore, depending upon the type of business, you can reach their cash flow if the cash flow flows through a financial institution subject to your local jurisdiction. We have one dentist located in upstate New York who takes American Express. Every few months, American Express sends us significant sums of money paying down that debt.

Here is the classic case of an offshore debtor and U.S. obligors who owe the judgment debtor. The Commonwealth of the Northern Mariana Islands is a U.S. protectorate and offered manufacturers of clothing a legal Disneyland. Manufacturers could label their products "Made in America," but pay their employees wages established by the Commonwealth, as opposed to prevailing rates in the U.S. mainland. Freed of prevailing wage constraints, but blessed with the "Made in the U.S. label," theses manufacturers snared a healthy portion of the U.S. garment market. All's well that ends well? No. How many of you are international economist? I wasn't, at least not until I took a crash course. Talk about a learning curve at a 90-degree angle. The General Agreement on Tariffs and Trade (GATT) limits the volume of products that a foreign country might import. During the 2000s, GATT freed China from certain import restrictions in the sale of garments consisting of women's clothing into the U.S. market. Chinese-made garments plummeted in wholesale price and beat out prices for products made in the Northern Mariana Islands. One by one the manufacturers in the North Marina Islands closed down and dumped on the streets thousands of unemployed Asian and Southeast Asian women. My case was a judgment against a manufacturer who had gone out of business. The case was pending the U.S. District Court, which followed the law of the state (the Commonwealth). After figuring out local law, we obtained an assignment order from the district court which we served the major U.S. retailers (Macy's, etc.). It was a great idea, but it was eight months too late. I did participate in one hearing through a telephone hookup. Given the date line and time difference, I appeared at the hour of about 7:00 p.m. for a hearing the *next day* at 10:00 a.m. Total *Back to the Future*. Very cool.

This remedy is important because an assignment order reaches current and future accounts. These orders are "evergreen" in reaching all accounts in the future. Service of 1,000 assignment orders would cost $0.48 per envelope, or $480.00. If the judgment wanted to levy the 1,000 garnishees through the sheriff, and assuming their presence in California and their agent is CT Corporation System, 818 West 7th Street, Los Angeles, 90017, the cost would be $35,000.00 or $35.00 per levy. Some sheriffs decline service of a routine levy, and parties are required to hire a private process server.

Spending $480 to collect a $50,000 account is credible, but spending $35,000 is incredible. Doctors, dentists, medical and health professionals, pharmaceutical makers, and convalescent care, acute care, and other facilities are vulnerable to this enforcement because their primary income is from insurance companies, which are generally national. The major insurers have a presence in nearly every state. An assignment order directed against a dentist is New York reaches the dentist's receivables due from Aetna, MetLife, United Concordia, Cigna, Humana, etc., all who have a presence in California.

Dentists are poor businesspeople and stumble over their commercial debts. Even though a good dentist might turn your teeth into a work of art, rivaling the statue of *David*, paying bills on time is like pulling teeth. The dentists bill insurance companies, which all have a nationwide presence. Serving the assignment order on insurance companies is like herding cattle: You are driving the accounts receivable away from the debtor to the plaintiff as assignee. "Get along, little doggie" is our motto. Did we have a winning hand here? Well yes, but this takes a number of hands, and a lot of effort, to get it right. Be careful in circulating assignment orders to 1,000 insurers. No, you won't get sued, but you can get your debtor mad and park himself at your front door as happened to us. Despite my repeated warnings, the front door was opened for this person who was enraged at me and much bigger and exceedingly angry. My life insurance was paid to date. After enormous screaming and shouting, he calmed down and we worked out the matter.

Any manufacturer, distributor, or importer is also vulnerable to assignment orders. Finding out the customers require a little detective work. Some debtors advertise their "customers" online. In other instances, if the debtor is a commercial importer of Indian food, the buyers are Indian restaurants, supermarkets or distributors. If the debtor imports bicycles, the buyers are bicycle shops, or distributors.

Chances are you have identified a few customers of the debtor who, for example, are offshore manufacturers That customer might be the company that bought the original defective products that injured the retail purchaser, now the plaintiff. You can presume that the debtor is selling to the competitors of the original wholesale buyer. How do you find the competitors? If the wholesale buyer is engaged in a specialty business, locate the trade association for the buyer. Many trade associations offer a comprehensive list of their members that includes phone, fax, and e-mail address. What will that information do for you? If the debtor sold the defective parts to the employer or the injured employee (e.g., a crane operator), you can cull through the trade association for all crane operators and locate the *online* membership list. You can append the membership list to your assignment motion as potential obligors (potential customers owing the debtor). Some judges push back on assignment motions unless you identify the obligor. Appending a list of potential obligors to the motion would identify the obligors. Maybe. Assuming that the debtor does not collapse when the debtor sees that the creditor is going to snap up the receivables due from all customers, the debtor will suffer enormous heartburn when you serve each customer by mail with the assignment order (Pay me, and not the debtor orders) and a broad-based subpoena for records. Enforcement is a campaign. Don't be shy. Call the president of the association, who might disclose the key competitors of the debtor. You might even score a membership list.

Always remember to post the order online. Make it easy. If the case name is "*Jones v. ABC Company,* United States District, Central District of California," and Case Number: CV11111, that case name would be the domain name for the website or the PDF title. Attach the assignment order as the sole document. Have a few dollars in your pocket? You can pay Google, or others, to ensure that the new website appears at the top of Google. Do I hear the phone ring? Is this defamatory? No, this is the publication of a court order, and in any event, truth is an absolute defense. Why is posting the order important? This is a court order, say, from a district court, which compels payment to the judgment creditor and not the debtor. Counsel for the customers (obligors of the debtor) might counsel the customers to withhold payment until the matter is resolved. Call this a constriction of the cash flow. The fact of posting on the Internet might compel the debtor to wake up from its slumber and resolve the case.

Parallel to customers are merchant accounts for the purpose of processing the credit cards and the credit card processors themselves. If you can identify the holder of the merchant account, you can reach the account through an assignment order. Maybe. You can serve the credit card processor likewise with an assignment order. The trick here is to make sure that the assignment order is drafted with enough particularity to reach these specialized accounts. The general counsel of the credit card processors is sensitive to enforcement against their accounts and expects great clarity in process.

If you cannot locate a trade association for the probable customers of the debtor, chances are the customers might bear similar names, and therefore, through the secretary of state, form the basis of a list. Try the online phone book for similar names ("Food Distributors"). If the customers are regulated (insurance companies and leasing companies, some of which are finance companies and necessarily are licensed), the state licensing boards offer a detailed list including addresses. Try the "top ten," of business, such as the "top ten" painting contractors if the debtor is a wholesale paint distributor. If the debtor is a contractor, cull through the city or county building department website that might disclose permits by the name of the contractor and, as the person "pulling down the permit." Serve the assignment order on the property owners, financiers of the project, or others to reach the revenue stream from the project.

If the debtor owns patents, cull through the USPTO to see if the debtor has assigned or licensed the patent, as that information might appear online. The assignee or licensee, if online, is probably paying a royalty or licensing fee to the debtor and is subject to the assignment order.

Rent control laws spawn an entire cottage industry of claims against landlords. Absent the smart landlord who would settle, or has oodles of insurance, the judgment creditor of the landlord can locate the debtor's units and rentals through the online grantor/grantee index of the recorder. You can serve an assignment order on the tenants. In one case, we did that. The tenants hated the landlord, our debtor. We had tenants calling us for confirmation of whose name should appear on the check. We had one tenant show up and pay us on the spot. The notion that somebody won a big judgment against the landlord, and needed to collect from the tenants, made the tenants smile. Slumlords do have to face justice through the barrel of civil enforcement.

Let's digress for a moment. The buyer of the product from the debtor might be a leasing company, if the debtor sells copiers, which are typically leased. Constructing a list of leasing companies is easy given the fact they belong to an association, and have easy to reconstruct names, as they use the name of "finance," or "leasing," or "lease" in their names. Serve an assignment order on the leasing and finance companies to reach any revenue due the debtors, as the leasing and finance company buy the "leased" equipment directly from the debtors.

Do you have to give notice to the debtor of who you are serving with the assignment order and notice to pay? Answer: no. No. Do you want to be clever? For sure. Your letter to the customer should explain who you are, why the obligor has to pay you, that the failure to pay might result in liability for double payment, enclose a copy of a certified copy of the order, and advise of the place of payment. You might want to include the name, address, telephone number, fax number, cell phone number, and e-mail address of the debtor, or the debtor's lawyer. Some obligors who get these letters that direct them to pay you and not the debtor are understandably concerned whether your demand letter is authentic and not a scam. Don't be shy, and embrace this expectation. Provide the obligors with the maximum amount of information. If the debtor, or debtor's counsel, gets 1,000 or more e-mails (or calls) from the customers that inquire whether the order is valid, and "what is going on," in turn you get a call from debtor's counsel as the opening gambit of settlement. The mass mailings of assignment orders, and accompanying subpoenas, is protected and privileged activity and free of any civil liability under the litigation privilege. The litigation privilege protects litigants from lawsuits against statements and actions arising in a judicial proceeding. Screaming "You are a liar," at the defendant at trial will not get you sued.

Do accompany a subpoena with the assignment order, as you might find that the debtor has pending sales, which the debtor seeks to advance payment to circumvent the assignment order (or levy). Best of all, you will get the debtor's banking information, new names, conduits, bank accounts, intermediaries. The obligor normally would pay for the goods or services, and necessarily would have information revealing the debtor's bank account or other (nontraditional) method of payment including payment to third parties. That third party might be a newly discovered successor in interest, fraudulent conveyance, the insiders of the debtors, or a new entity. The information that reveals the bank accounts will guide you to enforcement against those accounts.

If you are really clever, you can tie up the debtor's entire cash flow with assignment orders and subpoena the bank records of the debtor's lawyers. If the lawyers are getting paid from the debtor, you can sue the lawyers for conversion because the assignment orders encumbered the funds paid the lawyers, and their use of the funds for fees or settlements would be considered conversion. Case settled. Lay an assignment order on every bank near the debtor. Serve the assignment on prospective, probable, or potential customers. Try contempt against the debtor if he attempts to circumvent the assignment order. This is truly a crowd pleaser to hold your debtor in contempt of court.

Are you ready for a little craziness here? Let's go off the deep end. A bankruptcy trustee scored a $100,000 judgment against a paint retailer and distributor in a central California town. The defendant refused to pay the judgment, even though the judgment debtor clearly could write a check with enough money to still pay the utility bills. Letters and calls were a waste of time. We prosecuted an assignment motion, which was granted, after some opposition by the debtor's lawyer. This was a very broad-based order reaching all revenues, accounts, and bank accounts due the judgment debtor. Usually the judgment debtor sobers up and capitulates. No grander vision than the white flag at dawn. No, not this time. We served every paint store in town. Nope, no settlement. Nada. We served most of the local banks. Nope, that didn't work. We hit up the local city government and captured a few thousand dollars. No, no surrender. So you want to be a tough guy, I said to myself. I hired a couple of process servers to stand in front of the store and served every customer with a copy of the order. The debtor chased away the process servers. I told them to stand across the street and make themselves visible. That, among everything else, did it. The debtor, quite solvent, filed a Chapter 11, and after months later was dismissed on the condition of payment.

Chapter 31

Collecting from Movie Stars and Music Idols

Welcome to a crash course on movie and music residuals and royalties. Movie stars are entitled to residuals from the exhibition of their movies, which might last over the years or even decades. The studios pay the continuing residuals to the Screen Actors Guild (SAG), which routinely disburses the funds. Megastars walk away with big money, and the "little people" rake in three-figure checks, or even less. No matter the amount, the choke point is the SAG. Before serving a garnishment or assignment order on SAG, the studio owes the residual directly to the stars. Lay a garnishment or assignment order on the studio, and, absent any impediment, the residual will come your way.

Let's start with the tale of O. J. Simpson, who enjoyed a fair movie career. He starred in multiple versions of *Naked Gun*, *The Towering Inferno*, *Capricorn One*, *The Frogman*, and other bits and pieces. He was a member of SAG and entitled to movie residuals. IMDb offers the screen bibliography for every movie star and director and identifies the movie studio that produced the movie. The movie studio pays the residuals. After some fits and starts, Fred Goldman latched onto O. J.'s movie residuals courtesy of an assignment order that assigned to Goldman all of O. J.'s movie residuals. Without too much effort, we developed a list of every movie studio, and, bolstered by the information available through IMDb, we served the assignment order of everybody or anybody who might owe for the movie residuals, which included Paramount. Mind you, this was not too tough because O. J. had a modest catalogue and his big hits, which still appear on cable, were the *Naked Gun* movies. The checks from Paramount for O. J.'s residuals are really pretty.

Music idols ("artist" is another expression) are no different. Depending upon their status (owner of the song, performer, etc.), the artist is entitled to royalties. American Society of Composers, Authors and Publishers (ASCAP), Broadcast Music, Inc. (BMI), Society of European Stage Authors and Composers (SESAC), and others collect royalties arising out of the use of the composition, performance rights, and other rights, and pay over the royalties to the artist or agent for the artist. EMI Music publishing, Harry Fox Agency,

Universal Music Publishing Group, and Warner Chappell might likewise collect royalties due the artists or their agents. The rights due artists (or agents) are performance rights, mechanical royalties (i.e., record sales), digital performance rights, and foreign rights, among other rights. The recording label might owe money to the artists or in many cases the talent agency who represents the debtor ("the artist"). Serve the agent for moneys due the debtor. Defining these rights is helpful because you need to specify the obligation that is garnished, or assigned. Serving a subpoena upon the talent agent for the artist, the paying party (such as ASCAP, BMI etc.), and third parties would be helpful in refining what rights are garnished or assigned.

What about live venues? Where is the money, and how is the artist paid? If the artist is a mid-to major celebrity, the artist has retained a talent agent, lawyer, or third-party representative who books the events for the artist anywhere between six months to a year in advance. Depending upon the status of the artist, the agent will demand a guaranty equal to anywhere between 50 percent and 100 percent of the event fee, which is usually a percentage of the door. William Morris, CAA, and others have standardized contracts, wire instructions, and a very structured protocol in representing artists. Prepayment likewise applies in other entertainment venues, including television, movies, theater, and live venues given the status of the artist. Payment is typically due on the signing of the contract, and rarely upon performance unless the parties bargain for some type of "back end" revenues. Once the funds come into the hands of the agent, the agent will take its share and disburse the rest to the artist, or more likely a limited liability company serves as a conduit for the artist. Sometimes the agent will disburse to the artist's lawyer or accountant to hold the funds and pay monies over when requested. Expect multiple levels.

Reaching these funds requires a garnishment or an assignment order directed at the talent agent, who is probably holding a power of lawyer (lawyer-in-fact for the artist) and therefore would be the person who physically receives the funds. The garnishment order would reach also any funds in the hands of the special LLC and the lawyer (if known) to reach any funds in which the artist has a beneficial interest. Serving the venue might be somewhat productive but not too likely because the venue (or the promoter) is usually paying the talent agent and not the artist.

If the artist is a low-level celebrity and might not even have an agent, the venue (or promoter, if the case) would not offer a guaranty but would pay at the conclusion of the live event and usually in cash. Local bars and entertainment venues that host local and unknown bands fall into this category. The artists (or band) get the lion's share of the door, and the bar makes money on the liquor sales. Compliance with tax laws is a luxury and not a necessity. Reaching the funds would require a garnishment or assignment order to reach the payout due the artist and service upon the bar owner who is more accessible at 1:00 a.m., not 1:00 p.m. A garnishment might fail because typically a garnishment only reaches the any debt that is immediately due the judgment debtor. An assignment order reaches debts due the debtor (the artist) now and in the future, including debts that are conditional or contingent. An assignment orders debts owed to the debtor, which are conditional or subject to precedent and might include the payoff due from the venue. Serve the venue with an assignment order to reach the "door proceeds," which are payable to the artist. Likewise serve the agent (talent agent), if any, for the artist who might succeed in wresting the funds from the venue. Better yet, most bars and venues promote the artists at least for a week or more before the event, which offers sufficient time to serve the bar or venue owner with the assignment order.

How about a moment of cleverness. Google is your bird dog, detective, and scout. How so? Open Google now, and look at the top bar, slightly to the left. You will see News. Open News. Give it about 10 seconds. You will see a large space bar. Type in the name of the artist (Taylor Swift, etc.), and see what happens. You will get the following: "Add "Taylor Swift" section to my Google News homepage. Add Ms. Swift to your Google News Homepage. Voilá! You will get a daily report on news that features Ms. Taylor, which will include all upcoming concerts. With a little more effort you can find Ms. Taylor's booking agent and email the agent to put you on her concert list.

Of course many artists, ranging from the fellow who sells CDs out of the trunk of a car to someone who fills a Las Vegas venue, ride herd over social media, particularly an active Twitter feed and over active FaceBook page. If the artist performs at a live venue, the promoter of the event, or venue owner, typically pays the artist's booking agency, which in turn pays the artist. In some cases, an accountant, lawyer, or a limited liability company intercept the payments and redirect them to the artist.

The booking agencies (talent agencies, etc.) maintain an active web presence that features the artists. In some instances, the promoter might pay the artist directly. In many cases, the booking agent might be paid in advance of the performance. The number of major agencies that represent famous celebrities are less than a dozen. Lay an assignment on all of them. You might spring some money loose.

The U.S. Copyright Office might list the artist as the owner of the copyright, which is very helpful when seeking to identify what royalties are due the artist. The garnishment, or assignment order, might well reach the rights, which are described as follows: "Right to payment of money, revenues, stream of income, incomes from any musical composition, performance, digital right, or licensing thereof, any rights to income, accounts receivable, accounts, funds in escrow, and general intangibles." Add to his description the names of the obligor, such as ASCAP or BMI, the label, the promoter, the booking or talent agent, or the lawyer. Another option is to state "all rights to payment of money . . . that arise from the use, exploitation, sale, licensing, performance of the judgment debtor, otherwise from the following copyrighted properties, performance of the judgment debtor, licensing of any rights by the judgment debtor, or any other rights of the judgment debtor."

Chapter 32

Big Men Make Big Mistakes, Get Themselves into a World of Hurt, and How to Hide the Money

My favorite movies are *Lawrence of Arabia* first and *Casablanca* second. Omar Sharif made himself an international star and appeared in many blockbuster movies, such as *Funny Girl* with Barbra Streisand. He also spent a considerable amount of time in Hollywood. On June 11, 2005, he was dining with friends in Beverly Hills, had one drink too many, and after dinner exited the restaurant to retrieve his car. He only had a 20 Euro note, which was more than adequate for the parking charge, but the parking lot attendant refused to take the Euro note. Sharif became belligerent and punched out the attendant, who immediately called the Beverly Hills police, who arrested Sharif. Sharif pled guilty to battery, which should have ended the matter. The attendant hired lawyers who sued and won a $318,190 judgment. The case comes to us, and we are now collecting Sharif's movie money through an assignment order.

Getting Omar Sharif's royalties in my hands was an enormous hoot, given that I am a great fan of the movie *Lawrence of Arabia*. Getting the case in my hands was easy, easy compared to getting paid the judgment. If any of you are chasing any celebrities, sports figures, or entertainers of any type, they routinely form limited limitability companies that warehouse their "name, image, story, likeness, talent," etc.). The LLC enters into the contract with the producer who, in turn, pays the LLC. These entities are called FBOs ("for the benefit of") or FSOs ("for the services of"). For example, you would see a contract with a star in the name of the star's LLC. The LLC licenses on an irrevocable basis, but for a limited purpose, the star's name, likeness, story, image, voice, necessary in the making of the movie. The contract might read "Dawn Company LLC," for the benefit of "JOE BIG STAR." The studio writes a check payable to the order of "Dawn Company LLC for the benefit of Joe Big Star," or "for the services of (FSO)." The FSO and FBO monikers imply the existence of the limited liability company, which is the conduit that receives payment from the studio and channels the money directly to the star, or agent, in a circuitous path that hinders or delays enforcement. A levy on the studio might not reach the fees or residuals due the star because these amounts are payable to the limited liability company.

For years, we collected M. C. Hammer's music royalties on an assignment order. That was an interesting experience. The court gave me a broad-based assignment order reaching M. C. Hammer's royalties from his postbankruptcy music. If you don't know the story, I can tell you M. C. Hammer's life story in a few sentences. He was truly a heroic figure who started with near nothing and rose to the top of the pop charts. He was a groundbreaking artist, enjoyed a wonderful reputation, and exuded first-rate charm. His only flaw was that he didn't know when to stop. As the urban legend goes, he built a monstrosity of a house in the Fremont Hills. Fremont is on the East Bay of the San Francisco Bay Area, and about midway between Oakland and San Jose. Fremont is primarily a suburban town that caters to the local business community consisting of manufacturing and distribution. Fremont is very nice and is what you would call an upper-middle-class or middle-class neighborhood. Building a multimillion-dollar home in the Fremont Hills was insane. Whether the home or some other seismic event took M. C. Hammer down, I do not know, but M. C. Hammer filed bankruptcy, and the trustee captured his music catalogue, which was worth millions. I represented one of the creditors whose claim arose postbankruptcy, and I spent almost 10 years collecting his music royalties. We served the order on ASCAP and BMI, among others, and ended up with thousands a year cash flow. That was certainly better than nothing. I did learn that when you chase down a celebrity, the first place to look is the U.S. Copyright Office, as the celebrity might well own valuable copyrights. If the celebrity is a TV or movie star, you can latch onto their residuals, as we did with O. J. Simpson and Omar Sharif.

Chapter 33

You Gotta Make Them Believe

Are we done? No, you. You can march down the field of frenetic enforcement. You can fax the assignment order to the debtor's business neighbors, lawyers, accountants, local banks, vendors, or anybody else that might have a connection. As a result of that type of action, an Ohio manufacturer came to its senses and settled a $30,000 judgment.

The cell phone tower manufacturer is my favorite. Judgment in hand, I called the lawyer for the debtor. Both the debtor and the lawyer were located in Louisiana. Polite as punch, I got the lawyer on the phone. After the pleasantries, the call went like this: "Is the defendant going to pay?" "No, we are in Louisiana. No." I served the assignment motion. "Is your client going to pay?" "No, we are in Louisiana. I got the order." "Is your client going to pay?" "No. We are in Louisiana. No." I sent the assignment order to all phone companies, cell providers, and telecommunications carriers who might want to construct a cell phone tower. It was a mass mailing. I got a very angry phone call. The lawyer told me that my letter was misleading, which was not true. Okay. I rewrote the letter and told the reader that the debtor's lawyer called and complained about the contents, and therefore I made everything clearer. No problem. I copied the lawyer and put his name, address, and phone number at the bottom. I hit one of the Baby Bells who owed big money to the debtor. The accounts payable lady was very nice. "Well, we have your letter, and we owe a very large sum of money to the manufacturer, and what is the total due you?" Yes, I got paid. I also got a very unhappy phone call from you know who.

Be careful when engaging in a mass serve of assignment orders. Not everyone takes that lying down. Some folks might show up at your door, and this isn't the Fuller Brush Man. Rest assured, nobody younger than 40 has ever seen a Fuller Brush Man, and nobody younger than 25 has ever heard of the Fuller Brush Man.

Despite what the banker's association and their lawyers will tell you, an assignment order should reach the bank accounts. A bank account is debt that is owed by the bank to its customer and payable on demand through the presentment of a check, wire transfer request, or personal appearance to withdraw funds in cash (the title of these accounts is DDA, or demand deposit account). An assignment order reaches all funds owed to the debtor, which likewise would include all funds owed by the bank to its customers. Banks deplore these orders because nothing stops a judgment creditor from mass mailing an assignment order to every bank, and I mean hundreds or thousands. This discussion is somewhat moot in California because as of January 1, 2013, for all banks that have more than nine branches, a levy on one branch is a levy on every branch. This is a big deal. A levy on the 10 largest banks reaches probably 1,000 branches (a little guesswork here).

Sending out 1,000 assignment orders and bagging the debtor's accounts receivable is more treasure.

Here is another one: "Your honor. I have completed the debtor's examination. The debtor admits that he has $20 on him. Please direct the defendant to turn over the $20 to the judgment creditor." Judge: "Turn over the $20 to Mr. Cook." The debtor: "I need the money for gas." Judge: "What do you drive?" The debtor: "A Toyota." Judge: "Where do you live?" Debtor: "Windsor." Judge: "How far is that?" Debtor: "30 miles." Judge: "Give Mr. Cook the $20. And Mr. Cook will give you change of $5. That should be enough for gas money." The debtor sent payment to me overnight. The judgment amounted to $30,000, but the check was $29,985.

How about retrieving the documents you seek from the debtor? Might the preceding line of questioning work? Let's try this one for size. "Were you served with this subpoena for records?" "Yes, I guess." "I show you this subpoena, marked Exhibit 'A.' Do you see that you are obligated to bring today the bank statements?" "I guess so." "Did you bring the bank statements with you today?" "No." "Why not?" "I did not think that I had to." "Why was that?" "I don't know." "Mr. Smith, that's not an answer. That's an evasion. You are here under court order to answer questions and provide documents. This is not a deposition. Do you understand that?" "I am not sure. Am I?" "The law compels you to answer these questions truthfully. You are not giving me an answer. Here is your choice. I can hit the reset button here and we can start all over again, and you can start to answer these questions. Or you and I are going to appear before the judge and I will ask the judge to toss you in jail until you answer the answers. You can spend the next few hours with me, or spend your time in jail with someone else who finds you exceedingly attractive, notwithstanding the similarity of your gender. Enjoy yourself. By the way, your choice to answer the questions, or find yourself in jail. Sit here or sit there, I don't care." Trust me, you will get your answer, absent some nutcase on the other side of the table.

Chapter 34

The Creditor's Suit

A judgment creditor can file a lawsuit directly against the obligor of the debtor for the purpose of having the obligor pay the judgment creditor and not the judgment debtor. Some states freely allow this remedy, whereas others bar this remedy, unless and until other enforcement emedies are exhausted. A creditor's suit imposes a lien on the obligation owed to the judgment debtor and gives the creditor a lien interest in the debt. Moreover, with some effort and expenses the creditor can enjoin (stop) the third party from payment to the debtor. However, absent some collusion between the third-party obligor and the debtor, the service of the creditor's suit suspends the account owed to the debtor. Better yet, the relationship between the third party and the debtor goes in hiatus because the third party has no interest in becoming intertwined with the personal misery of the debtor (a vendor of the third party). In some, the service of the lawsuit, which announces the fact that the debtor has suffered a judgment, might even be grounds to terminate the debtor as a vendor and bring to bear enormous pressure upon the debtor to settle and to settle very soon.

Let's ratchet up the pressure some more. Remember, this is a business in instilling fear and dread in the heart of the debtor, and even the third party. Be polite but firm. No, be a fanatic. Before you sue every one of the debtor's customers, serve the debtor with the order of examination (OEX). The service of the OEX imposes a lien on the debtor's property no matter where located. This OEX lien offers you a stand alone lien, which means that you announce to the customer, whom you just sued, that the account owed to the debtor is secured by the creditor's lien. Absent a foolhardy customer, or someone aligned with the debtor, most customers now facing the butt of a lawsuit, claims of security from suit itself, and a liens from a valid legal process, are going to lock down the account. Why wade into a quagmire?

Does the locked down account do the creditor any good? Well, yes and no. This does quite a bit of good because the debtor does not have access to the funds and suffers a loss of income. You have now caused pain. Good job. You have inched the ball down the goal line. This is the exact mirror image of asset protection, which is to deprive the creditor access to the debtor's assets. Locking down the debtor's receivables from big customers deprives the debtor from access to its own assets. Call this tit for tat, retribution, or postdigital cosmic justice. The name does not matter, but what does matter is that the debtor is staring down the maw of financial destruction.

Let's talk about the "no," in our journey. If the third party defendant, the subject of this lawsuit, does not owe any money to the debtor, the defendant might push back and demand fees and costs. Maybe. To avoid a brushfire, accompany the lawsuit with a very polite letter that states that if no money is owed, and with some confirmation, the lawsuit will be dismissed promptly. No muss, no fuss.

The true impact is that the creditor can effectively lock down the debtor's receivables owed by customers who lack an agent for service of process in the domicile state. If the third party lacks an agent, a garnishment is tough. The creditor can reach accounts through a garnishment if and only if the creditor can serve the garnishment upon the obligor through an agent (or officer) in the domicile. This requirement of domicile service by the levying officer (the sheriff of the county) limits garnishments to obligors (the customers of the debtor) who have a local agent or officer. On the other hand, the creditor's suit reaches any customer who might be subject to the jurisdiction of the domicile state, which is a large class of potential obligors to reach.

If the judgment creditor wants to march the ball down the field, the creditor can reconstruct the debtor's entire customer base and sue all of them in one creditor's suit. Even though service of process through a process server is the norm, nothing stops the creditor from mailing the lawsuit to all of the debtor's customers, big and small, accompanied by a cover letter that accurately, truthfully, and completely describes the case. As long as the defendant in the creditor's suit is a bona fide customer of the debtor, at least a very good faith belief, the creditor is entitled to prosecute the lawsuit.

Creditor's suits are enormously corrosive. You get to sue the customers of your debtor to collect the debt owed by the customers in favor of the debtor. What does this mean in plain English? You get to name every customer in the lawsuit, serve the president of the customer, who in turn will leap out of his or her chair in total and complete shock that the customer has been named in an action solely involving one of its suppliers. Total gonzo moment. Creditor's suits are arcane and rare. Creditor's suits are expensive to defend, and, worse, the debtor owing the judgment to you probably lacks the ready financial ability to reimburse its customer's legal fees arising from the creditors suit. Federal and state law, along with common sense, prohibits you from threatening anybody, other than with a communication in furtherance of a legitimate civil right. However, the customer of the debtor, who now feels entrapped in a legal proceeding not of the customer's making, feels no such constraint and would not hesitate in "lowering the boom" on the errant supplier whose misdeeds will now cost the customer five figures in legal fees.

What is the difference between a creditor's suit and a levy upon the obligor? Answer: The creditor's suit can reach an obligor who might not have a local agent for service of process but probably does business in the domicile state.

The debtor might have entered into a contract with the third party that obligates the debtor to comply with noneconomic covenants, such as financial solvency, professional management of the business, and prompt payment of all liabilities. The fact is that a large judgment might constitute a breach of the noneconomic covenants and entitle the third party to suspend the debtor, or even terminate the contract. There is total coercion just by paying a filing fee and more treasure.

Were you lucky enough to obtain a copy of the debtor's customer list, or can you reconstruct the list by gosh and by golly? This list might offer the largest customers who owe large sums of money to the debtor. You can reach these customers with a garnishment, assuming that the customer is located in your jurisdiction. If not, you can sue the customers with a creditor's suit to reach this customer. What about the small-dollar customers who owe a few hundred to a few thousand dollars on a monthly basis. Let's say that the debtor has 500, 1,000, or 2,000 customers. At $35 a pop, plus $65 to serve the garnishment, nobody in their right mind would spend $100,000 in garnishing these small-dollar customers.

The creditor's suit might reach all sums due to the debtor at the time that the third party is sued, or maybe all sums owed by the third party for the next two years from date of service. If the answer is that the creditor suit reaches only those debts due the debtor at the time of service, nothing stops you from filing suit every month, say, on the 29th of each month, and to reach all debts that accrue at month's end. Pricey but fun.

Can you reach these small-dollar customers? Sue them all, and I mean every last one, in one creditor's suit. Name all the customers as defendants on one lawsuit, file the lawsuit, and serve the customers by mail. Enclose a nice cover letter that explains why the customer has been sued and include the accounts receivables listing from the debtor that proves that the customers owe something. Make sure that you have toll free phone and fax numbers and include your e-mail address. Expect that the customer will become irate and necessarily will want to contact the debtor and express deep anger that the customer has been a party to a lawsuit, filed in a far-off jurisdiction because the debtor refused to pay judgment. In that phone call, the customer will complain that the customer has been sued because the debtor has acted in an irresponsible manner, and that the customer might have to obtain a local lawyer at some expense and waste time in dealing with someone else's problem. Expect profanity. Expect that the customer will threaten to terminate the relationship with the customer. If the contract between the customer and debtor has a solvency clause (the debtor's solvency) the outstanding judgment is a potential breach under the contract. To enable the customer to expeditiously call the debtor and express displeasure in being named in a massive lawsuit, you should include in the cover letter to the customer the name, address, contact information, direct dial phone, cell phone (don't forget), and personal e-mail for the debtor. Don't forget to include the debtor's toll free phone and fax numbers. If you rustle up 100 customers, righteously sued, you can expect

50 irate phone calls, which is virtual picketing and community organizing. Saul Alinsky would love this.

What else will a creditor's suit offer you? Remember that information is the key in the door to unlock the debtor's treasure room. Some jurisdictions, such as California, bar unbridled discovery postjudgment and only authorize discovery if attached to the OEX. Why is this obstacle such a big deal? The answer is that the debtor might be inaccessible to compulsory discovery. The debtor might be offshore, out of state, uncooperative, or a downright liar. The debtor might resist turning over records, might have destroyed records, and might put up such a stink as to make a direct assault to reach the records financially prohibitive. If you cannot reconstruct the debtor's business and ferret out assets by using a Ouija board, you are going to saddle up with Moses and wander in the wilderness for the next 40 years and never reach the Promised Land. Don't fret now, and you need not reach for your Birkenstocks as we have a Chicken Delight solution to reach the promised land of unbridled broad-based discovery in state court. The creditor's suit opens up discovery because it is new stand-alone proceeding that entitles the judgment creditor to serve subpoenas on the debtor's other customers, banks, accountants, and lawyers. If the debtor is a brick wall, turn the car around, put the car in reverse, stick your head outside the window, take a deep breath, and go up the hill backwards. Sue every customer of the debtor, and you can launch a massive discovery campaign. You, too, will smell like fried chicken. That's really okay. You can do this.

Chapter 35

Receiverships

A receiver is a court-appointed officer who is authorized to take possession of the debtor's property for the purpose of an orderly sale. A receiver might be appointed to take possession of the debtor's farm, apartment building, professional practice, industrial facility, or unique personal property, such as artwork. Receivers are infrequent, given their enormous expense, and the necessity of retaining counsel for the receiver, and judicial sentiment that a receiver is a remedy of last resort. California law relaxed this rule, but generally receivers are rare, absent a substantial need for their participation. California Code of Civil Procedure §708.620 provides that the court can appoint a receiver as follows: "The court may appoint a receiver to enforce the judgment where the judgment creditor shows that, considering the interests of both the judgment creditor and the judgment debtor, the appointment of a receiver is a reasonable method to obtain the fair and orderly satisfaction of the judgment." No matter the flexibility afforded by the court in granting a receiver, you cannot use a receiver to eject Mother Hubbard out of her shoe sans homestead rights says *Wells Fargo Financial Leasing v. D& M Cabinets* (2009) 177 Cal App. 4th 59 (3rd Dist. 2009).

Receivers are typically bankruptcy trustees or other estate professionals. Dealt the hand that compels you to collect rent judgments? Commercial rent claims are tough. The person defaulting in rent usually crawls into bankruptcy court. The debtor can scrape by not paying nearly every other expense, except rent. Why would anyone take a rent judgment to collect? A bad round of cards, except when the judgment debtor is a contestant on *Next Iron Chef America*. You read that right. Elizabeth Falkner. She failed to pay rent on commercial space. The landlord filed suit which lead to money judgment against her. The case dropped into our lap while she was mid-cycle and beating out the better chefs. My wife and I were cheering her on. Go, Elizabeth, go. Well, she lost to Geoffery Zakarian. She shut down her two San Francisco restaurants, and her only known asset was the cookbook featuring her baking and pastry concoctions. What was the next round? A receivership motion for the cookbook, the copyright, and the recipes. The judge granted the order, and we made a deal, but only after I served the agent and publisher to pick up the book royalties. Adverse counsel told me that in partial payment of fees Ms. Falkner was giving baking lessons to his daughter. This round was a royal flush. We bought a copy of her cookbook from Amazon at retail, no less.

Postjudgment remedies allow the judgment creditor to record and file liens upon the debtor's real and personal property, encumber the debtor's lawsuit against third parties, and, as previously indicated, impose "broad blanket liens" upon the service of the OEX or third-party OEX. Sounds impressive, but sometimes only a receiver will bring home the bacon.

Nearly 30 years ago, we were chasing down an emerging high-tech company that refused to pay a $30,000 judgment. That was a lot of money then. Why the company refused to pay is beyond me. We went to court and got a receiver appointed. The receiver was an old-hand liquidator who spent an entire career taking over companies and converting their assets to cash. You can call these types of people the morticians of the business world. Right after the hearing, we drove over to the debtor's place of business with a court order authorizing our access. We gained access to the premises. At every office, we opened up the door and asked each person there if he or she had the checkbook. Each of the employees was enormously startled to see this lawyer and older man in tow literally rummaging through the place, barging into offices, and demanding the checkbook. After about 15 minutes, the debtor sobered up and paid off the judgment.

Patents, copyrights, trademarks, trade dresses, and domain names are solely reachable through a receiver. The U.S. Patent and Trademark Office lists the patents and trademarks in great detail. Most entertainment, literary, and commercial copyrighted properties are registered.

This means that a judgment creditor will have to file a motion before the judge and seek a court order appointing a receiver of the intellectual property. That doesn't sound too tough, and the Supreme Court established a receivership as the virtual sole remedy in the case of *Ager v. Murray*, 105 U.S. 126 (1881). Despite the age of this case, this is still good law. Getting a receiver of intellectual property appointed just cracks open the door for you. Assuming that you have a receivership, the question is what to do. Let's take a patent, for example. In the King's English, a patent gives the patent holder exclusive rights to an invention for a period of years. A patent does not make money by itself, but rather, it makes money by excluding others from making the same invention. A patent does make money if the patent is licensed to a manufacturer who would have the legal exclusive rights for manufacturing the product. A patent is, in effect, a right to sue others who infringe on the patent rather than something that has intrinsic value. About 80 percent of patents have no value one way or another, because the invention that is protected is not commercially viable. Postdigital, patents assume a disguised value, through patent portfolios or collections in which the collector would sue the alleged infringer whose product is subject to the patent. Silicon Valley is the home of these venture capitalists that are in possession of thousands of patents. The urban legend is that patent trolls all have offices on Sand Hill Road. The more common term is "patent troll."

If the debtor owns a patent and the court appoints a receiver, necessarily the receiver would seek to realize the value of the patent. In nearly all cases, the receiver would put the patent up for sale. In most instances, the judgment creditor would credit bid at the receiver's sale and become the owner of the patent. The judgment creditor could hold on to the patent, license the patent, or sell it outright. The buyer from the judgment creditor would pay good money for the patent only if the invention protected by the patent is commercially viable, or if the marketplace reveals another person infringing on the patent through their manufacture of a competing product. Absent indirect or even direct exploitation, the value of the patent becomes very speculative. Patents tend to be integral in the operation of a business.

Patent battles are company killers both in the outcome and expense to litigate and defend. At the time of the writing of this book, Apple was busy pulverizing Samsung and marching toward the victory line with a billion-dollar prize at the end. Patent battles tend to be "bet the company" scenarios. If the patent holder wins, the infringer is out of business. If the infringer wins the case, the patent holder is left with ashes in its hands. If the judgment creditor is serious about grabbing the patent, the judgment creditor may want to grab an intellectual properties (IP) lawyer to ensure that the legal process is perfect in ultimately titling the patent in the hands of the judgment creditor at the end of the legal process. In most infringement actions, the initial battle is the standing or title of the party seeking to recover under the infringement.

Given the high stakes in a patent battle, the infringer is going to fly speck the plaintiff's title. The slightest flaw, blemish, ding, or dent that might impair title would well derail the plaintiff and end the quest for big-money damages arising out of an infringement. For anyone contemplating law school and a career in law, forget wills and trusts and ignore insurance defense or criminal justice (absent a career dedicated to public service). Try a career in IP litigation, and particularly patent battles. Parties spend *hundreds* of millions in fees. Court filings in the *Barbie v. Bratz* fiasco suggest that total fees exceeded $250 million. The families of many lawyers attached to *Barbie v. Bratz* enjoy wonderful lifestyles. Therefore, before the judgment creditor spends a fair chunk of money in chasing down the patent, the business issue is whether or not the patent would protect an invention that is commercially viable or part of the marketplace. This might take some gumshoe work by the judgment creditor.

You can reach copyrights likewise through a receiver. Unlike a patent, a copyright might have greater value because a copyright is usually attached to a "work of art," such as a book, paintings or like image, musical compositions, songs, movies and movie scripts, video games, or virtually any other entertainment vehicle that would constitute "artwork" capable of being protected. The value in the copyright is the right of the person to sue for an infringement, but that right only has great value if the "artwork" has value in the marketplace. Therefore, in going through the entire machinery to appoint a receiver and purchase the copyright at a receiver's sale, the business issue facing the judgment creditor is whether or not the copyright protects a work of art subject to commercial exploitation.

Domain names are a close cousin to copyrights. A domain name has value given its commercial value to drive traffic to its site and, therefore, the ability of the site holder to sell goods or services or collect information. In a handful of cases, sites are valuable given their unique name, and some of the most famous are Sex.com, Money.com, Wallstreet.com, Flowers.com, and Dentists.com. These domain names, given their simplicity and clear message, have a stand-alone value beyond basic commercial exploitation. Other domain names have value because they attract traffic. Should your debtor own a domain name that is similar to the judgment creditor's business, that domain name would have enhanced value, given the ability of the judgment creditor to oust from the marketplace a competitor, or that the traffic going to the judgment debtor's domain name would be redirected to the judgment creditor. On the other hand, a domain name, such as SmithJonesJonesSmithLegalTeam@yahoo.com has no value. Again, before going through the expense from the receiver to the receiver's sale, you have to test the water to see if the domain name is worth anything.

The enforcement of a judgment should generate payment of the judgment by extracting from the judgment debtor property and subjecting it to sale through the judicial process. That's the whole point of this business. Does that sound about right to you? It should, but that's not complete. The more subtle answer is that the enforcement separates property from the debtor in which the property has intrinsic value to the debtor, that the property would be too expensive or impossible to replace, or that the property in and of itself would have great value to the creditor only by the fact that the creditor grabbed it from the debtor. The fact of separation itself can be very painful to the debtor. Do you intuit from this discussion that part of enforcement is to cause, or threaten to cause, pain and suffering upon the judgment debtor if you succeed in separating the debtor from the debtor's property? I hope so, and the fact of an involuntary separation, at the hands of a uniformed sheriff or marshal, can be absolutely catastrophic in a debtor's life. Intellectual properties, and particularly domain names, are very personal to the debtor, and extracting them from the debtor and cycling them through a receiver's sale and in the hands of the judgment creditor can cause enormous grief and pain. Taking other property, such as heirlooms, artwork, cars, office equipment, coins, watches, jewelry, or personal mementos, can cause great pain and discomfort. The fact that the debtor knows that the debtor is vulnerable to such enforcement and that the judgment creditor has the stomach, and paid up insurance policy to prosecute this strategy, might get the case settled. Maybe.

Trademarks are different than patents and copyrights. Let's review. A patent gives the patent holder the exclusive right to an invention. A copyright gives the holder exclusive ownership of a work of art. A domain name is nothing more than a exclusive nom de plume in the electronic age to the debtor. On the other hand, a trademark is a mark, symbol, artwork, sign, logo, or anything that identifies or distinguishes goods or services from other goods or services in the marketplace. One of the most famous trademarks is the Nike swoosh. The swoosh identifies the tennis shoes as the Nike brand.

The best example is purses. We are going shopping for a birthday gift for your wife. Purses are status symbols, accessories, or just leather bags that hold a bunch of stuff. What is the difference between the utilitarian pockets of one purse as opposed to another? Not much, despite the probable torrent of e-mails accusing me of fashion ignorance, purchasers distinguish one purse from another. Why? The brand name of the purse. Chanel runs through its entire stock of $1,000 handbags at Christmas, whereas Wal-Mart discounts its $50 bags on December 26.

Unlike patents and copyrights, a trademark cannot be sold detached from the goods or services associated with the mark or, alternatively, with the related goodwill. What does this really mean? The holder of a trademark cannot sell, license, or give away the mark unless the mark is attached to the goods or services associated with the mark. The technical term for the trademark mavens is called a transfer in gross. This is a pretty fancy way of saying, "You can't detach the trademark from the goods or services."

You should read *Marshak v. Green*, 746 F.2d 927 (2nd Cir. 1984). There is a big body of law in this area, and if you Google *Marshak* or "transfers in gross," and have a cup of coffee in hand, you can spend a lovely afternoon becoming an expert in this area. This is very interesting reading because you will learn that the purpose of the trademark is to communicate to the consumer that the mark is associated with the goods or services, and presumably ascribe value, uniqueness, or some special characteristic that is appealing to the consumer.

Every time I write about trademarks, I just feel smarter. This came from an even funnier joke. Two women spend the afternoon at the Museum of Modern Art in New York, as depicted in a cartoon in *The New Yorker* magazine. In the cartoon, you can see that these are very high-society ladies. One lady says to the other, "I just feel smarter walking through the place."

You should also read *Vittoria North America LLC v. Euro-Asia Imports Inc.*, 278 F.3d 1076 (10th Cir. 2001). This case is important because the court upheld an assignment if the assignee of the mark is producing a product or performing a service similar to the assignor and those consumers would not be deceived or harmed. The court clearly explained that the assignment will be upheld if the mark is attached to similar goods or services. What does that mean in the enforcement business? If the judgment creditor is in the hotdog business and has a mark in the shape of a hotdog and a bun, the judgment creditor could grab the mark, through a receiver, and use the mark in the operation of its own business. Clearly, this would not work if the judgment creditor is in the shoe business and the judgment debtor is in the hotdog business.

Are you interested in more bizarre examples? My only grief over this case is that it's not mine. The plaintiff sues defendant. The plaintiff gets tossed. The defendant wins big fees. The plaintiff appeals but doesn't get a bond. The defendant wants to collect and, better yet, dump the appeal. The stage is set. The defendant enforces the judgment against the plaintiff's right of an appeal. Through legal process (in Utah), which included a sheriff's sale, the defendant, with the big-money judgment in hand, acquired the plaintiff's right of appeal. With the right of appeal in hand, the defendant appears in the appellate court and files a dismissal of the appeal. Did you get that? The defendant, with the money judgment in hand, bought the plaintiff's right of appeal and dismissed it. The court's opinion is worth reading. (I am going to do some slight editing to get to the point.)

> We recognize the circumstances of this case present a degree of discomfort. . . [No kidding. Flushing the appeal down the toilet for a few bucks at a sheriff's sale would undermine any appeal. Utah law changed, but so what. What a tour de force.] Despite such concerns, we are unable to ignore the fact that a public execution sale took place in which Defendants purchased Plaintiff's legal right to continue this appeal for $10,000." *RMA Ventures California v. SunAmerica Life Ins. Co.* (10th Cir. 2009) 576 F.3d 1070, 1075–1076.

The appellate court was beside itself in dismissing the appeal at the hands of the judgment creditor who snapped up the appellate right through a sheriff's sale. Whether or not this case is good law is not important. What is conceptually important is that any judgment creditor could disentitle ("kicked to the curb" is the vernacular) a judgment debtor from appellate rights by acquiring the right of an appeal through legal process. The sheriff's sale is off the beaten path, and more likely the remedy would be a motion for appointment of receiver. Even the bankruptcy courts authorize the sale of appellate rights. You also may want to take a look at the case of *In re Mozer*, 302 B.R. 892 (C.D., Cal. 2003). In that case the trustee sold off the debtor's appellate rights, and the district court affirmed in holding under California law that appellate rights are property. Whether *RMA Ventures California v. SunAmerica Life Ins. Co.* is good law is another matter; however, Utah did change its postjudgment laws. More interesting is that the Salt Lake City deputy constable, not the U.S. marshal, executed upon the judgment in federal court.

Let me provide you with the keys to the kingdom. Your debtor has a domain name, say, AmericaTrucking.com. Your debtor also owns a registered trademark of America Trucking, Inc., in which the distinctive characteristics are red, white, and blue coloring, and an American eagle background. First, you move to appoint a receiver of *both* the trademark and the domain name. With any luck, you will find a buyer that will continue with the debtor's services, which are identified by the trademark. The buyer would own *both* the trademark and domain name. The buyer could effectively change its name. While the debtor might continue its business, the debtor necessarily would have to change its name, website address and name, and forfeit the trademark in light of the buyer's purchase of the trademark and domain name. This receivership motion would eviscerate the debtor's goodwill and going concern value. Facing this threat, most debtors would capitulate rather than face total destruction. Likewise, the motion for appointment of a receiver of the domain name, trademark, patents, copyrights (if attached to other intellectual property) is the *Merrimack* and *Monitor* war winner. The adage of that story: Pound and pound against the weakest armor on the ship's side until the cannon balls smash through and sink the ship.

Chapter 36

Abracadabra Jurisdiction

Intellectual property is the toast of the town. Unlike 30 years ago, today many businesses, no matter how common, frequently own a trademark (Ray's Pizza), domain names (nearly everybody), copyrights (key business material); (nearly universal), and, if a high-tech business of any type, a bushel of patents. A debtor might own a trademark, patent, copyright, a 1-800 number, and a domain name, all of which are related to each other, and, more importantly, they may represent the core of the business. You can find the patents and trademarks from the U.S. Patent and Trademark Office; you can find the domain name through Go Daddy, Google, or any other search engine and the copyright through the U.S. Copyright Office or by simply examining the debtor's written materials. This intellectual property is the core of the debtor's business.

Do you want to collect? That's easy. File a motion for appointment of receiver of the trademark, patent, copyright, domain name, and maybe the 1-800 number. These are called vanity numbers. Stuff these items in one motion, promptly file it, and proceed. Few debtors (or no debtors) could survive the appointment of a receiver of the intellectual property that is the core of their business. Call this a nuclear option, and if the motion is granted, the debtor either will file bankruptcy or write you the big check. There is virtually no exit, if at all, from these receivership orders if the debtor loses. The debtor faces nuclear winter.

As with every good solution, there is a backdoor escape. Most courts require anywhere between a 15- and a 33-day turnaround on a motion. This means that the debtor has between 15 and 30 days to respond to a motion such as this. In the enforcement of a judgment, this time period is an eternity. The debtor can easily transfer all of these assets to a related entity, create a new corporation or LLC to cloak these assets, or encumber these assets with some type of security interest. One way or another, don't expect the debtor to lay supine and run all over the debtor, turning the debtor into hamburger. This is not going to happen.

Let's go backwards. In a prior chapter, we told you that the filing and service of a debtor's examination order creates a lien upon the debtor's assets. Other states likewise provide for a broad-based lien on the debtor's assets. If you are going to charge up San

Juan Hill to breach the trademark, patent, copyright, 800 telephone number and domain name in one swoop by way of a receivership, serve the debtor with an order of examination (OEX) ASAP, that will encumber all of the debtor's assets. The OEX lien locks down all assets. If the debtor, as you expect, transfers these assets before the receiver is appointed, these assets would be transferred subject to a lien, and readily recovered against a transferee, who is usually the debtor cloaked in another name.

How do you reach these assets that are clearly a fraudulent conveyance subject to your execution lien and, moreover, subject to the receivership order? That's a good question. Do you have to file a brand-new expensive lawsuit and cycle through years of misery, including unbelievable expense before your judge slams down the gavel and says that the conveyance was fraudulent and that the assets must be turned over to the receiver? The answer is probably no. Serve the conveyee (the debtor's successor) who is probably an LLC, corporation, or family member, and who took title to the assets with a third-party OEX, and hail this purported third-party into court. Come to the hearing prepared, certified papers in hand, with a plan in mind and prepared orders in hand, and your courage skewed to the sticking post, along with a court reporter in tow. Sit there and grind at the conveyee (who is really your debtor masked in another LLC), and go through step by step the transfer of the assets. At the end of the hearing, drag the debtor in front of the judge, with the court reporter, and have the court reporter read into the record each one of your questions and each of the answers. At the end of the examination, and assuming that the transfer was subject to your execution lien, without any consideration at all, from the debtor to an entity created by the debtor, the judge will set aside the conveyance, and hand the assets over to the creditor. Voilá. You win, without filing a brand-new lawsuit. You must, and I repeat, you must be extremely well prepared, and have in hand an order, trial brief, and receiver in tow. Be quick, be nimble, jump over the fraudulent conveyance candlestick.

Facing a large judgment and nasty enforcement, the debtor cycles the real property through a half dozen conveyances. Think of the transfers in terms of badminton when the property flies like the birdie from one player to another. The plaintiff takes umbrage and moves for the appointment of a receiver of the property. The conveyees, who are the surrogates for the debtor, appear at the hearing and grouse that the plaintiff seeks to trample on their rights as owners of the property. The judge orders the plaintiff to file a fraudulent conveyance action in civil court and work it out, or the judge can call the conveyees' bluff and set the "kit and caboodle" for trial within 30 days. "I'll give you a chance to prove your ownership. Be prepared to bring in your witnesses and you will have your trial." The technical term is insta-jurisdiction. Everyone goes to trial.

Chapter 37

Passive Liens

Passive liens are liens on personal and real property. Filing a JL-1 lien with the secretary of state gets you a lien on personal property. A JL-1 is the cousin to a UCC Financing Statement, which is filed with the secretary of state to notify the world of the creditor's security interest in personal property. A UCC-1 is a JL-1 look alike. Think of Tweedle Dee and Tweedle Dum. Recording an abstract of judgment gets you a lien on the real property. Serving an OEX (debtor's exam) gets you a lien on personal property. Serving a third-party OEX gets you a lien on the third-party obligation. Serving a creditor's suit on the third party gets you a lien on the debt owed by the third party. Serving a charging order motion gets you a lien on the interest of the debtor in the partnership. Serving effective execution creates an execution lien. You can lien the crap out of your debtor. This advice will get you within yards of the goal line of enforcement.

However, unrecorded instruments, such as grant deeds and deeds of trust, take priority over recorded abstracts of judgment. *Bank of Ukiah v. Petaluma S. Bank* (1893) 100 Cal. 590; *Wells Fargo Bank v. Pal Investments Inc.* (1979) 96 Cal. App. 3d 431; *Boye v. Boerner* (1940) 38 Cal. App. 2d 567, 570; *Livingston v. Rice* (1955) 131 Cal. App. 2d 1, 2–3. The prior unrecorded deed or mortgage crushes the subsequently recorded abstracts.

These cases are worth reading (and online) because they teach that the debtor can execute a legitimate grant deed to a bona fide buyer, who can secret the document in the kitchen drawer and record the instrument and beat out the previously recorded abstract of judgment. This scenario assumes that the prior sale or lien is genuine and bona fide. The fact of the previously executed and unrecorded lien is very suspicious, and few would take this defeat lying down. Consider a fully notarized grant deed a wooden stake in the heart the ambitious creditor.

Do you want to make sure that your lien sticks to the property? If an abstract of judgment, purchase a litigation guaranty (another fancy word for a title report). Title companies are run by very smart people who worry that their customer or others can easily manipulate a title with hidden or unrecorded deeds. In buying a litigation guaranty, you will note the "effective date" "date through," or "Good through" date. What does this mean? The title company is only giving you a "snapshot" of the title as of a certain date, which is typically two to three weeks prior to the current date. Therefore the litigation guaranty is "ancient history" and does not intend to disclose the state of the title within the last two to three weeks. Why is this important? If you are chasing down the debtor, and the debtor is presumptively aware of this, the debtor is prone to transferring the property at or near the time that you are going to record your abstracts. Weeks, days, hours, and minutes count in this race. Chances are that the debtor sought to frustrate your efforts literally on the eve of the recording of your liens. If you don't know what happened in the last two weeks, you don't know anything. Call the title company and have them "date down" the title report to the current date. Or go online and see what got recorded. The online records of most recorders are very accurate and up to date. By the way, the buzzword is demanding that the title company "date down" the title report to the current date. Remember that most recorders are online. These online sites are accurate up to about 24 hours. With a smartphone and access to recorder grantor/grantee website that enables you to ferret out intervening liens and you can get ready to close the deal. Now you know what to do before you affix your name to the contract.

Another passive lien is a lien on a lawsuit. This might work. The judgment creditor can file a lien on the debtor's lawsuit, but the debtor might be motivated to work a "side deal" with the plaintiff for the purpose of defeating the creditor's lien. Remember the Middle East expression: The enemy of my enemy is my friend. Consider intervening in the lawsuit that would provide you with a seat at the counsel's settlement table. If you don't get a seat at the table, expect to get thrown under the table and forfeit any recovery at the hands of the rapacious debtor and a very conniving defendant in the lawsuit.

If the judgment debtor is a creditor of another debtor on a judgment, act aggressively to levy on the judgment itself, and levy the debtor's interest in the judgment by service of a garnishment on the judgment; serve a third-party debtor's examination, assignment order, and third-party lawsuit on the judgment debtor. Even though this levy is not quite a passive lien, at least you should be able to reach the proceeds of the judgment. You can always file a creditor's suit to reach the proceeds due under the judgment.

Chapter 38

Remedies

Reaching Embezzled Money

If you have suffered a loss because the debtor embezzled from you, swindled you, or took money arising out of a trust relationship, you can sue for more than just money. You can sue for a constructive trust, which is a remedy that seeks to impose upon the debtor's assets a lien to ensure payment to you. You can sue for unjust enrichment. You can seek an order tracing your property, such as money, into what the debtor has as "ill-gotten gains." These are all equitable remedies and entitle you to a restraining order, receiver, or injunction to effectively sequester this property pending the outcome of the case. Achieving this type of equitable relief is expensive and cumbersome, but if the debtor really stole from you and you can trace your money into the debtor's property, you might be able to tie up that property until trial.

Chapter 39

Platform Litigation Unlocks Access to Power

What does that mean? Let's talk about this. First, let's explain what the business of law is really about. Litigation means the delivery of paperwork to a judge to make a ruling, which is a fancy word for turning the wheels of power, in front of the other lawyer to ponder what the judge might do, and in front of others who are obligated to respond, such as to turn over money, produce records, or show up in court. Getting paperwork out the door and into the hands of the intended party makes a big splash or causes a tsunami. Whatever the effect, the debtor is going to feel the consequences. In collecting from a debtor and unearthing secret assets, you have to be efficient and well organized and retain the ability to pump out a lot of paper without the usual burden of starting from scratch.

The starting point is the lawsuit. The complaint seeks relief and a prayer for damages. The debtor files an answer to the lawsuit and that the plaintiff take nothing. Here you have it. The plaintiff wants money, and the defendant wants out. Conceivably, the two people who can decide whether the plaintiff gets any money, or gets nothing, are the judge and the jury. However, the real people who decide what the plaintiff gets paid, or skunked, are the parties and their lawyers. Clients and lawyers make this call based on their knowledge of the case. Sometimes this knowledge is based on the investigation into the fact of the case, the pretrial exchange of information, interviews with third parties, and exchanges between the lawyers. Cases settle for an amount that is the product of an efficient market for information. Whether the information is real or imagined is not the issue, but only that the settlement represents the total sum of all information. If the debtor claims that the debtor lacks assets, or is bankruptcy-prone and lacks any insurance, this information is fed into the hopper as part of the information cocktail.

In part, getting the lawyer for the plaintiff to talk to the judge or jury is now called platform litigation. If you, the lawyer, aren't talking to the judge or jury, you are not going to get them to sign their names to a piece of paper (i.e., the judgment) to win money or beat back the plaintiff. The settlement amount is the product of the total sum of all information, real or imagined. Of course, most cases are settled, and lawyers spend the bulk of their time talking to other lawyers about what they might say to the judge or jury on that platform as an act of intimidation or education—"I am going to win because I have evidence that will persuade the jury to award me millions." Among other purposes, platform litigation means that the entire purpose of the suit is to get the lawyer in front of the judge as the decision maker, which is the ostensible purpose. Getting there is more than physically standing up; it includes filing of papers, presenting physical evidence, and preparing.

Whatever the process, the outcome is the same: talking to the decision maker, which requires a platform. For the bulk of preliminary hearings, the judge decides the key issues on the papers (what the lawyers file), which imposes an enormous premium on the lawyers' writing skills. Federal courts routinely decide the matters on the "papers," and lawyer appearances for the routine pretrial motions are not guaranteed. Spelling counts and so does first-rate scholarship.

Postjudgment platform litigation also enables the judgment creditor to easily launch hundreds, or thousands, of subpoenas, a dozen assignment motions, a heap of receivership motions, to serve OEXs on everyone that creeps, crawls, moves and slithers, and to levy every bank in a five-mile radius. We are going to talk about baking pies and whether the pie tasted just as good if cooked at 57 minutes as opposed to 60 minutes. I can't tell the difference and better yet, every oven is different. The fact that the creditor can launch a massive campaign, even marred by imperfect, but not fatally flawed paper, is part of the Efficient Market Hypothesis. The debtor perceives an onslaught of motions, levies, liens, and examinations orders, and hundreds of subpoenas directed to third-parties customers. At some point, the debtor and lawyer no longer focus on whether the paperwork is perfect, good grammar and correct spelling have been used, or the staple is in the upper-left-hand corner. Coffee stains don't matter. After the 400th subpoena directed to the probable customers, somebody is going to pick up the phone. Or not. Just calling upon the debtor's counsel and stating that another 200 subpoenas are going out the door adds to the mix of information. Remember that, as discussed earlier, this is not extortion. Extortion is the threat of revelation or the accusation of a crime or wrongful conduct as a threat to compel payment of money, even though money is owed, and the threat might be lawful on its face. Saying that you will subpoena everyone doing business with the debtor to unearth any account and accounts receivables for purpose of a levy is the core of enforcement and not the revelation of a secret or disclosure of a shameful act. The message here: Better to get competent product out the door every day than super shiny product any day.

Chapter 40

Confirmation of Liens and Levies

Despite anyone's politics, President Reagan had a quick wit. You might not see his image on a dime or Mount Rushmore, but his witticisms have entered the American lexicon. "Trust but verify" is more than a catch phrase; it is a policy, military, and business imperative. In enforcement of judgments, this phrase is your mantra. You filed and recorded liens with the secretary of state, county recorders, and maybe elsewhere. The debtor lacks any liquid assets, which means that payment comes to you when the debtor sells or liquidates an asset. The usual suspects are the sale of real estate, subject to the recorded abstract, or the sale of the business, subject to the filed personal property lien.

How do you know that the liens were properly indexed that a third party, such as a buyer, would find them in doing a search? Forget the fact that the lien bears a filing or recording stamp. The answer is to run a search under the name of the judgment debtor as if you were a potential buyer. You would run a search under the name of the individual names of the judgment debtor, the trade name, the corporate or LLC name (if any), and all derivations and spellings. Put yourself it the position of the buyer to ensure that your liens appear in a third-party search.

You can search for the filed personal property by running a UCC search through the secretary of state. Commercial searches provide this service for less than a $100. Westlaw, D&B, LexisNexis, and others provide similar search features. The secretary of state is online and searchable for free or for a small fee. Other than Los Angeles, most county recorders are online. Title companies offer lot book guaranties, litigation guaranties, title reports, and similar products that show the recorded liens, and hopefully yours. The prices range from about $250 to thousands of dollars depending upon the title company, the type of product, and the amount of insurance.

Trust that your liens were filed and recorded, but verify with a title search. You will be able to sleep through the night under the blanket of third-party searches.

Chapter 41

The Boogeyman Is Coming to Get You

The Bankruptcy Preference

We are going to introduce you to bankruptcy preferences. Here is the state of the law, somewhat simplified. Absent the extreme set of facts, the bankruptcy trustee, or debtor in possession in a Chapter 11, can recover from creditor payments made to an antecedent debt, or void any liens, levies, and enforcement, if paid or undertaken within 90 days prior to the filing of bankruptcy. The major exception is that the creditor does not have to disgorge payments for the cash on delivery (COD) sales, contemporaneous exchange, or payments in the ordinary course of business. The trustee, or the debtor in possession, files these lawsuits in the bankruptcy court, which for larger cases means the bankruptcy court in Los Angeles, Chicago, New York City, or most likely Delaware. They are nice places to visit, but not to litigate.

If the debtor owes you, the debtor owes others. In plain English, if everyone rushes the debtor, the debtor will file bankruptcy. Embrace this risk or even expectation. What is the antidote, if any? Answer: Move quickly, don't dally, don't delay, and file or record liens as soon as possible to beat out the 90-day preference clock.

Preference risks, strategies, and litigation flood the Internet. Just punch up Bankruptcy Code Section 547 and you can spend a lovely afternoon becoming an expert.

Clients have a need to know. Bankruptcy preferences would unwind any enforcement within 90 days prior to filing, which would destroy the financial investment in prosecuting the enforcement strategy.

P.S. I started out as a bankruptcy attorney.

Section 9

Foolish and Very Stupid People

Chapter 1

What to Do About Jerks

You read that right. The most potent weapon in a collector's arsenal is the voice on the phone. What does that mean in plain English? Calling the debtor, writing the debtor, showing up on the debtor's doorstep, or even raising your voice at the debtor and cursing at the debtor? Read and reread the Fair Debt Collection Practices Act, both federal and state versions, and, yes, there are other limits. Don't get yourself sued if you curse at someone.

The summary of these laws: Don't call too early. Don't call too late. Don't call the employer unless to verify employment. Don't leave messages, unless "it's a personal call." Be nice. Don't be mean. Be direct. Be yourself, and not a cop, lawyer, or judge. Give the mini-Miranda warning if required. If you write letters, sanitize the envelope. Don't make claims, demands, or threats unless they are accurate, clear, and free of ambiguity. If the debtor tells you that the debtor has "lawyered-up," let it be. Be a pro. Avoid the mantra of teaching someone a lesson.

What if the debtor is a jerk or a violent jerk? The Efficient Market Hypothesis quantifies obnoxious, dangerous, menacing, or threatening phone calls. The EMH is the total sum of all knowledge that quantifies anything, i.e., risk or result. As most these individuals are interested in their own preservation and safety on all sides of the conflict divide, fostering a counterinsurgency strategy is the solution to the problem. When you receive a menacing call, this is the strategy, aside from yelling at the person:

First, say the following:

"Wait." Put the person on hold and transfer the call to an office (unless you have one already) with a speakerphone.

Second, continue the speakerphone call with your supervisor, boss, or other person in a management capacity or for that matter, anyone else. This person must be made of strong stuff and immune to fear, flight, or intimidation. Say the following to the caller. "I have transferred the call to an office with a speakerphone, and we are taping the call. My associates are present in the room, and they are also taking very copious notes. Whatever you say is being recorded. Do I have your permission to record this call?" Pause for effect. You will get a yes or no. "First, please tell me your name—and spell it out—your home address and work address, and your phone numbers where I can reach you. I need your date of birth and Social Security number so I can readily identify you. Do you have email? A Facebook page?" At about this moment, about 99 percent of the callers hang up, and you are done, and they are unlikely to ever call back. Should your caller persists, as they might, repeat lesson one but inform the caller: "You gave me your consent to record this call. I have done that. What is it you want? If you threaten me in the call, first, I am going to upload this call into YouTube, and, next, I am going to turn over this recording to the police or FBI. Have a good day." Hang up. Absent Charles Manson on the phone, this person will disappear. If Charles Manson lands on your doorstep, rethink your career choice, and do call the cops. If you are in the Deep South, Texas, or for that matter any other Red State, you can legally remind the caller that you carry. Please don't chamber a round. Even we alleged latte-loving limousine liberals know that.

Chapter 2

You Can Bluff Your Way Out

Is it important that you record the call? Yes and no. Yes, you can record the call with a smartphone, and depending on the state, you might or might not need the consent of the caller. You can use a handheld tape recorder. You can tell the caller that the call is being recorded, ask for his or her consent, and don't bother recording the call. Why not at all? You told the caller that you are legally recording the call, which escalates the caller's potential criminal liability for multiple crimes. The actual recording of the phone call, or threat to record, is a risk confronting the caller in weighing whether to continue the call or hang up. The belief by the debtor that you are recording the call might be enough to defuse the risk and eject him from the cusp of threat. Risk is weighed by the sum of all knowledge.

As long as scandalous language is not broadcast to third parties and part and parcel of a judicial proceeding, this is not actionable. "Sticks and stones might break my bones, but words will never harm me," unless you go off the grid. Why is this so? The California Supreme Court in *Rusheen v. Cohen*, 37 Cal. 4th 1048, 128 P.3d 713, 39 Cal. Rptr. 3d 516 (2006), says that the communications and conduct in the course and scope of civil litigation is privileged, as long as the communication had some connection to the litigation itself. This case is worth reading. What does this mean in plain English? If you or your lawyer call the debtor "a liar," "a big-time liar," or "an incredible liar" in court as part of the closing statement, you will not get sued for defamation. This is called the litigation privilege. You can botch a levy, file a bad proof of service, or do something equally stupid, and you will likewise get away with it. Malpractice rates for collection lawyers plummeted. *Rusheen v. Cohen* holds that communications, including postjudgment remedies, are not subject to an independent civil action.

When crazies do call, as they will in this line of work, keep in mind that most will walk away. They will call you during the day. They will call during the night. If your home phone is listed, they will call you at home. If your cell phone is listed, they will call you on the cell phone. They might lurk around your office. They might lurk around you home. As happened to me, they will break into your garage and vandalize your car. They will put nails or screws in the tires of your car or attempt to disable the car.

Chapter 3

Terror on the Kitchen Counter

"Oh. You Will Be. You Will Be."

Welcome to the new gothic horror of the legal profession. Here is the shocker. You are not immune from terror perpetrated by crazy people. Forget the riveting novels available on Amazon.com. Put aside *Dracula in the Courts,* (1897) 1 *Stoker* 1, pp. 1–200. *Rosemary's Baby,* looks cuddly compared to today's terror. Expect retaliation. Expect revenge. Expect retribution at the hands of a very deranged person. Liens are a cheap form of revenge.

Here is terror sitting in the office of the local county recorder or clerk, secretary of state, or your home mailbox waiting for your spouse to open the mail. Terror is in the face of your spouse with opened envelope lying on the kitchen counter, lien notice gripped in hand, asking you, "Are we losing our home?" The lien notice contains the address of the home, its legal description, and threats of criminal prosecution. Mirrors, necklaces of garlic, or religious symbols are useless in fending off this vampire.

Welcome to the sovereign citizens, the postdigital vampires, who attack anybody who has caused them some perceived harm, slight, wrong, or inconvenience. The weapon of choice is paper filings masquerading as liens.

For those who took Worker's Compensation as a third-year elective, a UCC is a preprinted form that requires the filer to fill in the name of the debtor, the name of the creditor, a description of the collateral, and the address for the return. The purpose of the UCC is to give notice that the secured creditor has an interest in the property of the debtor, such as a security interest, lease interest, or interest in assigned receivables. Here is the typical UCC: Lien Debtor: Jones, Jones and Jones PLC. Secured Creditor: First Bank and Trust. Collateral: "Furniture, fixtures, equipment, furnishings, accounts, accounts receivable, legal fees, bank accounts, and cash, now owned and hereinafter acquired, and proceeds." The filing fees are range from $5 to $20. Some secretaries of state allow for electronic filings.

Can Some Nutcase File Liens Against Me?

The origin of this terror is a quirk in the law of secured transactions. Article 9 of the Uniform Commercial Code permits the secured creditor to file with the secretary of state or record with the country recorder a UCC-1 without the "wet" signature of the debtor, or for that matter any proof to the filing agency that the creditor is authorized to file or record. Article 9 does not compel any verification by the secretary of state or county recorder that the secured party has a legal authority to file or record the financing statement. UCC § 9-509 (a)&(b) authorizes the creditor to file the financing statement if the debtor provided authority in the security agreement. In 99.99 percent of the cases, the debtor authorized the secured creditor to file the financing statement. The sovereign citizen filings are the 0.01 percent of unauthorized filings.

An aggrieved individual can file one or a hundred UCCs without the necessity of a court order, permission from the secretary of state or recorder, or permission from the listed "debtor's" in the filings. The fact that the debtor need not sign the UCC-1 and that no proof of authorization is required by the filing agency open the door to abuse. Nothing stops an aggrieved individual from filing or recording a UCC, which would name the client, lawyer, spouses, law firm, partners, associates, or paralegals as "debtors" in the financing statement and the aggrieved individuals who would be the "creditor." Here is a typical filing: Lien Debtor: "Jones and Jones, PLC, Fred Jones and Bob Jones, and Mary Smith Associates." Lien Creditor: "Ms. Aggrieved Defendant." Collateral: "All personal and real property" or "123 Oak Road, Anytown, Nevada 89501, and legal description of Lot 1, Block 1, Oak Street Development, Map 1, Washoe County Recorder." A recorded UCC might impose a colorable lien interest in real property. The filing or recording of these liens are predatory acts.

Disgruntled taxpayers, defendants facing collection lawsuits or enforcement, or former employees bent on retaliation for a workplace grievance are also frequent filers. Discharged employees sue for discrimination and other labor claims. To scare away witnesses and instill fear, these individuals will file liens against former supervisors, coworkers, department managers, or even the employer's lawyers. These liens terrify the lien debtors because the lien creditor identifies collateral at the personal residence of the lien debtor by street address and legal description.

The UCC is not the sole weapon. The sovereign citizen can record a Claim of Lien Affidavit with the county recorder or county clerk which appear in title reports and even credit reports. That is terrible.

These filers might file the bogus UCC with the secretary of state and moreover record the same document with the county recorder. These filings evidence a deliberate act to terrorize someone given multiple filings.

The Medium Is the Message

The sovereign citizen will ensure that the lien notice gets to the victim. Under local law, the county recorder might also mail the lien notices to the lien debtor at the address provided in the Affidavit of Lien. The envelope from the county recorder is innocuous at best, but rest assured the shock and terror befalling the victim or the spouse upon discovery of a recorded lien notice naming the victim as the putative "grantor" of their home. In other cases, the sovereign citizen will assuredly mail the lien notice, certified mail, return receipt requested, to the home address of the lien debtor and will enclose a legal-looking criminal complaint for total shock value. At first glance, the lien notice intimates that the "grantor" gave the title to their home to the sovereign citizen.

Lawyers, Clients, and Everyone Else Associated with the Filer Are All Targets

Lawyers perceive that they are immune from terror on the basis that their proclaimed image of the "chest bumping alpha" would insulate them from acts of terror ("Do you know who I am?" is the common salutation). This belief of self-imagined immunity is a false, and even dangerous, assumption and alarming in major urban jurisdictions such as Los Angeles County. The Los Angeles county recorder is the only major California recorder whose records are not readily available online, and absent effort, the lawyer would not readily know that some sovereign citizen recorded liens unless mailed by the recorder.

Will These Liens Surface?

For those lawyers whose memory of the Real Property course appears only in a rearview mirror, the county recorder maintains a current grantor/grantee index of real property transactions. For example, Mary sells her home to Joe. Mary executes a grant deed as the grantor, and Joe is the grantee. Upon recording, the recorder shows Mary as the grantor of the real property, and Joe as the grantee. For those who skipped secured transactions in law school in favor of advanced trial advocacy, the secretary of state (UCC Division) is the repository of filed financing statements. This is how a financing statement would appear: Mary Victim Lawyer as "grantor." Joe Sovereign Citizen as "grantee."

What Are the Financial and Personal Consequences of These Liens?

Bogus Liens Destroy Lawsuits

The threat of more liens intimidates parties to litigation, witnesses, lawyers, staff members of the firm, and employees of parties. Once a lien is filed against parties or lawyers, fear of additional liens metastasizes and dissuades others from participating in any facet of the litigation, including signing any papers, showing up in court, or even having names disclosed in discovery. Even though the liens are void filings, a potential participant fears any encumbrance on their home, threat of even bogus criminal prosecution, or smear of their good name.

Once this fear has permeated any litigation, key participants on behalf of a party, fearful of these personal attacks, assume an attitude of "make it go away." These liens advance the defense of any litigation borne by the sovereign citizen because the liens make prosecution of the case against them more painful, costly, and unattractive. While experienced counsel might find these liens nuisances, or barely a bump in the road to court, parties and witnesses find these liens very intimidating. These liens frighten everyone.

The Donut Hole in the Uniform Commercial Code

At best UCC § 9518(c) (now retitled effective 1/1/2014 as § 9518(e)) offers the lien debtor an opportunity to explain the bogus filing but not expunge the lien as matter of statute as follows: "The filing of a correction statement does not affect the effectiveness of an initial financing statement or other filed record." The UCC comment to original § 9518(c) tells the whole story:

> Resort to Other Law. *This Article cannot provide a satisfactory or complete solution to problems caused by misuse of the public records.* The problem of "bogus" filings is not limited to the UCC filing system but extends to the real-property records, as well. A summary judicial procedure for correcting the public record and criminal penalties for those who misuse the filing and recording systems are likely to be more effective and put less strain on the filing system than provisions authorizing or requiring action by filing and recording offices.

What does this quote mean? In the face of bogus and destructive filings, Article 9 abandons the lien debtor, on the UCC stone cold curb. The courts echo this tragic position. *In Gruber v. Tilton* CIV. 1:08-0524-JLS (2009 WL 3081829 Page *6, (E.D. Cal. 2009) aff'd, 405 Fed. Appx. 200 (9th Cir. 2010)(unpublished) the court stated as follows:

> There is no procedure for revoking or removing a UCC–1. The form stays filed over its life, typically five years, and Vasquez's office retains it for an additional year after that. A UCC–1 can be continued in a six-month window prior to its expiration date. A person can file a termination statement stating a lien has been terminated, but the original UCC–1 is still retained on record. A UCC–3 is an amendment document that can be used to continue the lien for an additional five years, to file a termination statement, to file an assignment, or to file a change in collateral. A UCC–5 is a correction statement filed by a person who believes the record is either in error or false.

Like all vampires who are undead immortals, sovereign citizens will persist, and even expand, the campaign of terror. Terror strikes fear and causes the greatest pain because terror is unexpected, unsettling, and unpredictable. Terror instills a strong sense of helplessness and vulnerability. Handling an injunction against some nutcase, a 30-year-old associate of the law firm confronts total terror in seeing her name on a recorded notice that identifies her residence, provides a legal description, and putatively imposes a lien.

These are the repercussions from this stunt. Upon coming to the office the next morning, the managing partner inquires about the associate. The office manager hands the partner an envelope from the partner. The note reads as follows: "I never thought that this job would endanger my security or property. I did not expect this. Am I being stalked? Do I need to move out of town? Did you know that this person was crazy or violent? I am resigning as a matter of personal safety. Please lift all liens against my property at your expense. I will tell all my alumni friends from law school to avoid your firm like the bubonic plague."

The UCC Excuse

Article 9 "cannot provide a satisfactory or complete solution to problems caused by misuses of public records. The problem of "bogus filings" is not limited to the UCC filings but extends to "real-property records as well" per the comment to § 9518. The cumbersome remedy is the civil action to expunge the liens, enjoin further liens, and award damages but at a steep cost. Section 9518 (n.3) expresses the UCC antipathy toward screening bogus filings by the secretary of state or county recorder. Absent a UCC solution, the § 9518 donut hole imperils lawyers, their staffs, and clients by refusing to offer summary expunging of bogus UCC filings or compels the filing agencies to screen for bogus filings.

Chapter 4

Blackmail

Lawyers write many threatening letters. Lawyers make many threatening statements. The butt end of these communications are sometimes, and many times, really bad people. This section lays down the basic ground rules of what the lawyer can and cannot state.

"If you don't pay me, I will tell the world that you are (a) cheating on your wife (with your partner's wife); (b) cheating on Uncle Sam; or (c) cheating on your partners and running a second set of books, etc. You get the picture.

What is wrong with this? This is out and out extortion, pure and simple. California Penal Code § 518 defines it as follows: "Extortion is the obtaining of property from another, with his consent, or the obtaining of an official act of a public officer, induced by a wrongful use of force or fear, or under color of official right. Fear, such as will constitute extortion, may be induced by a threat, either: 1. To do an unlawful injury to the person or property of the individual threatened or of a third person; or, 2. To accuse the individual threatened, or any relative of his, or member of his family, of any crime; or, 3. To expose, or to impute to him or them any deformity, disgrace or crime; or, 4. To expose any secret affecting him or them. This section reflects extortion statutes of nearly every other state."

Flatley v. Mauro (2006) 39 Cal. 4th 299, 326–327 teaches us blackmail. You need to read this case, not only for its salacious facts, but as a roadmap for incredible clarity.

> On the second page, a large caption announced "***NOTICE OF CLAIM & LAWYER'S LIEN.***" The letter continued: "Please consider this as Notice of our Lawyers' [*sic*] Liens. We hereby make a claim and lien in the amount of 40% of the Total Recovery of all funds obtained through trial or settlement, plus all costs of suit, and lawyer fees leveled against you." After urging Flatley to contact his insurance carrier, the letter states "Tell them to contact me directly." It warns that Flatley's failure to do so will result in the filing of a lawsuit and that "all judgment proceeds" will be sought "***directly from your personal assets.***" The letter then states: "***You are granted until January 30, 2002, [sic: 2003] to resolve this matter. . . .***" Mauro also advises Flatley that he has "worked at Lloyd's of London, and [is] familiar with International Law.

> These causes of action allow for PUNITIVE DAMAGES. Punitive Damages are non-dischargeable in bankruptcy, and are recognized under British Law. . . .
>
> The first paragraph of the third page of Mauro's letter refers Flatley to a "settlement of **$100,000,000.00**" awarded as punitive damages in an unidentified case. The second full paragraph then states that an investigation into Flatley's assets for purposes of determining an appropriate award of punitive damages will require "an in-depth investigation" and that any information would then "**BECOME A MATTER OF PUBLIC RECORD, AS IT MUST BE FILED WITH THE COURT**, as it will be part of the basis of several of our expert's [*sic*] testimony." The third paragraph states in its entirety: "**Any and all information, including Immigration, Social Security Issuances and Use, and IRS and various State Tax Levies and information will be exposed.** We are positive the media worldwide will enjoy what they find." . . . the fifth paragraph again warns that "**all pertinent information and documentation, if in violation of any U.S. Federal, Immigration, I.R.S., S.S. Admin., U.S. State, Local, Commonwealth U.K., or International Laws, shall immediately [be] turned over to any and all appropriate authorities.**" . . .
>
> . . . At the bottom of the page, beneath Mauro's signature, a final paragraph warns Flatley that, along with the filing of suit, press releases will be disseminated to various media sources, including but not limited to "**Fox News Chicago, Fox News Indiana, Fox News Wisconsin, and the U.S. National Fox News Network; WGN National U.S. Television; All Local Las Vegas Television, radio stations and newspapers; The Chicago Tribune, The Chicago Southern Economist, The News Sun, The Beacon News, The Daily Herald, The New York Times, The Washington Post; ALL National U.S. Television Networks of NBC, ABC and CBS; as well as INTERNET POSTINGS WORLDWIDE, including the BRITISH BROADCASTING COMPANY, and the Germany National News Network Stations.**" [I substantially shortened the quotes here, and you should read the entire decision as it is a tremendous eye-opener.]

Nobody could have made up this stuff. This guy really worked at this. I believe that the California Supreme Court took the case because the lawyer did such a good job in painting the perfect picture of extortion.

What does this mean to you? The court will not protect extortion, even if cloaked with the threat of a lawsuit. Here is valid threat: Pay me my just debt, or I will file a lawsuit that will be embarrassing. Well, sure, all lawsuits over money are embarrassing because the lawsuit suggests that the defendant is a deadbeat or dishonest. Here is another valid threat: "Pay me my just debt, or I will file a lawsuit and the public will learn that you are a deadbeat and untrustworthy." Is this extortion? No, because the filing of a lawsuit and ensuing disclosure of information is no more or no less than what a lawsuit would impart upon the world. How about this: "Pay my $100,000,000 (no typo's here) for the rape suffered by my client, or I will tell the world's media, and law enforcement, Mr. Celebrity, that you are a rapist and sex fiend. By the way, I will file a lawsuit."

Sticks and stones will break my bones, but words will never harm me as long as those words don't become an act of extortion. The acid test is that extortion is the demand for money coupled with the threat of revealing something that is a secret or is humiliating, embarrassing, or degrading to the person. "I know that you cheated on your wife by taking the floozy to Las Vegas. Worse you used the airline miles and points from your last *family* vacation." That's okay. It's okay to be a jerk or even a moron, but not an extortionist.

Well, that's not quite true, but at least you won't get sued or tossed into jail. Postdigital, federal court filings online through PACER, some state courts have online full dockets and even are accessible through a Google search. Finding your stupid remarks online, or part of a published decision, becomes debris in your slipstream.

The fact that the communication is privileged, again, will not save your bacon. Any stupid comment might creep into legal filings, letters, e-mails, online, or judicial comments on the bench or in written published decisions.

Blackmail and the Bright-Line Rule Test

Here is the test. Figure out which demands are protected and which demands are blackmail.

Group 1:

1. "Settle my client's case, or I will *file a lawsuit* against you that will air out your dirty laundry."
2. "Settle the community property dispute or the *divorce* will expose your bizarre personal life."
3. "Settle the visitation rights, or the *custody case* will air out that you smoke recreational marijuana and therefore you are not a fit parent. I cannot begin to tell what will happen to your career as a family entertainer."
4. "During a sexual liaison, you infected Ms. Doe with genital herpes. Ms. Doe is afflicted with an incurable sexually transmitted disease that has now damaged her prospects for marriage and children. The quality of her life has been damaged. Settle this claim or we file a lawsuit. Your prospect of marriage and children will be damaged."
5. "You have sexually molested my client, a minor. This is a legal, moral, and criminal wrong and a humiliating act by which you have shown no remorse. I intend to file a lawsuit against you, name the religious institution you serve and your direct superiors who failed to report your wrongful conduct to the police, all of which becomes a public record, and accessible to the press, as in all such lawsuits, unless this matter

is settled to my client's satisfaction. Worse, you are a person of great stature in the community, and this lawsuit will be very embarrassing to you. Making this situation even worse is that your stature and power that enabled you to earn the trust of my client, a minor, likely enhanced your unfettered accesses and opportunity to molest my client. My client trusted you because you are a person of stature and standing in the community."

6. "You impregnated your housekeeper when you were an elected official. You were also married at the time, and worse, you carried on the affair in the family bedroom. You are a person of enormous wealth. I hear that you live on $100,000 a month. You are a very famous person. You have a million-person Twitter following. You have your own Wikipedia page. Your Facebook page has millions of Friends. *Forbes* featured you on the front page. I will *file a suit* that spells the most graphic details that will flood social media."
7. "I represent the backers of Exotic-Exotic Bar & Restaurant. You are the operating manager. I will sue you for using my company money that was spent on sexual escapades with famous people whose names, and better yet color photos, will be revealed in the litigation . . . unless you settle the case. If you don't settle the case, the complaint filed in the Los Angeles County Superior Court will spell out the lurid details."

Group 2:

8. "I represent the backers of Exotic-Exotic Bar & Restaurant. You are the operating manager. I will sue you for using my company money that was spent on sexual escapades with famous people whose names, and color photos will be revealed in the litigation . . . unless you settle the case. If you don't settle the case, the complaint filed in the Los Angeles County Superior Court will spell out the lurid details. I will also publish the excruciating details on my website and attach the photos that certainly will go viral, send out a zillion press releases, and hold a press conference that will disclose your salacious conduct. The LASC website offers access if you have a case number, which I will publish on my website in blinking red. I intend to publish the suit and insure that every reporter has a copy of the suit and the steamy investigator's reports. Your wife and her very prominent family will find out your escapades in a nanosecond. We hear that her family money supports your lavish lifestyle including private education for your five children. Do you really want me to pick up the phone and start calling your family, including your children? Their cell phones are on Facebook. Kids today are so social media savvy. Call me to settle, now!"
9. "Pay my client a huge sum of money for your rape of my client or I will put out press releases and inform the mass media that you raped my client through the medium of a lawsuit. You are a big international star, and this information will

ruin your life. I will sue. I will make a point of *telling the world about this rape*, and *report this incident to tax, immigration, and law enforcement authorities*. We will follow you around and *picket your shows*. I will ensure that this campaign will go *viral and flood the social media*. I will not make a deal with you. Payment is what I demand."

10. "As you are aware, I have been retained to represent ABC Company. We are in the process of uncovering the substantial fraud, conversion, and breaches of contract that your client has committed on my client. . . . To date we have uncovered damages exceeding $75,000, not including interest applied thereto, punitive damages, and lawyers' fees. If your client does not agree to cooperate with our investigation and provide us with a repayment of such damages caused, we will be forced to proceed with filing a legal action against him, as well as *reporting him to the California Lawyer General, the Los Angeles District Lawyer, the Internal Revenue Service regarding tax fraud, the Better Business Bureau, as well as to customers and vendors upon whom he may be perpetrating the same fraud*."

Rules Now Written Far More Clearly

The gist of all extortion is that the "threats" are coercive, or, stated more simply, extortion is characterized by the risk or threat of injury, harm, fright, fears of humiliation, or community approbation that compel the victim to part with money. *People v. Beggs* (1918) 178 Cal. 79, 83. Unlike many other torts, extortion lacks finite lines and enters the lexicon of "But I know it when I see it," as stated by Justice Potter Stewart, concurring opinion in *Jacobellis v. State of Ohio* (1964) 378 U.S. 184, 84 S. Ct. 1676, 12 L. Ed. 2d 793.

The anvil of all presuit communication is anti-Slapp [CCP § 415.16(b)] ,which immunizes litigants for liability based on constitutionally protected activities, such as the filing of suit and presuit communications, unless the communication is extortion as a matter of law. Anti-Slapp, which is enacted in many states, permits the defendant, sued for conduct that might be constitutionally protected (i.e., picketing, writing letters to the editor, filings a lawsuit, etc.) to petition the court to dismiss the lawsuit unless the lawsuit has some legal merit. Anti-Slapp quickly dumps lawsuits that seek to punish people for the exercise of their constitutional rights. Most states have a variation of this statute.

The most recent treatment of extortion is found in *Mendoza v. Hamzeh* (2013) 215 Cal. App. 4th 799 in which the court stated as follows:

> In *Flatley, supra*, the California Supreme Court concluded the anti-SLAPP statute does not apply to communications which constitute criminal extortion as a matter of law because such communications are "unprotected by constitutional guarantees

of free speech or petition." (39 Cal. 4th at p. 305, 46 Cal. Rptr. 3d 606, 139 P.3d 2.) As the *Flatley* Court set forth:

"Extortion is the obtaining of property from another, with his consent . . . induced by a wrongful use of force or fear. . . ." (Pen.Code, § 518.) Fear, for purposes of extortion "may be induced by a threat, either: [¶] . . . [¶] 2. To accuse the individual threatened . . . of any crime; or, [¶] 3. To expose, or impute to him . . . any deformity, disgrace or crime[.]" (Pen.Code, § 519.) "Every person who, with intent to extort any money or other property from another, sends or delivers to any person any letter or other writing, whether subscribed or not, expressing or implying, or adapted to imply, any threat such as is specified in Section 519, is punishable in the same manner as if such money or property were actually obtained by means of such threat." (Pen.Code, § 523.) (*Flatley, supra*, 39 Cal. 4th at p. 326, 46 Cal. Rptr. 3d 606, 139 P.3d 2.) *Mendoza v. Hamzeh*, 155 Cal. Rptr. 3d 832, 835 (Cal. App. 2d Dist. 2013)

When does a demand letter leave the protections of anti-Slapp (§ 425.16(b)) and become extortion as a matter of law? In *Mendoza v. Hamzeh*, the court sought to lay down clear markers:

> We do not read *Flatley* to mean the anti-SLAPP statute applies to *some* litigation communications which satisfy the criteria for criminal extortion if such communications are not particularly extreme or egregious. The rule must be a bright line rule. The anti-SLAPP statute does not apply to litigation communications which constitute criminal extortion as a matter of law. (*Flatley, supra*, 39 Cal. 4th at p. 305, 46 Cal. Rptr. 3d 606, 139 P.3d 2.) *Mendoza v. Hamzeh*, 155 Cal. Rptr. 3d 832, 837 (Cal. App. 2d Dist. 2013)

Isn't the threat of filing a suit an act of extortion? Lawsuits are scary, but so what. Threatening a lawsuit is always coercive as stated by *Seidner v. 1551 Greenfield Owner's Association* (1980) 108 Cal. App. 3d 895, 904, 905:

> What, if anything else, did the respondents as defendants do except file its lawsuit? Is it not true that in any lawsuit there is an element of threat or coercion? It is difficult for us to determine the improper purpose to which the process, filing the corporate suit, is put so as to pressure the appellant to settle the partnership suit. If he feels pressure that may be his subjective feelings or thoughts.

The gist of extortion is the demand for money in consideration of keeping secret an embarrassing, secret, humiliating, or private act. The threat to reveal the "secret" causes fear, apprehension, and dread and induces the victim, when the threat is coupled with a demand for money, to comply and pay up. Lambasting a person with threats to go to the police, the press or even family members might be horrid or reprehensible, but it is not an act extortion, if untethered to a demand for payment of money. Conversely, a demand payment of money detached from a threat to reveal a secret is not actionable. That's just playing hardball.

Being a jerk is okay according to the California Supreme Court:

> Thus, our opinion should not be read to imply that rude, aggressive, or even belligerent prelitigation negotiations, whether verbal or written, that may include threats to file a lawsuit, report criminal behavior to authorities or publicize allegations of wrongdoing, necessarily constitute extortion. *Flatley v. Mauro*, 39 Cal. 4th 299, 332, 139 P.3d 2, 24 (2006) [footnote 16]

Where is that bright line? Lawyers, morning, noon, and night, write letters that accuse defendants of hideous, shameful, stupid, or horrific conduct as seen in examples #1 to #7. These examples bear one common denominator. The communications do not threaten the revelation of the shameful act except through the filing of a lawsuit or other process. The allegations in the lawsuit might well go viral, which is a near certainty if the defendant is a celebrity or well known but the threat in the letter does not state that the writer will facilitate, encourage, or enable the dissemination. Any lawsuit filed in the Los Angeles County Superior Court against a celebrity will find its way to a celebrity website within hours or even minutes: "Mr. Big Box Office celebrity sued by *pregnant* housekeeper!" or "Ms. Big Box Office celebrity sued by pool guy for unwanted advances!" is all common fodder.

What about examples #8 to #10? Are these letters acts of extortion and excluded from the protection of anti-Slapp (Section 426.16(b))? *Mendoza v. Hamzeh* answers this question and lays down the bright line case that holds that letters #8 to #10 are acts of extortion because they threatened to disseminate criminal, embarrassing, or private conduct unless a settlement was paid. These disclosures to third parties are separate and beyond the disclosure associated with the filing of a lawsuit.

The Line in the Judicial Sand

Mendoza v. Hamzeh is the bright line case. The lawyer should have stopped at the phrase "will file suit." The lawyer might have gotten away with "will file suit . . . that assuredly will become public knowledge." What went wrong was the threat to communicate to third parties, or threaten the dissemination of allegations of the lawsuit to third parties. *Mendoza v. Hamzeh* does not move the bright line up or down the field of extortion, but it does enunciate one simple rule: keep it simple, keep it short, and keep it in the courts.

Let's look at the mirror. Face it, many lawyers are first-rate jerks and scare the living daylights out of everyone. Not me, of course. Lawyers are professional intimidators, and sometimes threatening some poor soul gets them to capitulate.

You are in the enforcement business. Stay there.

The message: Learn from Jerry Brown. He taught us that "Less is More." Apply this rule to your letter writing: Don't say anything more than absolutely necessary. Remember: Mr. Judge is going to read whatever you write. Judges hate letters that are full of vitriolic statements, insults, nasty comments and venom.

Section 10

Settlements and Potholes in the Road to Money

Chapter 1

Cash Is King, and Everything Else Is a Joke

First, is the client really angry? Is the client embroiled in this quest to "teach the bastard a lesson," or recover the client's loss? Who is teaching whom? Did the debtor swindle the creditor? That is a lesson in self-protection and common sense in steering clear of crooks and cheats. Did the debtor physically abuse the creditor? That is a lesson in personal safety and care. Did the debtor default on a commercial transaction? That is a lesson in finance and credit.

Be wary of those clients seeking to "teach someone a lesson." This business is about money, and not vengeance. Judges offer judgments as paper justice. Lawyers turn those paper judgments into paper money. If you want money, read on. If you want your pound of flesh, skip this chapter. Clients who use litigation as a method to wreak vengeance lost sight of the fact that the debtor owes some money and that the debtor's sole legal obligation is to pay the money. If the debtor pays the money, the case is over, and there is no lesson ever to be learned. End of lesson.

This chapter teaches the rudiments of settlements. Coming to terms that you have to settle the case means that you are coming to terms with the end of the case. If the debtor pays the settlement, you are done and finished. That is both a good thing, Martha, and bad thing, Martha. Some people do not want to settle because they have dedicated their life to pummeling their debtor to death and maybe for a very good reason. That good reason is that the debtor caused some unspeakable loss to the plaintiff, such as the murder, rape, or maiming of a loved one. To the victim of a violent crime, settlement is an anathema because settlement necessarily entails closure, which is repugnant to victims of violent crime. Settlement is not an option to the seriously aggrieved.

Every case has a difficult settlement calculus. For example, what if you are offered a cash settlement to settle the embezzlement? What should you accept and how much? Why accept a settlement? Is "We will teach this guy a lesson" your battle hymn? Embezzlements are particularly opaque cases because you might have a good grip on the debtor's financial ability, whether the money from the embezzlement was stashed, or even a good idea of the total amount of the loss. Embezzlers usually (no, always) destroy the accounting records, which hinders reconstruction.

The answer to this question is a cocktail. No better moment than dinner at Gibson's Bar & Steakhouse in Chicago. The bartenders can entertain you with a blur of concocting colorful drinks, the contents of which are unknown to the natural world. What goes in that cocktail?

First, let's dial back the judgment and grip the real economic loss. Remember the good old days when the jury would render multimillion verdicts for a marginally damaged car. *BMW of North America, Inc. v. Gore*, 517 U.S. 559 (1996). This is a poster child for a jury gone crazy. This is the initial award: $4,000 compensatory damages for selling slightly damaged car, but $4,000,000 in punitive damages, reduced to $2,000,000 by the trial judge, but upset in the U.S. Supreme Court for a violation of due process. Due process? Let's try common sense. No wonder insurance companies settle cases.

Unless the judgment is airtight, and the defendant has deep pockets, unpeel the judgment to refine the true economic loss. If the defendant is a Fortune 100 company and the judgment is solid, skip this discussion. If somebody less than Bill Gates is your judgment debtor, contemplate what amount of money will make the judgment creditor whole. The next step is assessing how close you are to reaching an asset. Is the Hope Diamond on the sheriff's auction block? That sounds pretty good, absent the U.S. government filing suit to get its property back. Are you about to sell the defendant's free and clear apartment building? Why settle? Forget it. How about latching on to the big bank account? Hang up the phone on the debtor, assuming that the bank accounts will satisfy the writ of execution. Absent manna from heaven, you might walk back your expectations. Is the debtor engaging in a hard-fought campaign of asset protection and causing you to run up big expenses and fees? The purpose of asset protection is rarely to successfully immunize the asset, but muscle in front of you some roadblocks that you will run of out money pushing them aside. Let's open the *Godfather Handbook of Diplomacy*. "Tom, I'm a businessman. Blood is a big expense," intones Tom Sollozzo. He is right.

If you don't settle, expect to chase down some nutcase for years and spend a bunch of money. You could chase this person for months, years, or decades. You can play hide and seek from here to kingdom come. Forget fashioning yourself as Cortez, let's try Ponce de León.

You can spend an awful lot of money trying to serve this person with an order compelling an appearance in court. To prove this point, we had to serve a lawyer with an Order to Show Cause Re Contempt, and like an order of examination, it must be personally served. We hired six (6) (you read that right) process servers who jointly staked out the lawyer who holed up in his office and did not come out.. Trust me, your debtor will become an expert in dodging service of process. Your debtor won't answer the door but will close the blinds, hide in the bedroom or bathroom, relocate to a hotel or another city until the coast is clear. The debtor will drive a rental car.

Chapter 2

Rudiments of Payment Programs

What else is there to consider? The "when" of any settlement means everything. Is money at hand now, or is it the pitch? "I'll pay you 10 percent now and 40 percent in 180 days." Will you ever see the 40 percent? I don't think so. "Don't cry for me, Argentina," if the money never sets foot on this earth. What strategies can you use to make sure that the debtor coughs up the balance of the settlement? This chapter is important because many cases are settled for a million reasons. Debtors are willing to pay but just need time. Creditors are willing to accept payments to end the civil litigation and squeeze the lawyer fee spigot. Both parties see risk. Sometimes the debtor enters into a payment program with the express intention of defaulting and forcing the judgment creditor to jump through more legal hoops before scoring a judgment. Call this settlement a continuation of litigation by other means, Professor Clausewitz. Embrace the risk that the default will default because of the debtor's anger and hostility or the debtor's exhaustion in making payment over a long period of time.

Let's cycle through the rudiments of any settlement:

1. Get the deal in writing, signed by the parties, and not just the lawyers. You can get a binding settlement before the court (Men—or Women—in Black). If you are in federal court, federal law follows the law of the state, which might include any specialized statute that constitutes a "stand-alone" statute of fraud for a settlement, such as California Code of Civil Procedure § 664.6 (signed by the parties or stated by the parties before a judge), which is a fancy word for settlement epoxy.
2. Make sure that you include every term whether in writing or before the court. Perish the thought of a do-over. If the term is not in writing, the term does not exist. This is a major source of trouble in settlement land. If you and the debtor stand up in court and put the deal on the record, before Mr. Judge, you are done, you are finished, and you are deep-fried. You are not coming back. Many states have statutes that state that when you put a settlement on the record, and the judge says something like "Judgment entered" or "I approve" "or "This wraps up the case," your

case is deep fried. Whatever you put on the record is your settlement and maybe nothing more. If you don't put a release that payment is due by wire transfer, that the parties promise each other confidentiality, that the parties agree to mediation and arbitration as dispute resolution, or anything else on the records, these terms fall to the judicial cutting room floor, never to be resuscitated. Moral of this tale: Get your deal in writing and have everyone sign it. If you are going to show up in court and put the settlement on the record, read into the record every possible term you want. Take your time, don't rush, and don't fumble; otherwise, you might damage the case.

3. If a payment program, Round One, include an acceleration clause (all due on default or sale of an asset), limited notice of default, notice going solely to a designated fax number, accrual of interest at the maximum legal rate, payments applied first on account of interest and thereafter to principal, right to recover lawyer's fees in the event of enforcement, payments to a designated address or payments by ACH or wire transfer to a designated account, no waiver of conditions if a late payment is accepted, reaffirmation of debt, judgment and liens, tolling of any statute of limitations, representation that the parties are represented by counsel and did not rely on the other parties, and the exparte right to accelerate and enforce in the event of an uncured default and without notice. Don't forget to add that all disputes are resolved in the original court, that any relief is subject to shortened time, and that any obligation to renew the judgment is waived.
4. If a payment program, Round Two, expect the debtor to default. Embrace the fact that the debtor is going to default. Where does that leave you? All the prior sections in this book on insolvency, lies and half-truths, liens, and judgments now come to fruition and plunk down in your lap. Let's assume that the debtor made three payments and defaulted on payment number four. What do you find when you enter the scene? The debtor's other creditors have been more aggressive then you and sued, served, took judgment, and recorded liens. Now, mind you, some debtors are going to default because they suffer from payment fatigue. This is the technical terms when someone stops paying: They just poop out. We call them payment zombies. Expect the default bomb.
5. If you did not have a lien on the debtor's property, your liens is now junior to your competitors. If the debtor is horribly insolvent and your lien is on the bottom of the totem pole, and the debtor filed bankruptcy, the sale of property pays the senior (and probably priority claims, such as taxes) and leaves you holding the bag and empty bag at worse. Worse, the remaining assets, if at all, are gone, damaged, vandalized, stolen, or seized by other creditors and sold to pay their debts. So what if the debtor lied about the other more pressing claims to induce you to stand down? You already learned that you cannot sue the debtor (you already have a judgment and what's another judgment worth?) and that you cannot sue the lawyer. Rest assured

that the day you made your deal is the day that the debtor executed an exit strategy in which you appeared only in the debtor's rearview mirror. Embrace collateral or embrace defeat at the hands of the debtor, who will do everything to topple the deal and cheat you out of payment.

6. If you are unsecured you look down the shaft of an empty well. This is really bad. Let's solve the problem. A payment program means that the debtor lacks the financial ability to pay the debt in full. Why? Insolvency, bad business, business reversals, substance abuse, a corrosive divorce that bleeds the debtor to death, or just a refusal to hand over a big check? Who knows and who cares, because when the debtor defaults, the creditor will surely survey financial carnage and debris. Okay, we got that. What can you do to avoid this preordained disaster? Answer: First, you can recognize the risk and bargain for a steep discount. Cash in hand is better than no cash at all. If a bird in the hand is worth two in the bush, the question is, whether the bird is a goose and whether someone's goose is cooked, in duck fat, no less (Food Channel jab). If you do not have assurances of payment and expect a moonscape when entering the debtor's business upon default, reconsider the 50 percent per dollar offer. This is very rational.
7. Next, for round #3, bargain for deep security, which consists of a judgment lien, UCC or deed of trust. This means judgment and liens upon settlement, and not judgment and liens upon default. This is a very big deal because at the time of settlement, hopefully, the debtor was still treading water, rather than sinking like Jack Dawson to the bottom of the Atlantic. This is a big fact, maybe. You have another long shot: Secure a guaranty from the debtor's principal. Sometime this works, assuming that the debtor's principal is more solvent than the corporate debtor. This will take a financial statement, credit report, warranties that no properties are held in the name of another or in trust, a copy of the most recent URLA and attachments, three years of tax returns, and stock and bank statements. How about a deed of trust (mortgage) and security interest in the personal property? These remedies might work assuming that the real property has real equity (buzzword for title report and appraisal) and the personal property likewise has equity (UCC search and won't walk out the back door in the event of default).
8. If a payment program, Round Four, expect the debtor to offer a payment program but demand that the plaintiff dismiss the lawsuit with prejudice. Good idea or bad idea? That's a really bad idea. Why? If the debtor defaults, the plaintiff must file a brand-new suit. Filing and serving a new lawsuit will take time, incur a new round of lawyer's fees, and if the debtor in the interim liquidated all assets, and absent consensual liens, the lawsuit will culminate in an empty judgment. The debtor hired a lawyer who offers the TV dinner of representations, including the cooked peas. "I will represent for a fixed price, no matter the outcome,

but not after judgment." The lawyer can claim that the creditor filed the lawsuit in the wrong state, wrong court, or the wrong county. That ploy will burn up a few months. The debtor's lawyer can claim that the debtor never defaulted. That can easily chew up a bunch of time and money. This is a great deal for the debtor, who watches from the galleries while his prefab lawyer wastes everyone's time. The debtor still has unfettered control over his assets. To end this nightmare, the creditor renegotiates the first settlement for a new settlement, which is typically less advantageous than the first agreement and certainly comes at a higher price. If the settlement is in federal court, absent a clear and unequivocal retention of district court jurisdiction and the reopening of the dismissal, the plaintiff might have to file in state court to enforce the settlement ugly. Adding to this very sorry and sad brew are big-buck obstacles such as mediation and arbitration that compels the creditor to spend tens of thousands through private services as a precondition to reducing a written settlement agreement into a judgment. Never dismiss the lawsuit with prejudice because you will have to start over. Secure a judgment to end the case, and keep continuing jurisdiction. If you have to dismiss, dismiss without prejudice and engineer a stipulation and signed order to reopen the case, and enter judgment if a default. Better than nothing, but chances are you find nothing because the debtor cleared out the place upon default, and the judgment reaches only empty shelves or nonexistent equity in real property.

9. Round #5. If a payment program, the settlement agreement usually obligates the parties to mutually release each other from all claims, known and unknown, that arise from the claims and prosecution of the case. No doubt, the creditor seeks a release to dump any real or imagined claims that the debtor harbors and might sue at a later date, assuming that the claim survives the settlement itself. Why should the creditor release the debtor and its principals? Answer: No reason. In fact, the release is a disaster. Before we leave this topic, watch out for a two-for-one deal. These deals provide that the debtor pay $10,000 in installment, but if the debtor defaults, the judgment is in the amount of $20,000. These deals are probably void because the $10,000 plus kicker is penalty and void as a matter of law.
10. This book is about recovering secret and hidden assets. Assuming a settlement that obligates the creditor to release the debtor and the principals (officer, directors, shareholders, agents, lawyers, and employees) in the event of a default, the creditor can only pursue the residual claims against the debtor. Let's say, or no, let's predict that the insiders looted the company before the settlement is signed. Literally, they formed a new entity, pinned the old name on an fictional business name, and transferred the asset of the debtor into the new entity, changed bank accounts, new tax TIN numbers, and state board of equalization number (sales tax). The insiders wiped the old debtor company off the face of the earth. You'd think that the creditor had

a sure-fire lawsuit to unwind this skulduggery and sue the living daylights out of the corporate principals for this grievous act of dishonesty.

Great case? No, the court will dump this case because the creditor signed a release that might cover these shenanigans under the label "all claims and causes of action that arise from, related to, or are based on the claim in this lawsuit, or any other matter, claims, right, cause of action, charge, or chose by and among the parties to this release." Stock language, no doubt, but this language is sufficient to potentially immunize the insiders from liability for these machinations when they plunder the assets of the debtor and leave its corpse on the doorstep of the creditors. Whether or not this language is bulletproof is not the issue. The issue is that the insider can hide and conceal assets and fend off any claims of a fraudulent conveyance when the creditors reawaken from a heavy slumber. The creditor would be lucky to collect $0.10 on the dollar. In short, don't release anybody. The person with the release in one hand has the assets of the company in the other hand.

Remember that a payment program serves two purposes: money and relief from the rigor and expense of litigation. But a payment program only works if you have incorporated an enforcement mechanism that is simple and free of constraints. Don't swap one problem for another.

Chapter 3

Noneconomic Terms and Contempt

Let's face reality that your debtor denies ownership of any assets. You get the "I have nothing. I am broke. I live in a car. I have $10 in my pocket." You don't believe him because you discovered that the debtor over the years shed enormous assets, which you cannot readily find. The debtor is the heir to a family fortune, which produced a multimillion-dollar trust. The debtor denies any right of income and certainly any right to invade the trust. What can you do to keep the case alive?

Enter into a stand-still agreement with the debtor that obligates the debtor to turn over to you on an annual basis financial records. Here is a good list:

> Debtor shall turnover to the Creditor the following documents in their original form, which bears an original signature by the debtor as follows:

1. The complete federal and state returns of the Debtor, [and if married, the joint returns of the debtor and spouse], and every corporation, limited liability company, partnership (general or limited), or trust, in which the debtor, spouse, child, or trustee for any trust for the debtor, spouse or children who have any interest or status as an officer, agent or manager [all collectively the "debtor"], commencing for tax year 2013, and continuing until the judgment is paid, plus interest costs and fees. The returns shall include all schedules attached thereof, and tax working papers of the accountant, certified public accountant, or tax preparer and likewise bear their original signatures. The Creditor shall be entitled, and the Debtor shall so direct, the accountant, certified public accountant, or tax prepared to swear under penalty of perjury that the tax returns, and all working papers, are authentic, unaltered, completed and subject to filing. Should the amount of the income claimed by the Debtor or spouse constitute a sum in which the taxing authorities do not require a tax return, nonetheless, the debtor and spouse, if filing a joint return, shall so file a tax return for all taxing authorities. The Creditor shall be entitled to copy the tax

returns, all schedules thereto and all working papers thereof which shall be made available from and after date of the filing thereof and for a period of 60 days. The Debtor shall affirmatively notify the Creditor and current counsel by return receipt mail, post prepaid at the addresses set forth below.

2. In addition, the Debtor shall provide and permit the creditor the opportunity to copy all pay stubs from any employment, all W-2s and 1099s, all tax returns for any limited liability company, corporation, partnership, limited partnership, or any other entity in which the Debtor has any interest there including, but not limited to, any schedules and all working papers and copies of checks or receipts confirming payments for taxes, interest and penalties, all court ordered payments pursuant to any judgment, and all legal fees and unreimbursed business expenses. These records are due to be produced by the Debtor between October 1 to December 31 of every year.
3. The obligation to turn over these documents is an affirmative obligation of the Debtor, which obligation is incorporated into the order and judgment, if any, for settlement of the action by and between the Creditor and the Debtor. The failure of the Debtor to comply with the terms and conditions in this paragraph shall be deemed a contempt of court for each calendar year, and each document that the Debtor fails to announce their availability, make available, and in fact turn over true and original there for inspection, and copying. The court shall keep and retain continuing jurisdiction to hear and consider any order to show cause or other pleading seeking contempt. The Debtor stipulates to service by mail upon current counsel, as designated in writing, the address of the Debtor as set forth in this Agreement, of the application for the issuance of the order to show case, any order issued thereon, all moving papers for the hearing on the order to cause, the service of the OSC upon the Debtor, and any order, judgment or decree that the court may award at the conclusion of the contempt hearing. In the event of any action to charge the Debtor with contempt, in addition to any other relief, the Creditor may seek to incarcerate the Debtor until the Debtor complies, seek to incarcerate the Debtor as and for punishment, seek lawyer's fees and damages.
4. The statute of limitations for issuance of contempt, or any claim of laches, estoppel, or otherwise, is waived for the benefit of the Creditor in its entirety.

What is the purpose of these covenants to compel the debtor to turn over these records? You might find something in the records. The easy one is a 1099 from a bank that reveals $2,000 in interest, which in today's interest means $400,000 at .5% annual interest. The tax return would represent income from some source that would be subject to garnishment. You can email me if my math sucks.

The tax return would also reflect ownership of real property, if the returns show depreciation, which is commonly associated with real estate, deductions consisting of payment of interest charges to a bank, payment of property taxes, or payment of real estate insurance, maintenance, legal fees, and other business expense associated with property ownership. If the debtor does not turn over the tax return, you can proceed with civil contempt, which might land the debtor in jail for five days for each act of contempt plus a $1,000 fine and maybe jail until the debtor complies with the order itself.

The duty to report is classically called a noneconomic covenant that represents an affirmative demand upon the debtor to forward the tax returns and related financial records. Failure to comply with the covenant is an act of contempt and potential incarceration. In some cases, the risk of incarceration for the failure to turn over records that might reveal assets is the only means to collect a judgment. This is not debtor's prison but instead the machinery to compel the debtor to produce information that might aid the creditor in locating assets.

Does this really work? You are giving the case a rest because the debtor claims a total lack of assets and zero income for the last five years. The debtor claims to live off "friends." Chasing down the debtor for a debtor's examination is expensive because the debtor is busy dodging the process servers. The bad news arrives at your doorstep. Ever so diligent, the client tells you that the debtor suffered a recorded $200,000 IRS lien. You pull the lien and discover that the tax lien is for 1040 taxes (income taxes) for a single prior year. After deducting penalties and interest from the $200,000 and using a touch of high school algebra, you extrapolate that the debtor's annual income for that year was $500,000. Tax return in hand would have avoided this disaster. The failure to surrender the tax returns would have offered you contempt.

Chapter 4

Settlement Negotiations Are Games of Bluffs, Lies, Threats, and Blusters

The debtor can lie and fake his way through settlement negotiations. Embrace this song and dance, Mr. Gere. Whatever the debtor says, whether a lie, half-truth, or unbelievable whopper, will not support a new lawsuit against anybody. Whether you like to believe that you can't sue someone for lying even when that lie cost you a bunch of money, that is the state of the law, absent very few exceptions, not relevant in this book. You are stuck but might be able to unwind the settlement. But what good would that do other than to recycle the enforcement process? If the debtor is insolvent, the creditor would gauge what assets are available, and if the assets are sold, would senior creditors get paid first, which would leave nothing for the junior lien creditor and clearly shut out the unsecured creditors? If the debtor claims insolvency and threatens to file bankruptcy to unload the crushing debt, the trick is to "trust but verify" the financial condition of the debtor. Calling the debtor's bluff, packing up your stuff, and walking out of the negotiating room are a tried and true method of posturing. Be careful that the debtor does not call your bluff.

Let's say that you hone in on a number that means your criteria. That number might be the total amount of the judgment, including interest to date, or the principal amount of the judgment without interest. Depending on the state, interest accrues at anywhere between 7 percent and 13 percent, and some states (Kentucky) provide for compounding. Are you in federal court? That's bad news, fellow. Interest accrues at 1 percent or less. Chump change. Would you accept half of the judgment if paid now? Would you accept something more or less of the judgment? This deal only works if you get money in hand. If you don't get money in hand, the debtor might claim that you agreed to discount the judgment permanently and that you agreed to accept a lesser amount. That hurts. You'd think "I made a deal, the debtor's doesn't pay, and now he claims that discounted the judgment." Whether this flies legally is not the issue. The issue is that you gave the debtor leverage. Cash is king and everything else is a joke.

By the way, since I have your attention, here is a short story. Sometimes a debtor concludes that the roadblocks he constructed will bring the creditor's campaign to a halt. Facing buccoo-bucks to overcome these obstacles, the creditor is willing to accept pennies on the dollar. Here is the rejection letter directed to the lawyer for the debtor: "Thank you for your efforts to resolve this case. Your offer is rejected, and we decline to respond with a counteroffer. The reason is because you offered tiny money."

But don't forget to bargain and bargain hard. Let the other fellow make the first offer. You should let the other guy make the first offer because the first offer itself represents that person's assessment of the case, which might be radically different from yours. Earlier, we discussed the Efficient Market Hypothesis, which stands for the proposition that the value of anything represents the sum total of all knowledge, real or imagined. The faux Tiffany lamp that you find at a department store will set you back about $300. That same faux Tiffany lamp owned by Angelina Jolie will set you back about $10,000. Is there a difference between these lamps? Absolutely not, except the sum total of all knowledge, real or imagined, imbued in these two lamps represent the true market value (i.e., the Efficient Market Hypothesis). The first offer from the other side is likewise a product of the Efficient Market Hypothesis, which is the total sum of all knowledge of the other side, whether that knowledge is real, imagined, or warped. If the other side offers $100,000 to settle the case, that number represents their efficient market hypothesis knowledge of known risks, rights, and defenses to the case, whether real, imagined, or warped. Your counteroffer likewise represents your efficient market hypothesis total of like knowledge, whether real, imagined, or warped.

Part of the settlement brew is the motivation of the parties to end the case, for the normal reasons, such as reducing expense and mitigating risks. The other person has the same motivation as you and might be willing to pay more money (or accept less, depending on what side of the equation you are on) to meet his needs but reshaped by the efficient market hypothesis. Remember, their knowledge, real, imagined, or warped, of the case might be different from yours. Needless to say, spreading rumors, innuendo, propaganda, and bald-faced lies poisons the other side and becomes part of the adverse parties efficient market hypothesis and warp decision making. Here is a great example. The plaintiff sues the defendant. The plaintiff wins the big judgment. The defendant finally hires a lawyer. The defendant's lawyer advises the plaintiff's counsel that the defendant is broke, is going to file bankruptcy, and offers 10 cents on the dollar as a settlement. Counsel's representations are lies; the defendant's spouse is warehousing the family fortune. These representations, even if false, become part of the plaintiff's efficient market hypothesis in valuing the offer and necessarily deflate the value of the case.

Don't gloss over this. The other person seeks to settle the case to suit his interests, as you do. What is that person's interest? Lawyer's fees? Fear of a big judgment? Marital issues? Getting a big problem solved? Fear of the unknown? Whatever the reason, figure it out.

If the other side is more motivated than you to resolve the case, your settlement calculus has changes, and you might find yourself a little richer—or poorer. Find out what drives the other side to the settlement table first, and you might be able to generate a better plan.

Remember that I told you that you can't sue some lawyer for lying to you. That's right. What does that mean? Presume everyone is a liar. Boy, that's tough, but worse if you learn that you left a whole bunch of money on the table. That really hurts.

Chapter 5

Jumping Out of the Settlement Plane Without a Parachute

Let's reset the clock for a second here. You sued the defendant. Did the case settle? Moving a little off the beaten path here, settlements can offer the debtor additional layers of asset protection. If the creditor accepts a payment program and dismisses the case with prejudice, the creditor has to file a new lawsuit to collect on the settlement. If the case is in federal court, and the parties dismiss without prejudice without retaining jurisdiction, the second lawsuit ends up in state court. An independent basis is required for federal jurisdiction. See *Peacock v. Thomas* (1999) 516 U.S. 349 (limits on jurisdiction in judgment proceedings against third parties); *Kokkonen v. Guardian Life Ins. Co.* (1994) 511 U.S. 375, 379–380 (limits on jurisdiction to enforce "stand-alone" settlement agreement).

The parties might bicker over venue or jurisdiction or the nature of the settlement or its terms. Expect that misery. This second battle is very wasteful, time-consuming, and ultraexpensive. The trial lawyer in the first case might be a witness and compel the client to hire another lawyer. If the settlement provides for a long-term payment agreement without security, the debtor can dispose of assets, abscond with the cash, default in grand style, and disappear from the face of the earth. If the settlement lacks a personal guarantee, why not file bankruptcy for the company? If the settlement compels the plaintiff to provide notice of default, mediate, or arbitrate before filing a suit to collect or taking any coercive action, the debtor has the opportunity to finalize any asset protection and "get out of dodge." Mediation and arbitration are very expensive, which foists upon the creditor another financial disincentive. Some settlements provide for extensive releases. That's a bad deal; don't do it. During the settlement, the insiders might have looted the company and left an empty shell that actually obligated itself to make payments under the agreement. Upon default, the plaintiff discovers that the insiders transferred to themselves everything but trips and falls over the release language that bars a lawsuit against the insiders for anything. The settlement gave the debtor the opportunity to destroy the company. The settlement was as good as nearly winning the lawsuit itself. The debtor can claim total victory. Great job, guys. Somebody's lawyer is going to get sued.

Chapter 6

How Phony Liens Cower a Party in a Settlement Conference

In the midst of a settlement conference in which the plaintiff chased down his ne'er-do-well ex-partner for millions, the partner dumped 30 bogus financing statements (UCC-1 liens with the secretary of state) into the lap of the plaintiff. The partner claimed that every other creditor tied up his assets and that, therefore, the plaintiff should accept the proffered deal, which was awful. UCCs are reasonably inexpensive to file, do not require notary, and need not be signed by anyone. A debtor can file a UCC showing various parties as alleged secured creditors. Whether these UCCs are fictitious or not is not the point.

Article 9 of the Commercial Code offers potential filers an open drawer to file a financing statement. The secretary of state declines to confirm the legality of filings. Here is a short quote from the Indiana secretary of state: "Open drawer concept: A large part of the way RA9 [Article 9] relieves the filing officer from making judgments and incurring liability is by letting the customer decide what the status is of a particular UCC lien. Open drawer means all active filings are left on record, whether lapsed or terminated, for the customer to see and interpret on their own." In plain English: The secretary of state offers its filing drawers to anyone. Jody, can Little Green Men, Inc., (lien creditor) file a UCC that lists Little Blue Men, Inc., from the planet Vega as the lien debtor and the planet Mars as the collateral. Yes, Mars the planet, and not the candy bar. (Please don't do this. Why? You might get it filed. I don't want to hear from some secretary of state.)

From the debtor's point of view, the debtor has invested almost nothing and probably didn't need to consult a lawyer, particularly after reading this. The debtor doesn't need to hire an expensive asset-protection strategist or pay tens of thousands of dollars to an expensive lawyer. The creditor faces a blizzard of UCCs and, therefore, confronts the risk that some or all might be valid. If not valid, the creditor faces the burden of toppling them, even though the secured creditors might not seek to protect them, assuming that a secured creditor actually exists. For most creditors, or more specifically the creditor's lawyers, they would ponder the expense factor in seeking to dispose of these financing statements, which itself is its own deterrent.

The creditor might face 10, 20, or 100 UCCs, and therefore confronts the burden of setting them all aside in a legal proceeding. The scheme is a perfect paradigm of asset protection. Cheap, cumbersome, complex. To unwind these UCCs, the creditor would spend some real money.

Chapter 7

When Are You in Contract?

What does this gobbledgook mean? When you go to Safeway and load up the cart, can Safeway sue you for the groceries should you abandon the cart and leave the store? No, you and Safeway are not in contract. How about standing in line at the checkout counter? No, you are not in contract. How about putting the groceries on the conveyor belt? No, you are not in contract. How about when the cashier rings up the groceries? Can Safeway sue you if you walk out (without the groceries)? No, you are not in contract. When can Safeway sue? Answer: Never. When the cashier rings up the sale, say, $78.12, this is Safeway's offer to sell you the groceries for the price of $78.12. You can accept or reject. How do you accept? Answer: By tender of $78.12 (cash, electronic, or check). You accept Safeway's offer, represented by the total rung by the cashier, in the tender of money. You can say, morning, noon, and night, "I accept your offer to buy the groceries, Mr. Safeway, and I will take them home and pay you later." This is not acceptance of Safeway's offer. Safeway conditions the acceptance of its offer solely by performance (i.e., payment). If you walk out with the groceries, without paying, you might spend some time in the county jail for petty theft, or cleaning the streets for a few days.

Here is the Safeway solution: Do you want money or another promise to pay? You want money. Acceptance of the deal requires payment of money and nothing less. Here is the formula: "You can accept this offer solely by due and timely performance and any type of nonconforming tender shall be deemed a rejection of this offer without further notice. Time is of the essence. You are not entitled to grace, notice, notice of default, or notice of any nonconformity. Any payments received inconsistent with this offer shall be deemed payment on account, and the amounts received shall be first applied on account accrued interest and the balance to principal." If a cash deal, this is the magic language that conditions acceptance upon money. Saying "I promise to pay," is not acceptance.

No Deal is Perfect

How about the right number? What if you don't get exactly what you want? Is that important? Maybe or maybe not. First, you need to embrace basic business concepts of the law of diminishing returns. If the debt is $100,000 and the case is troublesome, but the debtor offers you $75,000 cash now, do you take it? Well maybe and probably, if the clawing at the remaining $25,000 is going to cost you $25,000.00 and screwing around for another year. We get calls like this: "The debtor owes me $10,000 and offered $6,000 right now. Shall I take it or sue? I tell everyone the following: "I am going to charge you 25 percent as a contingency fee. Your case is not worth $10,000 but $7,500.00. The spread is now $1,500. You will need to pay me in advance $1,500 as a deposit for court costs. I do not guarantee that I will collect your debt and don't guarantee that I will recover the court costs that I financed from your cash deposit. You might as well kiss the $1,500 good-bye. Cogitate hard on this offer."

Let's talk about pies. Yes, yes, pies, you read that right. Betty Crocker pies, Marie Callender pies, frozen pies, a homemade pie, or Pillsbury Doughboy pies, for all I know. What do pies have to do with collecting money? I knew you'd ask, and thank you, my mental health is good. Let's say that the cookbook advises that baking time for the pie is 60 minutes at 350 degrees. You cook the pie for 61 minutes. Is there any difference? No. How about 62 minutes? There's an imperceptible difference. How about 63 minutes? Ever so slightly, and you need to be a judge on Iron Chef America. How about 64 minutes? The judges on Chopped might complain, but you would move to the next round. How about 65 minutes? That might get you chopped unless one of the competitors screwed the pooch. How about 66 minutes? I might even notice. You can cycle through the same process if the cooking spread is between 55 to 60 minutes. These are all incremental differences, but the pie is cooked, on the table, ready to eat, and a treat for all as long as it was baked for 55 to 65 minutes, which is a full 10-minute spread. If your heart is set on $100,000, think of pies. Does it really make a difference if the final number is $97,000 given everything else involved in the process of delivering up the money? Call this process incrementalism, which means in simple English that you need to temper your goals with the imperative that you ensure yourself of something, some deliverable or some result, even though imperfect. It is better to eat a warm pie with a singed crust than to stare at an empty plate.

Chapter 8

The Settlement Is the Grand Bargain

Diplomats use the term "grand bargain" in striking a dramatic deal that resolves millennium-old conflicts between warring factions. This word first appeared in the Senator's George Mitchell's settlement of the conflict in Northern Ireland. A grand bargain means that the parties in conflict with each other hit the "reset button" in their negotiations and make dramatic and extraordinary offers that have never been made before. The parties will meet each other at the halfway point. The creditor claims that the debtor owes $100, and the debtor denies all liability. The parties settle halfway at $50. The grand bargain itself is obvious, but getting the parties to make a huge sacrifice is a big deal. Grand bargains work when parties face enormous litigation expense, the risk of loss, difficulty of collection, and the personal stress of conflict itself.

Chapter 9

Remediation in Grand Bargain Strategy

Remediation means restoring the person to his or her original condition before the financial or personal disaster. Remediation means making the victim whole or complete, if possible. Money and maybe a personal apology might do the trick. Lawsuits seek damages that go well beyond the true economic loss suffered by the plaintiff as these suits seek costs, interest, fees, and additional damages, such as lost profits or proceeds, penalties, fines, punitive damages, or treble damages. Nonpayment of labor claims accrue stupendous penalties that double or triple the loss. Sexual harassment claims, battery cases, drunken driving cases, and frauds spin out punitive damages that add thousands or millions to the loss itself.

These additional bells and whistles can turn a manageable loss into the company killer. From the viewpoint of remediation, which is making the person whole, the question is, what is the client's true loss? Let's take, for example, the standard sexual harassment claim. Doctors, dentists, medical professionals, and others in cloistered working environments face these claims. The great expression is that familiarity breeds contempt. No, this is wrong. Familiarity breeds lawsuits. Lawyers are not immune. Thinking about dumping every lawyer older than 63 to make way for the "younger generation"? Think about all those lawsuits from disgruntled partners shown the door. Age discrimination lawsuits are big and ugly and eat everything and everybody in sight. Yum, yum!

The employer, typically an older male, mistakes a business for a sexual playground and mistakes the female employees for a herd of animals subject to sexual predation at any time. You know what happens. The employer uses profane, sexually charged language, graduates to groping, unwarranted and excessive touching or pursues office dating that becomes oppressive. The claims are loaded spring guns, and few survive the discharge in front of a sympathetic jury. But what is the true loss? That's a tough one. $10,000? $50,000? $100,000? Who knows?

What amount of money is necessary to make this person whole? The shrewd lawyer, and rapidly sobering defendant, fix that number and make an offer at the earliest possible moment before the greed bug bites the plaintiff and sends the case careening in front of a jury who loves commas, many commas, in a number. The punch line is to divine the number that remediates the loss and to put that in front of the victim.

Before we move on to the next topic, let's chat about legal obituaries. What is that? A legal obituary is a jury verdict that kills off a party. The standard legal obit is that a plaintiff has a difficult but spectacular case: employment claims, such as sex, race, or age discrimination, wage and hour claims, sexual harassment, or whistle-blower cases. Other claims are commercial and banking claims in which the defendant claims that the bank victimized him or her. Right before the trial, somebody, either plaintiff or defendant, fails to grasp the reality of the case and the risk that he or she will lose. The plaintiff offers to accept cents on the dollar for the claim but the defendant seeks personal vindication before the jury. You know the outcome: The jury buries the defendant under millions of punitive damages. Or the plaintiffs have a righteous case, but the defendant believes himself be the next O. J. Simpson (at the least in the first trial) and immune from common sense and the paper that he signed. The defendants get buried under millions of dollars of damages. Throwing money at the other side, if it sticks, ends the case. Throwing money at your trial lawyer only gets you to the trial, if you seek personal vindication, which is never guaranteed.

Chapter 10

Making a Settlement Stick

Let's go through the basic rules of settlements. This is important because a settlement forgoes the "day in court." This is both very good and very bad. Why is forgoing the day in court a good thing, Martha? The answer is that trials are unpredictable. Rock solid witnesses collapse under withering cross-examinations. Jurors fall in love with, or learn to hate, lawyers or parties. Key documents turn out to be forgeries. Critical witnesses change their story. What can go wrong usually goes wrong. Certainty is worth something. On the other hand, a party might have a very meritorious case, and the perils of trial ought not to deter the just from seeking justice. Settlement offers certainty, assuming that the settlement is for cash. Trial offers risk and maybe a greater recovery than any settlement.

A settlement between two parties over a sum of money is enforceable, even though the settlement is not reduced to writing, assuming that the two parties communicated an acceptance and offer and reached a meeting of the minds. This is very scary. Should the plaintiff call up the defendant and settle the case on the phone, that's a deal, and no writing is required unless the deal was conditional upon a writing. Parties who sign pieces of paper that spell out a deal are stuck with that deal, no matter how bad. If parties go to court, and they put a settlement on the record, they are stuck with what is on the record. California Code of Civil Procedure § 664.6 states that if parties reduce their settlement to a writing signed by each and stand before a judge and put the terms on the record, the deal is done, but based on the writing or what was said on the record. You don't get a do-over.

What is the moral of the tale if one party later suffers settler's remorse? Loose lips sink ships. This means that if somebody opens his or her mouth and starts talking settlement, and the other side agrees, that might be a done deal. If parties are exchanging e-mails and letters and make a deal, that's a deal, and it will be enforced by the court. The antidote to this misery is to let the lawyers do the talking because the lawyers will do lawyer things and make sure that the deal conforms to everybody's reasonable expectations and that the deal has safeguards to protect parties in the event of a default. These safeguards are typically acceleration clauses in the event that a party defaults on an installment note, forum selection clauses to ensure that a particular forum can adjudicate the matter such as the home forum for a party, arbitration clauses that keep the case out of the courts, interest clauses to make a default expensive, lawyer's fees clauses to shift the risk of a default to the breaching party, and an integration clause that will hopefully, but not assuredly, preclude the parties from bringing in collateral promises and representations into the litigation to topple the deal. This list is for real. Getting the deal in writing through the lawyers compels the parties to think through the deal and not do anything rash or hasty.

We have all heard about the big man syndrome. In settling a lawsuit, the big man syndrome leads to big mistakes. Blowhards are inevitably fools.

Chapter 11

Potholes in Settlements

Every settlement is different, but all settlements share the same DNA. Learn the settlement DNA, and you will never go wrong.

Let's go through each strand:

Cash Settlements. A settlement for cash ends the case. The upside is that the defendant places a sum of money in the hands of the plaintiff, who finds payment satisfaction for the debt, and hopefully a personal satisfaction that the case is concluded. The defendant achieves his or her own victory by ending the litigation and discharging a significant liability for a lesser sum of money. Negotiation mavens frequently use the terms "getting them to say yes" or "win-win situations" or a more modern version of "sharing a commonality." These homilies all sound great, but they are buzzwords. Plaintiff simply agrees to accept a sum of money for a million reasons, and some are very irrational or even downright stupid. Likewise, a defendant agrees to pay a sum of money similarly for a whole host of reasons. Attempting to divine personal motivations on behalf of each party is helpful because the settlement comes to fruition when the parties reach a deal for whatever reason. In the end, the deal is done when the deal is done because the parties want to settle. Forget the psychobabble, just take the money.

Is a settlement an invitation to continue litigation by other means? The famous statement from Von Clausewitz is that "War is a continuation of politics by other means." Unfortunately, settlements sometimes are continuations of litigation by other means if the settlement provides for periodic, long-term payment programs, where the debtor defaults. Any payment program initiated by a financially distressed debtor is ripe for the risk that the debtor will collapse, which will lead either to the enforcement of a judgment or to the filing of a separate lawsuit. This is an enormous risk borne by the plaintiff because the plaintiff, instead of receiving finality (i.e., money in hand, and not later), embraces uncertainty in the event of a default. The debtor defaults because the debtor ran out of money, or the debtor allocated resources to a more pressing debtor, or the debtor stopped paying due to debtor fatigue or the debtor did not care. The lawyer for the plaintiff (the creditor) would do everything possible to ensure that the debtor pays, including a personal guaranty, a stipulated judgment and judgment entered, liens recorded, realistic security, monthly payments or sooner, an acceleration of the unpaid payments in the event of a default, a lawyer's fees clause, forum selection clause for the original jurisdiction in keeping the case open, and choice of law. These terms appear to be eye-glaze; however, the admission of any of these terms will turn the settlement into ashes, leaving the creditor without the slightest recourse. This is no joke. Settlements are like math problems, and any error in the midst of an equation leads to a bad result.

Who has the power in the settlement equation? Bankers have a wonderful adage: "You owe the bank $100. The bank owns you. You owe the bank $10 million. You own the bank." If the amount of money owed by the debtor to the creditor is so substantial that a failure to pay the debt would destroy the creditor (much less the debtor), the debtor has enormous control over the creditor. In effect, the outstanding debt owed to the creditor is the creditor's lifeline. This creates leverage in giving the debtor the opportunity to dictate terms. The sad corollary is that if the debtor files bankruptcy, the creditor likewise will file bankruptcy, leading both of them in the same tragic position.

Are there available options? Assume that the debtor is a wage earner who makes approximately $6,000 a month. For sake of efficiency, the net take home is $4,000 a month. In most cases, the debtor is entitled to a 75 percent automatic exemption in which only $1,000 is a payment each month for the outstanding debt. The creditor can "huff and puff and blow the house down," but the creditor is going to get no more than $1,000 a month or maybe less. If the creditor engages in a rambunctious, overly aggressive collection tactic, attempts to force the sale of the debtor's home, which has nonexempt personal property, and examines the debtor from here to kingdom come, the debtor is probably going to file bankruptcy, in which case the creditor would only get something, or potentially nothing at all. Given the debtor's limited portfolio of accessible assets (the $1,000 a month), the creditor ought to take the $1,000 a month by way of a negotiated wage levy, or a payment program. Call this a case of killing the goose that laid the golden egg. Not everybody is hiding assets under their mattresses.

How about the "two-for-one" deals? Let's take the standard business dispute. The vendor sells the customer $10,000 worth of goods. The debtor claims that the goods were defective and owes nothing. The creditor files suit, and after the to and fro of negotiations, the creditor and debtor enter into the following agreement: The debtor agrees to a stipulated judgment for $10,000, but pays $5,000 in increments of $500 a month, each month, for 10 months. Unfortunately, the debtor defaults on the last month's payment, and the creditor enters the judgment for $5,500. Will this judgment stick? No. This deal is a dead dog. Consider *Sybron Corporation v. Clark Medical Supply*, 765 Cal. App. 3d 896 (2 Dist. 1978). In Sybron, the court tossed the $100,000 award but ordered judgment entered for the unpaid balance of the settlement. Sybron still lives, thank you. See Greentree Financial Group v. Execute Sports Inc., 163 Cal. App. 4th 495 (2008). These cases teach that judgement based on a penalty might be void. The California courts and just about everybody else held that a judgment based upon a sum of money well in excess of the last payment is a penalty or forfeiture. Equity abhors forfeiture and will vacate the judgment. This comes as a shock to just about everybody, as these deals are extremely common. The creditor thinks that the leverage of the big judgment will compel the debtor to pay. In fact, this purported leverage is absolutely illusory.

Take any security? A debtor through a settlement will offer security, consisting of a UCC, security interest in the business personal property, deed of trust or mortgage upon a home, title in rolling stock, or pledge of personal property. This is common but also dangerous. Before accepting security of any type and closing out the deal, the creditor needs to run a title report of real property or a UCC search for personal property, or obtain a pledge to have the personal property (its original state, like a stock, bond, or cash) physically presented to the creditor. More than once, security has proven to be nothing more than a Trojan Horse, in which this horse is hollow and has nothing of value. Neglecting to run any type of title search on personal or real property is an invitation to the debtor to clean out the equity and hand over worthless or useless collateral.

Confidentiality. Most settlement agreements contain a confidentiality clause. These are both good and bad. These are good because sometimes the creditor does not want to broadcast to the world that he took a big discount, which might ultimately prompt other customers to engage in some type of fracas for the purpose of compelling the creditor likewise to discount a debt. On the other hand, the creditor (and of course the debtor) have to police confidentiality to make sure that everybody "keeps mum."

When should you settle? You should settle when you are ready to settle. Settlements end cases. Don't be too quick to end your case if you are uncertain of the facts, if you have yet to speak to key witnesses or obtain key documents, if you are under no particular pressure to settle, or if the continuation of the lawsuit might compel the debtor to pay even more money, or substantially more money at a later time. Settlements bring finality, and finality too early in the process could be a disaster. Settlements are best when the party seeking the settlement has the maximum amount of information to make a considered decision. As they say in the movies, "timing is everything."

What about fraud claims? The toughest claims to settle are fraud claims. Such fraud claims arise out of garden-variety matters, such as the sale of a car with a rolled back odometer, a ring claimed as a diamond but really cubic zirconium, investment on real estate deals in which the money never went to buy the real estate but went into the developer's pocket, and sometimes, tragically, loans to family members, business associates, and friends who have not the slightest intention of repayment. Fraud cases assume many colors and hues, but the bottom line is that the person never had the intention or ability to repay the amount of money or make good the loss. The standard settlement on any fraud case is about 50¢ on the dollar gross. Anything in excess of that would make you, as the lawyer, a hero. Individuals who engage in large-scale fraud rarely pocket the money; instead, they finance an extremely lavish lifestyle, or fritter the money away through gambling, drugs, horses, or other means. A financial recovery from these individuals through traditional means is very remote. Bankruptcy likewise looms extremely large.

Cocktail Party Lawyers. Watch out for these folks. On a Friday, the client accepts 50 percent on the dollar of a long-standing but large judgment. You are happy, and the client is initially happy. The client attends a cocktail party on Saturday night and runs into a local lawyer. Fueled by a little settlor's regret and a drink, or two, or more, the client tells the tale of woe to this lawyer. Sensing a new client over the rim of a high-octane martini, the lawyer suggests that another avenue might have been pursued to generate a better settlement and perhaps current attorney (you!) could have done a better job. Monday morning is the morning of reckoning. The client calls up the lawyer (you) and Mr. Twinkle Toes launches into a series of questions: Why wasn't this done? Why did you tell me to accept 50 percent on the dollar? When was the last time that you did an independent investigation of the debtor's assets? The telephone call ends badly. Blood is in the water. Your blood is in the water. By week's end, the letter hits the lawyer's desk, penned by the cocktail party lawyer, threatening the filing of suit for malpractice unless the total amount of the judgment is paid by the lawyer. This is terrible. This sucks. I hope I made my point clearly. No?

How can you protect yourself from the cocktail party lawyer? In the bazaar of high-end enforcement, everyone including the debtor, creditor, and the lawyer are haggling with each other, and some more obviously than others. The creditor wants money and as much as possible but does not spend any money to get there. The debtor wants to pay as little as possible either on account of the judgment or his or her own lawyer. Both lawyers want to see the case over. The motivation for the lawyers is to close out a hideous case, separate from rapacious or evil clients, start a new case, or avoid the risk of continuing a case without payment of fees. Settlements are the stuff of sausages: lots of stuff gets run through the grinder. Absent a settlement at par, plus interest, costs, and fees here is the letter that should accompany the settlement of any major case:

> Dear Client:
>
> You have retained our offices to collect a judgment due you in the amount of $1,000,000.00, entered on December 1, 2005. Six years have passed and the accrued interest at 10 percent per annum, simple, is $559,994.30, and interest continues to accrue at the rate of $273.97 per day. You have accrued postjudgment costs of $10,000, which is added to the judgment. You have a right to postjudgment lawyer's fees, which we conservatively calculate at about $250,000 with a 20 percent variance, either way. We, along with prior counsel, have undertaken over many years, investigations into the debtor's assets and liabilities. We have also retained the services of a third party who has provided us with a report, which is consistent with

our own analysis. We have served various financial institutions that have lent large sums of money to the debtor and retrieved loan files that included Uniform Residential Loan Applications and credit reports, commercial credit applications in the hands of vendors who have extended credit to the debtor's business. We subpoenaed the credit file of a leasing company that leased a luxury car to the debtor. We also served subpoenas upon a factor that purchased the receivables from the debtor's business as cash flow mechanism. We have come into possession of the debtor's tax returns over a five-year period.

From this information we opine that the debtor has committed multiple fraudulent conveyances including, but not limited to, transferring title to his multimillion-dollar house, changing ownership of his successful business, and moving bank accounts, stock accounts, and other valuable personal property to a trust. The trustee of the trust is the debtor's father-in-law, and the beneficiaries are the debtor's infant children. Posttransfer the debtor lacks any tangible assets. We opine that the conveyance is a fraudulent conveyance and that you can, through legal process, recover some or all of these assets. We do not guaranty that you will be successful, but rather advise you that you have a clear, cogent, and viable claim and cause of action to unwind these transfers. We have run a UCC search and "lot book guaranty" that suggest that these assets are not subject to valid liens or encumbrances. We have advised you in prior letters of these fraudulent conveyances and among your remedies would be the filing of suit against all parties involved including the debtor's family members, such as his wife and father-in-law, who, we have been told, is very solvent. We enclose copies of these letters. You have advised, and we have confirmed, that the debtor bears enormous ill will and hostility towards you. We presume that the basis predicated upon the fact that the debtor believes that he committed no wrong or harm and that the judgment against him is unfair. Whatever the reason, we advise you that the debtor is highly motivated to avoid payment and we perceive that he would avail himself of every opportunity to engage in asset protection to increase your expense and emotional commitment into nothing less than a personal quest or campaign.

We also address the risk of bankruptcy. We have determined that other creditors have filed suit and in some instances have obtained defaults in substantial amounts. The fact that the debtor has defaulted leads to a number of scenarios. The debtor is defaulting because the debtor is mismanaging its financial affairs and is unable to respond to litigation. Or, the debtor lacks the financial ability to pay its debts and likewise is unable to pay for legal counsel. Or, the debtor has engaged in a massive fraudulent conveyance and has no interest in defending against lawsuits seeking payment from an empty shell. Or, the debtor is about to file bankruptcy and all these liens and levies by virtue of this onslaught of litigation will evaporate given nearly all liens and levies within 90 days are avoided by the bankruptcy court as preferences.

If the debtor files bankruptcy, further enforcement would be stayed, absent suing the debtor to exempt the debt from the bankruptcy discharge; your rights to recover would be limited to bankruptcy dividend. We do not have enough information to advise you one way or another regarding any recovery you might achieve from a bankruptcy, but anecdotal evidence suggests that your expectations should be very limited.

Your engagement agreement with our offices provides for fees on an hourly basis at $250.00 an hour plus expenses, and you are generally current. You have indicated over a substantial period of time some dissatisfaction that we have not been working as quickly or expeditious as you would wish. You have also complained about our fees. In turn, we have discounted some of our bills. These fees are non-contingent. When you engaged us, we offered you an engagement at a contingency rate, which means that you have no obligation to pay us fees until and unless we collected. You declined.

We enclose a written offer of settlement that offers you $500,000 as settlement in full of your judgment and all ancillary claims, such as the claim for fraudulent conveyances. While the letter does not spell out the source of payment, we can only presume that the debtor (and his nominee—the trustee under the irrevocable trust) would like to refinance the residence and that the proceeds would come from the refinance. We have informally determined that the equity in the property is sufficient to pay your judgment in full, plus interest, costs, and fees to date. However, title is in the name of the "irrevocable trust," and, therefore, the lien by virtue of your judgment would not reach the real property. We suspect however that the title company who would insure title to the bank who is facilitating the refinance might demand title clear of the abstract given clear signs of fraud in the title. Maybe title companies are very conservative and decline to insure any title if a third party might have a valid claim against the title. You have the following options at this point:

You can file a suit, or proceed by levy and execution, to unwind the fraudulent conveyances, which, if successful, would topple the irrevocable trust, and retitle the real property in the name of the judgment debtor. Your lien would presumably affix to the real property. Moreover, with title in the name of the judgment debtor, and the amount of equity, you would have a credible claim to sell the entire property at a sheriff's sale. Given that the business is in the name of the irrevocable trust, a fraudulent conveyance action might reach those assets, whose net value might generate full or partial payment due you. We cannot give you a precise fee and cost quote at this time, but we are projecting fees and costs in the high five- or even six-figure levels. Given the debtor's recalcitrance, these are only estimates, and we would not be surprised if the fees exceeded these early estimates. We do not predict or guaranty any success, but advise you as to your rights and remedies.

Aside from discussion of bargaining, such as rejecting this offer, and putting forth a counteroffer (which we highly recommend and urge you to proceed down that path), you can accept this offer. The advantage, and inherent value, of this offer is that you would be recovering a substantial sum of money, ending the ongoing enforcement, curtail the accrual of lawyers' fees and costs, and extricate yourself from a time-consuming matter. The downside of this offer is that you are accepting 50 percent on the dollar, which in fact becomes less than 25 percent on the dollar after deducting your investments of past and present fees and costs. You are also foregoing the opportunity to recover the total amount due you with interest to date, should you decide to reject this offer and proceed. As in all matters, you might suffer "settlor's remorse" and perceive at a later date that you have made a serious error and "left money on the table." You have a very difficult decision ahead of you. We are advising you that you have a credible, and even successful, right and remedy to collect the judgment in full. This is a personal and business decision in which you are accepting a deep discount of your judgment and accepting what amounts to 25 percent on the dollar, when you have the option to pursue legal rights and remedies that might generate a far higher recovery and even full payment.

You have other options available to you. You have engaged us on an hourly basis. This means that you pay our fees for our efforts, time, and energy. You have the right to discharge at any time and engage the services of counsel who would undertake representation on a contingency fee basis with or without demanding costs. The fact that you might be able to engage counsel on a contingency fee basis might well alter your decision to accept or reject this offer or even to negotiate. Contingency counsel might charge you anywhere between 10 percent and 50 percent to collect this judgment, but whatever the rate, you would not bear a financial responsibility, other than for costs, unless and until the lawyer collected for you. The disadvantage, of course, is that your recovery would be substantially degraded by the fee due contingency counsel. It is possible that contingency counsel might collect some or all of his or her fees from the debtor, but this is a matter that you should discuss with counsel.

Therefore, we advise you to contact other lawyers who would take on the collection of your judgment on a contingency fee basis. If you find someone who is willing to represent you on a contingency fee basis and proceed to topple these asset protection schemes, you should consider that prospect a viable path for a successful resolution of this matter. We recommend that you locate a lawyer through the local bar association or attempt to find on through the specialized local, state, or national bar associations that specialize in collection and enforcement matters. If you find someone, we will posthaste turn the file over to the lawyer. If on the other hand, you are unable to find someone, or otherwise have made a decision to end this matter, you can contact us so we can discuss some type of strategy in responding to the offer.

We advise you that you have many options, and you are not obligated to continue with our offices. You are free to change lawyers. You are free to accept this offer or reject the offer and make a counteroffer. You are free to ignore this offer. You are free to do nothing. We do advise, however, that the statute of limitations for a fraudulent conveyance is four years, and will expire on ———. So we have the greatest clarity between us, we do not have an opinion that you accept or reject this offer given the multiple and viable options available to you. You have many choices, and this settlement offer is one choice of many. This settlement offer is close to a near sacrifice of your case. Given your options at this time, we advise you that settlement at $500,000 is one option of many. Other options might generate a better recovery. Your decision to accept this offer is yours solely. Given the mediocre nature of this offer, we do recommend that you see another lawyer should you believe another opinion is necessary.

We are providing you with the options at the bottom of this letter and request that you indicate how you wish to proceed. You are free to discuss this matter with me, and I look forward to hearing from you.

Very truly yours,

Mary Jones, Partner, Jones, Smith and Jones, Lawyer at Law

/_/ I accept this offer.

/_/ I reject this offer and direct you to proceed.

/_/ Please counter offer at 75 percent of the total judgment plus interest or $________.

I acknowledge that if I reject this offer, and the debtor rejects my counteroffer, that settlement is dead.

/_/ I am hiring another lawyer.

/_/ Do nothing at this time.

/_/ Other: ____

Signed: ___________________ [Client]

What does this letter do for you? This letter protects you from the earful of complaints stage-managed by the competitor who is dying to sue you for alleged misdeeds and ruin your reputation even though the lawyer is "buddy-buddy" with you. Henry Kissinger was right: We have no allies, only interests. This letter rearranges the chairs at the competitive bargaining table and imposes upon the client the personal and emotional responsibility to make a very considered decision and ratify the decision in writing. This letter compels the client to engage the cocktail party lawyer as the new advisor before, not after, accepting or rejecting the deal, negotiating, or finding a new lawyer. You want this letter, signed by the client in hand, for that terrible day when the cocktail lawyer forwards the demand letter.

Chapter 12

Risks Topple the Vigilant

This is important. Read this chapter and read it again. Memorize it. Tattoo it on whatever part of your body is little used.

Negotiating with a high-octane debtor shoves risk in your face. While you might wind down active enforcement, other creditors march toward Atlanta, and surely will burn everything along the way. State and federal taxing agencies rarely slow down. If the debtor promises you security, check, double-check, and triple-check that your competitor did not encumber, seize, lien, or levy the assets. Give that risk about 100 percent. Gone is 60 seconds, Mr. Cage.

You have stopped what you are doing so you can talk to the debtor's lawyer. Here is what the debtor's lawyer is telling the debtor: "Run for the hills, clear out the bank account, and hock everything to the hilt. Do not delay and do not tarry. Leave nothing behind. Make the first payment and flee." This is not a guess but a guaranty. Expect that counsel will exhort the clients to liquidate everything while they exit the courtroom where they just concluded the settlement conference.

Divorce court, postmarital separate agreements, formal or divisions of property, or family law machinations beckon the parties.

Expect that during the hiatus of the shooting war the debtor will sell all real property, encumber the property with family loans or hard money lenders, or convey mortgages to offshore fictitious entities. This is a certainty.

If you have not nailed down the assets, expect the assets to fly the coop and never return. Even after you consummate the settlement, please ensure that the settlement is not effective and do not give any concession, unless and until you can confirm your lien position.

You don't believe me. This is the sad tale of *Arthur Malcolm Hetzer* (Bkrtcy. N. D. Cal. 1998) 1998 WL 35315852; it shows the risks that accrue when the title report is not brought up to date at the time of the transactions or the debtor does not show up at the recorder's office. After the digital age, the grantor/grantee docket might mitigate this risk. The facts are the paradigm of the race to the recorder:

> [The] Debtor did not perform under the Settlement Agreement: he did not pay $100,000 (or any part of that amount) by ***September 1, 1992*** and he did not convey the Tahoe Lot to Creditor by ***September 30, 1992*** [as required under a settlement agreement between the Debtor and Creditor]. On ***October 6, 1992***, Creditor made an *ex parte* application to the State Court for judgment pursuant to the Settlement Agreement and judgment was issued that date by the Santa Cruz County Superior Court against Debtor and in favor of Creditor for the sum of $100,000. That judgment also provided that Creditor was entitled to receive the Tahoe Lot free and clear of encumbrances, and a deed conveying that property to Creditor was issued ***October 6, 1992***, signed in Debtor's stead by the Honorable Thomas A. Black, Judge of the Superior Court; the deed was recorded in Placer County on ***October 7, 1992***. . . . Prior to the State Court judgment and deed of ***October 6, 1992***, Debtor encumbered the Tahoe Lot with a deed of trust to Beneficial California, Inc. ("Beneficial"), as partial security for a loan of $200,000. The loan agreement between Debtor and Beneficial was dated ***September 16, 1992*** and the deed of trust was recorded on ***September 28, 1992***. Creditor was not informed directly of this encumbrance at the time it was made and did not learn of it until Beneficial commenced non-judicial foreclosure proceedings under its deed of trust approximately three years later. Beneficial took title at the foreclosure sale and later sold the property for approximately $125,000. *In re Hetzer* (Bankr. N.D. Cal., Mar. 31, 1998, 95-52710-ASW) 1998 WL 35315852. [Quote is shortened for sake of brevity, which is the soul of wit.] [My emphasis. Could not help myself.]

The flaw is simple. Two days before the debtor was required to turn over the deed to the property, the debtor scooped out the equity through a refinance with a hard money lender. Postdigital, the September 28 deed of trust would appear almost contemporaneously and perhaps the outcome of this debacle might have been different.

Is there saving grace from this disaster? If the debtor files bankruptcy within one year of making a fraudulent conveyance, and depending upon the egregiousness of the conveyance, the debtor might face the forfeiture of the discharge. *In re Bernard, Bernard, v. Shaeffer*, 96 F.3d 1279 (9th Cir. 1996), in which the Ninth Circuit ruled that a fraudulent conveyance can arise from converting the debtor's stock account into cash even though the debtor still had custody of the money.

Before you move on to the next section, do not forget that you are not alone. Other creditors, including the IRS, are after your debtor and sometimes in a very big way. Your debtor can dump everyone and everything over the side by filing bankruptcy. If the debtor paid any money, give or gave you a lien or collateral within 90 days prior to the filing of the bankruptcy, you will have to cough back everything that you got as a bankruptcy preference.

This is a total crisis. You have to hand everything back to the bankruptcy trustee, or worse even the debtor who paid you the money if the debtor filed a Chapter 11. Yes, you might have defenses to the preference action including the fact that you were secured outside the 90-day window. A bankruptcy, postsettlement, is a big nuclear winter. The debtor, or the trustee, gets back the settlement money, the creditor is enraged, and the lawyer for the creditor faces a risk of malpractice for the failure to advise, protect, or collateralize the settlement. Nobody will ever see the sun.

Section 11

No Money Is No Money

[Turnips!]

Chapter 1

The Money Is Gone and Learn to Take a Hike from the Case

If the Debtor Spent the Money, Is There Anything Left?

What if the money is gone? How could this happen? This is a "No money, Honey," moment. If the money is gone, the money is gone. More than one person lives for that Charlie Sheen weekend in Las Vegas. If the money is gone, settlement is a viable option even for chump change.

Face the facts: Your debtor might have blown the money. Your debtor might have nothing because the debtor expended the money to finance a lavish lifestyle which is common in a Ponzi scheme when the money from one victim pays off another, which chews up some money, but the rest fuels the lavish and even absurd spending. Other than the Madoff bankruptcy, which might recover something for the victims, victims in a Ponzi scheme rarely recover anything beyond pennies on the dollar, and sometimes nothing.

"Lavish" is a frequent visitor to the courts in theft, embezzlement, tax, and drug cases. Looking for the money? Go no further than examining the defendant's home, cars, or lifestyle. Open the closets and chest of drawers. You might find a rack of dresses that are haute couture. I'd bet that 99 percent of America has yet to lay its hands on any garment previously gracing a New York high-fashion runway. Who says so? The courts. The courts view an inexplicable lavish lifestyle as potential evidence of theft or embezzlement. See *U.S. v. Jackson-Randolph* (6th Cir. 2002) 282 F.3d 369, 376, in which the court stated as follows:

> The government argued at trial . . . that the evidence of Jackson-Randolph's lifestyle was relevant to her motive for committing the alleged crimes. According to the government, Jackson-Randolph needed large amounts of money to maintain her lifestyle and spending habits. . . . The district court agreed with the government and cited three cases to support its ruling that lifestyle evidence is admissible to

> show motive. . . . (holding that evidence of an accomplice's exorbitant lifestyle was relevant to the structure of a transaction to avoid currency reporting requirements and the accomplice's motive) . . . holding in a federal education loan fraud case that evidence of extravagant lifestyle was relevant to motive; . . . (agreeing with the district court that the prosecutor's references to the defendants' lifestyles were relevant to motive for committing bribery and misapplication of funds, especially in light of fact that the defendants opened the door to lifestyle evidence by referring to the lifestyle of a co-conspirator . . .).

What about embezzlements arising from the workplace or a trust relationship? Are these cases worth the effort? The usual culprit is the bookkeeper, accountant, midlevel manager, or someone else with easy access to funds and little or no supervision. Stolen funds are often used to finance European vacations, expensive cars, and massive home renovations and to purchase vacations or second homes, jewelry, extravagant clothing, and, believe it or not, an extensive horse collection. This is very common. A debtor might convert the two-bedroom split-level home into the next Taj Mahal, even though the improvements do not increase the property's inherent value. Pouring $1,000,000 into a house is common. The trick, of course, is to reach the $1,000,000 given that the debtor claims that the property is subject to a homestead. The answer is to impose a constructive trust and subordinate the homestead claim on the basis that the debtor cannot use stolen money to create equity in real estate. Maybe, and plan to spend six figures on a lawyer.

Stolen funds finance gambling and drug habits or an abusive lifestyle. What happened to the money? Let's try a whirlpool bath in the master bedroom, multiple $3,000 toilets, additional rooms, marble floors, and pricey kitchen appliances. When Sun Trust Bank went bust in the 1990s, federal agents recovered millions in art purchased with company funds. The purchase price for the art was seven figures, but the true value of the art was 10 percent of the purchase price. Why? When the money is illicitly taken, nothing stops the person from lavish spending.

Some money is traceable into hard assets, which are subject to seizure but usually the bulk of the money is gone or the person has nothing. Accept this outcome as justification to walk from the case. Expect that the records will be destroyed, which renders a recalculation of the loss very expensive and difficult. The embezzler is going to trash the bank statements, cancelled checks, wire transfers, invoices, and other commercial records to obfuscate and hinder the reconstruction process. Expect to spend a lot of money.

As a detour, embezzlement cases have their rhythm including the destruction of records, the clearing of computer memories, incomplete records, and fire or water damage in the accounting department. An embezzlement dawns on management when the bookkeeper wears Manolo Blahnik on casual Friday (about $600) and Jimmy Choo's on Monday ($900) but the books don't balance, cash flow dwindles, accounts receivables vanish, inventory shrinks, or rumors of drug use abound. On a $75,000 salary, does the bookkeeper wear haute couture from Nieman Marcus with a Chanel purse under the desk ($1,000)? Does she find Macy's "so last year"? Does the bookkeeper sport more than one Gucci purse? Is there something rotten in the company? You bet, but the bookkeeper, and others, are carrying on a grand lifestyle.

Can you spot the clues of lavish spending other than the coordinated Chanel dresses, purses, and shoes; the diamond-encrusted Rolex; and the single-carat earrings? You would think that this ensemble would be the "X" on the treasure matter. Well, maybe, but better proof stares you in the face. Literally, in the face. Most embezzlers are middle-aged women who enjoy a position of financial trust, such as controllers, bookkeepers, accounting clerks, or someone else in the finance department. Embezzlements spans years, or even decades, because the embezzler is a trusted employee, lacks any supervision, has total and unfettered access to the bank or stock accounts, and can conceal the theft. Concealing includes inadequate or nonexistent bookkeeping, the destruction of records, false entries and false billings, or years of personal dissembling and lies. Still, why is this embezzlement in your face? The answer is that the embezzler used the money to pay for a facelift. This cosmetic surgery goes well beyond Botox. Unlimited money at hand readily finances massive plastic surgery including a new nose, lips, cheeks, and best of all, resetting the ears. Frankenstein would look like a porker. Cosmetic surgery is additive, and embezzlers seek tune-ups, makeovers, and even overhauls.

Look for the "X" on this treasure map. Aside from the clothes, house, car, vacation homes, horses, trips, and jewelry, the "X" is the face of the debtor. You cannot miss this "X." Why? Because her ears touch.

What motivates someone to embezzle? The answer to this question is the answer, in part, to whether you can collect. All embezzlements start with unfettered and unsupervised access to money or property. The money has to be within reach. Once the money is on the table, the next ingredient is the lack of supervision or control. Embezzlers succeed because no one is looking over their shoulders, performing audits, or even reviewing cancelled checks. Most embezzlements are incremental. The first day, the person steals $.10, and nobody misses the money. The next day, the person steals $.20, and no one misses the money. About 36 months later, or longer, the embezzler steals $1,000 a week, and maybe, at that point in time, somebody wakes when the books do not balance, or cash flow careens out of control.

But why steal at all, aside from greed? Answer: Ego, an unrequited hunger to fuel inexhaustible consumption, arrogance, or anger. Whatever the motivation, the outcome is the same. The embezzler will consume everyone and everything in sight. Collecting these claims is not impossible, but it is typically limited to the hard assets, which were acquired with the embezzled money. Don't expect big bucks from the hard assets. Embezzlers are wasteful and foolish spenders and squander the money on extravagant purchases, whether it's a $10,000 camera and other photographic equipment that Ansel Adams would shun, marble floors from wall to wall in a working class neighborhood, or champion-level horses maintained by a mid-level department head.

Stolen money has no intrinsic value. Stolen money means nothing. Expect that the embezzler is going to burn through the money. If you can recover 50¢/dollar, call me and tell me how you did it. Better yet, patent your efforts and license it to me.

Chapter 2

Recognize the Debtor as a Thief and Recalibrate the Prospect of Collection

The most successful form of theft that works like a charm and is virtually sue-proof is the failure to pay secured debts and priority debts. Let's talk first about secured debts.

Let's start with a commercial building and two partners. What's the alternative definition of partners? Litigants, and it is only a matter of time before they sue each other. As tradition goes, one partner is running the back office and the books, and the other partner is out pounding the pavement for business and bringing in the revenues. The partners agree to refinance the company building. No problem. The inside partner is going to make payments to the bank, pay down the mortgage, and after 30 years, the building will be free and clear. Everybody lives on easy street. Sounds about right? Did I forget to tell you that the inside partner has a bad gambling habit? Gambling habits can consume billions. (No typo!) Gambling habits are worse than drugs because of their insatiable and unrequited demand for money. Why? A very bad drug habit usually kills the addict and ends the addiction. Unfortunately gambling is not life threatening.

What does the inside partner do? He steals the revenue in an amount equal to the mortgage payments, or he habitually short-pays the bank. This might go on for months, or even longer, depending upon the relationship with the bank. The bank debt gets bigger and bigger, and ultimately the bank calls the loan and proceeds to foreclosure. The foreclosure is certainly righteous, and the penalties and default interest ballooned the bank debt even further. However, this huge balance owed to the bank matches the money stolen by the inside partner. Match the due date of the missed installment with the deposit to the inside partner's personal bank account, payments on the inside partner's credit cards, payments to load up debit cards, or even wire transfers to the casinos. Given that this theft is incremental, and maybe out of cash flow, checks paid to dummy companies controlled by the inside partner, or intercepted accounts receivable collection checks, the outside partner would have a very tough time in tracing down this theft.

Nonpayment of secured debt and siphoning off the money imperils other parties. The tempting target is the evergreen cash flow picked off by the inside partner who defaults on the senior liens. The inside partner stops paying the bank, steals the money that would be used for debt service, lets the property go into foreclosure, and wipes out the junior liens. If the owner of the real property is a corporation, and the junior lien holders lack a personal guaranty, the loans in favor of the junior lien holders are wiped out. This is a very neat trick.

Chapter 3

Poor Man's Bankruptcy

Failure to Pay Taxes Followed by the Bulk Transfer

Ever heard of a poor man's bankruptcy? This is what we are going to do. Let's incorporate our business into ABC Inc. We open credit lines with wholesalers, pay the bills on time, and make ourselves great credit risks. The lines of credit expand, which inflates the business with greater product purchases, expanding retail sales, and a greater cash flow. Let's pick an end date for the business in about 90 days. During the last 90 days, the sales blossom because the inside partner runs crazy sales, but payments due vendors slow and even stop. None of these credit lines are guaranteed by the principals. Payments due the State Board of Equalization for sales tax, other state agencies for employment taxes, and trust funds due the IRS slow and grind to a halt. The business is now sold, and creditors file their claims with the escrow holder. The state taxing agencies and the IRS file their priority claims that consume the entirety of the sale proceeds and leave no money for unsecured creditors. Other than the taxes, the creditors get shafted. What is going on here?

Answer: The principals siphoned off the income that otherwise would have paid trade and tax liabilities in a timely fashion. The business was sold for a negotiated price equal to the taxes, and the unsecured creditors got nothing. The principals expertly skimmed the cash flow (i.e., an asset) by diverting the cash flow to themselves rather than to vendor bills and taxes. Rarely if ever would the creditor engage expert counsel and a team of CPAs to unwind this sophisticated fraud given the expense and complexity.

The euphemisms are "Borrowing from Uncle Sam" or "Making Uncle Sam into an involuntary creditor." A very shrewd businessperson would ensure that the proceeds paid the tax liabilities in full and left nothing for the "trades." There is no free lunch here. The reality is that nonpayment of trust fund taxes might impose steep penalties: a 100 percent penalty liability under the responsible officer, who might face criminal liability. Taxes are nondischargeable in bankruptcy.

Of course, the debtor and the buyer negotiated a deal in which only a small percentage went through escrow, equal to the tax liability. The balance is paid to the debtor's inside partner via a "long-term consulting agreement," which is outside the escrow and never sees the light of day. Sometimes the balance of the true price is paid in cash, a long-term note, outside of escrow, payment to third parties as nominees for the debtor (as sellers). Paying off the debtor's principal through a long-term employment agreement is credible on its face because the appearance is that the debtor's principal is rendering future service that is compensated under the consulting agreement. This, of course, is a total fiction.

Stupid conduct kills some businesses. Underpaying employees, sexually harassing the female (or male) staff, cheating customers, running glorified pyramid schemes, or selling shoddy products culminates in a very bad ending. Any of these stunts will guarantee an ugly lawsuit and an even uglier judgment for some obscene amount of money. Justice is preordained. Expect that the employer closes down the accounts, including the credit card processing accounts. The employer stops paying all taxes and pockets the money. The state entities are sometimes slow to recognize that the employer defaulted and might take months before tax liens are filed. These tax liens encumber the assets of the debtor and take priority over junior liens.

This is the perfect theft. The insider can loot the company by siphoning to himself funds that should have been paid to the taxing authorities, which would consist of payroll trust funds, sales tax, and other taxes. These taxing authorities encumber the company assets to provide for payment of the omitted taxes and wipe out any equity in the assets, which all renders the debtor judgment-proof. When you think through this, the process puts into the owner's hands the cash that should have been paid to the taxing authorities, when in turn the taxing authorities seize the company's assets and leaves nothing for creditors. Call this a swap out of the company cash to the inside partner, and a swap in the tax liens to grab the company assets, leaving an empty shell encumbered by the taxing authorities.

These thefts are bookends. The first bookend is the acknowledgment that the embezzler is bound and determined to loot the business, steal the money, or take the asset. This person is a predator who lacks any scruples. The successful theft is the success of his life. Embrace this person and even admire his or her skill. Great job, Jimmy, you cleaned out the bank account. The second bookend is that the person spent, hid, or squirreled away the money. This person is bound and determined to thwart any enforcement, absent an enormous effort and a war chest overfilling with cost money. Don Quixote and Poncho Sanchez at your service.

Chapter 4

Gone with the Wind Is a Generally Accepted Accounting Term

Confronting a truly ugly theft, the judgment creditor might be able to reach the hard assets, such as an overly renovated home, luxury car, artwork, jewelry, and other items of personal property. If the money has been spent on dental care, facelifts, vacations, or expensive meals and clothing, the money is truly gone. If you conclude that civil remedies are vacuous, without making any threats, go to the District Attorney or US Attorney with organized evidence in hand. Sometimes the law enforcement authorities will prosecute the case. The threat of a long prison sentence, more than any other potential consequence, might compel the debtor to make full and complete restitution. Maybe or maybe not.

Why are you in this fix? This is the time and place to ponder your predicament. Size up the person who caused you the loss. Why now? You are going to negotiate with this person. Maybe you might make a deal in which that person has to sign his or her name to a piece of paper. Chances are you are giving something of value to induce this person to pay money to compensate you for your staggering losses. In structuring your deal, should you get that far, hearken back to how the loss occurred. Did you take a financial beating because the defendant embezzled from you to feed a drug habit or fuel a lavish lifestyle (clothing, horses, houses, and trips)? Was the defendant so impaired that he or she ran down your relative and dragged the body 200 feet before coming to a halt? My personal favorite is the two partners who start a business and open up a line of credit with a bank based on the high net worth of one partner. The business craters when the other person illicitly exhausts the line of credit and sticks the high-net person with the bank's liability. Are you going to trust this person to comply with a settlement agreement?

Consider all settlements a Las Vegas show. Really, I am serious. You are my straight man and say, "Which show?" Answer: Siegfried and Roy. What would two Austrian showmen and a bunch of white, and very angry, tigers have to do with settlements? Siegfried and Roy built a spectacular act based on total adrenaline. Call these fellows risk junkies. In seeing the show, you'd think to yourself, this is dangerous, these tigers are wild animals, they roar, they like red meat, and Siegfried and Roy look like an appetizer. The tigers are looking at the daily menu of Roy Tartare and Siegfried al dente. Dijon mustard is good with any tartare.

When Siegfried and Roy took center stage in close proximity to the tigers, they placed themselves in a position of unbridled risk. The question was when would the tigers attack Siegfried and Roy and not whether they would attack. We cannot psychoanalyze the tigers, but if we could, they would tell you, after a drink or two, they're just biding their time. We're waiting for the best moment, they would tell you. Consider your debtors a white tiger. You are relying on the debtor's promises and warranties that he or she will pay as promised, will refrain from fraudulently conveying everything that is not bolted down, and will not liquidate anything else to pay off debts that would survive a bankruptcy such as tax debts. Like Siegfried and Roy, you might exit the show unharmed and ready to tackle the next show with the greatest of gusto and confidence in the air. God Bless these United States, you'd say in the morning. But one day, and one day for sure, this debtor will turn on you, engage in a massive fraud campaign, and you'll end up, like poor Roy, in the mouth of a white tiger.

You can breathe now. It's time for another break.

Section 12

The Battle to Save the Assets from Enforcement

The Soufflé Has Fallen

Chapter 1

Eating Your Lunch

Expect asset protection. Stop being you, and start being the other side. When you win a big case, and after the round of champagne-fueled celebrations, sober up to this question: What would I do if had I lost this case? When you answer that question, you start down the path of the debtor's asset protection strategy. No debtor is going to leave money on the table, no matter how righteous the claim. Expect asset flight.-

Facing a large claim, the debtor is not going to sit still, let the creditor scoop up valuable property, clean out bank accounts, or liquidate receivables. If the debtor possesses something of value, the debtor is going make that something inaccessible to the creditor. This is a not a guess or irrational belief. This is asset protection.

Asset protection is a settled expectation that the debtor is going to hide and conceal the accessible assets. Upon embracing this settled expectation that the debtor will hide, conceal, or secret away assets, and render them near judgment-proof, the judgment creditor can better adjust expectations to reshape a strategy to meet this challenge. This is more than a group of buzzwords. At a routine debtor's examination, the debtor revealed the name and address of his bank. A few days later, we levied on the account. We collected some $15,000, which was payment in full. I was happy to collect the judgment, but I kept thinking to myself: "Why did the debtor leave the money just hanging around and vulnerable to my levy?" My own expectation was that, after the examination, he would close the bank account and open a new account in an attempt to thwart my enforcement.

In dealing with the debtor, or probably the lawyer for the debtor, don't hesitate to mention that the fraudulent conveyance probably destroyed the debtor's right of a discharge in a bankruptcy, but better yet, that the conveyance between the debtor and the conveyee themselves is final. As a result of that conveyance, the debtor might have forfeited all exemption rights, including a homestead exemption. What does that mean in English? The creditor can grab the property fraudulently conveyed out of the hands of the conveyee, and that the debtor cannot seek to protect that property by way of an exemption, such as a homestead exemption. Over the years, we have had many a sad and sorry debtor seek to protect fraudulently conveyed property through an exemption, such as a homestead, when in fact the judge turned down the debtor because the debtor no longer owns the property. In *Slater v. Bielsky* (1960) 183 Cal. App. 2d 523, 526, the court stated as follows:

> ". . . a general rule that a conveyance in fraud of creditors vests title to the property transferred in the grantee except as against the creditors of the grantor. . . ."

Once it's gone, it's gone, and it will never return; the exemption rights will also be gone. Remember that the debtor can only claim an exemption if the debtor owns the property. A fraudulent conveyance action necessarily topples title held by the conveyee, but it does not restore the debtor to his or her homestead rights. Is this guaranteed? Well, mostly yes and sometimes no. A debtor facing the forfeiture of the homestead rights might compel the conveyee to reconvey the property to the debtor who will immediately invoke the homestead rights. Call this a purge. Some judges might let the debtor off the hook. Maybe, Mr. Chicken.

Recycling the homestead rights is a big deal. The homestead right compels the creditor to sell the property for cash at 90 percent of a court-approved appraisal and prove that the cash price would pay prior liens and encumbrances, restore the debtor's homestead, and leave some money to the creditor. Given that a sheriff's deed is difficult to insure for title insurance (but not impossible), the sheriff's sale is for cash and sold "as is, where is," a sale for 90 percent of the appraised value, getting the property sold is difficult. Absent the extreme, most speculators with real money in hand enjoy a banquet of investment opportunities, and a single-family dwelling, sold without marketable title, inspection, or financing, looks a little wilted on the banquet table, but not inedible.

Chapter 2

Hide Assets in a False or Misleading Name

Why are names important to you, or better stated, to the sheriff as the levying officer? Who? The answer here takes a slight journey into the legal process. The name on the contract that is in default is the liable party under the contract, presumptively. The liable party is the person who is named on the complaint and served with the lawsuit, and if failing to answer, the liable party is the name on the judgment. This is a seamless web from the deal, and deathbed of the deal, to the courthouse and resting in the judgment. Assuming that the judgment debtor does not respond to the lawsuit, and why should he, the clerk issues a writ of execution (an order directed to the sheriff to seize property), which names the judgment debtor, which echoes backward in time to the contract. This is a seamless thread, from the signature on the bottom line to the bank account being levied upon.

"What's in a name? That which we call a rose by any other name would smell as sweet." [*Romeo and Juliet* (II, ii, 1–2)]. No, Will, you got that wrong. Fuzzy names make great theater, but ineffectual enforcement, because the name on the judgment must match the name on the bank account, real property title, car, accounts receivable or notes receivable, or other assets. We are not talking about the slight misnomer between James Smith and Jim Smith (that might be a problem, no less). Maybe. We are talking about defendant James Smith and his LLC, Turnip LLC. The writ reaches property in the name of the judgment debtor and not the LLC. Serving a garnishment upon a bank that warehouses accounts in the name of Turnip, LLC will turn up, you guessed it, bupkis. Minor errors might not defeat the levy. Maybe.

Judgment in hand, you must learn what name the defendant draped over the assets. A newly inscribed name cloaks the asset with a veil of invisibility. Unknown to you, the new name imbues the asset with immunity from enforcement on two levels. First, the writ only reaches assets in the name of the judgment debtor who cycles back to the name on the defaulted contract. Second, the judgment creditor might not know (assuredly) of this new name. Here, we have a slight detour. Under fraudulent laws, if the plaintiff knows that the asset is warehoused in a dummy name, the judgment creditor can levy against the asset. In response, the surrogate (i.e., the entity that bears the name but is really the defendant) will file a third-party claim, which is a glorified lawsuit claiming that the surrogate is the lawful owner of the asset, and not the defendant.

Names have two properties. First, the name on the title, or the account, is a name, other than the defendant, and somebody, or something, owns that name. We are going to presume the somebody or something is a surrogate, an entity, or person, who stands in the shoes of the defendant.

Chapter 3

Comedy of Errors of First and Middle Names

Case law is full of comedies of errors over names. My favorite is *In re the Marriage of JAMES and DANA CLONEY*, 91 Cal. App. 4th 429, 432–433, 110 Cal. Rptr. 2d 615 (Cal. App. 1 Dist. 2001). The facts here are very illustrative, as follows:

> The facts are not in dispute. The marriage of James Michael Cloney (hereafter Cloney) and appellant Dana J. Gregg was terminated effective September 21, 1984, by a judgment of dissolution filed on September 26, 1984. The dissolution judgment ordered Cloney to pay appellant $100 per month in child support, plus $200 per month as spousal support for a period of three years. As of September 30, 1999, the total arrearages of child and spousal support owed by Cloney to appellant, including accrued interest, amounted to $17,279.61.
>
> At some point after his divorce from appellant, Cloney remarried. In April 1991, Cloney had title to a parcel of real property (the Property) located at 3222 High Street in the City of Eureka conveyed to himself and his new wife in joint tenancy, using the name "***Mike*** ***Cloney***" rather than his full name of ***James Michael Cloney***. On June 30, 1997, appellant recorded the dissolution judgment in the Humboldt County Recorder's Office at 1997-15460-7 of the Official Records of the County of Humboldt. The dissolution judgment was properly indexed and cross-indexed under the names of the two parties to the judgment as "***James Michael Cloney***" and "Dana J. Cloney."
>
> Prior to the end of July 1999, Cloney and his second wife entered into a purchase and sale agreement to sell respondent the Property. Respondent employed First American Title Company (First American), located in Eureka, California, as his title insurance company. The parties to the purchase and sale transaction (the Transaction) also agreed to have First American act as the escrow agent for the transfer of the Property." [I added the emphasis so you could follow the names.]

By the grace of the holding of the court, that notice of the name to the escrow holder was notice to the parties, and this abstract was deemed enforceable even though the property was held in the name of *MIKE* CLONEY, and not *JAMES* MICHAEL CLONEY. Therefore payment was due the judgment creditor. Had this property been sold without an escrow, conceivably the buyer would have taken the property, free of the abstract, and the judgment creditor would have been thrown under the bus. Names, therefore, if wrong, incomplete, misspelled, lacking a junior, senior, or other designation, impede all enforcement, including passive liens. Shakespeare should stick to playwriting, and not the practice of law.

Chapter 4

Children Can Hide Money

Because children can bear the same name as a parent and are pliable, and cooperative, they are a great choice to warehouse the title of property. Minors are no exception and stories abound of one-year-olds sitting as members of a board of directors or eight-year-olds owning a vintage Mercedes. If the defendant is Mary Jones and the daughter is Marie Jones, depositing checks and writing checks out of Marie's account is no problem. If the check is inscribed with the name M. Jones, merchants would rarely hesitate in accepting a check presented by Mary. Credit cards in the name of M. Jones work for Mary or Marie. This is always the best because Amex frequently uses an initial as the first name on the card.

Adult children are frequently conspirators with the debtor in setting up bank accounts in the children's name to facilitate the warehousing of money. Children will form LLCs and serve as members, or managers, or whatever, to hold funds. Sometimes this is done knowingly, and sometimes it is done unknowingly. Expect this risk.

The epitome of adult children's participation is O. J. Simpson. He really wanted to tell a story. O. J. formed a Florida corporation in the name of the two children he had with Nicole Brown Simpson. Whether or not these two kids knew that their names adorned a conduit to funnel the money that O. J. earned from telling the tale of the murder itself, we will never know. However, the president of this corporation was O. J.'s oldest daughter from a prior marriage, Arnelle, who did know. How do I know that? She was deposed in the Florida bankruptcy proceeding and had knowledge that her name was glued to the corporation.

As Judith Regan told the world, Simpson wanted to confess. I met Judith Regan, and I think that she was wrong. O. J. Simpson just wanted to make a bunch of money, as everybody else did off his story. Sorry to get off the track here, but O. J. Simpson's celebrity spawned the careers of Greta Van Susteren (Fox News), Jeff Toobin (CNN and author), Marcia Clark (CNN and author), Mark Fuhrman (TV and radio personality and author), Robert Shapiro (The Legal Zoom founder), Robert Kardashian, who incidentally is the father of the stars of *Keeping Up with the Kardashians*, as the top TV reality show, and most importantly, Daniel M. Petrocelli, as Fred Goldman's civil trial lawyer and now a big-cheese lawyer. Even more galling is that Petrocelli has his own Wikipedia page, and I don't, and I was the guy who collected the judgment in part. I guess winning is everything and collecting is nothing.

Children are a joy, they say, particularly when they can facilitate the movement of money.

Chapter 5

Parking Money with Spouses and Girlfriends

Expect that the real estate, money, accounts, instruments, cars, and title to anything else will migrate from the defendant to the spouse when the judgment looms large. This is a certainty and not a guess. The defendant and spouse are going to play soccer with assets to beat out the creditor. Collusive divorces are common, if expected. One divorce divested $3,000,000 worth of valuable real estate, including a working gas station from the husband as community property into the wife's name as sole and separate property. Upon examining the spouse (wife) and pointing out this is clear fraud, her comment was, "So what." Mejia v. Reed (2003) 31 Cal. 4th 657 says to the contrary [Marital Settlement Agreements, even if cycled through family law court, do not trump fraudulent conveyance protections afforded creditors].

Transmuting community property that is subject to creditors' claims, even though jointly owned by the spouses, into separate property, individually owned by the spouses, is a fraudulent conveyance. Why? Community property is subject to execution in its entirety. Chopping up the community property into two pieces reduced by 50 percent the equity in the property. Worse, a partial interest in the property has little or no intrinsic value, and therefore splitting the property into two halves of co-ownership renders the property unsalable. The MLS (Multiple Listing Service) has numerous ads for three-bedroom, two-bath houses, but virtually no listings for a partial interest in real property.

Upon the rendition of the judgment, the couple will spend all night and the next day, transferring everything out the defendant's name and into the spouse's name. Upon recording the abstract, immediately run a title search. Do not delay. While you were standing before the judge arguing for the million-dollar default, the defendant will be standing before the clerk in the recorder's office and tending grant deeds that fraudulently conveyed the million-dollar home. Count on this. We had one case in which the defendant recorded quitclaim deeds to her children at 8:34 a.m., in the face of a hearing at 9:00 a.m. in which she appeared to sign off on a restraining order to impound the property. No wonder she was 20 minutes late to the hearing.

Is this enforcement bulletproof? No, but this strategy will defeat the first round of enforcement because the assets are now titled in the name of the spouse and render the enforcement futile, unless the judgment creditors know from the outset that the spouse warehouses the account. This is very unlikely because this information comes later in the process upon service of the subpoena. Stashing money with the wife (or husband) is never foolproof because creditors anticipate this stunt and reach funds through turnover orders, fraudulent conveyance actions, and third-party examinations. However, these procedures take time, effort, and money and, therefore, serve as a natural barrier.

Unpeeling this onion is not too difficult, but unraveling the fraudulent conveyance takes effort and money. Most judges will sign off on an order authorizing an examination of the nondebtor spouse. You can bet that this person will deny the slightest involvement in warehousing funds. Therefore, to overcome this burden, you need to grab the bank records of the debtor spouse, the company records, and the records from key account debtors (i.e., people who pay the debtor), or other people who owe money to the debtor to start the process of tracing. Come in with hat in hand and ask the nondebtor spouse if she is holding any money, and you will walk out with hat in hand. Come in with proof that the wife is laundering funds, and you might walk out with a credible lawsuit against the wife.

Chasing down spouses and girlfriends might not endear you to a conservative judge. Let me share Judge 101, and there is no 102. We have a difficult, but not impossible case before a bankruptcy judge. I was taking an extreme, but not irrational position. I thought it was decent. I really did. At the hearing, and after explaining myself, I thought clearly, the judge responded something to the effect, "Very interesting, but I avoid making new law." In simple English: There's a difference between cutting edge and falling off the edge of the cliff. For the under-40 set, no judge will join the crew of Captain Kirk. Judges decline to "to boldly go where no man has gone before." The moral of this tale: When chasing down third parties who ostensibly have no direct liability to a creditor, work hard to assemble a thorough and credible case.

How do I know this? Prior counsel in a good-sized case did an excellent job of tracing money from the debtor to the spouse, who warehoused the funds until directed by the debtor to disburse to other creditors of the debtor. We sued the spouse on the basis of a conspiracy and fraudulent conveyance, among other claims, and in the end, they settled. This is a case of pure diligence.

No book would be complete without talking about girlfriends as a conduit for fraudulent conveyance. "He put the business, bank accounts, cars, or money in the girlfriend's name" is the typical refrain. The "girlfriend has the money," is more of the same. Is this true? Do girlfriends warehouse the debtor's assets and lend their name to real estate, banking, and other financial transactions? Is the girlfriend the surrogate for the debtor who cloaks her good name and credit upon the debtor's transactions for the purpose of defrauding creditors? Well, my friends, the answer is probably yes, but if I was the girlfriend's father, I would tell her that she is one dumb sh-t. How stupid could she be in lending her good name and credit as well as her safety and security and potentially exposing herself to criminal and civil liability (in the millions) because the guy makes her laugh? Did her brains spill out of her ears? What a fool. One day that bed will go cold and her boyfriend will rob her just like he robbed the other victims.

Spouses and girlfriends won't escape unscorched from this awful melee. If the businesses or assets were transferred from the debtor to the girlfriend like any other transfer, the fraudulent conveyance laws (UFTA and UFCA) permits you to topple these transfers and recover the assets. If the asset have been diminished in value, or torched and destroyed, you have a clear case of liability against the girlfriend who might emerge from this debacle burdened by a big money judgment and no future. "But he made me laugh" won't save the girlfriend from the bankruptcy court or the poorhouse.

Chapter 6

Bury the Money with Limited Liability Companies or Partnerships

Limited liability companies (LLCs) are easy to form, do not require the services of a lawyer to manage, bear less formalities than corporations, and are dirt cheap to form. Let me save the expense and time of reading the expensive asset protection tomes written by lawyers. To protect a business from creditors, these books suggest that, at the outset, each facet of the business be housed in a separate LLC. Dump the sales department in LLC #1, the manufacturing department in LLC #2, and the finance department in LLC #3.

Creditors whose claims arose after the formation of these separate entities would have a difficult time claiming a fraudulent conveyance because the "parsing" of the business arose before debt arose. The creditor might claim that the purpose of the separate LLC was to defraud future creditors. That is tough to prove unless the business immediately accrued the debt in questions or lacked insurance, or engaged in risky or reckless conduct. In fact, dividing up the business in LLCs creates a joint venture because one entity cannot operate without the other entity. Moreover, even though a debt arose later, the court can collapse the entity as one under alter ego theories.

What is the best forum? Nevada. LLCs are inexpensive to form, and there are no taxes. Managers are surrogates or other LLCs or dummy corporations. With a few thousand dollars, and some ingenuity, the defendant can construct a near impenetrable wedding case of an artifice, cloaking untold riches. Absent the FBI armed with search warrants and wire taps, mere mortals would walk from any enforcement. The defendant, as an employee of the member LLC, would have the ability to open a checking account and gain access to the assets, typically consisting of a bank account or receivables.

Chapter 7

Prosecuting the Debtor

Make no mistake. This is money laundering and a crime of significant proportions in the hands of a motivated prosecutor, or injured party who has a lot "juice" in getting law enforcement motivated. Hiring the former U.S. Attorney or district attorney to interface with law enforcement is the first step in getting law enforcement up and running. They all can "talk the talk." The second task, and most important one, is marshaling evidence, preserving and archiving the materials, and making a compelling presentation. Walking in with a shoebox full of financial debris is the ticket out the front door and the request to return more organized. You must prove to the prosecuting lawyer that the government can carry the burden of proof beyond a reasonable doubt.

Criminal prosecution offers the victim a free lawyer. At sentencing, the judge can render a civil judgment due the victim for the compensatory losses without the necessity of a civil trial and usually without further proceedings. State and federal law (California Penal Code § 214(b)), offers to the victim a civil restitution judgment. Let's not forget that the criminal judgment that provides for restitution to the county is not enforceable by the victim. Worse, if probation expires, so does the jurisdiction of the criminal court to enforce the restitution awards due the county.

Civil restitution judgments have really good days and really bad days. The good day for a civil restitution judgment is that the judgment is free. The judge physically fills out the form, inserts the name of the defendant and the amount, and hands the documents over to the victim. No muss, no fuss, and you win without spending a dime. It's very cool, and ever so convenient. This is a good day, and it's even better because you can record the judgment as a lien against the debtor's real property sooner rather than later and hopefully get paid when the debtor sells or refinances any real property.

Why would your civil restitution judgment have a bad day? The judgment is only for the damages that are "out of pocket," such as lost wages, damage to property, and stolen or embezzled money. These judgments do not encompass general damages claims, personal injuries such as pain and suffering, or punitive damages. These judgments do not encompass spouses, conspirators, enablers, or fraudulent conveyees. For general damages you have to file a new suit.

Chapter 8

Play Hide and Go Seek

Let's cycle back to the initial premise. Upon judgment, the plaintiff rarely does not know that the defendant warehoused key assets in the hands of a surrogate. That comes later (we shall see). The first round of any enforcement, such as levies on the bank account, liens on real and personal properties, and seizure of personal property, kicks off upon judgment when the judgment creditor lacks information that these assets are retitled in the name and hands off a surrogate. Of course, this enforcement is futile, inefficient, and wasteful because the judgment reaches assets of the precisely named defendant and not the surrogate. That comes later. Therefore, even though vulnerable to fraudulent conveyance relief, stuffing the property in the name of the LLC is a successful strategy to thwart the first round of enforcement. The defendant knew that the judgment was coming and had lots of time to plan for this eventuality. Embrace, not eschew, this outcome. A less bulky and more streamlined strategy is to establish even a California LLC and to employ the spouse as the manager and member.

Transferring property in the name of a partnership is useful, but the better strategy is to form a limited partnership. A limited partnership needs a general partner. So this is what we are going to do. We form a second limited partnership to serve as the general partner of the first partnership. The general partner of that second limited partnership is an out-of-state, limited liability company. The membership interests of the LLC are owned by out-of-state or offshore corporations that are domiciled in corporation-friendly states such as Delaware. Think of the title entering a galactic black hole and never coming out. It is near impossible to find and worse to unwind.

Setting up a Nevada LLC to warehouse money (or securities) is not a "shot in the dark" but an expectation. Asset protection schemes flood the Internet and are peddled by lawyers, accountants, authors, and even foreign countries. Amazing. Nearly every island country in the Pacific or Caribbean offers to shelter money and promises, even competitively, austere laws that bar local enforcement, invoke Draconian privacy rules, and shield the "banks," or "trustees," from any legal entanglements. Switzerland, Luxemburg, and Singapore, among other nations or city-states, likewise offer similar protection.

Discovering and locking down the names is important, as the spouse's name or ethnic name might appear as the manager member or members. This information is potentially accessible through commercial search services that disclose the names of managing members if they appear on the public records.

You will have no trouble finding well-written and well-researched books that offer fantastic strategies to hide money, conceal assets, or set up a million roadblocks to deter enforcement. Many of these tomes are written by gifted and smart lawyers. Not one of them is a fool. They all start their books off with the same warning: "None of these strategies is foolproof. None will keep the boogey man away from you. Nothing will stop the zealot, the nutcase, the crazy, or the well-financed, from breaking down your door and grabbing the pot of gold." But, these tomes will say, "Whatever we propose is going to make the process of collecting, enforcement of remedies, or any other legal process, so expensive, so complicated, and so risky, that most people would walk. Therefore, the strategies we offer just increase the levels of risk." This is in every book that I have read.

Nearly all of these books provide for a simple theme. Take the asset, business, real estate, expensive car, jewelry, bank account, stock account, or anything else, and chop up or change the ownership. If a business, divide the business into a gazillion LLCs, called cells by the asset protection folks. A cell is part of a business encased in its own title and name and therefore ostensibly immune from the reach of a writ of execution, which is name specific. If an apartment building, put everybody's name on the title. The piece is now a cell owned by different entities or people. If it is a rental, add the parents. If it's a home, encumber it with a bunch of deeds of trust. LLCs and corporations, and their cousins trusts or offshore trusts, are the entities that ostensibly hold title or claim title to the assets.

Legitimate trusts invoke their level of asset protection through a spendthrift provision that immunizes the trust assets and distribution from creditor's claims, assignment, and enforcement. Payments once made are fair game. When the trustee and the beneficiary are the same, the trust collapses under the doctrine of merger absent other potential beneficiaries. Merger is framed as follows: When the sole trustee of a trust and the sole beneficiary of the trust become one-and-the-same person, the duties of the person, in his or her role as trustee, and the interests of the person, in his or her role as beneficiary, 'merge,' meaning that the trust terminates as a matter of law, and the trust's assets irrevocably vest in the beneficiary. Determining whether the duties of a trustee and the interests of a beneficiary have become united in a single person is a question of law resolved by construction of the trust instrument. If the debtor is both the trustee and beneficiary, the trust craps out, maybe. Don't go too far. Don't forget that transfers to children in which the debtor is obligated to support is also a fraudulent conveyance per se.

This dividing, cleaving, and chopping of entities into cells or pasting of people's names on titles has no viable purpose other than to render property difficult to reach. If the property is in the name of a titular holder, and not the debtor, the creditor will be hobbled in reaching the debtor's interest and worse, the sheriff might balk in seeking to reach property held in the name of another person.

Chapter 9

Names Are the Best Asset-Protection Device

Who said America is a melting pot? This guy never left the 1960s fondue party and still wears a Nehru jacket. He is wrong, no, dead wrong. Not so, Joe DiMaggio. America is a salad bowl and each ingredient is separate and distinct. Let's take a tour of our cities. Little Havana. Little Saigon. Chinatown. Koreatown. Japantown. Little Odessa. The Mission. Little India. Little Manila. Little Italy. The list is endless. Other than tourist traps, you will encounter unique ethnic names. ForgetAmericanized names. Immigrants from the top of the 20th century hurriedly dumped their ethnic names and readily embraced Americanized versions, this is no more. Early 21st-century parents affix their grandparents' names on the children.

However, modern business conventions bevel the edge of ethnic names, and render Farad into Fred, Phuong into Harry, Mohammad into Moe, and Barack into Barry, but later, as you might know, Barry into Barack Hussein Obama, president of the United States. So you sued Joe Wong, age 65, who speaks with a significant Mandarin accent. Was he born here? No. Was he born in China or Taiwan? Probably. That is not his real name, but an American name for convenience. What is his real name? Wong Jintao. Is the judgment effective against the assets of Wong Jintao? Maybe not, and maybe not the bank account if the account is in the name of Wong Jintao and the bank lacks any record (uploaded and readily accessible) that Joe Wong is Wong Jintao.

This is a barn burner, and here is the story to prove it. The plaintiff sued the defendant whose name is (changes here) Jack Wong. Like my wife, Jack was born in China and raised in Taiwan. (I live in a Mandarin-speaking household.) Jack was not born Jack but given an ethnic name. The plaintiff was bent out shape because he believed that Jack cheated him out $2,000,000, or so he claimed and sued. Fearing a cataclysmic finale, Jack fraudulently conveyed his million home to himself as trustee in an alleged irrevocable trust for the benefit of his adult children. Boffo, Jack. Upon review of the judgment, I knew that the judgment was flawed. We bought a title report that showed the abstract to be an exception to the title in the name of the buyer. We levied the property that prompted the buyer to call (and scream) that he bought the property free of the abstract. Was he mad? The broker called next, somewhat belligerent, which was something of an understatement. After more chest beating, the broker informed us that the title company, aware of the potential blemish on the title, no fools were they, compelled Jack to indemnify the title company as a condition of insurance but collateralized the indemnification with a cash deposit. We sued the title company for the deposit, along with Jack. Jack dodged our depositions notices, leading to an order to appear for a deposition. On the day of the appearance, Jack flew to Taiwan (My wife knows the territory). We moved to strike the answer. The judge ordered Jack, again, to sit down and face a deposition or turn over the money.

Did I tell you that the case was still on appeal? Oops, silly me. Yup, Jack appealed the case, and since no case is appeal-proof, he sought to settle for good money. On the day of deposition, we were set to go: documents stacked neatly, fresh coffee and the court reporter in tow, all for the 10:00 a.m. show. Yes sirree. 10:00 a.m. came and 10:00 a.m. went, and no Jack, but the fax machine whirled and out popped copies of six receipts from the clerk of the Superior Court that showed the cash deposit (actually certificates of deposit) for the total cash deposit mooted out the enforcement action. The issuer of the certificate of deposit, we found, was a newly formed limited liability company established using Jack's wife ethnic name. It probably warehoused the sale proceeds, and, of course, rendered her and the LLC nearly invisible. The devil was in the details such as ethnic names. Worse, the bank that held the money was just down the street from us.

Does all end well? Winning is nothing, and collecting is everything. Right? No, wrong. Winning helps occasionally. Remember I told you about that pesky appeal. All appeals are pesky. Forget whistling, all you had to do was win. Hang on to the judgment. Win, Forrest, win. Right? Right. This was tried before a jury with an 11–1 verdict. The trial judge summarily denied posttrial motions. How much more appeal-proof can you get? The court of appeal didn't think so. The court of appeal hated the case, tossed the verdict, and deep-sixed the judgment over the side. Call this case judicial spam in a can. At least a handful survived the *Titanic*. Not this case. Other than the defendant, everyone on my side was settled on the ocean floor.

Ethnic names offer other permutations that can thwart enforcement. Hispanic names incorporate long extensions: José García Rodríguez, Mary Lopez Fuentes, Manuel Torres Domingo. Given that the Hispanic community is the largest nonwhite group in the United States, these names now enter the American lexicon. Even experienced lawyers fail to grip the entirety of somenames, and that the "middle name" of Lopez, Rodriquez, or Dias is part of the surname. An incomplete name is trouble. While the last four digits of the Social Security number might resolve this conundrum, the name "Jose Garcia" is potentially incomplete, but not necessarily ineffective.

The law of comparative advantage means that persons with a specific advantage can excel. Growing up in a bilingual home enables the child to excel at the foreign language. Children of college professors excel academically. Children of, say, sports figures, A-list celebrities, presidents of the United States, or billionaires have lots of advantages. Doors open at a touch. Getting your foot in the door is easy if dad owns the door. People with two sets of names, two passports, and foreign IDs in their own ethnic names can launder money from one name to another which is a classic fraudulent conveyance. Converting an account into cash, although still in the possession of a debtor, is a fraudulent conveyance. *In re Bernard*, 96 F.3d 1279 (9th Cir. 1996) [Fraudulent conveyance under bankruptcy when debtor converted accounts into cash, which rendered enforcement more cumbersome and difficult]. The purpose of a fraudulent conveyance is to hinder, delay, or defraud and not necessarily to "conceal" or "hide." Hiding money in a bank account in another name of the debtor, or debtor's spouse, is an expected fraudulent conveyance. Let's remember that the most common fraudulent conveyances are closing down the known bank account and reestablishing the account with a bank down the street, or closing down the account in the domicile state and relocating the account to an out-of-state bank.

Debtor's lawyers routinely, to a T, recommend that clients, facing the crush of lawsuits and judgments, launder money out of their known accounts into unknown or difficult to locate accounts. Lawyers defend that these transfers are nonfraudulent because the debtor still retains ownership of the account. *In re Bernard* rejects this advice because hiding the funds in an unknown account renders the money more difficult to reach due to the burden of discovery. Funds parked in out-of-state banks are even more difficult to reach given the burden of discovery and ancillary proceedings in the other state. Assuredly these funds have fled when the new proceedings blossom into enforcement, which might take months. This advice to hide the money might get the lawyers suspended or worse. See, e.g., *Townsend v. State Bar,* 32 Cal.2d 592. See also, *Allen v. State Bar of California* (1977) 20 Cal. 3d 172, 178 [Participating in a scheme to defraud creditors is a crime under California Penal Code §551 and the subject of discipline].

Parents name their kids after themselves, which is an act of total vanity or family pride. Jim Smith becomes Jim Smith II, or Jim Smith III. The name of the judgment debtor is not Jim Smith, but Jim Smith II. Omitting the "II" or "III" is potentially fatal. There is exception. The great Count Dracula was Bela Lugosi (the "I want to suck your blood" guy before HIV). Bela (and wife) had a son, named, you guessed it, Bela Lugosi Jr. who becomes a world class and famous intellectual property lawyer in Los Angeles. Mr. Lugosi Jr. would appear in court, and the court would ask for appearances. Mr. Lugosi would say, "Bela Lugosi for the Plaintiff." Inevitably the judge would look over the bench and ask? "Are you related?" Answer: Son.

Let us close in on ethnic names. Absent enforcement directed against the nondebtor (could be), or amending the judgment to show the true name of the defendant (could be, but will take some effort here), enforcement is directed against property precisely in the name of the defendant only. The judgment against Moe Gadiffi is not quite the same as the judgment against Muammar Muhammad Abu Minyar al-Gaddafi.

A misspelled name, incorrect name, or incomplete name might well protect the assets because levies and writs reach those assets who are specifically described. If the name is wrong, fix the judgment and writ, if you can. The court might give you a pass to correct a misspelled or incomplete name based on the inherent power of the court to correct a clerical error or to insert the debtor's complete name or names. However, if the judge believes that the error is substantive and not clerical or you are adding parties or seeking to change the status, capacity, or character of a party, the judge might turn you down because you are altering a final judgment. Accomplishing these more substantial changes will require the filing and service of detailed motion upon the debtor and new entities, who hopefully will default. Maybe. Some judges might require that you file a brand new lawsuit to change names if the original defendant was misnamed but properly sued and served. The lawsuit might even reach an alter ego. This should work. Let's keep in mind that the levy, even in a slightly wrong name, or even an incorrect name, might be effective if the third party has clear notice of the identity of the party.

Some of this information might be online, in part, or available through a commercial service. In other cases, some of this information can be readily downloaded.

Chapter 10

Safe Harbor Immunizes the Property from Later Attack

A BFP is a Laundromat to a Fraudulent Conveyance

Once title is in the name of another person, or even titled in another name for the debtor, the debtor can sell or refinance the property in favor of a bona fide buyer for value and in good faith. This is called laundering the title and is akin to money laundering. The buyer would take the assets free of the claims of the fraudulent conveyance claims of the creditors. According to California Civil Code Section 3439.08(a), "A transfer or an obligation is not voidable under paragraph (1) of subdivision (a) of Section 3439.04, against a person who took in good faith and for a reasonably equivalent value or against any subsequent transferee or obligee."

This is called safe harbor and protects the buyer from "buying a lawsuit," unless the buyer was acting in bad faith or did not pay fair and equivalent consideration. Let's say the creditor recorded a lien (i.e., abstract of judgment) against the property. If the lien was recorded with the correct name before the transfer, the creditor wins the battle over title. If the lien listed the facially incorrect name, and assuming that the buyer or financier was in good faith and with fair and equivalent consideration, the creditor will probably lose.

What about bad names? This is much tougher given the fact that the debtor probably did not broadcast to the world that the property is encumbered with a judgment. Worse, the debtor probably did not tell the world or lied about the judgment. The escrow holder did not demand a full statement of identity nor was a fool in failing to sense that the debtor was less than honest. Could the debtor get away with it and flee with money in hand and the creditor be left at the altar without a bride, regardless of the gender or life form? *Cloney* told you that story.

Are we safe? (Ask Dustin Hoffman in *Marathon Man*.) Sorry, Dustin, you are still screwed in that dentist chair at the hands of Lawrence Olivier. Because the property is titled in the name of the transferee (a probable family member), the transferee can sell or refinance the property potentially free of the creditor's abstract, which, if recorded post-transfer, would not show up on the title report.

Chapter 11

Mother Hubbard Beats Out the Fraudulent Conveyance Lawsuit

"Old Mother Hubbard went to the cupboard, to give the poor dog a bone: When she got there, the cupboard was bare, and so the poor dog had none." Nice, but what does this have to with collecting $12 million against pedophiles? To vacate a fraudulent conveyance, the creditor must show that the debtor had a leviable interest in the property. There must be something in the cupboard. What does that mean in English? It means that if the creditor grabbed the property and sold it through the sheriff, then after a probable exemption (i.e., homestead), the sale would produce a recovery (money) to the creditor. Money is left over. Let's say that the property is worth $300,000, that the prior lien (a bank loan) is for $250,000, and that the homestead is $75,000. For whatever stupid reason, the debtor transfers the property, and the creditor cries foul. Could the creditor avoid the transfer? Under *Mehrtash v. Mehrtash* (2001) 93 Cal. App. 4th 75, 81, the court killed a viable fraudulent conveyance action because the property was "underwater" after taking into consideration the homestead as follows:

> In the present case, the evidence showed the property was heavily mortgaged. When it was purchased for $540,000 (or $551,000 if the testimony about a "side" deal with the seller is believed), it was subject to first and second trust deed encumbrances of $510,000. Then plaintiff's own evidence revealed at least two judgment liens of other creditors, for about $42,000 and $58,000 (total $100,000). These creditors recorded abstracts of judgment in 1994 and thereby obtained judgment liens on Ata's real property in Los Angeles County. [Citations omitted.] In the absence of evidence, that plaintiff recorded an abstract of judgment prior to them and they obtained a priority in time. [Citations omitted.] Plaintiff did not obtain her execution lien until 2000. [Citations omitted.] . . .
>
> Even assuming the allegedly fraudulent conveyance were set aside and the property were hypothetically available to enforce plaintiff's money judgment, it could not be

> sold without a court order because it is Ata's dwelling, and could not be sold without a minimum bid equal to all encumbrances and senior liens plus the homestead exemption. [Citation omitted.] Plaintiff produced no evidence that the value of the property could support any ***net recovery*** for her in the event the conveyance was set aside. The trial court was authorized to consider this a failure by plaintiff to prove an essential element of her case (that the allegedly fraudulent conveyance injured her), and therefore was authorized to grant judgment for defendants denying plaintiff's requested relief. [My emphasis. I love marking pens.]

You have to show that the residence would produce net dollars to the judgment creditor if the enforcement ran its full course. These facts are worth reading, given the fact that some 30 percent or more of residential real property in some communities are "underwater," and therefore these equities are immune from enforcement. We talked about this earlier. This is called the 90 percent rule which means that the residential property cannot be sold unless the sale price is 90 percent of the appraiser value, for cash and payment of prior valid liens and the homestead. California Code of Civil Procedure §704.800(b): "If no bid is received at the sale of a homestead pursuant to a court order for sale that is 90 percent or more of the fair market value determined pursuant to Section 704.780, the homestead shall not be sold unless the court, upon motion of the judgment creditor, does one of the following: (1) Grants permission to accept the highest bid that exceeds the amount of the minimum bid required by subdivision (a). (2) Makes a new order for sale of the homestead."

Expect the debtor to bring in an appraiser who will opine that the property is worth millions in an attempt to score a benchmark number that the sheriff's sale will never attain. This is another form of very clever asset protection. However, this magic 90 percent rule is not cast is stone. If a buyer bids enough to pay the senior liens, the homestead, and some of the judgment, but fails to hit the 90 percent mark, the court can nonetheless order the sale. Be prepared to show that the home is the sole available asset, that you worked very hard to generate any buyers, that you advertised the property, and that the offer, whatever it might be, is the best that you have. Engage in intense prayer, but bring a very competitive appraiser. Who would testify that the offer on the table is the best offer and that under the circumstances no one could or would buy the property at the 90 percent cash mark. Be prepared. Be afraid, as Yoda would tell you. P.S.: Frank Oz does the voice for Miss Piggy and Yoda. Listen carefully and you will hear Miss Piggy from Yoda. This is a business of the quick and dead.

Chapter 12

Learn the Tricks of Truly Protecting Assets

The current bibliography on asset protection offers an entire catalogue of schemes to hide assets. They all start with the premise that funds can be transferred from the debtor to another entity that would warehouse the funds and ultimately render them immune from active enforcement. The trick in all of these schemes is to title the assets in the hands of a surrogate but repose in the debtor access to the money. Whether you label these as shell games, money laundering, or simply concealing the money in others' names, the outcome is the same: masking the money in a name other than the debtor, but with the debtor's hand on the checkbook.

All of these transactions begin with the initial act of transferring money or property away from the debtor. Let's stop the show right there. What is this transfer? Writing a check? Wire transfer? Cashing the debtor's check and parking the cash somewhere? Executing a bill of sale to another entity? Taking the current assets and vesting them in the name of a new corporation or LLC? Placing the assets by way of a transfer document in the hands of a trust? It doesn't matter. All of these transfers are fraudulent conveyances because the conveyances are all without any consideration, which is reasonably equivalent, and also done in bad faith. These transfers obviously are to other entities who are the debtor or debtor's surrogates.

Before launching any further into this discussion, let's briefly talk about reasonable equivalency. For example, we have a residence owned by Joe Smith. This house is worth $1,000,000 and has a first deed of trust of $500,000. Joe is the owner, and the property is in a good neighborhood and readily subject to sale or refinance. Joe can readily realize (i.e., put in his hand) $500,000, less costs of sale or refinance, in cold hard cash. This means that an established and well-recognized market that can convert equity in the house into cash for the full value of the equity without delay, big expense, or degradation might arise from converting a capital asset into cash. We call this a very efficient market.

Under exemption laws, the debtor can only protect $100,000, and therefore $400,000 is vulnerable to execution. The debtor says, "I'm going to transfer the $400,000 worth of equity to an LLC, and the LLC will give me a note for $400,000, payable in 30 years, unsecured, and no interest." A creditor levies on the property and claims a fraudulent conveyance. The debtor says, "No, I own a note for $400,000, and therefore I have suffered no diminution of value and still own the asset." The debtor would claim that the home equity is worth $400,000 but just in another form.

The conveyance of the equity in the home to an LLC that issues the debtor the note is a fraudulent conveyance because the conveyance transformed the cash equity due the debtor from an asset that had a recognized and efficient market into a worthless promissory note that could not be converted into cash, lacked any market place, and had zero current value. These fraudulent conveyances are called transformative, meaning that the conveyance is fraudulent to the creditor when the purpose of the conveyance is to transform the title, marketability, or character of the property.

Here is another classic conveyance. Joe owns the $1,000,000 home, subject to the $100,000 homeowner's exemption and subject to a $500,000 first mortgage. The debtor can readily sell or refinance the house and receive gross cash of $500,000. The creditor can reach the $400,000 in equity in execution sale. To thwart the creditor, the debtor forms a limited partnership with his children and conveys the property to the limited partnership in which the debtor's interest is now a partnership interest in the home. Banks do not lend on Joe's partnership interest in home. The partnership interest of Joe cannot be readily sold in the marketplace. The creditor would find it nearly impossible to convert the partnership interest into cash. Transforming the equity into a limited partnership interest is another act of transformation that renders the debtor's equity worthless to the creditor and potentially unsalable. The act of this title transformation is a fraudulent conveyance.

A transformative conveyance is a fraudulent conveyance because of two issues: (1) What is the true economic worth of the consideration received and exchanged? (2) What is the economic value of the consideration from the viewpoint of the creditor, not the debtor? Here, the $400,000 unsecured note, payable in 30 years, is worthless. The present value of this note is probably $10,000, or nothing. This note has no recognizable market, cannot be readily bought and sold, and is unsecured, and the obligor is not creditworthy. Therefore, this transaction diminished the debtor's net worth by $390,000. The second test is the viewpoint of the creditor. The debtor's equity was capable of supporting a lien and a levy. The property could be sold by way of a judicially supervised sale and produce hundreds of thousands of dollars to the creditor. Converting the equity to a note did not benefit the creditor but rather damaged the creditor's prospect of payment. Therefore, all of the schemes that transmute property in effect degrade the economic value of the property and render it nearly unsalable.

This is a time-honored trick confronting the IRS in valuing assets in large estates, assuming we still have an estate tax. If the debtor owns a home worth say, $10 million, and free and clear, the house can be sold for $10 million, the government would get its share. If over the years the taxpayer transferred partial interest to family members and effectively converted ownership to a family partnership, leaving the owner with a 20 percent fractional interest, and the owner dies, the claim would be that the 20 percent fractional interest is worthless, given the lack of a marketplace. In effect, chopping up ownership destroys it marketability because fractional interests have no market and will not support a refinance, sale, or other commercial disposition.

The typical schemes show "unbundling" which means taking a corporation and retitling assets into separate corporations or limited liability companies. How does this really work? Let's start with ABC Manufacturing Co., which makes fireworks. Fireworks are inherently dangerous. Occasionally, they explode at the wrong moment. The person standing nearby probably is going to walk away, at best, singed, and worse, fried, or worst, deep fried and crispy on the outside. We would all agree that this company would need an awful lot of insurance, and even that might not be enough. The clever business owner, understanding the risk, would form a half dozen limited liability companies and sign a series of bills of sale that would transfer the manufacturing section to one LLC, another bill of sale that would transfer the marketing and sales division to another LLC, and finally, the accounting, finance, and "treasury section" where the money is, to another LLC. The idea would be that manufacturing and sales might be the entity that accrues a liability, but if the cash is in another entity, that cash would be protected. This strategy is a fraud, and the sole purpose is to create an enormous expense burdened by the creditor to unwind this Byzantine structure. How do I know that? Potential clients call me up at least twice a day, and in every conversation, we have to quote fees and charges. When it becomes clear that their debtor has engaged in asset protection, such as this, I necessarily quote a contingency, or hourly, and a request for a cost retainer amounting to many thousands of dollars. The standard response is, "Thank you, but no thank you" because the client has suffered litigation fatigue and declines to invest more money in the quest, or maybe I am just quoting too high a price. Whatever the reason, the client walks. Asset protection, therefore, succeeds in protecting the assets because the cost factor in toppling these stunts necessarily drives the client out of the marketplace for accessible legal services. If people wanted to rectify this matter, they should write their assemblyman or state senator to request a change to the fraudulent conveyance laws that the creditor, in addition to any other relief, recovers lawyer's fees.

Intellectual property takes center stage here. The typical stunt is that the owner of the company, a corporation, is the owner and holder of the intellectual property (IP), such as the patent, trademark, or copyright. The owner enters into a revocable license with the corporation. This license can be revoked at will, and without this IP, the corporation is functionally deader than a doornail. Personally, I like this gimmick best of all, but the gimmick dies in the manger of the loan application for the commercial line of credit. If a lender is going to shell out millions to a corporate borrower whose primary asset is intellectual property, the lender is going to assure itself that the corporation owns the IP.

In the postmodern world (no joke here), the products bear enhanced value based on the associated IP which is owned by the borrower. Rest assured that the insider provided the lender with the irrevocable assignment or bill of sale to the corporate debtor. On the other hand, the insider has provided you with a "revocable license," as well as a fairy tale that the insider owns the IP and that the corporation has nothing. This is another efficient market hypothesis application because the creditor perceives the corporation as bereft of its key asset, the IP—being the trademark, copyright, or patent, and commensurately, the judgment is worthless and the quest to recover the judgment might die stillborn.

Standard stunts are domestic asset protection trusts. Here, the settler hands over property to a "trustee" and the settler is also the beneficiary. This is a dog. A person cannot transfer his property to another person in which the settlor is also the beneficiary. Settlor trusts are by themselves fraudulent conveyances. Making these trusts even more absurd is that a person renders himself or herself "asset-less" when in fact he or she needs to represent himself or herself as "asset-rich" in seeking consumer and commercial credit. These trusts are pure money laundering and nothing more. If people want to engage in money laundering by hiding property in an attempt to defraud the IRS, creditors, and angry spouses, among others, they should admit they are money launderers and face the consequences.

Chapter 13

Basic Earmarks of a Fraudulent Conveyance

What's wrong with all of these deals? Elizabeth Barrett Browning would say, "let me count the ways." These are the highpoints:

1. All of these transfers benefit the debtor by permitting the debtor access to cash or property, but retitle in the name of another closely related entity. This entity serves no independent purpose.
2. The assets by the transfer are diminished or drained in value and are not available to creditors.
3. The net worth of the debtor declines substantially or is reduced to zero.
4. The transfer is inconsistent with tax, estate, general business planning, or a routine reorganization.
5. The debtor is facing multiple claims without any adequate means of routine or normal payment.
6. The debtor is left without any adequate assets to pay these claims.
7. The transfers are without fair and equivalent consideration.
8. The transfers and creation of surrogate entities were done in haste.
9. The transfers solely benefited the debtor and family members.
10. The transfers were unduly complex and convoluted, without reason.

Each transfer is analyzed separately. If the debtor writes a check to a nearly formed LLC, that transfer is independently examined to determine whether it is a fraudulent conveyance. If that transfer is a fraudulent conveyance, the fraudulent character of that initial transfer would continue (i.e., percolate) through a transfer to another entity. Ultimately, all of these transfers would be collapsed, as they represent one continuous fraud. This is called collapsing the transactions. It is well established that multilateral transactions may under appropriate circumstances be collapsed and treated as phases of a single transaction for analysis under the Uniform Fraudulent Conveyance Act (UFCA). See, e.g., *Orr v. Kinderhill Corp.,* 991 F.2d 31, 35–36 (2d Cir.1993) and *HBE Leasing Corp. v. Frank* (2d Cir. 1995) 48 F.3d 623.

Fraudulent conveyance law is really old. You can check out the cases that go back 400 plus years.

Chapter 14

How to Unpeel the Onion of the Asset-Protection Scheme

Concealing assets is an open book. What book? Punch up asset protection on the Internet, and knock yourself out with endless options. Most state bars require continuing legal education (CLE). Many commercial services offer CLE courses in asset protection. These classes are not cheap.

You can spend days going through this vast bibliography of asset protection. The books, articles, website pitches, and personal advice all start with the same spiel: Protect your assets from pesky creditors, tax collectors, angry partners, nasty collection lawyers, and shrieking ex-spouses. The literature says the best asset protection is to dump the assets into an irrevocable trust before these liabilities arise. That way, they say, the transfer is not fraudulent because the conveyor has yet to accrue an unmanageable liability.

Asset protection preys on professionals, businesspeople, and entrepreneurs who engage in high-income but high-risk professions. The sales pitch is that asset protection is legitimate if undertaken before the claims accrue. Again, I have to remind everyone that asset protection lawyers and advisors charge a boatload of money, amounting to $20,000 to $50,000.00. Here is a typical pitch:

> What is clear is that doctors must protect their assets from aggressive litigants and plaintiffs' lawyers. Asset protection allows doctors to maintain reasonable levels of liability insurance. In the event that a patient is in fact injured, he or she can be compensated, but is unable to go after the doctor's personal assets to satisfy an unreasonable judgment. Asset protection is most effective when implemented prophylactically, before the patient's lawsuit, rather than as a reaction to the lawsuit. Doctors who plan ahead can feel secure that their personal assets are protected from all future threats.

The entire purpose of these machinations is to protect the assets from future creditors. None of these transfers serves any other purpose and in fact contravenes financial planning in offering a robust financial picture to a bank, leasing company, landlord, or vendor to justify a loan, lease, or credit on favorable terms. Nobody would extend credit to a doctor whose lacks any ostensible assets. Fraudulent conveyance law would unpeel these transfers: "A transfer made or obligation incurred by a debtor is fraudulent as to *a creditor, whether the creditor's claim arose before or **after** the transfer was made or the obligation was incurred,* if the debtor made the transfer or incurred the obligation as follows: (1) with actual intent to hinder, delay, or defraud any creditor of the debtor."

Does an irrevocable trust really work? Not in a million years because most businesspeople, or even the average consumer, engage in routine financial transactions that require the disclosure of financial information that reveals assets and liabilities. The typical transaction is a home loan, credit card application, residential refinance, car lease or loan, or a commercial loan. Postmeltdown, the lenders demand a detailed and verifiable loan application and three years of tax returns, unless you are running for president.

Telling the potential credit grantor (i.e., a credit card company) that the credit applicant owns nothing but the shirt on his back is telling the creditor off. The loan dies a quick but brutal death. No credit grantor is going to hand over a credit card or line of credit, make a secured loan, or finance a car if the credit applicant divested himself irrevocably of all nonexempt assets. Doing business with a turnip is bad business. Yes, it is true that the debtor might completely fall off the grid.

Businesspeople running a wholesale or retail business frequently issue personal guaranties for the trade debt. Vendors demand personal financial statements, do credit reports, and compel the businessperson to provide for financial disclosures embodied in the credit application, such as "Do you own your home?"

Are you chasing someone who claims that an irrevocable trust has title to his assets? Serve every vendor with a subpoena. If the debtor took out a business loan, serve the bank with a subpoena. If the loan with the bank reveals the name of the accountant, lawyer, partner, or affiliate, serve those people with subpoenas. All of these records would reveal bank accounts. Subpoena those records. If the financial statements reveal credit cards, such as American Express, go to town and subpoena those records.

Chapter 15

Irrevocable Trusts Destroyed

Let's once and forever blow up irrevocable trusts or other artificial devices that warehouse title and allow the debtor to deny ownership. Take the simple case: the equity in the house. The big bad boogeyman is breathing down the neck of the hapless defendant who fears the million-dollar judgment that would swallow in one bite the million-dollar equity in the home. This is very frightening because the house has sufficient equity to satisfy a judgment at the sheriff's sale. Furniture, clothing, and kids on the street are the defendant's personal vision. Begging on the corner? Soup kitchen? Homeless?

Consider irrevocable trusts a David Copperfield moment. Now you see the assets in the hands of the debtor, and now you don't. Personally, I always like the rabbit out of the hat and that might be occupational on my part.

What about assets held in trust or concealed in the face of a loan? In confronting any large-dollar judgment, the debtor inevitably claims that the assets are held in an irrevocable trust for the benefit of the children. This is an endless refrain. Count on it. Other family members are the trustee (father-in-law is typical).

What is wrong with the claim that all assets of the debtor are held by an irrevocable trust? Banks, vendors, leasing companies, factors, and financiers don't make loans or extend credit to persons who have transferred their assets irrevocably to trusts, or third parties, rendering the borrower insolvent at the outset of the loan. Banks lend to successful businesses, not turnips. A trust is not a separate legal entity says *Greenspan vs LADJ LLC* (2010) 191 Cal App 4th 486-521 J24.

What about this: "To summarize, in a perfect world, the absolute 'best' way to defend against a fraudulent transfer attack is to create and fund your asset protection trust with a transaction that includes fair consideration at a time when the seas are calm, the transfer does not render you insolvent, you have no judgments against you, you are not behind on payments, and you have no reason to believe that substantial liabilities or judgments are imminent. If you do so, the fraudulent transfer attack is avoided, and you can move on to the next phase of the analysis, but this tends to be an area where the great planners separate themselves from the good planners." If this person lives on cash, does not have or need a credit card, drives the same paid-up car forever, never borrows money from a bank, never refinances a property, and never signs off on a financial statement or credit application, or offers any statement of financial ability, such as a cosignor for a student loan, this strategy still craters. A fraudulent conveyance with the intent to hinder, delay, and defraud, protects present and *future* creditors.

All, and I repeat, all concealment strategies die on this anvil of reality. Concealing, hiding, encumbering, making half disclosures of assets kills every credit deal and renders the assets, other than cash, near valueless, unless sold for cash. If assets are subject to a concealment strategy, the defendant cannot represent the asset in order to secure a loan or use the assets as collateral. Nobody in their right mind would claim that they own nothing more than the clothes on their back when on the other hand, they seek consumer and commercial credit, including, but not limited to, credit cards, bank loans, lease arrangements, and car loans. Lenders do not lend to paupers. Is asset protection one big fan dance? Are we talking about burlesque?

In seeking a loan the borrower is obligated to come clean. Most states, including California, require the trustees of these trusts to disclose the terms of the trust. California Probate Code §18100.5(b) (1–4) compels the trustee to disclose the following:

> (1) The existence of the trust and date of execution of the trust instrument.
> (2) The identity of the settler(s) and the currently acting trustee(s) of the trust.
> (3) The powers of the trustee.
> (4) The *revocability or irrevocability* of the trust and the identity of any person holding any power to revoke the trust.

This is important. Probate puts most folks to sleep. Probate lawyers run around with bow ties and gray suits and talk about estates endlessly. They are super-duper boring. But look Suzie, wake up. This is important. Take note.

The Probate Code §18100.5 compels folks adorned with their phony-baloney trusts to come clean about their bogus trusts and save your bacon from a disaster. Rest assured (and after this book) that in culling through the financial disclosures that the defendant made to the lender, you are certain to find either (1) the defendant did not disclose the existence of the "irrevocable trust"; or (2) if disclosed, the lender demanded and received the Section 18100.5(b) statement that described the trust as revocable. Otherwise, the loan would have died on the vine. Subpoena title, loan, credit, or other files that compel the trustee of a bogus trust to make disclosure, and you should find the Section 18100.5.

Let's cobble this together. At some point in time, the debtor transferred the million-dollar home into an irrevocable trust. The transfer might have taken place well before the claim arose, or maybe took place as a result of the claim itself. The debtor sought to borrow money from a commercial lender, or enter into a long-term commercial lease or other credit transaction. If the debtor represented to the lender, lessor, or credit grantor, that the debtor transferred property into an irrevocable trust, the credit transaction would die. If the debtor sought to refinance the "trust assets," or any other assets, the lender would demand the Section 18100.5 certificate and determine the true character of the trust. The subpoena upon the lender would flush out the Section 18100.5 certificate, which effectively upended the claim of an irrevocable trust.

Dear reader, this is very important. Don't be bashful. When Mr. Foodle Doodle tells you that his assets are held in trust, you can conclude that Mr. Foodle Doodle is a cretin and crook and dangerous. For whatever reason, you chose to go into business with this person, lend money (don't call me if the deal goes bad), or give this person a plug nickel, you must demand that he fill out this statement. You are dealing with a predator.

Here is where these trusts self-destruct. If the house is transferred to the irrevocable trust, the trustee would have to take out insurance in its name. Necessarily the debtor would cancel the insurance policy under his name because the debtor is no longer the owner of the property. This change of policy would have repercussions. Under the secured loan, the bank is a named payee under the insurance policy. The insurance company would immediately notify the bank that the debtor canceled the homeowner's insurance, which includes fire coverage for the benefit of the bank. In response, the bank court acquires its own policy at a big expense, charges back the borrower (the debtor) the charges for the new policy in the bank's name, and in the event of a default in nonpayment, initiates foreclosure proceedings.

If the debtor informed the bank that the property was transferred to an irrevocable trust, the bank might take the position that the loan was due on sale and likewise commence foreclosure. Alternatively, the bank could demand that "trust assume" the loan and demand financials of which the trustee has none. What a mess. To avoid this brewing nightmare, the debtor would in turn advise the bank that the conveyance was to a revocable trust and that the transfer is for tax planning and not a sale of the beneficial interest. The bank would demand that the debtor complete a certificate under Probate Code §18100.5(b) to demonstrate that the transfer was to a revocable trust, along with a copy of the Preliminary Change of Ownership Report (PCOR), which likewise would show that the transfer was to a revocable trust.

If truly a transfer to an irrevocable trust, the property taxes go through the roof. The debtor bought the house in 1990 and paid, say, $100,000, and the property taxes were $1,500. The debtor transfers the property to an irrevocable trust and the country reassesses the property at, say, $1,000,000 and property taxes at $15,000 forever and a day.

In any examination of the debtor about a suspicious transfer, the first task is to point out to the debtor that the property taxes did not go up, that no transfer tax was paid, that the property was not reassessed, that neither the trust nor the bank took out new insurance, and that the debtor continued to deduct the interest and property taxes on his returns. The utilities were not changed. Certainly the debtor will come up with one excuse or another, all of which does not matter. Here, your best friend is the PCOR, if you lay your hands on it, and probably the certificate of trust (maybe) in the hands of the lender. If you were able to get your hands on the tax returns, you will surely find the debtor continued to deduct the interest of the debt service and the property taxes. In state court, don't count on tax returns.

Modern mortgages and deeds of trusts all have due-on-sale clauses. This enables the bank to call the loan due when the property is sold. Remember I told you that banks make the most money in the early part of the loan and not on the back end? Banks are highly motivated to see the loan turn over, sort of like watching your clothing in the washing machine. The loan or your clothing goes round and round. The bank is highly motivated to call the loan due and force the borrower to refinance the loan based upon the due-on-sale acceleration. Absent the most extreme circumstances, no debtor is going to communicate with the bank that her or she sold the house, absent a bona fide sale.

In fact, the assets exit the backdoor only when Mr. Process Server knocks on the front door. Mr. and Ms. Reader embrace this result as a settled expectation. Once again, I apologize. In my defense, we call a judge, Mr. Judge, and the jury, Mr. Jury no matter the gender. Asset-protection lore tells the reader that fraudulent conveyances cloak assets with a veil that can be lifted should the creditor hire a lawyer who would file suit (or execute) under the Uniform Fraudulent Transfer Act (UFTA). Asset protection is costly given the income, transfer, and property tax implication, plus the boatload of money paid to the lawyer. Experts charge $30,000 or more to set up high-class offshore trusts. For asset protectors, it's nice work if you can get it.

How about interest and property tax deductions on the debtor's home mortgage? Here is the answer from a quote from a the *CPA Journal* (The CPA Journal: *Trust Your Home*, by Michael Mingione; www.nysscpa.org/cpajournal/1996/0996/features/house.htm.): "For income tax purposes, the creation of a QPRT is considered a grantor trust governed by IRC Sec. 677. Accordingly, the grantor is treated as the owner of the income portion of the trust's property. As such, the trust's income and deductions for real estate taxes and mortgage interest are attributed to the grantor since the trust is ignored for income tax purposes. Therefore a parent in a high tax bracket will still obtain a deduction for mortgage interest and real estate taxes provided he or she continues to pay for them." A QPRT is a qualified personal residence trust.

What does this mean? More than meets the eye. Even though the debtor conveyed the property to an irrevocable trust, which is a fraudulent conveyance, the debtor continues to deduct interest payments and property taxes against the debtor's income as allowed by the IRS Code. That's no problem. However, we are in the Serengeti of predators, crooks, and charlatans where the rules are slightly different.

Work with me, Judge. The debtor tells you that he "sold" his home to his "irrevocable trust." The trustee is his father-in-law, and the beneficiaries are his minor children. The house bears a first deed of trust (mortgage), which bears a monthly debt service of $6,000 and annual taxes of $12,000 for a total out of pocket of $7,000 plus utilities and maintenance. As a matter of tax law, the debtor can still deduct the interest portion of the debt service and the property taxes based upon the IRS-authorized pass-through. However, under the fraudulent conveyance law, he allegedly no longer owns the property. He sold the home to the trust. However, the new "landlord" is the trustee of the trust who would receive rent payments from the debtor. The debtor would always claim that he is paying rent to his trustee of the trust and produce, if he can, monthly rent checks and a rental agreement that sets the rent equal to the debt service and property taxes. If on the other hand, he chooses to pay the bank and county collector directly, the conveyance would self-destruct as a total because payment of the debt service and property taxes constitutes an admission that the debtor still owns the property. The legal presumption is that the debtor makes payments because he owes the money to the bank and the property tax collection. If he pays the debt service and property taxes that support the property, the presumption is that he is the owner of the property. Owners keep up debt service and property taxes, not tenants.

Irrevocable trusts are all frauds because notwithstanding what the parties claim, the "trustee," which might be the debtor, debtor's spouse, debtor's family members, or an offshore bogus company, retains control over the property for the debtor's own use and benefit. The typical method of control is the power of the "grantor" (your debtor) to hire and fire the trustee, the power to invade the trust, if the debtor is a beneficiary, or the best, and I mean very best, is that the debtor controls the assets through a power of appointment.

This is super clever. A general or special power of appointment gives the holder (the appointee) the power to dispose of assets, designate trustees or beneficiaries, make distributions, invade the trust, and frankly do whatever he pleases with the property. Here is the legal drone: "A power of appointment is a power that enables the donee of the power to designate recipients of beneficial ownership interests in or powers of appointment over the appointive property." The debtor holds the "power of appointment," which means that the debtor owns and controls the assets held by the trust. The trust is no longer "irrevocable" given that the debtor retains control. Some lawyers attempt to escape these consequences by labeling the power as special. This is an enormous zero because the holder can do everything and anything with the asset of trust; the beneficiaries—the 3-month-old infant, the 4- and 6-year-old children, and the wife—are not going to complain. Many of these trusts provide that the discretion of the trustee is beyond judicial supervision and deemed final as a matter of law.

The beat goes on: If the trustee and the beneficiary are the same, the trust is merged. If the trustor, your debtor, can hire and fire the trustee, the trust is a sham. If the beneficiaries are the trustee's family members, the trust is a sham. The trustee is a family member of the trustor (your debtor), and the debtor retains control. If the debtor controls the trust with an LLC as the trustee, the trust is a sham. If one day the debtor owns the business, and the next day, the "trust" owns the business, and the trustee is an LLC in which the debtor is the manager, the trust is a sham. If the trustor can still control the assets through the power of appointment, the trust is a sham.

Remember the lesson from *In Re Bernard* and its many ugly children: The transfer of property from the debtor (the trustor) to the trust is always a fraudulent conveyance because the transfer is "transformative" by rendering the property inaccessible, more difficult to reach, or less valuable to the creditors. In every case, through some clever device, the debtor retains the beneficial control over the property.

Here is one comment that tells everything: "Although an asset protection trust is not discovered in the majority of cases, one should never rely solely on secrecy to defend against every attack. A sophisticated creditor can always get you under oath and ask enough of the right questions to discover the trust. If that happens to you, you should always answer honestly and with confidence that your trust was established for appropriate purposes and that it will hold up on its own merits. The best asset protection trust has the following characteristics: (1) it is funded in advance of a problem, (2) it is created for legitimate estate planning purposes, (3) it is an irrevocable trust that does not include the grantor as a beneficiary, (4) it includes an independent professional trustee in the State of Nevada (although it is possible to use a family member or friend in your home state as long as the parties respect the trust as a separate legal entity), and (5) *it includes a special power of appointment which provides flexibility to the trust despite the fact that the trust is irrevocable*." (*How to Attack an Asset Protection Trust and How to Defend Against Such an Attack* (http://www.assetprotectionatty.com/52-how-to-attack-an-asset-protection-trust-and-how-to-defend-against-such-an-attack/, accessed on May 1, 2014)

Priceless. I am speechless.

Every irrevocable trust is a fraudulent conveyance, and the debtor does everything possible to hide this "trust" when seeking credit, a loan, a lease, a credit card, or other financial accommodation. When the transaction craters, the debtor crawls into the irrevocable trust and waives the flag of immunity from enforcement, which is artfully constructed by expensive counsel. This battle rises and falls, based on the creditor's budget.

Victory carries the debtor off the playing field when the creditor declines to finance the battle. This tragic outcome is common in tort cases because the victim, now a judgment creditor, might not be a person of means, and trial counsel is rarely duty-bound to collect the judgment. Moreover, trial counsel disdains postjudgment enforcement that might take years. Absent an agreement, trial counsel bears no liability to collect the judgment. *Mizrahi v. Miscione* (1967) 252 Cal. App. 2d 673, 676, 60 Cal. Rptr. 680 and *Maxwell v. Cooltech, Inc.* (1997) 17 Cal. App. 4th 629, 632, 67 Cal. Rpr. 2d 293. This fact is well known and well understood, which means that the creditor necessarily incurs a second fee to collect the judgment.

Call asset protection schadenfreude, which means malicious satisfaction at the misery of others. All asset schemes are vulnerable to toppling, but the expense, effort, and commitment to topple these schemes dissuade everyone except the zealots, aggrieved or well healed. Even though vulnerable to a UFTA action, fraudulent conveyances render the assets immune from enforcement because the creditor declines to finance another round of litigation to reach that asset. Call this litigation fatigue.

The asset protection folks claim that the transfer from the debtor to the irrevocable is for "fair and equivalent value" What does that mean? Is this financial gobbly-gook? Courts measure "fair and equivalent value," from the viewpoint of the creditor and not the debtor. Let's take a simple business. Our debtor, Mr. Foodle Doodle, runs a jewelry store. You look up the websites for the sale tax agency, and the fictitious business name division of the clerk, check out a handful of lawsuits, and look through the secretary of state who confirms that Mr. Foodle Doodle is the sole proprietor. By guess and by golly, you figure out that his inventory is worth $100,000.

Mr. Doodle cheated Ms. Ma Ligned when she consigned to him her mother's wedding ring (Mom is gone) and he kept the proceeds. Worse, you find out that the consignment sale netted $50,000, but Mr. Foodle Doodle fessed up only to $25,000. This is really bad. You suspect that Mr. Foodle Doodle has a gambling or drug problem, or is just greedy.

You sue, serve, and get judgment. Thinking that you have easy prey on your hands, you direct the local county sheriff to seize the inventory that the sheriff would sell for a pretty price on the sheriff's auction block. Hopefully, when Mr. Sheriff enters the premises with the writ of execution in one hand, badge in the other hand, and Glock on his Sam Browne belt. Call the sheriff the belle of the enforcement ball. "My name is Deputy Sheriff Doright, and I am here to seize this inventory to satisfy the amounts due this writ of execution," says the sheriff. Mr. Foodle Doodle hands over the new sale tax permit, city business license, and the signed papers that show the transfer of the store to the Doodle-Foodle Irrevocable Trust. Mr. Foodle Doodle tells Sheriff Doright that the inventory of the jewelry store belongs to the trust and that he is an employee and lacks any ownership. Fearful of civil liability for grabbing property that does not ostensibly belong to the judgment debtor, as identified in the writ (this is a very precise business), Deputy Doright exits the premises and reports that the debtor "no longer" operates the business.

What do you do? File suit and move to impound the store (and its inventory) because the transfer is a fraudulent conveyance. The debtor hires Mr. S. Whiplash, Esq. who argues that the transfer was in fact for fair and equivalent consideration because the trust agreed to the lifetime support of the children of Mr. Foodle Doodle payable through a guaranteed salary to Mr. Foodle Doodle. The inventory is worth $100,000, and the probable expenses for the children (all under 10) well exceeds $100,000. What a deal, you'd think. This transfer has a lot of problems. From the viewpoint of the creditor, this transfer converted $100,000 in near liquid into an obligation to make period salary payments to the debtor, which itself (if legitimate) is subject to a 75 percent exemption from enforcement. This "stream of income" has no stand-alone economic value. This stream of lifetime income is not salable; there is no marketplace; there are no buyers; the stream of income is not guaranteed; and nearly every state severely limits any wage assignment. The jewelry can be sold for cash, at once, with a recognized market and generate, say, $100,000 in one fell swoop. The lifetime stream of income has no marketplace, and no buyers, and its market value is zero or less than zero.

The judge would rule that the transfer to the trust is a fraudulent conveyance because, among other reasons, from the viewpoint of the creditor, the transfer converted the asset of $100,000 a worthless, inaccessible stream of income, which is untouchable by creditors through legal means.

The test of "value" from the viewpoint of the creditors means more than whether the asset can be sold and at what price. The value test is whether a creditor can reach the asset through enforcement, and if reached, what price the sheriff or receiver would generate if sold through legal process. Here is easiest. The debtor transfers the $20,000,000 home to an LLC in which the spouse and debtor as the trustees for his minor children are the newly minted members. The house is situated north of Santa Monica in Beverly Hills. The house was formerly graced by an A-level celebrity who can open a movie on seven continents. The house features the Charlie Sheen-influenced master bedroom and Adele private recording studio. Given rising values, and more notoriety for this home, how long do you think the house will remain on the market? Choose one: minutes, hours, or days. I have excluded weeks. This house is worth $20,000,000 in cash, just standing still in the hands of the debtor. Posttransfer, what is the worth of the debtor's membership in the LLC in cash? Zero, zero, and more zero. The interest of the debtor in the LLC has no stand-alone value, no market, no buyers, and no salability. Creditors cannot readily liquidate the interest of the debtor, if any, in the LLC.

Sorry about this long-winded explanation but this is important because every debtor, and his lawyer, Mr. S. Whiplash, will argue "fair and equivalent consideration."

This is a good moment for a bathroom break. I'll be right back. Don't go, and don't change the channel.

Some trusts are a joke. Really. The debtor claims that everything is in a trust. This is nonsense. You have to read and memorize *in re* Schwarzkopf (9th Cir, 2010) 626 F2nd 10321040. Try also, *Steinhart vs County of Los Angeles* (2010) 47 Cal 4th 1298, 1319.

Chapter 16

Some Assets Go Out the Back Door

Let me pass along other secrets. The purpose of all asset protection is to accrue an expense, risk, and burden befalling the creditor that deters further legal action. Asset protections are glorified chain-link fences, with razor wire on the top, that cause the creditor great pause before ascending that barrier. Case in point is the classic call: "How much is your judgment?" "$3 million." "How old is your judgment?" "10 days." "Well, congratulations on your victory. Did he put up a big fight?" "No, just a default." "What can I do for you?" "We fear that the debtor emptied out the bank accounts, and during the lawsuit transferred the business to a new entity under his wife's name, and worse, took out a big loan. Can you help us unwind this mess?" "I might, but I need all the paperwork, and you need to send me $5,000 to give you a preliminary opinion. If we agree to take the case, this is an hourly matter, plus costs, or a contingency matter at 33.3% plus costs, and I need a retainer for all costs up front. We are talking about $30,000 as an estimate." "Well, I already paid the first lawyer $50,000 to get the judgment, and now my expense might double or worse. Thanks for your time." This is a standard phone call. Does asset protection work? Well sure, because the asset protection accrued such an expense to unwind that the creditor, and more tragiclly the victim of a crime, is unwilling or unable to finance another round of enforcement or litigation. The secret is that asset protection is just smoke and mirrors, but very expensive smoke and mirrors.

How do you find a limited liability company set up by the debtor, whose sole purpose is to warehouse money? Some commercial services provide for a cross-referencing of a stated name with membership of an LLC, or as a manager of an LLC, through the records of the secretary of state. Florida, for example, provides for extensive cross-referencing of corporate agents, officers, incorporators, and other information. Depending upon the state and the commercial service available, you might be able to cross-reference the debtor's name, name of spouse, lawyer, adult children, adult children's middle names, or some other derivation, and discover a newly formed LLC attached to any of these people. Depending upon the state, this process would apply to a corporation or limited partnership. If the debtor is born offshore, you can cross-reference his or her original ethnic name.

Section 13

Here Is Where You Can Find the Money

Chapter 1

Here Are Your Treasure Maps

This book is about how to collect and how to find money. Given that the barrier to collecting is getting your hands on the debtor's assets, primarily cash or accounts, this book is about how to find the money. I am going to tell you where you can find the money (or assets) as follows:

1. Stashing money with the lawyer: Facing a judgment for unpaid wages due employees, the debtor after judgment, but before the abstract was recorded, sold real property and parked the proceeds with her lawyer ($200,000). The debtor had a reputation for being obstinate. The lawyer is now in everyone's crosshairs as an aider and abettor. Hiding money with lawyers, accountants, family members, spouses, children, and friends is very common. In many states, you do not need probable cause, or for that matter, any rationale to launch a levy upon a third party such as these culprits. When in doubt, levy on the lot. Always levy on the lawyer who might well hold money in the trust account due the judgment from an unrelated real estate transaction. Do it. This is very common. Lawyers are frequently complicit in manufacturing schemes to hide assets. The candidates are collusion divorces, fraudulent postjudgment separation agreements, parking money in trust accounts, and advising clients to move from one bank account to another, including out of county, out of state, and offshore.
2. Transferring property to a charity: Facing a seven-figure rent judgment (the entire floor of an office building), the debtor conveyed two properties to two newly formed corporations. One corporation was dedicated to the care of cancer-ridden children. The debtor produced pictures of the "dying children." My wife looked at the pictures and said: "Dying? Cancer? Chemotherapy? These kids hadn't missed a meal in their life. Some of the kids, for lack of a better expression, looked really healthy. Our kid doesn't even look that good." As a side note, the debtor organized a picket line in front of the courthouse. The picketeers carried signs that read "save our ranch for the dying children." Local press took lots of pictures. My unbelievable error was not going down to the picket line, buying everyone a soft drink and getting my picture

taken with the group. This was pre-O. J. Check with the secretary of state to see if the debtor recently filed for a new nonprofit corporation, or a limited liability company. Some secretaries of state offer cross-referencing by individual names, or offer indexes under the name of agents, officers, or members.

3. Transferring the failing restaurant to the children: Restaurant owners drove their restaurant into the ground, ignored tax and trade bills, and defaulted on everything else. As a Hail Mary, they transferred the business to their son and posted it on their website. Didn't require much digging on that case. Google beats out Sherlock Holmes every day. You can unwind this transfer by going through the state Alcoholic Beverage Control Department, which will show the transfer from one licensed person to another, the state sale tax records that might show a new sale tax permit at the same location, and the county recorder that will show the transfer of the assets through a recorded bulk sale notice. Try also the county clerk who will reveal a new fictitious business license, and the county health department for a new permit in the name of the transferee. Drop a subpoena or two on the landlord, utility company, major purveyors, phone company, and neighborhood association to confirm the transfer and new owner.
4. Transferring failing boutiques to serial holding companies: Unable to pay shopping mall rents, a women's clothing store owner created serial holding companies and for good measure encumbered each successor entity with security interests in favor of his minor children no less. Now don't run off on me. Personal property security is the shield of choice in defeating enforcement. Cheap, easy-to-file records and a lack of formalities makes this remedy the frontline defense. Most states have bulk sale laws that require the recording and publication of notices of transfer of businesses.
5. Sending financing statements (UCCs) to the rescue: Some debtors transfer assets from corporation #1 to corporation #2. Upon the transfer, the debtor loads up corporation #2 with secured debt, all imagined. If you are quick on the draw, and when your debt goes bad, check the loan agreement, credit application, invoice, or purchase order to see if you can file a financing statement (UCC). If so, file away, and record a financing statement to pick up the trade fixtures against corporation #1. If corporation #1 transfers the assets to corporation #2 (or limited liability company), file the UCC against the transferee. Use a filing service to file your UCC, and maybe you can beat the flood of ensuing fraudulent liens.
6. Creating liens in favor of offshore creditors: What, there's no proof that the offshore creditors exist or that they are owed money or that the paperwork is bona fide? Does this matter? No, because the creditor and lawyer have to work through this misery, which creates another expense. In chasing down a very determined debtor, we cycled through five separate third-party claims asserted by parties claiming an ownership or lien interest in the assets. This guy really didn't want to

pay. He only paid after we sold his Mendocino home at a sheriff's sale. We were within seconds (not minutes) of selling his Half Moon Bay home before he collapsed. Bring money to this table.

7. Transferring a gas station: Facing a fraud claim (which is meritorious) arising from the sale of the business, a gas station owner transferred the business to his adult sons, who in turn conveyed station to the debtor's spouse. Facing another claim for the fees from the first litigation, the debtor and his wife cycled through a collusive divorce. You have to sue everyone to unwind this zoo, including the conveyee.
8. Parking the money in the second wife's bank account: Facing investors nearly armed with pitchforks and a partner belligerent over an unconscionable loss, an investment guru parked his cash with his second wife who in turn disbursed money at the husband's requests. You have to examine the wife, confirm that she laundered the money, and sue her for a fraudulent conveyance and damages.
9. Transferring title to the adult son: Building a home on a San Francisco hillside requires enormous skill. Installing windows that ramp up and down three stories compels craftsmanship, not shoddy construction, lest rain and moisture enter the premises. Fending off the irate homeowner stuck with a leaky home, the builder transferred his own home to his 21-year-old son to fend off collection of the damage award for bad work. Upon the judge pinning the badge of fraud upon the son in a hearing to unwind this transaction, the debtor capitulated and paid off the debt.
10. Transferring the Mercedes to the 8-year-old son: Facing a small-dollar debt but burdened with a supersize ego, the debtor owned a paid-off Mercedes-Benz. He transferred the car to his 8-year-old son. I asked him in the debtor's examination if his son drove the car. The answer was yes, but the kid needed a phone book to reach the steering wheel. Facing a fraud lawsuit, the debtor collapsed.
11. Creating a new entity but bearing the name of the debtor: Facing an eight (8) figure class action for unpaid wages (those penalties double the damages), the debtor created another entity that promptly filed a fictitious business name bearing the same name as the debtor. The debtor quietly vanished overseas. The business continues and wires the money to overseas (China) bank accounts controlled by the new entity and its principals. (I know because I traced the money from the credit card collections that were creditor to the new bank account and that were then transferred monthly to an account in China.)
12. Hiding ownership of a business to evade an injunction and children as recipients of a large-dollar largesse: Facing an injunction arising from a breach of a noncompete agreement and a bar against operating a similar business, the former manager of the aggrieved corporation continued to operate a competitive business, but parked his ownership in a trust for the benefit of the children, claimed the wife as the president, and installed the minor children (toddlers) as board members.

13. Transferring the home to avoid a restraining order: Facing civil claims for looting a trust, the disgraced (ex-)trustee faced a blanket restraining order tying up assets. Minutes before the order was entered, she conveyed her real property to family members. Within 30 days, she reconveyed the property back.
14. Transferring a home to avoid payment of a big money judgment: Facing a million-dollar-plus judgment for lewd and lascivious conduct, the defendant conveyed her or her home to an offshore trust. Unwinding this transfer took a contested trial, leading to a judgment that was upheld on appeal. The debtor filed bankruptcy. The trustee sold the house.
15. Transferring the property before the murder: Enraged at a tenant for reporting the landlord to the police as the town pedophile, the landlord fraudulently transferred two properties and cash. About a week later, he pumps three shots into the tenant's head, at close range. What a mess.
16. Escaping sanctions: Even foreign states engage in asset protection. Facing strangulating sanctions and restrictions against the state's fleet of freighters and bulk carriers, Iran retitled its Islamic Republic of Iran Shipping Lines (IRISL group) under shell companies. Iran declined to rename any ship "The Peacock Throne." You read that right. Changing the name and apparent title to its ships is a fraudulent conveyance, perpetrated by a sovereign state to escape sanctions. Billions of dollars in judgments have been rendered against Iran, and an entire army of lawyers is chasing down this rogue nation in federal court.
17. Beating out Mr. Boogeyman with bogus deeds of trust: Upon receiving a call that legal proceedings were initiated to tie up valuable real property, the debtor on the eve of the hearing records a bogus deed of trust with a fictitious beneficiary. This took a lawsuit to unwind.
18. Having difficulty telling the good guys from the bad guys: Facing exploding insolvency, a corporate debtor engages a "work out" credit agency to deal directly with the creditors. To fend off the creditors, the credit agency files a UCC encumbering the debtor's assets, designating the agency as the "trustee" for the creditors. Individual creditors file suit and seek to attach the assets of the debtor, and the agency intervenes as a third party claiming superior title. This stunt is a total fraud because the "creditors" did not hire the agency. The debtor hired the agent, and the security interest is illusory.
19. Dabbling in debt: Real property equities in California ballooned in the 1990s and hit stratospheric heights that started in 2000. Housewives, entrepreneurs, real estate operators, and retail merchants all caught the real estate bug. No fools, the bank demanded that the newly minted moguls form LLCs that would buy and finance the megaprojects and that the individuals sign personal guaranties. Upon default, the bank would foreclose on the real property, and generate small dollars from the

foreclosure, but charge the guarantors for the huge deficiencies in the tens of millions or far more. These deficiencies routinely broke the $10,000,000 barrier. Upon judgment, the guarantors engaged in massive asset protection by transferring everything in their name to family members, though newly formed LLCs. The remaining equities fled on the magic carpet of fraudulent conveyances.

20. Using phony deeds of trust to defraud the bankruptcy trustees: If the debtor filed bankruptcy on the eve of, but more than 90 days before the filing date, the debtor would sign phony notes and record a phony deed of trust to protect the equity in the home from being liquidated by the trustee. The loan is equally phony along with the promissory note. This is very common.
21. Leaving the liens on the property: The debtor would claim that he or she owed a large secured debt and leave the deed of trust on the property. These false liens include paid judgments. This awful person, puerile to say the least, left a string of debt.

    We were offered enforcement of another judgment, but that went nowhere. This person was not destitute and owned multiple parcels of good-quality but ostensibly burdened, San Francisco real estate. A one million-dollar parcel was burdened with a junior lien from a local savings and loan and recorded through a lawyer whom I knew. I knew that the debtor was keen on litigation. The secured debt, if unpaid, would have sopped up the equity in the property. I called the lawyer who sounded as if he expected the call. After the usual pleasantries, and when I told him that the property appeared to be encumbered by the savings and loan, he told me that the debt was settled and paid. Why did the debtor leave the lien on the property? Answer: Absent the telephone call, most creditors would have concluded that the property was oversecured and worthless and abandoned any attempt to enforce the judgment. The moral of this tale, folks, is always call and confirm whether the senior debt has been paid down or paid off. There is money in those encumbered assets, but only if you ask. The judgment creditor serves the judgment debtor with the release of the abstract. Many a smart and crafty debtor has declined to record the lien release in order to look hopelessly insolvent.
22. Stashing money with the lawyer (Round #2). One of the best-kept secrets is stashing money with the lawyer, specifically in the lawyer-client trust account. The debtor believes that when her or she parks money with the lawyer, the lawyer-client privilege shields disclosure of the funds to third parties. Call this the legal moat. First, the lawyer (and client) will decline to answer any questions about whether the client turned over funds, and while the turnover is not subject to attorney-client privilege, you can expect a day in court in prying this information from either one. The best solution is to serve a levy on the lawyer If money is there, the money is yours. If the lawyer or debtor objects on the basis of lawyer-client privilege, chances are money

is parked in the account, and you are off and running through the judicial gauntlet to compel the lawyer to turn over the money.

The moral of this tale: Serve the lawyer with a subpoena and levy and remember that lawyer-client privilege does not immunize the lawyer from disclosing the existence of funds in his or her hands. The levy is good, and money held by the lawyer should be turned over to the sheriff or marshal. The louder they scream, the more money the lawyer holds. Every year we hear the same story that a financially distressed debtor sells valuable property and parks the money with the lawyer. The lawyer buries it in the lawyer-client trust account. I hear these stories because the client, through discovery, finds out that the money was parked with the lawyer who later released the funds back to the client "when the coast is clear." The client is beside himself. The moral of that tale is judgment should always levy upon the defendant's lawyer.

23. Insulating contractors from debt: Most experienced owners in hiring a contractor will always demand retention of between 5 percent and 15 percent of the job. The purpose is to enable the owner to compel the contractor to properly finish the job by holding a significant amount of money as hostage. Alternatively, many contractors fail to take care of the residual items on the proverbial "punch list," and the retention enables the owner to hire a substitute contractor at little or no cost. You might be able to find all the contractor's jobs through the Permit Database, if the contractor took out a permit. If you find the permit, you might find the retention, and therefore a levy or subpoena. Levy everyone.

    Even ancient societies hated contractors. The Code of Hammurabi spelled out the consequences for shoddy work as follows in Line 229: "If a builder builds a house for someone, and does not construct it properly, and the house which he built fall in and kill its owner, then that builder shall be put to death." If you have experienced the misery of slipshod work at the hands of a contractor, the death penalty is generous.

24. Using storage lockers to hide property: Did you ever see *Storage Wars* on cable? Sometimes, and like *Pawn Stars,* this show features blue collar predicators snapping up the possessions of the dispossessed, depressed, and despondent. There is total bottom feeding here. But this show tells you that a debtor might store valuable personal property in storage lockers under his or her own name and the names of children, wives, and confederates. If you have the time, and money, levy on all of them in 100 miles. It's pricey but interesting.

25. Redirecting accounts offshore: Expect that every bank account is going to be closed, and that the funds remitted as a cashier's check or wired to another account in the name of the debtor, the debtor's relatives, the new LLC, or an entity offshore. Assume that all funds will be redirected to another offshore account. Expect that every securities account will be retitled in the name of a nondebtor spouse. Embrace this outcome.

26. Hiding the accounts receivable stash: Expect that accounts receivable, which are paid by way of check, will be deposited into the account of the successor entity. Watch for AR checks that are cashed. Watch for AR checks that are endorsed and paid over to key creditors, such as American Express, to pay for a personal bill. Watch for AR obligors (the people who owe the money) to pay checks with an abbreviated name of the debtor, or its initials, and the checks deposited in new accounts. The most common is the debtor closes one bank account and opens up another bank account in the same town, or state, or uses the same bank, but reestablishes the account in another state, such as Nevada. Unwinding this problem will take a lot of subpoenas.
27. Hiding money in an overfunded IRA: Chasing down a dentist about 20 years ago was an eye-opener. The plaintiff scored a nondischargeability judgment for fraud arising from a botched real estate transaction and was bent on collecting no matter what. We started the process of enforcement when the debtor offered to settle for 50 percent on the dollar and claimed that this was his first, final, and last offer. The client took it but later discovered that the debtor stuffed excess earnings in his pension account and hid the money in plain sight. You can ratchet up this trick by prepaying or overpaying every consumer bill, credit card bill such as American Express, or interest payment under the mortgage or just prepaying taxes and letting Uncle Sam hold the funds for a year.
28. Leaving title in names of dead people: The running joke near final exam time is the wave of grandparents who magically die of old age necessitating that little Johnny or Mary miss the exam. The same grandparents die every year. Some grandparents do die, regrettably so, but their names remain on utility, cable, trash, and credit card bills for years. Some parents remain on title to real property. If nobody is carping, burying bank accounts and other title in the name of the dead parent is just asset protection planning and good estate planning.

    Dead parents offer asset protection. The classic is that the parents create a living trust, such as Ma and Pa Living Trust, which takes title to the Beverly Hills mansion. Money was never the strong suit for the son, who squandered every nickel and ran up debts all over town. The son is the beneficiary under the living trust (more complicated than that but not important for this discussion) and files bankruptcy to unload $500,000 worth of credit card debt, personal loan debt, and debts from luxury vendors. The son does not schedule "Châteu Le Extreme" because title remains in the name of his parents' living trust. The bankruptcy comes and goes, and he sits tight for years. Might this strategy enable the son to escape his debts, defraud the bankruptcy court, commit a bunch of serious crimes, and walk away a wealthy, but debt-free, guy? Answer: Maybe.
29. Leasing the employees to hide the payroll account: In the late 1980s and going forward, the concept of employee leasing became popular. Company A, instead

of employing the hundreds of employees, would lease its workforce (already in place) from a "leasing company." The employer would send one check to the leasing company who in turn would take care of human resources, taxes, and worker's compensation. Getting rid of disgruntled employees would be easier and faster. Can you hide money here? You bet. Payroll is remitted to the leasing company who writes the payroll check. The payroll money sits with the leasing company and not the debtor and deflects a levy on the payroll account because the account is superfluous. Levy on the payroll service company, the employee leasing company, or even the corporate president of the debtor, any of whom could warehouse the company treasury.

30. Hiding money in the tax returns: Real property is sold at a loss, a business takes a beating, or the debtor loses his shirt in a bad business deal. The taxpayer (your debtor) now earns a loss carryback, which entitled the owners to file an amended tax return and a tax refund of previously paid taxes. Money is in"them thar hills," and the debtor can file an amended return. Under the Worker, Homeownership, and Business Assistance Act of 2009, taxpayers may elect to carry back net operating losses arising in a 2008 or 2009 tax year for up to five years. This is also available to certain small business taxpayers as part of the Emergency Economic Stabilization Act of 2008 (EESA), but it is limited to taxpayers with gross receipts averaging $15 million or less over a three-year period. Prior to these changes, the net operating losses generally could be carried back only two years. The new legislation applies to net operating losses of a taxpayer for any taxable year ending after December 31, 2007, and beginning before January 1, 2010. The carryback election, however, may be made only with respect to one taxable year within such period. A taxpayer that makes an election under the new legislation may extend the net operating loss carryback period to three, four, or five years subject to certain limits.

    A taxpayer who makes a carryback election under the new legislation generally will be able to apply the net operating loss carryback deductions against the taxpayer's entire regular taxable income and alternative minimum taxable income for each year in the carry back period (other than the fifth preceding taxable year), again subject to certain limits. I had a small piece of debtor defense in which the battle was over the disclosure of the debtor's tax returns to see if the debtor was entitled to loss carryback, whether the debtor filed a refund, got paid, and, more to the point, what happened to the refund. Try an assignment order, turnover, or receivership to reach the secret refunds.

31. Hiding money in tax returns: In retrieving the tax returns either through a subpoena upon third parties, or a voluntary turnover, the creditor should retain the services of a tax CPA or tax lawyer to cull through the return to determine if the debtor is entitled to refunds based on the tax carrybacks. Let's presume that the CPA (or lawyer) comes to that conclusion. The next step, and not to be missed, is asking

the debtor whether an amended return and claim for a refund has been filed with the IRS. A straight answer to this question is paramount. If nothing has been filed, and a big refund is due, the creditor has found a pile of money. If the debtor filed a claim for a refund, presume that the IRS paid on the refund. We are talking about appreciable amounts. The refund is sitting in someone's bank account.

32. Hiding the tax refunds: Here comes into play the 1099INT. If the debtor's return does not show a 1099INT in an amount that would approximate the refund, or the refund was not banked in the debtor's bank accounts, the creditor must presume that the refund is sitting with the debtor's spouse, lawyer, or accountant, or is parked in an LLC or corporation or even with an adult child, or sent offshore or out of state. It's there, somewhere. If you see a big 1099INT you see money.
33. Hiding money in tax refunds due from the counties: Counties, such as those through the Central Valley of California, have issued new and lower assessments of property values and, therefore, offered refunds or property taxes paid based on the higher valuations. Property values in certain counties dropped by 60 percent to 75 percent and generated significant refunds. Refunds equalling or exceeding $100,000 on major developments were common.
34. Looking for the bankruptcy proofs of claims: Your debtor might have filed a bankruptcy proof of claim, participated in a bankruptcy proceeding, or been a party to a lawsuit in which the debtor or trustee seeks to determine the interest of the debtor in real or personal property. Run the debtor's name through PACER, and you might well find your debtor as a claimant. You also might find the debtor as a claimant in a district court proceeding, including but not limited to, a plaintiff, among other plaintiffs, seeking significant damages. Check court dockets for lawsuits and judgments.
35. Looking for the money in secured transactions: The old saw is that security follows the debt. This means that the debt, or the debt instrument, is the property, and that the purpose of security is to secure that debt. Cull through the recorder's office or the secretary of state, and you might well find a deed of trust in favor of the debtor, or a UCC listing the debtor as the secured creditor. That means that the security secures a debt in which that debtor is identified under the deed of trust or the financing statement. This "debtor" who owes money to your debtor is properly the subject of a levy, assignment order, third-party examination, or creditor's suit. For every recorded or filed lien, whether a deed of trust, mortgage, or UCC, you would necessarily find the debt instrument (i.e. the note) which in favor of the debtor. Levy, or take possession of the note, and redirect the stream of payments to the creditor.
36. Wearing two hats as a debtor and a claimant: Somebody might owe money to your debtor. This information might be accessible through a public records search. If the case is big enough, you could hire a skip tracer or an investigator to start culling through court records, whether electronically or at the courthouse. As explained

elsewhere, nearly all courts are online, and with a little persistence, you might be able to find this lawsuit. In slapping a lien on the lawsuit, you might be assured of payment assuming that the plaintiff, your debtor, and the defendant don't enter into conspiracy to enter into a collusive settlement providing for payment of chump change, which would cheat the judgment creditor. After that collusive settlement, the defendant would write a check for the full amount of the settlement. If you believe that the debtor (as plaintiff) and defendant will conspire against you, you can intervene and secure yourself a seat at the bargaining table. If you are lucky enough to find that pot of gold, rest assured that the debtor is going to engage counsel to cull through your file and fly-speck every detail to see whether or not he prosecuted the case correctly. Counsel for the debtor is looking for jurisdictional errors that might render the judgment void, and therefore you are crap out of luck (SOL being the technical term).

Upon gratuitous circumstances, we heard that our debtor scored big time in a class action lawsuit and pasted a lien on his recovery. Within weeks, the debtor hired a lawyer who filed a motion, claiming that service of process was faulty because the proof of service showed an address which was not the debtor's place of business. The accusation was called "gutter service." The lawyer attached this proof of service, which was about nine years old. My file was in deep storage, which we pulled, and that proof of service showed the correct address. We had dueling proofs of service, signed by the same person. The judge calls the case for a hearing to determine which proof of service was correct and what was done. The judge rules for us, the judgment is good, and we collected. I guess we all sweated a little, but the moral of this tale is that when a lot of money is at stake, anticipate that the defendant will not hesitate in altering documents in the court file or, in another case, removing documents from the court's file, such as proofs of service. In the electronic age, we would see less of this, but to preserve the file, you necessarily would have to archive and protect proofs of service and other jurisdictional documents.

37. Hiding money in overpayment of common household bills: Credit companies, utilities, home lenders, cable companies, phone companies, and just about everyone else will accept overpayment of a bill. Nothing stops the debtor from overpaying department store, gas, or bank credit cards and living off the credit balance. Sometimes the debtor would overpay the credit card, file bankruptcy, decline to schedule the card issuer (usually a bank), and after the bankruptcy is closed, get a big refund. Call this warehousing the liquid assets. Home lenders will gladly accept and warehouse overpayments. Overpayment of bills is very common. Expect overpayment of the spouse's adult children, company (LLC or corporation) credit cards, or trade bills.
38. Conveying property to a Bahamian trust: In the face of spirited enforcement, debtors will convey their multimillion-dollar home to a Bahamian trust in which the trustee

is an offshore Bahamian trust officer, corporation, or third party as a trust protector. These are all frauds, but they are expensive to set aside. These are near certainties if the judgment against the debtor is based upon some type of major personal injury, property damage, or embezzlement. Expect this outcome. You can topple this trust because the borrower, your debtor, still deducts the interest payments on the IRS tax return, continues to pay property taxes, doesn't pay rent to the trustee, retains utility service in his or her name, and represents the property as his or her own in third-party financial statements. Notwithstanding this outcome, these transfers are nearly guaranteed.

Chapter 2

Capturing Real Estate

Flaws in Real Property Titles

Let's go through the telltale signs of a fraudulent deed. Unwinding the bad deed to property enables the creditor to reach the property and compel its sale. The bad deed, or bad transaction, is full of clues and arrows. Unwind the bad deed, and you find the salable assets. Let's get to work.

The deed shows that no transfer taxes have been paid. What does this mean?

State law imposes transfer taxes, which are calculated based on the consideration (i.e., money) paid for the property and paid to the city or county. The rate is about 1.2 percent to 1.5 percent of the total "new" (real money) consideration. The transfer tax section is found at the top of the deed or in the upper right-hand corner. The claimed exemption from the transfer taxes evidences a lack of consideration. No taxes paid means the buyer paid nothing.

The second risk of any transfer is a reassessment under Proposition 13. Proposition 13, as part of California law (and many other states), keeps the property taxes (about 1.5 percent of the value) at their original assessment unless the property is sold to a bona fide buyer who would pay property taxes based on the "new value," which is nearly the purchase in every transaction. For example, property held by the same person in 1950 (ignoring everything else) for $50,000 accrues annual property taxes of $750. Today that property is worth $5,000,000, but the taxes are $750 (not quite but close for this analysis). When the property is sold for $5 million, the buyer pays transfer taxes at $1.10 per thousand against the purchase price or $75,000. Protected transfers such as transfer from the original owner to a trust in which the owner retains his beneficial interest (living trust) would not trigger a transfer tax or a new assessment.

If the transfer does not prompt a substantial property transfer tax and does not compel a steep reassessment in taxable value, the only conclusion is that the debtor transferred the property to an entity that he represented as a "transferee in name only" and as "no change of beneficial interest" to the county tax collector and assessor. Presto gizmo! You have solid proof of a fraudulent conveyance. Call this a wobbling star moment. If you don't see the transfer taxes and don't see the Proposition 13 reassessment, you can conclude that the transfer is fraudulent. The presence of bona fide taxes and a market-based reassessment is the hidden planet that makes the star wobble. Love this every time.

Let's keep in mind that some county tax assessors will reassess property if the transfer is to a new entity (unless there are claims of the identical beneficial interest between the transferor and transferee). This is bad news for the debtor because the transfer is going to trigger at least a new market-based assessment with staggering property taxes, which are "forever." To avoid this reassessment, the debtor will engineer a putative sale to a stranger, but in fact spell out in the Preliminary Change of Ownership Report (PCOR) that the debtor is still the owner.

Chapter 3

Transfer to a Closely Related Entity Is Always Fraudulent

Aside from transfers to family members, business associates, and spouses, the defendant may also transfer the property to a limited liability company or limited partnership. The word *family* as an adjective to *partnership* usually signifies that the purpose of the partnership is to repose an asset in the hands of family members for the purpose of rendering it invulnerable to enforcement. The defendant or family members are the members of the limited liability company or the general partner of the limited partnership or even form an LLC to be the general partner of the limited partnership. Again to avoid transfer taxes, the face of the deed will claim an exemption. This is a guaranty.

Family partnerships are a favorite among asset protection specialists because the debtor can transfer the asset to an entity in which the debtor is the sole general partner, and therefore retains total control and enjoys the beneficial use of the asset. The limited partners are family members and ever minor children. In a debtor's examination, the debtor always states that the transfer to the family partnership was part of "estate planning," or "gift giving" and that the debtor was talking about this for "years." The transfer to the partnership transforms the title from the debtor as the sole owner and substitutes in place a partnership, in which the debtor's interest is in a partnership. Although the real property might have been freely salable in the open market and had a known market value, the interest in the partnership has no market value. The interest is not transferable under the partnership and is difficult to reach by levy. Many family partnership agreements preclude the free transferability of the partnership interest, which would destroy any value at all. The judgment creditor would have a difficult time reaching the partnership asset through a charging order (the method to reach a partnership interest), and even if successful, the partnership might spin off negative tax treatment, which is akin to a poison pill.

Rendering family partnerships even more ugly and pernicious is when the judgment debtor is the ex-husband who transfers assets to a family partnership in which the limited partners are minors from the marriage of the husband and wife. This is puerile. If the wife seeks to unwind the transfer as a fraudulent conveyance, conceivably, the wife would have to sue her minor children to unwind the transaction as they might be "necessary and indispensable parties" to the lawsuit. Certainly no ex-wife is going to sue her own children to unwind a fraudulent transfer. Just the idea of suing one's own children or even appointing the suing parent as guardian ad litem is repulsive.

Again, the key here is to transfer the property to the same parties with their beneficial ownership intact to avoid payment of transfer taxes.

Chapter 4

Badges of Fraud

These are the typical badges of fraud in a real estate transaction:

1. When was the conveyance consummated—on the date of the incident, the filing of the suit, when the process was served, the key deposition, the summary judgment, the trial, or the entry of judgment?
   As the milestones of litigation, these events represent the plaintiff's drive to judgment. At every turn, the defendant is likewise motivated to hide assets. Line up the docket from the court with the recorder's office. The day that you seek the lawsuit to be served might be the date that you see the new "mortgage" on the house in which the mortgage holder is the wife, minor child, or father-in-law. Repeatedly (and I mean many times), we match the litigation docket with the recorder records and find that events in the litigation track transfers and liens. Fraudulent deeds or mortgages precede the entry of judgment by days, hours, or minutes.
2. Is the defendant or family member a principal of the conveyee? Again check names, and don't forget maiden names, ethnic names, or the natures of in-laws.
3. Was the transaction consummated in haste using, for example, handwritten corrections or changes to the documents? Watch for white outs, cross outs, misspellings, handwritten descriptions, and coffee stains.
4. Does the conveyor have a separate business existence, books or files, office, or existence other than to warehouse the title to the property? Are the conveyor and the conveyee at the same address?
5. Did the conveyor assume, as opposed to take subject to, the prior consensual secured defendant, maintain a bank account to pay insurance, maintenance, property taxes, and accounting charges? Subpoena the records of the conveyor to see if (a) this entity has records and (b) who is paying these routine charges for maintaining the property.
6. What is the place of business, or mailing address for the conveyee, such as the address for the defendant or commercial post office box established by the defendant? A post office box address for the conveyee is the tip-off that the conveyee is a fraud.

7. Has the defendant executed deeds of trusts, or other instruments as attorney-in-fact, or as the officer, member, or agent for the conveyee? Is the defendant's name in too many places?
8. Was the conveyee formed during the pendency of a tort action and, if so, by whom? Start pulling records from the secretary of state.
9. Is the entity created out of state such as in Nevada or Florida? (Nevada is a haven for phony LLCs.)
10. Has the defendant consummated multiple conveyances to all closely related entities? Upon judgment did the defendant convey everything away—think of the last 3 minutes of the *Titanic*.
11. Was the conveyance recorded after claims arose from other lawsuits, the filing of those lawsuits, or the recording of liens arising from other judgments? Timing is everything. If the accident is today and the transfer is tomorrow, you've got a fraudulent conveyance on your hands. Most real property transactions are done deliberately even given the expense, income tax repercussions, and significance of any transactions in a lifetime.
12. Routine deeds of trust (or mortgages) [or grant deed] might reveal a 10-digit order number for the title company, an 8- to 15-digit loan number for the bank, or an 8-digit escrow number for the escrow holder. The deeds of trust might show that the lender is located out of state, that the loan is for an amount near 70 percent to 80 percent of loan to value, and the face the deed of trust shows a 10-, 14-, 20-, or 30-year maturity. The transaction was facilitated through, and recorded by, a professional escrow company. "Recording Requested by: XXXX Title Company." The recording of the document is usually early morning (8:00 a.m.). This is important because the title company is always fearful of last-minute judgment or tax liens that might impair title. If you want to take the extra step, you can locate the place of work for the notary. The fact that the notary is an employee of the escrow company suggests that the transaction is legitimate. If the notary works out of the UPS or FedEx store, the transaction was notarized over the weekend, and records weeks or months later suggests the deed is fraudulent. The deed of trust (or mortgage) might constitute a series of recorded documents, including other recorded documents such as an interspousal deed, or other routine filings. A grant deed for a bona fide sale might reveal much of this information, and all this information is routine. The absence of this information suggests a fraudulent transaction. Going backwards a little bit, if the transaction is for the sale of property, the face of the deed reveals the amount of the transfer tax.
13. Eagle badge for fraud.`

A transfer to a trustee of an irrevocable trust is the key badge of a fraudulent conveyance. The purpose of this conveyance is to cloak title in the name of another entity (i.e., the trustee of the trust) and repose the beneficial interest in the hands of the defendant. Some trustees are offshore entities (usually created in an offshore island nation), family members (common), or sometimes the ethnic name of the defendant itself. Any irrevocable trust is a fraudulent transfer per se. Any transfer to a trust entity where the trustee is "offshore," a "trust protector," a Nevada corporation, or any entity controlled by the debtor is a fraudulent conveyance.

Chapter 5

The Preliminary Change of Ownership Report

Another source of information that reveals a transaction's true nature is the Preliminary Change of Ownership Report (PCOR) (signed by the buyer), which explains the transaction. If taxes have not been paid on the transaction given any of these exceptions, you have a fraudulent conveyance on your hand.

The PCOR compels the buyer to disclose whether the transfer is to a revocable or irrevocable trust, whether the transfer is a change of title only and not beneficial interest, or whether the transfer is for a name change only and not a change of party. The PCOR also compels the buyer to disclose the purchase terms, such as a purchase, foreclosure, gift, trade, merger of companies, contract of sale, or leaseback. The PCOR likewise compels the buyer to provide the financial terms of the transfer, if a purchase, including the purchase price, down payment, mortgage information, total consideration, and terms of sale. The PCOR compels the buyer to generally describe the property.

The form would unwind any fraudulent transfer of real property because the debtor who is in disguise as the buyer would never tell the county that the sale was to a stranger because the county would reassess the transfer to the current value. The buyer would never disclose a purchase price because the county would demand transfer taxes. To avoid the reassessment (and therefore high property taxes in perpetuity) and transfer taxes, the buyer (who is the debtor) would claim that that the transfer is a change of title and not ownership. The PCOR is a treasure map. Congratulations on finding this map.

Chapter 6

Bad Deal for the Debtor

Holding title in the name of a conveyee is financially adverse to the defendant as follows:

If a home, the defendant forfeited all homestead protection because the defendant is no longer the owner; the conveyee (e.g., LLC) is not entitled to the homestead exemption. This is a major disaster because the judgment creditor, if able to unwind the transaction, can proceed with the sale of home and credit bid part of the judgment. A credit bid means that the judgment creditor does not have to bid money but only a credit against the judgment. If the equity in the property is $500,000 and the judgment is for $10 million, the judgment creditor can bid in $500,000 (or any amount), and beat out any competitor bidders who must bid real money.

The defendant is not the owner and cannot deduct from incomes taxes the interest expenses or county property taxes, because the defendant claims to be a renter.

The defendant probably continues to make payments to the senior lenders and taxes, but without any purpose given that the defendant no longer owns the home. The standard repartee is that the defendant is paying rent equal to the mortgage. This claim collapses because the defendant, if believed, is now paying rent equal to a mortgage, after giving up equity in a home for no economic value in return. (See later discussion on tax implications.) A subpoena served upon the lender would reveal this information. Bank records show that the debtor is paying the debt service, taxes, and normal maintenance.

If the conveyance is the change of title, not beneficial interest, the transfer passes without the tax consequence courtesy of California Proposition 13 and other state equivalents (California Revenue and Taxation Code §11923(d) or the tax gnomes). On the other hand, if the defendant conveys the property to an irrevocable trust, the county could seek a reassessment that would increase the property taxes in perpetuity because this is a transfer of title and beneficial interest.

Let's stop the show here. A bona fide transfer might accrue transfer taxes at about 1.2 to 1.5% of the purchase price. That's bad enough. This transfer also enables the county tax assessor to reassess the property in light with current values. Property values have skyrocketed in the last 24 months.

The risk of this tax reassessment prompts many conveyees as the surrogates of the debtors to claim on the Preliminary Change of Ownership Report (PCOR) that the transfer is to a revocable trust, while telling the creditors that the transfer is to an irrevocable trust. California Probate Code §18100.5(b)(4) (and other state equivalents) Certificates of Trust reveals whether the transfer is revocable, which means that the assets are subject to creditors, or irrevocable, which means that the transfer is a fraudulent conveyance. Probate Code §18200 states that assets held in a revocable trust are subject to the claims of creditors.

The tax collector-assessor requires that the buyer file a PCOR that explains the transaction in great detail and compel the disclosure of what consideration has been paid. These forms are online. Lawfully obtaining the PCOR unwinds claims of an irrevocable trust or true change of title because the conveyee will claim the transfer was to a revocable trust to beat out the Proposition 13 reassessment and bump, much less the city and county transfer taxes.

Transfer to an LLC, partnership, or corporation kicks off an insurance nightmare. Lenders demand the debtor carry at least fire insurance. Most insurance companies offer a comprehensive general liability policy to the homeownership which of course provides for fire insurance coverage to the lender. This is near universal. When the debtor transfers the property to an LLC, partnership, corporation, or family members, these putative buyers need to take out a new policy of insurance at great expense and cancel the old policy. If not, and assuming some terrible accident, such as the delivery person or postal employee slipping and falling, the current homeowner is uninsured and subject to massive lawsuit without coverage. This new tort plaintiff, if victorious, can reach the home to satisfy the judgment.

If the prior coverage in the name of the debtor and protecting the lender is canceled, and the new owner gets coverage, the insurance company will immediately notify the lender who in turn can buy its own policy insurance at an enormous price. The lender will charge back the new homeowner with the premium, who is obviously the debtor's surrogate, or even foreclose in the event of nonpayment. Worse, once the lender finds out about the transfer, the lender might invoke the due-on-sale clause and commence foreclosure.

When Was the Conveyance Made?

The deed might reflect three dates for the conveyance: the date the defendant executed the deed, the date the deed was notarized, and the date it was recorded. These dates probably track the prosecution of the tort action, or even the tort itself.

Conveyances in Groups or Batches

The defendant might convey multiple properties in batches to the same or multiple entities or to family members. The fact of multiple conveyances to entities controlled by the defendant is the badge of fraudulent conveyances, if linked to the parallel tort litigation. These conveyances might take place on one day in which the deeds bear sequential order. This means that the defendant probably personally appeared in the recorder's office and handed the front desk clerk the deeds, and cash for the recording charges, and then signed. This is strong evidence that there was no consideration and that transfer was title only and not the beneficial interest. The tip-off to sequential recording is the dates, times (actual time stamp), and actual recording sequence. Presumptively, the defendant had property in other counties and is likewise engaged in serial recordings. This also applies to batch filings of UCC-1 (personal property liens) with the secretary of state that might accompany batch filings with the recorder.

What Is Wrong with the Transaction?

Escrow companies handle most real property transfers. The name of the escrow company appears at the upper left-hand corner of the deed as "Recorded at the Request of." The deed shows the escrow company's "order" number and, if a deed of trust for the loan, the loan number, and the "transaction number," followed by the initials of the escrow officer. A transfer, outside of escrow, shows that the buyer and seller abandoned this routine safeguard to ensure that the seller got paid before title changed hands and that the buyer got "good title" before paying the seller. Escrows protect parties from real estate fraud. The lack of an escrow shows that the parties are not concerned about fraud because they are related to each other or, one in the same, no money is changing hands or the beneficial interest in the title was not changing hands.

The defendant did not engage a real estate broker, did not receive multiple offers, did not list the property through the multiple listing services (MLS), did not post the property online for sale, did not put a "for sale" sign on the house, or did not advertise through online brokerage sites. The defendant did not engage in cosmetic repairs to increase the value of the property. The defendant has no interest in maximizing the beneficial interest because the defendant or surrogate continued to retain the beneficial interest. This evidence is found through the MLS (Internet today), onsite investigations, or talking to the neighbors.

Deeds are important documents and retain their viability through generations. Title companies and lawyers draft deeds with enormous care given their longevity through many generations. On the other hand, deeds that bear handwritten corrections, are done in pen and so are not typed, bear inconsistent statements, or lack a correct legal description, parcel number, even address, show haste. Sloppy deeds suggest that the parties did not care whether the grantee (conveyee) could ever enforce the deed or for that matter has sufficient earmarks of good title to sell the property to a bona find purchaser.

Deeds that show the address to which to return the deed as the defendant (the conveyor) suggest that the conveyees never took delivery at all and might not know that they are the owners of the property. All buyers of real property through a bona fide transaction ensure that their names appear on the "return to" blank. This is common practice, and it makes good sense that the buyer of any property should have physical possession of the grant deed to a home or commercial property. The fact that the seller (defendant) retains possession of the deed implies that the buyer did not care whether he or she had possession of the actual deed and, importantly, never saw the deed, knew of its existence, or even participated in the transaction in the first place. The fact that the deed never gets into the hand of the buyer postrecording is strong evidence that the defendant, as the transferor, never delivered the deed and that the transaction is therefore void. California Civil Code Section 1054 and *Miller v. Jansen*, 21 Cal. 3d 473, 477 (1943) (big cheese case and worth reading—"big cheese" is a well-known and judicially accepted term for "this is the big case").

The parties forego other incidents of a sale, such as the execution of a standard real estate "deposit receipt and contract for sale," earnest money deposit, termite reports, inspections, financing, state and federal mandated disclosures and representations, covenants to bring the property up to code, and, most importantly, title insurance. Modern real estate closings require nearly a dozen signed disclosure statements concerning the condition of the house.

The lack of the standard "deposit receipt" and the accompanying earnest money deposit suggests a great irregularity and a badge of fraud as nearly all California (and West Coast) real estate transactions cycle through these ubiquitous documents. The lack of title insurance evidences that the buyer was assured of good title because the buyer and seller are practically the same entity, the transaction is illusionary, or the buyer did not care because the equitable interest in the property remains with the seller.

The lack of an inspection and termite report dooms the legitimacy of nearly every transaction because no buyer would spend millions to buy a "pig in poke," unless the buyer and the seller are the same people. ("Subject to final inspection" is the usual language.) The lack of financing the transaction suggests that the buyer is acquiring the net equity without commensurate payment, a key indicator of a fraudulent conveyance. ("Subject to financing" is likewise another common term.) The recorder's office would show new (or nonexistent) financing.

A change of ownership prompts the change of customer for gas and electric, telephone, water, garbage, cable, sewer, septic tank service, which is common in rural and semirural communities, phone (landline), and Internet services. Changing routine utility services accompanies all real estate transactions without exception. Mom and dad tell every college-age student, "When you move out of the apartment, get the utility service out of your name. If you don't, you are going to pay for it, and I don't care."

Given enough time, the subpoena of these records (or a search through the trash) reveals that the defendant is still the utility customer on record and presumptively the occupant or the owner of the property. Double-check with the county tax assessor to see who is the assessed owner for purposes of property taxes. The archenemy in real estate transactions is the county tax assessor collector who will readily assess county transfer taxes in the event of a nonprotected transfer and moreover will reassess to the current fair market value under Proposition 13. Nobody is stupid in this business: therefore, the debtor as the conveyor will do everything possible to represent to the taxing authorities that the debtor is still the owner in an attempt to fend off transfer taxes and a reassessment.

As you will read in another section, you can directly levy on the property, but don't cry if the third-party conveyee files a third-party claim that catapults you into a trial, without discovery, and might even be tried by declarations. Bring Perry Mason. The leading case is *Whitehouse v. Six Corporation* (1995) 40 Cal App. 4th 527. If you are going to battle a third-party claim, memorize this case. If you are the creditor, you bear the burden of proof by a preponderance of the evidence to prove a fraudulent conveyance without the benefit of discovery and maybe a very short trial.

Section 14

Trial

Yikes, we have to put on a case

Chapter 1

The Easy Enforcement

Just Take the Money and Run

Standard enforcement permits you to seize the debtor's property. Let's go through the most basic scenarios. If the money is in the name of the defendant, you can levy on the money by serving the garnishee (usually the bank) with a writ of execution package; it is done every day and is no big deal. If the debtor owns a retail or wholesale business, you can have the sheriff seize the contents and put it up for sale. This is very expensive, and can run you thousands of dollars, but the shock effect is worth it. You can send the sheriff into the debtor's place of business to take money out of the cash register, open up the mail, pull money out of the sale, or seize checks. Generally, this is called a keeper if the sheriff is there for some period of time, or a till tap.

If the debtor owns a car, grab the car. If the debtor owns a home with equity over the homestead, sell the home. If the debtor owns nonexempt property, you can sell this property without the misery of dealing with the homestead. You can sell intellectual property through a receiver, and you can liquidate notes and receivables through a garnishment, assignment, or actual seizure of the note. This is all straightforward, and the Internet is full of practice guides to teach you the nuts and bolts. Try the sheriff's website, collection lawyer's tomes, and every practice guide offered by judgment professionals. In English: beat a hasty retreat.

Chapter 2

Get Ready to Go to Court

How do you grab the property of the debtor when it is in the name or title of another? This is the crux of the problem. The answer is found in the law of fraudulent conveyance and the resulting trust. Facing a fraudulent conveyance perpetrated by the debtor, the creditor has multiple options, each with their "pluses and minuses."

The first cousin to fraudulent conveyance law is the law of resulting trusts. This means that the person holding title, or even possession of the property, holds the property for the benefit of the debtor and that the transfer was illusory. The property always belongs to the debtor. The simple explanation of a resulting trust is that the debtor parks title, but not ownership, in the name of another. This is a classic form of fraudulent conveyance as transformative of title, but not ownership. The leading California case is *Fidelity National Title Insurance Company v. Gordon Schoeder etc. et al.* (2009) 179 Cal. App. 4th 834 and *In re Schwarzkopf* (9th Cir. 2010) 626 F. 3d 1032 (both are online). These cases permit the judgment creditor to reach assets held by the debtor apart from fraudulent conveyance remedies. These cases are worth reading. Also, if the conveyance is illusory and the property is always owned by the debtor, the statute of limitations never runs.

Most states allow prejudgment writs of attachment that enable a creditor to lien a debtor's property. A lien can include encumbering the debtor's personal or real property, impounding a bank account or accounts receivable, or taking possession of inventory or other valuable personal property. The creditor files a lawsuit and an application that proves up the debt that the amount is fixed and readily ascertainable and, in nearly all cases, that the debt is based on a contract express or implied. Every state is different, and some states are more (or less) restrictive.

If the court grants the attachment, the creditor can enforce the writ against the debtor's property. The creditor would place the writ of attachment in the hands of the service with precise instructions of what property to seize and how to seize the property. The creditor has to prepay the sheriff for the services. Some states require a small-dollar bond such as $10,000, whereas other states require a bond in the amount of the debt. These large-dollar bond are difficult, but not impossible, to post. If the creditor loses the case for whatever reason and attaches the debtor's property, the debtor can recover damages under the bond. The creditor is the indemnitor under the bond and stuck paying the damages. Most states authorize an immediate attachment if the debtor threatens to abscond, commit a fraudulent conveyance, or leave the state. Other states allow attachment against out-of-state residents, such as a foreign corporation or limited liability company.

Should your case lie in federal court, you follow the rules of the state, as federal law does not `generally provide a prejudgment relief, such as an asset freeze, unless authorized by a specific federal statute. In most states, the state sheriff is far more adept in the enforcement of the writ of attachment than the U.S. marshal. If the attachment of the debtor's property is going to be difficult task, or you expect that the debtor will engage in a some type of expeditious stunt or maneuver to escape the attachment lien, such as a introducing a fraudulent conveyance or liquidating the property in a flash, suing in state court expedites attachment process. Let's attach the property before it vanishes.

Chapter 3

Introduction to Litigation of Claims by Third Parties

The creditor can instruct the sheriff to levy on the asset, even though ostensibly in the name of the third party. Sometimes the property is in the name of the defendant, but upon the levy, a third party claims ownership or lien, and hence, it is a third-party claim. In other cases, if the property is in the name of the third party, the sheriff might balk and compel you to get a court order. The sheriff will seize the property. Maybe. In response, the third party, being the conveyee, will inevitably file a third-party claim with the sheriff.

What is a third-party claim? A third-party claim is a sworn statement by the third party that the third party is the righteous owner. Upon the filing of the claim, the creditor must post a bond or get a restraining order to prevent the sheriff from releasing the property back to the debtor. This release is self-executing, whether or not the third-party claim has any viability. What does this mean to you? This means that the third party can file anything, as long as the statement claims "ownership," "under penalty of perjury," and is signed by the third party. This could be an entire pack of lies, but the contents are not important. From an asset-protection point of view, the third-party claim filing is a total winner. File the claim, and get back the property.

Chapter 4

The Third-Party Claim

The third-party claim effectively protects an asset from enforcement sought by the creditor through the risk that the creditor accrues in posting of the bond or the restraining order. Call this a bet-your-ranch moment. The fact that the creditor or the creditor's lawyer might bear a financial expense, should the third-party claim prevail, acts as an independent deterrent against litigating the third-party claim. As in all facets of asset protection, the trick is not necessarily shielding the asset, but rather creating a counterrisk that dissuades nearly everybody, other than zealots or the well heeled. Third-party claim practice is also expensive, which itself serves as another deterrent against a plaintiff who lacks the resources to litigate the case. Third-party claim is the province of state courts that have more experience.

In response, the creditor must post a bond or get a restraining order. This doesn't sound too tough. Is this a free lunch? No. Let's presume that the third-party claim is valid, or for some insane reason, the creditor loses the trial, as set forth later. The third-party-claimant now has a righteous claim against the creditor for lawyer's fees and damages based upon the alleged unlawful restraint of the personal property. Lawyers' fees claims after a third party claim battle frequently exceed $50,000 or more. Creditor's counsel must necessarily advise the client that a loss in the third-party claim proceeding might be costly and compel the client to write the "big check" to the third party. This is tough pill to swallow for anybody, and few informed clients would readily assume this risk. This is the second line of asset protection, being the threat of lawyers' fees, if the case goes bad.

Bad news continues. Third-party claim proceedings amount to a minitrial, which is relatively rare in the courts. The third party claims that the asset is "mine," or subject to "my lien as security for my cash loan." The third-party claimant probably comes to court with manufactured documents and offers perjured or distorted testimony. Rest assured, this is a settled expectation. Third-party claim proceedings, however, do not permit discovery; therefore, the creditor's counsel is facing this testimony with limited advance notice, and worse, no discovery, which otherwise would enable the creditor to frontally confront this perjured testimony and evidence. Discovery means that you can depose (question) the adversary before a court reporter and ask tough questions. Interrogatories are long questionnaires that stretch the facts of the claims or defenses. A document request forces the other side to turn over the key documents. The discovery process enables a party to prepare for trial and protect against surprise, fraud, or "sandbagging." With good information at hand, the lawyer can do a bang-up job at cross-examination. Your lawyer might be the cat's meow, but sorry to say he is no Abe Lincoln, Clarence Darrow, or Perry Mason. They set the standards for cross-examination, but unfortunately these folks have other engagements. You will have to do with what you have. The fact that the party must go to trial without discovery is an enormously daunting challenge and would dissuade everybody but the most skilled or foolish. Of course, the fallback position is to engage in an examination of the debtor or third parties and subpoena related records prior to the levy process in order to build a record. Absent this diligence, the lack of discovery is another barrier.

Chapter 5

Third-Party Claim Trials

Did you think this was bad? No. It gets worse. After hearing the evidence in the third-party claim trial, assuming that you get a trial, the judge doesn't have to make findings. My favorite movie is *Gladiator* with Russell Crowe. Thumbs-up or thumbs-down judgement is for the crowd. Third-party claim practice is pretty close. Thumbs-up, and the creditor walks away with the property; thumbs-down is a total disaster. Big money is paid to the third party's lawyer, and the creditor gets zip. This presumes, of course, that you have a trial in the first place. Third-party proceedings do not guarantee a trial, only a hearing, such as it may be. What does that mean to you? That means that the trial judge can rule on the papers, or limit the evidence and stop the trial when the judge has made up his or her mind. A limited trial favors the third party because the creditor bears the affirmative burden of proof by a preponderance of evidence to proof up a fraudulent conveyance. Fraudulent conveyances are proven by circumstantial evidence. What this means in plain English is that the lawyer for the creditor is going to "huff and puff," to prove the case and create a vast record of circumstantial evidence.

Enforcement is asset driven. What does that really mean? If you lose the asset to a third party, your case died on the operating table, and nobody, even Dr. Kildare, is going to bring the case back to life.

Chapter 6

Expert Testimony at a Fraudulent Conveyance Trial

Here is standard testimony in a fraudulent conveyance trial or third-party claim trial in which the creditor seeks to topple a fraudulent conveyance. Counsel: "Mr. Expert, you have been asked today to given an opinion why the transfer is fraudulent. Can you render such as opinion?" Adverse lawyer: "Expert cannot offer opinion on legal matter nor legal conclusion." Objection: "This is a bench trial (i.e., no jury), and I will listen to what he has to say. You may proceed." Expert: "Well the facts are the following: On April 1, while drunk, the defendant struck and ran over the plaintiff. As I understand the facts, he was so drunk that after running over his body the first time, that he backed up the car and ran over the body again, crushing his skull. The defendant fled on foot, but was apprehended by the police. On June 1, the defendant pled guilty to vehicular manslaughter, was sentenced to 10 years, and is currently incarcerated. The plaintiff, the spouse to the decedent, filed suit on May 1 and seeks, I presume, substantial damages. I am informed that the insurance is in the amount of $500,000 and with no umbrella coverage. The decedent was a resident at University Hospital in the orthopedic department. One year to go before completing his residency. Between the accident and plea, the defendant transferred to his wife his interest in a free and clear $5,000,000 home."

"First, the transfer of the house to the wife did not serve any type of legitimate estate planning given the high deduction for federal estate taxes. The property was held in joint tenancy, and, therefore, probate fees and costs were not an immediate consideration. The transfer is not for charitable purposes because the wife received the property as opposed to a charity, which anyway would have been unusual. Next, I viewed the transfer for the viewpoint of fairness in a community property division. Commonly the wife ends up with the house, and the husband ends up with the business, assuming an appraisal and proof that the business is functional and bears a real value equal to the house. The parties did not do an appraisal, and, in any event, the husband pled guilty to a felony and therefore forfeited his law license. The law firm collapsed given the egregiousness of the accident. Therefore the transfer does not serve any legitimate family law purpose. This is transfer between two individuals, and I could not find any type of business purpose such as a business reorganization as this property is a single-family house. This transfer did not serve any state or federal income tax planning purpose. The transfer did not serve to reduce, or ameliorate, property taxes. The fact of the transfer did not alter insurance coverage. I could not find any pending financing transactions such as a refinance, potential sale, or renovation that might require the transfer of title. Although it is true that husbands and wives transfer title from the less credit worthy to the more creditworthy spouse to secure a refinance, I did not see any type of traditional home loan or refinance encumbering the property."

"Therefore I could not find any viable or legitimate purpose to this transfer other than to retitle a key valuable asset in the name of the wife, a nondebtor, out of the title in the names of the husband and wife as community property, which was subject to the ostensible claim of the victim's family." Adverse counsel: "Are you opining that the transfer is fraudulent?" Expert: "Not necessarily. I am opining that the transfer did not serve any viable purpose under estate tax, charitable, business reorganization, income tax, insurance, lending, property tax, or family law principles. Therefore, I conclude, given the lack of any legitimacy, the transfer is fraudulent."

Chapter 7

The Family Law Code Offers Many Tricks

The Family Law Code is chock-full of asset-protection devices. The usual suspect is the immunity of separate property from the debt of another spouse, absent joint liability and agency, among other grounds. Upon the entry of judgment, the spouse cloaks the title of separate on every scratch of property or reshuffles the deck through a collusive divorce. Premarital agreements drop from the sky to rescue some property in the grip of the enforcement.

Family law sneaks in the separate property trick. Property held in joint tenancy is deemed to be separate property and not subject to the claims of creditors of the nondebtor unless the parties intended the property to be held as community property. I told you to subpoena every lender, creditor, car-leasing company, and anybody else in possession of the debtor financials, or a URLA. This is the payoff. These documents should reveal that the parties intended to hold the property as community and not joint. In California, community property is subject to the claims of creditors of either spouse. Converting community property in separate property (i.e., converting the deed from "community property" to "joint tenancy") is a fraudulent conveyance.

If you win the big judgment against the spouse and the sole source of recovery is the community property, expect and even embrace that the debtor and spouse will file for divorce. They will concoct a marital settlement agreement that gives the husband nothing and the wife everything. Is the fraudulent marital settlement vulnerable to a lawsuit to unwind and compel the liquidation of the community assets for payment of the judgment? Yes, so says the California Supreme court in *Mejia v. Reed* (2003) 31 Cal. 4th 657, which holds that family law court is not another form of bankruptcy.

Most community property states provide that community property is subject to the debts of either spouse (California). When one spouse runs down, or runs over, the hapless bicycle rider, the day after, the husband and wife engage an asset-protection lawyer who inevitably advises the couple to divorce. At least, goes the thinking, the postdivorce earnings will not be subject to an eternal garnishment because the postdivorce earnings are separate property. This might work.

Let's go back to the Efficient Market Hypothesis. Can the judgment creditor unwind a fraudulent MSA and recover community property that has been transmuted into separate property? Yes. Is that expensive? Yes, that will cost a lot of money. The issue is not winning the battle but gauging the going-forward expenses and effort, which creates a patina of "concern" and "worry" and infuses information in the decision to go forward. The face of the collusion divorce is part of the market value of the recovery, that, by the expense, risk, and misery involved, depreciates the value of the case. More than one debtor has told the creditor: "Sure you can unwind this deal. Sure you can win. Sure you can get back the property, assuming that the conveyee has not sold everything to the walls and given me the cash that I will spend in more than one Charlie Sheen Las Vegas weekend (the deluxe suite, please—three nights). You are now facing $100,000 in legal fees to unravel this mess I made, and the lawsuits will take you three or four years. So, my offer to you is cash 10 cents on the dollar and be happy."

The other variation is the postdisaster marital separation proceeding and related agreement in which the parties allegedly split up their assets and transmute community property into separate property. This is another scam, but an expensive one to unwind. Does this stunt become part of the marketplace of information that depreciates the judgment? For sure, and the creditor faces the efforts of unwinding a judicial proceedings in which the husband and wife, as in the divorce, are aligned against the creditor. They will get their story straight and read from the same prayer book at the trial that seeks to unwind the fraudulent transfers.

Make no mistake. If post debt (usually the big tax debt, tort, or judgment) husband and wife cycle through a post marital separation agreement, which converts community property into separate property, even future wages, they committed a fraudulent conveyance. Right on the money is *State Board of Equalization v. Woo* (2000) 82 Cal. App. 4th 481, 484. In that case, the husband and wife signed a post marital separation agreement to protect the wife's wages from garnishment. The court of appeal tossed the agreement, stating the following:

> Further, appellant's attempt to transmute the community property earnings to her separate property constituted a fraudulent transfer. Family Code section 851 provides that "[a] transmutation is subject to the laws governing fraudulent transfers." Civil Code section 3439.04, subdivision (a) provides that a transfer is fraudulent as to a creditor if it is made "[w]ith actual intent to hinder, delay, or defraud any creditor of the debtor." Here, appellant does not dispute that the community estate was liable for Ho's tax debt. (See Fam. Code, § 910 ["community estate is liable for a debt incurred by either spouse before or during marriage"].) Nor does she dispute that she entered into the marital agreement after learning that respondent intended to garnish her wages. Given these facts, the trial court did not err in rejecting

> appellant's argument that there was no fraudulent transfer. Ho had a present interest in appellant's earnings at the time the agreement was executed. Appellant's attempt to transmute that interest to avoid Ho's tax debt constituted a fraudulent transfer in violation of Family Code section 851 and Civil Code section 3439.04, subdivision (a).

This is worth the long quote. In plain English: Husband and wife cannot launder their asset through a washing machine to launder out the community character of the property.

The moral of this tale is easy. Community property is subject to the claims of the creditors of either spouse. An agreement that destroys the community property and converts, transmutes, the community into separate property for the purpose of shielding the wife's wages, postdebt, from enforcement is a fraudulent conveyance.

Dividing up the family home from its prior intact status as community into two halves of separate property is a fraudulent conveyance. Dividing up the bank accounts, stock accounts, or any other remaining community property is likewise a fraudulent conveyance because the judgment creditor has the right to reach all the community property. Playing footsie-wootsie with community property is a fraud. These are bad people.

The creditor is going to face a near-impossible burden of selling the debtor's separate property interest in the residence and effectively render the residence "sale proof." The fact that the creditor cannot force a sale of the property does not immunize the property generally from enforcement. The lien by virtue of the recorded abstract encumbers the real property, and absent the bizarre outcome, a title company will not insure title in the name of the bona fide buyer unless judgment liens are cleared, no matter whose title is encumbered.

The next variation is that the husband and wife get divorced or cycle through a legal separation, which is very common. In fact, upon the filing of the million-dollar tort lawsuit, expect that within seven days the husband and wife will hire an asset-protection lawyer who will advise the couple to file for divorce. Count on it, Pollyanna. The lawyer will advise that the divorce will destroy the community property and protect the nondebtor from a future wage garnishment. The divorce can award to the spouses half the property and therefore render any enforcement impossible because the sheriff would be effectively unable to sell a half a residence and reach the 90 percent mark, or even reach a sufficient price to pay the senior liens, deeds of trust, the homestead, or even the judgment. Are these divorces, or legal separations sure-fire strategies to foil any fraudulent conveyance actions? No, not in a million years. The husband and wife who continue to cohabitate, conduct themselves as husband and wife, and share the same bank account and same credit and same expenses (e.g., the household expenses) do not tell their creditors that they are divorced, take out home loans and commercial and consumer credit in the name of husband and wife, and otherwise act as if married are still married under fraudulent conveyance law. The trick in nearly all of these cases is that the parties do not engage in the normal disposition of community property, which provides for the actual sale and division. The reason for this reticence is that lenders will not extend credit on property in which the title is split. Most legitimate divorces end up with spousal and child support, stay-away orders, rights of visitation, the sale of property, equalization payments, and alternating holidays. A collusive divorce leaves everyone in place. Modern divorces let the wife take back her maiden name, which is very common for most professionals.

The best evidence is the state and federal income tax return. Married couples inevitably file joint returns because they would be able to more equitably enjoy deductions and the economy of scale. It is rare that collusively divorced parties files separate returns, although sometimes the parties get that far. Try the home insurance, auto insurance, or any other insurance policy to see who is insured. Are the insured still listed as husband and wife? Try serving a subpoena upon the school where their kids attend and see if they notified the school of the alleged joint custody agreement.

Most collusive divorces collapse as a fraudulent conveyance if the nondebtor spouse gets all of the community property or even the separate property of the debtor spouse, and, in return, the debtor spouse got nothing but liabilities. Even if the court determines that the divorce is noncollusive in determining the status of the parties, the court can still hold that the property division is fraudulent and apply the property to the claims of the creditor.

You can sue the husband and the wife to unwind these transfers, obtain an injunction against any further disposition, and seek $1,000,000 in punitive damages.

Chapter 8

New Lawsuits and More Lawyers

The next remedy is to file a civil lawsuit for a fraudulent conveyance. The lawsuit to grab the asset is no big deal. Getting it served is no big deal. Cycling through discovery is routine. Millions of lawsuits are filed every day, and nobody breaks a sweat. Why should you break a sweat here? The answer is that the lawsuit is like BBs against a battleship because the debtor or third party still has possession of the asset, and therefore may dispose of the asset by sale, transfer, or refinance. A lawsuit to recover the fraudulent transfer is only good as the ability of the creditor to tie up the assets.

This is as a good a place as any for this seminal story of death and degradation. John and Mary own a nice home. John, a drunk, bashes into a pedestrian whose broken body flips over twice before smashing into the curb, head first. Fearing the lawsuit, John transfers title of their home to Mary only which is the first fraudulent conveyance. The house has big equity. Before judgment, and after reading this book, they refinance the home. John is the breadwinner and the bank demands that he appear on the title. They transfer the property back to John, who signs for the refinance and sucks out all the equity and renders the property immune from a forced sale. After the refinance is completed, John transfers this interest to Mary. The transfer by John to Mary, postrefinance, is the second fraudulent conveyance. John transferred his interest in the house with the intent to hinder, delay, and defraud in the face of the large-dollar tort claim. However, the victory in peeling away this transfer is pyrrhic because the bank that refinances the home beats out the creditor-based "safe harbor."

These lawsuits only have teeth when the creditor gets a restraining order or receiver records a lis pendens. Getting a restraining order or a receiver means that at the outset of the filing, you have to prove up your entire case by a near preponderance of the evidence. Typically, you have not even done discovery unless you are lucky enough to have cycled through postjudgment discovery in the prior case. This is enormously expensive, which is the first barrier.

Let's say you score the restraining order or receiver. You have to post a bond, which is not particularly expensive, but should you lose the case, the bonding company is obligated to pay off the defendant for the lawyers' fees and damages. Should the bond be inadequate, the plaintiff is on the hook for these damages. The client must sign off on that risk and might balk. This is another barrier.

If the fraudulently conveyed property is real estate, the creditor is going to file and record a lis pendens. That does not take a court order. In response, a third party can file a motion to expunge the lis pendens. This shifts the burden to the creditor to prove up the case by way of a probability of success on the merits. Lis pendens are frequently filed at the outset of the case, where the parties have yet to engage in discovery. If the lis pendens goes down the drain, the creditor might be on the hook for big-time lawyers' fees, which is another level of asset protection. Let's stop the show. Charging up San Juan Hill is fabulous until your wingman gets shot in the face. A pucker look. It's messy, ugly and stains the uniform. Clients are shocked to confront a five-figure award of fees when the judge topples the lis pendens. You cannot spend enough time explaining the risks of a blown lis pendens. Again, this is another barrier.

The final barrier is the judge. Depending upon your locale, you might find that some judges have little or no experience in handling fraudulent conveyance cases. The briefs, oral argument, and the presentation itself must be predicated upon the fact that the judge is a "blank slate," but not a dummy. Take nothing for granted and presume that the judge has no prior knowledge or exposure in this body of law. Take your time to explain the statutory law and lay out the case law in detail. Who has the burden of proof? What needs to be proved? If the plaintiff proves up the fraudulence, what are the remedies?

Chasing down the debtor rarely rattles a judge. Chasing down third parties compel the judges to view the case more conservatively, given that the plaintiff is attempting to foist the judgment upon a third party. Explain to the judge exactly what you plan to do in the lawsuit. Make it simple. Do not expect that the judge has a legacy understanding of this body of law. If you are suing to vacate the transfer, conveyance, or lien and impress the property with the judgment, you might not face a huge wall of judicial resistance. On the other hand, if you are seeking big-time damages because the property has been sold or liquidated and want money out of the third party's personal hide, you are going to huff and puff. I hope you had a good breakfast because you will be sweating through your Hugo Boss all day. I am not saying that these cases are impossible, but your chances of winning increase if you can show that the conveyee conspired with the conveyor to cheat the creditor or acted as an enabler.

Section 15

Hide and Seek for Wandering Money

Chapter 1

The Repositories

Where is the debtor typically going to hide money? The first option is that the debtor is going abandon the banking system completely and convert accounts with financial institutions into cash. Pay cash for everything. This is very common and as one debtor told me, "I closed out every account so that you cannot reach my money." Expect that the debtor is going to flee the banking system and convert cash into prepaid credit and debit cards in the name of another entity so expect the debtor to form LLC's on or offshore, to warehouse funds. With an out-of-state or offshore account, the LLC's can cause the bank to issue a debit or credit card, tied to account, which is loaded, or tethered to the account itself. Cash is good, but it requires a home safe. Prepaid credit or debit cards are better, particularly if issued in the name of an LLC.

The debtor will inevitably wire funds to an offshore or out-of-state account. Let's figure this out. Let's read the wire confirmation. You will see the line item of originator (5000). The first line is the ID code; the next line is the identifier, which is a 10-digit number. The next line requests a name. What name? The name of the person who is wiring the money. That person might not be your debtor, but the person (or entity) who has possession of the debtor's money and therefore, the "surrogate," hiding the money from you. When you subpoena records from the vendors, leasing companies, landlord, utility, or anybody else that the debtor is paying, always ask for the wire confirmations that reveal the person (or entity) who is holding the debtor's money. Chances are that the entity is a limited liability company whose agent is LegalZoom.com, which is the do-it-yourself legal service founded by Robert Shapiro, O.J. Simpson's criminal trial lawyer.

Let's cycle through the usual and unusual suspects, Captain Renault.

Chapter 2

Nontraditional Online Banking

PayPal, Square One, Strip, Google Wallet, OboPay, PaymentOne, Billmelater, WePay, and many others establish an account that enables the customer to pay for goods or service by debiting the account through the use of a smartphone, Internet purchase, or wire transfer. This is for real. Let me explain. Shellie Zimmerman, wife to George Zimmerman who allegedly shot to death Trayvon Martin, testified at the first bail hearing that the couple was indigent, which prompted the judge to grant bail set in the amount of $150,000 ($15,000 charge to post the bond). Jailhouse recordings shows that she was holding about $200,000 in a PayPal account arising from the donations for the legal defense. Had she done a little (very small) legal research online, she would have immediately learned that jailhouse phones are bugged. Loose lips might not sink ships today, but loose lips spilled the beans on the PayPal account and sent her packing to jail, facing a perjury charge, a felony no less.

Let's take a quick tour of PayPal. PayPal will establish an account with a user name, address, password, and funding source. Others can transmit funds to this account, and the account holder can likewise disburse funds to other accounts, including banks and other PayPal accounts. PayPal will issue a physical "check card," which is encoded with the PayPal account. The card enables the holder to purchase goods at retail locations or online, or to use the account code, or account, to purchase goods and services online. PayPal premium accounts authorize the buying and selling of goods and services and the collection of payments. For example, I can establish a PayPal account in the name of DAVID COOK LLC (a Nevada limited liability company), with an e-mail address of DAVIDCOOK@DAVIDCOOKLLC.com. I can fund the PayPal account with funds emanating offshore, family accounts, accounts in the names of other LLCs controlled by myself, or accounts in the names of obligors who are obligated to make payments (rents, note payments, product, or goods purchases). I can transfer funds in personal bank accounts that I control or vice a versa. I can have customers pay me through the PayPal account.

With the check card or account number in hand, the account holder has access to funds warehoused in another name at PayPal and therefore is immune to enforcement directed to the *named* defendant. Whereas a bank might offer a similar service, PayPal is far less demanding of information and better permits the establishment of an account without a face-to-face meeting.

PayPal, Google Wallet, and others warehouse money accessible to the account holder outside traditional banking. Given PayPal's ease and familiarity, an account holder can receive and disburse funds to other PayPal and bank accounts outside banking channels.

PayPal will respond to garnishments. I called and confirmed. This is important.

Nontraditional financial institutions include repositories that issue cards, hold funds, and might have information that would reveal the existence of accounts. Now before spending good money to chase down these potential garnishees, some of these folks might actually hold money in the name of the debtor, assuming that you have the debtor's social security number, URL, e-mail address, or other identifying information. Some of these potential garnishees do not hold an account in the name of the debtor, but only issue the card that is tied to a specific bank account. The account might be in the name of the garnishee, or in the name of the issuer or third party bank. Don't get too excited if you lay process on these folks, who in turn bounce back your enforcement with the statement "we do not hold the account. . . . First National Bank of Podunk, Iowa, might hold the account." I have served many of these potential repositories, and the standard response is "no money held under the named party." The best target is PayPal.

These are the most prevalent third parties who offer nontraditional banking. So no one goes out and blows a bunch of money chasing down these folks, many do not hold an account for the debtor, although they have issued a card, whether plastic or electronic, in the debtor's name. Banks are subject to strict antilaundering rules, which preclude the laundering of cash or the deposit of funds from unknown or anonymous sources, and therefore would maintain an account in the name of an identifiable person.

Let me repeat: These are *possible* targets. Don't get bent out of shape if some turnout to be duds. I will not listen to you complaining.

- ACCOUNTNOW INC., c/o National Corporation Research Inc., 523 West Sixth Street, Suite 544, Los Angeles, California 90014 (prepaid debit cards).
- AMERICAN EXPRESS COMPANY, c/o CT Corporation System, 818 West Seventh Street, Los Angeles, California 90017 (prepaid debit cards and credit balances).
- DISCOVER BANK, c/o CT Corporation System, 818 West Seventh Street, Los Angeles, California 90017 (major issuers of cards in which customers frequently retain credit balances).
- ELAVON INC., c/o CT Corporation System, 818 West Seventh Street, Los Angeles, California 90017 (major credit card processor who might hold funds due a commercial business who is processing credit cards). This is one of many credit card processors and clearing houses that operates as a conduit to clear credit card drafts.

For example, a consumer would offer a VISA, MasterCard, or an American Express card to a merchant, who in turn would process the draft and obtain payment from the issuing card. The credit card processor would pay or deposit the amount of the draft in the customer's account. Accordingly, at any given time, the credit card processor has in its possession accounts waiting to be processed and funds paid over to the debtor.

- GREEN DOT CORPORATION, c/o Corporation Service Company, 2710 Gateway Oaks Drive, Suite 150-N, Sacramento, California 95833 (prepaid debit cards). These cards can be acquired without a social security number.
- JPMORGAN CHASE BANK, c/o CT Corporation System, 818 West Seventh Street, Los Angeles, California 90017 (prepaid debit cards and issuer of credit cards on a major basis). Personal information is required to obtain prepaid cards.
- NETSPEND CORPORATION, c/o CT Corporation System, 818 West Seventh Street, Los Angeles, California 90017 (issuer of debit cards). This is an issuer of prepaid debit and/or credit cards. These issuers necessarily hold on account funds that are disbursed electronically when the customer uses the card.
- PAYPAL INC., c/o National Registered Agents, 818 West Seventh Street, Los Angeles, California 90017. PayPal is the largest of the online financial repositories. PayPal may hold on its books funds due for a customer. PayPal accounts are tied to a bank. Personal information is required to obtain prepaid cards or establish an account.
- SQUARE INC., c/o CT Corporation System, 818 West Seventh Street, Los Angeles, California 90017. Square Inc. accepts credit cards and therefore is a repository of credit cards. These folks just announced that they move money through an e-mailing process. Personal information is required to obtain prepaid cards or establish an account.
- WAL-MART STORES, INC. c/o CT Corporation System, 818 West Seventh Street, Los Angeles, California 90017 (debit cards). Personal information is required to obtain prepaid cards or establish an account.
- WEPAY, INC., c/o CT Corporation System, 818 West Seventh Street, Los Angeles, California 90017. Wepay accepts payment online and therefore is an online repository.
- WESTERN UNION FINANCIAL SERVICES INC., c/o CT Corporation System, 818 West Seventh Street, Los Angeles, California 90017. Western Union operates account transfer and might constitute a repository of customer funds available for online disposition. Western Union Financial is part of First Data Corporation.
- CAPITAL ONE, NATIONAL ASSOCIATION, c/o Corporation Service Company, 2710 Gateway Oaks Drive, Suite 150-N, Sacramento, California 95833 (major issuer of debit and like instruments).
- CHECKFREE SERVICES CORPORATION, c/o Corporation Service Company, 2710 Gateway Oaks Drive, Suite 150-N, Sacramento, California 95833 (online repository of funds).
- GOOGLE INC., c/o Corporation Service Company, 2710 Gateway Oaks Drive, Suite

150-N, Sacramento, California 95833. (Like PayPal, Google Inc. and related entities are online repositories of funds under the name of Google Wallet.)

- GOOGLE PAYMENT CORP., c/o Corporation Service Company, 2710 Gateway Oaks Drive, Suite 150-N, Sacramento, California 95833. (Google Payment Corporation, doing business as Google Checkout, offers online payment services. This entity appears to be an online repository of funds.)
- ACE CASH EXPRESS, INC., c/o CT Corporation System, 818 West Seventh Street, Los Angeles, California 90017 (prepaid debit cards).
- ALLY FINANCIAL INC., c/o CT Corporation System, 818 West Seventh Street, Los Angeles, California 90017 (online banking).

This list is illustrative and not exhaustive. Debit cards are issued by many other financial institutions. Out-of-state and offshore banks offer prepaid credit cards, debit cards, and accounts that may be electronically accessed. In making online purchase, the customer need only maintain an active account with a financial institution that can e-mail, or wire, through an electronic means to the vendor. CT Corporation System and CSC as professional agents have branches in nearly every major city. Many of these potential targets might have a presence in most major jurisdictions.

For purpose of enormous clarity, some of these entities sell the card but do not hold the debtor's funds. The funds might be held by an intermediary in the customer's name, but the funds are held by a financial institution, either in the customer's name or in the intermediary's name. Therefore, the levy on the issuer would be futile, but a subpoena might be very helpful. Some of these repositories are less than cordial in responding to process.

Online and digital repositories tend to hold accounts in the name of an e-mail address. For example, a debtor can establish an account under the name of BinLadenRIP@TerrorizeUS.com, URL, or other digital identifier. If the account is solely listed on the name of the e-mail address, or some other artificial name (i.e., anonymous if possible), and on the notice of levy is the name of OSAMA BIN LADEN, the digital bank will bounce the levy (i.e., not honor) by claiming "not found," "inadequate information," "no account in the name of the debtor identified on the notice of levy," or "accounts held only in the name of the e-mail address." Some digital services offer their customers multiple account names, or might accept accounts under multiple e-mail addresses, URLs, or other marks. Nearly all, but not all, digital services require social security numbers. Nobody stops anyone from forming a Nevada limited liability company that establishes a bank account in Nevada, accompanied by a valid TIN in the name of the Nevada LLC to establish a digital account. This is first-rate barrier to enforcement because the Social Security or TIN number on file with the digital bank is not the social security or TIN number of the debtor.

This list consists of some online major financial institutions such as PayPal; financial institutions, such as American Express, that necessarily act as a "merchant bank" and therefore hold funds for a debtor; issuers of prepaid credit cards; third-party credit card processors such as Elavon, Square Inc., and related entities; and issuers of prepaid credit and debit cards. All of these entities are a debtor in a debtor-creditor relationship with the underlying debtor, and therefore a levy on them would necessarily be a levy upon a surrogate financial institution. Postdigital, PayPal has become the number one recipient of broad-based subpoenas and process for funds held on account. American Express is frequently garnished. Elavon, First Data, and other credit card processors hold large sums of money due a debtor. Other credit card process servicers are Flagship Merchant Services, Merchant Warehouse, and National Bankcard, among others.

Under California law and related federal process that adopts the domicile state, the creditor is free to levy any of these accounts, without "good cause," or any prelevy discovery. In short, every one of these entities is subject to enforcement at the price of $35 for the sheriff's levy fee and about $75 to $125 for the process server fee.

Issuers of debit cards are now the paradigm of online banking that replaces the brick-and-mortar check-cashing services. Debit cards, or their first cousin, prepaid credit cards, enable a person to walk around with significant funds and potentially with a total balance at any time of $10,000. A person can establish an account and load up the card with wired funds, a cash deposit through Western Union, or other repositories. The card holder can use the card to pay for retail purchases and online purchase; it can even be used through other venues to pay bills, acquire goods or services, and establish an offshore (or out-of-state account). The issuer of the card will pay upon demand the charges incurred by the holder just like a credit card, but only up to the limit of the card. The issuer of the card (or the person holding the credit balance) is an "obligor" to the judgment debtor who is the creditor and has the right to draw down the credit balance. This relation is nearly the same as the relation between a bank holding a bank account and the customer who has the right to write checks on the bank account.

The relationship between the issuer of these cards and the debtor is that the card issuer is a debtor who owes money to the judgment debtor. The judgment debtor can access the funds through a swipe of the card in a retail purchase or typically through an online purchase. Assuming that the card has a credit balance, the issuer (or bank) will pay the merchant for the amount of the charge as the direction of the card holder. This process of the issuer paying for the charge is the same as the bank paying a check when presented for payment by the collecting bank. The credit balance held by the card issuer constitutes funds that can be drawn upon by the judgment debtor, assuming that the account owner is the debtor.

Do you want to collect? You have many options. You can levy upon every issuer of a debit card which might be successful if the account is in the name of the debtor. Recall that you will not get sued because the levy is a privileged act and free of any liability. What is the downside? Answer: About $125.00 per levy. What is the upside? Imagine the face of the debtor when he discovers that a restaurant declined his debit card and demands cash for the meal. You can file a creditor's suit against the entities and reach the account owed to the debtor. What's the upside? This is straightforward but will cost about $400 for the filing fee, and worse, if no money is owed, you will have mud on your face and a very angry defendant. You can serve an order to appear against a third party and compel the issuer to show in court. This is very effective, but it will cost about $60 to issue the order, another $100 to serve the order, and the potential costs of a court reporter. The downside is that the issuer owes nothing, and you will have a very irate person on your hands. The last remedy is to serve an assignment order that reaches the accounts. These are cheap ($.48 cent stamp) and won't cause the issuer to show up in court, but some issuers blow off these orders based on principle and might demand that you serve a levy. Whatever the process, accompany the enforcement with a subpoena for records. You might or might not get resistance, and your chances of scoring some decent records will go up exponentially if you furnish the debtor's social security number or TIN (at least the last four digits), the e-mail address or other digital identifier, the last known address, and all names. Postdigital, these online repositories are now frequent targets of enforcement by collection agencies, commercial collection and enforcement lawyers, the IRS, and other aggressive tax collectors. These entities will respond but only if you properly format the enforcement tools. Also be sure to serve these entities through their agent for service of process. This will ensure that you have effective proper service of process, but better yet, the process will go to the law department, which can best evaluate what department will respond to your enforcement.

Debit cards require a lot of financial machinery. A customer (your debtor) has $500 (or more) at hand. The customer goes to a brick-and-mortar store for the check-cashing service, bank, or other entity that sells the card. For the $500 (less the service fee), the retailer, such as the check-cashing service, hands over the card to the customer. The check-cashing service banks the cash in its bank account but wires (or EFT—electronic funds transfer) the funds to the card issuer. The funds go through the card issuer and are deposited in a financial institution, such as MetaBank, who holds the account for either the issuer or the customer. The creditor can reach the balance on the card by a levy upon the issuer (if the funds are held in the issuer's name) or the financial institution of the funds (if held in the customer's name with the financial institution).

Chapter 3

Reverse Credit Card Balances

My older sister, Phyllis, had an awful end of her life. A lifelong smoker, lung cancer snared her at age 63. She labored through one year of a gloomy horror. She named me executor and before her death, I inherited her banking and financial records, which included her American Express account. Upon her passing (she was a criminal defense lawyer and the funeral emptied out the Washington, D.C., criminal courts, prosecutors and judges included), I noticed an $8,000 balance on the Amex account. First, I wondered what would my sister purchase on the Amex account when facing death. What? An online casket? Well, I read the statement wrong. This is credit balance, and we discovered that, postlucidity, she accidentally wrote an $8,000 check to Amex, who was happier than a clam to hold these funds, interest free. Absent an escheat to the state, those funds would have sat around for months, or years. Moral of this tale: Seeking to hide money, the defendant will overpay the credit card companies, all of whom will gladly carry a credit balance that enables the card holder to pay for purchases through the physical card, purchase goods or services through the phone, or buy products (or services) online.

The first cousin to reverse credit card balances is overpayment of bills, consumer credit card balances, home lenders, utility companies, and the IRS or state taxing agencies. These routine creditors will usually accept the overpayment and charge accruing expenses to the credit balances. Finding the credit balance is not too tough. The credit report might reflect the credit balance, or you might find a $10,000 check written to Macy's from the check registrar.

Chapter 4

Portable Wealth

Near the conclusion of *Schindler's List,* with the end of the war looming large, a high-ranking Nazi marveled at a cache of diamonds, which Schindler offered as "portable wealth." Diamonds and gold are for a guy (or girl) a new best friend (BFF), they say, but postmodern, portable wealth resides in prepaid Amex cards, credit cards, debit cards, cashier's checks, traveler's checks, or, for those who have seen *Casino* too many times (forget the shop scene), casino chips. Casino chips are money. You read that right. In fairness to the casinos who are subject to the same anti money-laundering regulations as banks, casinos serve as a natural haven to warehouse stolen money, "money on the lam" from the pursuit by angry creditors, funds that are the subject of an embezzlement, or otherwise. These funds end up in an account maintained by the casino acting as a near bank. These funds are converted into casino chips, or gambling credits, or other financial accommodations.

Would you like to find the casino chips? Where are they? Who has them? I am sure that is the question in your mind. The debtor keeps casino chips in one of three places: (1) they are in a safety deposit box, and chances are the bank that holds the safety deposit box is in Las Vegas or the town where the casino sits; (2) the debtor has the casino chips locked away in a home safe. I would give this about a 50 percent probability. The problem with home safes, or any cash on the premises is the risk of a home-invasion robbery; Finally, and I kid you not, (3) the debtor buried the casino chips in a tin can in the back yard. You might laugh and giggle at me, but here is the story. A local daily newspaper scored a tremendous victory against a competitor and won tens of millions of dollars. The defendant did not post a bond. The plaintiff hired a competent collection lawyer from southern California. The battle between these two newspapers and the enforcement gained great notoriety and became a lead story with *The California Lawyer* magazine. Obviously, I read the article, and with a little bit of righteous envy. The magazine featured the lawyer on the front page. Most lawyer magazines present lawyers who are wearing business suits, in front or behind their desks, and typically with the rows of casebooks as the background. It's pretty standard stuff. This picture was different. This picture depicted the lawyer in work clothing, and in the background appeared to be a residential backyard.

On the lawyer's shoulders around which his hands were draped was a shovel, probably courtesy of Home Depot. Mind you, I've been at this business for a long time, and I was looking at that picture for more than a few seconds trying to figure out the message. The collection of that judgment was tough. I could see that. After about a microsecond, I got it. He had the shovel so he could dig up the tin can in the backyard of the debtor. Very clever, and the subsequent news story reported that the case settled, probably based upon his efforts looking for the tin can.

Going backwards a bit, a smartphone linked to a PayPal or other electronic funds transfer account is portable wealth. Always levy on the safety deposit boxes of the debtor and spouse. Accompany the levy with a subpoena for the safety deposit account card and the "sign" slip to see who has access and when.

Once in a blue moon and I mean very blue, your debtor might have parked portable wealth in the safety deposit box. Common occupants of the box, aside from wills and trusts, are gold coins, watches, stocks and bonds, cash money, personal letters, and sometimes guns and dope. When I was age 28, I was chasing down a ski instructor in Tahoe. These guys worked freelance and do not have steady or recognizable income. We did have his bank account information and levied on everything including the safety deposit box. Five days later, he gave up the ghost and paid the judgment in full with all costs and interest. Why? I suspect that the stuff in the box was white stuff, and not the same kind found on the slopes.

The smartphone enables the holder to make account transfers where less than 10 years ago, the task required at least a laptop with a direct Internet connection. These cards are generally bearer cards, which the person with the card in hand and, if necessary, a pin number can use to access the account that is tied to the card. Starbucks takes smartphone payments. It's still weird to me to see someone waive a smartphone in front of a reader in payment for the cappuccino.

For the more sophisticated folks who wish to conceal their ownership of the card, that Nevada LLC can deposit funds with the card issuer who would produce a fully loaded card to a user. To a person on the move or on the lam, the next level is to form an offshore entity (corporation, trust, indigenous LLC, etc.) in which ownership resides with a local "trustee," immune from any legal process, or the stock ownership resides with a bearer, but the name appearing on the stock and therefore the corporation records is "bearer" only. This is very pricey and only for those wanted for big-time crimes. Of course, with the advent of electronic transfers through a smartphone, transferring money from one account to another, held in separate LLC names is nearly foolproof. We assisted in part in the defense of a bankruptcy nondischargeability action in which the claim was that the defendant was engaged in offshore money laundering. The chart listed 37 bank transactions—predigital. In another case, we saw money move from Argentina to a New York bank account and thereafter to a Cook Islands account. That was total money laundering, and the transaction represented a bribe.

Money laundering is not tough. Form a dozen or more offshore entities that warehouse offshore accounts and move the money from account to account. The offshore jurisdictions forbid peering beyond the corporate veil of these entities and stifle any further investigation.

The subset, of course, is offshore bank accounts. The IRS demands disclosure of these accounts, which does not really matter. The person with an offshore account (other than presidential candidates) has greater problems than annoying the IRS. The two purposes of an offshore account are (1) to warehouse profits and proceeds, subject to taxes, but unreported or underreported and (2) to warehouse the funds in a jurisdiction immune from all legal process and shield the fund from tax, family, civil, or even criminal seizure or enforcement against the money. Offshore banks are cranky, cumbersome, expensive, and inconvenient. Don't expect the TV, toaster, or free gun when opening an account (the first scene in *Bowling for Columbine,* which is the opening scene of the movie).

This does matter to the government, and many sad and sorry fools stare at four walls of a federal jail cell for tax fraud. Overseas accounts serve no viable business purpose other than to hide money from the IRS, spouses, the government, or angry creditors. Offshore accounts warehouse profits and proceeds from offshore transactions. For example, the U.S. citizen who liquidates an offshore asset (i.e., house, stock, personal property, or other investment) would have the proceeds wired to the offshore account and thereby cloak the transaction and profit invisible to the IRS. Swiss banks advertise themselves as havens from U.S. tax laws.

A more convenient and common subset of warehousing money is simple: Close the local bank account and move the funds to an out of state locale. Postdigital, parking funds out-of-state poses little burden, given the ability to move money electronically or access it through credit cards, prepaid cards, or payment via electronic check. This works if the bank that holds the funds requires a levy upon the individual branch. Some banks, on the other hand, have a centralized levy-processing unit, which means that a levy on one branch is a levy on all branches. In the bad old days, and for some banks, you had to levy branch by branch. As of January 1, 2013, California law provides that banks establish a centralized levy department. Currently, most banks generally provide that a levy upon one branch is a levy on all branches. This significantly alters the calculus in favor of a creditor. What does this mean to you if you are the creditor? You can levy upon the 10 largest banks by a levy upon any branch of these banks, and therefore reach every branch.

Chapter 5

One-Stop Shopping

Too many words? Let me simplify this. Let's presume that each of these megabanks has 100 branches. We are talking about 10 banks, and therefore 1,000 branches. Let's presume that a San Francisco or Los Angeles sheriff will perform levies. The sheriff charges $35 per levy. Therefore, for a $350 investment, a judgment creditor can reach 1,000 branches. This means that the debtor's assets, if consisting of a bank account, are clearly more vulnerable, given the change of the law. A levy upon a law will also reach a safety deposit box if the notice of levy covers safety deposit boxes.

Reaching every branch with a single levy is a big smash. The power of enforcement expands exponentially. Miracle from Heaven. This is the good news. The very bad news is that the sheriffs are getting much busier. In fact, the sheriffs are so busy that they are unable to process levies within the six-month time limit to execute under a writ. Private process servers can serve a levy, but the price of process servers ranges from $50 to $150 per levy. A levy on 10 banks runs about $500 to $1,500 just for the process servers. Are these numbers deal breakers? Maybe and maybe not. If your client is willing to invest in this strategy, and you perceive that a mass levy might snare some real dollars, do it and don't hesitate.

On its website, the California Department of Business Oversight provides a complete directory of the centralized levy departments for all reporting banks. Presume that if a bank has not reported a centralized levy department, a levy on one branch is a levy on every branch. Now, before you levy every bank in town, this is the law in California and may not work in your state.

Safety deposit boxes are key repositories for cash, jewelry, coins, key documents, and other valuables. The new law would allow a creditor to reach a safety deposit box if in the hands of one of these banks and the notice of levy includes safety deposit boxes. Some banks even take the position that a levy might even reach branches outside the State of California, which necessarily would include safety deposit boxes. The trick here of course is drafting up the levy papers.

New York law is even better. A levy on the branch is a levy on the bank and even reaches assets that are offshore. *Koehler v. Bank of Bermuda Ltd.*, 12 NY 3d 533, 541

[2009].["In short, the principle that a New York court may issue a judgment ordering the turnover of out-of-state assets is not limited to judgment debtors, but applies equally to garnishees. Consequently, we conclude that a court sitting in New York that has personal jurisdiction over a garnishee bank can order the bank to produce stock certificates located outside New York, pursuant to CPLR 5225(b)."]

What does this means to you? This is a very big deal. Assuming that you can domesticate the judgment in New York, and believe that you have reasonably identified the bank, a levy on the bank would reach assets that are worldwide. This of course demolishes the barrier represented by offshore retention of funds, assuming that the funds are held in the name of the judgment debtor.

Don't rush off to New York too fast. First, New York does not authorize the enforcement of default judgment through the Sister State Judgment Act. You have to file suit in New York and, in part, "recycle" the case again. Under the Sister State Judgment Act (as in California), you must file the out-of-state judgment in the California court and then convert the out-of-state judgment into a California judgment. Serve the debtor with the notice of entry, application to enter, and copy of the California judgment, and, absent an objection, assuming the jurisdiction of the sister state, and absent a motion within 30 days, you now have a California judgment. Also, the judgment debtor isn't too stupid. Offshore banks are less picky in identifying customers.

For about $1500 you levy just about every major bank in town.

Chapter 6

Captive Insurance Is the Latest and Greatest

What is captive insurance? Instead of my explaining it to you, here is the pitch (www.captiveinsurancesolutions.com/captive_asset_protection_benefits.htm.) (Accessed on May 8, 2014):

> **Captive insurance companies** can have significant **Asset Protection** benefits for their affiliated insureds and owners. The list below contains a number of the critical features which make **Captive Insurance Companies** excellent **Asset Protection** vehicles for high net worth businesses and their owners.
>
> **Formed as Corporations or Limited Liability Companies**—Since most **Captive Insurance Companies** are formed as either a **Corporation** or a **Limited Liability Company,** they provide their shareholders or members (owners) with limited liability up to the extent of their investment in the **Captive.**
>
> **Captive Ownership is Confidential—Captive Insurance Company** ownership information is kept in strict confidence by the insurance regulators and corporate registrars of the various domiciles that permit **Captives** to be formed and operated in their jurisdiction.
>
> **Protected Premiums Accounts**—Some **Captive Insurance Domiciles** have **Captive Insurance** legislation which prevents premiums paid to a **Captive** from attack by creditors. For example, **Anguilla** has excellent **Captive Insurance** legislation which provides for "**Protected Premium Accounts.**" **Anguilla** insurance law ***protects*** the premiums paid by an insured to an insurance company from being challenged by creditors, unless the payment of such premiums was made with the intent to defraud the creditor. In addition, premiums are protected against any legal actions, provided such premiums are maintained in an account separate from any other. This **Protected Premium Accounts** legislation makes **Anguilla** an excellent domicile for **Captives** concerned with **Asset Protection.**

> **Choice of Laws and Venue**— . . . Creditors wishing to bring an action against the **Captive** would have to use the foreign domicile's courts and laws in order to pursue their claim. **Moving the Captive's assets to an account in the foreign country where the Captive is domiciled and forcing creditors to bring legal actions in the domicile's courts using its law creates a formidable if not insurmountable obstacle for even the most aggressive creditors.**

A captive "insurance company" is one big fat lie. No, I am sorry. It is a really fat, gargantuan lie. A captive insurance company is an offshore bank account. That's it, folks, and nothing else. I'd love to charge Dr. Doodle-Noodle $50,000 to set up an offshore bank account. I'd do it for $5,000 and keep the change, Mister.

If asset protection is a pig, captive insurances wear nice lipstick. Regulated by who, or what? The man in the moon? Worse, the bedraggled doctor, the usual mark for these deals, might believe this lie. Some doctor is taking umbrage at these remarks. The issue with doctors is that they exist in a high-risk cloud buzzed by vultures. These birds of prey include patients and their rapacious lawyers, current and past screaming wives, dishonest partners and bookkeepers, and other predators. This is a Ponce de Leon moment. First, let's deconstruct "captive insurance company." This is not insurance. A captive insurance company is a bank account, and nothing more. Call captive insurance the hocus-pocus of asset protection. "Hocus-pocus, the bank accounts disappeared!" But find the captive insurer, and you have found the money.

The entire purpose of asset protection is to retitle the assets in another name, hopefully with the patina of legitimacy, but to retain control. Here is the punch-line quote: "While the physician's concerns are certainly justified, the proper CIC structure allows for complete control by the physician. There is no need for the physician to trust any other person or entity with their assets—a drawback of some of the other asset protection structures we use as planning professionals, such as irrevocable trusts. Further, while the CIC may be established outside the U.S. to keep administrative costs low (although certain U.S. states can also be used), the CIC funds can remain in the U.S., in American stocks, mutual funds, money management accounts, etc." This is language of classic asset protection that offers to shield an asset in the name of another asset, enjoy the benefits of the U.S. financial market, and retain beneficial control in the hands of the debtors. Very cool and good job. Find the captive insurer, and you will find the money. As a matter of law, insurance will never cover an intentional tort, but it usually provides the costs of defense. Insurance typically covers most negligence and personal injury claims, and it never covers routine contractual matters. Insurance rarely covers employment disputes absent a personal injury.

Insurance is issued on a yearly basis in which premiums go up or down. Insurance is highly regulated by state law including capital reserves, claims practices, and methods of operation. Insurance companies file annual reports with the state. Insurers are admitted, (i.e., do business in the state) or nonadmitted. Nearly all insurance companies are rated by Bests, among others. Real property leases, supply contract, construction, transportation, wholesale distribution, and manufacturing require that a person maintain million-dollar insurance policies that name others as loss payees or just proof of insurance as part of the deal. The capital (reserves) for most insurers is in the (many) billions, and the risk covered is in the trillions. This is the general summary of insurance, and its core is an unbreakable contract by a solvent person to pay expenses or compensate another arising from a contractually defined risk. In some cases, the insurance company will pay the total of the policy limits with or without the cooperation of the insured. Individuals, businesses, and governments stake their existence upon these services offered by solvent, reliable, and professional insurance companies. The U.S. government did not hesitate in saving AIG, but it let Lehman Brothers go down the drain. Banks can come and go, but big insurance companies must stay. In every case, bar none, the state department of insurance regulates this entity.

Captive insurance is none of these when the sole purpose is to enable the doctor (or others) to park large sums of money in offshore bank accounts that are controlled by the doctor or surrogates, or even here but held out of state or in another name. Captive insurance is not insurance. Captive insurance does not define risk, set premiums, and have deductibles, nor is it regulated by the state. Captive insurance is another bank account with a new name, but holding the debtor's money. The debtor, usually a doctor in a high-risk practice, loves these deals because the debtor thinks, foolishly, that the captive insurance is "insurance" when he or she is doing is dumping money equal to traditional premium in another account. I had one case in which millions of dollars flowed from a real estate Ponzi scheme to an offshore captive insurer. The money was never seen again.

This is a fraudulent conveyance because the intent of the debtor is to transfer the money (i.e., the supposed "premium") to another repository, which renders enforcement against those funds more difficult, arduous, or nearly impossible, which is the core of fraudulent conveyance. Many asset protection professionals opine that preplanning for a future contingency is not a fraudulent conveyance because the claim has not arisen. This is complete baloney. If a debtor transfers assets and is "engaged in, or was about to engage in a business or a transaction for which the remaining assets of the debtor were unreasonably small in relation to the business or transaction or . . . intended to incur, or believed, or reasonably should have believed that he or she would incur debts beyond his or her ability to pay as they became due," the transfer is a fraudulent conveyance.

If you lay your hands on a Uniform Residential Loan Application for the debtor, the captive insurer disappears from the URLA and reappears as a stock or bank account, housed in a local financial institution. Why? An offshore account is nearly immune from routine enforcement, and the lender in qualifying the borrower would disallow the account in determining the borrower's net worth. The negative shrinkage of the debtor's net worth might compel the lender to demand additional collateral, raise the rate of interest or other terms, or even reject the credit altogether. This is very bad.

When a traditional lender rejects a borrower, the borrower might find other lenders likewise disinterested and might resort to the next tier of lenders, such as hard money lenders, and even factors. This second and declining level of lender would demand larger chunks of collateral and clearly at much higher rates. In finance, there is no free lunch.

Section 16

The Story of *If I Did It*

All beginnings have an innocuous start. In November 2006 my wife, Lilly, and I, were sitting on the couch watching CNN when the news broke that O. J. Simpson was going to publish his book *IF I Did It*. In its reigning glory, the media reported that O. J. was going publish his book that would spell out the lurid details of the murders of Nicole Brown Simpson and Ronald Goldman and any money would go around Fred Goldman. I watched and said to myself, "I can collect that judgment. I can do this." I pointed my finger at the TV. "This is doable," I said. The next morning I culled through the Los Angeles County Superior Court website and located the original lawyers. I sent them a package of my materials. No response. Dead silence. Not so good. I located the current lawyers and likewise sent them a package. No immediate response. Not so good. I called. I called. And I called again. After another call, I arranged for a meeting in Los Angeles and met Peter Haven, who was the local counsel for Fred. I met Peter who was an associate with a major Los Angeles law firm and kicked off the quest to join this case. After an hour of presenting myself, Peter and I went out to dinner at a she-she restaurant in Los Angeles. This place was packed with young professionals, offered a bar that was packed three deep, and had a menu that catered to the type A crowd. Heavy on steak and low on tofu. I was fortunate, or very lucky, because I met Kim Goldman, Fred's daughter, who was sitting with her party at the same restaurant. Luck favored me, and, after the meeting, I was on board. All I remember about the food was that the steak I ordered came out very rare. I should have ordered the chicken.

I finally got on board to represent Fred. I told my wife, Lilly, that life would change.

This was (and is) in Fred's historic quest to recover his $38 million judgment against O. J. Simpson for the murder of his son who became an innocent victim to a horrid act of aggression perpetrated upon Nicole Brown Simpson. O. J.'s book stood to profit from this blood fest. The near publication by HarperCollins of the O. J. authored book, under the imprint of Judith Regan of Regan Books caused a national uproar, including protests by Bill O'Reilly of the *O'Reilly Factor* and other conservative figures. As a result, Rupert Murdoch, Chairman of the Board of News Corporation, which owned HarperCollins, caused the recall of the book and had it pulped. At the time that I joined the legal team, the book had already been pulled, and I became aware that on the day the book was announced to be published, HarperCollins wired $800,000 to Mr. Simpson through intermediaries, which was the local agent who wired the funds to Leonardo Da Vinci Stark, who was Simpson's local lawyer. Mr. Simpson was residing in Florida, a state well known as a debtor-friendly haven. Seeking to recover against a debtor in Florida is enormously difficult, and Simpson was even more problematical given his implacable hatred of Fred. Moreover, Mr. Simpson was represented by Ronald Slates, a well-known and capable collection lawyer who had been practicing as many years as myself.

Shortly after my engagement, I determined that the HarperCollins book contract provided for the reversion of the book rights to the "author," should the book not go to publication. Well, this was the clear case that the book never got published at all (with the exception of one copy) given the pulping of some 300,000 plus copies. In this case, the holder of the book rights was Lorraine Brooke Associates, Inc., a Florida corporation, in which the two names represent the middle names of Nicole Brown Simpson's children by Mr. Simpson, and Arnelle Simpson, Simpson's daughter from his first marriage, was "the managing member." HarperCollins maintained an agent for service of process through Corporate Service Company (CSC) at 2710 Gateway Oaks Drive, Sacramento, California 95833, which means that a litigant could serve HarperCollins by leaving papers with the CSC.

Let's digress here and go through Publishing 101. Under a publishing contract, the author hands over the rights to the work to the publisher who has an exclusive license to publish, or disseminate the work. This is an exclusive license in favor of the publisher and bars the author from any efforts to disseminate, or exploit, the work. It's mine, says the publisher and for good reason because the publisher is going to invest big money in promoting the book or other medium. This license entitles the publisher to publish a book, distribute the work through an electronic medium, such as e-book, serialize the book, or cycle the work through another medium, such as tapes, presentations, or even movies, television, or digital medium. The author also licenses his or her name, and likewise, signature, personal history and story, and image and right of celebrity to the publisher who can promote the book. These licenses of the personal rights of publicity are common in the publishing business.

What happens if the publisher declines or fails to get the work "out the door" and the work remains dormant? The publisher might halt the project if the market is not ready, is saturated with competing works, or dies on the vine for a particular work. How many books about the Navy Seals can the marketplace tolerate? Can an unknown author offer works that compete with the *Harry Potter* book series? Do we think that the *Life and*

Glory of Osama bin Laden would be a best seller? The obligation to bounce back the right to publish in favor of the author are called "reversionary rights," with the typical language "In the event that the publisher does not publish or exploit the WORK within 12 months from date of contract, all rights revert to the AUTHOR who is free to publish, exploit, license or assign the WORK." Under the publishing agreement, these reversionary rights constituted a general intangible, which means a property right capable of ownership. For example, a trade name, business goodwill, right to do business, or business opportunity is a general intangible, and all have value. You reach the general intangible by serving legal process (a levy consisting of the writ of execution, notice of levy, and memorandum of garnishee) upon the person who is obligated to provide the general intangible (the obligor), which in this case was HarperCollins, who was obligated to restore the book rights to the original holder. I personally typed up the notice of levy to reach Simpson's reversionary rights under the HarperCollins book contract. If a bank account is levied, the notice describes the assets as "deposit accounts, savings accounts, safety deposit boxes and general intangibles. . ." Here, I described the reversionary rights for the book as "general intangibles due, any residual rights, all rights to contract or veto any business transaction . . . all due and in favor of Orenthal James Simpson, Lorraine Brooke Associates from . . . HarperCollins Publishers, Inc." This levy on HarperCollins would be identical to a levy on a bank account held by a financial institution. The only difference is that the creditor is reaching book rights, and not money on deposit. So far so good? I hope that I didn't lose you.

Legalese, a private process server, served the levy package upon HarperCollins. This levy vested in Fred the reversionary rights to in the HarperCollins book contact, which consisted of the story rights, book contract, copyright, and intellectual property consisting of the work known as *If I Did It*. Make no mistake, the book described in gruesome detail the murder of both Nicole Brown Simpson and Ronald Goldman. Call this gore porn. To get the book rights actually sold through the sheriff took a court order that necessitated frequent appearances before the Honorable Gerald Rosenberg, Judge of the Superior Court (Santa Monica Courthouse). The primary battleground was the fact that the book rights were in the name of Lorraine Brooke Associates, Inc. (hereinafter "LBA"), and not O. J. Simpson. This took some time and effort to conflate (collapse) the LBA title holder into O. J. and make them one in the same. The Simpson legal teams including LBA's own lawyer, Tappan Zee, argued that the levy was improper and that LBA was really a separate entity. Even before Mr. Zee's appearance, the court made short shrift of that argument and held that LBA was O. J. Simpson's surrogate and held the book rights as his property and for his benefit. This is another glorified way of calling LBA O. J. Simpson's alter ego. Judge Rosenberg at the hearings had enough evidence to come to the conclusion that the story of Ron Goldman's murder and Nicole Brown Simpson's decapitation belonged to O. J. Simpson, and impressed the book rights, held by LBA, with the Fred Goldman judgment.

Is this a big deal or a legal technicality? Both. This is a big deal because the court permitted Fred to reach the book rights, which were shrouded in a Florida corporation, bearing the middle names of the children of one victim, for purpose of compensating the father of the other victim. After Judge Rosenberg came to that conclusion, the court ordered the Sacramento sheriff to sell the book rights at a public auction. The reason why the Sacramento sheriff was the levying officer to sell the rights is that CSC is located in Sacramento. The order for sale of *If I Did It* to compensate Fred was a big deal, particularly since early in the battle, Fred, among others, objected to the publication of the book.

The Sacramento sheriff was uncooperative and initially balked at auctioning off the book rights. Even though the sheriff's reluctance was not earthshaking, the media pounced on the sheriff, and that led, of course, to more press statements. Why is the sheriff balking at selling the debtor's property? We went around and around with the sheriff, until we delivered up the court order that they demanded and set the date for a sale. This was not a big deal.

The sale was set for April 17, 2007. We did a mass mailing to drum up interest and attract buyers. On April 13, 2007, the Friday before, lawyers for the family of Nicole Brown Simpson appeared before Judge Rosenberg to stay the sale. I should tell you that the hearing was set for 8:30 a.m., and I was stuck in downtown Los Angeles on another matter and arrived at about 10:00 a.m. No harm, as Peter was holding down the fort. I remember walking in to Judge Rosenberg's chambers with a roller cart that unceremoniously fell out of my hands and tumbled on the ground. I nearly tripped myself. Great start for a seminal hearing on the eve of selling the book that launched thousands of news stories. I picked myself up, and sat down at the judge's conference. The Nicole Brown Simpson family hired first-rate counsel (Greg Hafif of the Hafif firm who are legendary trial lawyers), and for this appearance, they came in twos. He was about age 40 with movie star good looks and wore a very expensive suit. He made a first-rate presentation. Initially, Hafif argued that the court should quash the sale because the sale and publication of the book would demoralize the children. That was a total nonstarter. Absent the brouhaha when HarperCollins was ready to launch the book with 300,000 copies, the book entered American consciences under the eternal rubric of "if I did it," as a punch line on *Saturday Night Live*, the late-night pundits, the blogosphere, print media, editorials, and radio commentators. With 300,000 copies already printed, the original incarnation of the book would have flooded the bookstores in 2006. The judge's visceral reaction: Denied. Not a tough decision. That didn't stop the Brown family lawyer. No siree. Hafif asked for half of the proceeds. That was another total nonstarter. The Brown family had no basis for that pitch. Let's not forget that Denise Brown blasted Fred Goldman for years. To prove my point, through the entire publication process through HarperCollins and our campaign, Denise Brown demanded a boycott for the book through a dedicated website. I didn't need to check with Fred on the Brown demand. I said no. The judge said no. Case closed. The sale of the book rights was set for April 17, 2007. We were done, I thought. I physically walked out of the courthouse (Santa Monica branch) at 10:35 a.m. and talked to the Associated Press and local reporters. At about 10:45 a.m., I got a screaming call from the office (in San Francisco). The litigation paralegal yells "stop, Stop. Don't do anything. O. J. filed bankruptcy." That wasn't quite correct, but at 10:45 a.m., Lorraine Brooks Associates, the titleholder of the book rights, filed a Chapter 7 bankruptcy in the bankruptcy court in Miami. Was that bad? Was the bankruptcy a disaster? Was it time to hang up the spurs and go home? No. The bankruptcy was a godsend. Why, you might ask? Doesn't everyone walk out of bankruptcy with pennies on the dollar, if they are so lucky? Not this time. As they say in the movies, "Nope."

Let's answer that question here. The *If I Did It* book, or any book, sits on the legal concrete pad of the legally protected copyright. To summarize, a copyright gives the holder of the right to sue anybody else who copies the "work of art." A copyright is the power of exclusion, and therefore the sole monopoly to exploit the "work of art," and hopefully for money. Can the state court sheriff sell the copyright and offer the buyer good and marketable title? Maybe or maybe not. Title might be "iffy" at best or scrap at worst. By the way, Fred would have credit bid and acquired the book at the sheriff's sale and ended up with the book rights. The answer to the title question is not so clear, and even if we could muddle through that nightmare, the sheriff's deed might be worthless and breed lawsuits. Is that important? For sure. I can clone myself to be the next Stephen King. Great. My wife would love that. Take all personal horror stories and turn them into money. But my manuscripts would die in the manger unless I can warrant that I have good and marketable title to the work (meaning that I wrote the tomes). If I acquired the "work of art" from someone else, I need to show full and complete title and warrant (promise) to the publisher that I owned the rights. The sheriff's deed might have conveyed nothing. Zippo. It was bad enough that the book suffered awful press, that the book was leaked in part online, and that the pundits were accusing Fred of profiting over the murder of his son, but it was worse that Fred could not peddle the book. Bad, Bad & Bad, PLC. The bankruptcy was our salvation because the bankruptcy trustee stands in the shoes of the debtor, and in part the creditors, and can sell the debtor's interest supported by the Good Housekeeping judicial seal of approval of the bankruptcy court. That works. Thank you, O. J., for dumping Lorraine Brooks Associates into bankruptcy because you invested good title in the trustee and made the book saleable. What a relief. It cost a bunch of money, but still the bankruptcy court gave the book a second life and bulletproof title.

After Lorraine Brooke Associates, Inc., the holder of the book rights and copyright to *If I Did It*, filed its Chapter 7 bankruptcy, we struck a deal with the trustee to title the rights in the hands of Fred Goldman. Together with local bankruptcy counsel, we drafted the sales agreement to ensure that the trustee would sell and assign the book rights, copyright, or any licenses, and any of Mr. Simpson's associated celebrity rights, which he contractually transferred to Lorraine Brooke Associates, who transferred to HarperCollins under the publishing contract. Talk about drilling into the copyright shale strata. (Case law bars the transfer of a copyright license without consent of the copyright owner.) This bankruptcy forced me to take a complete crash course in the area of salability of copyrights and licenses. *Gardner v. Nike, Inc.*, 279 F. 3d 774 (9th Cir. 2002) [Absent agreement to the contrary, licensee of copyright cannot transfer license to a third party.]. This was important to make sure that we had complete title if we were to get a book publisher to stick out its neck and bring the book to market.

Let's remember that as part of the deal, or any deal, a celebrity license of the name, photo, likeness, signature, and personal story is standard practice in publishing and entertainment and allows the licensee (HarperCollins, in this case) to exploit the celebrity status of the author as the key marketing tool. While the California courts barred Fred from directly grabbing O. J. Simpson's right of publicity in August 2006, the bankruptcy court, honoring the deal between the trustee and Goldman, ordered the transfer of the rights of publicity. That was very cool because O. J. Simpson granted away his celebrity rights to Lorraine Brooke Associates, his surrogate, and with the bankrupt entity, the publicity rights became a bankruptcy asset and controlled by the trustee. I gave the following statement to the press: "Ron Goldman LLC will own Simpson's name, likeness, signature, story, and hawk it to satisfy this terrible judgment. Justice has arrived in Miami." It was very good drama: One victim's namesake acquired the story of his own murder as recompense from the namesake of the children of the other victim, who was the estranged wife of the murderer.

After protracted proceedings in the Florida Bankruptcy Court before Judge Cristol, the trustee inked a deal with Fred Goldman, turning over the book based upon my levy on HarperCollins through the agent for service of process of January 2007, and the bankruptcy was in March 2007. The deal provided that Fred would publish the book and remit 10 percent of the sales of the book to the estate. You can do a deal in bankruptcy court with court approval. That means that the court conducts a hearing that entitles disgruntled parties to argue complaints or vent their spleen. Absent the billion-dollar cases in Delaware, hearings to approve a business deal are nonstarters, and few show up. Not this time, friend. Fred, Kim, Peter Haven, and I walked over to the bankruptcy court, which was located in the U.S. Courthouse. We got in line and immediately saw the cavalcade of press and their cameras. All U.S. courts have tight security ("shoes and belts," folks); we exited through security and made our way up to the court. When we got out of the elevator, another U.S. marshal greeted us and said, "Good morning Mr. Goldman." Normally, we don't receive a personal greeting from a U.S. marshal. We went through another metal detector. We got here about 45 minutes early, and the place was packed with press. We spotted Arnelle Simpson, O. J.'s oldest daughter, the managing agent of the Lorraine Brooke Associates. She had counsel in tow, who was Leonardo Da Vinci Stark. I could not make up that name for the life of me.

The Brown family filed papers that objected to the trustee's sale to Fred. In their filings, they carped about my legal process. Talk about picky people. That did not make me happy. No sir. Great, I had to defend my enforcement that seized the most famous book in the later part of 20th century in front of the national and international media. Talk about a career ender. I would have to go back to collecting for pawn shops and repossessing copiers. I would never hear the end of it from my wife. That frightened me most. "You did what!" Brown's lawyers addressed Judge Cristol and said that Cook did that wrong. Cook missed that. Cook didn't comply with California law. If Cook screwed up, Your Honor, Goldman has nothing, and the book doesn't go to Goldman, but stays with the trustee. I took the podium and addressed Judge Cristol. Remember those offerings in the *Reader's Digest*, such as "What are your last thoughts before you die?" Stuff like that. When walking up to the podium with the press of the free world behind me, my only thoughts were about pawn shops. I explained what I did. I told the judge that I did the right thing. You know what? I don't think the court cared what I said. The judge was attentive and asked me a few questions, and I sat down. Judge Cristol said, "I am going to take this matter under submission for about 30 minutes and come out with a decision." Judge Cristol exited, and we ambled around the courtroom. Everyone was chatting up everyone else, a typical old-time movie intermission.

Judge Cristol returned, took the bench, and paused for a second. He went through the cases that talked about the standards in approving deals proposed by the bankruptcy trustees. His favorite, he told everyone, was one case in which he was the author of the opinion. That brought the house down. Judge Cristol said that his job was to approve the deal if the deal was fair and reasonable. He said that the estate had no money to pay creditors, and that deal was the best deal (or the only deal) to turn the book into money and pay creditors. He intimated (or suggested) that the trustee was not about to publish the book. He ordered that the sale to Fred was conditional upon Fred publishing the book, and gave Fred 18 months to get the book published. If not, the book might come back to the estate. Call this order, "Publish or perish." The judge stated, "I need to have Mr. Goldman come to the lectern." Fred was beside himself, and our local bankruptcy lawyer, Paul Bautista, who could double as a linebacker for the Green Bay Packers, escorted Fred to the lectern and held him by the arm. Fred was slightly wobbly. Fred took the lectern. Judge Cristol said, "Mr. Goldman, I am going to approve this deal. You are obligated to publish this book. You cannot bury this matter. You understand this?" Fred said, "Yes." Fred paused. "Thank you. This is the first time that I have really received justice." Fred broke down in tears. Judge Cristol was staring at Fred, and Fred was crying in front of the judge. Judge Cristol paused for Fred to regain his composure. As you know, Fred has a white mustache. Judge Cristol has a white handlebar mustache. Judge Cristol looked at Fred and said, "You have the better mustache." The courtroom broke down in total laughter, and we exited the building to the side portico for a press conference. Having matriculated from Press

101 to Advanced Press 303, I had a much better idea how to respond in a press conference, which was to deliver the sound bite, speak in small sentences, dump the legal lingo, and skip the details. I told them that we would find a publisher and get the book out the door. Yes, I said that. Did I have any idea who to get the book published? Not a clue. No idea. Nothing. I had total sawdust in my brain.

I flew back to San Francisco. Great. With the help of others, we put the book *If I Did It* in Fred's hands. He has good and marketable title. Are we done? Can I write my own book? The pawn shop nightmare receded but was never gone. Now, I had to get the book published. How do you get a book published? How to get *If I Did It* published as one of the most reviled book in the last 20 years? My first bright idea was calling Judith Regan.

Let me introduce you to this story. Upon the implosion of *If I Did It,* Rupert Murdoch, who ran HarperCollins and News Corporation, fired Ms. Regan and closed her Los Angeles-based imprint. At the time, Ms. Regan was the world's most successful publisher, introducing the public to such titles as Jenna Jameson's, *How to Make Love Like a Porn Star* (2004). Through a local lawyer, we were able to arrange for Ms. Regan to come to my office. Peter Haven, my cocounsel, and I met Ms. Regan for a two-hour meeting. She came dressed casually in jeans and a jacket. She is very petite. In meeting with her, we asked for her help. She turned us down flat. Okay, that was not the end of it. We found out that she was very insightful, smart, and extremely erudite. This is one very smart person. She was also extremely profane. I didn't know that certain profanities could be nouns, verbs, adjectives, adverbs, commas, semicolons, or periods, or even one-word sentences. I also didn't know that one human being could evacuate the air out of an entire building. She expressed deep outrage in being thrown under the Murdoch bus, and she told us that the *If I Did It* book had approval from the highest levels, that she believed the book was a confession, and that she had personally conducted taped interviews with Mr. Simpson. She also complained that Rupert Murdoch treated her unfairly as she has sold "thousands of *pallets*" of books. We knew about the tapes and asked that they be turned over us. We got turned down, many, many times.

Okay, that cratered. I called one of the big Hollywood agencies. That went nowhere and I could not get past the receptionist. I bought the "how to publish" books from Borders. They were helpful. The *Los Angeles Times* ran an article that stated that the book is dead and virtually labeled the book as toxic. RIP. That pawn shop opportunity was creeping again in my head. Worse, I was nearing a long trial in the Marin County Superior Court. Remember that I told you about mass mailing the assignment orders to every insurance company? Remember the story of driving backwards up the hill to deliver $2.50 worth of fried chicken (at least the chicken was not soggy)? This was another Chicken Delight story. I composed a letter seeking a publisher and enclosed the court order. I concocted a list of all U.S. publishers (which I still have—see later comment), and did, you guessed it, a mass mailing to every publisher, just like the assignment orders. Did I get a hit? Two out of about 400. So much for my direct marketing campaign. I got one inquiry from Hachette, which was a major mass publisher and another small-time publisher (that went nowhere). Hachette's interest died on the vine. Too bad. I don't think that they wanted to get their hands dirty. I started the Marin County trial and was still getting calls from the press. My cell phone was primitive at the time. The phone was a small Nokia with only voice. During the trial, I would get calls during lunch. I got one call after leaving the restaurant walking through the parking lot. My client was in tow. The phone slipped out of my hands and shattered in four pieces on the pavement. I scrambled to pick up the pieces and snapped them in place. Miracle of miracles, the phone still worked, and better, I did not lose the call. I had the court reporter repeat the question. This was an out-of-body experience, and my client had the show of a lifetime.

Let's hit the Chicken Delight reset button. I got a list of all literary agents. I did another mass mailing. I got two or three desultory phone calls. That looked very bad at the time, and I might have blood on my hands if I couldn't find a publisher or agent. During the trial, I got a phone call from Sharlene Martin of Martin Literary Management (Encino). She introduced herself and stated words to effect that she handled difficult projects and was interested. Okay. That was a start. Peter Haven, local to her, took the lead. Within weeks, we had ourselves a literary agent. She placed the book with Beaufort Books (in New York City) and we had a contract. Interestingly enough, Beaufort Books publishes lots of Christian devotional books. I guess crime pays better.

The book was ready to be launched and Fred and Kim Goldman appeared on the *Oprah Winfrey Show* to "launch the book" at the hour of 4:00 p.m. on a Thursday. I knew that Oprah Winfrey was no great friend of the Goldmans and told her 20 million viewers that she had not read the book, and that she would not buy the book. That might be true, but her staff did read the book. We knew that. Getting Fred and Kim on the *Oprah Winfrey Show* was a big deal, given what was said in the vein of Calvin Klein, that any publicity is better than no publicity—just spell my name right. Oprah said that it was the choice of the viewers to buy the book. Oprah also had Denise Brown on the show by way of video. Denise Brown again condemned Fred and the book. Denise essentially accused Fred of profiting off his son's murder and asserted that any money he earned would be "blood money." This person was an unhappy camper, but let's not forget that the publication of that book put money in the hands of the Brown family. The bankruptcy court docket does not show that their money was returned.

The next morning, September 14, 2007, I was making coffee at home and turned on CNN. The crawl at the bottom of the screen says: "O. J. Simpson is a person of interest for a Las Vegas robbery." Little did I know that the night before, at the hour of 7:30 p.m., Mr. Simpson and his confederates robbed memorabilia from two dealers who were situated in the Palace Hotel in Las Vegas. Some of this memorabilia was O. J.'s pictures, plaques, game books, ties, and other stuff, including Joe Montana memorabilia and baseballs.

When I got into the office, the press called me for comment as to whether the memorabilia was subject to Fred's turnover orders. Later in the afternoon, I received a frantic phone call from the AP reporter who ramped through a very extensive interview of what O. J. might have had, what might have been taken, and what I would do about it. During this heated AP call, Andy Murr of *Newsweek* called for a story. My receptionist put the message in front of me and I told the AP reporter that Andy Murr of *Newsweek* just called me. The AP guy took a second and screamed in the phone: "Don't tell him anything." We finished, and I called Andy Murr back. I got him on the phone and told him exactly what the AP guy said. Murr screamed back: "Tell me everything." Within a few days, I got a court order for turnover of the sports memorabilia when the criminal trial was over. Again, Judge Rosenberg signed off on this order. Even though Judge Rosenberg might have quibbled with what he said (unless we had a record), his comment was, "I do not know whether or not this order is going to be any good." That is my recollection of what he said. If I am wrong, I apologize, but this is the gist of his statement. We will get there in a minute, if you need a bathroom break. I do.

Life entered the surreal. I hit the TV circuit. What did I know about TV before? Jack, zip, and nothing. I learned fast. First, pack your pockets with sound bites. Don't talk too fast. Speak up. Smile. Look into the camera. Say something intelligent, but not intellectual. Above all else, be funny. I walked into Fox News' San Francisco studio with those tips in hand. This taping was for Bill O'Reilly, no slouch and the chief critic of HarperCollins for publishing *If I Did It*. I gave O'Reilly a lot of credit, given that News Corporation owns Fox. Unlike other interviewers who plop you down in the chair and start the camera, this show required makeup. Makeup? Never in a million years have I ever worn makeup. Total guy thing. I walked into the makeup booth at the back of the studio and was greeted by a short, white-haired older lady. She had a wonderful touch. She told me to sit down, and draped over my shoulders a makeup gown. She looked at me, and seeing my discomfort, said, "Let's see what we can do." She applied everything. The works. I was age 57 at the time. She looked at her handiwork, stood back, and pronounced her creation, my reconstructed face, as "Autumn Glow." She handed me her business card and told me if I needed her help to give her a call. Telling my wife this story was even more bizarre because my wife did professional makeup. I ran into another lawyer who had an appearance before me on the airing of another TV show. I told him the story. He responded that he got used to TV makeup and one evening he came home without washing off the makeup. He said to his wife, "Let's go out to dinner." She refused by stating that she wouldn't go out with anyone that looked like a French hooker. This guy could double for another fullback.

The book virtually retitled as "*I Did It*," with the "*If*" in very small print. *If I Did It* reached number #2 on the New York Times Best Seller list and beat out Mother Teresa's book. Who says crime doesn't pay, even if acquitted? Editorials in newspaper condemned the publication, and nascent blogs went berserk.

Peter Haven was my partner in chasing down O. J. Simpson. Peter is a graduate of Stanford University and UCLA Law School and a first-rate lawyer. There is more. There is a lot more. Peter is about 6'2", thin, and extremely handsome. He has movie star good looks and a wonderful demeanor. This is not a case of jealousy, but a fact. How do I know this? We are in the Santa Monica Courthouse, on the first floor, in which the courthouse has long and wide hallways. As you walk up and down the spine of the court, the benches are on your left and of course interspersed by the doorways to the individual courtrooms. We were waiting to go into court, and like most type A folks, we are walking up and down the hallway. That's not a problem. Many lawyers pace up and down hallways. When I do it, I'm just another fellow pacing up and down the hallway. When Peter paces up and down the hallway, heads turn, especially those belonging to women who are sitting on the benches waiting to go into court. They all turn their heads in unison. At least we didn't have people throwing their phone numbers at him, or at least as far as I could see. This is so weird to walk by a group of women who turn their heads at your partner.

Peter picks me up at the airport with his new car, which was a leased, late-model Lincoln. It was a great car, beautiful ride, and had the new car smell. Here is the story of Lincoln cars. When the police would arrest small-time criminals and throw them in jail, bail was a realistic option. These criminals, or more politely, the defendant, would contact a bail bondsman who was able to get them out of jail for a modest price. However, the defendant needed a lawyer, and needed one very soon at the bail hearing. The point of contact, of course, was the bail bondsman and not the lawyer. The defendant would routinely ask the bail bondsman for the name of a lawyer, who in turn would make the hearing. Papers needed to be filled out by hand. Lawyers would necessarily complete the paperwork in order to present before the judge to spring the defendant loose. Obviously, the lawyer did not have an office, or desk, or any other writing surface, except one: the hood of the car. What was the premiere car, with a flat hood? A Lincoln Continental. The hood of this car was big enough to seat eight for a big dinner. These lawyers would fill out their paperwork by using the hood of the car as a writing surface. You would see lawyers leaning over the hoods of the cars by the droves in completing the bail paperwork. These lawyers forever were known as "Lincoln lawyers," being forever associated with small-time criminals who needed to be sprung from jail. When I got into the car with Peter, recognized that the car was a Lincoln, and without being unkind, all I could say was, "Lincoln lawyer." The latest incarnation of the Lincoln lawyer was a movie with Matthew McConaughey named *Lincoln Lawyer,* but it failed to explain the origin of this term.

The jury acquitted O. J. because of the jury total calculation of what was available to the jury in making that decision, which in part had little connection with the weight of the evidence. The acquittal was a market-based decision and nothing more. Whether the jury felt bad for Goldman and Brown family is not the issue. Did the jury love O. J.? Not too likely. Did the jury hate the prosecutors, the D.A.'s office, and police? In their mind, they didn't care. Why should they? They were entering immortality. The jury verdict, acquitting O. J. Simpson, represented the total sum of all knowledge of the murders, whether this information was real or imagined, and what the value of that acquittal would have to the jury. The jury verdict is the product of the Efficient Market Hypothesis because the jury weighed the total sum of all information, no matter the source, reliability, rational foundation, or just sheer fantasy inside and outside the court, including the future of the jury members. Whether the jury believed that O. J. Simpson murdered these people was not relevant to the jury. The fact of the murders was only the numerator in the equation, and not the product of the equation. The denominator was, of course, the jury trial for criminal cases, guaranteed by our Founding Fathers.

Section 17

Secrets of the Chef

Chapter 1

Star Trek Convention

Ever attend a convention of collection professionals? Collection agencies? Collection lawyers? Skip tracers? Private investigators? Everyone is swapping war stories.

Private investigators do a booming business in locating assets. Going through garbage is popular among the private eye set. In many instances, PIs are hired in big-time civil cases to discover millions in hidden assets. PIs are major players in big divorce cases and likewise look for the hidden stash including the dumpster dives. The plaintiff's lawyer calls in the PIs to verify the bona fides of financial statements offered to settle million-dollar personal injury claims for just the policy limits. The charge of the PI is to ensure that the financial statements are accurate. If you are going to hire a private investigator and want more than a regurgitation of the public records, be prepared to pay somewhere between $5,000 and $10,000 or far more. Don't forget to show the client the photo of your PI sorting through the debtor's garbage.

After the drone of speeches, all these folks hit the local watering house and after a round or two, or more, the war stories take center stage. Real or imagined, these stories have a kernel of truth. This is the best they have to offer, sans the cheap bar food and well liquor. You might even find some "Xs" on the treasure map.

Chapter 2

Do You Really Want to Find the Bank Account?

Let's go down the list:

A. Rummage through the client's file and locate any payment on account to the client. This might include getting from the client the deposit slip for the check. The client might have a credit application, sales contract, credit report, Dun &Bradstreet report that lists the bank accounts.
B. Pull a D&B report for about $20, which might list a current bank account. D&B canvases business and one of the routine questions is a banking reference.
C. Most banks demand a compensating balance as part of any loan to a customer. Find the recorded mortgage or deed of trust, or UCC in favor of the bank, and find the bank account.
D. Cull through every lawsuit filed by competing creditors and chances are that you will find that the other creditor filed with the court the credit application.
E. Serve a subpoena upon the debtor's primary vendors, such as the landlord, utilities, many trade vendors, suppliers, or third parties. The debtor probably pays with a check or wire transfer. With a copy of that check or wire transfer information in hand, you have the bank in hand.
F. Serve a subpoena upon the debtor's customers who pay the debtor with a check or wire transfer. The debtor endorses the customer's check, and the stamped endorsement identifies the depositing bank. The wire transfer information from the customer identifies the debtor's accounts.
G. Depending upon the state, if the banks have a centralized levy department, levy on every big bank. A bank that has a centralized levy department means that a levy on one branch (or the centralized levy department) is a levy on every branch. A levy on the 10 largest banks with a centralized levy department is a de facto levy on 1,000 branches.

H. Levy on the closest banks to the debtor's place of business, or if a small town, levy on every bank.
I. Serve the financial institution that refinanced the debtor's home, business, or other major assets. The debtor gave the lender a detailed loan application, URLA, or other financials that included bank statements.

This list is endless and had the best ways of reaching a bank account.

Chapter 3

Random Levies for Bank

If the debtor is a cash business or needs extensive customer service from a brick-and-mortar bank, such as cashier's checks, the debtor might select a bank as close as possible to the place of business. If the bank is on the first floor of the building where the debtor maintains an office, assume that the bank holds the debtor's accounts. The banks next door, nearby, or the only one in the area are tempting targets.

Before the advent of remote deposit, we found bank accounts by locating the bank nearest to the debtor's place of business. The theory is that the debtor needs to make a physical deposit of cash through a "live teller" and purchase cashier's checks and other bank services. Maybe. The debtor, a dentist, maintained an office at 123 Main Street, 4th Floor, Los Angeles, California. We punched up the address on Google Maps and found the bank at "123 Main Street, 1st Floor, Los Angeles, California. We got most of the money due on the judgment.

Here is another story. In San Francisco, and particularly downtown, people walk to their banks. You can find the bank by measuring the distance between the business and the actual branch. We had won a judgment against a very tiny restaurant that was in the middle of a good-sized block. We had hit the bank listed on the credit application, which was a few blocks down and came up with nothing. The restaurant did a fair volume, and we presumed that the restaurant constantly needed cashier's checks to pay for its supplies, given its declining fortunes. We literally counted feet, and hit the bank that was physically closest, which turned out to be 50 feet away. The bank did have the account, and the judgment was paid in full.

Let's keep in mind that Los Angeles is different. Other than downtown, Beverly Hills, Westwood, and other dense areas, few people walk as a routine matter, and everybody drives. Finding a bank account means that you find the bank most convenient by car, or the nearest off-ramp on the freeway. Sure. But levies are very expensive at $35 per bank and about $100 (or less) to get them actually served. See prior note that some banks have centralized their levy departments. Remember, stockbrokers are different. A levy on one branch is a levy on every branch. Post-January 2013, hit every bank.

Here is another story. This fellow was facing the twin barrels of a deficiency judgment arising from a real estate deal gone bad. Many mortgage and some deed-of-trust states burden the borrower with a deficiency. The risk of a zillion-dollar deficiency came as a shock to many investors seeking bigger returns when snapping up small shopping centers and apartment buildings in modest growth states. Disaster struck between 2007 and 2011 when the market cratered and rents plummeted, creating unbearable negative cash flows that drove many of these borrowers into a judicial foreclosure.

This one fellow was confronted by a six-figure judgment but refused to pay. This guy was not broke. This guy was not financially distressed. He just did not want to pay. I was the third lawyer. We served every major bank in his community (about 15), the major mutual funds (the top five), and the five top discount stockbrokers. We got $12,000 from one bank account, $9,000 from another account and locked down his mutual funds. Five days later, and unannounced, his lawyer mailed us the balance of $89,000 in one check. We did hit up the credit union in town, but that did not work. Better luck next time.

Random bank levies is just another version of roulette. The bet is $35.

Chapter 4

How to Find a Bank Account

In making a loan, the banker demands that the borrower maintains the accounts with the lender. The reason is that the banker offers a lower rate of interest, given the depository account as compensating balances and has the right of offset. Find the bank as lender, and you will probably find the bank holding the accounts for the debtor. These banks are identified through the UCC filings (liens on personal property) or deeds of trust [mortgages] on file with the county recorder. If you find the recorded UCC or deed of trust, chances are that you found the depository bank.

Bank accounts are usually linked to lines of credit, both unsecured and secured. You can identify a line-of-credit facility through recorded documents, such as deed of trust or mortgage, which bear the legend "Line of Credit" or "Equity Line of Credit." The bank will file a UCC that provides for a blanket lien. You can make an educated guess that the UCC represents the lien in favor of the bank securing advances on a line of credit. The yoke between security and debt (security follows the debt) is paramount because once you see the security (the recorded deed of trust or mortgage or filed UCC), you have found a debt.

Google and PayPal accounts are necessarily tethered to a bank account, line of credit, or other source of funds. Laying a subpoena upon these online services should reveal the source of funds, which in most cases is a bank account, but could be a credit card or offshore account.

PayPal does hold accounts in the name of its customers and will respond to levies.

D&B and other commercial credit reporting services (Trans Union, Experian, Equifax, services provided by Westlaw and Lexis-Nexis, among others). Some of these services might disclose the bank for the debtor. These records are available for a fee, for a service charge, or by subscription. You can buy a D&B report for a very modest price.

Absent the unusual, the plaintiff is not alone, and others are suing the debtor. This is an expectation. Other litigants might have attached a credit application or even a financial statement to the lawsuit, attachment application or declaration that discloses the bank, branch, or even the account number. Many court dockets are now online, and allow for the downloading of these documents without a charge. Vendors, banks, and hard money lenders might have filed suit. These commercial credit grantors probably have an extensive file accessible through a subpoena.

Did you garnish the known bank account and receive the response, "Account closed" or collection of a marginal recovery (less than $100) when the recovery should have been in the thousands? That tells you that the debtor emptied out the bank account by writing a check, wire transferring the funds to another account, or drawing out the funds through a cashier's check. This information is critical in pointing out the new repository for the funds.

Let's presume that the debtor closed out the account by drawing out a cashier's check. No problem. Subpoena the canceled cashier's check and look at the backside that might identify the new bank. Expect that the new bank is potentially out of state, and commonly another branch of the original depository bank. Depositing a cashier's check drawn on Chase (Los Angeles) in a Bank of America account in Las Vegas will delay access to the fund, given that Bank of America is going to wait until the check clears. Depositing the check (or cashing the check) in Chase (Las Vegas) will be much quicker.

Chapter 5

Fictitious Business Names Mask Money

Customers are attracted to the business, given familiarity, or knowledge, of the name. "A name that you can trust," is the mantra of every business. Let's assume that the defendant is facing a meritorious and massive lawsuit and, bearing malice toward the plaintiffs, decides that cycling assets into another entity is the best defense. If the business is primarily a service business, the defendant need not comply with the Bulk Sales Act, which requires the buyer to publish and record a notice of sale and establish an escrow. Upon service of the lawsuit, the defendant (or its principals) will form a new corporate or LLC entity that will file a fictitious business name very close or identical to the defendant's name. To all appearances, the business continues to operate under the same name, but it is reposed in another entity. Given the absence of a bulk sales notice, the plaintiff would not necessarily disclose this change of business, absent extreme diligence.

To further mask this charade, the defendant will continue to defend the following lawsuit and fabricate the illusion that the defendant is expending money because the defendant has something to defend (i.e., assets) in the first place. The day that the suit is filed, the case is set for trial, the case goes to trial, judgment is entered, liens are issued, enforcement is afoot, or when anything else happens that advances the collection ball, stop what you are doing. Constantly check with the clerk to determine if a new fictitious business name (FBN) has been filed, and whether the FBN is in the name of the debtor, the debtor's own FBN, or something very close. Here's one for the ages. Shortly after the filing of a class action for unpaid wages, and in the face of a million-dollar case, the debtor's confederates file a FBN with the debtor's business name, but attach it to another corporation that immediately takes out the required permits and license to operate. The new entity opened up fresh bank accounts. Of course, the lease probably did not get transferred; therefore, the remedy to topple this scheme is to subpoena the landlord and key vendors to see who is writing them checks. The money is in the hands of the new entity. The new FBN is the "X" on the treasure map because the FBN identifies the new owner of the business and the repository of assets.

What is the remedy? Subpoena the records of the new entity, including the key vendors, and most importantly, the bank (probably the same bank) and the landlord. Double-check with the finance department of the city for the city business license, the state board of equalization permit (sales tax), or other licenses (city business permit, health permit etc.) that might identify the successor entity.

Expect the successor will file a fictitious business name certificate that bears the name as the debtor. FBN filings are online. Sit down and look at the legal name of the successor, the phone number, the e-mail address, the fax number, the logo, the advertising, the name on the door, the color scheme of the facility, and the advertising or letterhead. If you are trying to pin the tail on the successor donkey, these indices of ownership are important. If the name of the debtor is American Broadway Corporation, and the successor is American Broadway Company, and hence duplicate initials of "ABC," the striking similarity and same initials suggests common ownership. Why? First, the secretary of state might reject the incorporation of the successor without the consent of the predecessor, given the similarity of names. To avoid the perils of consents and further evidence of commonality, the successor is a limited liability company and not a corporation. The change of organization (assuming the same phone number, address, and principal) is the bull's-eye in proving successor liability. The secret here is more interesting. I spent 20-plus years representing banks. Customers write checks payable to the vendors based on the names on the invoices, whether the legal name or the trade name. If the debtor's invoice says "Pay to ABC, 123 Main Street, Anytown, California, U.S.A. 10000," the depositing bank for the successor would not hesitate in accepting checking payable to the initials of the company. The customer wouldn't think twice in looking at the endorsement that says, "Deposit to the Order of the Name Payee," or "ABC." Draping the successor with the name of the predecessor (the debtor) enables the successor to launder the predecessor's cash flow through the successor's bank account. How do I know? I know. In one large case, on the eve of filing the class action suit, the debtor's principals formed a new corporation, installed the "manager" as the corporate principal, filed a new FBN in the name of the debtor, closed the debtor's accounts, closed the merchant accounts, closed the credit card accounts, changed banks, and received, without missing a beat, the debtor's continuing cash flow. Great job, guys. Unpeeling the onion took money and time, but the subpoena upon the successor's bank accounts, successor's loan file, and the principal's loan file with a bank revealed this stunt.

Section 18

Bills of Lading

Chapter 1

Bills of Lading Are Treasure Maps

Bills of lading tell you everything. Bills of lading are the neon and ever-flashing signposts in the rabbit hole.

Bills of lading are the shipping documents that identity the shipper (the person who ships the goods and the probable seller) as the consignor and the recipient of the goods (the person who is buying the goods) as the consignee. The ship that transports the goods on the high seas is called the carrier. The shipper (consignor or your debtor) might have directly contracted with the carrier, sought the services of a freight forwarder (likely), used the services of a nonvessel operating common carrier (NVOCC), or ocean transportation intermediary (OTI). A vessel operating common carrier is called VOCC. Ocean-going carriers (usually ocean-going container ships), NVOCCs, OTIs, trucking companies, global, national, and regional package services (FedEx, UPS, USPS, DHL, etc.), or other common carriers issue bills of lading. These entities are readily subject to service of process, given their size and pervasiveness.

Laying a subpoena upon their carriers will reveal, if you are chasing the consignor, the identities of the consignees who are the probable customers of the consignor. After the consignees have been identified, you can garnish the consignees for the accounts receivable, or serve a subpoena for the consignee's records to ferret out bank accounts of the consignor who received the payment from the consignee, which appears on the backside of the cashed check or in the wire instructions. Alternatively, the creditor can reach the consignees with an assignment order, third-party order of examination and turnover order, or a stand-alone creditor's suit.

Better yet, the consignee probably has a raft of documentation that can better identify the consignor, which is the offshore debtor or maybe a successor to the debtor. If the debtor (consignor) committed a fraudulent transfer and started up a new entity, the bills of lading might reveal the new and successor entity. The subpoena therefore should cover all names that are associated with the debtor or successor entities. If you are close to striking pay dirt, expect a spirited motion to quash the levies and subpoenas, and even an appeal. Trolling through bills of lading to reach the accounts receivable due the offshore debtor is the postdigital equivalent of digging up a coffee can in the backyard. Instead of the backyard, the money is buried in the containers on the deck of the carrier.

Before running off to the next chapter, many commercial services will sell you bills of lading specific to your consignor or consignee, but keep in mind that some bills of lading are online. These charges are not cheap, but if you are chasing down a million-dollar judgment, spending a few thousand is "behind the couch" money.

Bills of lading might identify the previously unknown U.S. subsidiary or affiliate of the offshore debtor of the consignee. If the offshore debtor is selling to the U.S. subsidiary, you can levy the U.S. subsidiary for the amounts due the offshore debtor for the subsidiary's sale of the debtor's product line in the United States or even other offshore markets. You can file a creditor's suit against the U.S. subsidiary to reach the receivable due the offshore debtor arising from the subsidiary sales of the debtor's product line in the U.S. market. You can gin up an assignment order to reach the revenues that originate from the U.S. customer-buyer who pays the U.S. subsidiary as the intermediate seller to the U.S. buyer and distributor of the offshore debtor's products. Expect a big response.

Chapter 2

Reaching Offshore Debtors Through U.S. Subsidiaries

United States subsidiaries are big fat targets. Offshore entities frequently do business with their local subsidiaries to enable them to reach a greater market share through the subsidiaries' portfolio of customers. U.S. subsidiaries maintain marketing and sales staff, coordinate product deliveries and traffic, and promote the brand names. Subsidiaries assume the credit and collection risk of resale to the U.S. customers, and moreover purchase large quantities of products and arrange for shipping, warehousing, and distribution. Subsidiaries also maintain local repair facilities and are good credit risks. Subsidiaries are rarely secretive of the lines of products that they carry, and therefore finding the subsidiary is not too tough. Some subsidiaries are alter ego targets.

If you really want to makes friends and influence people, Mr. Carnegie, serve a subpoena on the customers of the U.S. subsidiary. You are certain to drawn a motion to quash the subpoena that claims that you are harassing the subsidiary, causing havoc, and abusing process from here to kingdom come. You expect that the lawyer for the subsidiary will ask for sanctions exceeding the GDP of most southern states. If the U.S. subsidiary is the sole conduit for the resale in the U.S. market of products manufactured and imported by the offshore judgment debtor, the defense to the motion is that the sales by the U.S. subsidiary is a mirror image of the products originating from the offshore debtor through the conduit of the U.S. subsidiary. Every sale accruing to a U.S. customer of the U.S. subsidiary is every dollar due the offshore debtor for the products through the U.S. subsidiary as a conduit.

For good measure, you might find the port of entry for the goods, and therefore subpoena and even levy every warehouse, trucking service, customs broker, or storage facility that has the debtor's goods. If you find the trucking services that transported the goods, you can find the final end customers through the trucking services own bills of lading. Let's look at this process a touch closer. If the offshore debtor is selling products in the United States and you served a subpoena on the ocean-going carriers and confirmed the probable port of destination, you should be able to identify the warehouse, terminals, trucking services, dock facilities, and other storage facilities that might warehouse the debtor's products.

Chapter 3

Grabbing Goods off the High Seas—Yo, Ho, Ho and Shiver Me Timbers

Can you grab the consignor's goods while in transit if the bill of lading is negotiable? Not so much, Martha. Not according to Commercial Code Section 7602 if the bill of lading is negotiable: "Unless a document of title was originally issued upon delivery of the goods by a person who did not have power to dispose of them, a lien does not attach by virtue of any judicial process to goods in the possession of a bailee for which a *negotiable* document of title is outstanding unless possession or control of the document is first surrendered to the bailee or the document's negotiation is enjoined. The bailee may not be compelled to deliver the goods pursuant to process until possession or control of the document is surrendered to the bailee or to the court. A purchaser of the document for value without notice of the process or injunction takes free of the lien imposed by judicial process." In plain English: Possession of the *negotiable* bill of lading is the right to sole possession and title of the goods. Possession of the bill of lading is effective possession and title to the goods. Section 7602 protects cargo in transit if the bill of lading is negotiable and nonnegotiable.

To add a touch of confusion, the goods that the carrier transports are interchangeably described as cargo, goods, or freight. "Freight" is the commonly accepted term.

Let's become a maritime lawyer and learn the lingo. A nonnegotiable bill of lading is called a straight bill of lading. The holder of a negotiable bill of lading is the holder of title to the cargo. A nonnegotiable bill of lading is marked conspicuously "nonnegotiable." A bill of lading is title, receipt for the cargo, and a contract to deliver the cargo to the consignee. The Carriage of Goods by Seas Act covers most legal aspects of the transportation of freight by sea.

First, let's start with an easier question before we get to the grand or booby prize here. We will start with seizing cargo if the judgment debtor is the consignee. Let's presume that the bill of lading provides for delivery (point of destination) to a U.S. port. We presume that the bill of lading is nonnegotiable and therefore the immunity from enforcement against the cargo does not apply under Commercial Code Section 7062 and the Federal Bills of Lading Act [49 U.S.C. § 80115(a).] Given this lack of immunity, the judgment creditor can garnish the cargo in the hands of the carrier, which is due to the consignee under the bill of lading because the consignee is entitled to goods under the bill of lading itself.

Could this really work? Is this fantasy, fantastic, or foolishness? Are you going to try this at home? The bill of lading obligates that the carrier will deliver the cargo to the consignee at the point of destination in the bill. If you garnish the cargo in the hands of the carrier, who is the custodian of the cargo, you might be able to reach the goods due the consignee. Given the volume of goods and burden imposed upon the sheriff by taking possession, you might have to arrange with the sheriff for warehouse and storage facilities. You can seek the appointment of a receiver to take possession of the cargo. This sounds credible, but, trust me, you will earn your keep convincing a court to appoint a receiver to stand in the place of a consignee under a bill of lading issued by an ocean-going carrier. Your scholarship must be perfect.

Are we done? Let's presume that your case is pending in state and not federal court. You read the section why the state court might offer advantages over federal court, such as more customer-friendly levying officers, more courthouses, a higher rate of interest on judgments, and judges who handle debt collection on a routine basis. In state court, you might snag an even patent license. Can you grab cargo off the high seas based on the status of the debtor as a consignee if the case is pending in state court? The answer is maybe or maybe. The U.S. Constitution imbues the federal court with admiralty and maritime jurisdiction. "The judicial Power shall extend to . . . all Cases of admiralty and maritime Jurisdiction." Article III, § 2, Clause 1. Congress, under the Judiciary Act of 1789, furnishes the district courts exclusive jurisdiction over admiralty and maritime cases. The statutory mandate is codified in 28 U.S.C. § 1333 as follows: "The district courts shall have original jurisdiction, exclusive of the courts of the States, of: (1) Any civil case of admiralty or maritime jurisdiction, saving to suitors in all cases all other remedies to which they are otherwise entitled." This discussion now harkens back to your choice, if possible, when to pursue enforcement in the federal or state court.

Whether the carrier could fend off the garnishment is not the issue, but rather which court you picked. If you have the choice of courts, and the debtor is offshore and engaged in overseas commerce, federal court is the better option given jurisdiction over admiralty and maritime matters and bypass a possible defense if the garnishment originates from a state court proceeding. Maybe.

What if the consignee, your debtor, is an offshore entity and the carrier seeks to carry the cargo from one offshore port to another offshore port (e.g., Taiwan to Chile)? We need to presume in these facts that the carrier maintains a presence in the United States and is also subject to the jurisdiction of the state in which the process was issued. We presume that the carrier issued a nonnegotiable bill of lading. The answer might be that the garnishment upon the carrier might reach the cargo on the high seas, even if the cargo originated in one foreign country and headed to another country because the issuing court had jurisdiction over the consignee and the carrier. Will this work? Maybe and maybe not, but you will find the answer in the following discussion. A garnishment can reach goods due the consignee in the hands of a common carrier, says *Chicago & Northwestern Railway Company v. Alvin B. Durham Company* (1926) 271 U.S. 251. Expect a big court battle. Don't expect anyone to surrender anytime soon, or probably never. Don't count your chickens before they hatch. In fact, forget the chicken counting.

You suspect that state court might lack the juice to reach the cargo due the consignee, given federal court jurisdiction over maritime and admiralty matters. The judgment is pending in state court. How can you get it into federal court? Answer: File in federal court a creditor's suit that seeks to reach the cargo that is in the hands of the ocean-going carrier. A creditor's suit enables a judgment creditor to reach a debt or property in the hands of a third party and seeks an order compelling the third party to pay to the creditor the debt, otherwise due the debtor, or turn over to a receiver or the levying officer the property due the debtor. This is an action that would qualify as a maritime matter. Before filing a creditor's suit in federal court to reach the cargo (or maybe the debt if the debtor asserts a damage claim against the carrier) owed by the ocean-going carrier, expect the district court judge, sua sponte (fancy word for "self-initiated") to prove up jurisdiction. Expect judicial heartburn when the hearing starts with, "Counsel, this is very interesting. Perhaps you can enlighten the court about your claims. I put your case on the bottom of the calendar to give you more than adequate time to explain yourself."

Let's stop the show and rethink this trip down the rabbit hole. You have this huge judgment against a judgment debtor for God only knows what. The debtor is importing products from overseas that you have identified through a mass service upon the carriers who produced bills of lading that identified the debtor as a consignee. You sue the carriers in federal court for turnover of the cargo (technical name "freight") to a receiver. Is this going to work? Will this stunt elevate you to a deity or a dunce? Maybe on either score, but the mechanics of this scheme are sound, unless the federal district court judge tells you to the contrary. Tell me how this turns out.

What if the judgment debtor is the consignor and not the consignee? Can you reach the cargo under a nonnegotiable bill of lading? This is much tougher, Rocky. The consignor is offshore. For the technical geeks, the word "offshore" means far, far away. The answer is maybe. On the one hand, the bill of lading as a contract obligates the carrier to delivery the cargo to the consignee (the buyer). On the other hand, if the consignor paid for the freight, the goods ostensibly belong to the consignor because the shipment is FOB point of destination and not point of origin. If the consignor has a right to redirect, store, cancel, or cause the return of the goods in transit, the garnishment might reach the goods. We have a big, fat, and ugly maybe. This "maybe" breaks the scales. Expect that the carrier is going to come out of the woodwork in the face of any enforcement. You can expect a motion to squash the enforcement, or file a separate action for an injunction and declaratory relief. You can expect a nuclear winter of litigation. Expect grief. Expect a long day in court.

Chapter 4

Who Owns the Cargo?

Before hunkering down after pulling that stunt, let's keep in mind that the consignor is generally the owner of the cargo. See *Satco, Inc. v. State Bd. of Equalization,* 144 Cal. App. 3d 12, 17–18, 192 Cal. Rptr. 449 (Ct. App. 1983), in which the court stated as follows:

> Shipment by the seller under a bill of lading to a consignee out-of-state insures delivery takes place outside of California. Interstate shipment by bill of lading is governed by federal law. (49 U.S.C. § 81 et seq.) ***The consignor of goods under an interstate bill of lading is presumptively the owner of the goods.*** [Cook's comment: This is a 1932 case cited for this proposition. The law is good but a tad dusty.] The requirement the seller be the shipper under a bill of lading assists in restricting the exemption to goods which are shipped out-of-state *as the property of the seller* [Cook's comment: too much detail—you can reach the case]. [Emphasis added.]

What a long quote, but it is worth the effort. What does this case means? Answer: The consignor owns the cargo that renders the cargo subject to enforcement by the judgment creditor.

Chapter 5

Getting a Lien on the Cargo

Let's try another avenue of attack. If the consignor, your offshore debtor, paid for the freight, the goods in the hands of the carrier still belong to the offshore debtor and technically might be subject to lien through the execution if the carrier is served with a writ of execution. Maybe. Service of the garnishment on the carrier imposes a lien on the cargo. Say this statement out loud and in the mirror because you are going to have to say this to a lot of people. Practice make perfect.

Let's explain this process in detail. Garnish (i.e., serve a notice of levy) the carrier who possesses the cargo shipped by the consignor, your offshore judgment debtor. The consignor (your debtor) paid for the freight (freight prepaid). No problem. The goods are still in transit. No problem. The levy gives you an execution lien that reaches the cargo of the consignor in transit. Does this procedure get you this cargo? Yes and no. Yes, if the cargo is offloaded, warehoused, and not sold or handed over to a "nonprotected person" because the debtor's rights in the cargo are undiminished. No, you don't get the cargo if the cargo is sold to a protected person such as a buyer in the ordinary course of business, a person who acquires the good for value and without notice of the lien, bona fide lien holder, person holding the document of title, or other protected persons. Absent transfer to a protected person, the execution lien remains affixed to the cargo. Many judges will ponder this claim. Serving the writ of execution and notice of levy upon the carrier gives you the all-important execution lien assuming the bill of lading is nonnegotiable, which is usually the case. A notice of levy must describe the goods with some particularity. The levy would seek "all goods, wares, merchandise, cargo, containers, bulk product, freight and other tangible items in the possession of, care, custody, control, in the hole of, on board, in transit by, or other under a bill of lading due to, owned by, for the benefit of, owed to, to be delivered to, payable to the order of the judgment debtor, or in which the judgment debtor is the consignor or consignee. All cash, deposits, accounts, general intangible rights to payment of money or other funds in the hands of the carrier for the benefit of the judgment debtor." "Gimme what you got. I'll take it all," would flunk the description test.

Serving the garnishment against an ocean-going carrier for the freight due the consignee (if your debtor), the debt owed to the consignor (if your debtor), or the freight of the consignor (if your debtor) will drive everyone crazy and make them mad at you, particularly if the cargo originally was headed to a foreign port. The idea that you can yank cargo from the hands of the shipper or snap up accounts receivable by the customers to the debtor might scare everybody, which tells you that this enforcement produces, in addition to money, lots of fear, angst, and anxiety.

The ocean-going carrier will usually contact the debtor (as consignor or consignee) and request a response, one way or another. For everyone swimming in this cocktail, the debtor, the carrier, the levying officer, and their lawyers will ponder this levy and contemplate whether the judgment creditor can actually reach the goods, particularly if the debtor is the consignee and entitled to receive the goods upon delivery, assuming that the bill of lading is nonnegotiable. I want to reiterate the word: contemplate.

This risk is further buttressed by the fact that that you might have obtained a turnover order from the court that directs the actual turnover of goods in the hand of the ocean-going carrier to the sheriff, absent a sale or transfer to a protected person. Better yet, if the judgment creditor scored a receivership order for the goods in transit, the carrier, if served with the order, is going to bolt up in its chair and contemplate compliance with the receivership order. The turnover order, receivership, and restraining order are very tall orders. Divine intervention is always an option.

The fact that the carrier faces financial risk and liability for the failure to properly respond to a legal process might compel the carrier to ponder a temporary sequester of the goods pending a resolution of the matter among the parties. This might take one hour, one day, one year, or never. The debtor intuitively knows that the carrier might lock down the goods or might even hand them over to the levying officer. The thought that the judgment creditor could legally hijack goods off a cargo ship on the open seas would deflate the sail of the debtor's campaign of resistance. "Are you kidding, can that nutcase of the creditor's lawyer grab our stuff while in transit under a nonnegotiable bill of lading?" Is the total sum of all knowledge, real or imagined, a threat facing the debtor? "This guy has gone off the deep end. Pay this judgment before he does any more damage or pulls some other crazy stunt." Call this legal piracy that might or might not work.

Let's imbue a little realism and maybe a touch of common sense here. Some cases are very tough or even impossible. Newly emerging economies in Asia and India have produced an enormous wealth of products at a tremendous discount that tempts the American consumer to acquire products that otherwise would have been financially inaccessible if made in the United States at U.S. domestic prices. Unfortunately, some of these vendors sell slipshod materials that injure, maim, or kill the consumer. The plaintiff might have recourse against the U.S. retailer and might score a judgment against the manufacturer; however, collection against offshore manufacturers located in Asia is very difficult, particularly if they do not sell into the U.S. market or don't sell to distributors, importers, or retailers that do have a U.S. presence. Big-dollar judgment claims against the lone wolf offshore manufacturers might end up as truly uncollectible, absent offshore enforcement or reaching products through enforcement against the shippers. These debtors are not immune from enforcement, but they are vulnerable through enforcement against their cargo in the hands of shippers who do have a U.S. presence.

Let's escape the earth's gravitational field. You are chasing down the standard offshore debtor who is selling products all over the world. The choke point is that ocean-going carriers must transport the products, sometime to a U.S. port and sometimes worldwide. Your judgment is domiciled in a state in which the carrier maintains a real presence and is presumptively subject to the jurisdiction of the state. In the preliminaries, you serve the carriers with subpoenas and learn that your debtor is a consignor (shipper) of products and prepays the freight. Taking everything that we have learned so far (and so good), terms of sale to the consignee (the recipient of the goods) is FOB destination. Under the Uniform Commercial Code, the consignor (shipper) has title to the goods because the consignor paid the freight and retains the contractual relationship with the carrier. The carrier issued a nonnegotiable bill of lading (waybill), Can you grab the cargo off the high seas? Can you legally hijack cargo off the high seas? By the way, the term "high seas" is an accepted maritime term that means the ship is surrounded by water on all sides. The answer is a big fat maybe because the garnishment reaches the personal property in the hands of the common carrier. Garnish the ocean-going carrier for the freight under a bill of lading in which the debtor is the consignor, and you might snare the freight. Engage in intense prayer if you want to succeed.

Now, you ask how I know this. How can I predict that a billion-dollar ocean-going carrier with unlimited resources would resist any enforcement unless the cow came home? We undertook enforcement of the $2.7 billion (no typo here) judgment against Iran and sought enforcement against various ocean-going carriers, financial institutions, and related parties. We filed papers, and the matter was set for hearing in the U.S. District Court, Northern District of California (San Francisco). The hearing was set for 2:00 p.m. The courtroom was at the end of the court's hallway so everyone headed to court would exit from the centrally located elevator and walk down the corridor to the courtroom. I, and my associate, got there at about 1:30 p.m. and sat on the hallway benches and prepared for the hearing. About 1:45 p.m. we saw a battalion of lawyers make their way to the courtroom. We started to count one, two, three, four, five, and so on. We stopped at nineteen. At nineteen, we could field a baseball game. In fact, we took a crack at reaching Iranian funds in a multinational bank that had branches in California. I had now no doubt that my adversaries were Harvard, Classes of '91, '92 and '93. That stunt drew multiple amicus briefs from state and national bankers associations. Moral of this tale: Be prepared to defend your treasure map. Eat a full breakfast.

Chapter 6

Looking for the Bank Account in Maritime Records

We are not done yet. If you want to escape the solar systems and head off to deep space and join Captain Kirk, here is your chance. Your offshore debtor is shipping products from its offshore domicile. The debtor might deal directly with the ocean-going carrier, a global logistics company, ocean transport intermediary, nonvessel operating common carrier, or a freight forwarder. Some of these players are large enough to have a U.S. presence and are subject to subpoena. None of these transportation players works for free. The debtor pays for the transportation services through a check or wire transfer. Subpoena the evidence of payment by the debtor in the hands of the transportation entity that deals nose to nose with the offshore debtor. Whether a check or wire transfer, this information reveals the name of the financial institution, the name of the account holder who might not be the debtor, and the account number. What do you have here? Answer: You have the debtor's bank account. Given true globalization, you might find that the financial institution does business in the United States and might have an agent for service of process in your state. Can you garnish the bank for the debtor's account that is probably domiciled in an offshore account? That depends upon local law. Some states (e.g., California) limit a garnishment to accounts domiciled in the state. Other states (e.g., New York) allow a garnishment to reach the accounts of the debtor no matter where located.

The alternative to a garnishment is an assignment order. An assignment order reaches all obligations that are due to the debtor, and certainly a bank account is an obligation due the debtor. You might succeed in scoring an assignment order that reaches the offshore bank accounts of the debtor. Serve the assignment orders on the bank and see what happens. If the bank that houses the offshore accounts is present in the state for all purposes, the bank might honor the order because the bank is subject to the court's jurisdiction. However, you can expect massive pushback and a stupendous battle because no bank is willing to concede that their offshore accounts are subject to enforcement of another jurisdiction. Warm up your briefing skills before the state supreme court because you will need all those justices voting unanimously for you before the banks turns over offshore money to you.

You have another arrow in your quiver. You can file a creditor's suit against the bank. This will wake up everyone. A creditor's suit reaches all obligations owed to the debtor by the defendant in the suit. The typical creditor's suit reaches the accounts receivable due from a third party to the judgment debtor. You typically would file a creditor's suit instead of a garnishment, when the obligor might lack an agent for service of process. File suit against the bank and claim that the bank account is an obligation owed to the debtor.

Expect the bank to move to quash because the bank will claim that it is not subject to the jurisdiction of the state. Believe it or not, you can beat that defense if you cull through the secretary of state and recorder's office and locate all the UCC filings (for the secretary of state) and recorded mortgages (or deeds of trust) to demonstrate the bank is doing business in your state. The UCC filings do reflect the dollar amount of the transaction, but the mortgages (or deeds of trust) does reflect the dollar amount of the transactions that might amount to millions or billions. These documents might evidence a sales office, the name and address of a local representative, or, for that matter, a close related entity, all of which support the fact that the bank is subject to your state's jurisdiction.

Section 19

Where Is the Money?

Face it. We all like to speak in our native tongue about intimate or private matters. Frenchmen like to speak French to French bankers. Russians like to speak Russian to Russian bankers. Successful Taiwanese business people bank with Taiwanese banks. I really know this because the bankers seek out ethnic speakers to enhance familiarity with their customers and better explain banking products. Trust me, if you want some potential customer to open a seven-figure deposit account and kick off an eight-figure line of credit, everyone needs to be speaking the same language.

Is this set in stone? Of course not. However, if the defendant is Korean, and there is one Korean bank in town, levy that bank first. If your debtor speaks only Korean, chances are the debtor banks with a Korean bank. The language is your "X" on the treasure map.

The under-30 set banks online. The under-40 set might have never set foot in a branch. The under-50 set are now accustomed to ATMs and rarely venture into a branch. What about the over-70 set? Online banking, ATMs, PayPal, and other modern conveniences are downright scary. Garnish the closest and oldest bank in town. Focus on local banks with great customer service (i.e., bank tellers). For older people, banking is a personal experience. The older the bank, the better.

Chapter 1

Retentions Due Contractors

Maybe nearly all experienced owners demand 10 percent to 15 percent retention of construction contract when the construction is completed. This retention secures the obligations to bring the work into compliance with the contract. This is commonly understood. The owner and the contractor survey the site with a "punch list" in hand. From the debtor's point of view, these retentions constitute funds due the debtor (i.e., the general contractor for most parts) and look like "money in the bank," assuming that the debtor's financial investment in resolving the "punch list" is less than the retention. Permits issued by the planning department in the name of the debtor are the "Xs" on the treasure map.

What does that tell you? Answer: Levy on every completed job to reach the retentions. Where to find the jobs? Most cities and counties have active online databases that identify permit holders for construction jobs. If the contractor recorded a lis pendens, you would find the jobs through recorder's office.

Chapter 2

Ponzi Schemes

You have had the Madoff tutorial by now. In a nutshell, a super-duper salesperson, with the apparent touch of Midas, promises customers fantastic and spectacular rates of return for common financial investments. These investments are "private promissory notes," "investments in accounts receivable financing," "offshore private banking," "offshore or private stock investments," or "managed stock trading." The swindler takes in money from a customer, and promises 10 percent to 100 percent per month. The swindler finds another customer whose "investment" funds the promised dividends to the first customer and down the line. Ultimately, the swindler runs out of victims and therefore runs out of money so the scheme collapses. Some customers upstream and earlier "investors," might have emerged with their original investment and even a handsome return, such as the promised 100 percent return on the dollar. These returns (or even the payments themselves of the principal) constitute a fraudulent conveyance. When the scheme collapses and the swindler files bankruptcy, the trustee sues everyone for a preference (claw back money if paid within 90 days of the date of filing) or for a fraudulent conveyance. The trustee collects millions or billions as in Madoff.

Before the bankruptcy, however, nothing stops a downstream victim who lost everything from suing the upstream participant who got paid in full. The downstream victim sues the upstream victim for a fraudulent conveyance because the money taken by the Ponzi operator from the downstream victims is used to pay the upstream victims, which is a fraudulent conveyance. Even though victims suing each other looks unsightly, at best, and resembles true carnage, at worst, that does not matter. Downstream victims can recover from upstream victims the same way that the bankruptcy trustee can likewise recover. Remember that the money received by the upstream person as partial, full, or complete payment is really the money from the downstream party and is, therefore, recoverable. Talk about a real bloodbath when one victim (the downstream person) sues the upstream person for disgorgement of their recovery from the perpetrator of the Ponzi scheme.

What do you call this outcome? Answer: fun.

Chapter 3

Odds and Ends

Here are the oddball items. Workers' compensation insurance offers dividends and rebates every year, or even more frequently, depending upon the insurer. Health insurance programs sometimes offer rebates. If the debtor is a distributor or wholesaler, car dealer, or sells through a leasing company, either the manufacturer or the leasing company might offer a rebate, bonus, or deferred compensation. This is very common in the operation of automotive dealerships, as the manufacturer offers big rebates if the deal exceeds the sales quota. Newspapers and other forms of media might owe a rebate. Check with the state controller's office for money held in escheat due the debtor.

In the agricultural business, packing houses, distributors, granaries, and other middlemen hold funds in trust and remit periodic payments over one to two years. In banking, the motto was "know your customer." In the enforcement of judgments, know your debtor. Money is out there. It's somewhere. Just look.

Judgments and Suits Due the Debtor

Always, and always, even though we said it elsewhere, cull through the state and federal records to see if your debtor is a plaintiff in a lawsuit, a judgment creditor in a case gone to judgment, or a claimant in a class action, antitrust, or other mass case. Always cycle the debtor through the probate court.

You can impose a lien or even levy the lawsuit or judgment due your debtor. The judgment creditor can file a lien, but the debtor (who is the plaintiff in the lawsuit) might be motivated to work a "side deal" with the plaintiff for the purpose of defeating the lien. Intervening in the lawsuit is much better.

If the judgment debtor is a creditor of another debtor on a judgment, act aggressively to levy on the judgment itself. You can levy the debtor's interest in the judgment by service of a garnishment on the judgment itself; serve a third-party debtor's examination order on the defendant in the suit or judgment, serve an assignment order, or go nuts and file a third-party lawsuit against the defendants in the lawsuit filed by the defendant or debtor in the judgment.

You can paint the town red with enforcement. Modern court dockets are online and searchable through names or case numbers. Find the lawsuit filed by the debtor, or the big judgment, and you have found the "X."

The smart money is to do everything. You are not the only person chasing down this person, and imposing a valid lien on your debtor's suit or judgment will beat your competitors.

The Recorded Deed of Trust, or UCC, in Favor of the Debtor

You find a deed of trust or UCC that reflects the debtor as the beneficiary or secured creditor and someone else as the obligor. What does that mean? It means that the other person, listed as the obligor, owes money to the debtor. The debtor might have lent money, or the obligor may owe money for some reason, including purchase money on acquiring the property, or for some other reason. You can levy on the obligor the debt owed to the debtor. You can examine the obligor and if the debt is undisputed, the judge will order the obligor to pay the creditor and not the debtor. If you are fairly certain that the obligor owes a substantial sum of money and is without a defense, you can file a creditor's suit against the obligor and get a judgment compelling direct payment. You can get an assignment order served on the obligor likewise compelling payment.

Security follows the debt. Find the security, and you have found the debt. If the debt is owing to the debtor, you can collect on the debt. The existence of the security is the "X" on the treasure map.

How Do I Rid Myself of Fraudulent Conveyances?

Facing the big judgment, the debtor transfers the $7,200,000 home to himself as trustee for his adult sons. What is the cost to facilitate this stunt? About $100 in recording and notary charges. This transfer is a blatant fraudulent conveyance and compels the creditor to spend big money to hire a lawyer and topple the transaction. Most lawyers would demand at least $10,000 as an upfront retainer for the case. The debtor did a great job because the debtor's miserable $100 investment created a $10,000 obstacle. Where else can you get 100 percent return on an investment? If the debtor as the trustee of the trust sold the property to a bona fide purchaser and pocketed the money, the lawyer would demand a $100,000 retainer and express disclaimer of any success. This is now a 1,000 percent return on the $100 investment, and the debtor gets the Uniform Fraudulent Transfer Act Award of the Year.

What can be done to rid yourself of this pestilence? The answer is found in common law, which is the body of judge-made law. A fraudulent conveyance is a tort that includes punitive damages. If the debtor fraudulently conveyed the property (or bank accounts) to family members, business associates, or other entities, sue to vacate the conveyance and ask for $1,000,000 in punitive damages per person. Will the punitive damage claim wipe away the conveyance from the debtor to children? Maybe not, but the punitive damage claim forces the conveyees (the debtor's children or business associates) to hire their own lawyers who might charge $10,000 or $100,000 upfront as a retainer to defend against the lawsuit. What does it costs to add the punitive damage claim to the fraudulent conveyance lawsuit? Answer: Nothing. While big-time tort claims might not guarantee success, these claims persuade the debtor and family members to unwind the conveyance and return the property or the debt, or alternatively to settle the case or otherwise accrue crushing legal fees and a huge damage award. What is good for the goose is good for the gander, Mr. Chicken.

Chapter 4

Baseline Information to Discover Assets

Here is the voice of Chicken Delight. You really have to be prepared. If you ask the person if they have a bank account the answer will be "No," "I am not sure," or "What do you mean?" If you shove under the debtor's nose a financial statement that discloses a bank accounts or a check written by the debtor to a third party, you have a place to start. Financial information from third parties establishes a *baseline* upon which you can conduct an examination. Everything else is a waste of time. Where can you get really useful information?

Absent the most bizarre or extreme, the defendant continues to function in borrowing money from a bank to a home or business loan, borrowing money to buy a car, paying the mortgage or lease payments, making lease or loan payments on the car, hardware, or other equipment, executing financial statements, and turning over tax returns to lenders and credit grantors. The defendant borrows money to start a business, pays routine vendors, and even pays the utility, phone, data, or telecommunications company. Whether besieged by creditors, and facing the zillion-dollar judgment, the defendant necessarily functions like everyone else and seeks basic credit. Basic credit mandates basic, or even complex, financial disclosures, particularly post real-estate meltdown. The defendant may also lease a car. Auto-leasing companies require far less paperwork and disclosures than a traditional car loan, but they charge rates that a shylock would envy.

Chapter 5

Credit Grantors Have Lots of Information—Just Ask

Let's put to use everything that you've read. Be persistent, and, more importantly, remember the story of the *Monitor* and *Merrimack:* Keep pounding away. You will find the treasure if you find your inner 12-inch Dahlgren.

The credit grantors, landlord, mortgage holders, leasing companies, banks, and third-party vendors demand and receive extensive financials, including the URLA, sworn loan applications, tax returns, financial statements, bank or stock statements, and detailed lists of real property holdings. These are your treasure maps. These credit grantors also receive payments via check, ACH, wire transfer, debit card, or even credit card, which would identify the account holder, the name on the account, the account number and domicile of the account, and the methodology of payments. These are the "Xs" on the treasure map. These records, as opposed to opaque results at the debtor's examination, will reveal every asset, every account, and every stock and bond. The debtor goes to Best Buy and purchases a television set, but due to unforeseen circumstances, files a Chapter 7 bankruptcy the next day. How does the debtor schedule that television set? A 15-inch, black-and-white television set, broken, and worth $100. Let's change the facts. Instead of filing bankruptcy, the debtor tragically suffers a catastrophic burglary in which the burglars steal the television. The debtor, no fool, purchased insurance for the replacement cost and files a $5,000 claim to replace the 60-inch, flat screen, liquid crystal set.

Subpoena the insurance company for the policy and see if the debtor obtain a "valuable" rider for expensive carpets, jewelry, watches, or antiques. If untaxed income paid for these valuables, many debtors hesitate to insure them for fear of creating a paper trail that might fall into the hands of the IRS. On the other hand, all valuables are tempting targets of theft and prompt the owner to insure them for their full value. Life is like a box of chocolates, and you never know what you will get. But first, you got to buy the box of chocolates, Forrest. Insurance riders that list high-end assets are another treasure map.

At the postjudgment debtor's examination, the debtor denies any source of revenue claiming to live off "friends," but the debtor can't remember their names, addresses, or telephone numbers. I've been there and heard that. You have in your hand the deed of trust, the URLA, the tax returns or accounting work papers, the financial statement or even a credit report that reflects an $8,000 monthly payment for the debt service, taxes, and insurance, which intimates, say, $24,000 to $32,000 *monthly* income. Money is coming in from some sources and certainly not friends and relatives. Confronted with this fact, the debtor is going to repeat the story. Hail the debtor in front of the judge on the basis that the statements are willful evasions, and ask for incarceration until you get a straight answer. You'd be surprised that the debtor might capitulate when you make your pitch to the judge. Are you really clever? You debtor is not stupid, nor should you be.

Chapter 6

The 1099INT Is the "X"

The 1099INT is the epitome of "X" marks the spot.

Banks, stockbrokers, mutual funds, and others issue 1099INTs, which show the interest paid on an account. If the bank reports $2,500 as interest, chances are that you would know that the prevailing rate is, say, 1 percent. Using a little high school algebra, you would know that the total funds held by the bank are about $250,000. What happens if you know how much the debtor got, by way of a theft, or even a legitimate payment, but don't see any report of interest? Nearly all banks pay some interest, even on a checking account. If you know that the debtor got $1,000,000 but you did not see any interest reported, you know that the debtor is hiding the money in another taxing-paying entity or converted the money to cash, gold, casino chips, cashier's check, debit cards, traveler's checks, or other "portable" wealth.

Chapter 7

Canceled Checks, PayPal Disbursements, and Credit Card Statements Are the Pottery Shards

At the debtor's examination, the debtor denies ownership of any assets, other than the clothes on his or her back. The financial statement provided to government or private examiners as part of other qualifications for financial aid, government grants, qualifications of programs, or the write-down of a loan deny ownership of real property. Bankruptcy schedules show the debtor as near indigent. Is this credible?

Wobbling stars suggest hidden planets and might suggest that we have intergalactic company, Jody. Pottery shards recreate ancient history and depict sermons on the mount. Dinosaur fingernails reconstruct paleontology and make T. rex into a hyena.

Let's take all the skills we learned and go through the debtor's canceled checks, PayPal account, credit card statements, or any other history of payments including the accounts of the spouse, closely held companies (corporations and LLCs that are controlled by the debtor), and "trusts" controlled by the debtor.

Payments to third parties are clues or arrows on the treasure map. Every one of these checks is an "X" as they reveal the existence and even location of the assets. Call the bank accounts pottery shards because they suggest, if not prove, the existence of assets, owned or controlled by the debtor. Spot a check payable to the Cocabana Home Owner's Association for $500, and you can spot the debtor vacation home in South Beach, Florida. Spot the payment for the property tax bill for County of Pitkin, and you have spotted the condo in Aspen, Colorado. Payments for property taxes, real estate loans, property maintenance, repairs, homeowner's association fees and charges, parking charges and, my total favorite, even parking tickets. These charges all show ownership of real property and a locale (the parking tickets).

Payments to supermarkets, gas stations, Trader Joe's, department stores, sporting goods stores, restaurants, and other consumer locales show a locale. These checks or payments show where the debtor is living that might be different from the place where the debtor claims.

Routine payments to the Whole Foods in Beverly Hills suggest that the person lives in Beverly Hills and not an apartment in Lancaster. (Top of Los Angeles County and on the other side of the moon. For movie buffs, here is the correct line: "If I were posted to the dark side of the moon, I could not be more isolated.".

Payments for gas are very helpful given their regularity and life's experience that many (including me) frequent the same gas station given its proximity to a home.

Transferring money to and from other accounts, receiving wire transfers, and forwarding wires all show the movement of money and money held in other accounts and subject to more subpoena. The movement of any money is per se suspicious.

Most people do not spend half their day moving money by and between companies or bank accounts or from state to state or country to country. Moving money, without a very rational basis, is money laundering.

A check for a few hundred dollars means nothing, but a check for $10,000 is something. Writing checks for cash on a routine basis is extraordinary, other than $200.00 or less (yes, this applies to ATM withdrawals); anything more is suspicious. What are unusual services? Joe's Porn site? Maybe, but so what. Starring a porn site might be sign of personal depravity but not money laundering. Credit card payments to LegalZoom.com or its competitors or to the secretary of state as payment for incorporation services suggests that someone is cooking up new entities.

Payments of secured debt mean that the creditor has a security interest (lien, deed of trust or mortgage) in property owned or controlled by the debtor. Subpoena the lender's credit file for the URLA and its equivalent, which is the treasure map. Lenders are your friends because the debtor gave the lender the treasure map.

I might love my daughter, but wiring the kid $20,000 is beyond a rational explanation.

Payments to offshore entities looks very bad. Nobody in their right mind would ever write a check that goes through the international mail. Checks in the mail are plucked, washed, and new payees and amounts are inserted. If you are a lawyer, businessperson, or anyone who handles money, don't ever mail a check overseas unless you want to give the money away. My introduction to washed checks was an eye opener. For whatever reason, one of the bank's customers was located offshore and wrote a check to someone in the United States. The check was stolen out of the mails (allegedly), and washed in favor of a new payee and for a larger amount. The bank cleared the check. The customer screamed and caused the bank to reverse the item. Litigation ensued. Next, if you give out your wire instructions, inscribe the wire information on a piece of paper and store the paper as a PDF in your computer. When asked to provide wire instructions, send the PDF as opposed to typing out a series of 5- to 10-digit numbers, which invites error.

Payments to insurance companies, including whole life insurers, are always suspicious. A whole life policy is subject to levy because it represents a glorified savings account.

Payments to liability insurers, worker's compensation, general liability and casualty insurers arouses suspicions. Insurers pay for losses arising from activities, such as driving a car, owning a home, or running a business. The fact that someone is writing checks to insurance companies suggests that the insurer owns the asset (i.e., business, car, home, rental, agricultural or industrial property). With the fact of payment to the insurance company in hand, you can subpoena the insurer and get the policy and underlying document that might reveal that the debtor owns the property insured.

Payments (or transfers) to other bank accounts, online accounts such as PayPal, accounts controlled by related entities, accounts in the name of LLCs, limited partnerships, or related corporations are always suspicious.

These payments are part of the treasure map because they identify by inference the hidden asset. These payments suggest the ownership, control or retention of accessible assets. Clearly payment for property taxes, a bank loan, transfer fees, and maintenance reflect ownership of real property that is hidden from the creditor. The charges might appear in a checking account, credit card account, and even American Express, PayPal, and others.

Let's walk through a tax return, another treasure map. Tax returns are perfect wobbling stars. Tax returns reflect assets through deductions and expenses. Let's start with real estate, whether a home or an investment property. Tax deductions and write-offs make real estate affordable for the bulk of Americans. Standard deductions are interest payments to the bank, property taxes, maintenance, insurance, and, most importantly, depreciation if a commercial property. Other deductions might be transfer taxes. At the order of examination, the debtor denies ownership of the property and claims that the wife, children, or, more likely, an irrevocable trust holds title to the real estate. Okay, no problem, but the debtor's tax returns reflects these deductions and write-offs, all which are an indicia of ownership and inconsistent with claims that another (i.e., the trust) owns the property. Taking the debtor at his or her word, the trust would have filed its own tax return, which is a very unlikely event. These generous deductions and write-offs make most real property affordable for the American middle class (or even those higher on the economic ladder) and constitute a necessity. Giving up these deductions in favor of another taxpayer renders the property unaffordable.

Getting into the weeds of real property ownership is the fact that the debtor made the down payment on the property. Premeltdown, that down payment might have been waived, but today the down payment is 20 percent to 30 percent of the purchase price. If the debtor recently acquired the property, using the loan of value ratio of the banks and identifying the debt secured by the first deed of trust (i.e., the mortgage) and confirmed by the amount of the transfer tax and Proposition 13 reassessment, you can intuit the purchase price. Where did that money come from? Banks are no longer fools nor buffoons in 2014 and demand proof that the down payment is "free capital," which means that the money for down payment is not borrowed from another source but belongs to the debtor. If you see that the debtor recently purchased real property, assume that the down payment came from savings, and therefore a source of funds. Again, the amount of the money payments represent a well-established percentage of the debtor's net income (about 33.3 percent) and gross income (25 percent), depending upon the bank and relationship of the borrower to the bank.

Chapter 8

Reconstructing the Revenue Streams

Is your debtor a wholesale distributor, offshore or out-of-state manufacturer, or importer or exporter? Does the debtor sell products (or services) locally, statewide, nationwide, or worldwide? Is the debtor a dentist, doctor, or in the health care professions and paid from insurance? Is your debtor engaged in transportation or storage? Is your debtor a film or movie star and entitled to receive residual through the Screen Actors Guild or through the release of new movies, television shows, or other entertainment? Does your debtor maintain solely an online presence and sell solely though the Internet? How do you collect? The answer is to reconstruct the debtor's customer base.

This will require the creditor to reconstruct the debtor and analyze what type, class, or census of customers is buying the debtor's goods or services. Let's talk about Texas. Texas has three main industries: oil and oil service, agriculture (including cattle and other livestock), and general manufacturing. We took an enforcement action against a trucking company. After culling through the California secretary of state, the Texas state website (our treasure map), and every list we could find, we reconstructed about 40 percent of the debtor's customer base. We turned out about 300-plus subpoenas and 30 levies on every big business in Texas that might need transportation services. In response to a served subpoena, Baker Hughes, a major oil service provider, called and told me that they had 10,000 pieces of paper with the debtor's name on it but were doing business through a logistic outfit, Ryder System. We picked Baker Hughes because we surmised that the trucking company provided trucking services to oil service businesses, and hence Baker Hughes. Baker Hughes became our "X." We filed a creditor's suit against Ryder who promptly impounded about $72,000. Through a subpoena, we found another major customer and likewise filed suit leading to a potential six-figure recovery. An offshore industrial company collapsed in part when faced with levies on its customer base in the United States. A pharmaceutical manufacturer, facing levies and subpoenas upon its reconstructed customer base, posted a large appeal bond that secured payment due the plaintiff.

Once you can identify a customer or class of customers, you can probably reconstruct the rest through trade groups, associations, the secretary of state website that would reveal common names, names of certificate or licensee holders in specialized industries, and, best yet, the debtor's own website with the list of "happy customers," or testimonials. With the census in hand, you can subpoena or levy on the lot or serve a motion for assignment of right to snare the accounts receivable due the debtor.

If the debtor is a dentist, doctor, or in health care, levy and subpoena every insurance company available through the Department of Insurance, or Department of Health. You can create a mailing list that can be reduced to Avery sticker sheets of 30 to a page of every major insurance company. With an assignment order or subpoena in hand, you can serve every insurance company at the cost of $20 in postage, and $3 in stickers. Of course, if the insurance companies balks, you costs might go up somewhat.

If the debtor or an offshore debtor who has a U.S. subsidiary has borrowed money from a bank, the banks demanded collateral, which necessitates the filing of a financing statement (UCC) with the secretary of state. If the debtor factored its receivables or entered into a hard money loan, the factor or lender filed a financing statement. If the debtor has a line of credit with a major vendor, the vendor has filed a financing statement. Find the lender, factor, or vendor, and you will find the financial statement, contract, or loan application that reveals the banking information. The bank itself might house the deposit accounts. To facilitate cash flow, banks, lenders, and factors require that the debtor establish a lock box account address that directs the debtor's customers to mail checks to "ABC COMPANY, P.O. Box 60000, Any town, USA 99000. The holder of the lock box is the bank, or factor, and not the debtor. A six digit PO box is a tipoff to a bank lock box.

Postdigital, the debtor offers its customers the ability to make wire payments to the debtor's bank account. Wire information is printed on the bottom of the debtor's invoices, statements, or even credit applications. Offshore or out-of-state customers routinely wire payments to the debtor, and paper checks are the exception. The wire information identifies the debtor's bank or third party, such as a lender or factor who receives payments on behalf of the vendor. This is common. Check the back of the invoice.

The bank account, which is the repository of the debtor's deposits, whether warehoused by the debtor's bank or third party, is the recipient of payments, by check or wire made by the debtor's customers. Absent payments by cash or payments that are intentionally misdirected, the deposits in these banks reveal the debtor's entire customer list, their annual volume, and, if a check, the name, address, and even the telephone number of each customer. Serve a subpoena for the deposits in theses bank accounts, and you will serve up the debtor's entire customer list. Tally ho, and away you go. File a creditor's suit that names all these customers. If local, you might lay a garnishment upon the customers, but why bother when you can name all of the customers in one lawsuit? You might or might not collect, but you will get everyone's attention.

Chapter 9

Dinosaur Fingernails Unwind Fraudulent Conveyances

About a zillion pages ago, I told you the story about dinosaur fingernails. I explained that the striations in a dinosaur fingernail might suggest that *T. rex* was a scavenger and not a predator. The paleontologist at the Museum of Natural History in New York would find my suggestion ridiculous, stupid, or just downright silly. Maybe that's true, but the methodology is the same. One little piece of evidence might suggest other evidence and lead to a startling conclusion. This is the stuff of CSI when the crime lab tech discovers some key piece of evidence that leads to the apprehension of the suspect. Always, on these shows, that little piece of evidence kicks off a chain of events, contrary to everybody else's embedded belief. In the land of fraudulent conveyances, money laundering, hidden assets, and concealment, we are always looking at some little piece of evidence that would unwind the transaction. Call this unraveling the knot.

Nearly every business sues for its bills. Check the clerk's docket to find every collection lawsuit filed on behalf of your debtor. You would be surprised that the debtor, or your debtor, to be exact, is still filing a lawsuit in its name, after the alleged transfer of the business of your debtor to the new entity. Courts are online, and many documents are accessible.

Subpoena the bank records of the new entity. Look for deposits, and more specifically, copies of the deposits that consist of checks paid by customers. For example, if your debtor's name is ABC, standing for American Broadway Corporation, which is written out, but the checks are deposited in the account of the successor, American Broadway Company, LLC, you might have proven a fraudulent conveyance of the accounts receivable collections, or proof that they are one and the same entity. For example, let's say that you won on the case on October 1. The insiders of your debtor form a new entity on October 2, and open a bank account on October 3. The insiders deposit big money on that date and on October 4 and continuing. What is the source of these funds? Answer: Probably account receivable collections. The balance in debtor's own account, routine refunds, and other payments due the debtor are parked in the bank account of the successor entity. How can you tell? Answer: The account receivable checks refer to invoices, which represent payment for the sale of goods or services delivered 30 to 60 days before, given normal credit terms. The checks might actually reveal invoices numbers and dates. If you extract from the successor their own invoice numbers (and dates), rest assured that the sequence started on October 1 and not before. The key here is the mass deposit of checks that pay for the accounts receivable of the debtor, as the predecessor entity, are evidenced by dates and numbering of the invoices numbers, which accrued prior to the change over.

Collection agencies are very good in retaining relationships with their clients. For whatever reason, you might be able to track the continuity through the agency, should they file suit in their own name, but on behalf of the client. If they file suit on behalf of the debtor after the transfer, you would show not only continuity but commonality.

Transfers of trademarks, patents, copyrights, domain names, trade dress, and other intellectual property disclose true ownership. These are expensive items of property to transfer and probably require a lawyer to do it right. Frequently, the transfer of this intellectual property is missed, and therefore you might find that the successor entity is effectively doing business under the debtor's trademark. If this was the case, the debtor certainly would sue the successor for trademark infringement. If you don't find a lawsuit, chances are that these entities are one and the same, no matter what you are told the contrary. A trademark is a symbol that identifies the products or services bearing the trademark and originates from the holder; it differentiates its products or services from those of other entities. The trademark brands the product with a symbol attached to the holder and differentiates the products from others. The flip side is that the person who makes the goods (with that mark) is the person identified in the trademark registration and no one else.

Nearly every commercial obligation, such as a note owed to a bank secured by real and personal property, real or personal property lease or obligation, or any other obligation, provides for an acceleration clause when the obligor (i.e., your debtor) sells its business ("due on sale"). Nearly every lease for real property requires the consent of the landlord for an assignment. Almost all loans secured by real property have a due on sale clause, entitling the lender to foreclose on the property. As a commercial matter, the change of ownership requires an updated credit file, the renegotiation of terms, a potential refinance, and a new debt instrument or a signed assumption agreement. Lay a subpoena upon every lender, leasing company, or other creditor doing business with your debtor. After service of the subpoena, you should contact the lenders and advise them of the change of ownership. If the response is "News to me," you found another dinosaur fingernail, wobbling star, or pottery shard. The factor that the lender has not pulled the loan, suggest that the debtor never told the lender. Why? There was never a transfer.

Certain key vendors demand a rewrite of any relationship, assuming a change of ownership. The utility companies, such as gas, electric, telecommunications, data, water, and sewer, would demand that the "new customer" open a new credit account, provide a deposit, fill out a credit application, or sign a contract. Governmental entities—including all taxing entities; state, county, and city licensing boards; city payroll tax division (San Francisco); permit departments; environmental agencies at all levels; county and city health departments; and any licensing such as the Department of Alcoholic Beverage Control—demand a new application, license, or certificate. Certain activities are subject to licensing, and only a licensee can conduct those activities (resale of goods, sale of liquor, sale of drugs, sale of foodstuff products, etc.). Licenses cannot be transferred, either at all or only on approval by the agency, after an application, background check, and onsite investigation. As the old saying goes, "the name on the license is the owner and operator."

Insurance is a goldmine of information. Absent the craziest people in the world, every business needs insurance, consisting of general liability, workers' compensation, automobile if separate from general liability, products liability if separate from general liability, and sometimes E&O (Error and Omission) insurance is people-specific. A change of ownership will necessitate a change of insureds. This rule is without exception. Absent a service business, the sale of a business must go through the Bulk Sales Act, which requires the recording and publication of a notice of bulk transfer and the establishment of an escrow for payment of creditor's claims. A transfer without compliance with the Bulk Sales Act might not necessarily constitute a fraudulent conveyance; on the other hand, it serves as a big red flashing light that something is deathly wrong. The whole point of the Bulk Sales Act is to protect the buyer from the seller's creditors.

Businesses are sold through the services of a business opportunity broker. Alternatively, businesses are listed through the multiple listing service or advertised, in the *Wall Street Journal, The New York Times,* or trade magazines. The entire purpose of these services is to enhance the marketability of the business and marshal competing bidders. Absent these marketing aids, the business presumption is that the debtor did not care one way or another what the sales price would be because there was no sales price. Moreover, if you see a sale to a related entity, you'll never find a fairness opinion, separate sets of lawyers representing each side, or the back-and-forth in drafting the sales contract. You won't see dueling indemnities in the sales contract, withholds, escrow agreements, disclosures of financials, warranties of financials, or any other machinery that would protect the seller and the buyer in a normal sales transaction. You will find unfair terms in the sales contract. These terms are (1) a very low price paid by the buyer, (2) immediate change in ownership, (3) no bulk sale compliance, (4) no escrow.

One of your best friends is one of the major vendors who are selling products to your debtor. These vendors all maintain professional credit files that maintain active and even accurate credit applications, personal guarantees, resale number certificates for sales tax purposes, financial statements, signed supply agreements, payment or wiring instructions, and other normal machinery of any credit relationship. Vendors offering a six- to seven-figure line of credit decline to extend credit to the alleged successor without a complete restructuring of the credit relationship. In the interim, the vendor would put its customer on a cash basis. This would be a total disaster for the debtor company. You therefore would find that the major vendors' files do not reflect a change of ownership, and in a deposition, you would encounter shock and surprise if you asked the vendors whether they knew that their prized customer changed hands. Keeping a secret from the vendor about the change of ownership would strongly suggest there was no change of ownership.

The new entity and the old entity probably share the same initials, the same content of ads in magazines or newspapers, the same logo, color design, fax number, phone number, domain name, physical location, and, most obviously, ownership, management, same trademark, same patents, employees, and even the name on the door. We had one case in which we knew that the successor entity ran ads that were copycats of the predecessor's (debtor's) ads and used the same initials. We had to work very hard to figure out that there was a change of ownership. Postdigital, you would find a pot of information from the website. If the debtor sells over the Internet, lay subpoenas upon electronic payments services, AMEX, Discover Card, Capital One, and credit card processors to determine the identity holder.

Employees always tell interesting tales. You can readily capture information from a disgruntled employee, who frequently will file through the Department of the Labor commissioner a claim for underemployment of wages or a claim for unemployment benefits. They said in World War II that "loose lips sink ships." Today it's "loose lips sink the company."

Section 20

The Final Frontier, Spock—Bankruptcy

Chapter 1

Ingredients of Bankruptcy

Enforcement of judgments crashes into bankruptcy. My personal vision is that the collision between high-end enforcement and a Chapter 7 looks like an insurance crash test. The dummy never makes it out alive. Even the dummy's relatives are shocked at the carnage.

Before getting into the weeds of bankruptcy, this chapter is the Billy Mays (OxiClean and KaBOOM) version of bankruptcy and is reasonably cringe free, your Honor. We take a lesson from Judge Harry Callahan (retired), U.S. Bankruptcy Court, Northern District California (San Francisco Division): "A man's got to know his limitations." Bankruptcy offers the limitations. Embrace this reality. Forget third grade, the earth is flat.

Bankruptcy is not a roadblock, nor is it the end of the road, but it is an alternative path taken by the debtor. Bankruptcy is a fact of life and gives the honest debtor a life raft to flee from the sinking financial ship, Ms. Rose DeWitt Bukater. Imagine enforcement of judgments as the pre-Columbian flat world. Bankruptcy is the place beyond the edge of the enforcement world where debtors fall, never to be seen again.

Bankruptcy is a grand, and legal, bargain offered to the financially distressed. Bankruptcy offers the debtor discharge (freedom) from most liabilities in exchange for disclosing and turning over nonexempt assets. This is worth repeating: full and complete disclosure and nothing less. The debtor retains the exempt assets and emerges from the process with a "fresh start." The trustee liquidates the nonexempt assets, pays secured creditors (maybe), administrative creditors, certain wage claims, taxes, and hopefully something to the unsecured creditors. Think pennies on the dollar.

Bankruptcy is a legal and moral pact: Be truthful and hand over nonexempts assets, and you can emerge free of debt, except taxes, alimony, child support, fines, penalties and forfeitures, drunk driving claims, and other claims arising from misconduct. The devil is in the details. Creditors should embrace bankruptcy as a settled expectation. Bankruptcy is a constitutional right and no more or less important than voting. In the last 20 years, corporate name icons, such as General Motors, Chrysler, Washington Mutual, Lehman Brothers, K-Mart, and Montgomery Ward all filed bankruptcy. A debtor can file a Chapter 7, which provides for a liquidation of assets (Lehman Bros. and Washington Mutual).

In other cases, large corporate debtors typically file Chapter 11 and hope to emerge with a plan that offers creditors some recovery. These recoveries range from 100 percent on the dollar (Texaco), a percentage of their claim (Winn Dixie), stock (K-Mart), or complex trust funds (nearly all asbestos bankruptcy cases, such as Johns Manville). Individuals can, and might have to, file a Chapter 13, which is a wage earner plan and compels the debtor to pay creditors a percentage of the income over a three- to five-year period.

Chapter 2

Paint by the Numbers: Chapters 7, 9, 11, 12, 13, and 15

Chapter 7 is a standard liquidation for most individuals and businesses. Chapter 9 is a municipal bankruptcy that was virtually forgotten until the real state meltdown and bad luck dragged many cities into bankruptcy, including the City of Detroit. Chapter 11 is reorganization for most medium and large businesses. The billion-dollar cases are filed in bankruptcy courts in Los Angeles, New York City, and Delaware. Chapter 12 is a work out for family farmers and fisherman. Chapter 13 is a wage earner plan that offers creditors payments from the debtor's discretionary income for up to 60 months. Debtors who make more than the median income of the state might have to file Chapter 13. Chapter 15 is for international insolvencies. The Internet offers an endless supply of academic articles, law journal analyses, and lawyer blogs on these subjects.

The rudiments are easy for creditors. If you are a creditor in a bankruptcy proceeding, your diligence is to (a) file the proof of claim if you are owed money, (b) file a request for special notice to ensure that you get copies of everything that is filed, (c) stop haranguing the debtor and call off the collection dogs (or cats), and (d) read your e-mail and mail, particularly the proposed plans, from Chapter 11s and Chapter 13s, or any paper from any proceedings that object to your claim. If you are a junior lien holder in a piece of real property, likewise file a proof of claim, serve a request for special notice to track the proceeding, for sure hire a lawyer to protect your interest, and read the mail. Hopefully, before the bankruptcy you recorded a request for notice that compelled the senior lien holder to serve with you with a notice of default and notice of sale, enabling you to track whether the senior lien holder might foreclose in the event that the debtor defaults. These are rudimentary to keeping you alive in these proceedings.

Sometimes, old or sick people file bankruptcy. Old and very sick people die. This is a settled expectation, Ponce de Leon. If an old and sick person dies after filing bankruptcy, the case still continues. In some instances, the bankruptcy might (a very big might) abstain from further proceedings and send the matter to the probate court. This is not too likely if the debtor left a pile of debt and some assets to marshal. Should the case return to the bosom of the probate court, and you are a creditor of the deceased, file a request for notice of all papers and proceedings and of course timely file the proof of claim. From a purely mercantile point of view, the likelihood of the creditor collecting from a dead and bankrupt debtor is mediocre.

Wait a second. Let's take breather. Enter our little story. The debtor ran a series of Asian restaurants. For reason unknown, she underpaid one of her employees. Instead of resolving the case, she battled the employment lawsuit until judgment, and even filed an appeal. After judgment, and on the cusp of looming enforcement, she sold one of her properties and parked the money with her lawyer. After more pushing and shoving, the debtor sold another one of her properties, which should have provided for payment of the judgment. The title company missed the abstract, but that case was settled. Facing enforcement of the judgment, she filed bankruptcy. During the bankruptcy, the debtor died. Apparently before and after her death, the debtor, and family, defaulted on her home loan, which cycled into foreclosure. The bank foreclosed. The property got sold on the courthouse steps for much more than was owed to the secured debtor. The excess proceeds paid the rest of the judgment plus interest to date.

Moral of this tale: Appreciation of the property trumps a judgment, bankruptcy, and death. As told to me, the better statement is appreciation cures all mistakes.

Chapter 3

When the Debtor Files Bankruptcy, Whoa Nelly!

The filing of a bankruptcy stays the collection of a debt, the filing of a lawsuit, the enforcement of a judgment, the foreclosure upon property, a sheriff's sale, or for that matter any act to collect.

Stop what you are doing, says Mr. Bankruptcy Judge. This is the law: Bankruptcy Code Section 362(a) says the following:

> Except as provided in . . . , a petition . . . operates as a stay, applicable to all entities, of—

1. The commencement or continuation, including the issuance or employment of process, of a judicial, administrative, or other action or proceeding against the debtor. . . ;
2. The enforcement, against the debtor or against property of the estate, of a judgment obtained before the commencement of the case . . . ;
3. Any act to obtain possession of property of the estate or of property from the estate or to exercise control over property of the estate;
4. Any act to create, perfect, or enforce any lien against property of the estate;
5. Any act to create, perfect, or enforce against property of the debtor any lien to the extent that such lien secures a claim that arose before the commencement of the case under this title;
6. Any act to collect, assess, or recover a claim against the debtor that arose before the commencement of the case under this title;
7. The setoff of any debt owing to the debtor that arose before the commencement of the case under this title against any claim against the debtor; and . . .

In plain English: Stop what you are doing. Hit the brakes! I would bet that some bankruptcy professionals are going to buy this book and expect that I launch into some type of academic discussion of the *nuances* and *penumbra* of the automatic stay. Or whether the automatic stay is a "*game changer*," in the *historic dialectic* between debtor and creditors. How about whether the automatic stay is *doctrinal*? (I had to look up that word, folks.)

Forget that. In plain English: Stop whatever you are doing and leave the debtor alone is what the automatic stay says in English. Bug off. Call the automatic stay a Greta Garbo moment: "I want to be alone." Any action in contravention of the automatic stay is stone cold dead, absent a court order by the bankruptcy judge annulling the automatic stay, nunc pro tunc (fancy words for "do over"). The 9th Circuit tells the story:

> Our decision today clarifies this area of the law by making clear that violations of the automatic stay are void, not voidable. [Citation omitted.] . . . Before addressing the interplay between various Code sections, we must emphasize that the automatic stay plays a vital role in bankruptcy. It is designed to protect debtors from all collection efforts while they attempt to regain their financial footing. . . .
>
> . . . If violations of the stay are merely voidable, debtors must spend a considerable amount of time and money policing and litigating creditor actions. If violations are void, however, debtors are afforded better protection and can focus their attention on reorganization.
>
> Given the important and fundamental purpose of the automatic stay and the broad debtor protections of the Bankruptcy Code, we find that Congress intended violations of the automatic stay to be void rather than voidable."[*In re Schwartz*, 954 F.2d 569, 571–572 (9th Cir. 1992).]

Bankruptcy means "Back off, Mister." So far so good, but what happens when the debtor files bankruptcy, but the creditor, with or without knowledge, continues to dun, demand, collect, or sue the debtor. Most stay violations start with the phone call, e-mail, or sometimes a letter that informs the creditor of the bankruptcy. Pre-cell-phone, making the call was "dropping the dime", which means ratting out the person. For years, you could make a phone call from a public phone with only a dime. Calls from public phones are no longer a dime, and few, if any, public telephones, are left.

Common sense dictates that the creditor confirms the fact of the filing, which is readily accessible through PACER, or a public records search through Westlaw, Lexis-Nexis, and all other services. Rest assured that the debtor (or lawyer) is going to raise a stink. Yes, I get these phone calls. I recognize trouble just from the identity of the lawyer. This is one call: "Law Offices." "Hi, I would like to speak to Mr. Cook. This is lawyer Joe Blowhard." (He is a well-know bankruptcy lawyer.) "So Joe, whose stay am I violating today? Did I tell you that I changed my name to "Violating the Stay Cook?" Sounds catchy.

This is what you, as the creditor, ought to do. Unwind the liens, levies, and collections. Return the money. Pay back the interest from the money that was taken. Pay the lawyer for the time and effort to arrange for the return of the money or property. Do this immediately and do not delay. *In Re Schwartz* compels you to cough back the money even if you were ignorant of the filings. So I don't get angry calls or e-mails, not all is lost if you can convince the judge to annul the automatic stay nunc pro tunc. What does this mean? This means that if you did not know of the bankruptcy, and particularly if the debtor did not tell you, and you cycled through enormous legal process, won the case, scored a lien, or even collected and the debtor didn't say "boo," the bankruptcy judge might cut you some slack, unwind the automatic stay and leave you in place. Maybe. A thousand maybes. Hopefully. *In re Soares*, 107 F.3d 969 (1st Cir 1997). Ignorance is total bliss.

Void is void. Stone cold dead is still pretty dead. It's not Zombie dead—those are the Chapter 13 debtors making payments for 60 months.

Bankruptcy judges impose substantial penalties for violating the automatic stay, including punitive damages. We were engaged to represent a major employer who failed to comply with a bankruptcy notice that would have ended a wage garnishment. Corporate counsel brought me in to unwind the levy and work with the debtor's lawyer. We returned the money that was taken out of the debtor's wages postbankruptcy, paid off the lawyer, and paid interest to the date of the return. The credit card company and its lawyers were very slow to unwind the levy themselves and in fact appeared to stumble. Our net loss was about $1,200 consisting of fees due the other lawyer; the credit card company and counsel got hit for about $9,000. Getting stuck for violating the stay, failing to take action to unwind the damages, and, worse, getting the judge's ruling published warrants the dunce hat. It's bad enough to pay money to the debtor, but it's worse to find yourself burdened by stocks and pillars. Unlike state court, bankruptcy and federal court are like living in glass houses in which Westlaw supplies the Windex and judges gleefully keep the glass sparkling.

Can the angry debtor bury the creditor with lawyers fees accrued in the stay violation litigation? The answer is no. This makes a big difference here. The creditor pays fees arising from the efforts to restore the property to the debtor. Before the debtor files suit, return the property and pay off the lawyer. Even though the debtor might have a decent damage claim, the debtor is not entitled to recover fees in that litigation. Permitting a debtor to collect lawyer fees incurred in prosecuting a damages action would further neither the financial nor the nonfinancial goals of the automatic stay. With regard to the financial goals, we have explained that "the stay gives the debtor time to put finances back in order, offers the debtor an opportunity to reorganize so that creditors can be satisfied to the greatest extent possible, and prevents creditors from racing to devour the debtor's estate. . . . The stay, then, is meant to help the debtor deal with his bankruptcy for the benefit of himself and his creditors alike. We have never said the stay should aid the debtor in pursuing his creditors, even those creditors who violate the stay. The stay is a shield, not a sword. . . . We conclude, therefore, that a damages action for a stay violation is akin to an ordinary damages action, for which lawyer fees are not available under the American Rule." *Sternberg v. Johnston,* 595 F.3d 937, 948 (9th Cir. 2010). That's painful, but helpful to know. It is better to emerge singed and not deep fried.

Chapter 4

Secret Bankruptcies and Beauty Contests

Ever heard of the secret bankruptcy? Shocker that term might be, but some bankruptcies are conducted in secret even though ostensibly public proceedings. The reason why a bankruptcy can be conducted in secret is that the debtor fails to notify the creditor. The failure to provide notice might be accidental or intentional. Why intentional? Answer: The creditor might file a lawsuit in the bankruptcy court to exempt the debt form the discharge because the debtor is based on a fraud, false financial statement, breach of fiduciary duty, willful and malicious conduct, and so on. Typically, the creditor discovers the bankruptcy when the creditor levies a bank account, and in response, the debtor complains that a prior bankruptcy discharged the judgment. In *In re Beezley,* 994 F.2d 1433 (9th Cir. 1993), the Ninth Circuit applied the "no harm, no foul," rule. The court held that the debt is still discharged, even though the creditor did not get notice, if the case is a no-asset dividend case or the debt is dischargeable. However, the creditor must file a lawsuit in bankruptcy court to prove ignorance of the bankruptcy and the debt is independently nonchargeable. Call this the judicial "see no evil, hear no evil, speak no evil," moment.

Let's have a cocktail. Instead of gin and vermouth, let's pour one part *In Re Beezley* and one part *In Re Schwartz* and what do you get? What you get is a big disaster. This is a *Bride of Chucky* moment. *Beezley* tells you that your debt is extinguished including a judgment if the debt is commercial (nontort) and the case is no asset (no money for creditors). You are deep fried without even knowing it. *Schwartz* voids your liens and levies, even if you did not know about the bankruptcy. In plain English: You sued, served, got judgment, and recorded liens in total good faith. The debtor is sitting on a boatload of equity. If the debtor is ready to sell the property and pick up your lien, you'd think that happy days are here again. Nope. The debtor is going to inform you that the he or she filed bankruptcy, did not give you notice, that your lawsuit, service, judgment, and lien are stone cold dead. Forget Lazarus from the dead. You can move for a motion to void the automatic stay nunc pro tunc. The bankruptcy judge can reaffirm your suit, service, and lien that rescue you from bankruptcy's Scylla and Charybdis, assuming that you were in total ignorance of the bankruptcy. Maybe or maybe not. Don't count your chickens before they hatch.

Ignorance is bliss, but it is a bitterly contested issue. Embrace the "dropping a dime" battle. Once a creditor is informed that the debtor filed bankruptcy, the creditor is on notice for all due dates including the date to file a proof of claim in order to receive a dividend, and the due date to file a lawsuit to exempt the debt from the discharge. Notice can be informal, including a telephone call to the lawyer for the creditor. "Are you the lawyer for Mr. Snoodle?" "Yes." "Well, this is Joe Padoodle, and I just filed bankruptcy (click!)" might be enough. Dropping a dime for the post-millennial set means that someone uses a pay phone (bet you never have seen one of these except in a movie).

What is required only is actual notice, which means that the debtor or lawyer can drop a dime and communicate informal notice of the bankruptcy. The debtor prays that the lawyer for the creditor fails to grasp the significance of the informal notice and blows it off. No kidding. This becomes a battle of "he said, and she said." This is a big deal. The creditor is going to file a suit to exempt the debt from the discharge and prove up total ignorance of the bankruptcy proceeding. The debtor will claim "dropping a dime." Expect a spirited battle.

Moral of this tale: Whoever had the best character-acting lessons is going to win this battle.

Chapter 5

Embrace Bankruptcy, Martha, and Save Yourself a Crockpot of Dough

Like Martha Stewart might say, bankruptcy is a good thing. Bankruptcy ends the expensive but futile quest to collect. In the moonscape of debtors and creditors, bankruptcy always looms over the horizon. Expect this outcome and the machinations that follow. Bankruptcy serves another purpose: It ends this messy quest to collect a judgment against someone who has nothing.

Embrace bankruptcy as part of information that contours what you should or should not do. Absent the most extreme cases or valid liens encumbering nonexempt equity imbued in the debtor's property, bankruptcy pancakes the value of the judgment to near zero. If you know that the debtor is filing bankruptcy, which is the best outcome for the debtor, the judgment and claim have marginal and even negative values if the creditor is going to invest real money in fees and expenses in chasing down this person. If anticipated, and embraced, bankruptcy protects the creditor from needlessly investing further money in a lost cause and bottomless pit of expenses without any promise of return or gain. Making the situation even worse is the fact that the trustee can claw back any collections or recoveries, and upset all liens, levies, and enforcement if undertaken within 90 days preceding the filing date. Don't hesitate to ask the debtor the following: "When are you going to file?" "Have you filed?" "Where did you file?" "Why don't you file bankruptcy, and end this misery?" Ask these questions, and make the creditor's decision more efficient.

Chapter 6

Chasing People Down in Bankruptcy Court

Do you have money to burn and are you really angry? Read on, sport.

Here is the law that carves out debts from the discharge. This is important because many state court lawsuits come to fruition on the eve of the bankruptcy. If the litigant wins the case by default and frames the requirements for nondischargeability clearly in the state court default, the state court litigation can unlock the door to the bankruptcy court and readily prove up nondischargeability. This is also a big deal because the creditor ,who might win handily the nondischargeability lawsuit and breathe life into the claim postbankruptcy, can pursue collection for all eternity. Facing an enforcement of a claim, bearing Dracula's longevity, the debtor might settle for something. Something is better than nothing. Please read Bankruptcy Code § 523(a)(2) [common-law fraud and fraud through a financial statement], Section 523(a) (4) [defalcation or breach of fiduciary duty], or Section 523(a)(6) [willful and malicious injury—creditor must show intent to injure and subjective malice directed at the plaintiff.] See also *In re Barboza,* 545 F.3d 702 (9th Cir. 2008) (copyright infringement case) ["willful" and "malicious" are separate]; *In re Sicroff,* 401 F.3d 1101 (9th Cir. 2005), cert. denied, 545 U.S. 1139, 125 S.Ct. 2964 (2005) [letter written by graduate student that libeled tenured professor held nondischargeable]; *In re Peck,* 295 B.R. 353 (9th Cir. B.A.P. 2003) [false accusations of child molestation were slanderous, and nondischargeable]; *In re Thiara,* 285 B.R. 420 (9th Cir. B.A.P. 2002) [subjective intent to harm required in conversion case]; *In re Su,* 290 F.3d 1140 (9th Cir. 2002) [a subjective intent to harm, or a subjective belief that harm is substantially certain].

Forget this case legalese here. *In re Su* is worth reading: "On August 21, 1997, shortly before 8 a.m., Carrillo was lawfully crossing a major downtown San Francisco intersection while walking to work. Su, who was driving a 14-passenger van, sped into the intersection against a red light, traveling 37 miles-per-hour in a 25-mile-per-hour zone, ***nearly five seconds after the light had turned red.*** He crashed into a car that was lawfully in the intersection and then careened into Carrillo, severely injuring her."

After I read *In re Su,* I look both ways before crossing a street. Talk about a destruction derby without the bankruptcy judge as the referee. *In re Su* means that idiots can run down pedestrians, leave them for road kill, and rinse themselves of legal and moral responsibility through a bankruptcy. This is the law. In plain English, what does this really mean? Bad people cause horrific injuries that prompt the victim to win a very big judgment. Call this Chapter 1. Chapter 2 is hiring a lawyer to enforce the judgment. Chapter 3 is the debtor filing bankruptcy. Chapter 4 is seeing whether the bankruptcy judge will find that the findings in the state court judgment meet the requirements of nondischargeability in the adversary proceeding, that you have to start from scratch, or that, absent the right proof, you get kicked out of court.

Maliciousness requires proof of a wrongful act that was done intentionally and causes injury, without just cause or excuse. Bankruptcy judges demand proof of each element, and unlike state court jury trials, sympathy gets you nowhere. A victim's tears generate lots of tissue paper and not victory. Expect to spend $25,000 on your lawyer in chasing someone down in bankruptcy court. If you are the debtor, take acting lessons. "Cry, weep, cry" is the new mantra. "I am sorry, I am sorry and by the way I blame my lawyer." Did I forget to tell you that the lawyer takes the witness stand? "Yes, I represented my client. I loved my client. I believed in my client. I might have been wrong, but don't blame my client, blame my zeal, and devotion to justice." Dear God, where is the Academy Award®? These cases are a cross between a confessional (you read that right) and a pantomime in blaming someone else, or coming up with some excuse, whether rational or otherwise, that the debtor was not acting with the intent to injure the plaintiff but to protect some other interest or person.

Remember, the decision by the bankruptcy judge on credibility and demeanor is nearly appeal-proof. If you are the creditor, you have 60 days from the date of the first meeting to file the lawsuit. One day late kills the case, no matter how righteous. Bankruptcy has a lot of detailed rules and deadlines that compel strict adherence. You can find these cases online through Google, as most federal cases are posted online and are free of charge. For some unknown reason, bankruptcy lawyers routinely post online decent articles that discuss these cases. Some of these articles are even readable. This case might make good reading because they usually pit the vulnerable or stupid against the venal or stupid.

Chapter 7

Debris in the Judicial Slipstream

Let's learn the secrets of hearsay and judicial and collateral estoppel. This is important stuff.

Hearsay means that a court will not let into evidence any statement that is made "out of court." This might include e-mails, letters, and other writings. Hearsay has a zillion exceptions. The most important is that when a party testifies in court, or gives a deposition, or even otherwise, that person's statements are admissible in another proceeding. We call this exception a party admission. Whatever you say in one court, deposition, e-mail, letter, or well-remembered conversation follows you forever. FaceBook, Twitter, and your website are eternal. God forbid indiscrete pictures, personal rants, and flaming anybody is the mark of "A."

The moral of the tale: Diarrhea of the mouth is fatal.

Judicial estoppel is a little different. A position taken by a party in one proceeding might bind the person to that position in another proceeding. Call this "planting a flag in judicial cement." If the debtor sues a customer for nonpayment of a business debt, the debtor cannot escape the election that the debtor owns the business. If the debtor sues the insurance company for damage to the home, chances are the debtor owns the home, notwithstanding the claims in court that the family trust owns the home. Call this a judicial echo that reverberates through many courts under the fancy title of judicial estoppel. In plain English: The decision is tattooed on your forehead.

Collateral estoppel means that a decision in one court binds the party in other proceedings. Stuck with deficient goods or services, a plaintiff sues the merchant for fraud. For one reason or another, the merchant blows off the lawsuit, does not answer the lawsuit, and the plaintiff wins the case by default. The judge makes a specific finding of fraud based on the uncontested evidence. Let's presume that the rulings are very precise, and that the damages are segregated for the fraud finding. Facing now a big-time judgment, the merchant tumbles into bankruptcy court in anticipation of dumping the fraud judgment as part of the bankruptcy discharge.

Not so fast here, partner. A specific ruling even arising from a default judgment in state court, or better yet, a default in an arbitration proceeding, reemerges in a bankruptcy nondischargeability proceeding. Bankruptcy will not discharge debts for fraud, willful and malicious injury, and breach of trust claims, among other claims. Getting stuck with a judgment for a malevolent wrongs ruling reverberates down the line. This is a well-understood law. Parklane Hosiery Co., Inc. v. Shore, 439 U.S. 322 (1979) and *Bank of America v. Bernhard* (1942) 19 Cal.2d 807 [a specific ruling in one court migrates into another court]. In English: Collateral estoppel is the perfect echo chamber. You will read down the line that hiring any lawyer to defend you is better than no lawyer at all. Ask my cousin Vinny.

A bad result in state court bleeds into bankruptcy court. Yuck! If you defaulted on the state court case, you are forever stuck with the bad result, says *Grogan v. Garner,* 498 U.S. 279, 285 fn. 11, 111 S.Ct. 654 (1991). In the Ninth Circuit, collateral estoppel principles are applied in nondischargeability litigation to the extent that they would apply were the litigation being held in a court of the state where the original judgment was entered. *In re Nourbakhsh,* 67 F.3d 798, 800 (9th Cir. 1995), citing *Marrese v. American Academy of Orthopaedic Surgeons,* 470 U.S. 373, 380 (1985). This is true in the Ninth Circuit, even in default cases. *Nourbaksh,* supra, 67 F.3d at 800. Blowing off the fraud lawsuit and suffering a default is bad strategy. These cases are online. Consider a default judgment a forever echo that reverberates in courtroom after courtroom. A defaulted arbitration award likewise reverberates right down the line of courthouses. What is really collateral estoppel, post-Zen? What comes around goes around.

If you are the plaintiff's counsel, plead each claim separate and distinctly, and track the statutory language for nondischargeability. Word for word, letter for letter, and comma for comma, if you make it so, Captain Picard. The prayer of the complaint must specify the damages attached to the fraud, defalcation, or "willful and malicious" claim. The prove-up hearing must evidence separate evidence and separating filing of those claims. The judgment must spell out the claim and the precise damages associated with each claim. The end product (the default judgment) looks like a platter of sushi and not a mess of low-carb spaghetti. Think paint-by-the-numbers pleading.

Is the debtor really stuck with a horrific default in the state court that frames the debtor as Attila the Hun? What is the exit? Upon the suit to exempt the debt from the discharge, the debtor can stay the bankruptcy lawsuit on the grounds that the debtor wants to go back to state court and reopen the case. The grounds to reopen the case might be excusable neglect, inadvertence or surprise, mishandling by the state court lawyer for the debtor, a void judgment, or any number of other reasons. Who knows? The state court judge might bend over backwards and give the debtor a pass on the default judgment that would enable the debtor to meaningfully oppose the bankruptcy nondischargeability lawsuit.

Let's say that the creditor files suit in bankruptcy court to exempt the debt from the discharge and emerge with an enforceable judgment in hand. Is the judgment collectable? Yes, as to future earnings, and no to prepetition assets, which belong to the trustee. Can you collect? No, if the debtor lives like Gandhi for the rest of his or her life; yes, if the debtor wins the lottery. The moral of this story: Buy lottery tickets for the debtor. Learn how to spell pyrrhic. Expect the lawyer to demand a big and very fat deposit for all fees and costs before accepting the case.

Let's get back to collateral estoppel. These echoes are also the "Xs" and arrows on the treasure map. If the debtor testifies in court that the debtor owns a home, business, or other assets, that testimony is admissible in another proceeding. The testimony is proof of ownership and entitles you to grab the asset, even if in the name of another entity, name, or relative. If the first court held that the debtor owned, controlled, or had a beneficial interest in the assets, the ruling is admissible in your enforcement to likewise grab the asset. Finding assets means that you first find every lawsuit or other proceeding (IRS or property tax proceedings) where the debtor was a party. Pull the transcripts, read the file, and seek any discovery (disclosure) responses. If the debtor sought and won damages for a toppled fence, the judicial inference is that the debtor owned the home.

Chapter 8

Asset Protection in a Mega-Chapter 11

Aladdin: Wish fulfillment?
Genie: Three wishes, to be exact. And ixnay on the wishing for more wishes. That's it. Three. Uno, dos, tres. No substitutions, exchanges, or refunds.

We were in a T-shirt stall in the Grand Bazaar in Istanbul. We were shuffling through the layers of shirts and came upon the Blue Mosque, the Hagia Sofia, and the Sea of Marmara. My wife, Lilly, intoned, "Yes, so so, no, and no way." The store clerks were all young people and very chatty. "Where are you from?" "How do you like Turkey?" and "How long are you staying?"

These young people were ever so enchanting. Like many people inhabiting the crossroads of Europe and Asia, their faces bore a near-olive color, their hair was jet black, and they spoke English like a young Omar Sharif. I asked them where they came from, and I received a tour of the Balkans, such as Macedonia, Montenegro, Thessaly, and Thrace. We Americans had little clue that these places existed until Tito died and Yugoslavia disintegrated. For most Americans the only recognizable Macedonian is Alexander the Great who is somewhat past his prime.

If you saw *Skyfall,* the latest James Bond movie, you enjoyed a brief but hyper-exciting travelogue of the Grand Bazaar when Bond and his current nemesis crashed through the upper story window and drove their motorcycles through stalls. Surely they passed a stall that sold copper and metal products, including olive oil lamps and vessels. These lamps take center stage in the story of "The Fisherman and the Genie" from *1001 Arabian Nights*. The impoverished fisherman fished out a vessel of yellow copper, broke the leaden seal, and out popped the Jinni who offered the fisherman three wishes. For the purists, the true name is Jinni and not genie.

While I recall my magical visit to the Grand Bazaar, with T-shirts in hand, spending hours drinking tea from a Turkish samovar, I ponder whether I missed the stall that sold olive oil lamps that bore a leaden stopper. Am I out of luck?

Not quite. Let's leave the Grand Bazaar and return to the land of enforcement of judgments and collection of debts. Hope you enjoyed the side trip. Who is the Jinni in this business? Is it true that if you rub the lamp, out pops Robin Williams who will grant you three wishes? What is the lamp called? Does the lamp have a name or title? Come on folks, this is important.

In this chapter, the lamp is Chapter 11, and the Jinni is the bankruptcy judge. Call this person Judge Jinni. The three wishes are in the Chapter 11. The first two wishes are surviving the rigors of Chapter 11 and filing a successful plan of reorganization. Most plans range from 20 pages for Joe's Hot Dog Parlor to 300-plus pages for American Airlines, plus a 500-page disclosure statement that must be read in paper. First, you want to print out the plan and disclosure statement. Forget loading up the paper in the printer. First install a brand new printer cartridge.

Hunt through these plans, and somewhere right above the final miscellaneous section you will find the "Discharge, Injunctions, and Release" sections. These provisions spell out what debts, claims, and obligations that the plan will discharge, enjoin, and release. What does the word "discharge" mean in a plan? The word "discharge" means to extinguish or to terminate, or for those with a sense of humor and the obligation to translate legalese into English for clients: "Dead as a doornail." For those whose sense of humor is uncontrollable, try "kaput."

The purpose of the plan is to pay creditors something, whether cash, stock, or even coupons, which is required under Bankruptcy Code § 1129(a)(7)(A)(ii) [creditor gets at least what a Chapter 7 would generate, which must be something]. In exchange for the payment under the plan, the discharge wipes out the creditor's prepetition claim. In plain English: Chapter 11 doles out to creditors what they get in Chapter 7 liquidation. Oliver Twist offers the best explanation: "Please sir, can I have some more?" Answer: "No. You got every nickel, dime, and quarter under Section 1129(a)(7)(A)(ii). Too bad." I remind everybody that some Chapter 11s produce very small dividends.

We still have a third wish for the Judge Jinni. The third wish is a discharge, accompanied by an injunction and release provision that extinguishes the claims of creditors *against* third parties for the debts of the debtor. The claims are personal guaranties, indemnity agreements, or liability under some theory of law. Did I forget to define a personal guaranty for you? Oops, I am sorry. A guarantor is the person with a pen in his hand. How can you avoid liability under a guarantor? Leave the pen at home. E-ZEE does it: No pen, no guaranty. By the way, what is the definition of conflict of interest? Answer: Seeing your name in too many places.

This discharge provision endeavors to extinguish the following liabilities:

A. A claim held by a creditor against third parties, under a guaranty, or for common-law fraud, or against another entity for conspiracy to defraud, or maybe an "alter ego" claim.

B. A claim held by a creditor against the spouse of the debtor if based on independent liability.
C. A claim for civil damages owed by the debtor or a third party arising from a continuing loss, such as toxic contamination, attractive nuisance, dangerous or unsafe structure, or riparian rights (water and irrigation).
D. A claim held by a creditor who has a right to seek indemnity, "hold harmless," contribution or other legal or equitable rights against the third party for the loss sustained as a result of nonpayment of any claim, debt, or suit. This is common in complex financial transactions, major property damage or personal injury, or negotiable instruments.
E. Or some other hare-brained claims concocted by a nutcase lawyer. These claims barely survive the pretrial challenges and threaten the defendant with big-time damages. In the face of colorable risk, most defendants would shell out a settlement. The winning hand is getting the stinker to trial, and not necessarily winning.

The third wish, which is the all-encompassing discharge, extinguishes the rights of the creditors against third parties to collect on an anagram of debts, obligations, and claims that are owed by the debtor. The focus here is to discharge personal guarantees of corporate insiders for company debts.

This third wish can be granted by Judge Jinni. A confirmed Chapter 11 is a unique cocktail of a judgment, contract, and consent decree. When the bankruptcy judge slams down the gavel and pronounces, "Confirmed!" the plan spells out the entire trip down the Yellow Brick Road that leads to the Land of Oz as financial redemption. Upon confirmation, the terms of the plan are both collateral estoppel and res judicata. Judge Jinni grants this wish if the debtor incorporates this broad discharge, *the creditors do not object,* and the judge declines to excise the third-party discharge.

Well, what happens if some creditor objects to this broad discharge and wants to raise a big stink? Raising a stink is a commonly known and highly technical term. This is how you raise a stink in bankruptcy court: File and serve objections before the final "drop dead date," and not a second later, serve electronically or by paper copy (or both) upon the debtor, and if in paper, accompany the paper filing with a CD in Word that is searchable upon the debtor, debtor's lawyer, the creditor's committee and its counsel, other committees and their counsel, the U.S. trustee, parties requesting special notice, the court, and probably the senior lenders. This list is typical. This is a must-do list and some orders compel the creditor to fax the objections in addition to mailing (over 20 on a page). Do everything by 9:00 a.m. EST. Should something go wrong, the technical bankruptcy jargon is "Do not pass Go. Do not collect $200. Engage in intense prayer."

Is this wish for a third-party discharge real? Let's apply this lesson. In opening up a commercial credit account, the creditor offered the customer, usually a corporation or

LLC, standard 30-day credit terms, but subject to a personal guaranty executed by the corporate principal. Believing tomorrow would never bring a cloud in the sky, the principal signs the guaranty that spawns a contingent liability of millions should the customer collapse. Lo and behold, the market shifts under everyone's feet, which compels the customer to stumble in Chapter 11 in a last-ditch effort to rehabilitate itself and shed gobs of flesh-eating debt. The debtor hires Ms. Sharpie, who successfully shepherds the debtor through Chapter 11. Quickly gripping that the corporate principals signed guaranties for millions in trade debt, the lawyer drafts the following discharge language: "This plan discharges the claims of all creditors, including, but not limited to, the claims of any creditors to enforce any personal guaranty executed by any person, sue any nondebtor for breach of contract, fraud or conspiracy, any other claim either in law or equity, pursue any claim in equity, arbitration or otherwise any person if connected with the claim owed by the debtor to the creditor, or any claim for indemnity, equitable or contractual, or contribution, owed by any person. Under this paragraphs claims include, but are not limited to, any claims arising from any written or oral agreement, claims arising from law or equity, claims that are reduced to suit or judgment, or otherwise."

What a terrible run-on sentence, but this broad discharge is a near-settled expectation. If incorporated into a confirmed plan, this language bars creditors from suing the guarantor, indemnitor, or conspirator on a fraud claim, or any other third party, even though the third parties are not the debtor. These third-party discharges work, assuming that the creditors are asleep at the switch. In *Levy v. Cohen* (1977) 19 C. 3rd. 165, 172, the confirmed plan discharged the personal liability of the general partners of a limited partnership which ran a Los Angeles-based convalescent hospital. The creditors sued the general partners, who asserted the plan discharge as a complete defense under collateral estoppel. The court stated: "An arrangement confirmed by a bankruptcy court has the effect of a judgment rendered by a federal district court. [Citation omitted.] The federal rule is that a judgment or order, once rendered, is final for purposes of res judicata until reversed on appeal or modified or set aside in the court of rendition. [Citation omitted.] The record does not indicate that the order confirming plan of arrangement was reversed, modified or set aside. Hence, that order is final."

This next quote from *Levy v. Cohen* knocks the ball out of the park, Bud: "Full faith and credit must be given to a final order or judgment of a federal court. [Citation omitted.] Such an order or judgment has the same effect in the courts of this state as it would have in a federal court. [Citation omitted.] In the federal jurisdiction, the doctrine of res judicata prevents the readjudication of all matters (including jurisdiction) which were, or might have been, litigated in a prior proceeding between the same parties. [Citation omitted.] Here, the trial court found, as a fact, that the question of defendants' liability for the debts and obligations of the limited partnership owed by plaintiff was not litigated in the bankruptcy proceeding. Nevertheless, if plaintiff had an opportunity to litigate such question in that proceeding, his failure to do so would not eliminate, in the present action, the conclusive effect of the bankruptcy court's determination that defendants are not liable for debts of the limited partnership." *Levy v. Cohen,* pp. 172–173.

In plain English: You snooze, you lose.

The third wish, embodied by *Levy v. Cohen,* is the broad discharge that frees the corporate principals from their personal liability owed to the creditors even though the corporate principals did not file bankruptcy and subject their assets to liquidation and distribution to the creditors.

Section 21

You Can't Eat Soup with a Knife

"Making war upon insurgents is messy and slow, like eating soup with a knife." T. E. Lawrence coined this expression, which U.S. tacticians embraced in the second Iraq war and Afghanistan. Enforcement of high-end judgment is usually messy, sometimes slow, and very nonlinear.

Thank you for taking this trip with me. At least I kept you company in this epic river trip, Kurtz. I hope that you are not suffering from a little PTSD after the highs and lows of this experience. Assuming that you have survived, here is the parting lesson. In undertaking the collection of a larger-dollar judgment, you will run into the buzz saw of some very determined individuals who have worked very hard and spent a whole bunch of money in an attempt to thwart your efforts. You are expected in the lion cage, and everyone is waiting for you. If your debtor is offshore, you are dealing with a debtor who perceives itself immune from enforcement. "Come and get me!" is the battle cry. If you are dealing with an individual who has buried a pile of assets in asset-protection trusts, offshore entities, and out-of-state limited liabilities companies, expect a long and tedious struggle. Eat lots of Wheaties for breakfast.

Let's get back to the premise of this book. You want to collect. You need a treasure map. You need determination. You need to convince your adversary that you will stop at nothing, other than violating the law. You have unlimited resources, and a brilliant strategy at hand. You will leave no stone unturned and confront any crisis with courage and intelligence. Face it, the defendant declined to defend or invest even nominal money in the defense because the defendant intuited that his assets were successfully concealed and that the judgment creditor would decline enforcement based on the expense and effort (or intimidation). The debtor priced the judgment at zero. Your job is to price the judgment at par and, better yet, collect the judgment at par.

On the other hand, other information resets the price of the judgment at 100 percent on the dollar. What is this other information? This is the information in this book that enables the judgment creditor to lift the veil of asset protection and follow the clues on the map until you reach the treasure. This information is that you have the wherewithal to latch onto the treasure map and unearth the treasure. The stated and express commitment by the creditor to serve hundreds of subpoenas, levy every bank account or customer, seize any property, pull cargo from open-going carriers while on the open sea, mail out thousands of assignment orders to an entire anagram of obligors, and set the price of judgment at par because, God forbid, you might and will collect, or at least the debtor thinks so.

Hopefully, you found the treasure map, and for less than $100, you found your $1,000,000 prize. While these steps might not always reach an asset or discover the buried treasure, the issue is that the debtor believes that the creditor will stop at nothing in hunting down the money. This belief by the debtor, based on information both real and imagined that the creditor will stop at nothing and therefore should pay the judgment at full price, is the sum and substance of this book.

Sorry to leave you so soon. Hope you enjoyed the trip and the pork sandwiches, but I have to go. I have more freight bills to collect, bad guys to chase down, treasures to find, and another book to write. See you soon. Have fun.

I still have not gotten over that awful person who posted that appeal bond and took away my toy. Too much fun.

By the way, dear reader. Pray that I make a big hit. Pray that I have a bestseller. Pray the books fly off the shelves. Why, oh why? Money, fortune or fame? No, but nice. Why? So I can clean up the typos and awful grammar.

Index